UFO

UNIDENTIFIED FLYING OBJECT FOR CONTEMPORARY ARCHITECTURE: UFO'S EXPERIMENTS BETWEEN POLITICAL ACTIVISM AND THE ARTISTIC AVANT-GARDE

Table of Contents

Beyond the Rejection of Explanation

Beatrice Lampariello, False Mirror Office (Andrea Anselmo, Boris Hamzeian)

UFO. Under this short and expressive name, a group of students from the Faculty of Architecture of the University of Florence (Carlo Bachi, Lapo Binazzi, Patrizia Cammeo, Riccardo Foresi, and Titti Maschietto, accompanied at the outset by Sandro Gioli) began to discuss and collaborate at the end of 1967, producing works that they wanted to appear obscure in their origin, in their content, and in their aims. They even wanted them to remain "unidentified" in order to establish a complete coincidence between the group's name and its work or, to use the semiological terms of which UFO was so fond, between "signifier, signified, and referent."[1] At a distance of almost sixty years and after a limited number of studies,[2] this book, accompanied by an exhibition at the FRAC Centre-Val de Loire (Orléans, France),[3] explores the twists and turns in the story of UFO, examining letters, notes, published essays, and photographs in an attempt to uncover the creative intentions of the group. The aim of the book, therefore, is to surmount the barrier that UFO itself had erected between its work and its interpretation through a "rejection of explanation,"[4] in order to keep it "unidentified," so as to provide, for the first time, a critical reading of UFO's entire body of work. Thus in going beyond that "rejection," the book has assumed the position of the "gate-crasher" in the film *The Swimmer* (1968),[5] which the group had adopted as a symbol in order to explore territories to which entry has been "forbidden" up until now.[6] And just as UFO had upset the established rhythms of the city and the holding of exhibitions with the aim of liberating architecture—and thus human beings—from any limitation, from the dimensional constraints of function, from the power of technology, and from any kind of construction that sought to last forever in order to bring architecture back to its essence of "pure creativity"[7]—and human beings to the condition of "operators/users"[8]—the book sets out to provide historians, theorists, architects, and designers with new fields of inquiry. The picture that emerges from it is a complex one, with multiple references ranging from art to semiotics and from politics to the Carnival. It sketches the outlines of an architecture that aimed at its "de-architecturization"[9] in rejection of the figure of the demiurge in favour of a community

1 See, among others, Umberto Eco, *Appunti per una semiologia delle comunicazioni visive* (Milan: Bompiani, 1967).

2 Among them it is worth citing the exhibition held at the Centro per l'arte contemporanea Luigi Pecci (Prato) from 29 September 2012 to 24 February 2013 and its catalogue: Stefano Pezzato (ed.), *Ufo story: dall'architettura radicale al design globale* (Prato: Centro per l'arte contemporanea Luigi Pecci, 2012). See too Amit Wolf, 'Superurbeffimero no. 7: Umberto Eco's Semiologia and the Architectural Rituals of the U.F.O.', *California Italian Studies*, no. 2, 2011; Alessandra Acocella, 'Scenografie radicali. San Giovanni Valdarno 1968', in Acocella, *Avanguardia diffusa. Luoghi di sperimentazione artistica in Italia 1967-1970* (Milan: Fondazione Passaré/Macerata: Quodlibet, 2016), pp. 73-94; Agata Knapik, 'Radykalne projekty grupy UFO jako przyklad architektury narracyjnej', *Quart: Kwartalnik Instytutu Historii Sztuki Uniwersytetu Wroclawskiego*, no. 2, 2018, pp. 88-106; and False Mirror Office (Andrea Anselmo and Boris Hamzeian), 'L'assemblaggio come testo figurativo per l'architettura. Un dialogo tra UFO e False Mirror Office', *PianoB*, no. 2, 2019, pp. 88-118.

3 The exhibition, entitled *Unidentified Flying Object (UFO), performer l'architecture* and curated by Beatrice Lampariello, Andrea Anselmo and Boris Hamzeian (False Mirror Office) and Nabila Metaïr and Abdelkader Damani (FRAC Centre-Val de Loire), was held from 15 April 2022 to 15 January 2023.

4 Lapo Binazzi (UFO), *Ufo. Discontinuità e territorio* (Milan: Centro internazionale di Brera, 1977).

of "operators/users"; of industrial production in favour of a process of construction that was a theatre of life; of building materials in favour of polyethylene, polyurethane, and papier-mâché; and finally of buildings in favour of happenings that were intended to provide environments to stimulate people's fantasy and imagination. In stripping itself of all those characteristics that it has been laden with over the centuries, architecture as understood by UFO was also set free of its original connotation of providing shelter for human beings and became a message to be delivered in squares, in streets, in shops, and in the countryside. In this approach, entailing a progressive destruction of the work, the object, and the city,[10] UFO seems to fall into line with Superstudio, Archizoom, and 9999. Despite their common position of rejection, however, it is possible to identify substantial differences between the exponents of the so-called Radical Architecture. What UFO set out to destroy was the very concept of the project as it had become entrenched in the 20th century, that of a prefiguration of the future, whether critical or visionary; whether on the scale of the object, the building, or the city; whether elaborated through plans, elevations, and sections or through collages, diagrams, and models. UFO distanced itself from the figurative character of the works of Superstudio, Archizoom, and 9999, as well as from their representations of objects, buildings, or cities, even if they were realised through a process of progressive graphic subtraction. In UFO's work, that figurative character became action on reality that pushed the project to the verge of a comprehension of what exists, and a revelation of its hidden dimension. UFO never crossed that line, never lapsed into the beauty of perspective, into the essentiality of the ideogram, into the materiality of the model, and thus never lapsed into a prefiguration of the future.

Adopting the position of the "gate-crasher," the book also takes from UFO its collective dimension of "operators/users," inasmuch as it is made up of essays written by different people and of different nature. The first part of the book, "History," reconstructs for the first time the entire body of UFO's work, from the years of its future

5 This is the name used to describe the character played by Burt Lancaster in the film, one of UFO's cinematic references.

6 See the photographs taken by Bachi in 1973 of Foresi, from the back, about to trespass on private property.

7 Lapo Binazzi, *Global Tools - Gruppo "Teoria". Relazione di Lapo Binazzi*, 10 October 1974 (Lapo Binazzi Archives, Florence).

8 Lapo Binazzi, Lapo (sic) Cammeo, Riccardo Foresi, Sandro Gioli and Titti Maschietto, 'Effimero Urbanistico scala 1/1', *Marcatrè*, no. 37-40, May 1968, pp. 198-209.

9 Binazzi (UFO), *Ufo. Discontinuità e territorio*.

10 "The Destruction of the Object," "The Elimination of the City," and "The Disappearance of the Work" were the themes that Superstudio and Archizoom proposed in January 1971 to the editor of the magazine *in. Argomenti e immagini di design*, Pierpaolo Saporito, as the subjects of three monographic issues.

members' university studies to the breakup of the group in 1978. The second, "Context," sets that work against the background of the sixties and seventies, between semiotic theories, political activism, neo-avant-gardes, artistic experimentation, and urban actions. The third, "Legacy," looks at the relevance of that work to the current production of the young generation of architects, asking them about some of the "things the UFOS really likes,"[11] from community to the use of colour, from celebration to accumulation, from narration to change of scale, and from disturbance to the icon and the happening. The fourth and final part of the book, "Anthology," brings together for the first time all the texts written by the members of UFO over the eleven years of its existence, in a collection that has been compiled maintaining total fidelity to the original publications. Texts that should be read in the light of the process of "de-architecturization" to which the group subjected the discipline as another opportunity for experimentation in which to involve architecture as language. It is only with the generous support of the Directorate-General for Contemporary Creativity of the Italian Ministry of Culture (Italian Council, 9th edition, 2020) that this book has been able to make the work of UFO "identified", revealing the secret messages that were imparted from 1967 onward behind its "rejection of explanation."

11 UFO, 'Urboeffimeri avvenenti 1:1', *Marcatrè*, no. 41-42, June 1968, pp. 52-73.

VIETATO
ENTRARE

HIST
1 ORY

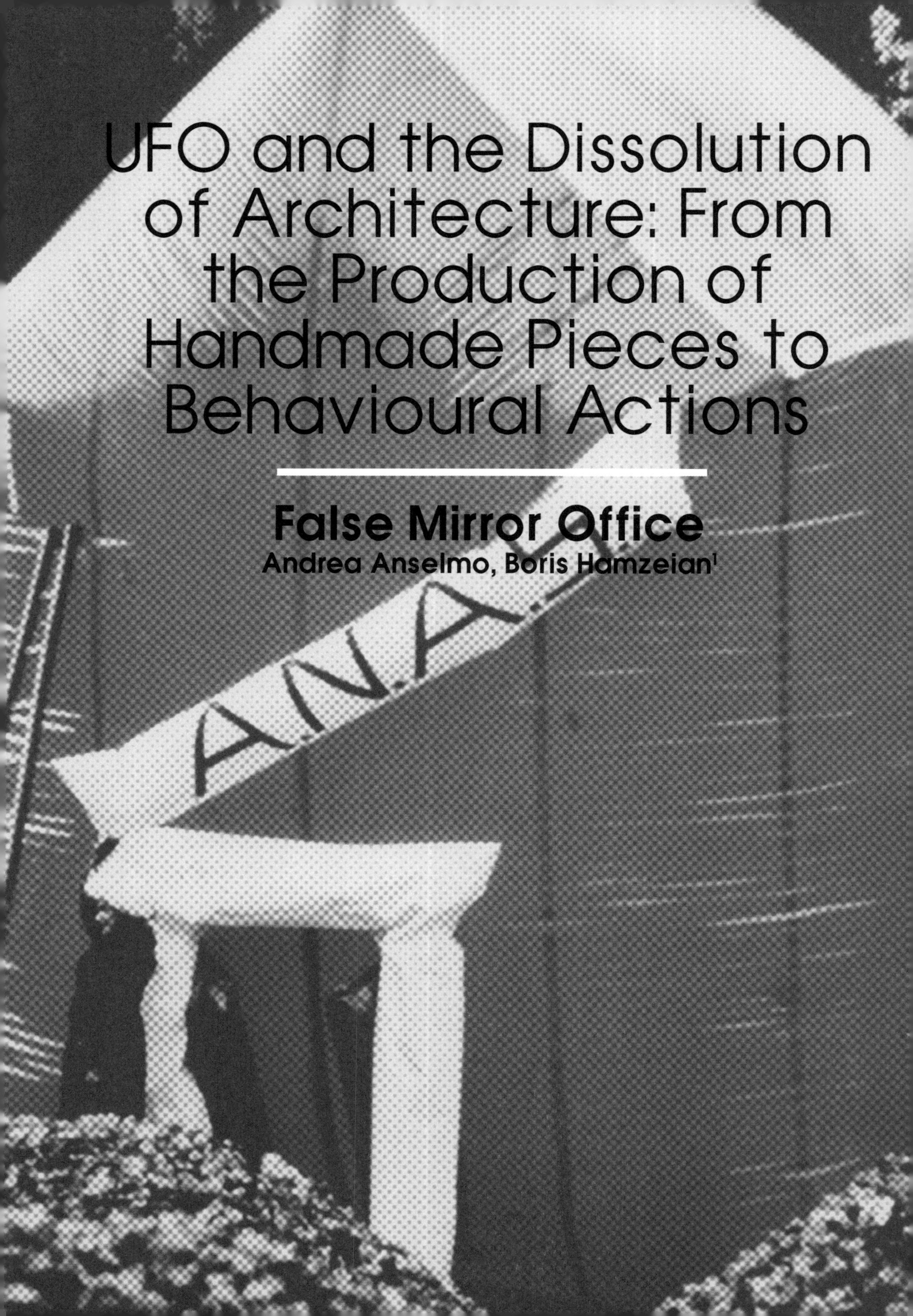

UFO and the Dissolution of Architecture: From the Production of Handmade Pieces to Behavioural Actions

False Mirror Office

Andrea Anselmo, Boris Hamzeian[1]

1 Chapters 1, 2, 5, 6 and 8 are by Anselmo while the introduction and chapters 3, 4, 7, 9 and 10 are by Hamzeian. The authors would like to thank Beatrice Lampariello and Roberto Gargiani.

Between 1959 and 1961, Carlo Bachi, Lapo Binazzi, Patrizia Cammeo, Riccardo Foresi, and Titti Maschietto, who would go on to form the group known by the name of Unidentified Flying Object and more simply the acronym UFO, enrolled in the Faculty of Architecture at the University of Florence, engaged since the beginning of the sixties in a revision of the theoretical and practical foundations of architecture.

During the education of the future members of UFO, the Faculty had transformed into a dynamic and cutting-edge research platform: Gillo Dorfles set the last trends of contemporary artistic avant-gardes as a tool for architecture design; Umberto Eco attempted to fit architecture into his interpretation of reality as a complex system of signs and significances; Leonardo Savioli experimented with a kind of space centred on its use and on the perception of it by users. Conceived in an educational environment expected to teach the rudiments of design, all this research aimed at developing a form of architecture intended to supersede the assumptions of the Modern Movement and include more recent tendencies originated in literature and the visual arts. Traced by some young protagonists of the international debate like Hans Hollein and Archigram, this was the direction in which Florence was looking, first of all by some students a few years older than the future members of UFO, among them Andrea Branzi, Paolo Deganello, and Adolfo Natalini. From their experience as students to the experiments conducted by Archizoom and Superstudio from the mid-sixties onwards, the research developed by the future exponents of so-called Radical Architecture was destined to become an inescapable model for UFO's experiences.

The experiments conducted by Carlo Bachi, Lapo Binazzi, Patrizia Cammeo, Riccardo Foresi, and Titti Maschietto, between the constitution of UFO in the context of the occupation of the Faculty at the beginning of 1968 and their last intervention in Venice in the summer of 1978, followed in the footsteps of the research that Archizoom and Superstudio had carried out in an effort to under-

UFO, Inflatable A.N.A.S. roadhouse, Palazzo di San Clemente, Florence, 1970, Patrizia Cammeo/Riccardo Foresi Archives, Florence mine the fundamental principles of architecture. While this research would lead Archizoom to *Dressing Design* and Superstudio to the celebration of the *Fundamental Acts* of human life, for UFO it would entail the metamorphosis of architecture into interventions with peculiar objects that no longer had anything to do with the elements of architecture. At first, these were ephemeral pieces made by hand out of polyethylene and then inflated for manipulation in particular ways. Subsequently they were transformed into iconic pieces made of polyurethane and papier-mâché and drawn from the collective imagination, which were utilised for the construction of original environments/performances. Finally, they dissolved completely into actions intended to encourage the expression of individual creativity.

The fact of resorting to procedures that ranged from the production of devices with open meanings to aggregations of human bodies in action, but always on the assumption that architecture is never a creative act but a combination of existing elements—be they artisanal artefacts or modes of behaviour—is perhaps the most distinctive aspect of the course taken by UFO. Through this peculiar course, UFO stood out in the context of the aim shared by all the exponents of Radical Architecture, the dissolution of architecture.

Bachi, Binazzi, Cammeo, Foresi, and Maschietto's Education: Beyond Architecture

The formative experiences of each of the future members of UFO represent the premise for the construction of the group's world of references and already reflect interests that went beyond architecture. In the sixties, in fact, Florence was part of a cultural revolution that had started in art and gone on to involve literature and the nascent studies of communication theory and semiotics, following a line of research that would also embrace architecture. Hence the young students at the Florentine Faculty of Architecture were prompted to look to experimental forms of architecture, such as those of Archigram, Utopie, and Hans Hollein, leading to the formation, just over a year before that of UFO, of the Archizoom and Superstudio groups, which would go on to become celebrated exponents of Radical Architecture. For these protagonists of the neo-avant-garde, the mass culture that was reappraised by artists and theorists at the turn of the sixties[2] became a source for the definition of an alternative form of architecture that would challenge the traditional assumptions of design and construction. Carlo Bachi, Lapo Binazzi, Patrizia Cammeo, Riccardo Foresi, and Titti Maschietto would begin, in the early sixties, to shape an imagery of their own through figures drawn from the world of cartoons, tele-

2 For the distinction between "high culture" and "popular culture", and the emerging concept of "mass culture" see Umberto Eco, *Apocalittici e integrati* (Milan: Bompiani, 1964).

vision and cinema, glossy magazines, and politics. These included protagonists of comic strips (Mickey Mouse, Flash Gordon, and the Phantom) and fables (Little Red Riding Hood, Alice in Wonderland, the Wizard of Oz), a number of TV and glossy magazine celebrities (the man who performed the first heart transplant—Christiaan Barnard—and his patient Philip Blaiberg, the Kennedy family and Pope Paul VI) and icons of international politics (Che Guevara, Fidel Castro, Mao Zedong, Ho Chi Minh, and one of the leader of the German student movement, Rudi Dutschke).

In the youthful experiences and personal interests of the future members of UFO we can already recognise what were going to be the fundamental themes of the group's work. Binazzi's passion for the cinema, which led him to organise film clubs, one for the regional branch of a trade union, and one for students called *I sabati dello studente*, and Cammeo's enthusiasm for epic films and their sets.[3] Then there was the interest in literature. Maschietto loved hermetic poetry and Samuel Beckett's Theatre of the Absurd, while Binazzi's was interested in existentialist literature—something instilled in him by his secondary school professor, the hermetic poet Mario Luzi—and in political commentary like that of the magazine *La Cina*—discovered through his father, a card-carrying and engaged member of the Communist Party.[4] All the members shared a passion for the irreverent poems of the group called the Novissimi, for the experimentalism of James Joyce's *Ulysses* and *Finnegans Wake*, and for the literary experiments of the Gruppo 63.[5] Another element that left an incisive mark on UFO was the active participation of its future members in artistic experimentation. Bachi joined the circle of figurative painters that gravitated around Giuseppe Bartolini, Gianfranco Ferroni, and Sandro Luporini,[6] before going on to specialise in photography.[7] Foresi practised drawing and painting in tempera in an expressionistic and sensual style that held a dialogue with the motifs of Ossianic poetry, such as wild landscapes, tombs, and death.[8] Maschietto experimented with Action Painting on expanded polystyrene and was so enthusiastic about contemporary American artistic experiences that, in the autumn of 1967, spent a long time in New York, where he visited Andy Warhol's Factory, discovering his feature films and pop silkscreens, as well as the happenings of Allan Kaprow and Claes Oldenburg. Right from their years of study, in addition to their interests in painting, the future members of UFO made objects by hand. Foresi and Cammeo produced jewellery by welding, bending, and sculpting metal;[9] Binazzi made wooden and metal furniture for shops and homes; finally, Maschietto had some experience of the way floats were constructed for the Viareggio Carnival[10] thanks to his father, who held the post of its vice president for years.

3 The information on the early years of the future members of UFO has been collected through a series of interviews with Binazzi, Cammeo and Maschietto: Patrizia Cammeo and Titti Maschietto, conversation with Gloria Castellini and Boris Hamzeian, 11 October 2019; Lapo Binazzi, conversation with Andrea Anselmo, 23 February 2020; Lapo Binazzi, conversation with Beatrice Lampariello, 19 March 2021; Titti Maschietto, conversation with Gloria Castellini, 22 May 2021; Patrizia Cammeo, conversation with Andrea Anselmo, 8 April 2022.

4 Binazzi took part in and organised the cultural activities of the Youth Federation of the Italian Communist Party in Florence.

5 See Umberto Eco, 'Dalla summa al Finnegans Wake. Le poetiche di Joyce', in Eco, *Opera aperta* (Milan: Bompiani, 1962), pp. 215-361; this chapter from the first edition of *Opera aperta* was not included in the English translation and has been published separately, as *The Aesthetics of Chaosmos: The Middle Ages of James Joyce* (Cambridge, MA: Harvard University Press, 1989). See too Alfredo Giuliani (ed.), *I Novissimi: poesie per gli anni '60* (Milan: Rusconi e Paolazzi, 1961). Many of the Novissimi writers would join the Gruppo 63. On these themes see Giovanni Galli's essay in this volume.

6 In the sixties these artists, and Ferroni in particular, were close to the current known as "Nuova figurazione." See Pia Ferrari and Sonia Paini (eds.), *La Nuova Figurazione: dagli anni Cinquanta agli anni Settanta nelle collezioni bresciane* (Brescia: AAB, 2006).

7 Biographical information on Bachi, who died in December 1991, is limited. We know that he was involved in the photographic documentation of the flood in Florence and the student protests of 1968 that would be published in the book Carlo Bachi, Nicola Bovoli, Riccardo Mariani and Giovanni Spinoso (eds.), *Firenze Piazza San Marco 30 gennaio 1968. Libro Bianco* (Florence: Cooperativa Libraria, 1968). His interest in the world of the performing arts would lead to him playing the part of Jesus Christ in Paolo Benvenuti's film *Il bacio di Giuda* (1988).

A decisive contribution to shaping the interests of the group came from some courses taught at the Faculty of Architecture in Florence by Gillo Dorfles and then Umberto Eco[11] on language and communication in the visual arts. The former was attended by Binazzi and Maschietto, and the latter by all the future members of UFO. It was through these courses that the young students acquired the basic tools for an understanding of society in the age of mass communication, seen as a producer of "new myths and new rites."[12] It was from their reading of Dorfles's writings that Bachi, Binazzi, Cammeo, Foresi, and Maschietto grasped the artistic potential of the use of new forms of visual language—like the comic strip, advertising, and the cinema—discovered kitsch, and realised the importance of aspects like perception and ambiguity in the relationship between the artwork and its viewer.[13] In Eco's lectures on the semiotics of visual communications, on the other hand, architecture was presented as "a system of signs" to be transformed and enriched to produce a design endowed with more than one meaning and therefore open to different interpretations.

Avant-garde literature and the works of some members of Gruppo 63, viewed from the perspective of Eco's lectures and the magazine *Marcatrè*, where Dorfles and Eco were on the editorial staff, proved to be decisive in showing the future members of UFO the possibility of a different kind of architecture.[14] Eco's semiotics, whose lectures were published in July 1967 in the book *Appunti per una semiologia delle comunicazioni visive*,[15] were studied in depth by the future members of UFO, to the point where Binazzi was persuaded to teach courses in semiotics at the Accademia d'Arte Leonetto Cappiello in Florence.[16] Binazzi's underlinings and annotations in his copy of the *Appunti* show his interest in making semiotics a discipline that "applied" to architecture, but not necessarily along the lines advocated by Eco. According to Binazzi, Eco was proposing a traditional genre of architecture from which the future members of UFO would soon distance themselves.[17] Binazzi was more interested in the passages of the *Appunti* that illustrate the mechanisms behind the codes of the avant-garde visual arts, which he intended to "master."[18] And he understood that to generate "polysemous messages" and therefore ones "open" to ever different interpretations it was necessary to define a "repertoire of symbols" with high degrees of "ambiguity," "redundancy," and "complication."[19] It was only through these semiological procedures that Binazzi thought it possible to modify the pre-established linguistic codes of architecture and the ideologies that they represented, in a strategy that was destined to provide a backdrop to the whole of UFO's work.[20]

8 See the pamphlet titled *Foresi Riccardo, Rilievo I, 1957* (Patrizia Cammeo/Riccardo Foresi Archives, Florence).

9 Cammeo and Foresi carried out every stage in the process of making this jewellery, from the production of models in wood, clay and wax to the final phases of its working, apart from the casting. Cammeo still makes jewellery today, calling her pieces "Wearable Landscapes."

10 Maschietto learned to draw from the artist Uberto Bonetti, designer of the communication icons for the Viareggio Carnival. Photographs of the Viareggio Carnival can be found in Binazzi and Maschietto's Archives.

11 Dorfles taught the course of Decoration at the Faculty of Architecture from 1964 to 1966, when his place was taken by Eco, who remained there until 1969. Eco's course on the Semiotics of Visual Communication began in March 1967. See Gabriele Corsani, 'Premessa', in Gabriele Corsani and Marco Bini (eds.), *La Facoltà di Architettura di Firenze fra tradizione e cambiamento: atti del convegno di studi: Firenze, 29-30 aprile 2004* (Florence: Firenze University Press, 2007), pp. XV-XXVI: XX.

12 See Gillo Dorfles, *Nuovi riti, nuovi miti* (Turin: Giulio Einaudi Editore, 1965); and Roland Barthes, *Mythologies* (New York: Farrar, Straus and Giroux, 1972).

13 In Binazzi's library one can find the first edition of the book *Il Kitsch. Antologia del cattivo gusto*, (Milan: Gabriele Mazzotta, 1968); in Maschietto's one can find the first editions of: *Simbolo, comunicazione, consumo* (1962), *Nuovi riti, nuovi miti* (1965), and *Artificio e natura* (1968); and Cammeo and Foresi's library contains the book *Le oscillazioni del gusto* (Milan: Lerici, 1966).

14 Among the members of Gruppo 63 whose writings were published in *Marcatrè* were Nanni Balestrini, Alfredo Giuliani, Elio Pagliarani, Antonio Porta, and Edoardo Sanguineti. See Dorfles, *Nuovi riti, nuovi miti*, pp. 210-211.

The Invention of "Usage-tools" for an Amplified Perception

The future members of UFO were given their first opportunities for experimentation with design by a series of exams and competitions over the years 1966 and 1967. As with the teachings of Dorfles and Eco, the themes tackled by two of the Faculty's professors of Composition, Elements of Architecture, and Urbanism, Leonardo Ricci and Leonardo Savioli, would have a decisive influence on the future members of UFO's approach to the design of architecture. It was in the light of Ricci's research into the scale of the city and the territory, and following the example of the projects for megastructures and visionary cities drawn up in the Faculty by other fellow students,[21] that Cammeo, Foresi, and Maschietto, who had formed what they called a "Gruppo Omogeneo" ("Homogeneous Group"),[22] chose to focus on the project of a new city to be laid out amongst the hills of Chianti.[23] The decision to combine an urban program with residences and services in a single building of a linear shape defined as a "macrostructure,"[24] together with the choice to locate it in an area given over to one of Tuscany's most important products, wine, turned the project into a means of criticising the intensive exploitation of the Chianti hills. Historically divided into plots occupied by different crops, the area had by this time been taken over by an increasingly intensive and monocultural form of cultivation. The Gruppo Omogeneo proposed a project that was intended as a denunciation of the industrial production of wine and the exploitation of the countryside with its definitive invasion by industry. And it is precisely by its critical nature that the macrostructure in Chianti revealed its descent from another city, the *Città Estrusa* ("Extruded City"), conceived by some of the future members of Archizoom and Superstudio.[25] The difference between the *Città Estrusa* and the macrostructure in Chianti lay in the Gruppo Omogeneo's choice to give its linear city a sinuous form, so that it could blend in with the hills on the model of Le Corbusier's *Plan Obus*.[26] That sinuous form distanced the Gruppo Omogeneo's macrostructure from the image of the assembly line pursued in the *Città Estrusa* and made it an expression of a territory whose spell Cammeo, Foresi, and Maschietto seem still to have been under, as if they wished to redeem it through a form that set out to replicate its natural topography.[27]

The possibility of intervening in the territory through a kind of architecture like the macrostructure remained an isolated experience for the future members of UFO, and its surpassing was connected with Savioli's teaching. After experimenting with the potentialities of a "macro" project, he began in the second half of the sixties to break down that sort of design into prefabricated and temporary structures that could therefore be dismantled, like the ones that were being tried out for the Universal Exhibitions in Brussels and Mon-

15 See Umberto Eco, *Appunti per una semiologia delle comunicazioni visive* (Milan: Bompiani, 1967). The third section of the book would be republished in Umberto Eco, 'Proposte per una semiologia dell'architettura', *Marcatrè*, no. 34-36, December 1967, pp. 58-76; and in Umberto Eco, *La struttura assente* (Milan: Bompiani, 1968).

16 Binazzi would give several lectures on Semiotics and the Psychology of Advertising at the Accademia Leonetto Cappiello in the first few months of 1968. Lapo Binazzi, *Curriculum Vitae*, 1974 (Lapo Binazzi Archives, Florence).

17 In this connection see Galli's essay in this volume. Binazzi's copy of the *Appunti* is annotated in sections "A" and "B" which deal with "general semiotics" and "visual messages," and not in "Section C" devoted to architecture. With respect to Eco's reflections on architecture in section "C," Binazzi noted: "it's not true at all," "the variations are infinite." See Eco, *Appunti per una semiologia delle comunicazioni visive*, p. 196 (Lapo Binazzi Archives, Florence).

18 Eco, *Appunti per una semiologia*, p. 148.

19 Eco, *Appunti per una semiologia*, pp. 10, 21 and 53.

20 Binazzi underlined forcefully the sentence: "Any real subversion of ideological expectations is effective to the extent to which *it is done in messages that also subvert the systems of rhetorical expectations and every profound subversion of rhetorical expectations is also a reduction in ideological expectations.* And it is on this principle that avant-garde art is based (...) when (...) it makes it necessary to reconsider in the crisis of the code the crisis of the ideologies with which it is identified." Eco, *Appunti per una semiologia*, p. 87.

21 These urban proposals on a large scale, as well as the association of students in groups, were the result of the revision of teaching practices following the student protests of 1963. On this subject see Roberto Gargiani, *Archizoom associati, 1966-1974. Dall'onda pop alla superficie neutra* (Milan: Electa, 2007), p. 8.

treal.[28] In the framework of the Interior Design course, followed by Bachi[29] (among the assistants were the future members of Superstudio and Archizoom Adolfo Natalini and Paolo Deganello), these temporary structures became the means for the definition of a "space of involvement" in which people were both "users" and "operators" participating in the construction of their own living environment. The conception of this kind of space passed through "pop processes" borrowed from contemporary artistic experimentation—from magnification to contamination and assemblage—and from the semiotic research crystallised by Eco in his *Open Work*.[30]

Temporary structures for the construction of an environment in which human beings can be "users" and "operators" became the decisive ingredients in a series of projects drawn up sometimes by Foresi and Cammeo, at others by Maschietto, but always with Marco Dezzi Bardeschi, Savioli's assistant:[31] the project for the competition for the seat of the National Centre of the Crafts in the Fortezza da Basso, in Florence, announced in January 1967, drawn up by Foresi and Cammeo in the group led by Dezzi Bardeschi;[32] Maschietto's project for the course of Restoration taught by Piero Sanpaolesi with the assistance of Dezzi Bardeschi;[33] and finally the project drawn up by Foresi in the group headed by Dezzi Bardeschi for the competition for the design of the Italian section of the 14th Milan Triennale, announced in August 1967.[34] The collaboration with Dezzi Bardeschi proved decisive in orienting the interests of Cammeo, Foresi, and Maschietto towards an architecture of involvement that spilled over into festivities, like at the funfair, but with a critical value. So a route was installed in the Fortezza da Basso that took the form of a rollercoaster linking the different parts of the project located in the fort and then emerging from it to connect up with the city. It too turned into a playful event

22 The group was made up of around thirty students, including Edoardo Negroni, Gianfranco Gorelli and Houchang Amirpour.

23 Cammeo and Maschietto, conversation with Castellini and Hamzeian. No record of the project has been found. Cammeo and Maschietto say they had made large models out of wood, plaster and cardboard.

24 Ibid. The term macrostructure was linked to some of Ricci and Savioli's works and in particular Ricci's building called *La Nave* ("The Ship"), in the district of Sorgane (1962-1966). See Giovanni Bartolozzi, *Leonardo Ricci: nuovi modelli urbani* (Macerata: Quodlibet, 2013), pp. 19-20; and Emiliano Romagnoli, *Leonardo Ricci: un pensiero che si fa spazio* (Macerata: Quodlibet, 2021), pp. 48-49, 101.

25 The provocative aspects of the intervention were explained by Maschietto (conversation with Castellini). For the *Città Estrusa* project (1964), drawn up by some of the future members of Archizoom and Superstudio (Cristiano Toraldo di Francia, Andrea Branzi, Gilberto Corretti, Massimo Morozzi, Alì Navai, Sergio Pastorini, and Pietro Spagna), see Gargiani, *Archizoom associati, 1966-1974. Dall'onda pop alla superficie neutra*; and Roberto Gargiani and Beatrice Lampariello, *Superstudio* (Rome: Laterza, 2010), p. 3. The idea of the linear city as megastructure was adopted in the same years by a group of students, among them

1. Marco Dezzi Bardeschi, Francesco Cafarella, Pierluigi Pieralli, Mario Bertolà, Gianni Cacciarini, Gianfranco Censini, Riccardo Foresi, and Patrizia Cammeo, Competition project for the seat of the National Centre of the Crafts in the Fortezza da Basso, Florence, *Ouroboros*, 1967

thanks to the presence of "facilities for play and leisure (merry-go-rounds, funfairs, Las Vegas, etc.)"[35]—*Ouroboros*, the rollercoaster that looped back on itself, also became the motto of the project (fig. 1).[36] The various activities, revolving around the crafts, play, and recreation,[37] were contained in primary volumes—a pyramid and a sphere—embedded in a three-dimensional metal structure or "(permanent) primary matrix" as the report put it,[38] on the model of the ones conceived by Yona Friedman, Archigram, and the Metabolism Group. If the playful event was re-created in the *Ouroboros* through metal structures, the sphere, the pyramid, and routes turned into rollercoasters, in the other projects drawn up over the course of 1967 Maschietto and Foresi made use of means of mass communication to offer the user completely new and alternative perceptions of reality. Thus Maschietto's project for the course of Restoration, drawn up together with members of the Gruppo Omogeneo, became an opportunity to propose the restoration not of historic buildings, but of the perception of people, and in particular tourists, who were invading Florence in ever greater numbers for a "rapid consumption" of the city—not coincidentally *Restauro dell'utenza* ("Restoration of the User") was the name given to the project.[39] There was no room for any building in the project of Maschietto and his fellow students because what interested them was the concept of "usage-tools" scattered around the city in such a way as to trigger different sensory stimuli in people, as if they too wished to participate in the "bombardment by the mass media."[40] Imagined as "a physical extension of the work of art onto the user,"[41] they were conceived not through an act of invention, but through the recovery of existing figures modified by means of those pop operations that Savioli was developing in his course (magnification and transposition of the figure into new materials and technologies—polyethylene, polystyrene and polyurethane, projections, and mobile components that could be assembled). Thus the "Attic base" and the "Corinthian capital" were imagined in polyurethane and PVC, while works of Optical Art and by artists like Warhol, Christo, and Jeanne-Claude generated "distorting mirrors," "serial reproductions," *empaquetage monumental*, and "urboTUBO" (figs. 2-3). All participated in the construction of what was intended to be a "great modern circus, an extension of the media."[42] The words of Maschietto and his fellow students make clear the objective of the project, which they wanted to act as a "disturbance and demystification of the city's rites and myths" and therefore of mass tourism in Florence. So the "bombardment by the mass media" in which the usage-tools were supposed to take part became a critical means of creating another reality. The idea of intervening in what existed through devices of semiotic disturbance,[43] which owed such a debt to Dorfles's lectures that it adopted the title of one of his essays (*Nuovi riti, nuovi miti*),

Sandro Gioli—a future member of UFO for the year 1968 alone—for a project of regeneration of the district of San Frediano, drawn up with Remo Buti, Riccardo Corazzi, V. Sasia, and Riccardo Segoni for Savioli's Urbanism II course in 1965-1966. See Patrizia Mello, *Firenze e le avanguardie Radicali* (Florence: DIDA Press, 2017), pp. 82-83, 121-123.

26 Cammeo and Maschietto have indicated the books and works of Le Corbusier, including the Ville Radieuse and the Unité d'Habitation, as important references for the macrostructure in Chianti and for their formation. Cammeo and Maschietto, conversation with Castellini and Hamzeian. This interest was shared by Binazzi, who was struck not only by the visit he paid to the exhibition on Le Corbusier held at Palazzo Strozzi in 1963, but also by the Unité d'Habitation in Marseille, which he went to see. Binazzi, conversation with Lampariello.

27 This interest in the territory is attested by the presence of some books on the subject in Cammeo and Foresi's library, including Giuseppe Susani (ed.), *Scienza e progetto* (Padua: Marsilio, 1967) and the Italian edition of William Alonso, *Location and Land Use: Toward a General Theory of Land Rent* (Cambridge, MA: Harvard University Press, 1964).

28 In addition to the discotheques known as Pipers, "the seminar of research and documentation" of the course of Interior Design was devoted to the exhibitions in Montreal, Brussels, and Lausanne. (Leonardo Savioli), *Corso di Architettura degli interni I, anno acc. 1966-1967*, n.p. (Archivio di Stato di Firenze, Fondo Leonardo Savioli, Florence).

29 Bachi is listed among the students attending the course but nothing is known of his project. See the *Elenco studenti corso architettura degli interni* (Archivio di Stato di Firenze, Fondo Leonardo Savioli, Florence).

30 Leonardo Savioli and Adolfo Natalini, 'Spazio di Coinvolgimento', *Casabella*, no. 326, 1968, pp. 32-45: 32, 34; Leonardo Savioli (ed.), *Ipotesi di Spazio* (Florence: G&G, 1972). For the reference to Eco's "open work" see (Leonardo

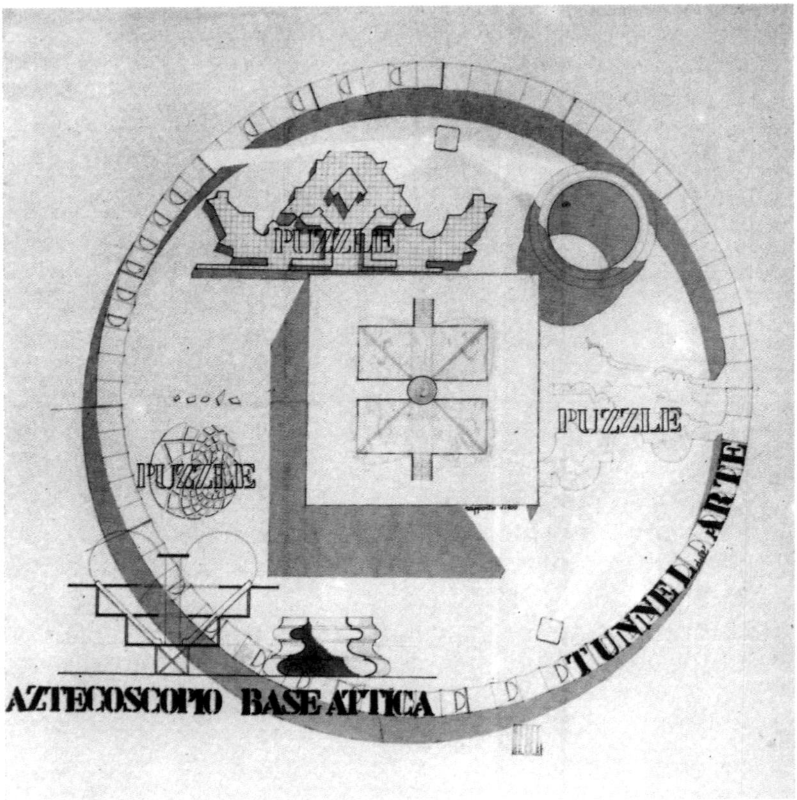

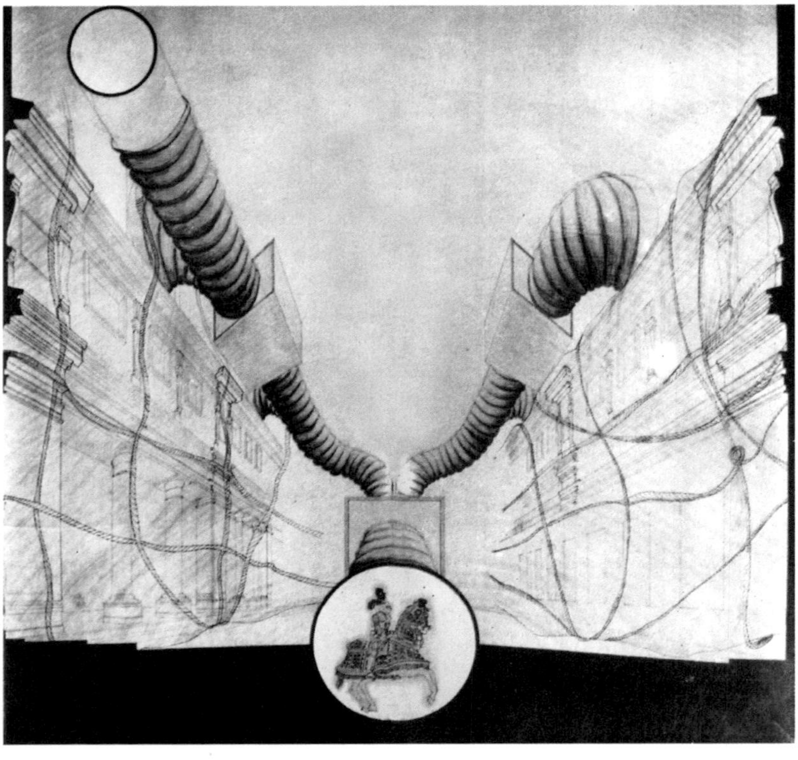

2-3. Houchang Amirpour, Rodolfo Bracci, Gianfranco Gorelli, and Titti Maschietto, Course in Restoration, *Il restauro dell'utenza*, 1967

was destined to guide the experimentation of the group over the following years.[44]

The last act in the formative experiences of the future members of UFO was effected in Foresi's project for the design of the Italian section of the 14th Milan Triennale. The usage-tools were now condensed into an "acculturating machine" conceived to re-educate human beings and turn them into disalienated "users" aware of the risks posed by monopoly of the means of production and communication.[45] The machine consisted of "pneumatic organs" made of PVC with a markedly erotic character (two "mammillary containers" and a "peristaltic tube" with a blow-up of the mouth of the protagonist of the erotic comic strip *The Adventures of Jodelle* as a backdrop[46]), each designed to carry out a process of "washing of inhibitions," "identification," "understanding," and "fixing of memory" with the aim of "acculturating" the visitors to the "most decisive contradictions" of contemporary society. The user was forced to enter the machine, channelled into it by two barriers: a pile of wrecked cars and a colossal papier-mâché washing machine which is "evidently handmade" (fig. 4).[47] The criticism of bombardment by the media in mass society that relied on a complex process in the acculturating machine would be reduced, in the pavilion devoted to "Italian expressions and productions," to a single means of communication and some pieces of furniture and decorative objects, assembled to symbolise "The Minimum for Survival" in the contemporary era.[48] In a space enclosed by a transparent curtain with vertical stripes on which an image of Jodelle's

Savioli), *Relazione sul significato del Piper. Corso interni 66/67*, n.d., p. 7 (Archivio di Stato di Firenze, Fondo Leonardo Savioli, Florence). In this document we read: "In this new space the user has to be operator and receiver at the same time: Piper open work. U. Eco: open work is form made up of a constellation of elements (we have said objects) in which the observer (we have said user) identifies through a precise choice his inclination in all directions, senses, ways."

31 Dezzi Bardeschi worked on Savioli's project for Sorgane. See Marco Dezzi Bardeschi, 'Leonardo Savioli. Una metodologia di progettazione', *Marcatrè*, no. 26-29, December 1966, pp. 36-71.

32 Although Cammeo and Foresi do not appear in the project report, their participation is attested by Cammeo. Patrizia Cammeo, conversation with Gloria Castellini, 24 June 2021. See Marco Dezzi Bardeschi, Francesco Cafarella, Pierluigi Pieralli, Mario Bertolà, Gianni Cacciarini and Gianfranco Censini, 'Ouroboros', in *Per la nuova sede della Mostra dell'Artigianato alla Fortezza da Basso. L'esito del concorso nazionale di idee per la Fortezza da Basso. 12 Progetti per la Fortezza da Basso* (Florence: Arti Grafiche Giorgi & Gambi, 1968).

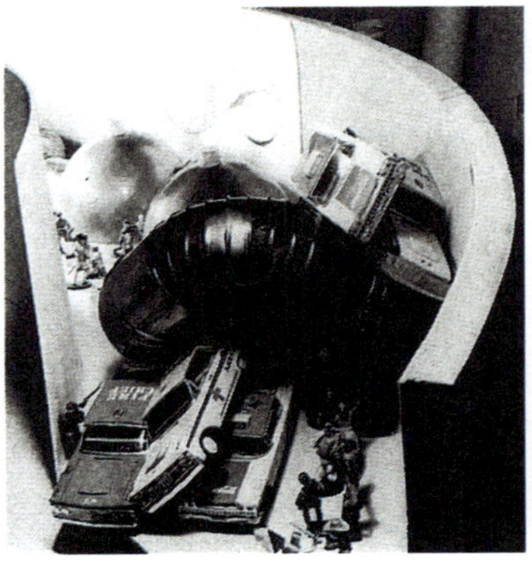

4. Marco Dezzi Bardeschi, Gianfranco Censini, and Riccardo Foresi, Competition project for the design of the Italian section of the 14th Milan Triennale, *La macchina acculturante*, 1967-1968

5-6. Marco Dezzi Bardeschi, Gianfranco Censini, and Riccardo Foresi, Installation for the pavilion of "Italian expressions and productions" in the Parco Sempione at the 14th Milan Triennale, *Il minimo per sopravvivere*, 1968

mouth was printed, stood a television set, framed by a visual cone with an Op Art decoration, topped by a souvenir gondola and faced by an office chair (figs. 5-6).

In the passage from the macrostructure to the usage-tools and acculturating machines, the future members of UFO had already grasped the possibility of interventions that, no longer ascribable to the traditional sense of architecture and building, became handmade and temporary objects for the perception of human beings now elevated to the status of active users.

Unidentified Flying Object: Inflatable Objects for a Collective Participation

In December 1967, Binazzi, Foresi, and Maschietto, soon to be joined by Cammeo and then Bachi, at the time all still students, started to think about the possibility of working together on joint projects.[49] Against the background of their common fascination with the cinematic medium, and even before formally constituting UFO group,[50] its future members made a several hours long film based on static shooting of everyday activities in the entrance hall of the Palazzo di San Clemente at the Faculty of Architecture in Florence.[51] In an experiment inspired by the long film that Warhol had made a few years earlier to capture the imperceptible changes in perception of the Empire State Building produced by the weather and the passage of time, the future members of UFO laid the foundations for a reflection that would underpin all the experiences of the following years, culminating eventually in their rejection of drawing.[52] Instead of going in for the usual student practice of the architectural competition, the future members of UFO joined up to record the use of a space with an act that, as avid

33 Cammeo and Maschietto, conversation with Castellini and Hamzeian.

34 Marco Dezzi Bardeschi, Gianfranco Censini and Riccardo Foresi, 'Proposta per il concorso per l'allestimento della sezione italiana alla XIV Triennale di Milano', in Carlo Guenzi, 'Una selezione difficile', *Casabella*, no. 325, June 1968, pp. 4-21: 9. For the results see 'Programma (15 maggio-14 luglio 1968, XIV Triennale, "Il grande numero", Milano)', *Casabella*, no. 323, February 1968, pp. 62-64.

35 Dezzi Bardeschi, Cafarella, Pieralli, Bertolà, Cacciarini and Censini, 'Ouroboros', p. 12.

36 Ibid.

37 Ibid.

38 Dezzi Bardeschi, Cafarella, Pieralli, Bertolà, Cacciarini and Censini, 'Ouroboros', p. 11.

39 "Do we in this way run the risk of consuming the work of art like a hit pop song just because we have the direct possibility of playing it ourselves? It is not a risk because an open work always presents a functional alternative. In any case you won't find us mourning the death of art." Houchang Amirpour, Rodolfo Bracci, Gianfranco Gorelli and Titti Maschietto, 'Il restauro dell'utenza', *Marcatrè*, no. 46-49, October 1968, pp. 52-71: 59.

40 Ibid.

7. UFO, Photography, Faculty of Architecture of University of Florence, February-April 1968, Patrizia Cammeo/Riccardo Foresi Archives, Florence

admirers of Eco's semiotic ideas, has to be understood as a preparatory analysis of its complex system of signs and meanings—the same space that a few weeks later they were going to alter with the creation of those usage-tools that Foresi and Maschietto had only been able to imagine up until that moment.

The transition from observation of the space to its physical and semiotic alteration was made possible by the occupation of the Faculty of Architecture. From 23 January to 24 April 1968, the courses were interrupted by alternative activities that involved students and professors, and that included a debate over the broadening of the right to higher education and a complete refounding of the modes and content of teaching that also involved the inclusion of social and political issues in the programme of study (fig. 7).[53] These aspirations shifted the still conceptual and artistic research that had led to the experiment of filming the entrance hall of San Clemente towards more engaged forms of intervention, remote even from the ones tried out in competitions and university projects over the course of 1967. The idea put forward by the General Assembly of students, held in the occupied Faculty, of carrying out an "analysis of the use of the territory by capital," the basic theme of the research to be undertaken for a new approach to teaching, induced Binazzi, Cammeo, Foresi, and Maschietto to view the city and the surrounding region as the theatre for exploitation on the part of capitalist power.[54]

With these premises, Binazzi, Cammeo, Foresi, and Maschietto, now joined by Bachi and, for a limited period, by fellow students like Sandro Gioli, Massimo Giovannini, and Mario Spinella, in concomitance with the start of the debate by the student Assembly at the beginning of February, set up a site for the production of special objects in the Faculty.[55] The decision to go for objects might be seen as reflecting an interest in industrial design on the part of the future members of UFO. However, the group made it clear right from the launch of their "construction site" that those objects were to be on a large scale—"macro-dimension" and "life-size" were the terms offered by Maschietto—in order to tackle architecture and the city but without replicating their form and substance.[56] That the objects of the San Clemente construction site had nothing to do with industrial design, as the discipline was emerging in the Italy of the economic boom, is also evident from the idea of making them by hand in the Faculty, out of papier-mâché and sheets of polyethylene held together with sticky tape to produce objects which could be inflated by pumping air into them. Following in the footsteps of Foresi and Maschietto's usage-tools, UFO was creating a kind of object whose handmade character was poles apart from mass-produced industrial ob-

41 Amirpour, Bracci, Gorelli and Maschietto, 'Il restauro dell'utenza', p. 58.

42 "The great modern circus, an extension of the media, is Montreal: we are proposing it monographically on art and on a Florentine scale." Ibid.

43 "Our proposal, our intervention hinge on the presentation of some examples of usage-tools at the semiotic rather than constructive level." Ibid.

44 Dorfles, *Nuovi riti, nuovi miti.*

45 Dezzi Bardeschi, Censini and Foresi, 'Proposta per il concorso per l'allestimento della sezione italiana alla XIV Triennale di Milano', p. 9.

46 Ibid. For the character of Jodelle see Guy Peellaert and Pierre Bartier, *The Adventures of Jodelle* (Seattle, WE: Fantagraphics Books, 2013).

47 Dezzi Bardeschi, Censini and Foresi, 'Proposta per il concorso per l'allestimento della sezione italiana alla XIV Triennale di Milano', p. 9.

48 Gianfranco Censini, Marco Dezzi Bardeschi and Riccardo Foresi, 'Il minimo per sopravvivere', in *Quattordicesima triennale di Milano: esposizione delle arti decorative industriali moderne dell'architettura moderna* (Milan: Arti grafiche Crespi & Occhipinti, 1968), pp. 134-135, LXV.

49 Cammeo and Maschietto, conversation with Castellini and Hamzeian. Binazzi, conversation with Lampariello.

50 Titti Maschietto, conversation with Boris Hamzeian, 23 April 2022.

51 The project was never completed due to a technical problem with the film used for the shooting. Cammeo and Maschietto, conversation with Castellini and Hamzeian.

52 Ibid.

53 For a first-hand account of the occupation of the Faculty see Maschietto's article in *Quindici*, a magazine founded against the background of the protests of 1968 and based on an idea of Gruppo 63. Vittorio Maschietto, 'Facoltà di

jects that were always identical and, in doing so, taking a stand against the capitalist system that manufactured them.[57] In any case, papier-mâché and polyethylene stuck together with adhesive tape had different characteristics. Papier-mâché allowed them to conceive works similar to those of the Viareggio Carnival floats or the magnified objects typical of American Pop Art, but finished and permanent.[58] Polyethylene, another material with which artistic and architectural avant-gardes were experimenting in those years for the production of works known to UFO,[59] offered the group the possibility of creating an intrinsically dynamic object. Its volume expanded and contracted on inflation and deflation, and even when under its greatest tension could be pushed around and manipulated. Not coincidentally, "pneumatic" was the term Foresi used for the inflatable PVC breasts of his acculturating machine, in an anatomical metaphor destined to recur several times in the production of the construction site in San Clemente.[60] While the example of the inflatable breasts might suggest that UFO was on the point of producing pop objects like the ones that made up the acculturating machine, the products of the San Clemente construction site were already something else. They were objects for an intervention that had nothing to do with the restoration of perception highlighted by Foresi and Maschietto's usage-tools. UFO now wanted to embark on militant and dissenting interventions of disturbance of spaces and the actions that traditionally took place in them—"major elements of disturbance and demystification of the city's rites and myths" was the definition that Maschietto took from the project for the *Restauro dell'utenza*.[61]

On the other hand, UFO members were moving towards a kind of object that they intended to be a break from pop icons and other figures of the collective imagination; an object that exploited the softness and malleability of the inflatable to lend itself to the free interpretation of whoever observed it, turning it into one of Eco's open works. UFO's decision to call it a "piece" reflected its nature as an indecipherable and unidentifiable fragment.[62] The absence of any iconography and thus the fact of their being "unidentified," together with their handmade and ephemeral character, which when the polyethylene was inflated allowed them to float, turned these pieces filled with air into Unidentified Flying Objects, or more simply UFOs. Stripped of its aerospace and science-fiction connotations, this was the name which Bachi, Binazzi, Cammeo, Foresi, and Maschietto gave not only to the objects from the San Clemente construction site but to their group as well. In this way they were able to leave the nature and objectives of the group and its work in suspense, just as had happened in the group's first collective experiment, the film in the entrance hall of San Clemente.[63] The identification of the group with its production may also have allud-

architettura di Firenze 85 giorni di occupazione', *Quindici*, no. 10, 15 April-15 May 1968, p. VI.

54 Maschietto, 'Facoltà di architettura di Firenze 85 giorni di occupazione'. On UFO's political engagement see too Jacopo Galimberti's essay in this volume.

55 A classmate of Binazzi's at secondary school, Gioli, is mentioned as a member of UFO in Lapo Binazzi, Lapo (sic) Cammeo, Riccardo Foresi, Sandro Gioli and Titti Maschietto, 'Effimero Urbanistico scala 1/1', *Marcatrè*, no. 37-40, May 1968, pp. 198-209: 198-199. In the next article in *Marcatrè*, Giovannini and Spinella were also included in the group: UFO, 'Urboeffimeri avvenenti 1:1', p. 53. UFO's nature as an open grouping in this early phase of its activity is confirmed by Binazzi and Gioli's participation in the blowing up of the model of Renata Galli's graduate thesis, together with Bracci, co-author of the *Restauro dell'utenza*, Francesco Pirera, and Alessandro Magris, future member of Superstudio. G. S., 'Scatenata a Firenze la repressione antistudentesca', *l'Unità*, no. 170, 26 June 1968, p. 5; 'Presidiata la procura generale per gli studenti', *l'Unità*, no. 171, 27 June 1968, p. 6.

56 "Since February a construction site has been opened in the Faculty itself: work is being done 'life-size' or on a macro-dimension with inflatable materials and papier-mâché. The pieces produced are dropped with surprise actions, as 'concrete' elements of rupture and disturbance, into the typical rites of the historic centre, such as afternoon shopping, the Sunday Mass-stroll, vehicular traffic and tourist itineraries." Maschietto, 'Facoltà di architettura di Firenze 85 giorni di occupazione'.

57 Ibid.

58 On the relations between the pieces from the construction site in San Clemente and the Viareggio Carnival see Beatrice Lampariello's essay in this volume.

59 On the genealogy of the pieces from the construction site in the artistic field see Alessandra Acocella's essay in this volume.

ed to the search for an interaction between object, creator, and user that would make the latter an integral part of the intervention.

It is likely that the first thing to be produced by the group now known as UFO was a promotional manifesto, put up in February to announce the opening of the construction site and invite students to take part.[64] Located in the entrance hall of San Clemente that was at the centre of the group's film, the manifesto took the form of a text written with a marker on strips of polyethylene similar to the ones in the installation proposed by Foresi for the Triennale.[65] Right from its name—*Giornale murario* ("Wall Newspaper") was the way it was presented to the press—the manifesto revealed its complex nature. In being a "newspaper" used to invite student participation and in the form of its support, it showed that its origin lay in the political manifestos that were being produced in those years and that the students of the Florentine Faculty of Architecture were themselves drawing up to incite their fellows to join the struggle. And yet instead of political slogans like the ones in the mural that Foresi painted on the university facade,[66] the *Giornale* was covered with letters and words that combined political content, mocking tones, and literary experimentation which owed a debt to the work of Gruppo 63 and the hermetic poetry dear to Binazzi and Maschietto.[67] Not so remote from what could be seen at the Viareggio Carnival since 1967, the juxtaposition of political slogans with ironic ones that took shape in the *Giornale murario* was destined to become a distinctive trait of UFO's production in the future.

Above and beyond its dimension as a text and manifesto, it was to architecture that the *Giornale murario* was addressed. As was underlined by its name, UFO wanted to associate the "newspaper" with a "wall," but in this case too it was an atypical wall given that the transparency of the polyethylene allowed people to see through it, while its division into strips allowed them to pass through as well. And so the refusal to deal with architecture that could be sensed in the film was now transformed into the idea of appealing to architecture but in order to turn it into something different from its traditional image and substance. In the *Giornale murario* this intention was made clear in the idea of transfiguring the wall into a curtain or—better still—a screen, whose role was to interact with users by means of the messages written on its surface and the shapes of people and the columns of the entrance hall that could be glimpsed through it. The change of tack represented by the *Giornale murario* was also a way stressing UFO's aim of doing away with modern architecture, considered mute ("atrophy of the objective" were the words written on the *Giornale murario*), in favour of an *architettura parlante* open to free interpretation by its observer in a dimension that was intended to be collective.

60 Dezzi Bardeschi, Censini and Foresi, 'Proposta per il concorso per l'allestimento della sezione italiana alla XIV Triennale di Milano', p. 9.

61 Maschietto, 'Facoltà di architettura di Firenze 85 giorni di occupazione'.

62 Ibid.

63 The first mentions of the acronym for the group, "U.F.O." and "ufo," were made in the article published in *Marcatrè* in May 1968. In some passages of the article the acronym seems to allude not only to the members of the group but also to their production. "WHAT THE UFOS ARE NOT AND WHAT THEY ARE," wrote UFO, "THEY ARE NOT FLYING SAUCERS, THEY ARE UNIDENTIFIED FLYING OBJECTS." UFO, 'Urboeffimeri avvenenti 1:1', p. 52.

64 The *Giornale murario* was published for the first time in *Marcatrè* in a version that only reproduced some parts of the text. Binazzi, Cammeo, Foresi, Gioli and Maschietto, 'Effimero Urbanistico scala 1/1', pp. 198-199. A different version of the *Giornale Murario* can be retraced in the photographs portraying the exhibition that UFO realised at the 14th Milan Triennale. See UFO, 'Urboeffimeri avvenenti 1:1', pp. 71-72.

65 Dezzi Bardeschi, Censini and Foresi, 'Proposta per il concorso per l'allestimento della sezione italiana alla XIV Triennale di Milano'.

66 On this see Lampariello's essay in this volume.

67 The sentences that make up the text are constructed using devices ranging from deformation of the phrase to its reduction to disjointed fragments that challenge the syntactic nature of conventional writing.

8-10. Carlo Bachi, Lapo Binazzi, Patrizia Cammeo, Riccardo Foresi, Sandro Gioli, and Titti Maschietto (UFO), *Urbanistic Ephemeron* (ephemera 1, 2, and 3), Palazzo di San Clemente, Florence, 12 February 1968

From the concerted conception of phrases and words written in different ways on its surface to the fact that it was possible to pass through it, and the peculiar optical effects produced by the semi-transparent polyethylene, the *Giornale murario* generated participatory interventions that had something to do with the production of the pieces, with their manipulation, and with their interaction with the space in which they were inserted—a sort of interaction that owed a debt to Savioli's teachings on the space of involvement.

After the *Giornale murario*, UFO devoted themselves to the production of pieces which turned the unexpected interactions that could be achieved with the space in which they were placed into actions of disturbance of the usability of that space. Thus UFO imagined an intervention to be located in the occupied Faculty again, on the occasion of the General Assembly of the students planned for 12 February.[68] Identified as the first "socio-urban rite and myth" to be undermined, the Assembly became an occasion on which to show the students an alternative strategy of struggle to the ideological and theoretical initiatives that were taking shape within the Assembly itself. UFO's intentions found expression in the production of an inflatable tube of white, semi-transparent polyethylene, 50 centimetres in diameter and 100 metres long, made out of the material used by the Pastucol company for the production of shopping bags.[69] The tube was kept in tension by sealing one end and inserting the nozzle of a vacuum cleaner with its function reversed into the other.

68 Maschietto, 'Facoltà di architettura di Firenze 85 giorni di occupazione'.

69 Binazzi, Cammeo, Foresi, Gioli and Maschietto, 'Effimero Urbanistico scala 1/1', pp. 200-201. Pastucol was owned by Gioli's brother-in-law.

On the morning of 12 February, the tube was unrolled on the floor of the entrance hall and then inflated until it took the form of a laby-

rinthine tangle (fig. 8). Made out of the same material as the *Giornale murario*, the tube made the transformation from manifesto to three-dimensional object. In its nature as a soft, semi-transparent cylinder, bent to adapt it to the space that contained it, the tube had an abstract form, lacking even the eloquent character that UFO had given to the *Giornale murario* through recourse to words. Rather than by the search for a figure, the choice of the tube was guided by the desire to find an element that would prevent people from crossing the entrance hall—an element used to disturb the very Assembly that was to be held a few hours later in the great hall on the upper floor of the Palazzo di San Clemente. In its nature as a barrier, the tube participated in the students action from which it originated, almost as if it were a symbolic representation of the occupation of the Faculty.

On the afternoon of 12 February, at that Assembly held in the great hall, two members of UFO proposed to their fellow students an alternative strategy of protest based on the concept of "operation and/or production" and, as a demonstration of it, brought the tube into the great hall. Passed from hand to hand over the students' heads, the tube hovered lightly in the air, interrupting the proceedings of the Assembly and confirming its efficacy as an element of disturbance (fig. 9). In its length and lack of handles, the tube became the protagonist of an atypical sequence of events that came close to that of the artistic performance.[70]

70 Binazzi, Cammeo, Foresi, Gioli and Maschietto, 'Effimero Urbanistico scala 1/1', pp. 202-203.

At a certain point someone pushed the still inflated tube out of the window and someone else went down to grab hold of it. With this act the Assembly was brought to an end; the students gathered in the street around the tube, and, just as had happened with the *Giornale murario*, it sparked spontaneous interventions. On its surface the students wrote a series of slogans, "Power to the Workers," "Control of Power," "Blackpower," "Hochiminh," and "Che," and in this way gave it a new identity.[71] As with the *Giornale murario*, the tube was turned into a special device that combined the engaged nature of a political manifesto and the playful character of literary word games or the popular ones broadcast on TV.

71 Binazzi, Cammeo, Foresi, Gioli and Maschietto, 'Effimero Urbanistico scala 1/1', p. 204.

The tube was carried through the streets of the city along a route that touched on the crucial points of the protest marches in order to generate an intervention of disturbance to its monuments and to the activities that were traditionally carried out in these places (fig. 10). With the appearance of the slogans and its passage through the streets, the tube was turned into an unusual kind of banner. Its unpredictable and irregular motion negated the disciplined character required by a banner, thereby destroying the orderly ritual of the march. Its place was taken by an alternative kind of organisation that upset the relationship between banner and march and in which the crowd, between the disorderly fluctuations of the tube and the pauses needed to re-inflate it, seemed to be guided by the tube.

Although activity at the San Clemente construction site would continue with the production of new pieces, the tube created on 12 February, between an unplanned manipulation and an abstract iconography open to different interpretations on the part of those who observed it, reflected a level of experimentation that would not be matched in subsequent production at the site.

The Figures of the "Ephemera" Between Icons and Words

After the tube, the members of UFO continued down the road of architecture transformed into an ephemeral intervention for open interpretation. Between March and May of 1968, the streets and squares in which protests were staged became the preferred location in which to parade three new pieces with the crowd, producing what the group described as "urbanistic terrorism."[72] Made for events that were going to last for several hours, these interventions offered the tube a new connotation, turning it into an icon that changed each time, depending on the message to be delivered. The abstraction that the tube still possessed was now adapted to serve as different symbols: a missile representing the American bombing under way in Vietnam (fig. 11), a dollar sign as an expression of contemporary capitalism (fig. 12), and Jodelle's mouth with a papier-mâché fork and inflatable spaghetti, to ridicule the ritual of Sunday lunch and denounce the "bingeing" of the Catholic church (fig. 13).[73] The transition from the abstraction of the tube to the icons marked a fundamental stage in the evolution of UFO's pieces that had to do with both their degree of interaction with the crowd and their nature as open works.

72 The term appeared in April, i.e. in coincidence with the start of production of the new series of pieces. Maschietto, 'Facoltà di architettura di Firenze 85 giorni di occupazione'. It returned in *Marcatrè*, in June, in the form of "terrorist urbanists." UFO, 'Urboeffimeri avvenenti 1:1', p. 52.

73 Cammeo and Maschietto, conversation with Castellini and Hamzeian.

From joint production on the construction site to their parading through the streets and squares of Florence and manipulation in front of the places of power to deliver political messages, UFO's new pieces continued to involve the crowd, but with a different degree of interaction. The atypical rhythm of the march that the tube had imposed with the pauses for its re-inflation were replaced by more orderly parades; the free and spontaneous manipulation that still occurred with the missile and the dollar sign gave way instead, in the *spaghettata*, to a kind of intervention that required a particular staging in order to convey the message

11-12. UFO, *Urboeffimero 5* and *6*, Florence, 26 April and 12 May 1968

13. Carlo Bachi, Lapo Binazzi, Patrizia Cammeo, Riccardo Foresi, Sandro Gioli, and Titti Maschietto (UFO), *Urbanistic Ephemeron* (ephemeron 4), Sagrato del Duomo, Florence, 5 March 1968

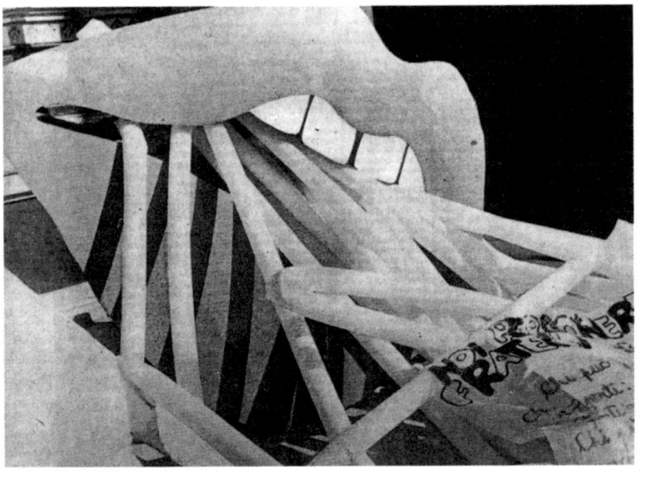

of "binge eating." Among the new pieces from the construction site, the *spaghettata* already paved the way for a sort of involvement of users that shifted from unplanned action towards actions not very different from the performances of contemporary art. The evolution that UFO's new pieces was undergoing also had something to do with their nature as objects used to disturb "socio-urban architectural rites and myths." If with the tube the disturbance had entailed interaction and the undermining of space, now that same disturbance was entrusted to the icons of the dollar sign, the missile, and the *spaghettata*. In UFO's works, the resort to icons also marked a limitation on the openness of the interpretation that had been sought in the abstraction of the tube, even though the new pieces continued to have an ambiguous character, halfway between an instrument of militancy and a playful object verging on the childish—not unlike the inflatable tube of lipstick mounted on a tank that Oldenburg would conceive in 1969 and which, like UFO's pieces, would attempt to combine the horror of war and the sensuality of Pop Art. However, those icons ensured the transmission of concepts and words as had been proposed by the *Giornale murario*—"architecture is language" was the message that UFO seems to have wanted to drum home with its pieces—along the same lines as another iconic and symbolic device that Robert Venturi and Denise Scott Brown would conceptualise in the years to come, that of the "duck."[74] In order to give the new pieces the nature of open works, UFO turned to the word, which was no longer limited to slogans written on the surface of the inflatable but included more complex forms of writing and texts to be drawn up following interventions.[75] And so between May and June, UFO reconstructed in the pages of *Marcatrè* the interventions relating to the production of the Florentine construction site through interpretations that ranged from the various attributions offered by the crowd during the parading of the pieces to ones proposed by UFO where the pieces assumed connotations that had to do with architecture and with the sensual and erotic dimension of the human body.[76]

The resemanticisation of the pieces in *Marcatrè* started from the definition of the intervention itself. UFO defined its pieces as *Urboeffimeri* ("Urban Ephemera"). The significance of the term *effimero* ("ephemeron") was twofold: it referred to the short duration of the intervention for which UFO's piece was used, but also to the nature of the intervention in the city with an "unidentified flying object."

Describing its inflation in the entrance hall of San Clemente in *Marcatrè*, UFO sought parallels between the tube and architecture, turning it into a "structural shape" that vied with the columns, to the point of attempting actual operations of "shoring and substi-

74 Robert Venturi, Denise Scott Brown and Steven Izenour, *Learning from Las Vegas* (Cambridge, MA: MIT Press, 1972), pp. 89-90.

75 In the missile and the dollar sign the surface of the piece continued to be the support for the written word, but in a more ironic and experimental fashion. The militant slogans that were typical of street protests in 1968 gave way to linguistic games poised between intellectualism and mockery that even sent up protest, finding the gall to translate the death of the Vietcong, the yoke of bourgeois imperialism and the control exercised over the media into mottos worthy of Eco: "Potele agli studenti," "pacco ti spacco," "Colgate con Vietcong," "giocagiocimin," and "magozurlinpiao." See UFO, 'Urboeffimeri avvenenti 1:1', p. 61.

76 Binazzi, Cammeo, Foresi, Gioli and Maschietto, 'Effimero Urbanistico scala 1/1'; UFO, 'Urboeffimeri avvenenti 1:1'.

tution" of those very columns.[77] In similar fashion, UFO rediscovered in the manipulation of the tube and its softness to the touch the erotic dimension that Foresi had bestowed on the acculturating machine. The tube was presented both as a phallus that, after a "first phase of stiffening," proceeded by "rubbing, pressing, wrinkling, poking, mounting" before reaching its "phase of maximum erection" and "penetrating the Mannerist pointed arches" of San Clemente's entrance hall, and as a "tube-foetus" that "evaginated at the big north window" of the great hall.[78] The search for new meanings of the tube in *Marcatrè* can also be traced in the recording of the descriptions that the crowd made of the tube as it passed through the city—"big snake," "Chinese dragon," "tube," "crap worm," "turd," "pop phallagogy," and "communists" were the names cited by UFO.[79] The narrative framework constructed in *Marcatrè* is an indication of the desire to overload the *effimero* with meanings to turn it into a semiotic device that probed architecture and its communicative nature, always following in the wake of Eco's research into codes of communication.

If the semiotic experiment attempted in *Marcatrè* for the piece created on 12 February assigned complementary meanings to a device for which the crowd had already offered a variety of interpretations, for the new pieces this experiment grew more complex, given that, with the transformation of the pieces into inflatable icons, now it was UFO that had to suggest new keys to their interpretation which went beyond the meanings that those icons offered in themselves. With these premises, UFO constructed a dialogue between a member of the group and an American tourist based on linguistic misunderstandings, as well as a fictional letter in which, this time, it was UFO and not the crowd that assigned new significances to the inflatable in the form of a dollar sign, turning it into the initial of the Salvarani cycling team, a symbol of the supermarket, and the logo of the Esselunga retail chain.[80] The interpretations that UFO presented in *Marcatrè* were accompanied by a series of photographs taken by Bachi during the interventions. Somewhere between journalistic reportage of an event and flawless reconstructions that seem to elevate the *Urboeffimeri* to works of art, these photographs remain the only tangible record of the ephemeral interventions of the San Clemente construction site—"Fond *memories* (...) for a *prudent historical use*," in the words of UFO (fig. 14).[81]

After two isolated attempts in which the tube seems to have regained its original nature as a means of disturbance,[82] and with the experience of the occupation of the Faculty at an end, the members of UFO carried on with the staging of interventions centred on inflatable polyethylene icons for at least two years, but aban-

77 Binazzi, Cammeo, Foresi, Gioli and Maschietto, 'Effimero Urbanistico scala 1/1', p. 201.

78 Binazzi, Cammeo, Foresi, Gioli and Maschietto, 'Effimero Urbanistico scala 1/1', pp. 200-204.

79 Binazzi, Cammeo, Foresi, Gioli and Maschietto, 'Effimero Urbanistico scala 1/1', p. 204.

80 UFO, 'Urboeffimeri avvenenti 1:1', p. 60.

81 In these games of resemanticisation can also be placed an installation for the Milan Triennale, at which UFO was invited to give voice to the student protests. Here a series of blow-ups of photographs of the pieces from the construction site taken by Bachi were plastered around the perimeter of a room in which a revised version of the *Giornale murario* was displayed (fig. 15). UFO, 'Urboeffimeri avvenenti 1:1', p. 73.

82 In September 1968, on the occasion of the Festa de l'Unità and at the Parco delle Cascine in Florence, the tube was multiplied to form a high wall. See UFO, 'Paramount', in Achille Bonito Oliva (ed.), *7e Biennale De Paris (catalogo della mostra, Parc Floral de Paris)* (Florence: Centro Di, 1971), n.p., and the photos in the Binazzi Archives. In the same period the tube reappeared to disturb the presentation of a book by Eco at the Feltrinelli bookshop in Milan. Amit Wolf, *Superarchitecture: Experimental Architectural Practices in Italy, 1963-1973*, PhD dissertation, University of California, Los Angeles 2012, p. 113.

14. UFO, *Urboeffimero 6*, Florence, April-May 1968

doned the streets and the student marches to seek new places and new forms of interaction with users. For the conception of this new series of inflatables, UFO again looked to the collective imagination, drawing icons sometimes from a playful and fabulous context (Walt Disney's mushroom), at others from current affairs and contemporary politics (the missile, the dollar sign, the keys of the Papal States modified to represent Russia and the United States, the two superpowers of the Cold War), and at yet others from the history of architecture (the Roman aqueduct and the roadhouse of the A.N.A.S.). In turning to those figures, UFO went back to reflecting on architecture, just as they had done with the *Giornale murario*, in order to distort its fundamental elements. And so it was that after a wall that was no longer a wall, UFO started to look at monuments and utilitarian constructions of the State in order to turn them into something else.

In the conception of these new pieces, UFO was aware that, now that the student occupation was over, it was necessary to come up with a new kind of intervention. In their discussions—Binazzi recalls—UFO considered the option of turning celebrated competition projects that had never been realised into other inflatable icons, in confirmation of the group's thesis that the only possible form of architecture entailed the repurposing of elements that already existed, whether actually built or only on paper.[83] Although this hypothesis never found concrete application, between 1969 and 1970, UFO produced two of its new inflatable icons in a courtyard of the Palazzo di San Clemente: a roadhouse of the A.N.A.S. government body and a Roman aqueduct. Both in the absence of any interaction with the public—it was inflated and deflated solely in the presence of the people involved in its creation—and in its form—it was three metres high and flaunted the gaudy red and green colours typical of this building—the inflatable in the shape of an A.N.A.S. roadhouse

83 Lapo Binazzi (UFO), *Ufo. Discontinuità e territorio* (Milan: Centro Internazionale di Brera, 1977) and Binazzi, conversation with Lampariello.

had the character of the gigantic replicas of objects created by Pop Art and was destined to become the conceptual core of a reflection on the control exercised by the Italian State over the territory (fig. 16). While the A.N.A.S. roadhouse did not establish a real relationship with the entrance hall of San Clemente, UFO rediscovered a dialogue between piece and place with the aqueduct, on a scale similar to that of the aqueducts of Rome, that was conceived within the framework of the course of the Restoration of Monuments taught by Sanpaolesi with the assistance of Dezzi Bardeschi (fig. 17).[84] The fact of having turned a historic monument into an inflatable, soft, and handmade structure can only be understood in terms of a critique not just of that monument but of the discipline of restoration itself.[85]

84 The published and archival sources diverge on the dates of the inflatables of the aqueduct, the A.N.A.S. roadhouse and the installation *Rebus Viventi all'Isolotto di Don Mazzi*. The projects were all conceived to sometime between 1969 and 1970.

85 For the photos of the installation, see the documentation in Cammeo, Foresi, and Binazzi's Archives. Some photos of the project have been published in Stefano Pezzato (ed.), *Ufo story: dall'architettura radicale al design globale* (Prato: Centro per l'arte contemporanea Luigi Pecci, 2012).

The last occasion for experimentation with the inflatable icons was staged by UFO with the arrangement of those icons in a courtyard of one of the rehabilitation centres run by Don Mazzi, a well-known member of the Catholic clergy whom the group admired for his work on behalf of drug addicts and the marginalised. In combination, the inflatable icons became the words of a text of a political nature to be deciphered through a puzzle, the *Rebus*, transposed in space and thus "living" as the group put it. Looking through a View-Master stereoscope, the observer, who was also a user, could read militant messages expressed through the inflatable icons that ranged from a critique of American imperialism to a protest against the war in Vietnam (fig. 18), again uniting politics and play. This made it clear that the objective of all UFO's inflatable icons was to deliver messages of a break with the past, in order to generate a new, ephemeral, penetrable, and eloquent architecture, ready to fight against the established discipline and power.

15. UFO, Installation for the 14th Milan Triennale, Art Section, 1968

16. UFO, Inflatable A.N.A.S. roadhouse, Palazzo di San Clemente, Florence, 1970, Patrizia Cammeo/Riccardo Foresi Archives, Florence

17. UFO, Inflatable aqueduct, Palazzo di San Clemente, Florence, Course of Restoration of Monuments, Florence, 1970-1971, Patrizia Cammeo/Riccardo Foresi Archives, Florence

18. UFO, *Rebus Viventi all'Isolotto di Don Mazzi*, Florence, 1970-1971

"Happenvironment": From the "Non-matrix" Performance to the Participatory Space

The inflatable icons were not the only products of UFO's efforts to propose a different kind of architecture. In the very same period in which it was engaged in that experimentation, the group turned to the invention of a performance of artistic derivation in which the one-off pieces interacted with the crowd and with the members of UFO, who became actors and therefore co-stars of the intervention. This combination of objects and acting found concrete expression for the first time at the 6th Masaccio National Painting Prize promoted by the Municipality of San Giovanni Valdarno.[86] UFO took part with an intervention of a subversive and participatory nature, thus resembling that of the *Urboeffimeri*, which set out to ridicule the location of the intervention (the square in front of the town hall), its monuments (the Palazzo d'Arnolfo di Cambio and the statues of the Marzocco and Garibaldi), the procession held there, and San Giovanni Valdarno's speciality (roast chicken). And yet, with the pieces presented, the new intervention by UFO differed from the ones with the *Urboeffimeri* right from the invitation card prepared by the group, as part of a happening (fig. 19).[87] Calling it a happening identified UFO's intervention as one of those forms of performance developed by American artists like John Cage, Kaprow, and Oldenburg, presented in Italy over the course of 1968 by Michael Kirby in the pages of *Marcatrè*, in the very same issue as the first of UFO's works had appeared.[88] That happening, in Kirby's words, was a performance that had degrees of indetermi-

86 See Furio Colombo, 'Un'astronave carica di polli', *L'Espresso*, vol. XIV, no. 30, 28 July 1968, p. 15. Tommaso Trini, 'Masaccio a Ufo', *Domus*, no. 466, September 1968, pp. 55-56; Cammeo and Maschietto, conversation with Castellini and Hamzeian.

87 See the document in the Archivio Premio Masaccio di San Giovanni Valdarno.

88 See Michael Kirby, 'The New Theatre', *Marcatrè*, no. 37-40, May 1968, pp. 210-217; the essay was originally published in English in *The Tuale Drama Review*, no. 2, winter 1965, pp. 23-43. See too Michael Kirby (ed.), *Happenings: An Illustrated Anthology* (New York: Dutton, 1965). On this theme see too Alessandra Acocella, 'Scenografie radicali. San Giovanni Valdarno 1968', in Acocella, *Avanguardia diffusa. Luoghi di sperimentazione artistica in Italia 1967-1970* (Milan: Fondazione Passaré/Macerata: Quodlibet, 2016), pp. 73-94, and Acocella's essay in this volume.

19. UFO, Invitation at the Premio Masaccio exhibition, *Chicken Circus Circulation, ovvero heppenveironment [sic], ovvero superurbeffimero n. 7*, San Giovanni Valdarno, June 1968, Lapo Binazzi Archives, Florence, Courtesy Alessandra Acocella

20-21. UFO, *Chicken Circus Circulation, ovvero heppenveironment [sic], ovvero superurbeffimero n. 7*, Premio Masaccio exhibition, San Giovanni Valdarno, June 1968

nacy and improvisation in which UFO must have discerned traits of the open work and that, unlike in traditional theatre, bestowed on the performance a "matrix" so weak and rudimentary that it disappeared—"non-matrixed," as Kirby put it. With its recourse to the happening, UFO transferred into the sphere of the "non-matrixed" performance the polysemous experiments that in *Marcatrè*, the *Giornale murario*, and the *Urboeffimeri* had been limited to plays between figure and written word.

UFO's happening constructed a fantastic narrative with a complex plot that combined the invasion of an ideal Venusian society with the figures of the "myths" of San Giovanni Valdarno, Italian history, and the civilisation of consumption,[89] with the aim of staging a critique of contemporary capitalist society. These figures included "Uncle Sam" (representing the military dominance of American society), "virgins" (the media that control the masses), "technicians" (workers exploited by capitalism), and "heroes" (Mao and Dutschke),[90] which performed between the statues of Garibaldi and the Marzocco, and amongst "throwing chickens," "porphyry chickens," and "Jacobin chickens."[91] Those chickens, whether made of polyester or in the natural and free-range form typical of San

89 The landing of the extra-terrestrials may have been inspired by Gioli's graduation thesis, dedicated to the arrival on Earth of aliens from Jupiter. Binazzi, conversation with Lampariello.

90 A photo of Dutschke also appeared on the inflatable icon in the form of a missile.

91 UFO, 'Chicken Circus Circulation ovvero heppenveironment (sic) ovvero superurbeffimero n. 7', *Marcatrè*, no. 41-42, June 1968, pp. 76-91: 77. The political connotation of the performance was made even clearer in the memorandum prepared by Binazzi for the article that Trini devoted to the happening (Lapo Binazzi Archives, Florence). Trini, 'Masaccio a UFO'. On this theme see too Acocella, 'Scenografie radicali. San Giovanni Valdarno 1968', p. 86.

Giovanni Valdarno, were an emblem of industrial production, not coincidentally referred to as a "prefabricated product for a new Tuscan architecture." It is clear that those chickens were intended as a reflection of local tradition, but it should not be forgotten that a few months prior to UFO's happening, Archizoom had presented the chicken as a symbol of the system of production, the "marble chicken."[92] But while Archizoom had used marble to indicate the risk of uselessness faced by products of design in the civilisation of consumption,[93] for UFO the chicken was no longer pointless decoration but another usage-tool aimed at unsettling contemporary "rites and myths" and a weapon to be turned against the injustices of contemporary imperialism.

The happening commenced with the appearance of a "Grand Alchemist" who, emerging from an inflatable tube lodged in the tower of the Palazzo d'Arnolfo di Cambio, oversaw the distribution of polyester chickens, called "Venusians" because they came from a remote world, that of America.[94] Ready to receive these gifts were some members of UFO who, dressed as "virgins" in bikinis and transparent cloaks, painted the chickens and threw them down another tube towards other members of the group, the "technicians" in white coats who in turn handed them out to the crowd (figs. 20-21). In a *coup de théâtre*, local roast chickens entered the scene and were tasted by the technicians before being thrown back to the virgins and the Grand Alchemist, and then against the Palazzo d'Arnolfo di Cambio. Just as the chicken had been ridiculed by making it out of polyester and then painting it and exchanging it with free-range chickens, UFO attacked the local historical monuments: spraying shaving foam on the statue of the Marzocco and covering the statue of Garibaldi with tin foil to marry it to a gigantic papier-mâché "Anitona" disguised as a pin-up of the Viareggio Carnival. The performance concluded with the "National Front of Saigon in Valdarno," which unleashed its "secret weapon": a tens of metres long polyethylene tube filled with air on which the three most famous members of the Kennedy family were portrayed.[95] To reinforce the complexity of the narrative, UFO multiplied the meanings of the pieces. Whereas with the *Urboeffimeri* it had relied on reworkings after the event in *Marcatrè*, the resemanticisation was now an integral part of the intervention. Through their "un-matrixed" performance and costumes, it was now the actors who multiplied the meanings of the story. Bachi transformed himself from Grand Alchemist into UFO Robot Grendizer and Hamlet while the encounter between Garibaldi and the Anitona became one between Robin Hood and *Italietta* ("little Italy"), between the "Happy Prince" and "sex," or between Mao and the American pin-up.[96]

92 Mentioned in an interview of February 1968, it was the title of the competition project for the Italian pavilion of the 14th Milan Triennale. Marco Fini, 'Arrivano gli Archizoom', *Panorama*, no. 94, 1 February 1968, pp. 52-57: 52. See also Gargiani, *Archizoom associati, 1966-1974. Dall'onda pop alla superficie neutra*, pp. 56, 95.

93 Fini, 'Arrivano gli Archizoom'.

94 UFO, 'Chicken Circus Circulation ovvero heppenveironment (sic)'.

95 UFO, 'Chicken Circus Circulation ovvero heppenveironment (sic)', p. 79. See Lapo Binazzi, conversation with Postcards from Beirut, https://www.youtube.com/watch?v=yr8PJvrD7Pg.

96 The different linguistic codes of fashion, radio, cooking and comic strips were used to amplify the meanings of the happening. UFO, 'Chicken Circus Circulation ovvero heppenveironment (sic)', p. 79.

22. UFO, Sherwood Restaurant, Florence, 1969, Patrizia Cammeo/Riccardo Foresi Archives, Florence

23-24. UFO, Mago di Oz Boutique, Viareggio, 1969, Titti Maschietto Archives, Florence

25. UFO, Re di Puglia Herbalist's Shop, Florence, 1970, Patrizia Cammeo/Riccardo Foresi Archives, Florence

The happening allowed UFO to experiment with a different form of participation, that of a crowd which could grasp the message of the intervention as they watched it and which, as in some of Kaprow and Oldenburg's happenings,[97] felt so provoked by the action that they were driven to take part in it. It is no surprise that the happening ended in clashes between the members of the group and the local community, while over the following days the youth groups of the Christian Democratic Party demanded the dissolution of the town council, guilty of having allowed UFO to stage its happening. The debate would continue with the organisation of an event to explain the meaning and value of the group's intervention, which was attended by members of UFO, Furio Colombo, and Eco.[98] It was Eco himself, on this occasion, who pointed out that UFO's happening consisted of a unique combination of elements open to the interpretation of the observer with the aim of generating an awareness in the audience of their own alienated condition.[99]

Despite UFO's intentions, *Marcatrè* probably remained the only means of fully grasping the meanings of the happening and understanding the evolution of the group's reflections with regard to the production of the construction site in San Clemente. The title of UFO's new article published in the magazine[100] is emblematic of what the group had discovered in the intervention at San Giovanni Valdarno. In addition to the designation *Superurbeffimero n. 7*, in continuity with the other *Urboeffimeri*, two more definitions appeared, *Chicken Circus Circulation* and *happenvironment*.[101] The former referred to the iconic figure of the chicken, central to the happening and that of the circus, which had already appeared in the report on the *Restauro dell'utenza*, but was now charged with a new significance seeing that Kirby had described the circus as another form of happening.[102] The latter was a neologism that united happening and environment. This combination is emblematic of the invention of an intervention that set out to bring together two dimensions—that of an involving action and that of a space made up of different objects—that combined in the manner of a collage, were intended to include spectators, in order to stimulate their critical and creative capacities, and make them active users in that action and that space.[103] This idea of a collage of elements—be they characters, words, figures, or objects—that according to Kaprow's happening, environment and assemblage all have in common,[104] guided UFO's conception of the *happenenvironment*, which between 1969 and 1971 would find new applications in the fitting-out of shops and a discotheque in Florence and Viareggio (the Sherwood restaurant, Saga de Xam clothing boutique, and the Re di Puglia herbalist's shop in Florence, the Mago di Oz boutique in Viareggio, and the Bamba Issa discotheque in Forte dei Marmi).[105]

97 Encouraging the public to take part in the event is one of the fundamental traits of the happening. Kirby (ed.), *Happenings*, pp. 10, 49. See for example Oldenburg's happening *World's Fair II* at which the onlookers were pushed and pressed by cardboard panels. Kirby (ed.), *Happenings*, pp. 25, 221.

98 See the photographs of the posters of protest put up by the Movimento Giovanile DC (Lapo Binazzi Archives, Florence).

99 See the transcription of Umberto Eco's speech at a debate about the topic "art and provocation" (Archivio Premio Masaccio, San Giovanni Valdarno). On this theme see too Acocella, 'Scenografie radicali. San Giovanni Valdarno 1968', p. 91.

100 UFO, 'Chicken Circus Circulation ovvero heppenveironment (sic)'.

101 The word originally used by UFO ("heppenveironment") has been modified here to eliminate the misprint.

102 Kirby, 'The New Theatre', *The Tuale Drama Review*, p. 30. See too Acocella, 'Scenografie radicali. San Giovanni Valdarno 1968', p. 82. Circus figures like the "man shot out of a cannon" and the "lion tamer" would return in UFO's subsequent interventions.

103 According to Kirby, in contemporary happenings the environment, whose origins lie in Kurt Schwitters's *Merzbau* (1924) as a derivation of the collage, "surrounds or encloses the viewer on all sides." See Kirby (ed.), *Happenings*, pp. 22-24, 29.

104 "(G) The composition of a Happening proceeds exactly as in Assemblages and Environments, that is, it is evolved as a collage of events in certain spans of time and in certain spaces." Allan Kaprow, *Assemblage, Environments and Happenings* (New York: Abrams, 1966), p. 266. It is interesting to note that Binazzi himself cited Kaprow's

26-27. UFO, Bamba Issa Discotheque, Forte dei Marmi, second and third season, 1970-1971, Titti Maschietto Archives, Florence

"Greenwich Village happenings" in a text now in his archive.

105 These fitting-outs all date from 1969, apart from the Re di Puglia herbalist's shop, which is from 1970. Two more shops, Forza John and You Tarzan Me Jane, fitted out by Binazzi and Maschietto respectively, were not venues of performances and so cannot be ascribed to the *happenvironments* realised between 1969 and 1970.

106 UFO used drawing only rarely and almost exclusively during the phase of construction. See the drawings in the Patrizia Cammeo/Riccardo Foresi Archives.

107 See the photo titled *UFO foto al cinematografo (B-Movies), 1968* with an army of skeletons, drawn from the 1963 mythological film *Jason and the Argonauts* (Lapo Binazzi Archives, Florence).

108 See Tommaso Trini, 'L'ufo della parodia', *Domus*, no. 495, February 1971, pp. 46-48; 'Dining can be a way-out experience in Florence', *Interior Design*, December 1972, pp. 80-81; Simone Micheli, 'Incontro con Lapo Binazzi. La discontinuità come punto di forza', in Micheli, *I negozi. Vita, morte e miracoli* (Flo-

In the passage from the streets to interiors, UFO's pieces underwent a new evolution, given that for room to be found for them in shops they could no longer be magnified but had to be reduced to the scale of objects. Polyethylene and papier-mâché were now joined by expanded polyurethane. Like papier-mâché, it allowed the pieces to assume a permanent air, but its malleability and lightness guaranteed the memory of the precarious character of the products of the construction site in San Clemente.[106]

The pieces imagined by UFO for the shops pertained to the world of fairy stories and the cinema, not the engaged kind but that of the American B-movie and epic.[107] They included a staircase disguised as a gigantic tree from *Jack and the Beanstalk*, a tavern located in the belly of Pinocchio's whale which had swallowed the ship from *Moby-Dick* (Sherwood), a colossal table with neon legs, and a shop window dressed as a Rube Goldberg machine for out-of-scale hamsters (*The Wizard of Oz*) (figs. 23-25).[108] The members of UFO themselves, in continuity with the happening in San Giovanni Valdarno, became actors playing the parts of Tarzan and Jane, the Three Musketeers, Captain Ahab, and Little Red Riding Hood.[109] The fittings-out for Bamba Issa, handled in different ways for the summer seasons of 1969, 1970, and 1971 ("western-caravanserai," roadworks in Africa, and Orientalising funfair)[110] made UFO's critique of capitalist industry and imperialism clearer than those of other shops (figs. 26-27).[111] Emblematic of this are the DJ booth which, af-

28. UFO, Bamba Issa Discotheque, Forte dei Marmi, second season, 1970, Titti Maschietto Archives, Florence

ter taking the form of a fabulous flying carpet, became a bomber disguised as a giant dove,[112] or the motorways that ran through the discotheque, interrupting an archaeological dig peopled with alligators and hippopotamuses, emblems of the colonisation to which Africa was subject (fig. 28). Above the excavation, an A.N.A.S. roadhouse, enigmatically suspended and in ruin, with workmen on the point of carrying out gymnastic exercises.[113] When tackling architecture, even if only on the scale of the fitting-out of interiors, UFO stuck to its belief that the only possible creative process was that of giving new meanings to icons for the ephemeral construction of *happenvironments* designed for the transmission of messages.

Squeezed into the restricted spaces of boutiques, the *happenvironments* were stripped of the natural crowd of the streets and reduced to solo performances with the participation of the members of UFO and occasional extras.[114] Only photographic features, endowed with the communicative and connotative force up until then entrusted to the articles in *Marcatrè* and to the "non-matrixed performance," restored a collective value to the actions staged in shops and the discotheque, enabling them to carry UFO's message to a wider public.[115] In any case, the small section of the public that had experienced those *happenvironments* had not grasped their significance, contributing to their rapid dismantling and therefore ensuring that their nature was as temporary as the *Urboeffimeri*.[116]

"Reproducible ad Infinitum" Handmade Objects for a "Non-design"

While engaged in the creation of *happenvironments* for shops and other commercial activities, UFO considered the possibility of

rence: Angelo Pontecorboli Editore, 1992), pp. 40-51.

109 Some of these figures are in line with the photographs of View-Master backgrounds present in the Binazzi Archives and dated 1970, portraying figures like Tarzan, Gulliver, lions and skeletons. Tarzan and Jane, the Phantom, Mandrake and Diana Palmer would people the You Tarzan Me Jane boutique that Maschietto designed for fashion designer Chiara Boni, his partner (Titti Maschietto Archives, Florence). Chiara Boni, 'La ricerca flessibile', in Alessia Galimberti, *Intrecci creativi: città, design e moda* (Rimini: Maggioli, 2013), pp. 103-115.

110 Cammeo and Maschietto, conversation with Castellini and Hamzeian. See UFO, 'Le cammelle di salvataggio', *Domus*, no. 483, February 1970, pp. 50-51; Titti Maschietto, 'Bamba Issa', in Marco Delogu (ed.), *Primo autunno. Conversazioni a Belgrave Square* (Macerata: Quodlibet, 2016), pp. 125-127; Trini, 'L'ufo della parodia'; Alexis Petridis, 'Build, baby, build: when radical architects did disco', *The Guardian*, 22 November 2015, https://www.theguardian.com/artanddesign/2015/nov/22/radical-disco-architects-italy-nightclub-design-60s-70s-ica. In this connection see too Simon Sadler's essay in this volume.

111 See *Topolino*, no. 25, March 1951. Maschietto, 'Bamba Issa'.

29. UFO, *Dollaro* lamp, 1969, Patrizia Cammeo/Riccardo Foresi Archives, Florence

turning what had been decorative objects needed for the construction of its narratives into functional objects for use not only in the home but also in gardens and swimming pools, as if to preserve the identity of those first pieces as Unidentified Flying Objects of the Faculty of Architecture, then transported into the open spaces of Florence.[117] In the hypothesis that the group was considering, it is possible to find traces of what Archizoom and Superstudio had just done, between 1967 and 1968, in their shift from the apparently useless objects made of cardboard show in the exhibition *Superarchitettura*, to lamps, sofas, and armchairs produced by Poltronova.[118] But in UFO's case, this passage appeared problematic as it seemed to contradict the critique of industrial production inherent in the setting up of the construction site in San Clemente, and yet was necessary to ensure the group's survival in the years in which its members were still students. Poltronova, contacted by Bachi and Cammeo to produce drums of columns and mushrooms in polyurethane, would not accept UFO's proposal—"too avant-garde to be understood" was, according to Cammeo, Poltronova's comment.[119]

In a way, their rejection by Poltronova saved UFO's pieces from the risk of being swallowed up by the design industry which the group would continue to fight until the conclusion of the collective experience. And UFO had already found an alternative to industrial production with the realisation of a table lamp called *Dollaro* ("Dollar"). That lamp had been intended from the outset as a one-off piece as it had been conceived as a birthday present for Foresi's brother-in-law, Franco Gori,[120] and as a handmade object that consisted of a base of pietra serena, vertical rods, and others bent to form the S-shape of the dollar sign[121] and a semicylindri-

112 Titti Maschietto, conversation with Andrea Anselmo, 26 April 2022. Cammeo and Maschietto, conversation with Castellini and Hamzeian. As for the choice to dedicate Bamba Issa to Africa, it is interesting to note that in 1968 there was also a float at the Viareggio Carnival, entitled *Africa addio*, that offered a critique of the colonisation of Africa. For a more thorough analysis of the dissenting dimension of the Viareggio Carnival see Lampariello's essay in this volume. See too Petridis, 'Build, baby, build: when radical architects did disco'.

113 Cammeo and Maschietto, conversation with Castellini and Hamzeian.

114 Binazzi declared that "these actions are used to transform the user (...), the public, (which) is identified with the members of the group themselves." See Emanuele Piccardo, 'Intervista a Lapo Binazzi', in Piccardo, *Dopo la rivoluzione. Azioni e protagonisti dell'Architettura Radicale italiana 1963-1973* (Busalla: plug_in, 2009).

115 In addition to publication in architecture magazines the photos were meant to be used to illustrate posters and menus. For example, the menu of the Sherwood restaurant was based on the model of the children's magazine *Corriere dei Piccoli*. Cammeo, conversation with Anselmo.

cal shade surmounted by a crown, all in gilded metal. The crown decorated with laurels might be an allusion to Gori's occupation as a teacher,[122] but there can be no doubt that at the same time it conveyed yet another political message against American imperialism symbolised by the S of the dollar sign.

The lamp's nature as a one-off piece would be preserved even when the group made seven more of them because each was different from the next (fig. 29). In these other pieces, the rods of the first version were made with a hollow wooden frame[123] and the proportions of all the parts were altered to accentuate the iconic and monumental character of the lamp. The elements added to the shade were icons drawn from UFO's imagery, what Binazzi would describe as the "frozen memories" of the group's history.[124] From the thunderbolt and the cemetery with a cross and a field full of flowers dear to Foresi to the classicising crown of Napoleon, the Volkswagen Beetle, and the palm tree, those different icons gave each lamp a particular connotation. It was a useful object since it illuminated and it was "reproducible ad infinitum,"[125] but, thanks to the innumerable variations made possible by substitution of the icons, rejected an industrial character, continuing the tradition ushered in with the production of the one-off pieces of San Clemente.

Just as with the Bamba Issa *happenvironment*, it is clear that the message concealed in the *Dollaro* lamp is anything but the fairy-tale "And they lived happily ever after" that some of its icons might suggest. The palm tree is a warning against neo-colonialism in Africa; the Volkswagen Beetle is a protest against the idea of mass production based on the exploitation of workers, and so is broken in half;[126] the cross of the cemetery is a reminder of the dead in the Vietnam War;[127] and the crown of Napoleon, finally, is a metaphor for power. As well as being made by hand, it was these subversive messages that meant the *Dollaro* lamp was a direct heir of the one-off pieces UFO had paraded through the streets of Florence and it is precisely in continuity with that "urbanistic terrorism" that we should see the definition that UFO provided of its lamp, describing it as "terroristic design." In its nature as a means of criticising the capitalist economy, the *Dollaro* lamp held a dialogue with Archizoom's "Trojan horses,"[128] but precisely because, unlike Archizoom's furniture, it did not enter the circuit of industrial production and the middle-class drawing room, it remained an unexploded bomb. Excluded even from the Sherwood restaurant, from which it would soon be removed along with the rest of the *happenvironment*, the *Dollaro* lamp remained nothing but a one-off piece to be carried around and manipulated the way the *Urboeffimeri* had been, at the celebrations of those who had participated in the militant marches of '68. And so it appeared

116 The short-lived nature of the set-ups was also due to their non-functional nature. For instance the Z-shape of the tables of the Sherwood restaurant, intended as a parody of the division of humanity between rich and poor, did not allow diners to share their meals. Micheli, 'Incontro con Lapo Binazzi. La discontinuità come punto di forza'.

117 The idea of an outdoor use was so deep-rooted that it prompted UFO to develop a waterproof paint in collaboration with a Florentine paint factory. The paint was given the ironic name "arcivernice," an evocation of the one that had the power of bringing things to life in the comic strip *Pier Cloruro de' Lambicchi*. See 'UFO', in Bonito Oliva (ed.), *7e Biennale de Paris*, n.p.

118 Patrizia Cammeo, conversation with Andrea Anselmo, 23 March 2022. Archizoom and Superstudio's objects had just been produced by Poltronova (*Passiflora*, in 1967; *Sofo*, in 1968; *Superonda*, between 1967 and 1968), those of Gaetano Pesce by C&B (*UP7*, in 1969) and of Piero Gilardi by Gufram (*Sassi*, in 1968). On this subject see Gargiani and Lampariello, *Superstudio*, pp. 8-9, 20-21, 115; Gabriele Mastrigli (ed.), *Superstudio, Opere 1966-1978* (Macerata: Quodlibet, 2016), pp. XXXII, 24, 32; Gianni Pettena, *Radical design. Ricerca e progetto dagli anni '60 a oggi* (Florence: Maschietto Editore, 2004), p. 38.

119 Cammeo and Maschietto, conversation with Castellini and Hamzeian.

120 Cammeo, conversation with Anselmo.

121 The dollar sign was made from a thin sheet of metal in the shape of an S welded onto two vertical rods, almost a memory of the "golden wires" used to compress the tube of the *Urboeffimero* in the form of a missile. See UFO, 'Urboeffimeri avvenenti scala 1:1', p. 61.

122 In considering the political significance of this gift we should not underestimate the fact that Gori was a member of the radical left-wing group Potere Operaio. Cammeo, conversation with Anselmo.

123 UFO originally conducted trials in which the lamp was coloured

30. UFO, Installation for the Salone del Mobile, Milan, 1971, Patrizia Cammeo/Riccardo Foresi Archives, Florence

between the legs of Chiara Boni at the wedding of the man who had been one of the leaders of the Student Movement, Michelangelo Caponetto.[129]

After the dollar sign, the world of Hollywood movies became the source for the invention of other lamps: the *Paramount*,[130] based on the logo of the film studio of that name, and the *MGM*, based on that of Metro-Goldwyn-Mayer.[131] Designed by UFO probably at the beginning of the seventies, these lamps would be produced after the dissolution of the group thanks to Binazzi's initiative of inserting them in the catalogue of Alessandro Guerriero's Studio Alchimia.[132] Without the *Dollaro* lamp's variations of figures and conceived for mass-production, *Paramount* and *MGM* lost the character of the one-off piece that the *Dollaro* had retained.[133]

It is again in the context of UFO's reflection on the one-off piece and its reproducibility ad infinitum that we can place two other realisations of the group: the furnishings of its studio, in Palazzo Uguccioni, and an installation for the 1971 Salone del Mobile in Milan. Some of the pieces made of polyurethane for the *happenvironments*, once those fittings had been dismantled, were rearranged by the group to create what looked like a new "renaissance" of classical architecture, consisting of a Doric column made up of drums of polyurethane interspersed with huge pieces of cheese and the head of a mushroom, and a trilithon with its lintel broken in the middle (fig. 30). It is obvious that, in the hands of UFO, such a renaissance could only lead to ungainly and sensual, home-made and subversive forms, oriented not towards a pop commercial production[134] but towards that "destruction of the object" which would characterise certain reflections of the Global Tools.[135] With

blue and different combinations of tints depending on the icons of the shade. Ibid.

124 See the mural painted by Foresi during the student protests of 1968 (Patrizia Cammeo/ Riccardo Foresi Archives, Florence) and the sketches with thunderbolts in the Binazzi Archives. The definition of "frozen memories," which had appeared in Lapo Binazzi, *Manifesto del discontinuo*, n.d. (FRAC Archives, Orléans) would only be explained in 1975. See UFO, 'L'oggetto storico riproducibile all'infinito', in Giovanni Maria Accame and Carlo Guenzi (eds.), *Avanguardie e cultura popolare* (Bologna: Galleria d'Arte Moderna, 1975), pp. 216-217.

125 UFO, 'L'oggetto storico riproducibile all'infinito'.

126 Cammeo, conversation with Anselmo. The version of the lamp with the VW Beetle and the palm tree would be given the name "Capitalism in Africa" and, in the pages of *Vogue*, "Long Live the Negus" of the series "Italy in Africa." In this connection see 'Dove va il design', *Vogue Italia*, January 1971, pp. 76-81: 77.

127 See UFO's photographic feature on the American cemetery in Florence where the war dead are buried, published in Pezzato (ed.), *Ufo story: dall'architettura radicale al design globale*, pp. 214-215.

128 Laura Barile, 'Architettura e

the assembly of these pieces in polyurethane, UFO reached an important stage in the process of dissolution of architecture. At the moment when the group had been on the point of turning the one-off piece into an object of design for mass production, UFO reacted with the invention of a handmade and militant object like the *Dollaro* lamp and polyurethane objects that, by the nature of their material and their non-functional character, were a negation of the very essence of design, sketching the outlines of another discipline that was not industrial but artisanal, that did not set out to sell things, and that did not want to produce functional objects but solely decorative ones: what Binazzi would define as "non-design,"[136] aimed not at buyers but at users capable of grasping the messages delivered by UFO.

Fantastic Narratives for the Investigation of the Territory

Against the background of the conception of the *happenvironments*, between dreamlike atmospheres and icons of a clumsy and playful appearance, UFO had never set aside the proposition with which it had started up the construction site in San Clemente: that of a struggle against the exploitation of the city and the territory perpetrated by capitalist industry.[137] With these premises, after concluding its experimentation with interiors, UFO turned its attention to the territory and, just as had happened for the city with the film made in the entrance hall of San Clemente, decided to precede the action proper with an activity of investigation that, in this case, aimed at a comprehension of what UFO saw as the obscure significance of some of the State works of infrastructure scattered around the Italian territory. After the media of film and polyethylene that UFO had used to investigate the space produced by architecture when its research was still confined to the entrance hall of San Clemente, UFO decided, now that it was convinced that architecture was a language, to rely on narration to conduct the new inquiry. The members of UFO declared themselves ready to tell "tender stories around campfires," outlining the traits of a new kind of architect who was no longer a professional figure seated at the drafting machine but a storyteller travelling around the territory.[138] "Architetti tzigani" ("Gypsy architects") and "cowboys" were the names that UFO gave to its metaphorical itinerant condition, now turning the aerial movement of the Flying Objects into the terrestrial one of nomadic communities.[139] In its discovery of the occupation of the land by power, the only cores of physical and mental resistance to that power appeared to UFO to be the villages. Instead of to futuristic cities that UFO dismissed as all-encompassing visions in the service of capitalist industry and not of their inhabitants, the group looked to Amerindian pueblos, aggregations of tribes and nomads, and rustic villages in the countryside.[140]

gioia di vivere. Le esperienze di un gruppo di neolaureati fiorentini. Un cavallo di troia nella civiltà dei superconsumi', *Il Corriere della Sera*, no. 80, Wednesday 5 April 1967, p. 11. On this theme see Gargiani, *Archizoom associati, 1966-1974. Dall'onda pop alla superficie neutra*, pp. 23, 43, 45, 48.

129 This was the marriage of Caponetto and Dominique Papi, celebrated in 1972.

130 See the drawing in UFO, 'Paramount'. See too Lapo Binazzi, 'Ghiribizzi di luce', *Interni annual: Luce '90-'91*, 1990, pp. 47-52.

131 Along the same lines, Binazzi conceived the *20th Century Fox* lamp, which never went into production. http://www.italian.it/lapobinazzi/start.html.

132 The lamps would become part of the *Bau Haus* collection. Alessandro Guerriero, 'Bau-haus I. II', in Kazuko Sato (ed.), *Alchimia: Never-Ending Italian Design* (Tokyo: Rikuyo-sha, 1985), pp. 16-27. Binazzi would create many other lamps and objects of design. See Lapo Binazzi, 'Luci nervose', *Modo*, no. 45, December 1981, p. 29.

133 The variations in these lamps were limited to the colouring of their surfaces.

134 The pop resurrection of classical elements, prefigured in UFO by Maschietto's usage-tools, would lead to the production of commercial objects of design by other exponents of the neo-avant-garde. See Gabriella D'Amato, 'Il design tra 'radicale' e 'commerciale'', *Op. cit.*, no. 53, January 1982, pp. 5-21.

135 See UFO, 'Produzione industriale e creatività individuale', *Casabella*, no. 379, July 1973, pp. 46-47; and Lapo Binazzi (UFO), 'Non-design. Dall'oggetto alla sopravvivenza', in Achille Bonito Oliva (ed.), *Contemporanea. Roma, Parcheggio di Villa Borghese 11. 1973 / 2. 1974* (Florence: Centro Di, 1973), pp. 301-303: 301.

136 See 'UFO', in Bonito Oliva (ed.), *7e Biennale de Paris*; and Binazzi, 'Non-design. Dall'oggetto alla sopravvivenza.

31-33. UFO, Investigation of the control of the State over the territory, 1971-1973, Patrizia Cammeo/ Riccardo Foresi Archives, Florence

In this exploration of the narrative form, Archizoom and Superstudio undoubtedly continued to play the part of an indispensable model with their illustrated stories of the *Discorsi per immagini* and the *Twelve Ideal Cities*. Unlike these models, however, UFO's narration never came to take on the character of a story. It was always rather presented in the forms of texts or images that, despite being combined, never defined an autonomous and complete corpus. They always remained fragments of an often cryptic nature and already anticipated an increasingly evident rejection of explanation that, in the years to come, would become a genuine poetic premise. With these texts, therefore, UFO transferred to narration as well the nature of an open work that it had bestowed on all its previous interventions.

Among the narrative experiments conducted by the group at the beginning of the seventies, there were texts that would only be finished, or at any rate published, in the following years and surveys for the identification of infrastructures that became emblematic icons of the occupation of the territory by capital. To this period belong three interventions, drawn up between 1969 and 1972, in which the narration either took the form of a sociological questionnaire or of a sort of illustrated account. The presence of drawing, up until then never utilised by UFO, led the group to formulate genuine proposals for the territory.[141] But it is important to stress that these proposals continued to possess the critical aspects of all of UFO's other one-off pieces and, once drawn, were already imagined by the group as on the point of being destroyed.

In the framework of its investigation of the territory, UFO identified several infrastructures as emanations of the power of industry as it expanded beyond the factory through the privatisation of services. To the A.N.A.S. roadhouse and the aqueduct, already turned into inflatable icons, were now added electricity pylons, barracks, and railway tracks. Whether this imagery came from the collective experiences of the group or the personal ones of its members,[142] these infrastructures of the territory were imbued with completely new meanings that turned them into true ideological figures (figs. 31-33). The most significant is the A.N.A.S. roadhouse. In 1969, some photographs that members of UFO had taken on journeys along Italian roads were assembled to form "a systematic cataloguing of the typological variations of A.N.A.S. buildings scattered around the country."[143] Once again, it was with the word that, through recourse to imaginative associations, UFO gave the roadman's house new meanings, from architectural ones that ennobled it as an "inn," "motel," "shop," and "villa," and those that made it an expression of the power of the State ("observation post," "hideout," "keep," and "blockhouse").[144]

137 For a deeper analysis of the question of the territory see Lampariello's essay in this volume.

138 UFO, 'Una lettera dagli UFO a Domus', *Domus*, no. 495, February 1971, p. 48.

139 For these names see Lapo Binazzi, *Architetti tzigani* (1969) (Lapo Binazzi Archives, Florence) and UFO, 'Una lettera dagli UFO a Domus'.

140 "...the aim of bigger NOVELINGSTORIES (sic)," declared Binazzi, "got hold of ARCHITECTURE that becomes UTOPIA of THEORETICAL THOUGHT. A big big STORY same for everybody tries to cancel the RIGHT of little little tribes to invent daily on THEIR OWN STORY to build a PERSONAL 'CIVITAS'. (...) We understood a thing boy, boxes guy, VILLAGES exist!". Binazzi, *Manifesto del discontinuo*.

141 Attributable in most cases to Binazzi, UFO's first stories, from *Architetti tzigani* to the narrations included in the *Manifesto del discontinuo*, were compiled in 1969 but would remain unpublished for many years. *Architetti tzigani* was published in 1983 and the *Manifesto del discontinuo* in 2013: Lapo Binazzi, 'Architetti Tzigani (1969)', in Gianni Pettena (ed.), *La città invisibile. Architettura sperimentale 1965/1975* (Florence: Associazione Intercomunale N.10, 1983), p. 96; UFO, 'Manifesto del discontinuo (1969)', in Marie-Ange Brayer (ed.), *Architectures expérimentales 1950-2012: collection du FRAC Centre* (Orléans: Éditions HYX, 2013), p. 599. The texts written in 1969 would however be revised and published as well in UFO, 'Una lettera dagli UFO a Domus'; UFO and Lapo Binazzi, 'Album di profezie', *Harck*, no. 1, 1971, pp. 30-31. Not unlike the *Giornale murario* or the *happenvironments*, UFO's stories were embellished with all sorts of wordplays and literary virtuosities, from semantic combinations verging on the absurd to hermetic passages of poetic origin.

142 The origin of the interest in the A.N.A.S. roadhouse is not clear. Cammeo traces it back to the journeys she and Foresi made by car to Civitavecchia and then Sardinia (Cammeo and Maschietto, conversation with Castellini and Hamzeian). Binazzi on the other hand says it stemmed from an epiphanic vision he had on journey

34. UFO, Design of installation, Eurodomus, Milan, 1970, Titti Maschietto Archives, Florence

to take part in the *Karnhoval degli artisti* in Rieti in February 1969. Patrizia Mello, 'Interviste a Lapo Binazzi (UFO)', in *Neoavanguardie e controcultura a Firenze* (Florence: Angelo Pontecorboli, 2017), pp. 107-115: 109.

143 UFO, 'Architettura della burocrazia', *Casabella*, no. 378, June 1973, pp. 30-31.

144 Ibid.

145 Maschietto, conversation with Castellini. For the questionnaire see UFO, 'Elementi di prossemica territoriale: questionario', *King Kong*, no. 2, June 1972, pp. 10-11.

146 Umberto Eco, 'Dopo i poeti', in Eco, *Dalla periferia dell'impero* (Milan: Bompiani, 1976), pp. 297-316: 308; Umberto Eco, 'Le nuove forme espressive', in Associazione Internazionale per gli Studi di Lingua e Letteratura Italiana (ed.), *Innovazioni tematiche espressive e linguistiche della letteratura italiana del Novecento: atti dell'VIII Congresso dell'associazione internazionale per gli studi di lingua e letteratura italiana, New York,*

Still in the context of the investigation of the territory, UFO followed up the identification of its aspects of control through photography by probing the secret and hidden value of the same figures in a sociological questionnaire. "Elements of Territorial Proxemics: Questionnaire" was its title. In turning the narration into a questionnaire, UFO was harking back to Eco's teaching at the Faculty of Architecture in Florence, when he had illustrated the semiotic potential inherent in the combination of different linguistic and communicative codes, from those of novels to those of sociological questionnaires and political manifestos—it is no coincidence that the original version of the questionnaire was drawn up by the members of UFO when they were following Eco's course.[145] And so the tone of the scientific enquiry was combined with an element of the fantastic that UFO derived from Franz Kafka's novel *The Castle*, which not coincidentally centred on the alienation of the individual in the bureaucratic machinery of the State. Although Eco would describe the questionnaire as an experiment in avant-garde literature capable of generating a "semiotic cluster," UFO's text was a manifesto in the form of a false questionnaire—inasmuch as the answers were already contained in the questions—aimed at revealing the real role of the infrastructures.[146] In a tone lying somewhere between the conspiracy and an ironic send-up, the A.N.A.S. roadhouses and the barracks became places of "psychological violence" and "abuse of the imaginary," "emissaries of these hidden powers" and "mimetic prostheses of exits, entrances, secret hatchways."[147] "Have you ever noticed," wrote UFO, "that in the vicinity of particular repressive institutions of the BOURGEOIS STATE: PRISONS MONASTERIES BARRACKS (secret bases) police stations (even neighbourhood ones), there is a sort of permanent protective psychological ring, a magnetic field of a special kind determined by what are usually strange circumstances?".[148]

After the identification of territorial infrastructures and study of their hidden meaning through the questionnaire, UFO continued its investigation with the design of an installation for Eurodomus, at the Palazzo dell'Arte of the Milan Triennale in 1970, and with the graduation thesis project presented in 1971 under the supervision of Ricci and Eco.[149] These were the first and only occasions on which UFO produced drawings that represented a work of architecture with apparently traditional forms. And yet that work was not the outcome of processes of composition that defined the configuration of the interiors, the design of the facades, or the structural details. Just as had happened with the wall and the aqueduct, the architecture designed by UFO was composed of existing figures drawn from its own imagery and recombined in a new unity. With these projects, therefore, UFO did not limit itself to undermining the material substance of architecture through its dematerialisation into inflatable polythene. The new message underlying UFO's interventions was that architecture is not the result of an act of invention, but at the most of a recycling of what already exists in different aggregations that can only be those of an ideal village laid out along a road (at the Triennale) or on the slopes of a mountain (for the graduation thesis).

For the Triennale, the village was made up of A.N.A.S. roadhouses fitted with signs that revealed their hidden content, that of an American N.A.S.A. base—another semantic game, this time the anagram—; a Greek temple erected to protect not the statue of a deity but a tent; a cemetery at whose entrance were set three letters "HCE," the initials of "Here Comes Everybody" from *Finnegans Wake*, an ironic revelation of every human being's fate; a Disney fairy castle; 16th-century stables; industrial silos, wigwams, a telephone box, and the theatrical background of an epic film (fig. 34).[150] All these elements are ranged along two railway tracks that come to an end at the village's monument: the one the group erected to itself, a building in the form of the word UFO, as if to say that the Unidentified Flying Object, after being identified with the members of the group, after having been turned into an ambiguous object, has now become a gilded monument, just as the *Dollaro* lamp had been gilded, able to unite architecture, word, object,

25-28 aprile 1973 (Florence: Olschki, 1976), pp. 227-244.

147 UFO, 'Elementi di prossemica territoriale: questionario', pp. 10-11.

148 UFO, 'Elementi di prossemica territoriale: questionario', p. 10.

149 For the design of an installation at Eurodomus and for the graduation thesis see the text R. B., 'UFO', *Caleidoscopio*, no. 11, January 1972, pp. 10-14.

150 The architectural figures that UFO laid out at the sides of the tracks for the installation at Eurodomus belonged to a much broader pantheon of figures that UFO mentioned in the text written to set the image of that railway village in a proper story. "IT WAS AN ARCHITECTURE," wrote UFO, "OF FACADES OF RAILWAY HOUSES OF INDIAN TENTS OF ROAD WORKERS' HOUSES OF COUNTRY GRAVEYARDS OF 16TH-CENTURY STABLES OF NEO-NEOREALIST FACTORIES OF LITTLE TEMPLES OF CASTLES OF FAIRY CASTLES OF ROMAN AQUEDUCTS OF TELEPHONE BOXES OF PINEWOODS OF BEACHES OF MONUMENTS AND AN URBANISM MADE UP OF CUL-DE-SACS DEAD-END TRACKS DESERTS PRAIRIES COLLAPSED TRENCHES MAIN STREETS CINEMATIC VILLAGES KASBAHS GHETTOES PUEBLOS BIG ESTATES SMALL TOWNS TENEMENT HOUSES TOWERS OF BABEL INDIAN CAMPS TENT CITIES SHANTIES ON A WORLDWIDE SCALE..." R. B., 'UFO', p. 12.

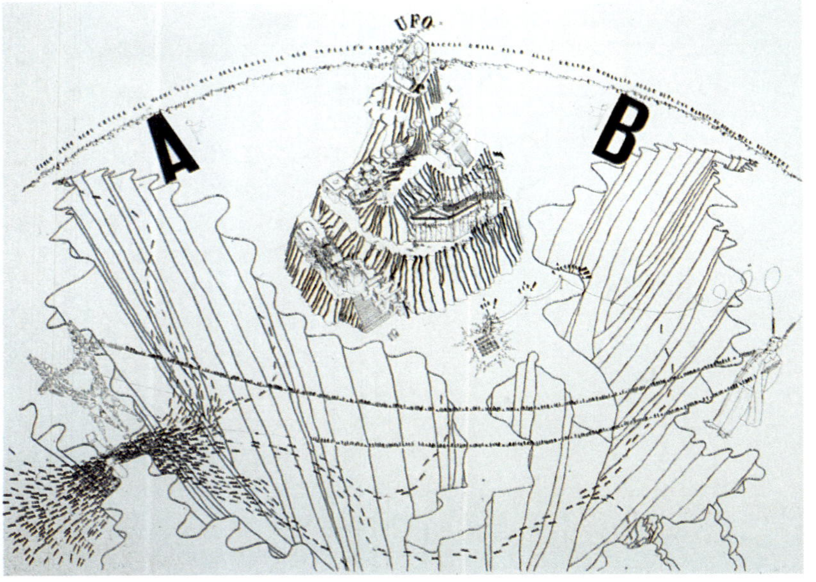

35. UFO, Graduation thesis project, *L'ingegnosa conquista della montagna della tigre*, supervisor Leonardo Ricci, assistant supervisor Umberto Eco, Faculty of Architecture at University of Florence, 1970-1971, Patrizia Cammeo/Riccardo Foresi Archives, Florence

36-40. UFO, Graduation thesis project, *L'ingegnosa conquista della montagna della tigre,* supervisor Leonardo Ricci, assistant supervisor Umberto Eco, Faculty of Architecture at University of Florence, 1970-1971, preparatory drawings, FRAC Archives, Orléans

form, and language. In the background of the composition stands an aqueduct that imitates the forms of the portico of Giovanni Muzio's Palazzo dell'Arte, but is now broken, emblem of an architecture which has been destroyed and replaced by an arrangement of eloquent fragments. With an image somewhere between that of an American-style Main Street and the set of a Spaghetti Western, UFO's road belongs to the same lineage as another celebrated street composed of eloquent bits and pieces, the *Strada Novissima* conceived by Paolo Portoghesi for the first Venice Biennale of Architecture, contributing to the semiotic shift that would distinguish Postmodern architecture.

In the graduation thesis, a single drawing represents a village made up of projects that the members of UFO had drawn up individually over the preceding years:[151] a villa designed by Foresi for his father, the fitting-out of a shop commissioned from UFO by a friend of Cammeo's, two villas conceived by Binazzi for Diacceto and Maiori, and the conversion of a barn commissioned from Cammeo (figs. 35-40).[152] Perched on the slopes of an imaginary mountain located at the centre of the Italian peninsula, the projects are arranged to form an ascending route that, as in the case of the village for the Triennale, has an apex on the summit of the mountain, where UFO placed the barn. Each of those buildings is a transfiguration of a historic work of architecture, as if they were trying to retrace the main stages in the history of the discipline, from the Greek temple to the Aztec monument, from the Roman villa to the Amerindian pueblo.[153] The fact that at the climax of that history of architecture there is an enclosure containing individual "nest boxes" is another of UFO's criticisms of contemporary architecture, reduced to "minimal housing units" for people who have themselves been reduced to birds.[154] UFO's spirit of dissent did not stop at contemporary architecture though, but addressed the essence of the architectural project itself. In the drawing prepared for the defence of the thesis, giants and blocks of kryptonite appeared,[155] both of them ascribable to the imagery of the comic strip, hurled against UFO's village as an expression of the history of architecture. So the group's only attempt to give architecture the form of the building and the village was destroyed by UFO itself, in confirmation of the impossibility of accepting any new construction, be it dwelling or monument. UFO's act takes on even more radical tones if we think that that project was presented as the conclusion of its members' training, elevating it to a critique of the teaching of architecture at the university. So it is no surprise that, alongside the drawing, UFO organised a series of performances, the ones that for the group were the only kind of architecture still possible: the multiplication of the drawing in many copies to simulate an ample graphic production, something usually expected for graduation theses; a screening of the film *Gone with*

151 Cammeo and Maschietto, conversation with Castellini and Hamzeian.

152 The shop, Foresi's villa, and the barn were recalled by Cammeo and Maschietto in the above conversation with Castellini and Hamzeian, while Binazzi's villas were mentioned in a conversation with Lampariello.

153 Cammeo and Maschietto, conversation with Castellini and Hamzeian.

154 Ibid.

155 Ibid.

41-42. UFO (with Antonio Infantino), *Ipotesi di sopravvivenza*, giugno 1971, Patrizia Cammeo/ Riccardo Foresi Archives, Florence

the Wind, accompanied by refreshments and a commentary by one of the waiters from the restaurant I 4 Leoni; the reading by someone from outside the group of an invented text that could only be deciphered with the aid of a mirror; finally the hurling of a brick against that mirror by Binazzi. The group was conscious that the propensity for protest had become its distinguishing characteristic, and so it represented itself in the thesis drawing in a new disguise, no longer that of Unidentified Flying Objects, but of eels swimming against the current, in order to go and die in the Sargasso Sea.

While the central theme of the thesis appears to be that of the destruction of architecture and its spilling over into performance, it is still possible to find in it an interest in the territory. In the drawing made by the group we also see the imposing figure of Mao, represented in the form of words, distributing energy to salad growing in a vegetable garden through a high-tension pylon that, emerging from his ears, spans the globe.[156] The fascination exercised by China, which was also reflected in the choice to give the project the title *L'ingegnosa conquista della montagna della tigre* ("Taking Tiger Mountain by Strategy"), based on that of a Chinese opera of the fifties, produced an image with a complex significance.[157] On the one hand, the flow of energy that runs along the pylon as words, whether onomatopoeic ones or the lyrics of a folksong inspired by communist poetry, is yet another representation of the spread of power around the territory—a lesson, this, that UFO had learned in part through the publications about China in the group's possession. On the other, it is precisely in those waves of energy in the form of written words that it is already possible to glimpse the premises of a kind of performative intervention that, once the investigation was concluded, would lead UFO into an effective confrontation with other power structures.

156 The title of the project is borrowed from one of the Chinese and communist "revolutionary model operas" of the fifties: *Zhi qu wei hu shan*, or *Taking Tiger Mountain by Strategy*. See the libretto of the opera in the Maschietto Archives.

157 UFO's fascination with China is also attested by the sentences written on the drawing of the thesis, including: "The true heroes are the masses when the masses have mastered maozedongthought they are endowed with an inexhaustible creative capacity."

43. UFO, Competition project for the new campus of the University of Florence, 1971, Musée National d'Art Moderne, Centre Pompidou, Paris

44. UFO, *Giro d'Italia, S-Space Mondial Festival*, Florence, November 1971, 9999 Archives, Florence, Courtesy Elettra Fiumi

UFO's exit from the Faculty of Architecture with *L'ingegnosa conquista della montagna della tigre* represents an important stage in its history. Although the group would formally continue its joint activity for several more years, after the thesis the members of UFO began to carry out individual actions, and in so doing undermined the concerted and participatory dimension that had always distinguished UFO, to the point where its voice would soon be reduced to the single one of Binazzi.[158]

Actions of Disturbance Against the Control of the Territory

What had been territorial projects to be tackled through storytelling and drawing were transformed, from 1971 onwards, into performances centred on behaviour. Although easily traced back to the ones staged at San Giovanni Valdarno and in the *happenvironments,* the territorial performances were a different matter, both because acting was now almost completely absent and the action became dynamic and athletic, and because there were no more inflatables and polyurethane figures, just objects of everyday use. UFO was conscious of this conceptual shift from one-off pieces to action based in behaviour, to the point where the group defined this sort of action as one of the few forms of architecture still possible.[159] UFO's new focus on behaviour reflected the group's interest in kinesics, the books of Desmond Morris, and Gustav Bally's research into human behaviour.[160] In the context of this research, UFO studied different forms of behaviour, ranging from the paramilitary to the aural or athletic.

The objective of these "behavioural actions" was to contest the presence of the State in the territory. At times they took the form

158 Although between 1972 and 1973 the participation of the other members of the group in the performances linked to the *Giro d'Italia* and in the drafting of texts like *Coccoina* was still evident, from the time of UFO's participation in Global Tools the group's activity would essentially be carried out by Binazzi alone.

159 UFO, 'Il Giro d'Italia', in *Argomenti e immagini di design*, no. 6, July-August 1972, pp. 66-67.

160 Lapo Binazzi, conversation with Beatrice Lampariello, 23 July 2021. Not coincidentally an article by Bally was published in the same issue of *Harck* as Binazzi's text 'Album di profezie'. See Gustav Bally, 'Il margine della libertà. Il significato del gioco negli animali e negli umani', *Harck*, no. 1, 1971, pp. 7-9. Desmond Morris, *The Naked Ape* (London: Jonathan Cape, 1967); Edward Hall, *The Hidden Dimension* (Garden City, NY: Doubleday, 1966). The Italian editions of both these books can be found in Binazzi and Maschietto's libraries.

45-46. UFO, *Giro d'Italia*, *Contemporanea* exhibition, Villa Borghese Car Park, Rome, 1973, Lapo Binazzi Archives, Florence

of "paramilitary exercises"[161] to be conducted by the group, at others with other colleagues in the countryside around Castel Ruggero, from the "parallel climbing" of trees to the "swim in 'AV' formation", and the assault on an electricity substation (figs. 41-42).[162] In other cases the behavioural research was reduced to actions carried out by Foresi alone, photographed by Bachi as he trespassed on property to which entry was forbidden, urinated on gas pipelines, and occupied railway tracks.[163] In all cases, though, UFO's actions represented an intervention in the territory that was of a peculiar urbanistic nature, one that Binazzi not coincidentally referred to as *fantaurbanistica*.[164]

Sometimes the actions involved the use of sound, as in the case of the performance staged for the competition for the new campus of the Faculty of Architecture on the plain of Sesto Fiorentino, an occasion which UFO decided to exploit for an attempt to ensure the preservation of the local environment and fauna. So the group drove in a car across the plain to warn with a megaphone the animals and inhabitants of the future destruction of the area.[165] The photographs taken during the performance were retouched by the group through the addition of "energy fluxus of communication" to produce a gigantic and monstrous creature, the *ID Monster*,[166] which was nothing but an allegorical representation of the oppression that the buildings of power were destined to exercise over the territory.[167] While in the drawing for the thesis UFO had employed onomatopoeic words to signify the flow of energy from the figure of Mao, for the

161 See UFO, 'Paramount'. These-actions were also entitled *Ipotesi di sopravvivenza* ("Hypotheses of Survival"). See the cover of *Casabella*, no. 386, February 1974.

162 Quoted in UFO, 'Risposta al questionario di "in" sui problemi della Facoltà di Architettura', *in. Argomenti e immagini di design*, no. 9, February-March 1973, pp. 78-80. These actions retained a fanciful character for the members of UFO that was able to turn the "swim in 'AV' formation" into the crossing of the Yangtze river under the guidance of Chairman Mao. Maschietto, conversation with Castellini.

163 For the significance of those infrastructures see UFO and Daniela Palazzoli (eds.), *Controllo colonizzazione e fascismo sul territorio: Milano, Galleria 291, maggio/giugno 1974* (Florence: Centro Di, 1974).

164 UFO, 'Appunti per una ridefinizione del concetto di fantaurbanistica', *Progettare inpiù*, no. 8, February-March 1975, pp. 24-27.

165 Patrizia Cammeo, conversation with Gloria Castellini, 24 June 2021.

47. UFO, *Casa a ostacoli sul territorio*, Eurodomus, Turin, 1972, Lapo Binazzi Archives, Florence

competition sound was represented in the form of graphic symbols such as arrows, stars, and other stylised drawings that were placed alongside words and letters ("No!," "A," "B"), turning these photographs into yet another of Eco's "semiotic clusters" (fig. 43).[168]

On other occasions, UFO's actions took on a sporting character, steeped in a playful dimension, perhaps even the atmosphere of a circus. At first these were staged indoors and then in the open—two aspects that made these actions variations on the interventions in Florence in 1968. One of the earliest athletic actions organised by UFO was a cycle race along the lines of the *Giro d'Italia* and held in the discotheque run by the 9999, Space Electronic, on the occasion of the architecture festival *S-space Mondial*, in November 1971.[169] Staged inside the discotheque, the *Giro* became a simulation of an athletic action, in which UFO replaced the handmade one-off pieces of the previous years with everyday objects like a bicycle and a tricolour jersey, of which UFO exorcised the symbolism that still associated them with Fascism in those years (fig. 44).[170] With the *Giro d'Italia*, UFO reduced the performance to those simple sporting and routine actions whose performative capacities had been recognised by Kirby himself.[171]

With the progressive abandonment of the interiors of the Space Electronic for the outdoors, the bicycle performance of the *Giro d'Italia* was transformed into a game played with Coca-Cola bottle tops in Bologna's Piazza Santo Stefano for the performance

166 UFO, 'The ID Monster', *On Site on Energy*, no. 7, 1975, p. 37. The name *Mostro dell'ID* ("ID Monster") referred to the "emanations of the subconscious" in the film *Forbidden Planet*, something which had already been a source of inspiration for the Independent Group in the exhibition *This Is Tomorrow*, held at the Whitechapel Art Gallery in London in 1956.

167 See UFO's description of the "repressive institutions of the BOURGEOIS STATE" as "a sort of monster of enormous size that eats, ruminates, spits fire, shits" in UFO, 'Elementi di prossemica territoriale: questionario', p. 10.

168 The arrows and stars were added to the photographs using a method of retouching similar to the one developed for the *Rebus Viventi all'Isolotto di Don Mazzi*.

169 The "Separate School for Expanded Conceptual Architecture" was held from 9 to 11 November 1971 with "happenings, declarations, and documents." 'Gli UFO', in 9999 and Superstudio (eds.), *Vita, morte e miracoli dell'architettura = Life, Death and Miracles of Architecture* (Florence: G&G, 1971), n.p.

170 UFO, 'Il Giro d'Italia'.

Coccoina,[172] and then a realistic bicycle race, first in Chianti, to reach an A.N.A.S. roadhouse that became the new target of a para-military exercise with the attempt by the members of the group to climb on top of it, get inside it, and even lift it up,[173] and then on the outskirts of Rome, to liberate the territory by crossing it in a variety of means, including clambering over pylons and monuments, passing through greenhouses, and trespassing on private property until they reached the venue of the exhibition *Contemporanea*, curated by Achille Bonito Oliva and held in the car park of Villa Borghese in the centre of Rome (figs. 45-46).[174] It was on this occasion that the group came up with a new form of representation that differed from the photographs which up until then had been the favoured means of disseminating UFO's work to a broader swathe of the public. The group intended to film its performance in Rome with a "super 8" film camera,[175] projecting it in real time, and so "live," on a screen set up in the exhibition.[176] We cannot escape the impression that the group appropriated the theme of the exhibition in an act of "video art" that was intended to disseminate instantaneous metaphorical meanings, with a different take on the role that photography had played in the *happenvironments*.

In addition to the sporting and irreverent actions in the framework of the *Giro d'Italia* performance, others were carried out by the group in Bologna and for the installation at "Eurodomus 4" in Turin devoted to a *Casa a ostacoli sul territorio* ("Obstacle House on the Territory").[177] In the first case, it involved shooting someone out of a cannon and gluing trading cards with portraits of sports champions onto the paving of Piazza Santo Stefano;[178] in the second case, the incursion of a horse into the "Eurodomus 4" exhibition (fig. 47).[179] That horse brought the experiments conducted by UFO to outline another sort of architecture that turned into performances aimed at mocking not just the discipline, but also its presentation at trade fairs, in line with the most recent artistic experimentations, such as the event staged by Jannis Kounellis with twelve horses at the Galleria L'Attico in Rome, in 1969.

Binazzi's Conceptualisation of UFO's Interventions

With the behavioural actions carried out on the territory, UFO arrived at a full awareness of the content and objective of its interventions. Since 1970, the group had given up on its one-off pieces and turned instead to the use of existing objects, such as the bicycle and the tricolour jersey, bringing to a logical conclusion the process of destruction of the object stemming from the original idea of rebelling against industrial production through the artisanal production of San Clemente. UFO was equally conscious of having destroyed the idea of architecture as project and creative act in favour of interventions

171 Kirby, 'The New Theatre', *The Tuale Drama Review*, pp. 29, 31. It was Binazzi who in the following years would conceptualise the analogy between UFO's actions and the "'non-matrixed' of everyday life" illustrated by Kirby. See Lapo Binazzi (UFO), "Senza titolo", in Andrea Granchi and Maurizio Nannucci (eds.), *Zona Film. Documenti di cinema d'artista* (Florence: Zona, 1977), n.p.

172 *Coccoina* was part of the event *Pollution* that was held in Bologna from 8 to 14 October 1972. In the action "Il Giro d'Italia a tappini" the members of UFO played the game on a track drawn in chalk on the paving of Piazza Santo Stefano, simulating a stage in the *Giro*. The concept of the game was based on a play of words between *tappini* ("bottle tops") and *tappe* ("stages" in the bicycle race). UFO, 'Coccoina', in Daniela Palazzoli (ed.), *Pollution: Per una nuova estetica dell'inquinamento* (Bologna: Fondazione Iris, 1972), pp. 46-47.

173 See UFO, 'Giro d'Italia', in *Architecture Player*, https://www.architectureplayer.com/clips/giro-d-italia.

174 Bonito Oliva (ed.), *Contemporanea. Roma, Parcheggio di Villa Borghese 11. 1973 / 2. 1974*. See Binazzi's testimony in Alessandra Acocella and Caterina Toschi (eds.), 'Firenze sperimentale: gli anni Settanta attraverso le testimonianze di Bruno Corà, Lapo Binazzi e Paolo Masi', in Anna Mazzanti (ed.), *Art/Tapes/22. Le origini della videoarte* (Cinisello Balsamo, MI: Silvana Editoriale, 2017), pp. 44-48.

175 UFO had experimented with film ever since the construction site in San Clemente. For a list of UFO's films see Binazzi (UFO), 'Senza titolo'.

176 Due to the failure to clean the camera heads the film was not recorded, but a sequence of photos does bear witness to the action. See the interview with Binazzi in Acocella and Toschi (eds.), 'Firenze sperimentale', p. 47.

177 In the event staged in Turin, on 27 May 1972, Bracci also took part. See UFO, 'La provocazione degli UFO: happening all'Eurodomus',

Domus, no. 512, July 1972, p. 34, and the photo on the cover of *Domus* no. 513, August 1972.

178 Despite the sporting and circus air of these actions, UFO did not lose its habit of imbuing them with ideological significance and turning the three performances into the same number of metaphors for Italian society and politics. See UFO, 'Coccoina'.

179 UFO, 'La provocazione degli UFO: happening all'Eurodomus'.

180 The idea of this kind of teaching experience was derived from the experiment that between 1970 and 1972 had led Superstudio and 9999 to invent the *S-Space* festival and the performances organised at Space Electronic.

181 *Una scuola di arti e tecniche popolari*, n.d. (Ugo La Pietra Archives, Milan).

182 For a closer examination of the relations between UFO and Global Tools see the essay by Sadler in this volume.

183 The magazine devoted issues 2 and 3 of 1971 to the destruction of the object and issues 5, 6, and 7 of 1972 to the destruction of the city.

184 UFO, 'Produzione industriale e creatività individuale', *Casabella*, no. 379, July 1973, pp. 46-47.

that had now become actions. The group condensed these reflections into a proper theory in a series of texts written between 1973 and 1974, chiefly by Binazzi in the context of UFO's participation in Global Tools, an alternative form of teaching aimed at replacing the construction of architecture with the elaboration of theoretical, conceptual, and performative operations in which the exponents of the Italian neo-avant-garde (9999, Archizoom, Ugo La Pietra, Gianni Pettena, Ettore Sottsass Jr., Superstudio, and the then editor of *Casabella* Alessandro Mendini) took part.[180] From the way that the experience of Global Tools was seen as an experimental laboratory devoted to manual and artisanal activity and centred on the free expression of individual creativity in contrast with the industrial object and the alienation inherent in its production, it is clear that in this phase of UFO's history, the collaboration with the other groups of the neo-avant-garde resulted in a mutual influence between the activities of Global Tools and the work of UFO.[181]

Just as Global Tools proclaimed that it was aiming at a de-intellectualisation and a de-culturalisation in order to free itself from the so-called "disciplinary specifics," the industrial product was targeted by UFO, clarifying the position it had already assumed at the construction site in San Clemente.[182] It was a position that, in the same period, was emerging among the neo-avant-gardes with the proposal of Archizoom and Superstudio to devote several monographic issues of the magazine *in. Argomenti e immagini di design* to the destruction of the object and the city.[183]

It was against this background that in the summer of 1973 Binazzi came up with another narration,[184] this time in the form of an illustrated account similar in appearance to Superstudio's *A Journey*

48. Lapo Binazzi and Isa Baldi, *Ladro d'albergo II, Annunciazione*, Galleria Schema, Florence, 1976, Lapo Binazzi Archives, Florence

49. Lapo Binazzi and Marino Vismara, *Catastrofi leggere ecc.*, Cortile di Palazzo Strozzi, Florence, 1978, Lapo Binazzi Archives, Florence

into the Realm of Reason, but with elements of science-fiction and the adventure story present in the recourse to figures drawn from the *Flash Gordon* and *Jungle Jim* comic strips.[185] Binazzi told the tale of an unnamed object that over the course of human evolution has lost its ability to function and communicate and thus has been abandoned, overrun by nature as if it were a new version of the *Moving City* represented by Sottsass Jr., in ruins and in a natural environment that has gained the upper hand over historical and modern architecture and even that of the neo-avant-garde.[186] Yet in Binazzi's story that nature does not restore the Earth to its original paradisiacal condition because on its surface "pay power sockets" continue to appear for new forms of State control of the territory. So it becomes clear why Binazzi declared that, with the object destroyed, nothing was left but to intervene in the territory through performances that consisted of modes of behaviour entailing the use of body and action.[187] With this sort of intervention, Binazzi also altered the objective of his and UFO's research, which was now less and less a matter of investigating and reconquering the territory. Binazzi's interventions remained acts of subversion, but de-intellectualised in order to sanction the creative freedom of the individual through "simple" "modes of behaviour" and "actions," and "elementary" "techniques" and "thoughts."[188] The processes of "discontinuity" and "disconnection" that UFO had developed out of Eco's reflections on semiotics, and applied to the interventions of disturbance through complex combinations of continually changing images, objects, sounds, and meanings were simplified into immediate processes like "thinking or doing two or more things at once," "comparing elements, more and more distant from each other," and "giving rise to deliberately imperfect systems."[189] And it was in the context of the posthumous conceptualisation of UFO's work that Binazzi defined the semantic short-circuits between signified and signifier and the ambiguous juxtaposition of ideas and objects that the group had always sought in terms of a "rejection of explanation."[190]

A Celibate Machine for the Production of Symbols: the Death of UFO

Between 1975 and 1978, UFO's production found concrete expression in a series of theoretical reflections and interventions formulated for the most part by Binazzi.[191] This period of experimentation proved to be an opportunity to examine more closely the actions that in the framework of Global Tools had remained generic formulations of "relations between architecture and magic," "sport analogy," and "pure creativity";[192] actions that had been staged at certain institutions linked to contemporary art (the Spazio Zona and Galleria Schema in Florence, and the Centro Internazionale di Brera in Milan).[193] With the destruction of the object and the formulation of the theory of the

185 See Alex Raymond's comic strips *Jungle Jim* and *Flash Gordon*.

186 "The explosive decentralization of consumer goods distribution has pulverized the cities, has eliminated them from the face of the earth. They have been consumed by the jungle, by the silk-cotton trees, by the desert." These are the premises that Sottsass Jr. enunciated to present his idea of architecture in an artisanal, post-industrial world that has rediscovered a balance between nature and the human psyche. Ettore Sottsass Jr., 'Il Pianeta come festival', *Casabella*, no. 365, May 1972, pp. 41-47: 42.

187 This reasoning was again formulated in the context of the works of Global Tools, at the moment when, in 1974, its participants divided themselves into five research and work groups: "Communication," "Body," "Construction," "Survival," and "Theory." The non-disciplinary groupings were organised to outline the work programme of the school, with seminars, experiments, and performances which reflected the fact that learning through doing was the basis of Global Tools. On the constitution of the work groups see *Bozza dei rapporti tra i gruppi Global Tools*, 22 September 1974 (Adolfo Natalini Archives, Florence).

188 Lapo Binazzi, *Global Tools - Gruppo "Teoria". Relazione di Lapo Binazzi*, Florence, 10 October 1974 (Lapo Binazzi Archives, Florence).

189 Ibid.

190 See Lapo Binazzi (UFO), Alberto Breschi, Roberto Pecchioli (Zziggurat) and Remo Buti, 'T-h-eor-y-ia', in *Bollettino Global Tools n. 1* (Milan: Edizioni l'uomo e l'arte, 1975), n.p.

191 In this period, Binazzi re-examined UFO's activity through writings that ranged from a reworking of the earlier investigations of the territory to an analysis of the reflections on the discontinuous

"discontinuous," the earlier performances devoted to the territory or to the manipulation of objects were reduced to actions devoid of any participation by the public or interaction with it; all of them were centred on an athletic effort (Binazzi's furtive nocturnal bursting into an imaginary hotel room to surprise Isa Baldi, his life partner; the archery practice accompanied by a violin sonata played by his friend, the musician Mino Vismara; and Binazzi's "dribble" around Vismara, who took part in the athletic action while still playing his violin) (figs. 48-49).[194] The few objects used by Binazzi—lamps, footballs, and violin—replaced the bicycle of the *Giro d'Italia*: they were tools needed for the expression of the performer's body and for the juxtaposition of incoherent operations in a Dada style, such as the fusion of a football move and a musical performance. "The institutional logic of intervention in the territory or the environment," wrote Binazzi, "is replaced by the poetic operation of discontinuous visual strategy and the connection of facts apparently remote from one another, comparable by relations of contiguity at the limits of the random theory of free associations."[195] In his pursuit of the "discontinuous visual strategy," Binazzi also revived the idea of the combination of different linguistic codes, making the notes of Vismara's violin a constant complement to the visual movement of the action.[196] It is in the context of Binazzi's performance that we have to place UFO's last collective action: the one staged by the group for the Venice Art Biennale of 1978, directed by Lara-Vinca Masini.[197] The group organised a crossing of the Venetian lagoon aboard a motorboat steered by a ferryman. During the crossing, against the backdrop of the facades of Venice's *palazzi* and with the musical accompaniment of Vismara, UFO displayed to the public lining the *fondamenta* ("quay") the blow-up of a framed photo of the A.N.A.S. roadhouse (fig. 50).[198] As had happened with the pieces of the San Clemente construction site, in the crossing of the lagoon UFO staged another parade, transforming the canals of Venice into streets and squares like those of the protest marches in Florence. But what in Florence had been a piece carried by people became in Venice a piece carried by a boat, a contrivance similar to the bikes of the *Giro d'Italia*. But that boat had a particular significance. The naming of it as a *b/arca* ("b/ark"), alluded to a container of precious objects for their preservation: the A.N.A.S. roadhouse, by now reduced to a screen for a new transmission of messages without any more need for the three-dimensional substance, although pared to a minimum, of the inflatable. In the combination of screen and boat, the performance in Venice seems to hold a dialogue with Foresi's installation *Ipotesi di sopravvivenza*. With respect to that model, however, screen and boat were now distorted in form and significance through a transfiguration that crystallised the evolution of UFO's work. In Milan the gondola had been an iconic object to be placed on top of the screen as a "fond memory" of the Italian

outlined with Global Tools and a historical reconstruction of UFO's activity that was poles apart from the de-intellectualization of the profession and the refusal to explain that Binazzi was theorising in those years. For the reflection on the territory see the *Controguida di Firenze (elementi di prossemica territoriale)*, n.d. (Lapo Binazzi Archives, Florence), Binazzi and Claudio Greppi's texts collected under the title *Programma di ricerca* (UFO, 'Appunti per una ridefinizione del concetto di fantaurbanistica', *Progettare inpiù*, no. 8, February-March 1975, pp. 24-27: 26), and a description of the *Mostro dell'ID* (UFO, 'The ID Monster'). On the theory of the discontinuous see UFO, 'Appunti per una ridefinizione del concetto di fantaurbanistica', p. 24; UFO, 'L'oggetto storico riproducibile all'infinito'; and 'L'architettura radicale è morta: viva l'architettura radicale', *Spazioarte*, vol. IV, no. 10-11, June-October 1977, pp. 17-20. On the rejection of explanation see Binazzi (UFO), *Ufo. Discontinuità e territorio*.

192 Binazzi, *Global Tools - Gruppo "Teoria". Relazione di Lapo Binazzi*.

193 See Pezzato (ed.), *Ufo story: dall'architettura radicale al design globale*; Acocella and Toschi (eds.), 'Firenze sperimentale', pp. 44, 46-48.

194 Lapo Binazzi (UFO) and Marino Vismara (violin), 'Scarto (performance serie "La metafora rovesciata" Milan 1977. Foto Carlo Bachi)', in Alberto Moretti, Carlo Bertocci, Raul Dominguez and Alessandro Vezzosi (eds.), *schema informazione 3. Politic-art (Le contraddizioni sono ovunque. Contradictions are everywhere)* (Florence: Schema, (1978)), n.p.

195 Binazzi (UFO), *Ufo. Discontinuità e territorio*.

196 Ibid.

197 See Lapo Binazzi (UFO), 'UFO' and 'Performance in barca UFO-Mino Vismara (violino)', in Lara-Vinca Masini (ed.), *Topologia e morfogenesi. Utopia e crisi dell'antinatura. Momenti delle intenzioni architettoniche in Italia* (Venice: Edizioni la Biennale di Venezia, 1978), pp. 56-59.

home, and a sign of resistance to the alienating bombardment by the media issuing from that screen. On the contrary, in Venice the gondola was no longer carried but was the carrier of the screen, while the screen became in turn a bearer of different messages. Right from the conception of the screen that was the *Giornale murario*, UFO had been drawn to the idea of an *architettura parlante*, and after experimenting with its potentialities through the production of eloquent three-dimensional objects, had now returned to the idea of a screen for the transmission not of words but of a photograph of the A.N.A.S. roadhouse. What had been identified as an icon of the power of the State over the territory, had now been reduced to an image, lost the ideological value of which it had been the bearer. It was transformed into a symbolic device for the transmission of immediate and not necessarily ideological messages, as demonstrated by the visual juxtaposition of the A.N.A.S. roadhouse and the facades of the Venetian *palazzi* in the background, which was as much a mockery of traditional architecture as a surreal optical game.[199] As it is demonstrated by Binazzi dressing up as Hemingway in the manner of the *happenvironments*, as well as by Vismara's musical accompaniment, UFO's last screen took on board Binazzi's reflections on the de-intellectualisation of the artistic operation and the random theory of discontinuity, and so it was turned into a symbolic device that more than any other rejected explanation and was presented as a truly open work—a "useless mechanism for the exit from the system of art and its disciplinary specifics: visual arts/architecture," was how Binazzi put it.[200] It is no accident that UFO identified as a model for this final performance *The Bride Stripped Bare by Her Bachelors, Even*, the Dada work of art with which, through a screen on which he arranged enigmatic forms, Marcel Duchamp had conceived a work open to different interpretations, paving the way for the emergence of Conceptual Art.[201] As a symbolic machine for the generation of open meanings, the Venetian parade of the screen on a "b/ark" also took on the character of a procession, but one that no longer had anything in common with the vitalistic march of the students in Florence, but assumed the guise of a dramatic funeral in which that "b/ark" revealed its other significance as an imaginary sarcophagus. In fact, it marked the end of UFO's collective experience, which came to a conclusion with this project and was continued afterwards solely through the personal and poetic reworking of Binazzi. It also marked the death of traditional architecture which, transformed first into an environment of meaningful iconic objects, and then dissolved into a performance, was reduced to a celibate machine for the free production of meanings that transferred the creative force once possessed by architecture to the eyes of its observer.

198 As with the actions of disturbance in 1968, the enigmatic performance was completed by a photographic feature by Bachi that set the A.N.A.S. roadhouse against facades along the Grand Canal and with some texts that, as in San Giovanni Valdarno, questioned the elements of the performance, nullifying its traditional meanings in a polysemous decoding. Among the texts there was one devoted to the theory of discontinuity that offered a key to the interpretation of UFO's actions and, in this sense, once again contradicted the principle of the refusal to explain. Vinca Masini (ed.), *Topologia e morfogenesi*, pp. 57-59.

199 "The b/ark is viewed on the same scale as the fronts-backdrops of Venice," wrote Binazzi. Binazzi (UFO), 'UFO' and 'Performance in barca UFO-Mino Vismara (violino)', p. 57.

200 Binazzi (UFO), *Ufo. Discontinuità e territorio*.

201 Binazzi made clear the derivation of the performance from Duchamp's work through numerous references in the text published in the catalogue of the Biennale. Binazzi (UFO), 'UFO' and 'Performance in barca UFO-Mino Vismara (violino)', pp. 57, 59.

50. UFO and Marino Vismara, Performance for the Venice Art Biennale, *B/arca A.N.A.S.*, Venice Art Biennale, Venice, 1978, Lapo Binazzi Archives, Florence

RISTORANTE

2 CO

NTEXT

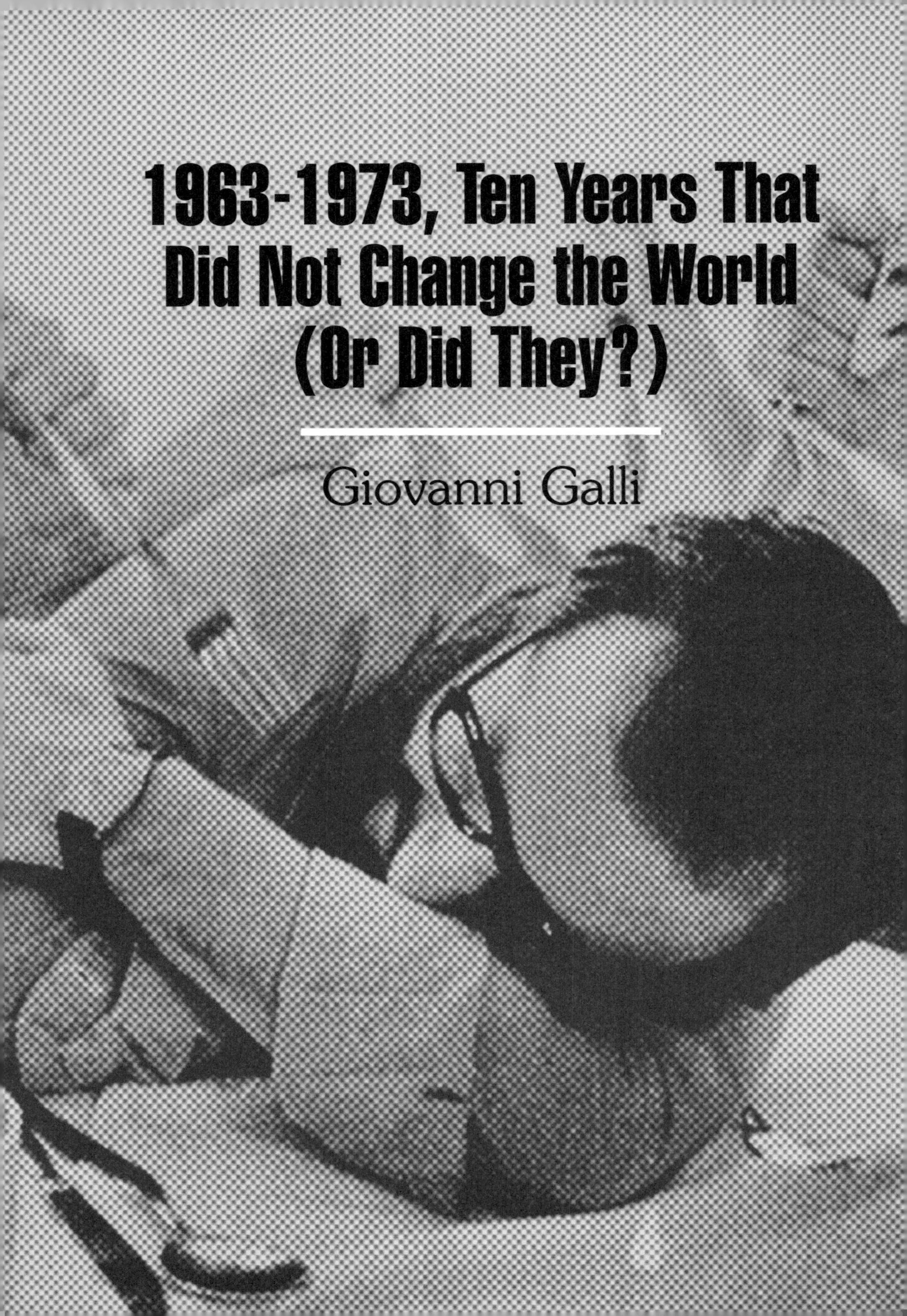
1963-1973, Ten Years That
Did Not Change the World
(Or Did They?)
Giovanni Galli

Between the mid-sixties and the mid-seventies of the last century, modernity held a *rendez-vous* with itself. It came out transfigured. Seen in hindsight, the whole affair appears a postmodern conspiracy against modernity, not to end it but to bring it to its final, logical outcome. Literature and architecture, with semiotics on the background, are the principal characters of the story told here, proposed as a synecdoche of a more general cultural phenomenon. The setting is Italy, in turn presented as a hyperbole of a global phenomenon. As the title suggests, 1963 and 1973 are the *termini post quem* and *ante quem*. Many reasons recommended the choice of this time-frame: ten is a round number (which is good for a tale); two avant-garde radical groups were born at this time: the literary movement Gruppo 63 and the architectural movement Global Tools (1973)—a stillborn attempt to group various radical architects into a sort of all-star team; and, last but certainly not least, the two dates mark, respectively, the peak of Italy's so-called "Economic Miracle," and October 1973's oil crisis, in turn triggering the first economic recession post World War II. Between the two, "68"—a number become a hallmark—is there as a placeholder for the peak of the first global cultural phenomenon in history, setting the mood for the whole decade in question.

UFO, Photograph, *Umberto Eco fatto segno a numerosi colpi di forchetta dai suoi discepoli* ("Umberto Eco turned into the target of numerous fork-stabs by his disciples"), n.d.

Intro

April 26, 1968: the centre of Florence is occupied by rallying students. Not just one of the usual '68 rallies the city is used to by now. The students are carrying an inflated plastic rocket, with an inscription in capital letters reading "Colgate con Vietcong": the rocket, it would seem, is both a weapon and a huge tube of toothpaste. The students, of course, are the members of the architectural group UFO, and the tube is one of their trademarks *Urboeffimeri*, the fifth in a series of seven: gigantic, ephemeral props at the centre of happenings mixing objects, provocations, and free use of words. UFO are considered one of the most significant "conspirators" of Radical Architecture, and *Urboeffimeri* probably their quintessential work. Not buildings, nor plans: just inflatables. Among other things, the adjective "radical" seems to qualify the capacity to transform the very concept of "architecture." Those rallies were specimens of a more general attitude (the first real architectonical avant-garde, we will argue), out there to change architecture and, with it, the world. After the past masters, using subtler weapons. Preparing the revolution, the one that never came.

1. Avant-garde, Neo-Avant-garde, and Radicalism

The concept of avant-garde is freighted with contradictions: it must forever struggle to defeat all kinds of tradition and *status quos*, but its greatest victory equals its worst defeat, in terms of integration in the common sensibility to become the new tradition.[1] This accounts for avant-gardes' nihilistic drive: the ever-growing reductionism, the race to arrive at the blank page in literature, the white canvas in painting, total silence in music; in the end it accounts for avant-gardes' suicidal drive: their thirst of destruction turned the other way round, against themselves and art itself.[2]

Or, instead of committing suicide, avant-garde can forever stall on the edge of the abyss, forever turning around the *beinahe nichts* ("almost nothing") separating from it, shifting a little nothing here, turning a little nothing there. The problem is, over a brief span outrage becomes routine and shock veers to boredom.[3] Worse: outrage and shock become acceptable, still a little boring perhaps, but acceptable. The sixties thrive on books about the crisis of modernity (which is the name avant-garde gets when accepted as normal).[4] But, in those same sixties, a new phenomenon emerged: new artistic movements self-consciously presenting themselves as *neo*-avant-gardes, looking back for inspiration at historical avant-gardes

1 See Peter Bürger, *Teoria dell'avanguardia* (Turin: Bollati Boringhieri, 1990 (1974)), pp. 43-64.

2 See Renato Poggioli, *Teoria dell'arte d'avanguardia* (Bologna: Il Mulino, 1962), pp. 76-79.

3 See Roger Kimball, 'The Trivialization of Outrage', in Kimball, *Experiments Against Reality* (Chicago: Ivan R. Dee, 2000), pp. 277-304.

4 See, for example, Daniel Bell, *The Cultural Contradictions of Capitalism* (New York: Basic Books, 1976), p. 20; Lionel Trilling, *Beyond*

Culture: Essays on Literature and Learning (New York: Viking Press, 1965), pp. IX-XVIII; Irving Howe, 'The Idea of the Modern', in Howe (ed.), *The Idea of the Modern in Literature and the Arts* (New York: Horizon Press, 1967), pp. 11-40.

5 It wasn't a phenomenon limited to Italy, nor to literature and architecture: suffice to mention the French Nouveau Roman literary movement, and the international arts movement Fluxus.

while trying to keep running forward. Putting a new paradox on top of the other. This is where both Gruppo 63 and the vast and heterogeneous phenomenon of Italian Radical Architecture came in,[5] suffering different levels of impact from the paradoxical quality of the "neo-" prefix. The different ontological status of the disciplines respectively implied accounts for that, as it does for all the other divergences and affinities between the two that we will encounter along the road.

1.1 Gruppo 63

The members of Gruppo 63 were mostly poets, writers, and art and literary critics who gathered for six days in Palermo in 1963. Hence the name of the group. They were "committed intellectuals," but preferred to call themselves "cultural workers": at the time, the heart of any intellectual worthy of the name beat to the left. As stated several times by themselves,[6] they had little in common apart from a clear idea of what they opposed: Benedetto Croce's idealism, still informing the aesthetical inclinations of both conservative and—amazingly—progressive "official" Italian culture; and the mimetic, naturalistic nature of contemporary Italian literature. They had a quote to define it: "The Marquise went out at five o'clock," taken from—not by chance—the first *Surrealist Manifesto* (1924), in which André Breton used it as an epitome of the *incipit* a real artist would never deign to begin a novel with.[7] The stale smell reeking from that line stood for all the mindless, unproblematic, self-assured, and, in the end, *petit bourgeois* "realism" lounging on the surface of the things it is supposed to describe. What Gruppo 63 could not condone in naturalism was the idea that there exists such a non-problematic concept as "nature"—one, in any case, that could be described via the referential language of traditional literature. As good avant-gardists, Gruppo 63 based much of its notoriety on making enemies: as a case in point, by famously dubbing decent traditional writers, such as Giorgio Bassani and Carlo Cassola, as "Liale."[8]

In the sixties, Italy was discovering the joys of consumerism, a rural country about to become, in the span of a few years, the world's fifth largest economy.[9] The cultural imbalances only to be expected from industrialization were magnified by such an abruptness. The coexistence of backwardness and forwardness could account for this will to provoke: where there still are *bourgeois* à épater, there can still be avant-garde. Nonetheless, the question of being an avant-garde *after* the avant-garde was at the centre of the first gathering's debate.

6 See Umberto Eco, 'Prolusione', in *Il Gruppo 63 quarant'anni dopo*, conference proceedings, Bologna, 8-11 May 2003 (Bologna: Pendragon, 2005), pp. 20-43.

7 "That kind of voiceover, which is the pure and simple transcendent voice of the true, omnipotent and omniscient (…) the convention of the narrator who knows everything, the thoughts of the famous heroine who comes out at five, is, today, the first thing to throw out the window." Edoardo Sanguineti, 'Il trattamento del materiale verbale nei testi narrativi della nuova avanguardia', in Sanguineti, *Ideologia e linguaggio* (Milan: Feltrinelli, 1965), pp. 84-85.

8 Liala was the *nom de plume* of Amalia Liana Negretti Odescalchi (1897-1995), the most successful Italian writer of popular romantic novels, the sixties equivalent of today's Harper-Collins' *Harmony* series.

9 See Valerio Castronovo, *L'Italia del miracolo economico* (Rome, Bari: Laterza, 2010).

Angelo Guglielmi expressed then what today appears as the most lucid and farsighted position: to survive, the avant-garde must give up its status (its judgemental, privileged position) to become a thing among all the other things, renouncing the expression of any idea about "others": any kind of dialectic denied, and with it the possibility of the very idea of history. He argued for a "visceral" avant-garde: "a-ideological, dis-engaged, a-historical, a-temporal," without "messages nor general meanings" to give. What he recommended, after all this carving up, was the artistic device of *pastiche*, "which, insofar as it casually intertwines contrasting cognitive plans, it decrees the death of ideologies by refusing them, precisely, as plans of knowledge."[10] Guglielmi's paradoxical way to keep the avant-garde alive was to kill the avant-garde itself. He later preferred to use the word "experimentalism,"[11] but the impression we retain—reading his words today—is that, to define what he preached, he lacked a key term: "postmodern."[12] He was too much ahead. Or was he too much behind? This is the kind of paradox implied when such deictic concepts as "modernity" and "avant-garde" become self-referential.

Needless to say, many of his fellows disagreed: since the revolution was on its way, they couldn't accept his description of the world as "a neutral space," where "things lie real and still, not even waiting."[13] Then again, in the true spirit of avant-garde, they all reciprocally disagreed about many other things. What they all agreed, apart from naturalism-loathing, was that, both from an artistic and a political point of view, the true battleground was language. The subject of a novel or a poem, its "plot," was deemed irrelevant in itself. Beyond the "Liale," another major target of Gruppo 63's mockeries was Pier Paolo Pasolini, represented as a do-gooder grounding his civic and political commitment in pathetic subjects wrapped in banausic forms: Pasolini's attitude, as Guglielmi said in a poisonous article, was "comparable, at a lower level, with tabloids."[14] As a person, a writer's commitment can only take the form of political action; but as an artist, commitment to language "is the only true guarantee for his/her attention to reality."[15] Anticipating here a concept we shall delve into later on, what was unforgivable about Pasolini was not so much contents *per se*, but his conflating the contents with the *referent*.

10 'Il gruppo '63 a palermo (sic)', *Marcatrè*, no. 1, November 1963, pp. 5-13; 'Il dibattito in occasione del primo incontro del gruppo a Palermo nel 1963', in Nanni Balestrini and Alfredo Giuliani (eds.), *Gruppo 63* (Milan: Feltrinelli, 1964), pp. 371-406.

11 Angelo Guglielmi, *Avanguardia e sperimentalismo* (Milan: Feltrinelli, 1964).

12 Matteo Di Gesù, 'Una avanguardia postmoderna?', *Italianistica: Rivista di letteratura italiana*, no. 1, 2001, pp. 117-133.

13 'Il dibattito in occasione'.

14 Angelo Guglielmi, 'Pasolini, maestro di vita', *Il Verri*, no. 3, 1960. See Angelo Guglielmi, *Vero e falso* (Milan: Feltrinelli, 1968), pp. 79-84.

15 Ibid.

1.2 Radical Architecture

In his *Chronicles of Bustos Domecq*, a book devoted to fictional revolutionary artists, Jorge Luis Borges tells the story of the

Dutch architect H. H. Verdussen, who in 1952 built an "Uninhabitable": a house of five storeys containing only doors on the ground floor; staircases on the second; windows on the third; thresholds on the fourth; and floors and ceilings on the fifth. By making no concessions to utilitarianism, Verdussen had succeeded in the enterprise of building a masterwork where, at last, *tout n'est qu'ordre et beauté*.[16] Written in 1967, Borges' tale seems a *reductio ad absurdum* of why there cannot be such a thing as avant-garde in architecture. As a producer of—in Kantian terms—"adherent beauty," architecture could never reach the extremes all other arts can afford. Apart from that, architecture is always by its nature—if we may say so—*concrete & constructive*. Indeed, an architect reading about modernism, as shaped in the hands of authors such Tristan Tzara or Marcel Duchamp, James Joyce or Samuel Beckett, cannot but feel disoriented discovering a face of modernity so different from the one he used to know. There are, of course, many coincidences, but there are also some decisive, mutually exclusive features: irony, cynicism, self-criticism, and nihilism on one side, and hopeless seriousness and optimism on the other, just to mention the most macroscopic and crucial ones. Modern architecture has never been able, and has never actually willed, to radically push negation to extremes large enough to comprehend everything, itself included. It never really defied the establishment (on the contrary, it was in a perennial quest for complicity); never doubted its power to materially change the world, always had an answer for any demand, never showed any sign of uncertainty. In short: it always kept nihilism at a safe distance.[17] This is what makes Radical Architecture the first real avant-garde architecture has known, and the only one it ever had. And if "radical" is the name it chose,[18] so be it: this will enable us to distinguish between so-called avant-gardes that were just forward-looking (utopians) and those who *radically* accepted to burden themselves with the "dirty work" of a true avant-garde (nihilists).

Critics commonly agree in seeing Archigram as the first instalment of the sixties architectonical "new wave," the one giving the cue from which Italian radicalism was originated.[19] This is certainly true; in fact the opinion is endorsed by some radicals too.[20] When looking at the student projects of future radical architects,[21] it is impossible not to experience a striking similar vibe: that mix of cutting-edge technology and psychedelic pop (Cedric Price + Milton Glaser) is instantly recognizable. Yet, something else must have intervened in the short time between those school exercises and their first published

16 Jorge Luis Borges and Adolfo Bioy-Casares, *Chronicles of Bustos Domecq* (New York: Dutton & Co., 1976 (1967)), pp. 77-82.

17 On this, see the illuminating distinction between the "modern I" and the "Voltairean I" made by Stephen Spender in 'Modern and Contemporaries', in Howe (ed.), *The Idea of the Modern in Literature and the Arts*, pp. 43-49.

18 The concept of "Radical Architecture" first officially appeared in Germano Celant, 'Senza titolo', *in. Argomenti e immagini di design*, no. 2-3, March-June 1971, pp. 76-81. However, in a personal conversation, Andrea Branzi told me that he was the one who first suggested such denomination.

19 See Mirko Zardini, 'Domani, col senno di poi', in Pino Brugellis, Gianni Pettena and Alberto Salvadori (eds.), *Utopie radicali. Archizoom, Remo Buti, 9999, Gianni Pettena, Superstudio, UFO, Zziggurat* (Macerata: Quodlibet, 2017), pp. 14-17.

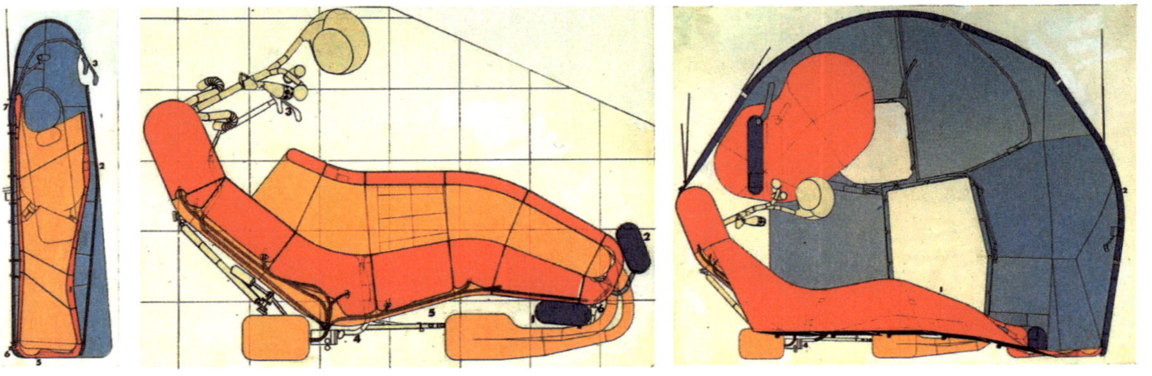

1. Michael Webb, *Cushicle and Suitaloon*, 1966-1967, Archigram Archives, London

projects in the magazines, because the latter completely lack that pop/tech look. Putting Michael Webb's *Cushicle and Suitaloon* and Ugo La Pietra's *Commutatore* side by side will suffice to measure the distance between Archigram and the radicals (figs. 1-2). Radicals have never shown a great interest in technology *per se*; moreover, following La Pietra's suggestion, we can understand how to them architecture is not so much a means to *change* the world, as to *look at* it in a different way. True, Archigram went way beyond the Modern Movement, but kept in its tracks, maintaining that same positive, redemptive attitude; radicals went further by taking their negative path; to reach the final destination, they were willing to do what for an architect is the ultimate sacrifice: to programmatically renounce building.

From the large and magmatic phenomenon going under the name Radical Architecture, we will select here just a few characters on the basis of their paradigmatic role as milestones along a radical path conducting to nothingness. Leafing through the pages of *Architettura "radicale,"*[22] the first retrospective book dedicated to the movement, the very first architects we find—not without surprise; moreover, in the chapter dedicated to "the *origins* of the Italian neo-avant-garde"—are Vittoriano Viganò and Aldo Rossi, mentioned as the first representing a real alternative to "the late-functionalism of the still active Italian 'masters'."[23] The first name we encounter afterwards is Andrea Branzi. Branzi himself, in an article of

20 "Archigram were the first fathers to relaunch the avant-garde issue in the dark days of the early sixties." Andrea Branzi, 'L'Africa è vicina. Il ruolo dell'avanguardia', *Casabella*, no. 364, April 1972, pp. 31-38.

21 Leonardo Savioli and Adolfo Natalini, 'Spazio di coinvolgimento', *Casabella*, no. 326, 1968, pp. 32-45.

22 Paola Navone and Bruno Orlandoni, *Architettura "radicale"* (Milan: Documenti di Casabella, 1974).

23 Navone and Orlandoni, *Architettura "radicale,"* p. 19.

1973, wrote that Rossi—if only he hadn't, at a certain point, gone astray—would had been for him "a brother, and a brilliant teacher."[24] Following their suggestions—and aware of the harsh *querelle* that, in that same 1973, opposed the Radical Movement and Rossi's Tendenza[25]—we will unorthodoxically begin our "radical path" with Rossi's work, as the first degree of a depletion process that will be taken to quite different levels by the radicals "proper" with their "no-building" move.[26] Mies van der Rohe had been the Modern Master who more than anyone else had reduced architecture to "almost nothing," but Rossi's first architectures have shown that less could still be done. Mies's curtain wall was still a *positive* statement, the last in a tradition going back at least to Viollet-le-Duc's championing of Gothic; compared to Mies' proud skeletons, Rossi's volumes—black holes on blank walls—are more like remains: "cuttlefish bones" weathered by the sea of history. Taking another cue from Branzi,[27] we could picture the road to nothingness as starting from *The Architecture of the City* of Rossi; passing through Superstudio's "architecture without the city" idea; then Archizoom's "city without architecture"; to arrive at its final destination: UFO's "objects," dispensing both with the city and architecture, and somewhat closing the circle opened by Archigram's *Instant City*, but with aggressiveness substituting for optimism.

What strikes more in these works, trying to see them as they must have appeared fifty years ago, is their "aloofness": the distance they put between them and everyday reality, while focusing on their "autonomous" laws of form and configuration. This is somewhat different from what could be expected from architects politically committed, moreover in the overheated political climate of that period. But, similarly to what happened with Gruppo 63, concentration on language is conceived here as the only real political commitment *as architects*, as opposed to direct action as militants. And, if the radicals' "Liala" was modernism, by now institutionalized and degraded to professionalism, they had their "Pasolini" too: intellectuals like Manfredo Tafuri or Italo Insolera, who argued for "dissolving" architecture into a wider and more direct activity of urban and political management of the territory.[28] Radicals' attention to form must be interpreted as a polemical revindication of architecture's political role within society. But, as for Gruppo 63, to understand why, we must first investigate the question of the "referent," as conceptualized by semiotics.

24 Andrea Branzi, 'Si scopron le tombe', *Casabella*, no. 383, 1973, pp. 10-11.

25 See Massimo Scolari, 'Avanguardia e nuova architettura', in Gianni Braghieri and Franco Raggi (eds.), *Architettura Razionale* (Milan: Franco Angeli, 1973), pp. 153-187.

26 It could be argued that at least some of Rossi's first projects were unbuildable, too: suffice to read the project report of *Locomotiva 2*, Rossi's proposal for Turin's Directional Centre, where he describes "free columns, rising 35 metres high." Then again, if those columns where not buildable *de facto*, they still where buildable *de jure*, contrary to what happens in Superstudio's and Archizoom's projects. I owe the knowledge about Turin's columns to Mariagabriella Lo Ricco, whom I thank for kindly letting me get some key information from her undisclosed doctoral dissertation *L'opera di Luca Meda nella cultura milanese (1957-1998). Il sogno dell'architettura*, Politecnico di Milano, XXI cycle, 2006-2009.

27 Andrea Branzi, *Una generazione esagerata* (Milan: Baldini+Castoldi, 2014), p. 93.

28 Insolera's entry in the competition for the new Chamber of Deputies' Palace in Rome (1967) was, symbolically enough, an urban plan. On Tafuri, Rossi, Branzi and autonomy of architecture, see Pier Vittorio Aureli, *The Project of Autonomy. Politics and Architecture within and against Capitalism* (Hudson, NY: Princeton Architectural Press, 2008).

2. Ugo La Pietra, *Il Commutatore*, from *Sistema Disequilibrante*, 1970, courtesy Ugo La Pietra Archives, Milan

2. Signrise

By usually associating the sixties with student uprising, the beat generation, the cold war, and race riots, we tend to forget that they were also the years of what could be called "the structuralist turn."[29] Slowly rising since 1945, by the sixties the structuralist paradigm had grown to dominate not just cultural circles, but people at large, as testified by the words of a soccer trainer announcing a "structuralist" team reorganization to improve results.[30] For a period, structuralism has been viewed as the promise of a *mathesis universalis*, gathering all disciplines under only one, scientific method. Step by step, structuralism had overflowed Saussurean linguistics to "colonize" nearly all humanities: from anthropology to philosophy, psychology, sociology, literary criticism, the list could continue. Given structuralism's linguistics ancestry, semiology came to the fore as the leading discipline, destined over time—at least in intention—to subsume all the others.[31]

Semiology was the "widespread feeling" and the "average theoretical orientation" of the period;[32] in fact, many of the period's cultural events are strictly interrelated with this common sensibility. So much so that we could even ask ourselves if semiology was the *cause* or the *effect* of those events. The second post-war period is the first in the world's history when we can properly talk of "mass society," giving a precise meaning to the term: a society where the majority of its compo-

29 See Eve Meltzer, *Systems We Have Loved* (Chicago, London: The University of Chicago Press, 2013), p. 13.

30 François Dosse, *Histoire du structuralisme, I. Le champ du signe, 1945-1966* (Paris: Éditions La Découverte, 1991), p. 9.

31 Since the cultural trend we are describing originally arose in France, to spread later in Italy, we shall henceforth prefer the French connoted term "semiology" to the American, and today more used, "semiotics."

32 Paolo D'Angelo, *L'estetica italiana del Novecento. Dal neoidealismo a oggi* (Rome, Bari: Laterza, 2007), p. 294.

nents have access to what economists call "discretionary income"—meaning above the basic needs—and can afford to *choose*.[33] Only then do the masses really begin to count in economy and, consequently, politics and culture. Because, in parallel, this is also when capitalism's major concerns shift from production to trade. So, for example, one of semiology's major accomplishments, the abolition of the high-culture/low-culture divide (since everything becomes a "text"),[34] appears particularly timely when the crucial problem becomes to understand—and eventually to predict and guide—the mass' economic, political and cultural choices. And again, semiology's mission to reduce natural facts—even erotic arousal—and cultural phenomena[35] seems quite appropriate in times when cultural tastes and lifestyles were substituting ancestry and class as tokens for self-identification.[36]

33 See Bell, *Cultural Contradictions of Capitalism*, p. 38.

34 Think of the *nonchalance* afforded by Roland Barthes' passing from high literature to mass tastes and vice-versa.

35 Umberto Eco, *La struttura assente* (Milan: Bompiani, 1998 (1968)), p. 147 and p. 152.

36 Bell, *Cultural Contradictions of Capitalism*, p. 38.

Then again, to downgrade semiology as a symptom of economic states of things would mean to over-submit to Marxist-imposed hierarchy between structural and superstructural phenomena, countering one of structuralism's major tenets, one having major consequences on the events we are talking about here. Anyway, the question "cause or effect" is already *en abîme* since we could simply argue—as we will see—that structuralism itself *is talked* by language.

2.1 Long-Term Strategies

Signification processes are usually illustrated with a triangular diagram, where the lower left vertex stands for the *signifier*, the top vertex for the *signified*, and the lower right vertex for the *referent*. Usually, the two legs are drawn with a continuous line, while the base is dotted.[37] So, to simplify a bit, the written word |dog| is the *signifier* of the *signified* "dog"—the concept mentally evoked. The *referent*, finally, should stand for the real dog "out there." Now, as far as semiology is concerned, the concept of referent should—as Roland Barthes once famously said—"be killed."[38] As the science of communication phenomena, semiology is only concerned with the left leg of the triangle, while the referent is just a hindrance. Worse, it is a red herring, giving the illusion of the possibility to jump from words to things without the mediation of semiosis. To semiology, communication remains within the realm of signs, words never actually "touching" reality. Furthermore, the referent—as says Umberto Eco—is not reality itself, but the shifting "ideological background" upon which our signification rests.[39]

37 This is what is generally known as the Ogden-Richards triangle; see C. K. Ogden and I. A. Richards, *The Meaning of Meaning: a study of the influence of language upon thought and of the science of symbolism* (New York: Harcourt, Brace & World, 1946 (1923)), p. 11. In this context, we have substituted Ogden-Richards' terms of the lower left and top vertices with Saussure's. The substitution is not entirely residue-free, but it was necessary for the sake of brevity and compatibility with what will be explained later.

38 "Il faut tuer le référent." Quoted in Umberto Eco, 'La maestria di Barthes', in Roland Barthes, *Miti d'oggi* (Turin: Einaudi, 1974), p. XIV.

39 Eco, *La struttura asssente*, pp. 93-94; Umberto Eco, *Theory of Semiotics* (Bloomington: Indiana University Press, 1976 (1975)), p. 61.

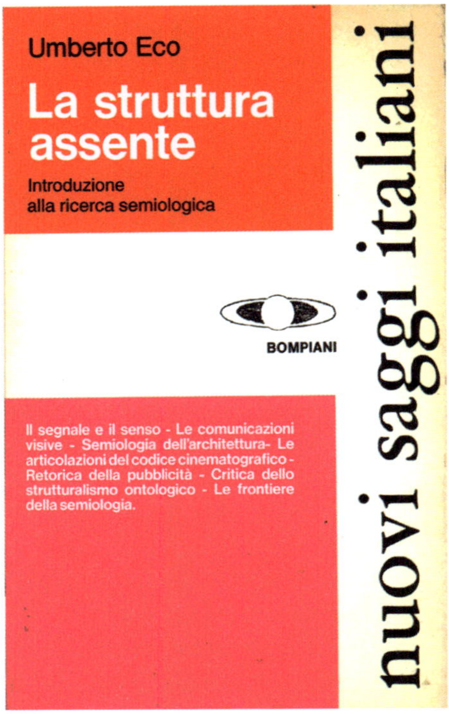

3. Umberto Eco, *La struttura assente* (Milan: Bompiani, 1968)

We can now understand how, in *this* cultural atmosphere, both Gruppo 63's and radical architects' refusal of "Liala" and of "Pasolini" were two sides of the same coin. If art is communication—and how could it not be—as artists they could only think of working on meanings via interventions on language. Direct intervention on reality implies another realm: it requires direct action. There remains to understand how, for the architects—who in principle *could* physically intervene on reality—work on form could be seen as more effective. And this is where we can measure the combined effect of semiology *and* structuralism.

One of the most disrupting effects of structuralism's inception was the turning down of a secular humanistic tradition, including its late forms of transcendentalist actualization, such as phenomenology and existentialism. Structure *precedes* man, the main idea now being that man *is talked* by language and not the other way around.[40] The corollary being that any real revolution passes through work on the structures, language not being just a symptom of them. According to structuralism, any form of a society's cultural life (taken in the broadest possible sense) is ruled by homologous structures bounded together by the existence of a deeper structure setting their transfor-

40 Eco, *Theory of Semiotics*, p. 10 and p. 237.

mation rules: for instance, the structure of a language talked in a primitive village is the same as the one ruling parental structure, political organization, and spatial organization.[41] Language is not a mirror of reality; it pre-exists knowledge and reality as a cultural phenomenon. And to work at the modification of language means—in the long run, since only very slow and collective processes can modify language—to contribute to society's transformation. And in a more effective way: any transformation that is not propitiated by a change in what, in the end, are the *structures of thought* (we are talked by language) is doomed to be superficial and easily reabsorbed by the system.

There is a catchphrase that is recurrent in the texts of Gruppo 63: *tempi lunghi* ("long-term"). Most certainly inspired by Fernand Braudel's *longue durée*,[42] it stands for the very long span required for deep, *structural* transformations, as opposed to the superficial ones obtained through short-term, direct action. The long term is what makes it preferable, for Eco, to work on "society's cultural values, through operations on language, on narrative structures, viewing patterns." On the contrary, "writing about peasant revolts, or painting partisans gunned down" is—in Eco's opinion—"ancient history."[43] And "A long-term strategy" is the title of an article of Branzi, the very first of the column "Radical Notes" he wrote for *Casabella* from 1972 to 1976, where he warned about the dangers of any rebellious attitude detached from the "reference points of structural laws."[44]

2.2 Absent Structures, Present Functions

One of semiology's leading figures in Italy, Eco, was a member of Gruppo 63, and taught semiology at the Faculty of Architecture of Florence in the years 1966-1967. It's only natural to think of him as the pivot of the literary and the architectonical avant-garde parallelism we are construing here. Moreover, his major influence on the Florentine section of Radical Architecture seems to be taken for granted.[45] Yet things can be more complicated than meets the eye.

Eco wrote some lecture notes for his class: first published as a standalone, then republished as an essay in "Section C" of *La struttura assente*, Eco's first official act as a semiologist. The essay is by far the most read and cited attempt to apply semiology's instruments to architecture.[46] Not a very felicitous one, as he himself later admitted.[47] "Section C"'s title, "The Function and the Sign," sets from the beginning Eco's overall

41 The example is drawn from Eco, *La struttura assente*, p. VIII.

42 Fernand Braudel, 'Histoire et sciences sociales: la longue durée', in *Écrits sur l'histoire* (Paris: Flammarion, 1969), pp. 44-83.

43 Umberto Eco, 'Vietando s'impara', *Quindici*, no. 12, September 1968, pp. 1-2.

44 Andrea Branzi, 'Strategia dei tempi lunghi', *Casabella*, no. 370, October 1972, p. 13. "(...) architecture, understood both as a physical and cultural structure. It is here that the experience of the avant-garde sets in motion lethal phenomena and long-term strategies." Andrea Branzi, 'Introduzione', in Navone and Orlandoni, *Architettura "radicale,"* pp. 2-15: 12.

45 Both direct influence (UFO's members were his pupils) and indirect (the leading Florentine radicals still gravitating around the Faculty in those years).

46 Many were tried in that period. Among the others, we remember here: Italo Gamberini, *Gli elementi dell'architettura come parole del linguaggio architettonico* (Florence: Coppini, 1959); Giovanni Klaus Koenig, *Analisi del linguaggio architettonico* (Florence: Libreria editrice fiorentina, 1964); Maria

approach, determined by his first gambit: equating architectural elements (doors, windows, stairs, etc.) with *signifiers* on one side; and the functions they enable with *signifieds* on the other.[48] A fatal decision, we could say, at least judging from the embarrassing conclusions he will be forced to reach at the end. It is not just the conclusions, obviously; the whole essay is conditioned by this approach, starting with its literary form: Eco's habitual logic and taxonomic exposition in-forms just the chapters' tree structure organization, while the overall discourse takes more the form of a spiralling, almost hermeneutical (and not very semiological) meandering, more than once seeming to arrive at a dead end, only to escape with what mostly seem sleights of hand.

With his function/signified equation, Eco conflates architecture with the act of building: according to him, the first architecture is the cave, signifying "shelter," while its front hole is the signifier of "entrance."[49] He then admits the possibility of second meanings—like "family," or "safety" (but, even so, we would still be in the realm of *private* meanings, not communication). Never for a moment does he consider the possibility that architecture may have been born when the transfiguring of the house into the temple, and the transmutation of forms from wood to stone, transformed a building into a *symbol*, recognized as such by the whole *community*. Sticking to his first move, he can only condemn architectural language to a purely denotative role. At times, he admits the possibility of connotative meanings (beyond function) for architectural signs:[50] in these moments he appears to intuit a way out of the conceptual prison he is stuck in, but in the long run denotation always takes over.

So strict is his submission to functions that at a certain point he seems to realize that, since the functions enabled are in fact "ways of living" (i.e., something pertaining with the world "out there" and not intrinsic to architectural language), architectural elements—as signifiers—*would relate directly with their referents*,[51] breaking the first rule of semiology and putting in crisis not just "Section C"'s arguments, but the whole book, *La struttura assente*, dedicated as it is to the explanation of all cultural phenomena as communication facts.[52] A real *coup de théâtre* from which to expect a sudden U-turn, but, via a long detour, function is transformed into a "relevant tract of a proxemic code."[53] Namely, a cultural signified: the book is safe (and there remains the mystery of why he gave the alarm in the first place).[54] Either way, he had already sanctioned architecture

Luisa Scalvini, *L'architettura come semiotica connotativa* (Milan: Bompiani, 1975).

47 Umberto Eco, 'Riflessioni 1980', in Eco, *La struttura assente*, pp. I-VIII.

48 Eco, *La struttura assente*, p. 200.

49 Eco, *La struttura assente*, pp. 192-193.

50 We use here the terms "denotation" and "connotation" according to the meaning they have in semiotics: in general, a *denotation* is the strict, dictionary-wise meaning of a word, while *connotation* stands for the ensemble of the additional, imaginative, and emotional meanings pertaining to that same word. For a more technical definition, see Roland Barthes, *Elements of Semiology* (New York: Hill and Wang, 1986 (1964)), ch. IV, pp. 89-94.

51 Eco, *La struttura assente*, p. 237.

52 Eco, *La struttura assente*, p. 238.

53 Eco, *La struttura assente*, p. 243.

54 See also Eco, *La struttura assente*, p. 238.

as an activity giving what society "prescribes": architecture is a "service," "like waste collection and water supply."[55] At best it can be a form of rhetoric, allowed to codify just what users already expect.[56] In no way can it be considered an art (never mind the manuals of art history), precisely because the role of art—according to semiology—is instead to generate new and unexpected meanings through unorthodox use of language. And, *if* architecture's meanings are functions, architecture cannot invent (that is, impose) new functions. It is difficult not to agree; the problem is all in that conditional "if."

55 Eco, *La struttura assente*, p. 225.

56 Ibid.

Only on the last page is Eco prepared to grant architecture the possibility of producing new meanings. At a price: it will have to be "built on wheels, or with prefabricated and demountable elements, or according to forms and orientations, so flexible that they could assume different meanings depending on the situation."[57] The conclusion makes us pause. We finally realize that the entire essay has been written under the spell of a strict, Modern Movement-like idea of "function." One he himself could have defined as a "dyadic relation of stimulus-response," as opposed to a "triadic relation of signification":[58] one where our ways of living, our lifestyles, can be modified only by *mechanical* action on space. The "proxemic trick," apparently, didn't work out. So, it's only natural that in the end he resorts to imagery inspired by Archigram, Cedric Price, and the Metabolism Group: the sixties release of the Modern Movement's idea of space *forging* (forcing) man's life.

57 Eco, *La struttura assente*, p. 249.

58 Umberto Eco, 'Trent'anni dopo: nuova (e più modesta) ricognizione della semiotica', Lecture at Sapienza University of Rome, 31 January 2010.

Indeed, to conclude a weighty sixty-page essay on architectural language's profound structures with ideas inspired by fashionable images, most certainly derived from the design studios at the Faculty of Florence, leaves something to be desired. Eco, it would seem, was influenced by architects much more than they were influenced by him. During the same years, his "pupils" were way ahead of him: in their works, Superstudio, Archizoom, and UFO treated architecture as a means of communication and as a critique of ideology (the ideology of "normalcy"), using uncommon forms to *communicate* evocative, axiological, "pathemic" *meanings*; they worked on "the long-terms" granting architecture with the possibility of doing precisely what Eco only allowed the other arts: "transposing on the plan of structural relationships (...) a way to see the world and to be in the world."[59]

59 Umberto Eco, *Opera aperta* (Milan: Bompiani, 1997 (1962)), p. 260.

In 1971, Eco published another essay on architecture: "For a semantic analysis of architectural signs," probably one of his least read, where he renewed his allegiance to the signified/function equation and criticized any other possible approach.[60] The essay's novelty was an attempt to codify an architectonical element (a classical column). The results were two Porphirian trees, some dozen labels each. To be fair, the impression is that of a "bachelor machine": the kind of overwhelming, and disappointing enterprises that finally buried semiology under its own ambitions.[61] But the experiment can perhaps give us an idea of why Eco's expertise was originally solicited by a Faculty of Architecture: perhaps the demand came from the desire to find a *new code* of architecture, after having accepted the fact that modern architecture couldn't produce a code comparable to the classical one. If so, his "Archigram-matical" suggestions must have been quite disappointing. Irony is, Rossi was the one who got nearer to an architectural codification, but Eco's Florentine "contractors"—Leonardo Savioli and Giovanni Klaus Koenig—weren't ready to accept it for "linguistic" reasons.

It is quite interesting, however, to point out what divides Rossi from the radicals, beyond ideologies and obvious differences of form, from a semiotic point of view. Rossi's adhesion to semiology is "technical": he doesn't seem primarily interested in communication, yet his treatment of form could be assimilated to language according to Saussurean terms: the "few objects" of his "rigid world"[62] can be read as "phonemes" assuming a different positional value on the syntagmatic axis (the cylinder, as "column," or as "part of a telescopic tower," depending on the relationship with adjacent "phonemes"). Quoting Ezio Bonfanti: "in the same forms the capacity to assume different values, meanings, and uses."[63] The Radicals' adhesion is much more "philosophical": in a specular way, they don't seem interested in language's technicalities *per se*, but in communication. Their projects are as many figural allegories: Superstudio's tales about the difference between architecture's ambition and its reality; Archizoom's about architecture's irrelevance in a modern world. From this point of view, we can also better understand their choice to design programmatically unbuildable architectures as a question of form/content fitting: were they buildable, the allegories would suddenly transform into utopias, the very opposite of their firm's nihilistic, avant-gardist stance.[64]

60 Umberto Eco, 'Per un'analisi semantica dei segni architettonici', in Eco, *Le forme del contenuto* (Milan: Bompiani, 1971), pp. 157-179.

61 On the demise of semiology, and in general what in France was called "Théorie" (comprising "nouvelle critique," "poétique," "structuralisme," "sémiologie," "narratologie"), see Antoine Compagnon, *Le démon de la théorie. Littérature et sens commun* (Paris: Éditions du Seuil, 1998).

62 "Un mondo architettonico rigido e di pochi oggetti." Aldo Rossi, 'Introduzione', in Braghieri and Raggi (eds.), *Architettura razionale*, p. 21.

63 Ezio Bonfanti, 'Elementi e costruzione. Note sull'architettura di Aldo Rossi', *Controspazio*, no. 10, October 1970, pp. 19-42. About Rossi structuralism see also: Francesco Samassa, 'Ferdinand De Saussure e Aldo Rossi. Teorie a confronto', in Riccardo Palma and Carlo Ravagnati (eds.), *Macchine nascoste* (Turin: Utet, 2004), pp. 77-90.

64 At the international congress *Rebel Matters Radical Patterns* (Genoa, 21-22 March 2013), Andrea Branzi and Gian Piero Frassinelli firmly denied any utopian connotation for their projects: "The utopians were the others," said Branzi. He didn't specify who these "others" were supposed to be, but there can be little doubt he was referring to La Tendenza.

2.3 Gruppo 73

In 1974, Lapo Binazzi—UFO's "frontman"—published a review of Eco's book *Segno*. He wrote it in the form of an affectionate letter to "Dear uncle Umberto," stating that their roads parted in 1968, "when practice and theory ceased to keep in step."[65]

65 Lapo Binazzi, 'Libri (recensione di Umberto Eco: "Segno". Enciclopedia filosofica ISEDI, Milano, 1973)', *Domus*, no. 530, January 1974, pp. 49-50.

May 1968 was history's first *generational* revolution: the one of the young generation that had all the impatience and, at least initially, the *joie de vivre* (*Travailleurs de tous les pays, amusez-vous!* ("Workers of the world, have fun!")), and the dreaminess (*Pouvoir à l'Imagination* ("Power to the imagination")). It acted as a detonator in the volatile period we are looking at. Slogans such as *On veut tout, tout de suite!* ("we want it all, we want it now!") wrong-footed any "long-term strategies" and forced many intellectuals to make choices. To adapt to the times, the magazine *Quindici*, born as Gruppo 63's "press organ," had become a sort of host magazine, publishing—alongside the usual reviews of literary books—the official press releases of the self-organized student groups guiding the revolt. But this kind of division of roles, between intellectuals' long-term strategy and students' short-term action, couldn't last. In June 1968, Eco published a polemical article against students' and artists' political occupation of Triennale di Milano exhibition, ironically commenting on the differences between a factory, a university, and a museum.[66] The article was followed by fellow "sixty-threers" Guido Davico-Bonino's and Edoardo Sanguineti's harsh reply, symptomatically titled "It is forbidden to forbid"[67] (after the '68 slogan, *Il est interdit d'interdire*), which discussed the "miserable pretext of long-term." Something had broken. Eco's further reply, "Learning by forbidding,"[68] still preached for a division of roles between words and acts, and concluded with an invitation "to forbid to forbid to forbid," and to avoid any kind of moralism: a symptom of the typical, end-of-the-road avant-garde loop in self-referentiality and a certification that, having once reached that point, moralism makes no more sense. Guglielmi's prophecy was coming true. Four months later, at the peak of its sales, *Quindici* ceased to exist and with it Gruppo 63 too. An avant-gardist suicidal act, as Eco proudly remembers.[69]

66 Umberto Eco, 'Il gioco dell'occupazione', *Quindici*, no. 11, 1968, p. 1.

67 Guido Davico Bonino and Edoardo Sanguineti, 'È vietato vietare', *Quindici*, no. 12, 1968, p. 1.

68 Eco, 'Vietando s'impara'.

69 Umberto Eco, 'The Death of the Gruppo 63', in Eco, *The Open Work* (Cambridge, MA: Harvard University Press, 1989), pp. 236-249.

UFO's work is thoroughly tinged by the heated atmosphere in which it made its debut. UFO had little more than a year gap with respect to Superstudio and Archizoom: in contracted times like these, a few months can mean everything. What probably weighed was also the direct and friendly relation with Eco: caught within the respect for the *lieber meister* and the strictures he had straitjacketed architecture into, they boldly stepped out of architecture, while conserving the master's lesson both at a superficial level ("Colgate con Vietcong" and "magozurlinpiao" are most likely recollections of Joycean calembours) and a deeper one: their happenings clearly owe something to the "open works" Eco most certainly had lectured about. They did "strange things" (inflatables, bicycle tours, reportages) and they called it "architecture": they could, because meanwhile Radical Architecture had succeeded not just in producing unexpected meanings, but in changing the meaning of architecture itself.

Eco, for his part, had defined "literature" a fake questionnaire written and publicly distributed by UFO." The first sentence read, "Have you ever noticed that in the vicinity of particular repressive institutions of the BOURGEOIS STATE (...) there is a sort of permanent protective psychological ring, a magnetic field of a special kind determined by what are usually strange circumstances? (yes) (no)."[70] The paranoiac humour deepened with each following question. Was it literature (since it was written), or architecture (since it was about space)? Under the combined attack of semiological levelling, and mass media pervasiveness, making distinctions was becoming difficult. Anyway, the questionnaire was, together with *Urboeffimeri*, UFO's attempt to step out the left leg of the signification triangle, and directly act on the referent (reality), while remaining *architectural* "cultural workers."

70 Umberto Eco, 'Dopo I poeti', in Eco, *Dalla periferia dell'impero* (Milan: Bompiani, 1976 (1973)), pp. 297-316.

By 1973, grassroots ideology had infected all the radicals. The Global Tools society was their attempt not to be left behind. It was a generous, if failed attempt.[71] Whatever the reasons, regardless of how little it lasted, it was from the start a suicidal act. Prompted by the proverbial "good intentions" (too good intentions), the idea was to go to the roots themselves of architecture, by delving into raw materiality, to promote "social creativity" through educational workshops for the young and the outcasts. Whatever opinion we may hold about it, it was the very antithesis of the relentless work of destruction accomplished until then. Worse, it was the attempt to make it naturally flow not even into a palingenetic primitivism, but into a neo-realist utopia of spontaneous creativity and untainted wisdom coming from below. Pasolini would probably have greatly appreciated it.

71 "The tiring and cumbersome (failed) project of Global Tools" (Branzi, *Una generazione esagerata*, p. 120).

The founding of Global Tools in January 1973 was particularly timely. Only ten months later, the oil crisis began, marking the first setback to the global economy since the war. Terms like "austerity" and "energy conservation" cropped up. The economy would know other ups and downs—the rollercoaster is still running—but 1973 marks the end of the idea of infinite growth. An old dream of radicalism, a society freed from labour thanks to technology progress, leaves the scene, accompanied by the nomadic tribes (hippies or "savages") populating their scenographies. In general, that atmosphere of general optimism, still colouring the whole scenario, yielded ground to harder feelings. The short-terms—after all—didn't seem to be short enough, and fights became impatient and nastier, bringing about one of the darkest periods of recent Italian history. They would reach their peak with the Movement of 1977, then what happened in May 1978—ten years after *the* symbol—worked like a sudden awakening from a nightmare that had begun as a beautiful dream.

3. Modernism for the Masses

In 1980, the Marquise resumed her five o'clock outings: bidding goodbye to semiology's universalistic ambitions, Eco put at work his semiological experience, and his unquestionable talent, to write the international best-seller *The Name of the Rose*: a "closed work," with a riveting plot, written in a traditional style. In an at times apologetic postscript written three years later, he openly talked about postmodernism, defining it as a *kunstwollen* more than a style, and materializing it as a man wanting to say, "I love you madly" to his beloved, cultivated woman; but he can't, because this is the kind of platitude you find in Liala's books. The solution is to say "As Liala would put it, I love you madly":[72] irony and awareness concede to a postmodern writer what was forbidden to poor Bassani and Cassola. The problem with irony, however, is that it lasts only as long as the memory sustaining it: one generation later, nobody gets the joke anymore. Released through Facebook today, in our forgetful times, UFO's questionnaire would join chemtrails and 5G conditioning in the inexhaustible reservoir of conspiracy theories.

72 Umberto Eco, *Postscript to The Name of the Rose* (San Diego: Harcourt Brace, 1984 (1983)), p. 67. In the English translation Liala has become its American counterpart Barbara Cartland.

In that same 1980, postmodern architecture was officially consecrated along the Venice Biennale's Strada Novissima, with much irony on Charles Jencks' part, and much seriousness on Paolo Portoghesi's. Architecture's constitutive backwardness explains the mix: modernist fundamentalism was still strong in Europe, classicism still a heresy, the eclectic facades along the Novissima still provocative. The vast polemics triggered by that Biennale[73] tell us that, despite appearances, postmodernism

73 See 'Il dibattito sulla Mostra e la Strada Novissima. Rassegna stampa', *Controspazio*, no. 1-6, July-November 1980, pp. 214-249.

was an architectural *neo*-avant-garde. The first, and the last possible one: in the catalogue introduction, titled "The end of Prohibition,"[74] Portoghesi preached for an "abandonment of Modern orthodoxy," talking about "young architects, no longer believing in totems and taboos," explicitly referring to Freud and implicitly to the '68 slogan, "it's forbidden to forbid." But, in the same Strada Novissima, Rem Koolhaas' hyper-modern facade openly demanded a tolerant attitude *also* towards modernism. As if to say, "it's forbidden to forbid to forbid." We already know where this was going: self-referentiality and the impossibility from then on of any viable moral stance.

74 Paolo Portoghesi, 'La fine del proibizionismo', in *La presenza del passato* (Venice: Edizioni La Biennale di Venezia, 1980), pp. 9-14.

Postmodernity is modernity explained to the masses. It happens when the idea of modernity has finally been firmly internalized in all society's *single individuals*. There is no such thing as the "unfinished project of modernity": every single point of its programme has been fulfilled, all the T's have been crossed. Those 1963-1973 years weren't preparing the *revolution*, they were just a significant part of an *evolution*: all the modern, avant-gardist, and semiology-oriented traits we have visited during our survey were united in preparing the ground for this mutation. The expression "cunning of reason" comes to mind.

Post-structuralism wasn't a reaction against structuralism: many of its protagonists were the same, the same people still talking about structures, only finally realizing that there is no ultimate structure, experimenting with the impossibility of really knowing structures always already deconstructing themselves. The question *cause* or *effect* could still be proposed. Whatever the answer, we cannot disagree that post-structuralism is *the* philosophy of what now we could call a "post-mass" society: where the *in-dividual* (an exact synonym of *a-tom*) has really become such. Everyone with *his own* ideas, slightly different from those of every other, and the means to express them in public, to make his/her voice heard, albeit in an indecipherable *rustle*: shifting clouds of opinions in the place of *a* "public opinion," or at least of *some* discernible movements of opposing opinions. Semiology lost its footing when the idea faded that such diversity could be coded. And when the *externality* of the referent became the *disappearance* of the referent. It couldn't be otherwise, since—as we saw—the referent is nothing but the ideological background of the meanings we construe through language. The impossibility of an ideology corresponds to the impossibility of the referent. Freed from that background, it's the signified that actually lost its footing, meanings forever ricocheting from signifiers to other signifiers.

Without an outer referent, the passage to self-referentiality is only natural.

Here we can finally understand an unsuspected synergy between the avant-gardes and the '68 revolution. Such a *singularization* of minds could never take place without a systematic destruction of all traditional values, both cultural and ethical. 1968 was much more a revolution of costumes than a political one, the transformation of elite's avant-gardism into a widespread habit. In the end, the "I," much more than the "we," was '68's champion: a non-alienated "I," freed in a society respectful of differences. As Dany Cohn-Bendit, charismatic leader of May '68, still maintained in '86, "the goal is no longer to reach an approximate consensus on a few general statements (...). What nonsense to pretend the same vision of things for immigrants, feminists, rockers, regionalists, pacifists, environmentalists and computer enthusiasts!".[75] The avant-gardes programme realized: the destruction of traditional values was just the beginning, the target then becoming *any general shared value*.

75 Félix Guattari and Dany Cohn-Bendit, 'Contribution pour le mouvement', *Autogestion*, no. 153, 24 November 1986, pp. 10-11.

Then again, true unadulterated singularity was in the DNA of modernity from the beginning: already there in Descartes' solipsistic *cogito* and in that wonderful "right to the pursuit of happiness" provided for in the first modern declaration of rights. It conflicted with another initial idea of modernity: progress, implying *direction, common purpose*; demised in 1973 and substituted with "innovation," implying just "new." A "new" relentlessly substituting other "new," no direction home: the avant-garde dream. Today we are all "visceral" avant-gardists: as consumers we can be "beat" in the morning and "punk" at night; as architects, parametricists this year, ecologists the next, and traditionalists the following.

It's good for economy too: the global market gets constantly renewed.

Born in the Occupied Universities: the Politics of Archizoom, Superstudio and UFO

Jacopo Galimberti

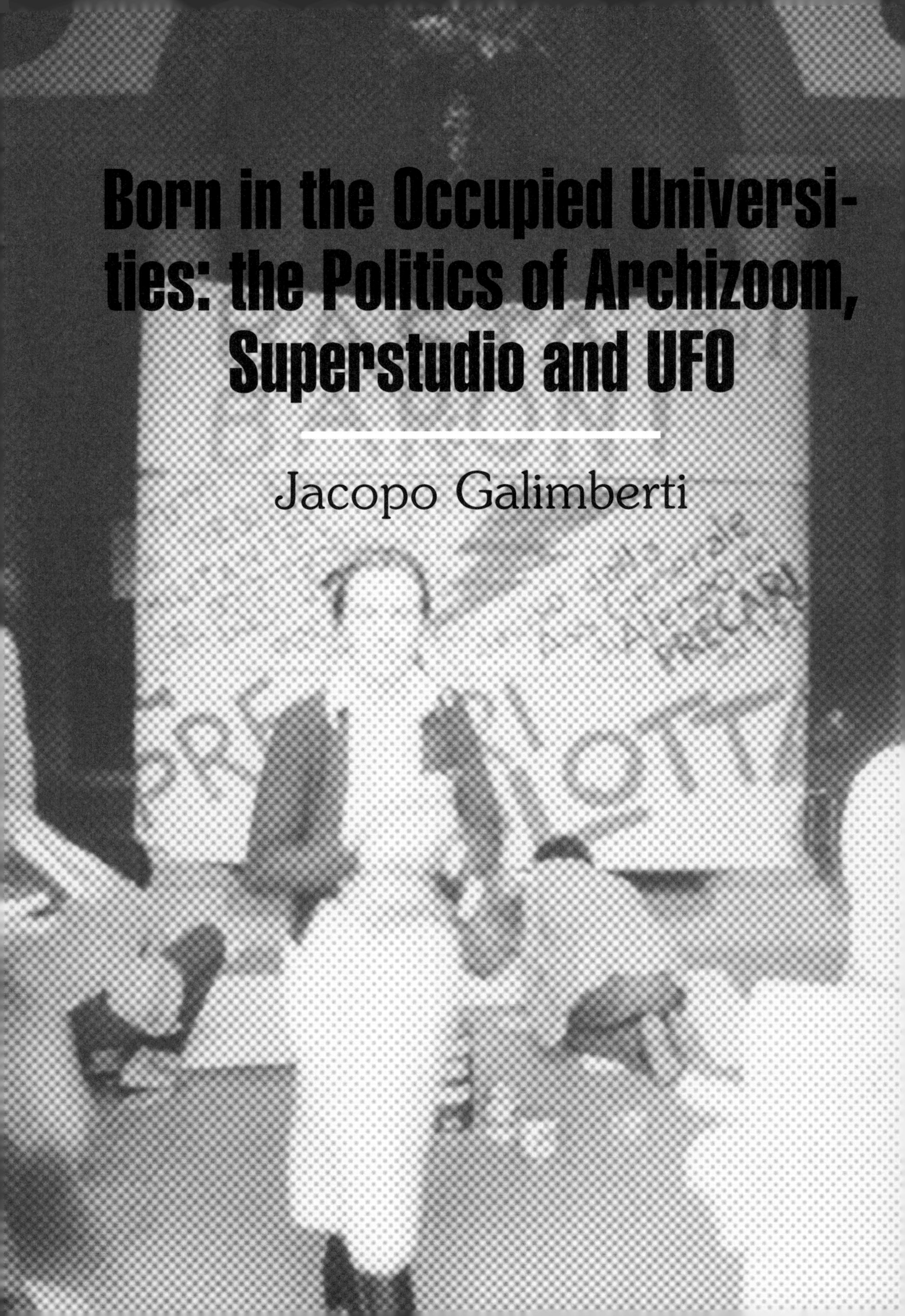

"Radical Architecture [was] born in the occupied university"[1]

Gian Piero Frassinelli

Now that half a century has passed, it seems clear that the Florence of the second half of the sixties was a ground-breaking cultural and political crossroads, and not just at a national level. If we confine our attention to one of the most dynamic components of this intellectual ferment, that of young architects, we find a proliferation of groups, publications, and meeting places that may seem almost disproportionate with respect to the size of the city. This essay sets out to plumb the Florentine architectural scene of those years by concentrating on one of its distinctive aspects, the relationship of its young exponents with politics. Certainly there is no intention to carry out an exhaustive analysis; this could only be done in a work of broader scope, one that would look at the intricate relations between national politics, local establishment, university, and public administration. More modestly, an attempt will be made to outline a political profile of three groups—Archizoom, Superstudio, and UFO—accepting the methodological suggestion, put forward by Roberto Gargiani and Beatrice Lampariello, to set aside the concept of "Radical Architecture."[2] Germano Celant's term was useful to identify a certain climate, but fifty years after the publication of his writings, and despite all the mutual influences between those whom Celant defined as "radicals," it has become necessary to make several distinctions. In November 1967, Celant had described Arte Povera as an art "of guerrilla warfare," creating a stir in an artistic milieu that was fascinated by the student movement and by a geopolitical situation riven by conflict. The term "radical"—meaning "politically extreme" (by implication, on the left), but also, to a certain extent, "fanatical," "hot-headed," "inflexible"—was Celant's second great critical coinage.[3] Vague enough to avoid causing an outcry, but at the same time intriguing and exotic, to the point where some, unaware of the meaning of "radical" in English, were initially perplexed, thinking that the adjective was in some way connected with the Radical Party.[4] Although only a few of the exponents of Radical Architecture were political extremists, the term had the merit of reflecting the centrality of a problem that many of them found inescapable, both in the sense of a reformulation of the specific nature of architecture—the political mission of the discipline and the architect—and in that of

1 Gian Piero Frassinelli, conversation with Peter Lang, 13 March 2002. Quoted in Peter Lang and William Menking, *Superstudio: A Life without Objects* (Milan: Skira/London: Thames & Hudson, 2003), p. 42.

2 Roberto Gargiani and Beatrice Lampariello, *Il Monumento Continuo di Superstudio. Eccesso del razionalismo e strategia del rifiuto* (Genoa: SAGEP, 2019).

3 Germano Celant, 'Radical Architecture', in Emilio Ambasz (ed.), *Italy: The New Domestic Landscape. Achievements and Problems of Italian Design* (Florence: Centro Di, 1972), pp. 380-387.

4 Gian Piero Frassinelli, conversation with Jacopo Galimberti, 8 June 2021.

UFO, Photograph of Palazzo di San Clemente, Florence, 1968, Patrizia Cammeo/Riccardo Foresi Archives, Florence an inclusion, within its own language of design, of the material cultures expressed by political groups, social movements, and the working class. It will be above all this second sense of the political that the essay will seek to explore.

At the outset, an attempt will be made to clarify the political dimension of what Archizoom, Superstudio, and UFO had in common more than anything else: teamwork. Later, the analysis will try to define the political coordinates of the three collectives on the basis of what can be discerned from their writings and in some of their works. The sensibilities of their members were diverse, but this essay posits the idea that it is methodologically appropriate to speak of the groups as entities that cannot be reduced to the sum of their components. Above and beyond the differences between Andrea Branzi and Paolo Deganello, between Adolfo Natalini and Gian Piero Frassinelli, between Lapo Binazzi and Riccardo Foresi, it is indeed possible to outline some of the political questions underpinning the work of the groups as a whole. What will be attempted here is a preliminary exploration of a vast and multifaceted topic that I hope may be the focus, in the future, of more detailed research that also embraces groups such as 9999.

Collective Authorship

With a labour market increasingly on the lookout for "teamwork skills," the concept of group work has been to some extent trivialised today, but in the artistic and architectural context it has not yet wholly lost the controversial undertones that it had, although with much greater force, in the sixties. To comprehend the decision to form collectives of architects, it is necessary to take into account the debate that arose in Western Europe over group work. Although networks of artists have always existed, it was only towards the end of the fifties and in the early sixties that groups of artists began to emerge that practised a deliberately "collectivist" choice, one which often implied a tendency to exhibit only as a group, to share a studio, to have a common fund of money and, more rarely, to move towards a collective signing of their works. As I tried to show in *Individuals against Individualism*, this propensity to politicise artistic authorship gave rise to a controversy that saw the involvement of critics like Giulio Carlo Argan and Aguilera Cerni and institutions like documenta in Kassel or the Paris Biennale.[5] What was the subject of the dispute? Nothing less than the figure of the individual in a context, that of the Cold War, in which the so-called "Soviet Bloc" was opposed by a self-styled "Free World" that saw the defence of individual liberty (understood, reductively, as freedom of expression and religion) as a bulwark against socialism. At a time when the artistic nature of an aesthetic object was often considered synonymous with its ability to express the inner life of the creative individual, the work of the Equipo 57, the Equipo Crónica

5 Jacopo Galimberti, *Individuals against Individualism: Art Collectives in Western Europe (1956-1969)* (Liverpool: Liverpool University Press, 2017).

(active under the Franco dictatorship) or the Gruppo N (in Padua) raised questions of a political and epistemological character that were of no little weight. What was the social function of the artist in the "Free World"? Was it possible to think of art in anti-individualistic terms? What kind of subjectivity did a group express? In the second half of the sixties the tendency to create groups became more widespread and a growing number of artists made the choice to work in strictly collective terms. Moreover, some of them, opposing what could be perceived as a fad, sought to emphasise the dissenting dimension of their authorship, insisting on the fact that, within the collective, there was no real division of labour. In so doing, they were stressing that collective work was a response to the desire not for a greater productive efficiency, but for the development of an alternative mode of production, and an anti-individualistic conception of the relationship between the single person and society.

It is not easy to determine to what extent the formation of groups of artists and the debate that ensued—which reached its height in Italy in 1963-1964—may have served as a stimulus. What is certain is that links can be demonstrated. Let us take the case of Deganello (Archizoom), who was from Este and presented his research into Cornelis van Eesteren's Town Plan (proposed to him by one of his professors, Leonardo Benevolo) in the studio of the Gruppo N in 1961. Another example concerns the Faculty of Architecture in Florence. Leonardo Savioli, with whom both Deganello and Natalini worked, invited his students to participate in the conferences of the MID group, one of the most resolute of collectives when it came to plural authorship.[6] Yet restricting a genealogy of the group work of Archizoom, Superstudio, and UFO solely to the artistic milieu, or to the architectural one (as in the case of Archigram), would be misleading. The request to take exams as a group—one of the recurrent themes of student protest at the Faculty of Architecture of Florence University in the early sixties—shows the long gestation of this aspiration and its already almost countercultural undertones. These impulses, moreover, cannot be dissociated from the model proposed by the groups of musicians who became one of the pillars of youth culture in the sixties. Linked not only to groups of artists, but also to student occupations and the early rock bands, the group work of the young architects of Florence was laden with (geo)political and ethical implications.

6 Roberto Gargiani, *Archizoom associati, 1966-1974. Dall'onda pop alla superficie neutra* (Milan: Electa, 2007), p. 26.

Archizoom

Of the three groups that will be analysed here, the political culture of Archizoom is the most complex and multifaceted, at times almost omnivorous, in its attempt to respond to stimuli coming from the Italian factories and from London, Oakland or Palestine. In part thanks to the meticulous research conducted by Pier Vittorio Aureli and Gargiani, it is now possible to reconstruct the multiplicity of indications and political allusions that had not been adequately examined in the pioneering studies of Dominique Rouillard and Marie Theres Stauffer.[7]

In the summer of 1964, Branzi, Deganello and Massimo Morozzi (who were between 23 and 26 years old) went to England, where they spent a fair amount of time in the heart of Swinging London. Between Carnaby Street and King's Road, the future members of Archizoom observed the miniskirts, the gaudy colours of the PVC raincoats (key for *Superonda*) and a working-class youth that made its own jewellery by hand. The provocative dress of this working-class youth seemed a long way from the bourgeois "decorum" that characterised the image that the official workers' movement often presented of itself in search of social legitimacy and mobility. Some of the people who flaunted their rebellious elegance in the streets of central London identified with mod culture, whose visual and political universe informed, however surreptitiously (as has been recently argued), a significant part of the British art of that decade.[8] In Florence, moreover, these were years of out-and-out anglophilia, especially where music and clothing were concerned. Moderate beatnicks and the first hippies listened to the "British sound" immersed in the stroboscopic lights of La Perla discotheque on Viale Guidoni. Brightly coloured sweaters and necklaces could be bought instead at the Fulgenzi shop, on Via dei Bardi. After the flood, the scene would change at least in part, with the opening of the *cantine* or "cellars" (fairly small places where people went to dance and listen to live music) and then, in 1969, with the inauguration of the legendary Space Electronic.[9] One of Archizoom's peculiarities, however, consists in the fact that, in the political and design culture of its members, countercultural hedonism was inseparable from a return to Marx—the less humanist Marx, the one of *Das Kapital* and of the *Grundrisse*, not yet published in Italian, but from which some extracts had been brought out by Raniero Panzieri in the *Quaderni Rossi* and by Mario Tronti in an anthology of texts.[10]

Gilberto Corretti, Branzi, Morozzi, and Deganello were personally acquainted with Tronti, and some of them with Panzieri, two militants who were at the heart of an ambitious attempt, which later came to be known as *operaismo* ("workerism"), to re-examine the life of the proletariat and revive the class struggle. One of the student leaders in Florence, Claudio Greppi, had in fact driven first Deganello and then Morozzi and Corretti to Turin so that they could attend a meeting of the *Quaderni Rossi*. Greppi was also one of the principal proponents of a renewal of Marxism at the Faculty of Architecture, where he distributed Engels's pamphlet *The Housing Question*.[11] With the other

7 Marie Theres Stauffer, *Figurationen des Utopischen theoretische Projekte von Archizoom und Superstudio* (Munich: Deutscher Kunstverlag, 2008); Dominique Rouillard, *Superarchitecture: le futur de l'architecture 1950-1970* (Paris: Éditions de la Villette, 2004).

8 Thomas Crow, *The Hidden Mod in Modern Art: London, 1957-1969* (London: Paul Mellon Centre, 2020).

9 For an impressionistic but effective reconstruction of this cultural context, see Bruno Casini, *Ribelli nello spazio: culture underground anni Settanta: lo Space Electronic a Firenze* (Arezzo: Zona, 2013).

10 Mario Tronti (ed.), *Scritti inediti di economia politica* (Rome: Editori Riuniti, 1963); Karl Marx, 'Il frammento delle macchine', trans. Renato Solmi, *Quaderni Rossi*, no. 4, 1964, pp. 289-300.

11 Claudio Greppi, 'Intervista a Claudio Greppi', in Guido Borio, Francesca Pozzi and Gigi Roggero (eds.), *Futuro anteriore. Dai 'Quaderni rossi' al movimento globale. Ricchezze e limiti dell'operaismo italiano* (Rome: DeriveApprodi, 2002). See https://www.autistici.org/operaismo/greppi/index_1.htm.

members of the studio of architects to which he belonged, the Lega Studenti Architetti, Greppi would follow Tronti when the latter broke with Panzieri in 1963 to found the magazine *classe operaia*. As Florence was located halfway between North Italy and Rome, some meetings between the various local editorial boards of *classe operaia* were held on the premises of the Lega, where the more prominent figures in the group voiced their own reflections on more than one occasion. Morozzi, Deganello, Branzi and Corretti attended these events and the workerism of *classe operaia* or *Contropiano* (a magazine founded in 1968 in which the contributions of Manfredo Tafuri, Asor Rosa and Massimo Cacciari stood out), was often cited in Archizoom's writings. As Gargiani and Aureli have shown, it is hard to comprehend the *No-Stop City* without taking into account its roots in *operaismo*, which can be discerned above all in the logic that presided over the conceptual operation.[12] In fact, the *No-Stop City* took as its formal model the supermarket, whose aniconic architecture, eminently oriented towards consumption, was seen by the group as "the true template of the city of the future."[13] But it was in the idea of outlining a "non-ideological" model of design—in other words, free from the deceptive humanistic and idealistic "veils" typical of the official workers' movement—that the endless expanses of apartments and car parks of the *No-Stop City* took up one of Tronti's insights, the need to exacerbate the contradictions of the system: "From the workers' point of view, capital's contradictions should neither be rejected nor resolved, but only used. And to make use of them, we have to exacerbate them, even when (...) they proceed under the banner of labour."[14] Between an aesthetics of exacerbation and a mocking statement of pop flavour (but inspired in its graphics by Mies van der Rohe and thus poles apart from Pop Art), *No-Stop City* articulated a *Discorso per immagini* ("Discourse in Images") in which political reflections and a complex visual semantics found a dialectic that it was rare to encounter in Italy in those years.

Nevertheless, Archizoom cannot be reduced to the *No-Stop City*'s critique of ideology. On several occasions, the group also sought to make a foray into non-Eurocentric political cultures. This included a reading of the theorist of anti-colonialism Frantz Fanon, who thought Archizoom (and Branzi in particular) tried to reconcile with Tronti, in an attempt to view the taste of the working classes and that of the "rebels" in a manner untinged by the moralism typical of the institutional left.[15] The "bad taste" of the proletariat ("exotic" souvenirs, leopard-skin patterned fabric, etc.) and its frustrated craving for consumption were seen by the group neither as a form of subjection to the dominant culture nor as a "reprehensible" *petit bourgeois* reflex on the part of the masses, but rather as the symbol of a legitimate ambition to possess what their wages did

12 Gargiani, *Archizoom associati, 1966-1974. Dall'onda pop alla superficie neutra*; Pier Vittorio Aureli, *The Project of Autonomy. Politics and Architecture within and against Capitalism* (Hudson, NY: Princeton Architectural Press, 2008).

13 Archizoom associati, 'Città, catena di montaggio del sociale. Ideologia e teoria della metropoli', *Casabella*, no. 350-351, July-August 1970, p. 51.

14 Mario Tronti, 'A Course of Action' (1966), in *Workers and Capital* (London-New York: Verso, 2019), pp. XXX. The translation has been slightly modified by the author to adhere more closely to the staccato rhythm of Tronti's prose. This passage is underlined in Deganello's copy of the book (Paolo Deganello Archives, Milan).

15 Archizoom, letter to Germano Celant, 3 April 1970. Quoted in Gargiani, *Archizoom associati, 1966-1974. Dall'onda pop alla superficie neutra*, p. 217.

not allow them to buy. Thus the garish eclecticism of the kitsch became, in Archizoom's eyes, an at least potential form of defiance and resistance. In the group's work, the proletarian desire of the "hippie" or the young "mass worker" (figures that could coincide) of *Quaderni Rossi* and *classe operaia*, also encountered the sort of people that Western Marxism found it difficult to fit into its paradigms. One thinks, for example, of the gazebos, which certainly embody a rejection of the conventions of Italian design, but whose orientalising atmospheres should also be seen as a provocative response to the anti-Arab and anti-Muslim rhetoric of much of the Italian press during the Six-Day War. These slender architectural structures parody the stereotyped Orient of Ettore Sottsass Jr., who published them in *Pianeta Fresco*, but they should also be associated conceptually with essays like Franco Fortini's *The Dogs of the Sinai*. Archizoom's was a sarcastic pan-Arabism, assimilated perhaps a little hastily to the Islam of some of the Black Panthers, but the political syncretism of Archizoom was fertile and wholly within the bounds of the Marxism of the sixties, although it was often loath to embrace the "intersectionality" (as it would be called today) that permeated the group's work.

Take the installation entitled *Centro di cospirazione eclettica* ("Centre of Eclectic Conspiracy") that Archizoom exhibited at the Milan Triennale in 1968 (fig. 1). Here the gazebo structure became an iconographic jumble of deliberate orientalism (the Kaaba), contemporary art (Rauschenberg's *Odalisk*), workerist symbols (the round door in the pronaos) and dreamlike objects (the bedside tables with "king-size" condoms), and was intended to celebrate the political radicalism of Malcolm X, assassinated shortly after his visit to Mecca. However, one not insignificant detail escaped the group's attention. What was supposed to be a pop cenotaph of the black leader did not reproduce his photo, but that of Rap Brown (alias Jamil Abdullah Al-Amin), a bellicose representative of Black Power, who was moreover still alive. Should this oversight, revealing perhaps of a still superficial knowledge of the Black Power movement struggles in America, lead us to speak of radical chic? I don't think so. While the relationship that the group had with rebels, the working-class, and anti-imperialist Islam was mediated by the market and by affluent buyers (in 1969 the *Superonda* costed about the same as the average monthly wages of a skilled worker[16]), Archizoom's objects and installations introduced political themes and players that still met widespread hostility in the world of Italian design at the dawn of 1968.

16 Centro Studi Poltronova, email to Paolo Deganello, 6 December 2017. The message was kindly forwarded to the author the following day.

In the seventies, the group carried on with its investigation of the potentialities inherent in the aesthetics of rebels and "radicals." While Deganello joined the revolutionaries of Potere Operaio and, in parallel, tried to obtain teaching posts at American universities where the students had a history of migration, Dario and Lucia Bartolini took part in

1. Archizoom, *Centro di cospirazione eclettica*, 1968, Musée National d'Art Moderne, Centre Pompidou, Paris

the competition for the National Arab-Islamic Dress staged by the young Gaddafi. In a classic operation of "soft power" in the Arab world shaken by the Yom Kippur War, Gaddafi presented himself as a second Nasser, anti-American, a defender of the Palestinian cause and promotor of a Muslim way to socialism. In a daring proposal that avoided both Western condescension and militant Orientalism, the Bartolinis came up with a style of dress that mediated between the ingeniousness of the draped Arab robe and cutting-edge technology in stitching. Thereby they created a hybrid work that was a manifesto of the political alliance between dissimilar political traditions, but ones that, in 1973, appeared capable of converging on a common "anti-imperialist" objective. The Faculty of Architecture of the University of Florence would become a real powder keg in the second half of the seventies, with "a tradition of teaching close to the positions of Potere Operaio" and a number of militants of the Prima Linea organisation.[17] Although Archizoom began to reduce its activity as a group in 1972 (bringing it officially to a conclusion in 1974), it would not be wholly extraneous to these political developments in so far as one of its collaborators would join Prima Linea and then have to flee to France in search of political asylum.[18]

17 Andrea Tanturli, *Prima linea: l'altra lotta armata (1974-1981)* (Rome: DeriveApprodi, 2018), p. 165.

18 Paolo Deganello, conversation with Jacopo Galimberti, 24 May 2021.

In spite of some naiveties, all too easy to perceive in hindsight, Archizoom remains one of the very few groups of artists/architects that was able to benefit fully from the great surge of political creativity that swept through the country before and after the protests of 1968 and 1969. Its ability to unite sophisticated political analysis, historical insights (undoubtedly partial in both senses of the word) and an unsettling visual language remains to some extent still unparalleled.

Superstudio

Unlike Archizoom, Superstudio's relationship with politics was fairly indirect. If Corretti, Morozzi and their colleagues disclosed their militant pantheon through the visual strategy of accumulation, Superstudio aspired to a perceptual rarefaction in search of impassive and hieratic forms, expressing a mathematical sublime in which rationality and transcendence seemed almost to become one and the same thing. The semantic and political shift from "architectural rationalism" to "rationality" and "reason" (in the Enlightenment sense of the concept) was typical of the sixties and can be found at the heart of Superstudio's work and its mystical journeys in the "regions of reason." One of the motives for the elusive nature of Superstudio's politics may lie in the diverse attitudes of its members. It suffices to single out three of them to understand the heterogeneous character of the group. Cristiano Toraldo di Francia was a man of the left but, as Frassinelli remembers him, did not have much to say about it and showed no sign of a desire to give the group a political slant. Close to the Italian Communist Party but without being a member, Frassinelli was an activist in the student movement in the mid-sixties and saw Deganello (of Archizoom) as one of his main political references at the Faculty of Architecture. During this period, which was marked by the protest against Saverio Muratori, a professor of architectural composition, Frassinelli collaborated on more than one occasion with Michelangelo Caponetto, a student leader at the Faculty in 1968 and, subsequently, a prominent exponent of Potere Operaio.[19] With the spread of the protests, however, Frassinelli distanced himself from the student movement, in which he saw what he considered a dangerous hardening of attitude. The fear of an authoritarian drift to the left also pervaded Frassinelli's criticism of the *Monumento Continuo* ("Continuous Monument"), which he viewed as a structure with totalitarian implications, and about which he expressed reservations not unlike the reflections to be found in Theodor Adorno and Max Horkheimer's *Dialectic of Enlightenment*. His *Dodici Città Ideali* ("Twelve Ideal Cities") were intended to reveal the belly of the beast, as it were, and show how what had been initially conceived as a monumental structure with emancipatory aims (the *Monumento Continuo* was also supposed to host some self-managed locations) could turn into a coercive and claustrophobic dystopia.[20] Natalini, for his part, was from a well-to-do family and had a father with far-right views; the name "Adolfo," given to his son in 1941, was a homage to the Nazi regime, then at its height. Unlike Toraldo di Francia and Frassinelli,

19 Gian Piero Frassinelli, conversation with Jacopo Galimberti, 8 June 2021.

20 'Intervista a Gian Piero Frassinelli', in Giovanni de Flego, *La fine della storia. Utopia critica nelle 12 città ideali di Superstudio*, PhD dissertation, University of Trieste, 2016, pp. 460-474.

who adhered at least in part to a certain kind of Marxism, Natalini was close to the youth wing of the Liberal Party and, in his private writings, expressed his doubts about Archizoom's radicalism; in a letter, Natalini disparaged the *Discorso per immagini* of his colleagues (a text that drew on the workerism of Tronti and *Contropiano*), describing it as founded on "obscure political bases."[21]

21 Adolfo Natalini, letter to Alì Navai, 22 November 1969. Quoted in Roberto Gargiani and Beatrice Lampariello, *Superstudio* (Rome, Bari: Laterza, 2010), p. 39.

An iconographic motif used by both groups is revealing of their divergences. The *Centre of Eclectic Conspiracy* was a cube surrounded by lengths of black cloth that alluded to the Kaaba. Although Archizoom saw it as an opportunity for a polemical response to Étienne-Louis Boullée's *Cenotaph to Newton*, praised by Aldo Rossi, this sacred place of Islam was primarily an icon of what the group understood as an opening towards the globalisation of struggle: the meeting of Pan-Africanism, the Black Panthers and factory strikes.[22] So the pop pilgrimage that the visitor was invited to make represented a challenge both to Italian design and to the modes of interpretation of Western Marxism. In Superstudio's photomontage *Saluti dalla Mecca* ("Greetings from Mecca"), the enigmatic forms of the *Monumento Continuo* take the place of the cube of the Kaaba (fig. 2). In this context, however, the Six-Day War and Pan-Arabism play no role; the impenetrable "black box" of the Kaaba constituted, for Superstudio, at once an architectural archetype and forebear of the *Monumento Continuo* and the place where the latter reached its "figurative dissolution."[23] For Natalini, the Kaaba symbolised a "controllable and measurable" space, a primary act that reflected "the surrounding confusion,"

22 For these themes, see Brenda Gayle Plummer, *In Search of Power: African Americans in the Era of Decolonization, 1956-1974* (New York-Cambridge, MA: Cambridge University Press, 2013).

23 Gargiani and Lampariello, *Superstudio*, p. 141.

2. Superstudio, *Saluti dalla Mecca*, [1969-1970], Musée National d'Art Moderne, Centre Pompidou, Paris

but was magically immune to it, even if the postcard-style rhetoric that gave the title to the photomontage carried a subtle hint of self-mockery.[24]

24 Gargiani and Lampariello, *Superstudio*, p. 16.

This levity only slightly attenuates the group's ambition to unite rationalism and cosmic forces, in an attempt that recalls the contemporary work of Sottsass Jr., and in particular his effort to meld his optimism with regard to the liberating potentialities of technology with a fascination with primordial forces that the designer/architect of Tyrolean origin sought to unleash in the space of the home. While Sottsass Jr., in the sixties, increasingly looked back to an immemorial past of vanished civilisations, Superstudio tried to get cutting-edge technique (theorising a "tecnomorphic architecture" where the technology was concealed inside pure forms) to coexist with a eulogy of autarky or self-sufficiency in its agricultural or hippie incarnations. If hippie nomadism is at the core of the photomontages of the *Atti Fondamentali* ("Fundamental Acts"), it was above all the first trend, the rural one, that was made the subject of detailed analysis in the "Extra-urban Material Culture" research project and of the figure of Zeno Fiaschi, a self-sufficient farmer and custodian, according to the group, of know-how and techniques by now doomed to extinction. The esteem in which Superstudio held agricultural society, which it saw as "a moment antecedent to the process of alienation of the urbanised individual," reflects, however, a dangerous positivism that marked a profound distance from their friends in Archizoom.[25] *No-Stop City* ascertained without nostalgia that the dichotomy between town and country was no longer in effect, as Archizoom construed these two cultural and economic worlds as subordinate to the processes of capitalist accumulation. Superstudio postulated instead a general absence of alienation in "agricultural society," often evoking it as if it were a homogeneous and timeless whole. Zeno became, from this perspective, a symbol of freedom, but a freedom that was conceived primarily as individual secession from industrialised society. Superstudio's vision of Zeno's proud self-exile would have undoubtedly appeared illusory, if not downright right-wing, in Archizoom's eyes—rather than an image of proletarian resistance, a "pastoral" figure, as Catharine Rossi has argued.[26] In 1979, when Deganello showed *Componenti edilizi* ("Building Components") at the Milan Triennale, the video in which Pietro Bianconi's wife describes the house that her husband built without planning permission out of waste materials should be juxtaposed with *La coscienza di Zeno* ("Zeno's Consciousness") that Superstudio had presented at the Venice Biennale the previous year. A former communist resistance fighter with ties to *classe operaia* and a "factory vanguard" at Italsider in Livorno, Bianconi embodied in *Componenti edilizi* not autarky but "worker autonomy," understood not only as the political extraneousness of the working class to the trade unions and

25 Adolfo Natalini, Alessandro Poli and Cristiano Toraldo di Francia, 'Viaggio con la matita tra gli artefatti del mondo contadino', *Modo*, no. 7, March 1978, pp. 49-53. See Gabriele Mastrigli (ed.), *Superstudio. Opere: 1966-1978* (Macerata: Quodlibet, 2016), p. 536.

26 Catharine Rossi, 'Crafting a Design Counterculture: the Pastoral and the Primitive in Italian Radical Design, 1972-1976', in Kjetil Fallan and Grace Lees-Maffei (eds.), *Made in Italy: Rethinking a Century of Italian Design* (London: Bloomsbury, 2014), pp. 145-160.

the "reformist" parties, but as its capacity to express an independence of design and construction through illegal self-building.

Perhaps Superstudio's most overtly political work is the graduation thesis of Alessandro Poli (drawn up in collaboration with Roberto Gherardi), that was supervised by Natalini and later submitted to the competition for a City Park Dedicated to the Resistance (fig. 3). The structure represented a gigantic rising sun, the symbol of Italian socialism from the late 19th century until the end of the seventies. In the project, however, the icon would have been constructed out of radial metal lattices on which neon lights would have created spectacles of "dawns and sunsets, rainbows, northern lights, etc." Gargiani and Lampariello have pointed out the influence of the "exalted rationalism" of the French architects Boullée, Claude-Nicolas Ledoux and Jean-Jacques Lequeu.[27] To this philologically incontrovertible derivation could be added a less demonstrable but stimulating observation; this "sun of the future" between lattices and neon lights made the material culture of Art Nouveau—omnipresent in the early days of the workers' movement—resonate with the Californian psychedelic graphics of the sixties, whose roots in Art Nouveau have been amply demonstrated. A meta-reflection on styles is moreover clearly present in the thesis. The massive reinforced-concrete structure was to stand on an imposing podium that alluded to defeated fascism. The monument would have been observed from the lawn in front, where the antifascist youth could lie down in the shade of trees. In Poli and Gherardi's thesis, the memory of the Resistance was not reactivated either through the generic rhetoric of civil martyrdom or by means of the vaguely nationalistic narrative of a new Risorgimento.

27 Gargiani and Lampariello, *Superstudio*, pp. 39-40.

3. Alessandro Poli and Roberto Gherardi, Urban park with social facilities for the municipality of Modena, graduation thesis project, supervisor Leonardo Savioli, Faculty of Architecture of University of Florence, 1970, courtesy Alessandro Poli Archives, Florence

At a time not long after the bomb in Piazza Fontana, Poli and Gherardi thought of the Resistance as a joyful collective ritual, as a solar cult fuelled by cannabis that, not unlike rock concerts, ought to be part of the history of socialism. But perhaps the most architecturally successful piece was located inside the structure. In the hall, a hemispherical cavity with no function or symbolic references had as its only purpose, according to Poli and Gherardi, that of "providing food for thought," and reiterated, in so doing, the proximity between the humanism of the Enlightenment and sapiential mysticism that constituted one of the stylistic characteristics of Superstudio.

UFO

Of the three groups analysed here, UFO (an acronym of Unidentified Flying Object) is the one most disengaged from the specifics of the discipline, although with their typological analysis of the A.N.A.S. roadhouse its members still situated themselves in the architectural field, but in its more paradoxical and conceptual dimension. The meta-discursive approach of UFO is inseparable, as Amit Wolf has shown, from the peculiarities of the teachers at the Faculty of Architecture of Florence University.[28] The analyses of Giovanni Klaus Koenig and of Gillo Dorfles (whose lectures were attended by Lapo Binazzi and Titti Maschietto), and above all the semiotics of Umberto Eco, with whom the entire group would have direct contact, helped to shape the culture of UFO and induced them to embark on a reflection—visual and performative—on the codes of architecture whose scope and quality had no precedent in the sixties in Italy. Eco's proximity allowed the group to articulate, in parallel, a meta-reflection on the language of politics, developing an approach that, in 1968, was not yet part of the movement. It would be necessary to wait until 1977 and the *Indiani Metropolitani* (whose "Italo-Indian" idiolect would promptly be analysed by Eco) to see something like what the slogans written on some of the *Urboeffimeri*—"Potele agli studenti," "magozurlinpiao," "Colgate con Vietcong"—had prefigured.[29] But there is a substantial difference. The parodies of the *Indiani Metropolitani* were situated at the end of a political cycle, after the categories of Marxism-Leninism had saturated the spaces of discourse for around a decade. Instead, UFO's inflatable polyethylene tubes appeared before a certain Marxist vulgate had become hackneyed jargon, and were still rooted, unlike the happenings of the *Indiani Metropolitani*, in the traditions of the Italian university fraternities and sororities known as *goliardia*.[30]

A striking example of the group's ability to criticise the codes is the Sherwood restaurant. UFO turned the interior design of the restaurant into an allegory of power, but the tone adopted by UFO was that of the fairy tale, which was used here to reveal the underlying structures of the imagination in relation to social hierarchies. While the waiter—

28 Amit Wolf, 'Superurbeffimero, n. 7: Umberto Eco's Semiologia and the Architectural Rituals of the U.F.O.', *California Italian Studies*, no. 2, 2011, http://dx.doi.org/10.5070/C322008956.

29 "There is another language, Italo-Indian" (10 April 1977). See the text reprinted as 'Il laboratorio in piazza' in Umberto Eco, *Sette anni di Desiderio* (Milan: Bompiani, 2000 (1983)). It is said that Eco, while working at the RAI, had played a part in the creation of the character of Mago Zurlì; see Wolf, 'Superurbeffimero, n. 7', n.p.

30 Tommaso Trini, 'Masaccio a Ufo', *Domus*, no. 466, September 1968. See Stefano Pezzato (ed.), *Ufo story: dall'architettura radicale al design globale* (Prato: Centro per l'arte contemporanea Luigi Pecci, 2012), p. 52.

the worker—moved around in what was literally a gilded cage, the customers were invited instead to take the place of those who exercised power, be it religious (one chair displayed papal symbols), political (one of the seats bore the Fascist symbol of the *fascio littorio*) or economic. It was at the Sherwood that appeared for the first time, as an indication of economic power, one of UFO's most celebrated objects of design, the *Dollaro* office lamp. The lamp, surmounted by a Volkswagen Beetle and a palm tree, is covered with a metal gilt that recalls an ingot. At a time when it was still possible to convert the dollar into gold, the "sign" of the American currency, arbitrary and contingent, became an "icon," i.e. an object whose form is connected by analogy with its referent. Here, the Moorish atmospheres of Archizoom's *Safari* are rendered more politically explicit; German industry, American imperialism and the petrodollars of the Middle Eastern kingdoms are united in the office of anyone who wished to illuminate his desk with a lamp that recalled how underdevelopment and development are two sides of the same coin, and not two successive stages in a process that leads incessantly towards progress, taken from the industrialised world to the rural one. Yet UFO's tone was never one of denunciation, but that of a distancing which allowed them not to lapse into the resignation of many "apocalyptics," as Eco defined them. In the furnishings of Sherwood, the positive pole was represented by three almost identical profiles cut out of plywood: those of Lenin, Robin Hood and Zorro. The irreverent association of the Bolshevik leader with two fictional characters was a way of debunking his mythical status. That being said, the parallel between the three figures can also be read differently, as the assertion that Lenin, like Robin Hood and Zorro (but the list could include Jesus Christ and Spartacus), embodied a desire for social justice and revenge against the authorities that has its roots in myth and, perhaps for this very reason, has the power to mobilise the masses at particular moments in history.

This relationship with the unconscious and the grand collective narratives was a characteristic feature of UFO. As False Mirror Office has rightly observed, the group's inflatables served to break with, and at the same time reveal, through an operation of demystification, "socio-urban myths and rites."[31] Objects at once phallic and playful, the *Urboeffimeri* managed to devise a language that not just in its content but also and above all in its forms—mobile, collective, fortuitous—echoed the meetings at the occupied Faculty of Architecture in Palazzo di San Clemente. The General Assembly of 12 February 1968 would be interrupted by the unexpected entry of the inflatable, whose simple presence shed a completely new light on the ritual of the Assembly, and on political engagement as a synonym for dismal and all-absorbing self-sacrifice. Once again

31 False Mirror Office (Andrea Anselmo, Boris Hamzeian), 'L'assemblaggio come testo figurativo per l'architettura. Un dialogo tra UFO e False Mirror Office', *PianoB*, no. 2, 2019, pp. 88-118: 100, https://doi.org/10.6092.

the inflatable seems almost to have been a satire on those confused "desiring assemblies" that would be analysed by Eco in 1977. However, the occupation of Palazzo di San Clemente preceded not only the Battle of Valle Giulia (a violent clash between students and the police that took place in Rome in March 1968), but also May '68 in France and its Atelier Populaire (the occupation of the École des Beaux-Arts and its transformation into a workshop for the production of militant posters). In hindsight, it can be argued that the happenings of 1968 that featured the *Urboeffimeri* were almost unique in Italy, where the occupations of the universities, as well as the Palazzo della Triennale in Milan, often got bogged down in interminable discussions and the drawing up of lists of demands, while failing to seek a language of protest that went beyond the political jargon of the time. But the festive reproach that UFO took through the *Urboeffimeri* should not be misunderstood as a rejection of the language of the left, but as constructive criticism expressed from within the movement. Nor is it a coincidence that the polyethylene inflatables, much like the manifesto that UFO showed at the Triennale of 1968, were confiscated by the police because they were found, during a search, stored on the premises of Potere Operaio in Florence.

Besides, the links with the extraparliamentary left of Potere Operaio were more than occasional. Some members of the group knew Greppi well and frequented both the Lega Studenti Architetti and the Centro Giovanni Francovich, the meeting place for the first generation of *operaisti* (Greppi, Lapo Berti, Franco Gori, etc.) in 1968, and now for the militants of the student movement who would join Potere Operaio, like Giancarlo Paba.[32] Paba collaborated on the drafting of UFO's questionnaire entitled *Elementi di prossemica territoriale* ("Elements of Territorial Proxemics"), a hilarious mock opinion poll that called acid trips to mind and whose copies would be duplicated at the Florentine branch of Potere Operaio.[33] One of the militants of Potere Operaio was the aforementioned Caponetto, at whose wedding in 1972 UFO staged a performance, *Partita a scacchi su territorio. Matrimonio Extraparlamentare* ("Chess Game on the Territory. Extraparliamentary Marriage"), in which the game of chess was not played between black and white, but between people dressed in red and people wearing the colours of the Italian flag. A similar dichotomy was at the centre of a performance entitled *Bamba Issa 2—Drive in*, where UFO presented a society split perfectly into two classes. It was a parody of a certain Marxist schematism, but not necessarily that of Potere Operaio, from whose work emerged, in the mid-seventies, magazines like *Quaderni del Territorio* (to which Paba contributed) and *Quaderni del Progetto* (edited in part by Deganello), which explored the expansion of the service industry and the complex subject of "class composition" outside the Taylorist paradigm. *Giro d'Italia. Evasione alla rovescia sul territorio*, the photographs of *Controllo colonizzazione e fascismo*

32 For these and other participants in the Centro Francovich, see Roggero, Pozzi and Borio (eds.), *Futuro anteriore*.

33 Lapo Binazzi, conversation with Jacopo Galimberti, 14 June 2021. For Giancarlo Paba, see http://archivio.commonware.org/index.php/neetwork//901-in-ricordo-di-giancarlo-paba; for Massimo Grandi and Francesco "Pancho" Pardi, two other key activists of Potere Operaio at the Faculty of Architecture, see their interviews in Aldo Grandi, *Insurrezione armata* (Milan: Rizzoli, 2005), pp. 148-156 and 279-285.

sul territorio and *Controguida di Firenze (elementi di prossemica territoriale)* can in part be viewed as responses to this political debate. Under these circumstances, UFO (and Binazzi in particular) had no difficulty in relying on irony and "conceptual urbanism" to investigate the interstitial and desolate spaces of peri-urban areas, dotted with electricity pylons, power stations, gas pipelines and A.N.A.S. roadhouses.

An "Indecorous" Generation

The work of Archizoom, Superstudio, and UFO was often enmeshed in national and international politics. While in Archizoom's case, the group was eager to include political and aesthetic appeals coming from the far-left in various parts of the world, Superstudio was intentionally reluctant to integrate the struggles of the sixties and seventies into its rationalist universe. Nevertheless, at times strictly political questions emerged in the work of its members, such as the ones regarding the reactivation of the Resistance in the post-1968 phase. The case of UFO is undoubtedly the least studied. The analyses presented in this essay suggest, however, that a thorough examination of its relations with the activists of the Faculty of Architecture and the extraparliamentary left would permit a deeper understanding of some of its performances and the attendant debates. Its light-hearted irony, its taste for the absurd and the paradoxical, cannot be dissociated from the political struggles of the sixties and seventies, from the tilt of the economy towards the service sector and from the "semiological" criticism of some categories of Marxism, an approach that would later be taken up by the more creative components of the movement of 1977, of which UFO represents, in some respects, a precursor.

Between the hippies and Greppi, between the teachings of Eco and neo-colonialism, between Caponetto and the occupations of the Faculty of Architecture, Archizoom, Superstudio, and UFO were born at a politically incandescent moment, one in which the far-left offered, sometimes unwittingly, fundamental cues for a reassessment of architectural design. At a time like the present, in which the city council of Florence, using the ideology of *decoro* or embellishment as a pretext, is turning some areas of the city into dystopian areas worthy of the *No-Stop City* or the grimmer of the *Ideal Cities*, it is important to remember the political radicalism of a part of this "over the top" generation (as Branzi has defined it), a generation that was first and foremost "indecorous"—to the extent to which it turned public spaces upside down, notably the university itself. It was the last generation of intellectuals that, from the viewpoint of architectural culture, once again made Florence, for a few years, one of the most influential cities in Europe.

Street, Party, Journey, Retreat: UFO's Constructed Situations, 1968-1975

Simon Sadler

Introduction

In its designs of the late sixties and early seventies, the Florentine architectural group UFO explored ways to occupy and live in spaces and relationships colonized by capitalism and the State. UFO chose sites like the street, party, journey, and retreat in which to construct *situations* rather than buildings or products: while vanguard architecture tended to exist on paper or as furniture, UFO's projects were *in situ*. This situation-constructing drew upon a main line of the 20th century avant-garde—Dada, Surrealism and Situationism—and drew too on popular expressions of civic life, communion, and pleasure outside of traditional architectural studio practice: processions, dancing, bike rides, picnics, and so on. UFO brought constructed situations into the architectural discipline, and half a century on, UFO's design—expanded as it was into habitat, bodies, politics, feeling, and entertainment—continues to invite a concomitantly expanded way of making and thinking about architecture and community. UFO's work alerts us, too, to our everyday complicity in late capitalism and to the possibilities of making it strange to our senses, emotions, and consciousness.

UFO, Bamba Issa Discoteque, Forte dei Marmi, first season, 1969, Titti Maschietto Archives, Florence

Towards Design Radicalism

UFO was what historians call a neo-avant-garde—one of the post-war West's second wave of experimental and radical creativity in the arts, after the inter-war first wave epitomized by the Bauhaus. For all the diversity of experimentation at the Bauhaus, its lessons had crystallized in a rationalism and functionalism exemplified by methodical problem-solving, efficiency-finding, and geometric form. This was a rationalism that spread through post-war architecture and product design. Management by reason started out as a deeply humanist project, championed by the left, and dedicated to the fostering of social progress and democracy. But the ascent of a sort of cultural managerialism became a provocation to the neo-avant-garde tendency portended by situationism, a cultural current of the fifties and sixties in Western Europe. Situationism renewed the struggle, inherited from surrealism, for the unleashing of repressed desire in politics, art, design and society.

Situationists wanted to intervene in what their erstwhile mentor and ally, philosopher Henri Lefebvre, described as "social space"—the way in which space organizes and is organized by relations of production and labour—and called for the "construction of situations" to reimagine and redirect those relations toward an improved future social life based upon encounter and play (fig. 1). Constructed situations would combine environment and people to produce a transcendent and revolutionary consciousness, situationists hoped. This sense of situation was detected by Lefebvre in the Paris Commune, and

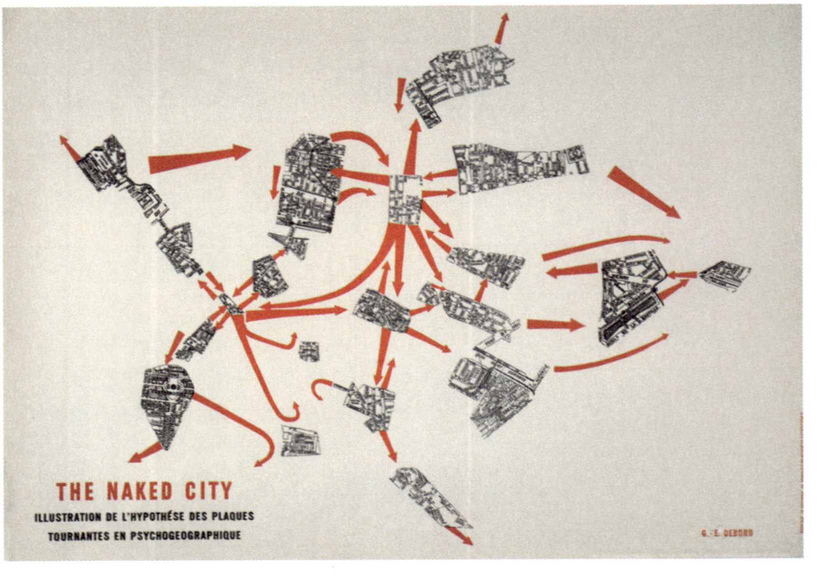

1. Guy Debord and Asger Jorn, *The Naked City—illustration de l'hypothèse des plaques tournantes en psychogeographique*, 1957, silkscreen printing

by situationists as they "drifted" through Paris and other cities, guided by intuition, and projecting the reconstruction of the entire city as a playful revolutionary situation. The implication was that architectural sensibility is innate to us all. Indeed, few of the main players in the formation of situationism were designers or architects by vocation, and core situationists didn't actively pursue the construction of situations after the early sixties, wanting instead nothing short of total urban revolution, a possibility seemingly ripened in the revolutionary May Events of 1968.

But the active contribution to revolutionary ferment remained a tantalizing possibility for some architects. UFO was aligned with so-called "Radical Architecture," formed alongside other groups like Superstudio and Archizoom at the University of Florence in the lead up to the May Events. And of the radical architects, UFO's work was probably the most redolent of something "ephemeral, without a future, passageways," as the situationists described constructed situations.[1] Radical Architecture became best known through its presentation in the landmark 1972 MoMA show *Italy: The New Domestic Landscape*, but UFO (absent from that show) offered little in the way of the crash pad comforts seen at MoMA. From its iconic *Dollaro* lamp (1969)—a cool light announcing the brutal economics of bourgeois comfort—to its situation-making, UFO drew attention to the peculiar lived experience of capitalism. With the waning of rationalist and countercultural utopianism alike, UFO turned to a popular, expansive lived environment.

1 Guy Debord, 'Rapport sur la construction des situations et sur les conditions de l'organisation et de l'action de la tendance situationniste internationale', trans. 'Report on the Construction of Situations and on the International Situationist Tendency's Conditions of Organization and Action', in Ken Knabb (ed.), *Situationist International Anthology* (Berkeley: Bureau of Public Secrets, 1981), pp. 17-25.

Constructed Situations

The best-known projects in which UFO were involved were bids to construct situations, of sorts, abandoning the formal and functional concerns of modern architecture and product design to focus on altered relations with the self, group, environment and time. In these projects UFO revisited "typologies" of social space—the street with the *Urboeffimeri* (1968) inflatables, the party with the Bamba Issa discotheque (1969-1971), the journey with the *Giro d'Italia* documentation (1971-1974), and the retreat with Global Tools workshops (1973-1975).

The *Urboeffimeri*, for which UFO is probably best known, connected traditional social spaces within the city—the school and the piazza—to revive their radical promise as spaces of "good disorder." In February 1968, UFO members joined the occupation of the Faculty of Architecture at the University of Florence, and cooperating Faculty provided a workshop for prototyping polyethylene tubular inflatable objects, becoming popular with neo-avant-gardes elsewhere (like Haus-Rucker-Co in Austria, and Utopie in France). These *Urboeffimeri* were deployed to help occupy Florence's piazza in a demonstration against the Vietnam War. The most iconic resembled a giant tube of toothpaste declaiming "Colgate con Vietcong," sporting a stylized American flag arrayed alongside images of political activist Rudi Dutschke, and declaring "Potele agli studenti" ("Power to the Students").

The Bamba Issa beach club discotheque in the resort of Forte dei Marmi the following year was fabulously incongruent with protest culture, but also blended art, surrealism, counterculture, and multidisciplinary experimentation with life. Pressed as to the look and feel of the constructed situation, situationists suggested as an initial model the party; its ambiance was born from lights, records, and stimulants, making the principle of the constructed situation comprehensible to anyone who had ever enjoyed gathering under the cover of darkness to decompress. The simplicity of the formula was suggested again by the Paris café that situationists Michèle Bernstein and Guy Debord operated for a few weeks in 1958. A decade later, UFO were at the cusp of clubbing's "golden age," with discotheque both an old and new type of social space traceable to the working-class dance halls or *bals de barrière* of mid-19th century Paris, London, and New York. Redolent of Dada and of the Berlin clubs of the twenties, discotheque promised a riposte to classical Italian culture.[2] Two 1966 American pop and counterculture events—San Francisco's psychedelic 1966 *Trips Festival*, and Andy Warhol's multimedia *Exploding Plastic Inevitable* in New York—served as models of this new environment. Trips Festival-style psychedelia offered its partygoers the dream of being "made one" through immersion in media; by contrast, the *Exploding Plastic Inevitable* induced a sense of near-dissociation.[3] Bamba Issa encouraged something in-between—an immersion cleaved open by self-lampooning. Bamba Issa's high-concept themed interiors (remade annually for the summer season) recreated an oasis with camels and sand, a radical adult Disneyland styled according to a fifties comic book, *Donald Duck and the Magic Hourglass*, in which Donald searches for the desert oasis of Bamba Issa in pursuit of supernatural sand for an hourglass to make him rich. Over three summers, recalls UFO's Titti Maschietto, from whose hotelier

2 See Tom Wilkinson, 'Typology: Nightclub', *The Architectural Review*, 13 April 2020. See https://www.architectural-review.com/essays/typology/typology-nightclub.

3 See Branden W. Joseph, '"My Mind Split Open": Andy Warhol's Exploding Plastic Inevitable', *Grey Room*, no. 8, Summer 2002, pp. 80-107.

father the commission came, the group offered "an allegory for capitalism, its arrogance, and shortcomings" as "a continuous, evolving story," from the search for oil (red sand) in the desert in the first year, to the colonization of the oasis in the second year, represented as an abandoned highway construction site in an African jungle, with unearthed archaeological finds. According to Maschietto, "in the third and final year," as the discotheque took the form of nearby Viareggio's Carnival tradition, "inevitable systematic exploitation is addressed,"[4] Maschietto explains. "Africa is rich in treasures, but now also filled with the colonizer's waste and the only way the natives can earn a living is by selling us unnecessary trinkets and exporting them back to our shores."[5]

Documenting bike rides and the road infrastructure that allows them, UFO's *Giro d'Italia* project seems to be at once its most arcane and most straightforward. Shaped by contemporaneous developments in performance and video art, *Giro* ranged from a 1971 "futurist reading" live performance at the appropriately futuristic Space Electronic discotheque in Florence (designed a couple of years earlier by UFO's friends 9999 group) (fig. 2), published by *in* magazine in July-August 1972 as an "urbanistic/architectural project," and followed that year by a (barely watchable) 30-minute video in which protagonists race, inexplicably, to an A.N.A.S. roadhouse, only to linger there. *Giro* was completed with a 1974 performance at the *Contemporanea* exhibition at the Villa Borghese in Rome, *Giro d'Italia. Evasione alla rovescia sul territorio*.[6] That "reverse escape to the territory" suggests *Giro*'s ultimate goal of encouraging the citizenry to chart and occupy its extra-urban territory. Other

4 Alexis Petridis, 'Build, baby, build: when radical architects did disco', *The Guardian*, 22 November 2015. See https://www.theguardian.com/artanddesign/2015/nov/22/radical-disco-architects-italy-nightclub-design-60s-70s-ica.

5 Ibid. See also Catharine Rossi, 'Bamba Issa, Forte dei Marmi, 1969', in Mateo Kries, Jochen Eisenbrand, Catharine Rossi and Kirsten Thietz (eds.), *Night Fever: Designing Club Culture, 1960-Today* (Weil am Rhein: Vitra Design Museum, 2018), p. 58.

6 See 'UFO, Giro d'Italia', on *Architecture Player*, https://www.architectureplayer.com/clips/giro-d-italia, and the documentation in Stefano Pezzato (ed.), *Ufo story: dall'architettura radicale al design globale* (Prato: Centro Luigi Pecci, 2012), p. 152 passim.

2. Carlo Caldini, Fabrizio Fiumi, Paolo Coggiola, Paolo Galli, Andrea Gigli, and Mario Presti, Space Electronic discotheque, 1969, Florence, 9999 Archives, Florence, courtesy Elettra Fiumi

than its project to construct situations, the situationists were most famous for their appropriation or "diversion" of existing materials and for "drifting" through space without aim or destination. In *Giro*, UFO members seem to be drifting through urban and rural territory and its in-between (the "A-B," as they call it), for pleasure but also as though on reconnaissance. The roads of the Tuscan countryside, so troubled by automobile traffic in the video—might these be diverted or reclaimed? Might cycling itself be reclaimed from its stigma as Fascism's preferred sport, and with it A.N.A.S., the State corporation founded by the fascists to maintain the roads, and a persistent symbol of bureaucracy and corruption? "We worked a lot on A.N.A.S., trying to re-appropriate a public symbol," Binazzi told the *New York Times* in 2016, explaining the presence of an A.N.A.S. roadhouse at Bamba Issa.[7] *Giro* dispassionately documented the terrain plotted by A.N.A.S. buildings and pylons in a photographic survey reminiscent of Hilla and Bernd Becher. All these A.N.A.S. roadhouses, many of them habitable—could they form something like a network of hostels? In his 1973 book *Tools for Conviviality*, anarchist philosopher Ivan Illich would identify the bicycle as one of those popular tools that "foster conviviality to the extent to which they can be easily used, by anybody, as often or as seldom as desired, for the accomplishment of a purpose chosen by the user."[8] In opposition to the disassociating effect of the automobiles in *Giro*, the bicycle and A.N.A.S.'s hostels-in-waiting were likely functioning for UFO as tools for conviviality; UFO's 1975-1985 *Laboratorio di Nuovo Artigianato Casa Anas* added lamps and picnic gear to the stockpile.

Illich's equally infamous book *Deschooling Society* (1971) was an influence on Global Tools, the multidisciplinary collective and experimental program of design education, an alternative design school in waiting, launched in the editorial office of *Casabella* magazine in 1973 with UFO among its founders.[9] Involvement with Global Tools' rusticity seemed to represent yet another pivot for UFO. But Global Tools' concern with lived environments, popularity, technology and the in-between, all beyond immediate monetary exchange, was just another natural progression for its UFO members. Illich argued that the industrial mode of production and its expertise, medicine, energy, and education had become irremediably damaging to people and the environment, and that the concentration of power, energy, and technical knowledge in bureaucratic systems disabled personal and collective autonomy and dignity. Global Tools followed suit by positioning design as an act of self-directed

7 Kat Herriman, 'The Artist-Architect Who Revolutionized Italian Design - With Humor', *The New York Times Style Magazine*, 27 September 2016. See https://www.nytimes.com/slideshow/2016/09/27/t-magazine/art/lapo-binazzis-radical-italian-design/s/lapo-bonazzi-slide-5RKR.html.

8 Ivan Illich, *Tools for Conviviality* (London: Marion Boyars, 1973), p. 26.

9 In addition to UFO, and other Radical Architecture groups such as Archizoom, 9999 and Superstudio, founding members included individual designers such as Ettore Sottsass Jr. and Gaetano Pesce and the magazines *Casabella* and *Rassegna*.

learning and community, "a new style of educational relationship between man and his environment" (to borrow Illich's vision).[10] *Giro* and Global Tools concurred with Illich that the physical environment was a freely available resource where people could learn on their own terms. Indeed, Global Tools' "Didactic Typology" in *Casabella* reads a little like a retroactive manifesto for UFO—"Global Tools takes form as a place, a repository of resources and a catalyst. The various elements of which it is composed (natural, urban, and human) constitute the various tools to use for the education process."[11]

Global Tools' "Didactic Typology" sought what it called "territorial proxemics,"[12] hailing the proto-discipline of environmental "proxemics" developed by anthropologist Edward Hall to track the interactive human choreography of crowds, workplaces, and the like.[13] Some architects were optimistic that proxemics could improve their capacity to design lived space, which was otherwise so ineffable—that tangle of actors, ideas, technologies, environments, context. Hall tried, and ultimately failed, to offer architects a scientific notation system, whereas UFO and their colleagues experimented, in effect, upon themselves, rescinding the possibility of an objective, predictive, behaviourist view of subject-environmental relations, or of a mind-body dualism. A memo from Global Tools' Survival Group explained the rationale for moving the group's 1974 workshop from Florence's Space Electronic to a country house between Florence and Siena, in Sambuca, as a way "that can lend itself to the organization of an encounter that keeps everyone in close contact. The organization of transportation and communications, cooking, cleaning and sleeping, becomes real-time action, and together with various other 'manual' activities (like construction and working with the earth), these activities constitute, with the reports and the discussions, the object/subject of the days of the workshop."[14] Sambuca in effect completed an arc of Italian neo-avant-garde workshop-situations beginning with the proto-situationism of the Imaginist Bauhaus in Alba in 1954. In these spaces creatives hung out, producing, maybe, but not much in particular.[15]

10 Ivan Illich, *Deschooling Society* (London: Marion Boyars Publishers Ltd, 1995 (1971)), p. 32, quoted in Sol Perez-Martinez, 'Deschooling Architecture', *e-flux*. See https://www.e-flux.com/architecture/education/322673/deschooling-architecture/. Global Tools' approach was also intended to counter the rationalist influence of the Hochschule für Gestaltung on one hand, and the typological influence of Aldo Rossi on other.

11 Global Tools, 'Didactic Typology Note 3', *Casabella*, no. 382, reprinted in Valerio Borgonuovo and Silvia Franceschini (eds.), *Global Tools 1973-1975* (Istanbul: SALT/Garanti Kültür A, 2015), p. 47.

12 Ibid.

13 See Larry D. Busbea, *The Responsive Environment: Design, Aesthetics, and the Human in the 1970s* (Minneapolis, London: University of Minnesota Press, 2020), p. 65 passim.

14 Superstudio and 9999 for Global Tools, 'First Survival Group Workshop: Sambuca Val di Pesa', reprinted in Borgonuovo and Franceschini (eds.), *Global Tools 1973-1975*, p. 148.

15 Indeed, Global Tools is generally regarded as marking the end of the Radical Architecture movement.

Open Work

The refusal to work for capitalism had been doctrine for the situationists and was imported into Global Tools from Italian *operaismo* ("workerism"), becoming central to a Global Tools report by UFO's Lapo Binazzi.[16] *Operaismo* refused the invasion of society by the Fordist logic and methods of the factory. Following suit, designers in Global Tools would decline to produce market fodder for society's "consumer force" pursuing predetermined "consumer choices." Further, Global Tools refused the invasion of *its* factory (so to speak) by the logic and methods of *society*.[17] After all, it is a commonplace that post-industrial work is based around *creativity*. By refusing to work for capitalism, Global Tools would be an instance of non-goal-oriented work, of "*pure* creativity," as Binazzi put it. Binazzi believed that in Global Tools there would be no difference between theory and practice. Imagine, instead, designing as itself a situation of sorts, conducted with fellow designers at a retreat, blissing out in a pure state of Being.[18]

Not in a *surrender* to the moment; this non-instrumental creativity was rather deemed to be a path to consciousness, praxis, life. After all, the refusal of work also implied the refusal of culture[19]—of society's prevailing moral, religious, economic, and aesthetic meanings and values. Binazzi posited creativity and communications without category or allegory, in which there was no longer a division of labour, nor an industrial system of communication. The name UFO (Unidentified Flying Object) had been intended to convey instead an anonymous and "open structure,"[20] and Binazzi, fresh from Bamba Issa and looking forward to Sambuca, was breathless in his memo to Global Tools about the revolutionary possibilities of this rupture in culture: "After the birth of information, the problem of DISCONTINUITY. We can think, define and spread about everything instantaneously. In order to CHANGE THE COURSE OF HISTORY, just a few words or thoughts are necessary."[21]

Was UFO being hopelessly optimistic—what good could come of a discontinuous informational and artifactual environment? Opinion among intellectuals about the emerging information society and artificial environment was a divided, changing, and complicated theoretical backdrop to UFO's situation-building activity. In the earlier part of the century, theorists like György Kepes and Siegfried Gideon claimed that design is a mechanistic, communicative, and rational extension for the human organism and its senses. By the mid-century, though,

16 See Lapo Binazzi, 'Global Tools - Theory group, Report by Lapo Binazzi, 10 October 1974', reprinted in Borgonuovo and Franceschini (eds.), *Global Tools 1973-1975*, pp. 167-169. The refusal of work, according to Andrea Branzi's report to Global Tools, was the "greatest discovery of the century" and "the fundamental law of all social dynamics." Andrea Branzi, 'La Gioconda senza Baffi', in Branzi, *Moderno postmoderno millenario* (Florence: Gruppo Editoriale Forma, 1980) quoted in Maurizio Lazzarato, 'The Conditions of a Radical Project: Refusal of Work as a Refusal of Culture', in Borgonuovo and Franceschini (eds.), *Global Tools 1973-1975*, p. 152.

17 See Lazzarato, 'The Conditions of a Radical Project: Refusal of Work as a Refusal of Culture', pp. 152-165.

18 See Binazzi, 'Global Tools - Theory group, Report by Lapo Binazzi, 10 October 1974', pp. 167-169.

19 See Lazzarato, 'The Conditions of a Radical Project: Refusal of Work as a Refusal of Culture', pp. 152-165.

20 See Paola Navone and Bruno Orlandoni, *Architettura "radicale"* (Milan: Documenti di Casabella, 1974), p. 32.

21 Binazzi, 'Global Tools - Theory group, Report by Lapo Binazzi, 10 October 1974', pp. 168-170. Preparing for the Sambuca workshop, Binazzi hoped to explore the mystery of design, proposing "three possible themes of discussion: 1. Relations between architecture and magic. Study of the cryptic relationships at the highest levels of professional organization. Pyramid of power. Magical objects. The problem of science. 2. Sports analogy. 3. Pure creativity."

this linear understanding of our extensions through design was being replaced by a less-predictable, less-directed feedback model. As Gillo Dorfles (one of the UFO members' professors at the Faculty of Architecture in Florence) argued in Kepes' 1966 book *The Man-Made Object*, the human subject becomes its own background, its own environment, an extension of its own will through its artificial extensions.[22] Kepes and Giedion were inspirations to the likes of Hall (the founder of proxemic study), and Hall's sometime correspondent, media theorist Marshall McLuhan. McLuhan excitedly anticipated our re-tribalization through the ecstatic swim of electronic communications in a shared "global village," but nonetheless cautioned that extensions always had reciprocal and unintended effects and, following Sigmund Freud, he remained skeptical about modernity's claims to omnipotence.[23] Semiologist Umberto Eco—another of the UFO members' professors at the Faculty of Architecture in Florence—criticized McLuhan's "global village" hypothesis, arguing that the expansion of communications would rather induce mere "narcotic passiveness."[24] While Anglo-American theorists of the informational and artifactual environment like Hall and McLuhan tended to lean on an "apolitical" cybernetics and evolutionary biology, Eco belonged to a more politically-engaged European school, shaped by Marxism and semiotics, and more encouraging of critical human agency.[25] What if the mass media didn't triumph, Eco wondered. Eco theorized what he termed the "open work," and in a celebrated lecture of 1967, "Towards a Semiological Guerrilla Warfare," he argued that "means of communication (...) unlike means of production, are not controllable either by private will or by the community." That being the case, he asked "the scholars and educators of tomorrow to abandon the TV studios or the offices of the newspapers, to fight a door-to-door guerrilla battle like provos of Critical Reception."[26]

This in effect was the task assumed by UFO, instigating critical reception through multimedia events founded, as Binazzi put it, in "discontinuity." Change the conditions of reception, and the meaning of the message changes, Eco explained of an approach reminiscent of situationist "diversion."[27] The *Urboeffimeri*—what did they mean? A form of Pop Art, for sure (the toothpaste tube), but the skein of signs—Colgate, Vietcong, the Stars and Stripes, Rudi Dutschke—was like a Marxian dream image; Bamba Issa's oasis still more so. UFO put meaning and ambiguity into a dialectic of modern life known to the cubists at the turn of the century as they navigated a flood of print

22 See Busbea, *The Responsive Environment: Design, Aesthetics, and the Human in the 1970s*, p. 201.

23 See Busbea, *The Responsive Environment: Design, Aesthetics, and the Human in the 1970s*, p. 206 passim.

24 Umberto Eco, 'Towards a Semiological Guerrilla Warfare', 1967. See http://www.kareneliot.de/downloads/UmbertoEco_Towards%20a%20Semiological%20Guerrilla%20Warfare.pdf.

25 See Busbea, *The Responsive Environment: Design, Aesthetics, and the Human in the 1970s*, p. 206.

26 Eco, 'Towards a Semiological Guerrilla Warfare'.

27 More artistically-oriented architects, like UFO, already knew that in aesthetic communication "the message is deliberately ambiguous precisely to foster the use of different codes by those who, in different times and places, will encounter the work of art" (Eco, 'Towards a Semiological Guerrilla Warfare').

media available in the cafe. Navigating media was not exactly work, nor exactly unadulterated pleasure, either. The discotheque oddly recalled something of the cafe's social space and space of reception, with no central image, activity, or narrative—unless, that is, the patron of Bamba Issa was sufficiently sober to see in the fake-oasis scenography a dependency on a glut of energy, derived from a global servitude of bodies and nature, under capitalism.

Communion

UFO's intense irony meanwhile served as a cover for seeking communion, love, and a secular godliness, one wonders. The Duomo was literally in the background of the *Urboeffimeri*—the perennial sacred heart of Florentine society. ("We were inspired by the feasts of Renaissance," Binazzi recently told the *New York Times*).[28] There was a quasi-monastic quality to Global Tools, its designers learning to till with one another. Bamba Issa hewed to a notably *soulful* playlist of records bought in London and delivered with the clarity afforded by expensive Swiss sound equipment.[29] The discotheque was a quasi-religious revival: congregation, light, sound, the ecstatic body, call-and-response—an altered consciousness known to churchgoers. In all of UFO's situations, a communality was aided by active audiences at one with the performance. Instead of live acts (a characteristic of other clubs being developed at the time by radical architects), Bamba Issa was driven by DJs, mitigating the spectacle of a band, diffusing attention to the crowd. Its spatial experience was not stable, Cartesian, nor exclusively visual, but corporeal as well, as sound penetrated the moving body.[30]

28 Lapo Binazzi, quoted in Herriman, 'The Artist-Architect Who Revolutionized Italian Design - With Humor'.

29 Patrizia Cammeo and Titti Maschietto, conversation with Boris Hamzeian and Gloria Castellini, 11 October 2019.

30 On the characteristics of the discotheque from Barcelona's pioneering Maddox club on, see Pol Esteve, 'Total Space', in Kries, Eisenbrand, Rossi and Thietz (eds.), *Night Fever: Designing Club Culture, 1960-Today*, p. 140.

In the street, and on bike rides, and with Global Tools, UFO tacitly opposed or withdrew from capitalist modernity. But Bamba Issa was in the belly of the beast, the forerunner of the orgy of consumption and hedonism that is today's Mediterranean club scene. Bamba Issa's pop iconography and music called out this unholy mix of capital, the popular, and the transcendent, which stretched back to Renaissance Florence's dependency on banking and forward to the venue's Motown playlist, the quintessential sound of Detroit, a city still enjoying its midwestern, and largely Black, American Renaissance. The uneasy intersection of godliness and secularism, community and commerce, is one way of interpreting the otherwise overwhelming irony of a space like Bamba Issa. It was an uneasy intersection inherent to the predominantly Black American music on Bamba Issa's playlist, too.[31] The secularization of gospel as soul—the expression of faithfulness to God repurposed as romantic and sexual devotion—had been the cause of some consternation among Black churchgoers in the fifties and sixties; complicating things further was the relationship of soul music to commerce, to capitalism. Was soul a transcendence of, and resistance to, racial capitalism, or a sell-out to it? Was Bamba Issa a transcendence of, and resistance to, racial capitalism, or a sell-out to it?

UFO projects were doing their best to mitigate life under capitalism and restore lived experience: try this, then this, then this, then this (street, party, bike, retreat). It was a romantic bid to reverse the repressive apparatus of modernity (Max Weber's "iron cage") into an apparatus of liberation. Was the discotheque and its pumping music an archetype of what Herbert Marcuse called "repressive desublimation"? In advanced industrial capitalism, Marcuse argued, culture is flattened out into a commodity and technology, denying its capacity for opposing and transcending society; as he put it in *One-Dimensional Man*, "The music of the soul is also the music of salesmanship."[32] Flip that, though—as Marcuse would imply was possible in *The Aesthetic Dimension*—and one might have instead a *liberating* sublimation. Michel Foucault, theorizing the ways that individual and social bodies are disciplined, might have considered the disco's hedonistic light and beat to be a mere *dispositif*, his term for the institutional, physical, technical, epistemological and administrative mechanisms that maintain and enhance power. But could these technologies of the self (to borrow another phrase from Foucault) become technologies of the non-self, of the communal? Could the discotheque be what Foucault described as a heterotopia, a space in which to live out something "other," a passage through crisis, a world within the world?

Probably all of the above: Bamba Issa foreshadows both the postmodern and our lives imbricated in an economy not necessarily of our choosing. It was an alternative state deconstructing global capitalism—*and* just a bar, just a pick-up joint, just somewhere to space out. We probably shouldn't underrate the importance of experiments like this, post-counterculture. The heterotopic refuge, often identity-based (youth, queer, Latinx, Black, punk, and so on) became the constructed situation with lineage traceable to the intimate clubs and safe

31 For a compilation of tracks played at Bamba Issa, see ICA, 'Bamba Issa Discotheque Playlist', https://www.youtube.com/playlist?list=PLHZc-7v6UhVITwpLX1C-uRV10GUdW2G0Z. Bamba Issa's playlist was peppered with folk revival and rock'n'roll, the staples of white counterculture—the Rolling Stones, the Beatles, Bob Dylan, Simon and Garfunkel, Janis Joplin, Creedence Clearwater Revival, tipping into some of the glitz of the seventies with Elton John, and including the key crossover acts of Santana and Hendrix. But with Hendrix, we see that the playlist was overwhelmingly African American—John Lee Hooker and Etta James at a bluesier and jazzier end, and at a more soulful end, Isaac Hayes, James Brown, Otis Redding, The Four Tops, Booker T. and the MG's, Jimmy Cliff, Al Green, Curtis Mayfield, Sam & Dave, The Bar-Kays, Aretha Franklin, The Supremes, imbuing Bamba Issa, and many other discotheques with something of the soulfulness of the Black church. On the relationship of music, race and capitalism, see for instance Brian Ward, *Just My Soul Responding: Rhythm and Blues, Black Consciousness, and Race Relations* (Berkeley: University of California Press, 1998).

32 Herbert Marcuse, *One-Dimensional Man: Studies in the ideology of advanced industrial society* (London, New York: Routledge, 1991 (1964)), p. 61.

spaces of Berlin, Harlem and Paris in the early 20th century and late 19th century, carving out space and time from the night, wrested by electricity from the old diurnal cycle. There is abundant testimony of the freeing experience of such spaces. Parties at this time were offering refuge to the oppressed and marginalized—Afro-Caribbean sound systems in the UK, for example, gay bars in San Francisco, and house music in Chicago and New York. In 1969, the same year as Bamba Issa first season, David Mancuso started his legendary Lower Manhattan loft party as an experiment in tripping: DJ Frankie Knuckles recalls it as being "a religious experience," in a space furnished with church pews. In what actually was Mancuso's own home, Knuckles "knew I was home. (...) There was all sorts of people in there: Black, white, gay, straight, Latino, this, that, and the other. (...) There was a rhythm that was moving through the room and you found that the minute you stepped into it you went right with the rhythm of the whole room."[33] Bamba Issa might be something like a Mediterranean variant of this "church," this "home," slipped laconically into the confluence of capitalism and Marxism. In the nightclub, everyone was on stage (not so far from the experience of the piazza, then), the caressing of light switching from the individual to the collective, self to non-self, subjectivity to intersubjectivity.[34]

Humanism, Romanticism, and capitalism have built the world around the individual, to which the alternative modernity in communitarianism and crowds has mostly existed adjacent; but in UFO's situations, the two states of individualism and communitarianism were superimposed. The partygoers at Bamba Issa were part of some collective performance wordlessly scripted and choreographed by the DJ and lighting technician in the booth. What narrative there was depended on lyrics, almost entirely in the foreign tongue of the Anglo-American empire, sung by those subaltern to it. It was a machine for a cosmopolitan space and future, an artificial holism (in Carl Jung's formulation, holistic therapy assists in the self's individuation, and the relationship of self to the group)—the pounding of an "archetypal" beat binding the crowd, the "critical" break in scenography reasserting the mind; a sense of home in tension with the brazen industrialization of affect. The iconography of industrial striping at Bamba Issa recurred the following decade at the legendary Manchester club The Hacienda (Ben Kelly, 1982), which name derived from a Situationist manifesto.

33 Frankie Knuckles, interview on the Benji B show, BBC radio, 17 January 2013, https://www.mixcloud.com/benjib/frankie-knuckles-special/. See too Tim Lawrence, 'Dance Floor Transformation: Counterculture, Post-Industrialism, and Environmental Design in New York City during the 1970s and Early 1980s', in Kries, Eisenbrand, Rossi and Thietz (eds.), *Night Fever: Designing Club Culture, 1960-Today*, pp. 88-96.

34 As a recent Instagram post by somatic therapist Tada Hozumi puts it, "Black music and dance is probably the most popularly accessible and provenly effective embodied transmutational / alchemical praxis that we know of." See https://www.instagram.com/tadahozumi/?hl=en.

Architectural aesthetics, then, *might* have a role in assisting its subjects toward some new subjectivity. American media theorist Gene Youngblood posited, in McLuhanite terms, that the *Expanded Cinema* (the title of his influential 1970 book) of new filmmaking technology, video, multi-media environments, special effects, and so on would not simply expand consciousness, but break through environmental equilibrium into teleological transformation. Under the shared influence of philosopher Pierre Teilhard de Chardin, American architect Paolo Soleri likewise sought the transformation of mass consciousness through his Arcology.[35] The Marxist cultural historian Raymond Williams had proposed that before a worldview is concretized as ideology—say, as an agenda for "community"—it is sensed in aesthetics, institutions, and experiences, as some "structure of feeling."[36] Williams focused his analysis on language and literature, but it might run through material and electronic culture, too. Were UFO's environments relays of sentiments and supports for behaviour? As philosopher Jacques Rancière has more recently proposed on the "politics of the sensible," social and political order is founded on "the distribution of the sensible," so that it matters what is audible and visible, as this defines what we know, think, and experience. Some groups and ideas can be sensed—heard, seen, and so on—while others remain outside of sensibility. Anthropologist Arturo Escobar now suggests that popular music is a test bed of lived relations, and pop musician David Byrne has argued that music, community and space are codependent.[37] UFO's scenes, pared down to wine and food shared with friends at Sambuca, or to the pulse of Detroit soul at Forte dei Marmi, invited guests to all look again, hear again, feel again, decode again, to become alert to what might be on the edges of our expectations.

35 See Busbea, *The Responsive Environment: Design, Aesthetics, and the Human in the 1970s*, p. 214 passim.

36 See Raymond Williams, *Marxism and Literature* (Oxford: Oxford University Press, 1977), pp. 128-135. For an adaptation of Williams' thesis to spatial and material culture, see too Ben Highmore, 'Feeling It: Habitat, Taste and the New Middle Class in 1970s Britain', *New Formations*, no. 88, Spring 2016.

37 See 'Design and the Relational Ontologies of Music', in Arturo Escobar, *Designs for the Pluriverse: Radical Interdependence, Autonomy, and the Making of Worlds* (Durham: Duke University Press, 2017), p. 129; and David Byrne, *How Music Works* (San Francisco: McSweeney's, 2012).

Conclusions

The archive of the neo-avant-garde has been revisited the last couple of decades as we find ourselves deeper and deeper into a postmodern, late capitalist condition, each time hoping to recover some better insight into its origins and inspirations for getting out of its most alienating impacts. What do we learn from UFO's construction of situations? The situationists themselves mostly concluded that constructing little situations was politically inadequate, and so insisted on nothing short of revolutionary change; at the time, the acerbic historian-critic Manfredo Tafuri would lump the Florentines in with the rest of the neo-avant-garde, as indulging in a performative radicalism. That arguably remains a fair assessment. In time, the experiences of the street, the party, journey, and retreat became just so much product for the experience economy.[38] The opportunity to curate and create became a standard neoliberal offer in the production and monetization of the self. UFO's scene was a rather privileged cosmopolitanism, we should also note. That oasis at Bamba Issa tried to embed into design what we might now refer to as a decoloniality, but within a bohemian and decadent Italian party scene, so that the Africans and African Americans being hailed were absent, nonetheless. Compared to the club scene of the *Exploding Plastic Inevitable* a few years earlier, UFO's space and playlist was trending toward something relatively comforting, and a long way from the sites of urban revolution.[39] UFO's was a somewhat adult male cosmopolitanism, too—UFO's Patrizia Cammeo was one of the few female participants at Sambuca, which also hosted just a few children.

That said, Italian Radical Architecture, UFO in particular, mostly remained truer to social change than did neo-avant-gardes elsewhere. There were at least three versions of the "autonomy" vaunted by the neo-avant-gardes. One was a disengagement with social revolution that became fashionable for those of them in the United States pursuing the neo-Kantian autonomy of formalism, like the New York Five architects (the influential New York architectural journal *Oppositions*, edited by one of the New York Five, pointedly lost interest in Global Tools).[40] Another was the autonomy of off-the-grid, ecological, belief-based, and survivalist settlement that took hold of counterculture and sent it inward, sometimes even to cultishness.[41] The casual presence of two guns on the lunch table at Sambuca seemed to be riffing on that outlaw spirit—especially as Italy was slipping after 1968 into the political terror of the Years of Lead (fig. 3).[42] But still, there seems to be an irony here, too: the lethal tool placed next to a corkscrew. Mostly we see around UFO a counterculture trying to remain *outward* turning (at Bamba Issa, space ran continually from inside to outside). *This* form of autonomy, stemming from *operaismo*, resolutely defined designers as "workers" like any other,[43] and in doing so claimed for themselves the dignity of socially-defined work. *Liberation* was more important than freedom (that is, the act of setting citizens free from oppression mattered more than the power to just act, speak, or think as one wanted).

38 Maschietto admitted to *The Guardian* newspaper that Radical Architecture was, to borrow the situationist term, recuperated by capitalism. "Some radicals became famous architects, and by that I mean the less radical they are, the more famous they become. I'm not even sure I'm 'radical' any more." Petridis, 'Build, baby, build: when radical architects did disco'.

39 "Though the forces unleashed there have occasionally erupted into the street—one has only to think of Stonewall—more frequently the nightclub acts as a pressure valve, allowing the controlled release of youthful energies that might otherwise be applied to more dangerous levers." Tom Wilkinson, 'Dark matters: The avant-garde and club culture since the 1960s', *The Architectural Review*, 16 May 2018. See https://www.architectural-review.com/essays/dark-matters-the-avant-garde-and-club-culture-since-the-1960s.

40 See the letter from Peter Eisenman to Global Tools reproduced in Borgonuovo and Franceschini (eds.), *Global Tools 1973-1975*, p. 30.

41 My thanks to Dr. Sampada Aranke for prompting this observation.

42 The seminar marked the beginning of the end of Global Tools, as disagreements between constituent groups from Florence and Milan prompted a participant to ironically set up the welcoming table with two guns. My thanks to Valerio Borgonuovo for explaining this.

43 Note who Global Tools self-identify as "workers" in 'Document-o No. 5 "Groups-Attivit-y-à-Dei Gruppi"', in *Bollettino Global Tools* (Milan: Edizioni L'uomo e l'arte, 1974), reproduced in Borgonuovo and Franceschini (eds.), *Global Tools 1973-1975*, p. 19.

In our own moment, studying the expanded architecture of UFO encourages a more expansive sense of what constitutes architecture. UFO's was an architecture of columns *and* beats, space *and* electronics, supplementing a white bourgeois university-based culture (the traditional domicile of the architectural discipline, and of the student uprisings) with inspiration from Black, queer and working-class cultures. It was an architecture that drew attention to the *apparatus* of architecture, to the patterns of the artifactual environment, and to their effect on thought, sentiment, politics, and motion.[44] That's of value now as our media tech becomes less public, and more eerie; its "architecture" ferreted away inside software. Meanwhile, the open work remains promising for *change*; schools of design are themselves constructed situations of sorts (Global Tools feels like a specter in design schools' ubiquitous makerspaces), schizophrenically serving the world as it is, while preparing preferred situations for a decolonized, decarbonized world to come.

44 Compare with Busbea, *The Responsive Environment: Design, Aesthetics, and the Human in the 1970s*, p. 238: "Is it possible to imagine an art history of the apparatus?".

3. Global Tools, first seminar, 1-4 November 1974, Sambuca Val di Pesa, Florence, courtesy Adolfo Natalini Archives, Florence

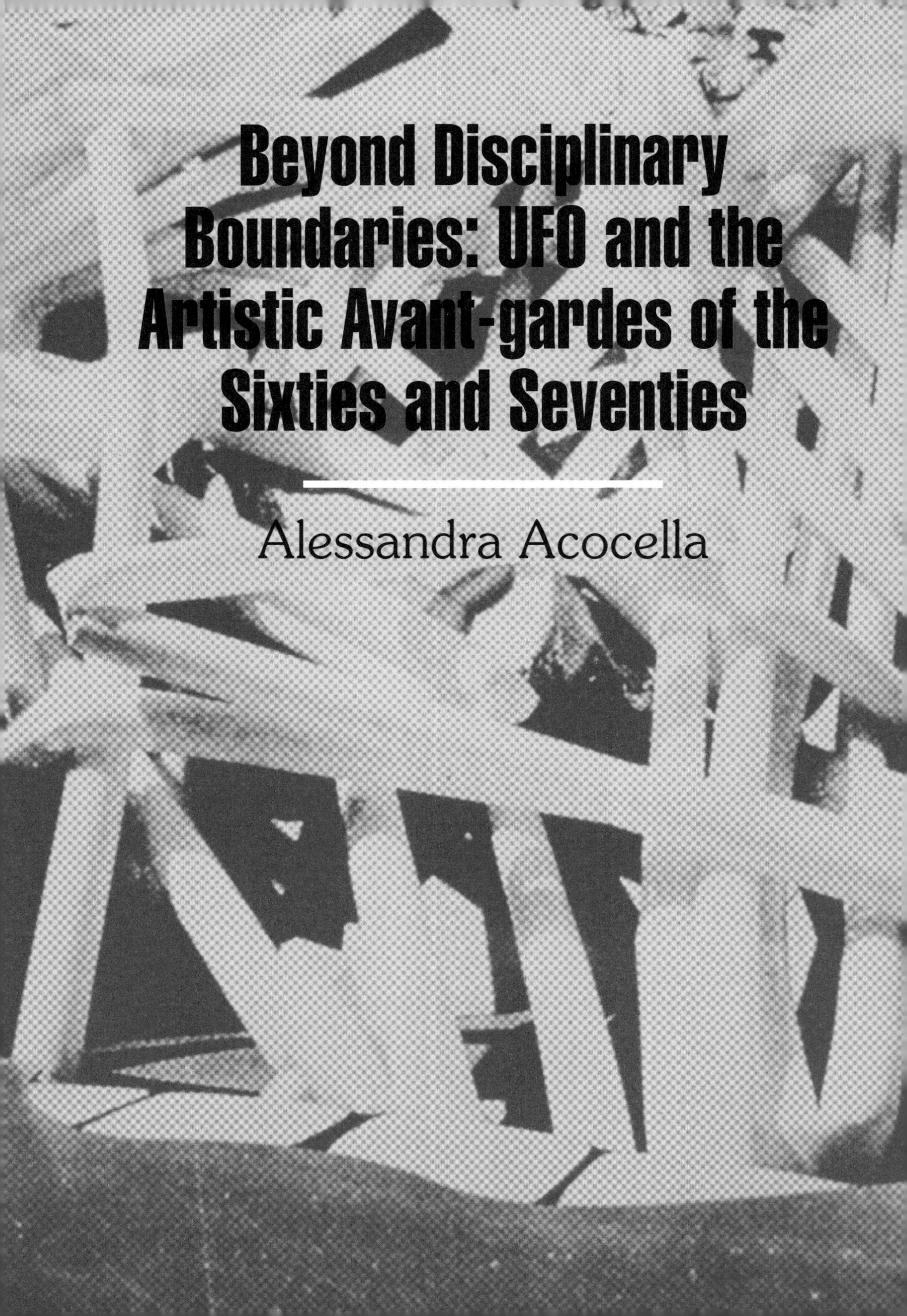

Beyond Disciplinary Boundaries: UFO and the Artistic Avant-gardes of the Sixties and Seventies

Alessandra Acocella

UFO, formed as a group by students in 1967 during the occupation of the Faculty of Architecture in Florence, and active until 1978, was one of the exponents of Italian Radical Architecture that devoted the most energy to the development of a line of research which had evident points of contact, both conceptually and linguistically, with the realm of the visual arts.[1] In their exploration of a form of creativity unconstrained by the discipline of architecture, its members produced an irreverent and anarchic range of imagery over the course of ten years of activity, appropriating the languages of the artistic avant-gardes of the day, and using them in an original manner. Inflatable objects, happenings, and art films and performances were the main means of communication through which UFO reshaped and invaded architectural, urban, and territorial space, with often playful and paradoxical results that were intended to challenge established codes.

This desire to break down disciplinary barriers is reflected in the participation of the group of young architects in many of the joint exhibitions that marked—in the big cities as well as in the livelier small cities and towns—the avant-garde art scene in the sixties and seventies: from the staging of the Premio Masaccio for the sixth time in renewed form at San Giovanni Valdarno (1968) to the Italian participation in the seventh Paris Biennale (1971), and from the urban happening *Pollution: Per una nuova estetica dell'inquinamento* (1972) in Bologna to the major interdisciplinary exhibition *Contemporanea* (1973-1974) in Rome and the recognition received on the international stage of the Venice Biennale in 1978 in the section coordinated by Lara-Vinca Masini.[2] Or again, the group's recurrent presence at festivals devoted to artist's films.[3]

The influence of Italian and foreign artistic neo-avant-gardes and their mutual contamination can be traced back to the first large inflatable structures made out of polyethylene from February 1968 in the occupied Faculty of Architecture and promptly used by the group during the student protests as "'concrete' elements

1 For a historical analysis of the UFO's work, see the essay by Andrea Anselmo and Boris Hamzeian in this volume. See too Stefano Pezzato (ed.), *Ufo story: dall'architettura radicale al design globale* (Prato: Centro per l'arte contemporanea Luigi Pecci, 2012).

2 *Premio nazionale di pittura Masaccio: 6. Edizione* (Florence: La Stamperia, 1968); Achille Bonito Oliva (ed.), *7e Biennale de Paris (catalogo della mostra, Parc Floral de Paris)* (Florence: Centro Di, 1971); Daniela Palazzoli (ed.), *Pollution: Per una nuova estetica dell'inquinamento* (Bologna: Fondazione Iris, 1972); Achille Bonito Oliva (ed.), *Contemporanea. Roma, Parcheggio di Villa Borghese 11. 1973 / 2. 1974* (Florence: Centro Di, 1973); Lara-Vinca Masini (ed.), *Topologia e morfogenesi. Utopia e crisi dell'antinatura. Momenti delle intenzioni architettoniche in Italia* (Venice: Edizioni La Biennale di Venezia, 1978).

3 They included: *Zona film. Documenti di cinema d'artista* (curated by Andrea Granchi and Maurizio Nannucci, Zona, Florence, April-June 1977) and *Cinema d'artista e cinema sperimentale in Italia 1960/1978* (curated by Andrea Granchi, Palais de Chaillot/Centre Pompidou, Paris, December 1978).

UFO, *Urbanistic Ephemeron 4*, Florence, 1968

interrupting and disrupting standard rites of the historic centre of Florence, such as afternoon shopping, the Sunday stroll after mass, vehicle traffic, tourist routes."[4]

4 UFO, 'Urboeffimeri avvenenti 1:1', *Marcatrè*, no. 41-42, June 1968, pp. 52-73: 53.

The idea of working with an immaterial and impalpable substance like air, which pumped into supple and lightweight envelopes became a visible structure and thus a new element with an aesthetic and communicative value, had already found a seminal application in the *Ambiente a volume variabile* ("Variable Volume Environment," later known as the *Grande oggetto pneumatico*, or "Large Pneumatic Object") presented by the Gruppo T in 1960 at the opening of their first exhibition *Miriorama 1*, held at the Galleria Pater in Milan. On this occasion the young Milanese artists had literally invaded the gallery with large tubes of transparent polyethylene that were continually inflated and deflated so as to activate a dynamic and many-sided experience in the exhibition space. "The visitors," wrote Bruno Munari in his description of reactions to the *Ambiente a volume variabile*, "were somewhat disoriented, not knowing 'how' to look at these objects."[5] The playful and participatory intentions underpinning the *Grande oggetto pneumatico* are evident from the photographs that picture the members of Gruppo T while they have fun in the spaces of the gallery with these light elements that could float and be manipulated (figs. 1-2).

5 Bruno Munari, 'I giovani del gruppo T', *Domus*, no. 378, May 1961, p. 53. For further information, see Lucilla Meloni, *Gli ambienti del Gruppo T. Arte immersiva e interattiva* (Cinisello Balsamo: Silvana Editoriale, 2004).

It was an experiential atmosphere that—from today's perspective—does not appear without parallels with what we see in the pictures taken and utilised several years later by UFO to document, in the cultural review *Marcatrè*, the unexpected and disruptive presence of the first two *Urboeffimeri* in the atrium and great hall of the Faculty in the days of the student protests and occupa-

1-2. Gruppo T, *Grande oggetto pneumatico–Ambiente a volume variabile*, made on the occasion of the exhibition *Miriorama 1*, Galleria Pater, Milan, 1960, courtesy Gabriele Devecchi Archives, Milan tion.[6] Supported and guided by the hands of their makers or other students, these long inflatable cylinders, put immediately to use, seemed to challenge the massive and static bulk of the traditional supports of the hall—"the diameter of tube and columns is now the same," pointed out their creators, offering themselves, not without irony, as an alternative model to architecture in masonry.[7]

The members of UFO were the only exponents of the Italian Radical avant-garde to make extensive creative use of the "technology of air,"[8] a type of experimentation that, explored by the Gruppo T well in advance, in the early sixties, found widespread application in the second half of the decade in the new forms of expression of European and American art, which showed an increasing tendency towards dematerialisation as a condition and consequence of conceptual, behavioural, and performative practices.

The ample illustrated feature that appeared in May 1968 in the pages of *Domus*—a magazine that in the early seventies would become one of the most important means of dissemination of Italian Radical research—offers an interesting cross-section, from a contemporary perspective, of this phenomenon that affected as much the field of art as those of architecture and experimental design.[9]

Outstanding among the works and events documented by the Milanese periodical were Andy Warhol's floating *Silver Clouds*, filled with helium and installed in 1966 at the Leo Castelli Gallery in New York; Christo's gigantic packaging lifted into the air by helicopter (*42,390 Cubic Feet Package*, 1966); and the exhibitions *Air Art* and *Structures Gonflables*, both held in March 1968, the former by Willoughby Sharp at the Arts Council in Philadelphia and the latter by the Utopie group at the Musée d'Art Moderne de la Ville de Paris.[10] And again, in relation to radical experiences close to UFO, the pneumatic, nomadic and temporary living structures created by the London-based group Archigram (with their celebrated *Cushicle*, 1966-1967) or those of the Austrian architects Hans Hollein, Walter Pichler and Haus-Rucker-Co.[11] With respect to the structural and housing aims underpinning these works, however, the inflatables of the Florentine collective had an avowed "their flimsily and clumsily handmade nature" that brought them closer to contemporary and more extemporaneous artistic proposals,[12] as means of disturbance aimed at stimulating critical and active participation in public space.

6 Lapo Binazzi, Lapo (sic) Cammeo, Riccardo Foresi, Sandro Gioli and Titti Maschietto, 'Effimero Urbanistico scala 1/1', *Marcatrè*, no. 37-40, May 1968, pp. 198-209: 200-203.

7 Binazzi, Cammeo, Foresi, Gioli and Maschietto, 'Effimero Urbanistico scala 1/1', p. 201.

8 On these aspects, see Emanuele Piccardo, 'UFO. Sperimentare la parodia nello spazio pubblico', in Pezzato (ed.), *UFO story: dall'architettura radicale al design globale*, pp. 16-18; Alessandra Acocella, 'L'immagine della piazza nelle azioni del gruppo UFO (1968)', in Stephanie Hanke, Brigitte Sölch (eds.), *Projektionen. Der Platz als Bildthema* (Munich: Deutscher Kunstverlag, 2019), pp. 197-210.

9 'Pneu: inflatable structures and forms', *Domus*, no. 462, May 1968, pp. 13-22.

10 Willoughby Sharp (ed.), *Air Art* (New York: Kineticism Press, 1968); Utopie (ed.), *Structures Gonflables* (Paris: Musée d'Art Moderne de la Ville de Paris, 1968).

11 On these aspects see Esther Choi, 'Atmosphere of Institutional Critique: Haus-Rucker-Co's Pneumatic Temporality', in Andrew Blauvelt (ed.), *Hippie Modernism: The Struggle for Utopia* (Minneapolis: Walker Art Center, 2016), pp. 31-43.

12 Binazzi, Cammeo, Foresi, Gioli and Maschietto, 'Effimero Urbanistico scala 1/1', p. 198.

1-2. Gruppo T, *Grande oggetto pneumatico–Ambiente a volume variabile*, made on the occasion of the exhibition *Miriorama 1*, Galleria Pater, Milan, 1960, courtesy Gabriele Devecchi Archives, Milan

In the revolutionary climate of 1968, pneumatic structures in the form of inflatables were widely used in ephemeral experiments carried out in the open air, outside the institutional settings of museums and galleries. The motives for this pervasive phenomenon can be found in such extrinsic characteristics as their cheapness, lightness and ease of transport, in addition to the way they could be expanded to generate the most varied volumes and shapes. Occupying very little space when uninflated, these elements were able to assume enormous dimensions in just a few minutes simply by filling them with compressed air, thereby resulting in a new perception of the urban or natural locations with which they interacted and, simultaneously, in a completely new and engaging mode of use.

Emblematic among the proposals presented at the events held in public space that enlivened the Italian avant-garde art scene between the sixties and seventies were the floating air-filled volumes of Hidetoshi Nagasawa and Jorrit Tornquist, installed in direct contact with the surface of Lake Idro for the festival *Un paese + l'avanguardia artistica* (Anfo, Brescia, 1968). These would be echoed by the large inflatables left for the public to use in unpredictable ways by Franco Mazzucchelli on the paving of the historic Piazza dei Priori, in Volterra, during the encounter between art and the city organised by Enrico Crispolti in 1973.[13]

In those same years, UFO also played a direct part in several experimental events that involved the urban environment, commencing with the 6th Premio Masaccio at San Giovanni Valdarno, in the province of Arezzo. This was a prize that in 1968 was opened up to interdisciplinarity and the most up-to-date artistic tendencies,

13 For further information on the artistic practices of intervention in urban spaces in Italy in the sixties and seventies, the reader is referred to Alessandra Pioselli, *L'arte nello spazio urbano. L'esperienza italiana dal 1968 a oggi* (Monza: Johan & Levi, 2015); Alessandra Acocella, *Avanguardia diffusa. Luoghi di sperimentazione artistica in Italia 1967-1970* (Milan: Fondazione Passaré/Macerata: Quodlibet, 2016).

from kinetic/programmed art to Arte Povera, with the presence of—among others—Alighiero Boetti, Giuseppe Chiari, Maurizio Nannucci, Giulio Paolini, Paolo Scheggi and Gilberto Zorio. On the opening night of the exhibition/prize, the Florentine collective put on a complex and disruptive mobile performance that, starting out from the tower of the 13th-century Palazzo d'Arnolfo di Cambio (reconfigured for the occasion by Gianni Pettena's installation/ camouflage), ended up in spectacular fashion, with large inflatables and papier-mâché figures taken directly from Viareggio Carnival, in the town's main square.[14]

14 On the story of the 6th Premio Masaccio see Acocella, *Avanguardia diffusa*. On the intervention proposed by UFO on this occasion, see too Amit Wolf, 'Superurbeffimero n. 7: Umberto Eco's Semiologia and the Architectural Rituals of the U.F.O.', *California Italian Studies*, no. 2, 2011, http://dx.doi.org/10.5070/ C322008956.

Interesting, in this context, is the definition of the *Superurbeffimero n. 7* intervention made by UFO at San Giovanni Valdarno, which the group presented as a "happening" (on the invitation) and a "happenvironment" (in the script).[15] Through this last formulation, the members of the group fused into a single concept the aesthetic categories of "happening" and "environment" that between the end of the fifties and the beginning of the following decade had become part of the vocabulary of contemporary art in the United States and then come into current use in Europe too. They were both forms of expression aimed at a break with the traditional genres of painting and sculpture: one through its character as a spectacle, the other through its encroachment on the surrounding space. In the experimentation and theorisation of these new practices, a primary role was played by Allan Kaprow, who in his essay *Assemblage, Environments & Happenings* (1965) had associated the "environment" and the "happening" through the principle of "extension," identifying a series of artists who—alongside himself—could be considered pioneers of this new art, from Jim Dine to Claes Oldenburg, and from Robert Whitman to the Gutai group and some of the exponents of Fluxus and Nouveau Réalisme.[16]

15 There is a copy of the invitation in the archives of the municipality of San Giovanni Valdarno, while the script of the performance was published in UFO, 'Chicken Circus Circulation ovvero heppenveironment (sic) ovvero superurbeffimero n. 7', *Marcatrè*, no. 41-42, June 1968, pp. 76-91.

16 Allan Kaprow, *Assemblage, Environments & Happenings* (New York: Harry N. Abrams, 1965).

Thus UFO showed, right from its earliest experiments, that the group was aware of and in tune with the forms of art-performance that had emerged in the context of the American avant-garde and become widely known over the course of 1968 in Italy thanks to the translation of Michael Kirby's illustrated anthology *Happenings*[17] (fig. 3) and the long essay "The New Theatre" by the same author, a translation of which was published by *Marcatrè* in the pages immediately following the first report on the activities of the Florentine collective.[18]

17 Michael Kirby (ed.), *Happenings: An Illustrated Anthology* (New York: E.P. Dutton & Co., 1965). Translated into Italian as *Happening* (Bari: De Donato, 1968).

18 Michael Kirby, 'The New Theatre', *Marcatrè*, no. 37-40, May 1968, pp. 210-217.

In the reports and reviews of the 6th Premio Masaccio that were written by critics and artists, it was precisely the word "happening" that came to be used to define the urban intervention by the

3. Michael Kirby (ed.), *Happening* (Bari: De Donato, 1968)

Florentine collective. Claudio Popovich, art critic and curator of the event, identified the concept of "happening" as one of the possible aesthetic categories into which the performance staged by UFO could be fitted, placing at the same time the accent on its character of indefinability. The UFO group, wrote Popovich, "has presented a form of 'spectacle—theatre—plastic operation—happening' (indefinable: but we have said that categories are not needed)."[19] An indeterminable character that it shared with many of the works in the exhibition that set out to break down traditional notions of art, such as the "Fluxus concert" performed by Giuseppe Chiari on the opening night, with a surreal montage of words and sounds lifted directly from everyday life. And Eugenio Miccini, visual poet and member of the Gruppo 70, identified in his review of the 6th Premio Masaccio the aspects that made the UFO's event an example of the practice of the "happening," equating them with the ones described by Kirby in his writings. On the one hand, a reliance on the logic of indeterminacy (even if roughly based on a script). On the other, the involvement of the public through gestures and words with a powerful impact, causing the action to go in unpredictable and unforeseen directions. "In front of the Palazzo," commented

19 Claudio Popovich, 'Polemiche e dibattiti intorno al Masaccio', *l'Unità*, Tuscan edition, 7 July 1968.

Miccini, "a performance was staged by architecture students from Florence that has been called a 'happening' at least in the sense that the action, planned and calculated in every detail, had that sense of precariousness, of approximation, of self-parody that involved everything in
the accident of time, in its own verbal violence, in its provisional nature."[20]

20 Eugenio Miccini, 'Nuovi interventi per il Premio Masaccio', *l'Unità*, Tuscan edition, 16 July 1968.

The concepts of fluidity, indefinability, and unpredictability of the action involving the public would characterise the whole of the successive research into "territorial appropriation" conducted by UFO through performances, artist's films and videos, writings and publications. Alternative experimentation to the practice of architecture and construction that—in line with what Ugo La Pietra had to say about his own "radical" vision of those years—turned architecture "into a recovery of hitherto unknown design forces, such as behaviour (the use of the body)" and "the ephemeral (occupation of space, transgression)."[21]

21 Ugo La Pietra, 'L'architettura radicale', in Marie-Ange Brayer (ed.), *Habiter la ville* (Orléans: Éditions HYX, 2009), pp. 12-15: 14.

In the early seventies, the ties with the avant-garde art scene, never interrupted, found further important moments of exchange and interaction, resulting from the contacts established by UFO—as well as by other protagonists of the "radical" scene in Florence—with international networks of artists and exhibition initiatives (between conceptual art and performance, video art and artist's publishing), promoted by the main centres of experimentation active in Florence at the time: Alessandra and Ferruccio Marchi's Centro Di publishing house, Maria Gloria Bicocchi's Art/Tapes/22 workshop for the production and distribution of videos, the Galleria Schema run by the artist Alberto Moretti and the Spazio Zona of the collective of artists headed by Nannucci.[22]

22 On the Florentine artistic context of the seventies, see Alessandra Acocella and Caterina Toschi (eds.), *Arte a Firenze 1970-2015. Una città in prospettiva* (Macerata: Quodlibet, 2016).

The Centro Di, a publishing house specialising in catalogues of contemporary art as well as a meeting place and source of the latest information on international avant-garde research, brought out, in 1974, the UFO's *Controllo colonizzazione e fascismo sul territorio*.[23] In the method of typological cataloguing through the medium of photography (with the aim of documenting road workers' houses, barbed-wire fences, level crossings, urban vegetable gardens, works of spontaneous architecture, gas pipelines, and power stations), there is an echo of the research of a conceptual character carried out in the sixties and seventies by Ed Ruscha and Dan Graham in the United States and Bernd and Hilla Becher in Germany.[24] A method that, for UFO, became a means of criticism used to assert the need for a reappropriation of the territory in order to free it from the logic of power and control.

23 UFO, Daniela Palazzoli (eds.), *Controllo colonizzazione e fascismo sul territorio, Milano, Galleria 291, maggio/giugno 1974* (Florence: Centro Di, 1974).

24 I am referring in particular to Ruscha's *Twentysix Gasoline Stations* (1963), Graham's *Homes for America* (1966-1967), and the Bechers' *Anonyme Skulpturen. Eine Typologie technischer Bauten* (1970).

4. Christo, *The Wall–Wrapped Roman Wall*, executed on the Aurelian Walls at Porta Pinciana on the occasion of the exhibition *Contemporanea*, Rome, 1974. Photo Massimo Piersanti. Archivi MAXXI Arte | Fondo Incontri Internazionali d'Arte (AIIA), courtesy Fondazione MAXXI. © CHRISTO by SIAE 2022

Linked to these themes, the series of works *Giro d'Italia* presents further points of contact with the more proactive artistic culture of the seventies. Developed on several occasions between 1971 and 1974 through performances, films, writings, and publications, *Giro d'Italia* expressed "the desire," as Lapo Binazzi (UFO) would recall, "to dominate the territory, to reclaim it, to establish geographical, physical boundaries in which liberated creativity could be exercised."[25]

For the major exhibition *Contemporanea* (1973-1974) curated by Achille Bonito Oliva and held in the underground car park of Villa Borghese in Rome,[26] the *Giro d'Italia* took on the dimensions of a collective performance. One that, more than any of the other works presented for the occasion, embodied the programmatic opening to an interdisciplinary exchange between visual arts and architecture, theatre and cinema, that underpinned the exhibition/event. An Italian cycle race seen as a project of *fantaurbanistica*[27] which, starting out from the car park, unfolded through a rapid succession of actions/performances in the surrounding area. From racing in the greenhouses to climbing on the trellises and crossings of restricted zones, the cycle race culminated in the return to the venue of the exhibition, where a videotape, made with equipment supplied by Maria Gloria Bicocchi, was supposed to show what the Florentine collective had staged outside.[28]

As much for its extension to an urban scale as for the deliberately temporary and ephemeral nature of this creative appropriation of physical space, the *Giro d'Italia* established a conceptual dialogue with the only other intervention made outside the spaces

25 Alessandra Acocella and Caterina Toschi (eds.), 'Firenze sperimentale: gli anni settanta attraverso le testimonianze di Bruno Corà, Lapo Binazzi e Paolo Masi', in Anna Mazzanti (ed.), *Art/Tapes/22. Le origini della videoarte* (Cinisello Balsamo: Silvana Editoriale, 2017), pp. 44-48: 46-47.

26 Bonito Oliva (ed.), *Contemporanea. Roma, Parcheggio di Villa Borghese 11. 1973 / 2. 1974.* See too Luigia Lonardelli, 'Sotterranea, Contemporanea', in Daniela Lancioni (ed.), *Anni 70. Arte a Roma* (Rome: Iacobelli, 2013), pp. 94-105.

27 UFO, 'Appunti per una ridefinizione del concetto di fantaurbanistica', *Progettare inpiù*, no. 8, February-March 1975, pp. 24-27: 24.

28 Binazzi would recall: "a videotape was supposed to show everything that had happened before our arrival (…). Unfortunately the equipment supplied to us by Maria Gloria Bicocchi had recording heads that should have

been cleaned with alcohol; but we found this out afterwards. So no one in the car park of *Contemporanea* saw what we had staged outside, and all we could do was present an account of what had happened, almost on an individual basis, to the visitors to the exhibition." Acocella and Toschi (eds.), *Firenze sperimentale*, p. 47.

of Villa Borghese's underground car park: the "wrapping" of a large stretch of the Aurelian Walls carried out for the occasion by Christo with long sheets of white polypropylene and thick orange ropes (fig. 4). Performative and behavioural the former; spectacular, scenic, and predominantly visual the latter. These works were both a response, although with different intentions and results, to the utopian propensity and process of renewal underway in those years, leading to the formulation of a new idea of anthropised space that "no longer coincided with the simple value of the sign or the finished object but instead with a sequence of actions and experiences."[29]

29 Gianni Pettena, 'Le ragioni di un'utopia', in Pino Brugellis, Gianni Pettena and Alberto Salvadori (eds.), *Utopie radicali. Archizoom, Remo Buti, 9999, Gianni Pettena, Superstudio, UFO, Zziggurat* (Macerata: Quodlibet, 2017), pp. 21-31: 24.

The frequencies of contemporary art resonated in a similar fashion in the UFO's last official production, staged on the occasion of the 1978 Venice Biennale at the invitation of Lara-Vinca Masini, a Florentine art historian and militant critic who, since the sixties, had been courageously supporting avant-garde experiences in her city (very little open to the new and to experimentation), always with an eye to collaborations and intersections between the languages of the visual arts, architecture, design, and new music.[30] For the Venice Biennale, UFO resorted once again to the dynamism of performance, ferrying through the city's canals—to the accompaniment of a violin played by Mino Vismara—a large reproduction of the A.N.A.S. roadhouse. An elementary and standardised structure, found all over the country, that during the lively procession on water staged by the Florentine collective contrasted both visually and symbolically with the monumental and varied architectural facades of the lagoon city.

30 Among the first significant articles written by Masini on the Florentine Radical architects, it is worth mentioning Lara-Vinca Masini, 'Archifirenze', *Domus*, no. 509, April 1972, p. 40, later in Alessandra Acocella and Angelika Stepken (eds.), *Lara-Vinca Masini. Scritti scelti 1961-2019. Arte Architettura Design Arti applicate* (Pistoia: Gli Ori, 2020), pp. 109-111.

Some photographs of those days, now preserved among the papers in the archives,[31] immortalise emblematically the performance entitled *B/arca A.N.A.S.* ("B/ark A.N.A.S.") together with the conceptual and ephemeral intervention—also set entirely in an urban dimension—by Nannucci: a long strip of transparent material, towed behind an aeroplane, on which the words *Image du ciel* referred allusively and implicitly to the infinite variety of the blue of the sky, progressively "selected" and "framed" by the strip. A dialogue with the cutting edge of artistic research, evoked by the members of UFO themselves in their contribution to the Venetian book-catalogue,[32] that brought to a close and summed up a whole decade of productions and inventions driven by the desire to overcome disciplinary boundaries, experimenting with a "radical" vision of architecture seen in the first place as a process of conceptual refounding, as a highly creative and communicative experience.

31 I examined the photographs in question personally in Lapo Binazzi's archive during my research into the 38th Venice Biennale, whose results were presented in Alessandra Acocella, 'Tra utopia e disincanto. Le mostre di Lara-Vinca Masini alla Biennale di Venezia del 1978', in Flavio Fergonzi (ed.), *Presenze toscane alla Biennale Internazionale d'Arte di Venezia* (Milan: Skira, 2016), pp. 133-147.

32 Lapo Binazzi (UFO), 'Performance in barca UFO-Mino Vismara (violino)', in Vinca Masini (ed.), *Topologia e morfogenesi*, pp. 57-59: 59.

Outlines of an Urbanism of Opposition: Terrorism and Liberation of the City According to UFO

Beatrice Lampariello

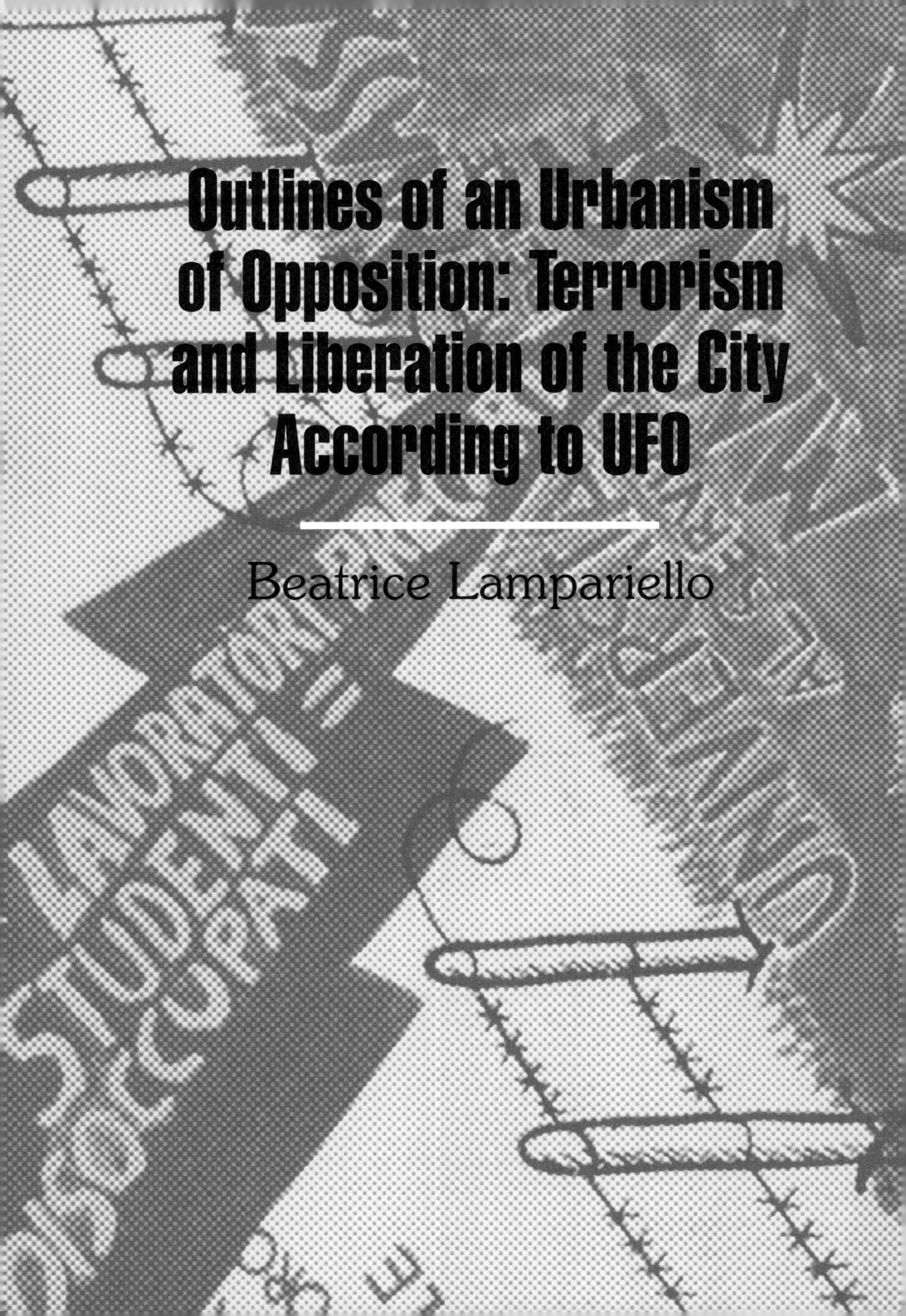

If there was a single phenomenon around which all the multifarious reflections of the young generation of architects and students in Florence turned from the second half of the sixties onwards, it was the city of the economic boom:[1] an agglomeration of production and accumulation of capital that, in search of the greatest profit, had crossed historical peripheries, cannibalised manufacturing and rural areas, and by this time assumed the scale of the territory to be governed through a single legislative act that covered the artistic, natural, and urban heritage, as had been outlined in a draft law of 1957.[2] A monster that had lost any "maternal" value as cradle and defence of human beings in order to take hold of the civilisation of the "large number,"[3] exercising such a degree of control over existence that it even held thought prisoner. It was against this city and the methods used to control and manage it as they were fixed in the discipline of urbanism that UFO railed, adopting a strategy that was subversive with respect not only to the most common professional practices, but even to the contemporary experimentation of the other neo-avant-garde groups in Florence. For one thing, because UFO refused to imagine alternative and critical futures and so rejected the project as it had been consolidated through drawing since the times of Renaissance Florence, in order to operate directly on the city by bringing another tradition into play; a tradition that, despite being rooted in the same historical culture, shifted the focus of the "imagination" onto the "crafts" and "poetry," as was celebrated in 1966 by the exhibition *Forma e Verità*.[4] From the square to the street, from the shop to the countryside, UFO intervened in the city on a "scale of 1:1." At first through an artisanal practice, organised into a process of construction in which materials like bricks, stone, concrete, and even the most advanced technologies were shunned to rely instead on the unconventional use of products of the society of the large number, and then through a behavioural approach that turned away from material and towards poetic acts, pure physical exercises. On the 1:1 scale, UFO rediscovered a dimension that the drawing, despite being a narrative manifesto, would never possess: the human presence of a community, that of

1 For Superstudio, see Roberto Gargiani and Beatrice Lampariello, *Il Monumento Continuo di Superstudio. Eccesso del razionalismo e strategia del rifiuto* (Genoa: Sagep, 2019). For Archizoom, see Roberto Gargiani, *Archizoom associati, 1966-1974. Dall'onda pop alla superficie neutra* (Milan: Electa, 2007); and Pier Vittorio Aureli, *Il progetto dell'autonomia. Politica e architettura dentro e contro il capitale* (Macerata: Quodlibet, 2016) (the Italian edition is cited here as it is more up-to-date than the English one). For UFO, see Emanuele Piccardo, 'UFO. Sperimentare la parodia nello spazio pubblico', in Stefano Pezzato (ed.), *Ufo story: dall'architettura radicale al design globale* (Prato: Centro per l'arte contemporanea Luigi Pecci, 2012), pp. 16-19; Alessandra Acocella, 'Effimero urbanistico. L'immagine della piazza nelle azioni del gruppo UFO (1968)', in Stephanie Hanke and Brigitte Sölch (eds.), *Projektionen. Der Platz als Bildthema* (Munich: Deutscher Kunstverlag, 2019), pp. 197-210; and False Mirror Office (Andrea Anselmo and Boris Hamzeian), 'L'assemblaggio come testo figurativo per l'architettura. Un dialogo tra UFO e False Mirror Office', *PianoB*, no. 2, 2019, pp. 88-118. For 9999, see Marco Ornella, *Rivoluzione 9999* (Busalla: Plug_in, 2020). For Gianni Pettena, see Gianni Pettena, *Le métier de l'architecte* (Orléans: Éditions HYX, 2009). For an examination of the interest shown by the European neo-avant-gardes in the city, see the monographic issue of *Archphoto* devoted to "Radical Cities."

UFO, Photograph of graffiti on the facade of the University of Florence, 1968, Patrizia Cammeo/Riccardo Foresi Archives, Florence an Assembly of students who talked, discussed, and exchanged ideas in order to produce an imaginary nuclear explosion whose radioactive material could descend on the city, the "fallout" of which UFO wrote in 1968[5]—"we are in a sense children of the atomic bomb," Lapo Binazzi, one of the members of the group, would recall.[6] It is no coincidence that, over the years, UFO, unlike the other Florentine neo-avant-gardes, would include, in addition to a consolidated and settled core (Carlo Bachi, Lapo Binazzi, Patrizia Cammeo, Riccardo Foresi, Titti Maschietto), a series of other people, as if wishing to reconstitute whenever possible the critical mass of the large number discovered in their time at university and seen as necessary by the generation of that urban fallout (Rodolfo Bracci, Sandro Gioli, Massimo Giovannini, Claudio Greppi, Antonio Infantino, Mario Spinella). And then the subversive nature of UFO's strategy found expression in the rejection of the fundamental disciplinary principles of *firmitas, venustas*, and *utilitas*. Its operations on a 1:1 scale would never take the concrete form of buildings, nor any kind of construction endowed with harmonious proportions and the functionality that had become central over the course of the 20th century. Those operations were, on the contrary, acts of terrorism against the city intended to undermine its decorum, to occupy it, obstruct its regular functioning, and finally sketch the outlines of an urbanism of opposition. Squares, streets, monuments, shops, and rural areas lost their connotation as the theatrical setting of the life of the large number, and became structures whose utilisation was distorted by human beings. These "operators/users" revealed the coercive function of squares, streets, monuments, shops, and rural areas through collective operations that were cultural "explosive devices" and "bombs," transmitting instantaneous messages of political revolt and social equality.[7] UFO's revolution took the form of peaceful and playful "battles" fought in the city, supported by arms that were those of the established disciplines, but now turned against them. The aim was to liberate it by unveiling its capitalist mechanisms, in line with Paul Klee's definition of an art that "does not reproduce the visible but makes visible." "The imaginary is not a mode of unreality, but indeed a mode of actuality, a way of approaching presence obliquely," Michel Foucault had written in 1954.[8]

Beyond the Faculty Walls: the Occupation of the Historic Centre

UFO's acts of terrorism against the city can only have had their origin in the occupation of the University of Florence. It was here, in what the students saw as the first stage on the assembly line of capital,[9] that the group, that had just formed, embarked on a series of experiments for the occupation of the city, understood as

2 See *Difesa e valorizzazione del paesaggio urbano e rurale*, Proceedings of the 6th INU Conference (Rome: Castaldi, 1958).

3 This was the theme of the 14th Milan Triennale in 1968. See Carlo Guenzi, 'Il grande numero', *Casabella*, no. 320, November 1967, pp. 58-63; and *Quattordicesima triennale di Milano: esposizione internazionale delle arti decorative industriali moderne dell'architettura moderna* (Milan: Arti grafiche Crespi & Occhipinti, 1968).

4 Studio Forte 63 (ed.), *Forma e verità* (Florence: Marchi, 1966), n.p. Binazzi visited the exhibition and bought the catalogue, still to be found in his Archives (Florence).

5 UFO, 'Urboeffimeri avvenenti 1:1', *Marcatrè*, no. 41-42, June 1968, pp. 52-73.

6 Lapo Binazzi, conversation with Beatrice Lampariello, 23 July 2021.

7 See Lapo Binazzi, letter to Magdalo Mussio, n.d. (Lapo Binazzi Archives, Florence).

8 Michel Foucault, 'Dream, Imagination and Existence: An Introduction to Ludwig Binswanger's "Dream and Existence"', in Ludwig Binswanger, *Dream and Existence* (Atlantic Highlands, NJ: Humanities Press, 1993), p. 70. A contribution to UFO's strategy of using the imaginary not to change reality but to add "new data" came from Edgar Morin's essays *Le Cinéma ou l'homme imaginaire*, published in English as *The Cinema, or the Imaginary Man* (Minneapolis, MN: University of Minnesota Press, 2005) and *L'Esprit du temps. Essai sur la culture de masse* (Paris, Grasset-Fasquelle, 1962), the Italian translations of which are both in Maschietto's Archives (Florence).

9 See the monographic issue of *in. Argomenti e immagini di design*, no. 9, February-March 1973, devoted to "The Faculty of Architecture in the Process of Downgrading."

a spatial projection of that capital. It was here, in the courtyard of the Palazzo di San Clemente and in its great hall, that the multitude of students freed themselves from academic magnates and isolated elites to create an Assembly in the form of an open, heterogeneous, and discontinuous community that saw discussion and action as the principles of the refounding of the discipline. "Correct ideas come from social practice," Mao Zedong had written.[10] So while Superstudio and Archizoom wrote and drew, shut up in their studios, and distanced themselves from the sometimes violent forms of the occupation in 1968, UFO was at home in that atmosphere, finding in it the origin and evolution of the group. And it was there, among the various operations in which its members took part, from film to "wall newspaper," that there was one that took on the status of a manifesto of UFO's terroristic intentions against the city. A group of students, amongst whom we can recognise Foresi, a member of UFO, photographed by another member, Cammeo, emerges from the Faculty and, armed with paint and brushes, sets to work on the facade of the seat of the University of Florence in Piazza San Marco. What had once been called *sgraffito*, a technique which had found important applications in Florence and was discussed theoretically by Giorgio Vasari as one means of decorating the city,[11] became political and social graffiti that, produced by a collective creative effort, were used to desecrate the historical heritage: it was the slogan shouted and amplified by megaphones at the demonstrations, fixed now in words and drawings; it was the voice of a society of revolution that was applied to the walls, not as a temporary poster, like the one for the exhibition *Superarchitettura* had been, or like the ones that were wrapped around the columns of San Clemente's entrance hall, constructing walls of paper between the bays, but as a permanent violation of the city's decorum. "The government wants to lock up the university. We want to open it" was one of these graffiti, which became part of a composition with the immediacy of an advertising slogan in its combination with other graffiti and two cartoon-like figures: a thunderbolt and an enclosure made of barbed wire and posts. The thunderbolt, already chosen by Archizoom as a symbol of a fast spurt, should be understood here as a violent and instant explosion taking place inside the Faculty and capable of destroying the enclosure and any other boundary to let that disruptive force go out into the city and occupy it, riding the wave of class struggle. There is nothing surprising about UFO's operation if we set it in the context of that Faculty, against the background of its first occupation in 1963, and the various disruptive actions carried out in European cities over the course of the sixties by groups like the Provos in the Netherlands, Roma 1 in Rome and Onda Verde in Milan. In his lecture *Per una guerriglia semiologica* given at a

10 In Maschietto's library there are the four volumes of the Italian translation of Mao Zedong's selected works: Mao Zedong, *Opere scelte*, the first two published by the Chinese Foreign Languages Press in 1969, the other two by Edizioni dell'Oriente between 1970 and 1971. In Binazzi's Archives instead there are many issues of the monthly magazine *La Cina*, starting from 1964.

11 See the chapter of *Le vite de' più eccellenti pittori, scultori e architettori* entitled 'Degli sgraffiti delle case che reggono all'acqua; quello che adoperi a farli; e come si lavorino le grottesche nelle mura'. It is not included in any of the English translations of the *Lives*, but has been published separately under the title 'Of the Sgraffiti for house decoration which withstand water; that which is used in their production; and how Grotesques are worked on the wall', in *Vasari on Technique* (New York: Dover, 2011).

1. Claes Oldenburg, *Proposed Monument for the Intersection of Canal Street and Broadway, N.Y.C.–Block on Concrete with the Names of War Heroes*, 1965, MoMA, New York

seminar in 1967, Umberto Eco urged his audience "to fight a door-to-door guerrilla battle."[12] On 1 February 1968, the members of Archizoom presented themselves in the pages of the weekly *Panorama* as "terrorists" preaching "revolution."[13] On 12 February of the same year, UFO installed a "construction site" in the Faculty that should be seen as a decisive device for the act of creation, allowing the involvement of the largest possible number of students in the generation of a "fission" that took the concrete form of a new operation of violation of the city that was no longer limited to graffiti. The starting point for this operation can be traced in the same historical heritage which had been violated: the seat of the university, more precisely the location of the construction site, the entrance hall of San Clemente with its monumental columns. Those columns were transfigured through an act of heretical "transubstantiation"[14] that charged the supporting structure of the Faculty, treated as an emblem of the structure of architecture itself, with a semantic interplay between signifier and signified. The tree trunk transformed into a stone column now became a "tubular profile"[15] with a diameter of 50 centimetres, made of

12 Umberto Eco, 'Per una guerriglia semiologica', in Eco, *Il costume di casa* (Milan: Bompiani, 1973), p. 291. Published in English as 'Towards a Semiological Guerrilla Warfare', in Umberto Eco, *Travels in Hyperreality* (New York: Harcourt Brace Jovanovich, 1986), p. 159. For the reference to this seminar, see too Simon Sadler's essay in this volume.

13 Marco Fini, 'Arrivano gli Archizoom', *Panorama*, no. 94, 1 February 1968, pp. 52-57.

14 This is the definition that Binazzi used for the Centre Pompidou, the transfiguration of the Archigram's projects into another substance. See Lapo Binazzi, 'L'arcangelo nudo', *Modo*, no. 76, January-February 1985, p. 75.

15 Lapo Binazzi, Lapo (sic) Cammeo, Riccardo Foresi, Sandro Gioli and Titti Maschietto, 'Effimero Urbanistico scala 1/1', *Marcatrè*, no. 37-40, May 1968, pp. 198-209: 200.

polyethylene in order to turn against the city of capital one of its fundamental materials—that of the shopping bag. Its height was magnified to 100 metres so that the profile could be turned into a bent tube and laid horizontally, turning it into a barricade. Thus it resembled the ones that were being constructed in the city streets by piling up the ready-mades of capital (cars, skips, advertising hoardings, and traffic signs) to block its usual flow and lay claim to spaces hitherto inaccessible to certain social classes, excluded from political representation and the prosperity of the economic boom. In the transubstantiation brought about by UFO we can recognise a reference to Claes Oldenburg's creation of an urban barrier by turning a pat of butter into a giant block of reinforced concrete, a "true obstacle"[16] that prevented people from crossing Canal Street and Broadway in Manhattan (fig. 1). It was as if the act of blowing up something out of proportion created the necessary conditions for a confrontation with the scale of the city—something that had been achieved in the barricades by piling objects on top of each other. But we can see that UFO's transubstantiation went a step farther than the magnification carried out by Oldenburg, since the group rejected the material substance of the column—the pat of butter turned into a block of reinforced concrete—and bestowed on it instead a lightness and evanescence whose origin lay in political revolt, if we consider that one of the definitions used to describe the "tubular profile" was that of its "precariousness"—the very "insecurity" against which the proletarians and students were protesting.[17] The polyethylene that one of the members of UFO, Maschietto, had already imagined as an *empaquetage* of the Colonna dell'Abbondanza in Florence to ensure its "conservative restoration,"[18] now became a wrapping of empty space, of air pumped out of the inverted nozzle of a Singer vacuum cleaner, elevated to an emblem of another kind of restoration: one for the purposes of "substitution."[19] "The columns are moved and take on the same diameter as that of the tube of milky white polyethylene" runs one of Binazzi's notes.[20] The transformation of the column into a tube, of mass into envelope, stone into air, was an act that made UFO's "profile" a precarious anti-monument, a symbol of social and political insecurity, laid on its side and bent as a material counterpoint to Adolf Loos's colossal column that was supposed to have scraped the sky of Chicago. So, if viewed from the perspective of *empaquetage*, the origin of UFO's anti-monument lay not just in balloons, in seats, in the inflatable coverings that had begun to invade cities in the sixties, but also and above all in the contemporary packaging of Christo's ambiguous "restorations." "Packaging means making a packet, the act of wrapping a parcel, in other words putting a wrapper around something: that thing is the important part of the packet, the wrapping is usually thrown

16 Barbara Haskell, *Claes Oldenburg. Object into Monument* (Pasadena: Pasadena Art Museum, 1972), p. 17.

17 Binazzi, Cammeo, Foresi, Gioli and Maschietto, 'Effimero Urbanistico scala 1/1', p. 198.

18 Houchang Amirpour, Rodolfo Bracci, Gianfranco Gorelli and Titti Maschietto, 'Il restauro dell'utenza', *Marcatrè*, no. 46-49, October 1968, pp. 52-71.

19 R. B., 'UFO', *Caleidoscopio*, no. 11, January 1972, pp. 10-14.

20 Lapo Binazzi, *Didascalie UFO*, 28 February 1990 (Lapo Binazzi Archives, Florence). See too Binazzi, Cammeo, Foresi, Gioli and Maschietto, 'Effimero Urbanistico scala 1/1', p. 201.

away,"[21] Ettore Sottsass Jr. had written in 1966, around the same time as Christo had begun carrying out his projects. The members of UFO were not the only ones not to throw away the wrapping and to elevate it to the status of an urban anti-monument. Christo himself would do this at the end of 1968 in Kassel[22], getting rid even of the coloured balloons that had been wrapped in his *42,390 Cubic Feet Empaquetage*.[23] Other architects would conceive wrappings of empty space installed in cities with the appearance of colossal monuments, but with the substance of inflatable structures or light curtain walls: Hans Hollein's coloured cylinders in Kapfenberg and Superstudio's *Continuous Monument* running through the Earth.[24]

After constructing a barricade in the entrance hall, the column transformed into tube emerged from the walls of the Faculty. For years, tubes and ducts had been invading the cities imagined by the young generation of Florentine architects in the wake of the projects of Archigram, Hollein, and Walter Pichler, among others, from Superstudio, with Adolfo Natalini's graduation thesis, to Archizoom, with Andrea Branzi's, both in 1966. UFO itself, through Maschietto and Foresi, had already designed enormous tubes.[25] And yet up until then those tubes had always been transfigurations of routes; roads in the air or on the land to be used for the movement of people assembled in a place that rejected the corridor of the *Existenzminimum*. UFO's tube, on the other hand—a wrapper of empty space—was uninhabitable. In emerging from the enclosure of the university and occupying the city without an apparent function, without a use value, and without an exchange value, it lost the connotation of an object and became a "tool."[26] Serving the needs of a moment in life, it was in line with the experiments carried out by Eliseo Mattiacci, who had ended up on the cover of *Domus* in August 1967 with the nickel-plated tube transported in a collective action from his studio in Via Laurina to Galleria La Tartaruga in Piazza del Popolo, Rome (fig. 2).[27] That *Tubo* ("Tube"), described by Tommaso Trini as a "true plastic boom" and by Germano Celant as a "despotic spatial tyrant" that "does not respect our privacy, (...) it listens to our conversations, it lives with us,"[28] showed UFO the potential of an operation that rejected the distinction between practice and contemplation, between individual and collective, between inside and outside, in a dimension that was intended to be that of an "open work." In the flurry of its meanings, outside the Faculty, the new "spatial tyrant" lost the connotation of a barricade and turned into a battering ram that lashed "the city with ever more violent writhings" and occupied space which had originally belonged to the community, but was in reality now reduced to just another element in the service of the capitalist system: that of the street and the square. Following a route in

21 Ettore Sottsass Jr., 'Viaggio a Occidente: Nr. 1. Che cosa fanno lì dentro?', *Domus*, no. 436, March 1966, pp. 42-44: 43-44.

22 T. T., 'Pneu-realtà', *Domus*, no. 467, October 1968, pp. 50-54.

23 Jan van der Marck, 'Un pacco di aria', *Domus*, no. 448, March 1967, pp. 50-53. For UFO's interest in the work of Oldenburg and Christo, see Lapo Binazzi (UFO), *Ufo. Discontinuità e territorio* (Milan: Centro internazionale di Brera, 1977).

24 See Beatrice Lampariello, 'The packaging of Superstudio: from technomorphism to neutral surfaces', in Rita Elvira Adamo, Cristiano Lippa and Federico Scaroni (eds.), *ARCHITETTURA INVISIBILE. Movimenti architettonici italiani e giapponesi degli anni '60 e '70 e il dibattito contemporaneo* (Cinisello Balsamo: Silvana Editoriale, 2017), pp. 168-173.

25 See Amirpour, Bracci, Gorelli and Maschietto, 'Il restauro dell'utenza'; and Marco Dezzi Bardeschi, Gianfranco Censini and Riccardo Foresi, 'Proposta per il concorso per l'allestimento della sezione italiana alla XIV Triennale di Milano', in Carlo Guenzi, 'Una selezione difficile', *Casabella*, no. 325, June 1968, pp. 4-21: 9.

26 Andrea Branzi (Archizoom), Lapo Binazzi (UFO), Gianni Pettena and Ettore Sottsass Jr., 'Conversazione a quattro sulla Global Tools', *Casabella*, no. 379, July 1973, pp. 45-48.

27 See Lara Conte, 'Eliseo Mattiacci. Processi di scultura a Roma tra anni Sessanta e Settanta', *L'uomo nero*, no. 17-18, February 2021, pp. 141-162. The contacts between UFO and Mattiacci would be intense throughout the seventies, with Binazzi acting as go-between.

28 See Tommaso Trini, 'Le mostre a Milano, Roma, Genova, Torino', *Domus*, no. 453, August 1967, p. 41; Germano Celant (ed.), *Arte Povera IM Spazio* (Genoa: Galleria La Bertesca-Masnata, 1967).

2. Eliseo Mattiacci, *Tubo*, 1967

stages that refused any kind of drift and went straight instead in order to occupy the places most closely associated with power and with Florence's historical heritage, the battering ram blocked traffic, and commercial activities. It re-established for a moment the conditions of life that had preceded the recent manifestations of consumerism and obliged passers-by to stop, not so much to gaze at that "big snake Chinese dragon"[29] as to reflect on what the students had spontaneously written on it ("Control of Power," "Power to the Workers," "Blackpower," "Hochiminh," "Che"). Thanks to those words, the battering ram not only served as a mobile post that upset the rhythms of the city, but at the same time carried messages and symbols, assuming the role of an evanescent diary of the protests by the students of architecture against the city of capital: a "sign" of amplified "communication" to produce "maximum information," as Eco would put it,[30] restoring the essence of architecture, not one of protection and shelter, but of language.

"'Concrete' elements interrupting" for an "urbanistic terrorism" were the words used by Maschietto to describe UFO's operation,[31] while the group called it an "urbanistic ephemeron."[32] In this concise designation is comprised the dual nature of the tube:

29 Against the background of UFO's experiments, other artists would propose a "big inflatable snake" at Anfo (Brescia) in the summer of 1968. See 'Un paese + l'avanguardia artistica', *Domus*, no. 468, November 1968, p. 48.

30 Umberto Eco, *Appunti per una semiologia delle comunicazioni visive* (Milan: Bompiani, 1967), p. 7. For the relationship between UFO and Eco, see Amit Wolf, 'Superurbeffimero n. 7: Umberto Eco's Semiologia and the Architectural Rituals of the U.F.O.', *California Italian Studies*, no. 2, 2011, http://dx.doi.org/10.5070/ C322008956.

31 Vittorio Maschietto, 'Facoltà di architettura di Firenze 85 giorni di occupazione', *Quindici*, no. 10, 15 April-15 May 1968, p. VI.

32 Binazzi, Cammeo, Foresi, Gioli and Maschietto, 'Effimero Urbanistico scala 1/1'.

3. Arnaldo Galli, *Conigli coraggiosi*, Viareggio Carnival, 1973, Titti Maschietto Archives, Florence

a tool born out of architecture (the column) to modify the city according to the principles of an urbanism which was not the academic kind that had become entrenched over the course of the 20th century, but its opposition as political and social activism against the stratification of capital. This activism could be defined as "action urbanism" along the lines of the well-known description of Jackson Pollock's work, another reference for the group.[33] It was by now clear to UFO that the only form of urbanism still possible was one that opposed functionality and perpetuity, and thus instantaneous and with a particular end in view, but without ever replicating the forms of an ideal city constructed with curtains, screens, robots and cranes, as Archigram had proposed. "Ephemeral, from the Greek: of a day, lasting a day. (...). It is replaceable, it rejects any sort of trappings that might turn it into a monument," declared an article published in *Domus* in 1967 devoted to "inflatable furniture."[34] Nothing would remain of that urbanistic ephemeron which, once deflated, "became a plan again," apart from the photographs taken during its occupation of the Faculty and the city, traces of a "frozen memory."[35] In the streets, over the cars, carried in triumph by the students, it was in the atmosphere of the Florentine night made up of points, lines, areas or volumes of light, and a black that erased everything that the tube revealed its last semantic play. The urbanistic ephemeron produced a "biennial flood,"[36] after the one in 1966, another phenomenon that had done violence to the city, temporarily occupying its fabric.[37]

After the column, in the spring of 1968, other figures would become the butt of the colossal, political and social transubstan-

33 Titti Maschietto, conversation with Gloria Castellini, 22 May 2021.

34 Costantino Corsini, 'I mobili gonfiabili', *Domus*, no. 457, December 1967, pp. 8-21: 9.

35 See UFO and Lapo Binazzi, 'Album di profezie', *Harck*, no. 1, 1971, pp. 30-31; and UFO, 'Risposta al questionario di "in" sui problemi della Facoltà di Architettura', in. *Argomenti e immagini di design*, no. 9, February-March 1973, pp. 78-80.

36 Amirpour, Bracci, Gorelli and Maschietto, 'Il restauro dell'utenza', p. 58. "Mestruo azzurro" was another definition of the urbanistic ephemeron in an undated typewritten text (Lapo Binazzi Archives, Florence). In confirmation of this interpretation, in the summer of 1968, UFO organised a new operation with the urbanistic ephemeron, on the occasion of the Festa de l'Unità, emblematically called "inflatable flood."

37 "Everything was destroyed. (...). The ground floor of the city was all destroyed," Binazzi would recall ('Lapo Binazzi. Interview by Maria Cristina Didero', *Apartamento Magazine*, spring-summer 2018, pp. 134-157).

tiation carried out by UFO, which now defined itself as a group of "urbanist terrorists,"[38] through new acts of urban desecration perpetrated in the same places as had been occupied by the urbanistic ephemeron. The mouth of the society of consumption, the S of the American dollar sign and the missile of the Vietnam war were the symbols of the civilisation of the large number chosen by UFO because they were part of the imagery of what was indeed the society of consumption, but also the one abused by those in power. The aim was to strip away every practical function in order to reveal its essence as an icon of capitalism. The Faculty continued to be the preferred location for the ephemeral concrete expression of UFO's imagination, developing the idea of a "construction site" that could be turned into a "museum" for the collection and preservation of pieces, materials and intuitions and then go back to being a "construction site" again.[39] After polyethylene, the use of papier-mâché, another material with which one of the members of UFO, Foresi, had experimented, to reproduce another emblem of consumer society (the washing machine) on a gigantic scale,[40] gave the group's operations a new connotation. Although that material had in fact already been brought back into favour by Oldenburg,[41] the parading of these papier-mâché tools around the city, along with a heterogeneous gathering of people, showed the new value that the urbanistic ephemera had assumed. In addition to the dimension of contemporary artistic experiments centred on the transformation of the sculptural object into a "total space" that would involve the city,[42] they had turned into floats like those of the Carnival of Viareggio (fig. 3).[43] The use of papier-mâché made it clear that the objective of the urbanistic ephemeron was to occupy the city in order to undermine its structure and unmask its consumption-driven character using instruments made out of cheap, light and short-lived materials; materials that were all centred on a practice of the crafts that denied the value of any form of contemporary technology and bestowed a new meaning on the act of colossal, political, and social transubstantiation; that of caricature, deriding the emblems of capital through an exaggeration of their proportions and replacement of their substance. What generated the mouth, the S, and the missile, just like the tube, was no longer the "labour force" of the factory, but the sort of workers to be found on a medieval construction site, a theatre of life of the community that relied on their imagination, their hands, and common materials, usually excluded from building. This kind of work brought into the realm of grass-roots initiatives what Christo was doing in Kassel, after obtaining permission from the town council, with two of the biggest cranes in Europe, a centrifugal blower run by a variable-speed electric motor and the collaboration of engineers from MIT and Frei Otto's studio. So we can understand why the urbanist terrorists

38 UFO, 'Urboeffimeri avvenenti 1:1'.

39 Binazzi, conversation with Lampariello.

40 Dezzi Bardeschi, Censini and Foresi, 'Proposta per il concorso per l'allestimento della sezione italiana alla XIV Triennale di Milano'.

41 See Sidney Janis, 'I mercanti d'arte', *Domus*, no. 403, June 1963, pp. 45-48.

42 For these experiments see Alessandra Pioselli, *L'arte nello spazio urbano. L'esperienza italiana dal 1968 a oggi* (Monza: Johan & Levi Editore, 2015); and Alessandra Acocella, *Avanguardia diffusa. Luoghi di sperimentazione artistica in Italia 1967-1970* (Milan: Fondazione Passaré/Macerata: Quodlibet, 2016).

43 For the origin of UFO's interest in the Carnival, see the essay of Andrea Anselmo and Boris Hamzeian in this volume.

also described themselves as urban "angels" in so far as they were the only people able to propose different forms of occupation of the city to liberate it from its capitalist functions by means that, born out of power, had at last unmasked and blocked it: *L'imagination au pouvoir* declared a well-known slogan of 1968 Paris that was dear to Binazzi.[44] Thus the rejection of the project as an emblem of the *longue durée* entailed not a withdrawal into silence or inaction, but a new way of working on the city in an unexpected move that brought social rules, functional paradigms, and daily repetitions back into play. What had happened during the occupation of the Faculty with the founding of a new form of community gathered in the Assembly seems to have been replicated in the occupation of the city. Through the artisanal culture of the Carnival of Viareggio, through the construction of the tube, mouth, dollar sign, or missile, and their parading in the streets and squares, a special form of urban community was created, one of "Rabelaisian" origin,[45] between people habitually divided by caste, income, profession, and age. *Homo faber* was superimposed on *Homo ludens* in the unprecedented combination of a human being who made celebration, disorder, and the practical joke a new condition of life.[46] This human being continued to rely on a particular kind of creation that rejected the assembly line, the object of the capitalist logic of production and the 20th-century approach to urbanism that was capable of giving concrete expression to projects or prefigure alternative futures, in order to generate a new form of nomadism in a new way of doing things; one that was free because construction was no longer a matter of building, workers were no longer proletarians, and architects were no longer the sole "operators/users." So in UFO's urbanism of opposition, the city could only be understood as the sum of the experiences of a community that lived through use of the imagination, the hands, and material on the construction site and in the streets and squares.

The outlines of UFO's urbanism of opposition were made clear in the texts that the group drew up to present its urban operations, even though they were carried out in order to stage a new rejection, that of the explanation.[47] Among the "things the UFOS really like" the group added, in addition to the Carnival, the "sixteenth-century street decorations" as other examples of the short-lived occupation of cities, and the revolts of Detroit and Newark in 1967, defined by the group as "urbanism initiatives." If we follow the reflections of UFO, then we should also include in the list of "things" which UFO "really likes" the revolt by young people at the nightclub La Bussola in Viareggio on New Year's Eve in 1967,[48] or that of the Florentine students in Piazza San Marco on 30 January 1968.[49] UFO's descriptions of its own urbanistic ephemera confirm

44 Binazzi, conversation with Lampariello.

45 Lapo Binazzi, 'Piacerebbe a Cambronne', *Modo*, no. 71-72, August-September 1984, p. 72.

46 UFO would find corroboration of its hypotheses regarding an alternative form of being human in the arguments put forward by Edgar Morin in his book *Le Paradigme perdu: la nature humaine* (Paris: Le Seuil, 1973), published in Italian by Bompiani in 1974 as *Il paradigma perduto*. For the festive dimension of UFO's actions, see too Sadler's essay in this volume.

47 Binazzi (UFO), *Ufo. Discontinuità e territorio*.

48 There is a cutting from a newspaper with a description of the events in Maschietto's Archives.

49 Photographs of these revolts were taken by Bachi and published in Carlo Bachi, Nicola Bovoli, Riccardo Mariani and Giovanni Spinoso (eds.), *Firenze Piazza San Marco 30 gennaio 1968. Libro Bianco* (Florence: Cooperativa Libraria, 1968).

their rebellious nature, with a continual resort to definitions like "guerrilla," "weapon," "sub-orbital bomb," and "explosive."[50] And yet that nature was toned down by other designations (above all, that of the phallus)[51] and by new slogans that appeared on the polyethylene which now shifted the tone from political protest to send-up ("Colgate con Vietcong," "Potele agli studenti," "gioca-giocimin"). In the dual register of the Carnival of Viareggio float, between the serious and the facetious, between denunciation and derision, between revolt and celebration, once taken out of the context of that institutionalised occasion on which things are turned upside down, the urbanistic ephemera would lead to genuine urban guerrilla warfare, waged by those who did not grasp their pacifist and playful dimension: among them, the inhabitants of San Giovanni Valdarno, as they watched the members of the group, amongst the usual urbanistic ephemera, now dubbed "super" because they had been strengthened by other operations,[52] like covering the town's statue of the Marzocco with foam and that of Garibaldi with tin foil to dress it up for a wedding with an "Anitona" made of papier-mâché; or the police, when, in Florence, worried that the polyethylene was in reality a wrapping filled with tear gas, made holes in the urbanistic ephemera with cigarettes (and alongside the mocking slogans was set a photograph of the man who had called for "controlled confrontations (...) with the power structure").[53] Their "memory" would be "frozen" on film and in photographs which the group used as propaganda tools. In the section devoted to "Youth Protest" at the 14th Milan Triennale, UFO plastered the walls of one room with blown-up photographs of their urbanistic ephemera, in order to participate in the construction of a "new imagination in urbanism" and immerse visitors in the atmosphere of the streets and squares of the revolt. The walls of the room next to it were also covered with photographs of large numbers of people and its floor with "paving that, at a certain point, was ripped up and interrupted by a barricade"[54]—an exemplary setting to host a new occupation, that of the Triennale itself. We should not underestimate the importance of the fact that Alison and Peter Smithson dedicated their own installation at that Triennale to the "transformations" of Florence, amongst which they included various "extraordinary and unexpected events," another "motive for temporary alteration of the urban appearance," from the flood of 1966 to wedding ceremonies.[55] Archigram instead arranged screens and mirrors inside a colossal transparent plastic "tube" to project and reflect images of cities in "perpetual motion."[56] In the Europe of the economic boom, the ephemeral and having fun became the foundation for new forms of urbanism of opposition, but distinguished by different goals and sets of cultural references.

50 UFO, 'Chicken Circus Circulation ovvero happenvironment (sic) ovvero superurbeffimero n. 7', *Marcatrè*, no. 41-42, June 1968, pp. 76-91; Binazzi, letter to Mussio.

51 UFO, 'Chicken Circus Circulation ovvero heppenveironment (sic) ovvero superurbeffimero n. 7'.

52 Ibid.

53 A photograph of Rudi Dutschke was stuck onto the polyethylene of the dollar sign with adhesive tape. Amongst the operations between the serious and the facetious carried out by UFO, it is worth mentioning the act of obstruction that Binazzi, Gioli, Bracci, Francesco Pirera, and Alessandro Magris, a future member of Superstudio, staged during a colleague's defence of his dissertation, throwing around firecrackers, sneezing powder and foul-smelling liquid (G. S., 'Scatenata a Firenze la repressione antistudentesca', *l'Unità*, no. 170, 26 June 1968, p. 5).

54 'La protesta dei giovani', in *Quattordicesima triennale di Milano: esposizione internazionale delle arti decorative industriali moderne dell'architettura moderna*, p. 47. See too Acocella, 'Effimero urbanistico. L'immagine della piazza nelle azioni del gruppo UFO (1968)'.

55 'Decorazione urbana', in *Quattordicesima triennale di Milano: esposizione internazionale delle arti decorative industriali moderne dell'architettura moderna*, pp. 53-54.

56 'Mutazioni dell'ambiente nell'epoca del "grande numero"', in *Quattordicesima triennale di Milano: esposizione internazionale delle arti decorative industriali moderne dell'architettura moderna*, pp. 70-71.

The "frozen memory" in the pages of the magazine *Marcatrè* in the same period in which the Triennale was due to be held adds other decisive details on the terrorist significance of the ephemera against the city. They were now photographed in front of the cathedral and the Palazzo della Signoria, and renamed *Urboeffimeri*, leaving in an ambiguous state that would always be sought by UFO[57] their origin in a generic "urbo-" that combined "urban" and "urbanistic."[58] Whoever worked on the photographs, whether it was Magdalo Mussio, the magazine's graphic designer, or Bachi,[59] revealed another meaning of the *Urboeffimeri*. As well as being obvious protests against capital as it had crystallised in the traffic and commerce of the city, they were acts of protest against the "legend of the historic centre,"[60] reduced to yet another mechanism of that capital, just as the foam on the Marzocco and the marriage between the statue of Garibaldi and the Anitona had been. A message conveyed by the way they hovered in the air, showing they did not belong to a specific site and cutting off the bases of the monuments like another flood that would even make those monuments free to move[61] (in the full-page photographs) or were aimed against them like new missiles, distorting their profiles and decorations (in the photographs symmetrically split on two pages). Thus in the same period in which Archizoom was criticising in the medium of drawing the reduction of monuments to machines of capitalist power through their invasion by tourists,[62] UFO was presenting the same critique on a scale of 1:1. In this sense, UFO's operations ought instead to be inserted between Gianni Pettena's experiments in San Giovanni Valdarno, when he enclosed Arnolfo di Cambio's loggia with screens made of wooden panels decorated with diagonal stripes of black and silver, and those of the 9999 group on the Ponte Vecchio in Florence, when they projected photographs of geometric patterns, motorways, and astronauts onto the bridge. And yet the *Urboeffimeri* had nothing of the pop language that could still be discerned in Pettena's polychrome decorations, nor of the 9999's electronic experimentation.[63] Finally, they never adhered to any pre-established scheme, not even that of the institutionalised occasions in which they participated, as befitted acts of transgression of the Duchampian kind. For their provocative character, ascribable to a cultural terrorism, the *Urboeffimeri* were instead "Trojan horses" that set out to remove the aura of "myth" surrounding the monuments, in keeping with the strategy developed by the members of Archizoom with their furniture.[64] But they had a scale that exceeded the domestic dimension in order to occupy the urban one, opposing pre-existent historic structures without overriding them, without tear gas, without violence, but just with empty envelopes or tools made of papier-mâché. And so UFO's positioning of its urbanistic ephemera to counter monuments assumed the value

57 "Ambiguous" is the adjective that accompanies any "message with an aesthetic function," underlined and circled in pencil by Binazzi in his copy of Eco's book *Appunti per una semiologia delle comunicazioni visive* (p. 8).

58 UFO, 'Urboeffimeri avvenenti 1:1', p. 61.

59 According to Cammeo, it was Bachi, according to Maschietto, Mussio (Patrizia Cammeo, conversation with Gloria Castellini, 14 February 2022; Titti Maschietto, conversation with Gloria Castellini, 14 February 2022).

60 UFO, 'Urboeffimeri avvenenti 1:1', p. 60.

61 "Ever seen or wished to see Palazzo Vecchio, that big object, put on wheels and move from its place, shaking out the clerks from its two-light windows, hauled with a thread of wool by a child dressed in a sailor suit?" asks one of the itineraries of the counter-guide to Florence drawn up by Binazzi (Lapo Binazzi Archives, Florence).

62 See the projects drawn up between 1966 and 1967 by Massimo Morozzi for Giotto's Campanile in Florence (with Alì Navai) and for the Castello dell'Imperatore in Prato. See Gargiani, *Archizoom associati, 1966-1974. Dall'onda Pop alla superficie neutra*, pp. 18, 26-29.

63 Mario Preti, Paolo Coggiola, Andrea Gigli, Paolo Galli, Fabrizio Fiumi, Carlo Caldini and Giovanni Sani, 'Happening progettuale', *Casabella*, no. 339-40, August 1969, pp. 98-99.

64 For the definition of Trojan horse see Fini, 'Arrivano gli Archizoom', p. 52. The designation would be utilised by Binazzi when he described the "super S gigantic dollar" as a "Trojan horse in front of the CHURCH" (Binazzi, *Didascalie UFO*).

of the flowers that pacifists had inserted in the guns of members of the American National Guard at the end of 1967. Turned into *Urboeffimeri*, those flowers became the emblem of an urbanism of opposition that wanted to be realist[65] in its occupation of the city with a playful and collective fantasy, but one with a political and social significance, that up until then had always been kept segregated. "You have to buy a ticket to go into (...) a circus or a place where they show pornographic films," wrote Bruno Zevi in an article kept by Binazzi. "(...) There is still a puritan mentality that the scenario of daily life should have merely functional aims, avoiding distractions and stimuli of a sensory or perceptual nature."[66]

65 Christo had been presented in the pages of *Domus* as a "neo-realist" artist. See Pierre Restany, 'Un giovane "neo realista" a Parigi', *Domus*, no. 402, May 1963, pp. 52-56.

66 Bruno Zevi, 'Un'anatra brutta ma rivoluzionaria', *L'Espresso*, 11 June 1972, p. 20 (Lapo Binazzi Archives, Florence).

Beyond the Historic Centre: the Occupation of the Countryside

The political aspect that had pervaded UFO's specific and instantaneous—or "discontinuous" as Binazzi put it[67]—strategy in occupying the historic centre of Florence with the grass-roots and artisanal character of the *Urboeffimeri*, took on new characteristics from 1969 onwards. At this moment, real terrorism emerged in Italy (the Piazza Fontana bombing, in Milan, took place in December 1969) and the impetus of the student revolts was institutionalised in extraparliamentary organisations, in which the group would never take part despite maintaining relations of friendship and collaboration with some of their protagonists, from Michelangelo Caponetto and Giancarlo Paba to Greppi. What in 1968 had been carnivalesque events with a political value of protest against the city, now turned into occupations of shops, historic buildings, squares, and rural areas. UFO persisted in the organisation of operations on the scale of the real. In the light of the contemporary graphic experiments of Superstudio and Archizoom for the occupation of town and country with models of the "perfect" city of capitalism with the dimensions of the megastructure, something which some members of UFO had also experimented with during the years of their studies,[68] UFO's operations assumed critical tones not only towards the contemporary city but even towards those experiments.

67 Lapo Binazzi, *Manifesto del discontinuo*, n.d. (FRAC Archives, Orléans). See too UFO, 'Manifesto del discontinuo (1969)', in Marie-Ange Brayer (ed.), *Architectures expérimentales 1950-2012, collection du FRAC Centre* (Orléans: Éditions HYX, 2013), p. 599.

68 See the project drawn up by the Gruppo Omogeneo, to which Cammeo, Foresi and Maschietto belonged, for a linear city in Chianti.

UFO's origin in the city of Florence continued to be reflected in operations on the scale of the urban fabric, making use of the skills of its artisans and generating, out of what were considered "minor" works of architecture, interferences, shocks and collisions that had the value of those "drum beats" described by Walter Benjamin in the life of the contemporary city. Continuing to operate on the real, UFO would occupy a shop to turn it into a subversive cell opposed to the rules of the market and traditional design, and so not conceptually different from the *Urboeffimeri*.

But in the evolution of UFO's thinking, shops offered the group the possibility to go beyond polyethylene and the event in the style of Viareggio Carnival and create other kinds of tools, functional in appearance (chairs, lamps, tables, cupboards) but in reality semantically charged with political and social meanings. In this sense, shop windows became decisive to the sending of messages of a break with the "atrophy" of the fabric of streets and squares and the efforts to subvert the city's equilibrium, transferring the precarious character of the *Urboeffimeri* into an interior that faced onto the world outside as another instrumental manifesto of the urbanism of opposition.[69] In those shops and their windows, UFO constructed poetic narrations that shunned any sort of coherent image in order to plunge customers into the vortex of an accumulation produced by imagination and fantasy out of "frozen memories"; memories that, once taken out of their context, became ambiguous fragments of an "absent structure" centred entirely on disconnections and fractures. Given the impossibility of operating on the kind of gigantic scale as had been done with the *Urboeffimeri* owing to the lack of room inside shops, that accumulation could only be seen as a piling up of things in the manner of the barricades of the 1968 protests, perpetrated now through other acts of transubstantiation. Columns, entablatures and aqueducts became ephemeral simulacra made of polyurethane, with drums replaced by rounds of cheese and capitals in the shape of mushrooms. They were left in ruins as signs of a "continuity" in the sense intended by Ernesto Nathan Rogers[70] that was now impossible to achieve, and devoid of any symbolic value, ideally "reproducible ad infinitum" for a "hypertrophy" of language[71] analogous to the one generated by Andy Warhol's series. So while Sottsass Jr., Superstudio, and Archizoom conceived objects as autonomous presences against white and nondescript backgrounds, and so potent as to become totems that ignore the rooms in which they are located to the point of destroying them,[72] UFO occupied shops with an environment. This environment involved the Rabelaisian community along with real actors in a happening, following a sort of script without words whose aim was to undermine the coupling of production and consumption by bringing to the surface repressions and fantasies belonging to the unconscious. What the group was doing in shops sheds new light on the *Urboeffimeri*, which therefore became the early forms of a happening of involvement for the construction of a new environment that was different from the city of capital, transfigured through the temporary occupation of streets and squares. The destruction of the room brought about by the totemic objects of Sottsass Jr., Superstudio, and Archizoom was accomplished, in UFO's shops, through the unprecedented combination of involvement and the fantastic ambience of a camp "decoration" like the one they had assimilated in the course

69 For the importance of shop windows in "conveying messages in real time" see Lapo Binazzi, 'Dove sono finite le avanguardie', *Controspazio*, no. 4, July-August 1993, pp. 39-47.

70 Lapo Binazzi, 'Alla ricerca dell'effetto città', no. 83, *Modo*, October 1985, pp. 37.

71 See Jean Baudrillard, *The System of Objects* (London: Verso, 2020). There is a copy of the Italian edition of the book, published in 1968, in Maschietto's Archives.

72 See Sottsass Jr.'s "katalogue of furniture" in white rooms (Tommaso Trini, 'Ettore Sottsass Jr.: katalogo di mobili. Studi per Poltronova in laminato plastico Print, 1966', *Domus*, no. 449, April 1967, pp. 37-44), Archizoom's series of drawings of "aggressive and eccentric" objects in an empty room (Archizoom associati, 'La distruzione degli oggetti', *in. Argomenti e immagini di design*, no. 2-3, March-June 1971, pp. 4-13), and finally the photographs of the furniture in Superstudio's *Misura* series taken in the open countryside.

4. *Edilizia Moderna*, 1965, n. 87-88

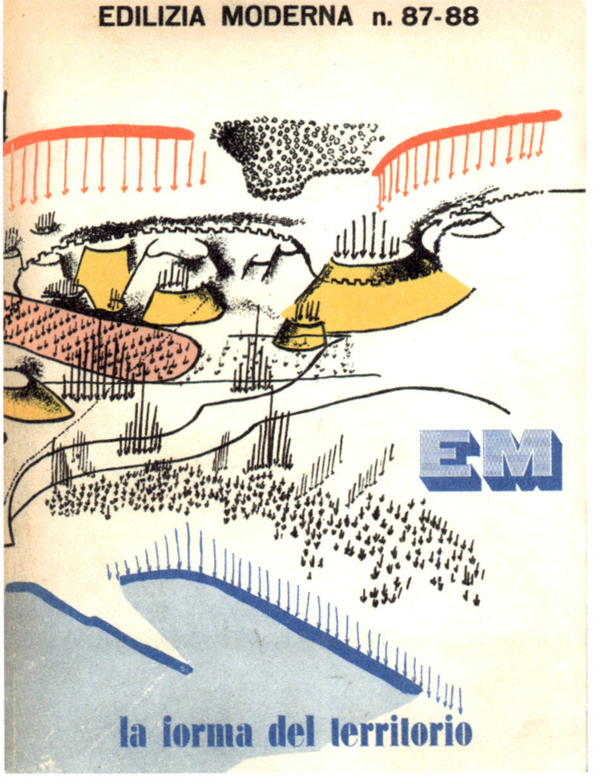

taught by Gillo Dorfles. In these shops the community doffed the guise of the "voluntary prisoner" to become operator/user of an account on which to project its own interpretation. Eco's words showed UFO the direction to go in: "design will have to realise that its problem is not so much one of constructing forms with a more precise, more limpid, more pregnant, and more profound meaning, as on the contrary, forms as open as possible to different meanings."[73] After destroying the room, the "high entropy" produced by the tools, people, and actors of that account burst into the city through a new fallout, and not just through shop windows. The historical heritage was occupied once again by tools that took the form of ephemeral urban decorations, masking its formal quality by emerging with carnivalesque excess from a window of Palazzo Uguccioni in the form of a "tricolour tongue." Or a "farming commune" was installed in Piazza della Signoria composed by polyurethane simulacra made by the group and salad plants to grow on the flagstones. The ironic act of foundation of an autonomous civic government based on agriculture was "mode of actuality" to "take a diagonal approach to the presence" of a city that had spilled over its historical limits to invade the countryside. This was, moreover, something the group had already had an inkling of in

73 Quoted in Virginia Gangemi, 'La prossemica: un nuovo apporto all'architettura?', *Op. cit.*, no. 14, January 1969, pp. 5-26: 21.

early 1968, when it had proposed, during the occupation of the Faculty, to study the "use of the territory by capital."[74]

UFO's interest in the territory cannot be understood without setting it against the background of the debates that had arisen in Italy at the end of the fifties over the new dimension of the city, culminating, first, in Giorgio Piccinato, Vieri Quilici, and Manfredo Tafuri's 1962 essay on the "city-territory" and then, between 1965 and 1967, in Vittorio Gregotti's publications on *La forma del territorio* and *Il territorio dell'architettura* (fig. 4).[75] It was against the backdrop of the discovery of the territorial dimension of the city, of a "switchboard into which it was possible, at any moment, to insert a plug" as Piccinato, Quilici, and Tafuri had pointed out, that UFO understood how the countryside, notwithstanding its different social and cultural structure and its different density of population, in reality possessed an urban essence, inasmuch as it too had been invaded by power and capital, becoming a place colonised and controlled by the bourgeois State. "At what moment do you stupidly believe you have left the city? Do you think that it depends on the warning signs of bourgeois geography? Or on the abrupt rejuvenation of the buildings? Or on unlet shops? Or on the unexpected appearance of a fleeing gardener?". This message run in a questionnaire drawn up by UFO in order to turn urbanism into a semiological tool that could be used to understand the "hidden dimension" of the countryside and thus the significance that individuals have bestowed on it through their behaviour, without any possibility of its concrete and permanent transformation: "territorial proxemics."[76] For UFO there was no "Garden of Eden filled with flowers"[77] and so the flight from the city to the country amongst "subordinate or marginalised cultures"[78] that some of the Florentine neo-avant-garde groups were imagining could have no value. By now, the "delirious" city of capital had cannibalised everything. All that was left for UFO to do was carry out explorations to reveal and denounce the urban nature of the countryside with new acts of occupation that, like the *Urboeffimeri*, were rooted in pure creativity in order to shun the logic of exploitation and invent new spontaneous and primitive modes of behaviour. In this sense, UFO's urbanism turned into territorial proxemics also became practical and critical opposition to what the Italian movement known as La Tendenza referred to as an "architecture of the city" that aimed to compose a new urban order on the scale of its new dimension.[79]

In its discovery of the city-territory, what were generally considered services provided to meet the needs of the community[80] became for UFO outposts of power like the monuments of Florence: electricity pylons and substations, telephone boxes, motorways, railway tracks. Among them, the roadhouses built along Italian

74 Maschietto, 'Facoltà di architettura di Firenze 85 giorni di occupazione'.

75 See Giorgio Piccinato, Vieri Quilici and Manfredo Tafuri, 'La città territorio. Verso una nuova dimensione', *Casabella continuità*, no. 270, December 1962, pp. 16-19; Vittorio Gregotti, 'La forma del territorio', *Edilizia moderna*, no. 87-88, 1965, pp. 1-146; Vittorio Gregotti, *Il territorio dell'architettura* (Milan: Feltrinelli, 1967).

76 UFO, 'Elementi di prossemica territoriale: questionario', *King Kong*, no. 2, June 1972, pp. 10-11. It was Edward Hall who coined the definition of proxemics in his book *The Hidden Dimension* (New York: Doubleday Anchor, 1969). There is a copy of the Italian edition of the book in Maschietto's Archives; Binazzi would cite the book several times. See, for example, Simone Micheli, 'Incontro con Lapo Binazzi. La discontinuità come punto di forza', in Micheli, *I negozi. Vita, morte e miracoli* (Florence: Angelo Pontecorboli, 1992), pp. 40-51.

77 Superstudio, 'Salvataggi di centri storici italiani', *in. Argomenti e immagini di design*, no. 5, May-June 1972, pp. 4-13.

78 Adolfo Natalini, Alessandro Poli and Cristiano Toraldo di Francia, 'Viaggio con la matita tra gli artefatti del mondo contadino', *Modo*, no. 7, March 1978, pp. 49-53: 52.

79 On these themes, see Beatrice Lampariello, 'L'"architettura del territorio" di Aldo Rossi, 1950-1970: per una teoria degli "elementi primari"', *ArcHistor*, no. 16, 2021, pp. 142-181.

80 UFO, 'Produzione industriale e creatività individuale', *Casabella*, July 1973, no. 379, pp. 46-47.

national highways by A.N.A.S., the government-owned company responsible for their maintenance, caught the imagination of UFO in particular. Buildings recognisable by their colours alone, they were ideal prototypes of the house, and yet extremely ambiguous in their always being enigmatically closed and their contents unknown. Thus, they were classified as simulacra of power[81] and transfigured in a new act of political and social transubstantiation that turned them into more wrappings of empty space, once again uninhabitable. They were even more distant from any other inflatable structure, be it that of Utopie, Archigram, or Ant Farm, in having transformed what were no longer figures (column, mouth, missile, dollar sign) but houses into emblems of denunciation in the form of non-functional tools.[82] Instead, the group railed against pylons, substations, and railway tracks with exercises of an apparently sporting character, but in reality "paramilitary" in nature,[83] for new activities of political denunciation, as always pervaded by a playful and pacifistic dimension. New acts of violation took the concrete form of urinating on billboards, trespassing on private property, opening the locks of gates, climbing pylons, and lying on railway tracks. A behavioural practice based on physical effort offered UFO the possibility to go beyond urban predictions and constructions, as it was now clear to the group that any project, independently of its scale and its realisation, was an accessory of capitalism. It was the body of the human being that became the means of the operation, but without there ever being any technological exaltation of it like the one Superstudio was imagining to boost the performance of the only envelope admitted in its idea of architecture from the seventies onwards: the skin of the human body.[84] The body for UFO was a means for acquiring knowledge of oneself and of the city-territory, of its visible and invisible dimensions. It made it possible to reach the limits of operations that, although always conducted collectively, started now to be centred on individuals, as an inevitable consequence of the new political and social scenario post-'68—it is no coincidence that what had been Assemblies now became group therapy in UFO's eyes.[85] The behavioural practice as it was being disseminated by magazines and books, by artistic experiments like Mattiacci's bicycle ride along the shore at Ostia, or Jannis Kounellis's picture-ballerina-violinist,[86] indicated to UFO the direction to follow, just as Land Art was taken by other groups of the Florentine neo-avant-garde as a model for the refounding of the discipline. UFO's imagination was also stirred by the impressions produced by the film *The Swimmer*,[87] in which a strapping Burt Lancaster leaps over obstacles, races against a horse, climbs a wall of rock, and swims from one pool to another of his wealthy upper middle-class neighbours to arrive at his own home, empty and abandoned. But the theoretical foundation of the practice on the scale of UFO's city-territory lies

81 The "typological" classification carried out by UFO was conceptually opposed to what La Tendenza had presented in the same years as an indispensable cognitive and compositional tool for the architecture of the city. No planimetric reconstruction could be used for UFO's cataloguing, both because the group rejected the graphic means of drawing and because those buildings were non-functional icons of power.

82 UFO, 'Architettura della burocrazia', *Casabella*, no. 378, June 1973, pp. 30-31.

83 UFO, 'Paramount', in Achille Bonito Oliva (ed.), *7e Biennale de Paris (catalogo della mostra, Parc Floral de Paris)* (Florence: Centro Di, 1971), n.p.

84 See the film *Supersurface: An alternative model for life on the earth*, produced by Superstudio on the occasion of the exhibition *Italy: The New Domestic Landscape* at the Museum of Modern Art, New York, 26 May-11 September 1972.

85 Lapo Binazzi, *Global Tools - Gruppo 'Teoria', Relazione di Lapo Binazzi*, 10 October 1974 (Lapo Binazzi Archives, Florence).

86 See, among others, Eliseo Mattiacci, 'Variazioni di movimenti terrestri', *Harck*, no. 1, 1971, n.p.; Pierre Restany, 'Les limites du comportement', *Domus*, no. 514, September 1972, pp. 53-55.

87 Binazzi, conversation with Lampariello.

in the books of Edward Hall, Desmond Morris, Giorgio Cesarano, and Gianni Collu, which showed them how patterns of behaviour should be seen as genuine systems of communication.[88] So it is no surprise that in the evolution of UFO's work, its urban operations, from 1971 onwards, got rid of polyethylene, papier-mâché, and polyurethane, shifting the territorial proxemics towards an exceptional physical effort that focused on exploration and intrusion: the man shot out of a cannon as the only possibility of reappropriation of the city-territory through the act of observation from above before crashing to the ground (on a mattress); and the *Giro d'Italia* for the reconnaissance of that same city-territory, whether acted out by the members of the group or reduced to the scale of a game played with Coca-Cola bottle tops and figurines of the riders on a natural setting in the form of a product—ceramic tiles from the Iris company reproducing a photograph of a clod of earth, used as a new paving for Piazza Santo Stefano, in Bologna, on the occasion of *Pollution*, another artistic event at which a sculptural object was temporarily transformed into a total space involving the city.[89] "The Giro d'Italia. It's really an urbanism scheme," explained the group. Its urbanism of opposition, given the impossibility of halting capital and therefore speculation, given the impossibility of solving the problems of the city and of human beings, had gone to their root, the body and its movement, along the lines of the nomadic community of the film *Glen and Randa*,[90] free from the city in a post-apocalyptic world and yet in frantic search of it in the form they have discovered in pictures from old comic books, where the people are dressed in white and able to fly: the *Metropolis* that will never be found, leaving Randa to her death.

Together with *Giro d'Italia*, another of UFO's urban operations constructed a new narration with elements of science fiction for an urbanism of opposition that became *fantaurbanistica*.[91] The competition for the design of the new campus of the University of Florence, with a deadline in the summer of 1971, became the occasion for a new invention of pure creativity whose starting point was the rejection of any kind of construction on the plain of Sesto Fiorentino, of any kind of transformation into another service and thus the umpteenth cornerstone of capital—"No!" wrote the group on the photograph of a new behavioural action carried out at the time of the competition. It was on this occasion that the contrasting strategies of the Florentine neo-avant-garde in their rejection of the city-territory of capital through different forms of denunciation were made plain: while Archizoom and Superstudio showed the image of that city taken to extremes with the continuous planes of the *No-Stop City* and *Supersuperficie*,[92] UFO set out to warn all the creatures—animals and plants—present on the

88 See Hall, *The Hidden Dimension*; Desmond Morris, *The Naked Ape* (London: Jonathan Cape, 1967); Desmond Morris, *Manwatching: A Field Guide to Human Behaviour* (London: Jonathan Cape, 1977); Giorgio Cesarano and Gianni Collu, *Apocalisse e rivoluzione* (Rome: Dedalo libri, 1973). There are copies of these books in the Archives of Maschietto and Binazzi.

89 For the man shot out of a cannon and the game with bottle tops, see UFO, 'Coccoina', in Daniela Palazzoli (ed.), *Pollution: Per una nuova estetica dell'inquinamento* (Bologna: Fondazione Iris, 1972), pp. 46-47. For the *Giro d'Italia*, see UFO, 'Il Giro d'Italia', *in*. *Argomenti e immagini di design*, no. 6, July-August 1972, pp. 66-67.

90 Binazzi, conversation with Lampariello.

91 UFO, 'Appunti per una ridefinizione del concetto di fantaurbanistica', *Progettare inpiù*, no. 8, February-March 1975, pp. 24-27.

92 See (Archizoom), 'Archizoom: progetto di concorso per l'università di Firenze', *Domus*, no. 509, April 1972, pp. 10-12. Superstudio did not take part in the competition, but the first sketches for the *Supersuperficie* were drawn up at the beginning of 1971, while the competition was underway, and set in a location with features resembling those of the plain of Sesto Fiorentino.

5. Madelon Vriesendorp, *Greed AKA New York Doom*, 1973, Madelon Vriesendorp Archives, London

plain, as significant as any architecture that could have been built there, of their imminent destruction, completing its reflection on the meaning of architecture as language. The "frozen memory" of the operation consists of five retouched and numbered photographs used to construct an orderly sequence with one of the members of the group sticking out of the rollback roof of a car and using the megaphone of the 1968 protests to communicate with the plain of Sesto Fiorentino through a coded language of arrows, stars and circles. The sequence of images that portrays a portion of the plain is defined between two extremes, A and B, which are to be understood as physical and conceptual limits of the operation, as the stages of the route taken by the urbanistic ephemera and those of the *Giro d'Italia* had been. In its effort to defend the natural world not so much from the generic pollution evoked by the first environmentalist protests,[93] but specifically from the city, UFO's proposal was in line with that of the 9999. The 9999 had represented the form of an alternative development of capital through a cutting-edge technology, the same as the one used to project images onto the Ponte Vecchio, which would

93 See 'New York', *Domus*, no. 487, June 1970, pp. 49-51. See too the publication of the *Whole Earth Catalog* between 1968 and 1971.

have guaranteed the survival of green fields and forests among people, historical monuments and data-processing monuments (servers).[94] But UFO took care not to prefigure any image of a future, whether critical or visionary, continuing down the road of denunciation as the only possible act of liberation and adhering to the ban placed by Italian Marxism on any sort of figurative avant-garde. Then the sequence of five photographs was condensed into a single image, obtained by a new and symmetrically split photograph that portrayed, on the ground of the plain, the car, and in the air, an aeroplane to mark out a new space opened up for fantastic explorations. The little arrows of the linguistic code of the plain, arranged in the sequence of images to form speech bubbles, now generated a colossal figure of human appearance that looms above the plain with its legs and arms spread wide. That figure is not an "Unidentified Flying Object," but a monster carrying out a new act of violation by urinating on an area that had already been converted for use by a service. Its origin is made clear by the title of the image, *ID Monster*, an allusion to the antagonist of the science-fiction film *Forbidden Planet*, produced by the subconscious of individuals to kill human beings and to trample on, mutilate, and do violence to territories. That the film was also taken as a reference in the exhibition *This Is Tomorrow* of 1956 is a coincidence that demonstrates, on the one hand, how the urbanism that emerged from the ashes of the CIAM fed on sources that went beyond the bounds of the discipline and, on the other, the full extent of the distance between the various positions assumed within that new urbanism. While in *This Is Tomorrow* what is celebrated from that film is Robby the Robot as a possible technological means of improving city life for human beings, UFO used the monster of the unconscious as a tool of its urbanism of opposition to demonstrate the psychanalytical force of a power, that of the city, which destroys itself in order to survive; another *Ouroboros* after the one imagined by Foresi and Cammeo in a project from 1968,[95] or the *Continuous Conveyor Belt City* that advanced at a constant speed, devouring nature to produce houses on an infinite cycle, while leaving a trail of waste in its wake,[96] but devoid of any figurative character that might lead to the image of a building or a city. The city became a being that moved and spoke like a living thing[97] to be psychoanalysed according to Freudian principles, as had already been done over the course of the sixties with other forms of capital[98] in order to reveal its imaginary and non-quantifiable dimension. In those years it was not just UFO that was imagining the destruction of the city. Others, across the Atlantic, were contemplating the destruction of that epitome of the metropolis, New York, by a monstrous figure driven by the greed of capital from the perspective of a psychoanalytical interpretation of the city: Madelon Vriesendorp, a future partner in OMA, with her

94 9999, 'Progetto di concorso per l'università di Firenze', *Domus*, no. 509, April 1972, p. 16.

95 This was the motto of the project submitted by Dezzi Bardeschi to the competition for the "layout and urbanistic and architectural restoration" of the Fortezza da Basso in Florence, in order to turn it into a National Centre of the Crafts. According to Cammeo, Foresi and Cammeo were also involved in drawing up the project, even though their names does not appear among its authors (Cesare Mattini, 'L'esito del Concorso Nazionale d'idee per la Fortezza da Basso di Firenze', *Bollettino degli Ingegneri*, no. 12, 1968, pp. 10-11).

96 This was one of the *Twelve Ideal Cities* invented by Gian Piero Frassinelli, a member of Superstudio, in 1971. Superstudio, 'Twelve Cautionary Tales for Christmas: Premonitions of the mystical rebirth of urbanism', *Architectural Design*, no. 12, December 1971, pp. 737-742 and 785.

97 UFO and Daniela Palazzoli (eds.), *Controllo colonizzazione e fascismo sul territorio: Milano, Galleria 291, maggio/giugno 1974* (Florence: Centro Di, 1974).

98 See Emilio Servadio, *La psicologia dell'attualità* (Milan: Longanesi, 1961). There is a copy of the book in Maschietto's Archives.

Greed AKA New York Doom (fig. 5).[99] The job of UFO's monster was to convey a new message of political and urban revolt that had now become an act of critical thinking which turned into mental strategy or "phantom urbanism"[100] as a means of struggle that no longer left any doubt as to its non-violent essence.

99 On Vriesendorp's early works, see Anna Rosellini, 'Il était une fois... La statue de la liberté et les gratte-ciels de New York', *Matières*, no. 15, 2019, pp. 91-109.

100 Binazzi, *Manifesto del discontinuo*.

Dead-end Track

Urbanism had become, in UFO's hands, a means of opposing capital and its concrete expression in the city. It had been turned into an ambiguous language of communication that took grass-roots activity as its conceptual basis. It freed itself from the predictions of the project to rely on an arbitrary approach, occupying streets, squares, and rural areas to use them for the founding of new modes of social conduct. It drew on the imagination to denounce its abuse by those in power and to produce cultural "bombs." It shunned feasibility and permanence to become a discourse conveyed through photographs or films. It was founded on discontinuity as an operation on reality that had the value of an unexpected move or oblique approach. It was used as a "cultural picklock" to break down any kind of delimitation in a declared "non-disciplinarity."[101] Finally it ventured into a psychoanalytic cultural domain from where it could generate sensitive and metaphorical operations on the city. In its various aspects of urbanistic terrorism, territorial proxemics, *fantaurbanistica*, and phantom urbanism, it became an ephemeral and conceptual action in order to produce operations that lasted for an instant, fixed in the memory of its participants or in the "frozen" one of films or photographs, falling back the moment after into the everyday life of capital. In its contestation and denunciation, in its rejection of drawing and any sort of transformation that went beyond the time frame of the instant, UFO's urbanism was a "dead-end track,"[102] like the one that the group represented in its design of an installation for Eurodomus in 1970, or photographed in its paramilitary incursions into the territory with a corpse lain over it. More than any other Florentine neo-avant-garde, UFO seems to have been conscious of the "tragic nature"[103] of its urbanism of opposition, which could only be rejected by the established discipline and was not understood by the large number "owing to the 'cultural' frailty of the receivers."[104] It became a concretisation of the human being who dies in the exceptional physical effort to control and rediscover the city, from the man shot out of a cannon to Randa. And, is tragedy not the flip side of the carnivalesque celebration that, without ever being able to transform the city-territory into a continuous festival,[105] after orgiastic excess and denunciation, left streets and squares once again at the mercy of the monster of the city-territory of capital, which endlessly repeats its mechanical gestures of survival and the conquest of new stretches of countryside?

101 Binazzi (UFO), *Ufo. Discontinuità e territorio*. The definition of *grimaldello* or "picklock" was suggested by Maschietto (Maschietto, conversation with Castellini).

102 R. B., 'UFO', *Caleidoscopio*.

103 Lapo Binazzi, 'Il Minotauro nella città', *Modo*, no. 87, March 1986, pp. 62-63.

104 Binazzi (UFO), *Ufo. Discontinuità e territorio*.

105 See Ettore Sottsass Jr., 'Il Pianeta come festival', *Casabella*, no. 365, May 1972, pp. 41-47.

HERITAGE

3

The Voice of the City

Point Supreme

On February 12, 1968, a 100 meter-long, semi-transparent, inflated plastic tube appeared in the city of Florence, carried by the students of the city's architecture school, then under occupation.

The labyrinthine tube, initiated by UFO, was inflated on the atrium floor of the Faculty of Architecture of the University of Florence. Held over the students' heads, moving from hand to hand, it soon penetrated the great hall, came out of a window, moved out to the street, and ended up parading the city, passing by its monuments, leading the crowd. People spontaneously wrote slogans on its surface, from plays on words to political statements, overloading it with meanings and turning it into a support for words, desires, and voices for all.

Some days before, a semi-transparent plastic sheet was hanging in the same Faculty entrance hall covered with messages, assemblages of words written in many hands. A screen of words against the rationalist architecture of the school, a fusion of words and space, that seemed to merge reality with communication as a true semantic device: an architecture that talks.

For UFO, the city is a place of history, traditions, and culture, where people live together, and where collective beliefs, desires, and creative energy exist. UFO projects always place the city and its people at their centres.

UFO projects give a voice to the city. What would the city say if it had a voice? For once, it becomes possible to hear it. People are not just users, or inhabitants, but mediators of the city's voice. UFO projects cannot exist if we try to think of them without the city or without the people. Words, objects, spaces, city, and people merge. They become equally important, and together they are able to create that language never spoken before or since. The projects are situations, mediums through which the city is revealed in new ways. They are definitely not simply about architecture, at all.

UFO, Festa de l'Unità, Parco delle Cascine, Florence, 1968, Patrizia Cammeo/Riccardo Foresi Archives, Florence

UFO, *Urboeffimero 5*, 1968

Point Supreme, *House of Resale Value*, 2010

Sometimes the voice of a city finds a way to be heard, usually applied to architecture in the form of banners or graffiti. It comes in opposition to the city and the involuntary host buildings; unwanted, antisocial, violent, even illegal. UFO's projects invented a way for the city's voice to be heard without the typical violence, and although more temporary and seemingly impermanent, it was far more playful, public, and effective.

UFO, *Linguaccia tricolore*, 1970

Point Supreme, Tiny Museum, Trbovlje, 2017

There are certain days when monuments and people together define the experience of the city; on feasts and festivals, people in costumes become small buildings, and buildings with flags and signs speak. UFO literally added a tongue with words to a building. The Tiny Museum in Trbovlje was offered to the people to freely showcase their talents, obsessions, desires. A monument made and operated by the people themselves.

UFO, *Giornale murario*, 1968

Point Supreme, *Half Real*
(after artists' interventions), 2010

Words in space 1: Space as language, language as architecture. In *Half Real*, a space was reproduced at half its scale and people were invited to act, write, and draw on it. In the end, the words and drawings became the space, the architecture disappeared.

UFO, *Urboeffimero 6*, 1968

Point Supreme, *Tag Mosaic*, 2014

Words in space 2: Text as form, the form of the text, the words of the city; the city communicating, beyond architecture, or creating a new kind of architecture, perhaps light, or temporary, or mobile, surely with a form of its own, anti-monumental, political, and playful at the same time.

UFO, *Casa a ostacoli sul territorio*, 1972

Point Supreme, *Faliro Pier*, 2012

Sometimes a new graphic language can add clarity to a situation, creating a bridge between disparate elements, between architecture and the city, connecting people and architecture.

Gianni Pettena, *Pettena-Arnolfo Dialogue*, 1968

Point Supreme, *Athens Heaven*, 2012

Offering a city its opposite, what it clearly and desperately misses: a pause from an omnipresent renaissance building typology, or an endless lava of concrete. Another scale, another form, another type of nature.

UFO and Mino Vismara, *Performance in b/arca*, 1978

Point Supreme, *Athens Ferry*, 2012

Boats and water in the city create dynamic and playful situations, like permanent urban happenings. Boats are often banal, everyday objects, tools in urban operational routines. In the *Performance Aboard a Boat* and *Athens Ferry*, a typical boat was used to create an extraordinary experience by a simple misplacement or new type of use.

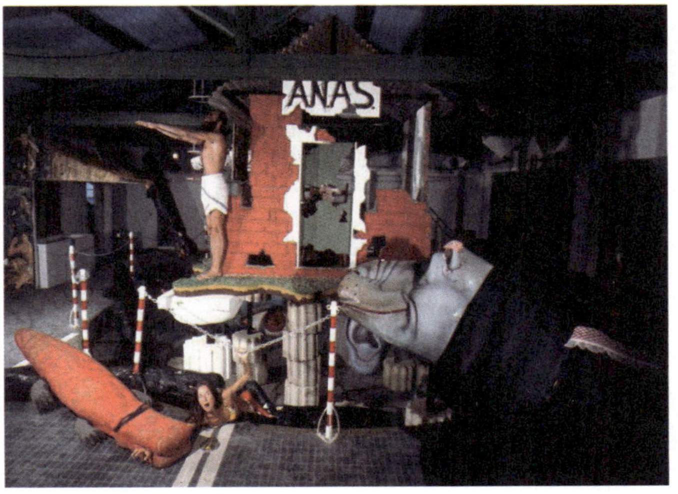

UFO, *Bamba Issa 2*, second season, 1970

Point Supreme (with Salottobuono), *"After Utopia" Characters*, from the *After Utopia Critical Set*, 2017

The city is made of elements, buildings, streets, stadiums, furniture; but also memories, stories, people and their unique personalities, fantasies, obsessions. It is revealing to imagine a city only through these elements, symbolic and ideological, seemingly ignoring architecture, for once.

Point Supreme, *Open Air Theater*, from *Only in Athens*, 2014

Urban happenings—hidden aspects of the city; the city as an empty canvas to be filled with people, words, spelled out desires.

Point Supreme, *Athens as an Island*, 2011

New myths; communicating the city's collective and subconscious desires. The city as made by people, the architect as operator.

Nick Hannes, Gas station Greek wedding, 8 October 2012, Rio, Greece ©Nick Hannes

FuelSave
V-Power
7
V-Power
FuelSave
Economy Fuels

The Radical
Sensuality
of Colour
Adam Nathaniel Furman

Colour is seen as shocking, confrontational, superficial, and dangerous because its absence has been so carefully constructed over the past century as being the embodiment of everything it is supposedly not, with the absence of colour coming to represent depth, sophistication, seriousness, and gravitas, while colour (unless supremely limited and controlled) was the embodiment of everything frivolous, or savage. It was, and still is, to be ridiculed, or feared. It is quite easy looking back now to see how the othering of colour was a vital ingredient in the separation of serious mainstream modernity in western culture from all of those troublesome queers, women, immigrants and colonial subjects who, because no doubt the upper echelons of colourless world culture were reserved only for a select few immensely dull but self-anointed-as-enlightened men, continued to utilise colour, pattern and the diversity of aesthetic expression that has always existed on this beautiful planet to express themselves. The absence of colour has, since the enlightenment, been a way for colonial culture to differentiate itself from the rest of the world, and internally, a way of keeping a clear separation between the difficult complexity and diversity of a rapidly evolving society, from those who see themselves as guiding it. Colour for the masses, let them watch Disney. Colour for the women, let them have their pastel kitchens. Colour for the queers, let them decorate the department stores. Colour for the immigrants, let them dress up for their weddings. But no respect. This relationship to colour has been drilled into us from the 18th century onwards, a form of social control and stratification that is reified through taste. There is a reason that protest movements harness the power of the rainbow to such powerful effect; it smashes through this. There is a reason why still to this day deploying an abundant and unapologetic range of colours in a manner beyond the accepted level of sophisticated restrain deemed tasteful is a shocking act that infuriates so many. Colour should not be radical, but unfortunately, it is.

UFO, Sherwood Restaurant, Florence, 1969, Titti Maschietto Archives, Florence

colour
is a
coalition

a collective
celebration
of difference

sometimes to be
radical
is simply to embrace
what has always been there

but which
you had been taught

was not allowed

"Moral puritanism and aesthetic austerity, along with resentment and old, stubborn, and underhanded desire to equate drabness with beauty ... make their righteous alliance and take delight in a constantly reiterated certainty: only what is insipid, odourless, and colourless may be said to be true, beautiful and good"

Jacqueline Lichtenstein

“You recognise these joys: to feel the generous belly of a vase, to caress its slender neck, and then to explore the subtleties of its contours. To thrust your hands into the deepest part of your pockets and, with eyes half closed, to give way to the slow intoxication of the fantastic glazes, the bursts of yellows, the velvet tones of the blues…”

Charles-Édouard Jeanneret

“Pompeian red: you are taken to a roman villa where lying men dressed in white peplum are served by young Egyptian slaves elaborate dishes, animals stuffed with animals stuffed with other animals, from the big ones to the small ones, and there is marble on the floor, outside the Mediterranean is blue but the walls of the room are red. That is all you see in a fraction when you hear Pompeian red”

Nathalie Du Pasquier

Welcome to UFOland!

False Mirror Office

Filippo Fanciotti, Giovanni Glorialanza

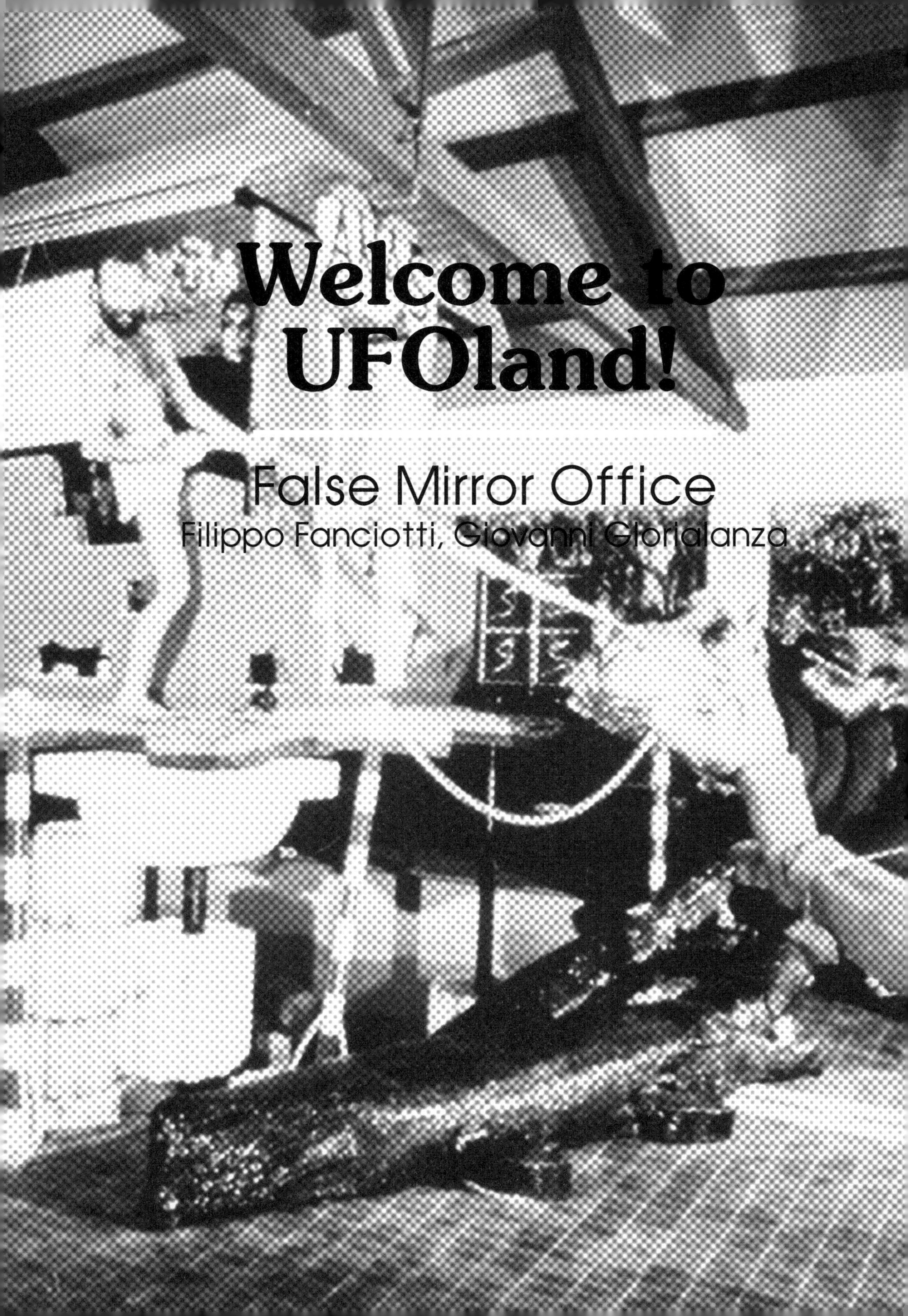

Author's Note

With rare exceptions, UFO provides no interpretations of its works; this so-called "rejection of explanation," as described by Lapo Binazzi, aims to apply the "amplifications of the sign" in architecture, simultaneously making the work of art available to multiple interpretations. If this practice jeopardizes UFO's productions by transforming them into cryptic devices that are borderline incommunicable, this risk is promptly averted through the use of a double-coded language capable of bringing together popular images and themes aimed at a more elitist audience; UFO directly involves the public in its works, leading the audience to participate in the provocative actions to which they are subjected, triggering a kind of playful intellectual competition with the authors.

This half-serious approach to architecture places UFO in a long-standing lineage that connects Giulio Romano's "joke" to Léon Krier's illustrated satire, caricatural symbols in Robert Venturi and Denise Scott Brown's architectures, the playful furniture of the Memphis Group, and Ugo La Pietra's disequilibrating systems.

We have catalogued various buildings and objects selected from the history of architecture and design and established a large laboratory of these works to celebrate the relevance and usefulness of a half-serious attitude in contemporary debate. This extraction of those fragments from their times, places, and socio-political contexts, and their later assemblage in a new composition are, in fact, acts of manipulation to verify and amplify their rhetorical value in today's culture.

Well are well aware that these procedures risk reducing architecture to a freak show. Nonetheless, we have decided to stage the outcomes in a phantasmagorical theme park—called *UFOland*—described and illustrated in the following informative booklet addressed to future visitors.

UFO, Bamba Issa Discoteque, Forte dei Marmi, second season, 1970, Titti Maschietto Archives, Florence

In the following pages you will find your personal map to an amusement park created just for you: *UFOland!*

Our entire staff are here to provide you with an enjoyable and unique experience, whether this is your first visit, or you are a die-hard UFOlander.

UFOland is divided into five macro-areas: *Playful Street*, *Caricatureville*, *Satirical Islands*, *Camp "Mountain,"* and, finally, the *Absurd Maze*. Within each one of these areas, you'll find forms that are distant in time and space, yet incredibly relatable in their purposes; the various rhetorical devices used here to convey the most varied messages were borrowed from the cheat book of the comedian, the court jester, or the revolutionary demonstrator.

Inside the park anything goes, but remember: the only word forbidden in *UFOland*'s dictionary is "sobriety."

Be careful not to get lost: boundaries between areas of the park are imprecise since they are constantly transforming! Fragments are initially stacked in a rather random way, but over time the consolidated connections have resulted in real assemblages with well-recognisable shapes; to orient and entertain you better they were promptly labelled as the main attractions here at *UFOland*.

Playful Street

You have arrived at *UFOland*'s entrance; on your right you will find the station, where you can hop on the cammella-train and reach all the attractions. Before you is the actual entrance: an assemblage of other architectures' entryways in which the structural elements have been semantically substituted. Once you have passed the portal, you will find yourself strolling along *Playful Street*, overlooked by an abundance of fragments devoted to an unrestrained libertinism: Radical beds, architectures caught red-handed, formalisms which are ends in themselves... Be careful not to lose your sense of decency: you're still an intellectual!

Camp "Mountain"

Right next to *Playful Street* stands *Camp "Mountain,"* where fragments of unnatural architecture and cheeky sculptures are experiencing a real pop renaissance, ironically re-appropriating current language; their unanticipated value comes from being queer parodies with a high rate of social, cultural, and ideological re-elaboration. Do not let the many phallic shapes or sexual references you encounter intimidate you: you are just penetrating the "colonnade" to the "cavity."

Satirical Islands

In the *Satirical Islands* archipelago, you can find architectures that ridicule authors or specific historical periods; of these complex critiques, however, only the bizarre shapes and garish colours remain. Besides sobriety indignation has also been neutralised at *UFOland*: only playfulness is welcome! From Satirical Islands you can see the *Parody Boat*: an irreverent pirate galleon composed of fragments that depend absolutely on pre-existing architectures. If this apparent lack of "originality" already makes it anti-modern in itself, legend has it that the *Parody Boat* sank a functionalist Lecorbusierian paquebot in a firefight: can you spot the shipwreck?

Caricatureville

In *Caricatureville* you will find yourself surrounded by fragments that deliberately imitate the style and features of other objects to spark hilarity in visitors. At the centre you will find the small, self-evident area of It's a *Redundant World*: a festival of paradoxical dysfunctional places where every form literally follows its function, celebrating it as a symbol. These pieces are just distant imitations of what they really should be, and it is this "lack of seriousness" that makes them effective caricatures. Don't miss the chance to buy a new hat or a donut—but always remember to smile: authors are very touchy.

Absurd Maze

The labyrinthine *Absurd Maze* is a mysterious place where you'll find elements of architecture extracted from their roles, elevated to symbols, and then abandoned to their fates; inflatable capitals, cheese moulds as benches... A surreal environment surrounded by the dense forest of the *Bizarre Columns*, coming from the four corners of the globe. To guide you through the labyrinth, the names and authors of the fragments have been deliberately omitted; you will have to forget any previous knowledge, celebrating everything you meet as if for the first time. Orienting oneself within the *Absurd Maze* will require a heuristic approach, proceeding by trial and error. If you choose to venture out on your own personal journey against the tide, the odds of emerging from the maze are slim; if you follow everyone else, you'll certainly find your way out, but you may miss the best bits!

Kitsch Castle

Before leaving us, take a minute to admire what is defined by many as *UFOland*'s central attraction; positioned in the centre of the park and forming the monumental crown of *Playful Street* stands spectacular *Kitsch Castle*. Here is where all the fragments in *UFOland* are first brought; once the area to which they belong is defined, each piece is then sorted and taken by a vertiginous system of cableways to the surrounding areas, there acquiring a role and a specific, although provisional, meaning. The castle is the result of the assembly of varied and ever-changing elements, but from a certain distance it will always appear recognisable and reassuring; if you look closely at its silhouette, you will be able to recognise leaning towers, miniaturised sailing ships, colossal lipsticks... At each blink of an eye, *Kitsch Castle* will offer you a view that is always new, but always sincere.

What are you waiting for? Start your journey... Welcome to *UFOland!*

Parody Boat
CAREFUL CHICKEN!
SATIRICAL ISLANDS
CAMP "MOUNTAIN"
WELCOME

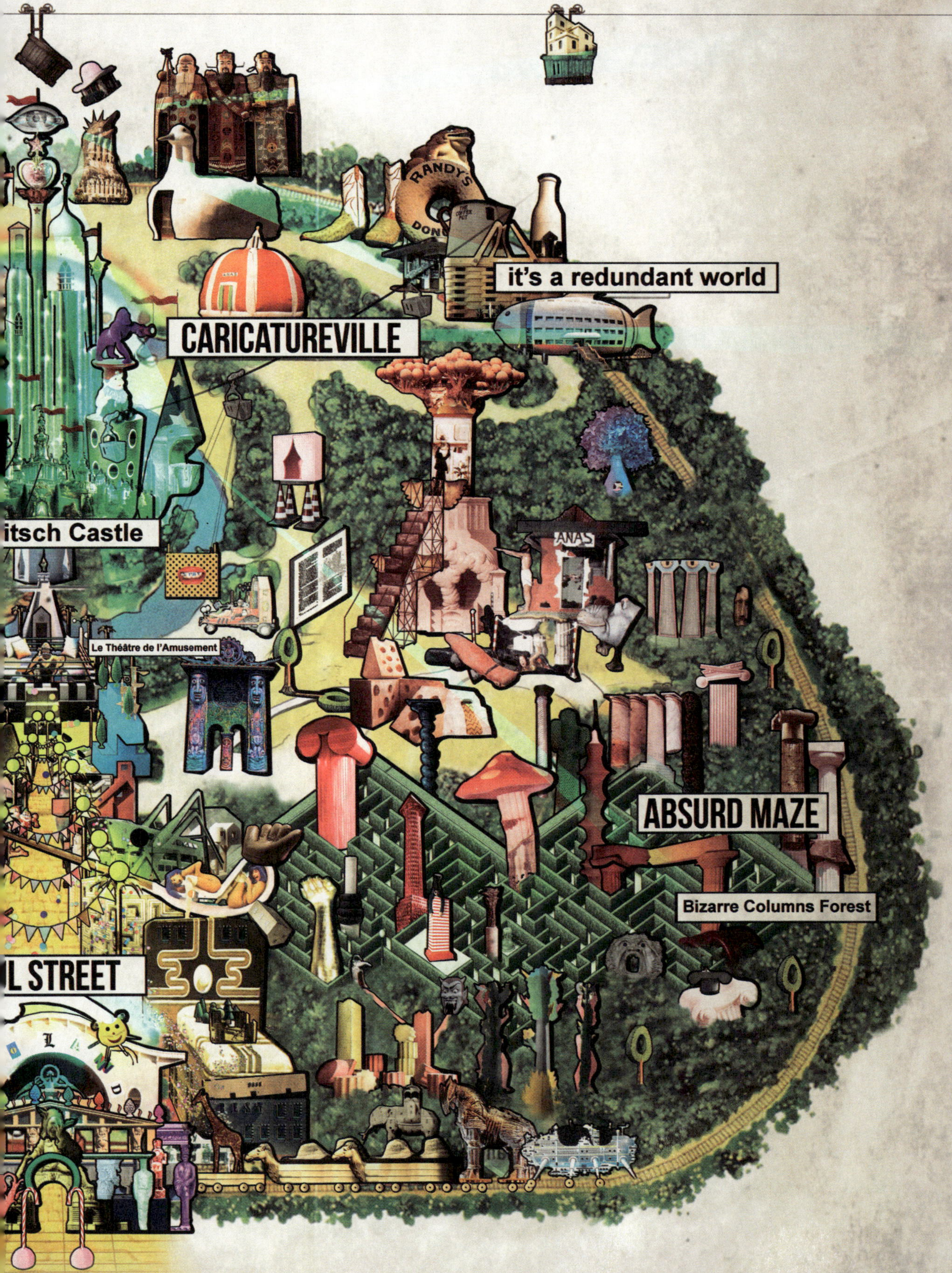

it's a redundant world
CARICATUREVILLE
itsch Castle
Le Théâtre de l'Amusement
ABSURD MAZE
Bizarre Columns Forest
L STREET
RANDY'S DONUTS

Five Practice Points
Andrew Kovacs

Introduction

Over the last twenty years, the so-called Radical Architecture and the experiments of its protagonists have been placed once again at the centre of the debate of architecture discipline, questioning both historians and the young generation of practitioners. Among the protagonists of the Florentine avant-garde, UFO group, with experiments ranging from their 1968 performances in agitated *piazzas* to irreverent installations for shops and discotheques, has called the profession of architect into question, shifting its areas of investigation, and coming to define a new and experimental way of doing architecture. An experimental approach to it—UFO must have understood this very well—can easily be seen as an anomaly. Indeed, it is necessary: only through this kind of approach can the very essence of architecture be questioned and the limits and contents of its scope renewed.

When we look at the most incisive and experimental techniques carried out by UFO, we immediately recognise that tendency, taken from the world of avant-garde art, to aggregate fragments and heterogeneous objects in order to build assemblages that are open to the interpretations of the user—what might be called "true three-dimensional collages." Fifty years after the UFO experiments, collage and assemblage have become once again an avenue of experimentation for the younger generation of architects. Their nature, however, cannot be the same. With the arrival of a digital era, new scanning technologies, and the appearance of the internet, collage and assemblage are evolving and are ready to push the boundaries of architecture even further.

UFO, Sherwood Restaurant, Florence, 1969, Titti Maschietto Archives, Florence

1. Folly

The folly is a disciplinary territory that exists at the intersection of art and architecture. Often produced by "amateur" architects, the folly exists on the periphery of the discipline. Oscillating between useful and useless architecture, the folly offers a space of architectural experimentation, the ability to be undisciplined, and the possibility of expanding the reaches and limits of architectural practice. The most famous folly in architecture in the second half of the 20th century was Bernard Tschumi's Parc de la Villette. In the first quarter of the 21st century, follies are often temporary and go by different names such as installations, pavilions, public art, design build workshops, etc. Unlike private work, these new types of follies are often quasi-public and collective in nature, and offer a space for "young architects" to generate a practice in and even turn into a practice itself.

2. Internet

Architecture once was something that you could only experience in person; today it can be experienced on the internet. The audience for architecture has instantly expanded to everyone with an internet connection. Clients now show you Pinterest pages as "inspo" for potential designs. Discourse across regions can be collapsed or expanded. The internet flattens our shared references as a discipline while opening up the possibility of expanding architecture's audience. Architecture has memes now: Instagram accounts such as @dank.lloyd.wright offer architectural criticism that happens in real time. The architects' publicity, a key aspect of practice, is now #WIP, architectural proposals, news and announcements, image collections, memories of past projects, realized projects, etc. Le Corbusier started a magazine before he made his most recognized buildings and today any architect can invent a practice on the internet and feed it content to demonstrate the activities of the practice. The internet has become a new arena for architects to disseminate their ideas and visions. One way "young architects" would generate a practice in the pre-internet world was through speculative and critical projects. Think of projects like the *Continuous Monument* by Superstudio and the resulting work of founder and member Adolfo Natalini. Speculative and critical projects in the discipline of architecture used to be called "paper architecture," but "young architects" can now produce "paper architecture" in a digital sphere. What is "paper" and what is "digital" in architecture is collapsed and "young architects" have endless opportunities to exploit this conflation.

3. Archive of Affinities

Archive of Affinities is primarily an image collection project that is disseminated on the internet. It is a form of practice in the sense that the project literally happens daily, as images of architecture are shared on various social media platforms. While Archive of Affinities is primarily an image collection project, it has also sparked architectural production at a speculative level. In this sense, one of the functions of Archive of Affinities is as a crucible for practice. The material collected through it is, at times, literally used to produce speculative architectural projects that are shared on the internet. One of the first instances of this was a series of speculative floor plans that were digitally collaged together from parts, fragments, and wholes that were shared on Archive of Affinities. Operating with this logic of collection and production, Archive of Affinities aims to expand the limits of the discipline of architecture.

4. Scanner

The overwhelming majority of content on Archive of Affinities are images scanned from old media. Part of it also consists of using a scanner to document physical objects that have been collected. Oftentimes, these physical objects are used to produce architectural models. The collection of physical objects as part of the project of Archive of Affinities also leads to a practice where the parts, fragments, and wholes of physical objects are digitally collaged into speculative architectural projects, conceptual sketches, and proposals. In this practice, the scanner helps push the project of Archive of Affinities from strictly a collection project into a production project. Since this is a daily form of practice, the scanner becomes the most useful tool when it comes to collecting objects. While the scanner is primarily thought of as a design tool rather than as a documentation tool, the scanner becomes productive in pushing the project of Archive of Affinities from a collection project into a production project. In this sense, when the scanner is pushed out of the realm of a collection tool and into the realm of a design tool, it becomes useful to the practice and work of Office Kovacs. The scanner is a tool that flattens and helps to collect and produce. The scanner primarily produces representation. The scanner makes plans. The scanner makes sections. The scanner makes elevations. The scanner makes views. The scanner makes axonometrics. The scanner makes collage. The scanner makes space. The scanner makes a catalog. The scanner makes a drawing. The scanner makes a rendering. The scanner takes a photograph. The scanner makes an archive. The scanner makes an advertisement. The scanner makes small things big. The scanner makes the physical world digital. The scanner makes old media new. The scanner makes pictures. The scanner makes images. The scanner makes file names. The scanner makes craft. The scanner makes architecture from architecture.

5. Collage

The more you collect the more you can collage. Collage is a form of architectural practice and thinking and, like the folly, it also exists at the intersection of art and architecture. According to Clement Greenberg, collage was invented in 1917 by either Pablo Picasso or Georges Braque when one of them decided to use sand as a material in a painting and subsequently invented synthetic cubism. Collage in architecture has taken many forms—from Mies van der Rohe's renderings, to Nils-Ole Lund's book *Collage Architecture*, to Colin Rowe and Fred Koetter's *Collage City*. Today, the "digital collage" is celebrated for its hyperrealism in books like Jesus Vassallo's *Seamless: Digital Collage and Dirty Realism in Contemporary Architecture*. In architecture, collage has been most useful as a form of generating new representation for either fictional or real projects. In the past, architects have deployed collage to generate speculative projects as part of their practice—from Kazimir Malevic's *Architekton* (1920s), to Hans Hollein's *Sparkplug* (1964), to Ben Nicholson's book *Appliance House* (1990), to Marshall Brown's contemporary perspective views. At the same time, collage has been useful in architecture as a form of criticism—just think of Stanley Tigerman's collage *The Titanic* (1979) as a proto-architectural meme. The internet amplifies and encourages a collage sensibility through its endlessness as a source for references. Collage is a critical design method that allows for disparate parts to live side by side in a new whole. If a collection can be used to generate comparisons, then a collage (that collapses comparison into contiguity) of that collection can lead to new architectural productions and practices. When collage becomes three-dimensional, it further reinforces its role in architecture. The assembly of parts, in real life, along with the ambition to make these parts a new totality becomes architecture. Three-dimensional collages can exist at the scale of a model or a building, yet it is ultimately a sensibility of assembly and composition of dissimilar parts.

"We're sitting here, and I'm supposed to be the franchise player, and we're talking about practice. I mean, listen, we're sitting here talking about practice, not a game, not a game, not a game, but we're talking about practice. Not the game that I go out there and die for and play every game like it's my last, but we're talking about practice, man. How silly is that?"
Allen Iverson, basketball player

Space Saloon 2019

Office Kovacs

176C
109C
323C
2191C
170C
2285C
563C
191C

Cochella
2019
Office
Kovacs

Alles Ist Fiktion

Traumnovelle

Fictions are the narratives which articulate human civilisations' cosmogonies. They are the foundational myths which describe and explain the creation of the world. These narratives serve as social binders, providing sense and meaning to human enterprise and core values to guide collective and individual behaviours. These myths rely on a series of devices, in particular artistic and cultural forms of expression, in order to be passed down and reinforced throughout generations. One of these devices is, of course, architecture.

By giving form to fictions through space, which is tangible, architecture makes them appear more durable, more permanent, more true. Myths, as any other social construct, are overlaid in space in order to give it a meaning that is consistent with a certain narrative, while rites are the codified ways in which spaces are inhabited according to their accompanying myths. These uses of architecture simultaneously translate and perpetuate their underlying narratives.

This text investigates three forms of fictions—the fiction of religion and the use of spatial symbolism, the fiction of the State and its relation to identity, and the fiction of the country and its interdependencies with the territory. By highlighting recurring architectural themes or language and their varying fictions through historical architectural examples, it aims to highlight architecture's political role and its ability to reinforce, subvert, or rewrite existing fictions. In doing so, it hopes to raise awareness and calls out space makers to seize the narrative power of architecture in order to construct other possible futures.

"To build is to serve"
Hendrik Petrus Berlage

Alles Ist Architektur

In a 1968 publication in *BAU Magazine*, Hans Hollein proclaimed that everything which constitutes the physical world can be considered as architecture. "Architecture must be freed from buildings," he says. In this 30-page manifesto comprising a selection of images at different scales reminiscent of landscapes or buildings and a short paragraph of text, Hollein invites readers to extend their understanding of architecture. "Everything is architecture."

In turn, we proclaim that "everything is fiction." We believe that the role of the architect, beyond creating spaces to serve society, is to represent, criticize and, ultimately, offer alternative fictions to the ones

UFO, *Rebus Viventi all'Isolotto di Don Mazzi*, Florence, 1970-1971 which form the basis of our societies. The word "fiction" derives from the Latin verb *fingere*, which means handle, touch, caress, compose, curl, shape, feign, pretend, invent, picture, and imagine. Everything is fiction.

One of the preconceptions that we have inherited from the modern movement is that fiction draws us away from the more noble quest for truth. This idea of a hegemonic truth has been contradicted in many fields including hard sciences, yet the concept of truth is upheld by the idea of rationality, which is a reassuring illusion to architects.

In 1911, German philosopher Hans Vaihinger published *Die Philosophie des Als Ob* (The Philosophy of the "As if"), in which he shows that fiction is an operative tool used by all fields of investigation, and in particular mathematics and most scientific reasoning. Vaihinger's "As if" philosophy states that human beings not knowing the underlying truths of the world construct systems of thought and then assume that these match reality. He even states that we can only perceive those phenomena of which we have mastered the fictions. We behave "as if" the world matches our models. A strong admirer of mathematics, Vaihinger mostly uses references to mathematics and physics, but he also refers to this syllogism:

All men are mortal.
Socrates is a man.
Therefore, Socrates is mortal.

In this unique case, we attribute Socrates a fictional filter of analysis: "man." This category is a construct. There exists no general "man," as all men are individuals. This syllogism leads to a truth, which is that Socrates is mortal. According to Vaihinger, fictions bear a positive role because they contribute to identifying the truth.

By bringing to light the fictions which underline a series of some of history's most prevalent architectural projects, this essay aims to shed light on the evolutive nature of the societal fictions which saw them built. Fictions, therefore, appear as operative tools which shape and are shaped by political, religious, or any other social structure.

Everything is architecture.
Architecture is fiction.
Therefore, everything is fiction.

Changing My Religion

The Athenian Parthenon (430 BC) is considered to be one of the founding buildings of western architectural culture—although recent research led on the Sumerian people contradicts this. It can be considered the very essence of the white purity of European architecture, even though it was probably painted very vividly. This building is a temple dedicated to goddess Athena. Though most of us probably agree that Athena is one of the constitutive fictions of Ancient Greece, at that time, the Olympian Gods were considered a general truth and largely uncontested. When we use the word "fiction," we are tempted to associate it with terms such as "fake," "untruth," or "deception," which, in turn, question the authenticity of a work. In that sense, it is interesting to remind ourselves that Greek temples were the stone abstractions of historical wooden temples.

The Mosque-Cathedral of Córdoba, in southern Spain, was at first a Visigoth church (600) until it was divided in two halves to be shared with Muslims (710). It was then purchased by an emir and became solely a mosque (784) until a cathedral was constructed inside (1236) and it became Catholic. This building has been vested with numerous truths which cohabit and accommodate to the space.

Another building testifying to such an imbrication of beliefs is the Roman Pantheon. This antique building was first a pagan temple, then a Catholic church, and now a temple to mass tourism. Every architecture is constructed through fiction and its contradictions. The Pantheon is one of those buildings, which can accommodate various stories, and contributes to writing new ones.

Bruno Latour is one of the thinkers of sociology of scientific knowledge, which deals with the social conditions and effects of science and with the social structures and processes of scientific activity. To put things differently, we could say that sociology of scientific knowledge aims at reasserting the myths behind scientific processes. In his 1991 essay *We Have Never Been Modern*, Latour questions the differences between pre-modern and modern understandings of the world. Modernity assumes nature and culture as two opposing and contradictory forces. According to Latour, not only does this "rationality" of science not exist, but rather fiction and experiments are the founding elements of science. The first of our modern fictions is that of progress, which supposedly eases humanity towards a better future.

Thanks to Latour and other cultural studies, we now know that there is no universal truth. Each culture develops its own stories, its own myths that we should strive to identify and question. Humans are cultural animals, and architecture is a cultural product.

Birth of a Nation

The People's Hall is an unrealised project by the Nazi Third Reich architect Albert Speer. Its aim was to inscribe Germany in the long course of history. For this, Speer put forward his theory of ruins, asserting that, even thousands of years after the collapse of the Reich, these buildings would testify to the greatness of this empire. This project belongs to a long tradition of nascent nations inventing their history, inventing their fictions. In order to write this fiction, Speer draws his inspiration from classical architecture—almost as if a few columns were enough to bring to life an eternal people.

In his *Perverted Guide to Ideology*, Slovenian philosopher Slavoj Žižek uses Beethoven's 9th Symphony *Ode to Joy* to illustrate works which have supported very different, even contradictory, fictions. *Ode to Joy* was played at Adolf Hitler's birthday as well as during communist rallies. Today, it is the official anthem of the European Union and was lately used at Emmanuel Macron's investiture. According to Žižek, *Ode to Joy* is able to maintain its unity despite these contradictory readings because it withholds a deep contradiction of its own, embodied by a Turkish march which unexpectedly manifests at the end of the second movement of the piece.

Classical architecture has the same power as Beethoven's Turkish march: it embodies the hopes and dreams of authoritarian regimes from both extremes as well as democratic ideals. Architecture is an evolving fiction, coloured by the values it is expected to convey.

The Danteum is a monument dedicated to the Italian poet Dante Alighieri, designed by Giuseppe Terragni for the Rome World Fair in 1942. Its ambition was to promote the grandeur of Benito Mussolini's new fascist nation. The Italian rationalists were the architects at Mussolini's service, and they too referred to classical architecture, as well as fictions and myths to construct the Italy Mussolini dreamed of. Terragni's project relates Dante's *Divine Comedy*. The visitor follows the route from Hell to Heaven through the geometric composition of the space. Terragni transposes the poem into sequences, rhythms, and proportions. It is not an illustration of the poem; it is the poem.

As opposed to Speer's architecture, entangled in grandiose, Italian rationalist architecture is more specifically destined to host crowds—and not the abstraction of a crowd. The Casa del Fascio, constructed in 1936 by Terragni, was the headquarters of the fascist party in the small city of Como in northern Italy. It draws its references from the Palazzo Farnese, a Roman palace from the renaissance which is remarkable for its balanced geometry and strict proportions, both in facade and in plan. The Casa del Fascio references this historical building twice; it narrates a common history for Italy and offers an interpretation of a transparent regime through architecture that is receptive to its people. The facade and the plan, with their systems of emptiness, testify to this openness. In the background, a powerful fascist fiction lingers: a new man, freed from his chains, under a new, unified Italian nation.

Leaving the realm of epicness and going back to a fiction that is closer to home, to us, but that should also sound familiar to most people, there is the fiction of the Belgian Nation. This is not the story of the creation of this small country which, nearly 200 years on, is still structured around a monarch, but of the question of the reconstruction of its cities after World War I. The book *Resurgam*, published in 1985, sheds light upon the moment of reconstruction during which Belgium invented a new architectural myth for itself: that of the bourgeois mansion. Although it was an uncharacteristic housing typology, it was used as a founding block for new urban developments; the results of which is the Flemish-style pitched-roof house.

The reconstruction of a nation is a difficult task in that it requires the creation of a new and artificial identity based on historical myths.

This project is a characteristic strategy of the movement known as ARAU, which is an architectural movement from the eighties. Its members rose to oppose the so-called destruction of the historical fabric of the city. They proposed a project as a manifesto for continuing the construction of European cities based on the typology of bourgeois housing and classical architecture with the aim of making them more human. Their urban model refers to undefined dreams for a traditional, authentic, anti-modern and peaceful city. One of their leading thinkers, Léon Krier, indeed contributed to this dream by building a few residential suburbs in the United States. On the surface, ARAU opposed the international and transversal ideals of the modern movement by referring to the fiction of small medieval bourgeois towns. In reality though, the modern fictions were not challenged but merely camouflaged behind cute brick facades.

Along the line of urban fictions, the garden-cities that were implemented in Belgium following Ebenezer Howard's theories oppose the model of the industrial city, mother of all vices. The garden city offers a retreat in the countryside for working-class families, not in the form of an autarkic retreat but rather as a community organised around a civic centre. Consequently, the garden-city model was very soon stifled in Belgium based on the fear of the emergence of communist worker communities, also named "red suburbs."

Subjecting the Territory

Fictions are not only expressed through architectural objects, but are also embodied in landscapes, cities, and territorial planning.

"Atlantropa" was first presented by German architect Herman Sörgel in the twenties. This unrealised plan projected the construction of several massive dams across the Mediterranean Sea, resulting in a significant lowering of sea levels, thus creating new arable lands for agriculture, and allowing increased connections between Europe and Africa. It also planned on installing large-scale infrastructure connecting the two continents, hence facilitating trade. This project is a fiction, the fiction of two united continents. It is fascinating in the fact that it depicts an alternative future. It opens new lands of investigation and contests what we take for granted in international relations.

Across the Atlantic, Thomas Jefferson developed his grid system in 1796. Architect and President of the United States, Jefferson imagined a territorial management tool which reflected this new nation's democratic ideals. Jefferson's grid is applied all over the United States landscape and inscribes upon it the principle of equality. The grid, according to Jefferson, makes each point equal to all others. This system is tangible in many American cities, and still supports the discourse of the American dream and its equality of chances. However, the grid system can also convey the complimentary values of total control and alienation through extreme rationalisation. The exact same territorial typology expresses, in China, radically different values. The grid creates a hierarchy upon the emperor's territory by emanating from its centre, the Imperial Palace of Beijing. Each point is measured in relation to its distance from the centre. The grid, like any model, is fiction.

Alles Ist Fiktion

Everything is fiction, which means that all the elements which make up human societies have been constructed and, as such, can and should be questioned. Nothing is more frightening than the pretense of an absolute truth. Fictions can be deconstructed and rebuilt, which is why first we need to be aware of how they permeate our perceptions of the world. In the "post-truth" era, we might also call fiction "ultra-realism."

Fiction is present at every step of project-making. Every thought emerges from a particular individual's mind bearing the fictions of their culture and societies. The users of a space will in turn appropriate the space and layer it with their own fictions.

Alles ist Fiktion. Everything is fiction. There is no universal truth. Architecture is a cultural act and, as such, conveys its own fictions. Fiction is an operative device which allows us to question contemporaneity and it is a constructive device allowing us to impact our culture. It allows us to be aware of the cultural framework in which actions and ideas take place. Fictions are everywhere and we need more fictions in which we, actually, want to believe.

Everything is fiction.

ABOLISH
POLICE
NO JUSTICE
NO PEACE
BLACK
LIVES
MATTER

SMATTER
BLACK LIVES MATTER
BLACK LIVES MATT
BLACK LIVES MATTER
NO JUSTICE
NO PEACE
KNOW JUSTICE
KNOW PEACE

Zoom of a Zoom of a Zoom

Jimenez Lai

One Wilshire, an edifice located in Downtown Los Angeles, tells the fiction of office space inside a building with the appearance of an office building. Around the turn of the 21st century, One Wilshire became more of a data center than a clerical workplace for people. As we transition from processing paperwork with stacks of physical paper into a society where data is digital, the idea of storing "paperwork" gradually becomes an action without the participation of humans.[1]

COVID-19, a global pandemic that transformed how people work, emptied out downtowns of many major metropolitan areas around the world into husks of office buildings without humans. Furthermore, the idea of digital paperwork became the only contactless paperwork that matters in a new and mysophobic reality—all administrative processes are kept as non-physical as possible. The office meetings are now on Zoom, framed within screens that zoom in and out of the private spaces where residential activities happen. One Wilshire is not an office building—yet the digital matter that makes up the human bureaucratic functions are now passed through and stored inside of a building that looks like an office space.

As a new reality stranger than fiction, the world we live in now collapses layers of experiences that are simultaneously factual and fictional. This short story, "Zoom of a Zoom of a Zoom", zooms in and out the spaces that used to be real, but are still real in an immaterial way, omnipresent between multiple scales.

1 Varnelis Kazys, *The Centripetal City*. See https://www.cabinetmagazine.org/issues/17/varnelis.php.

UFO, Investigation of the control of the State over the territory, 1971-1973, Patrizia Cammeo/Riccardo Foresi Archives, Florence

The data center is inside of One Wilshire

One Wilshire is inside the skyline of DTLA

The skyline of DTLA is inside a window

This window is inside of a room

This room is inside of an architectural model

This architectural model is inside a photo shoot

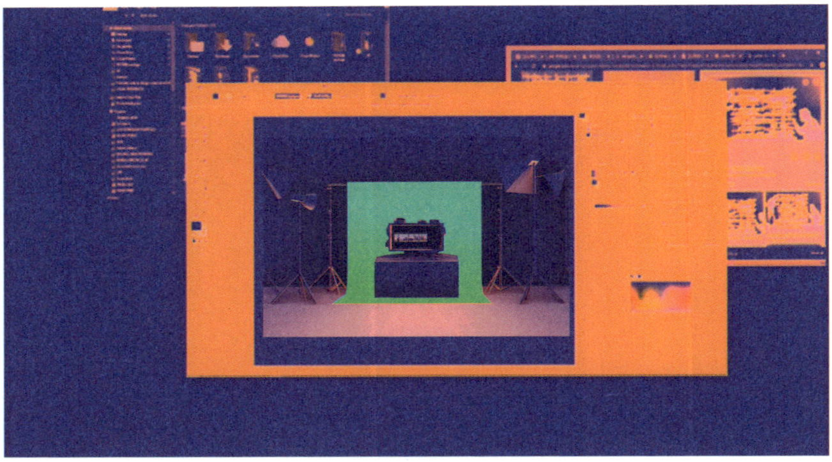

This photo shoot is inside of a computer

This computer is on a desk

This desk is inside an office

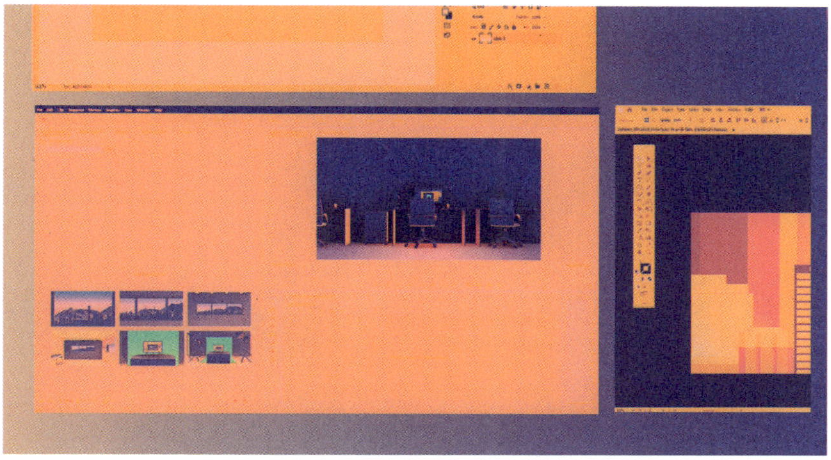

This office is a file

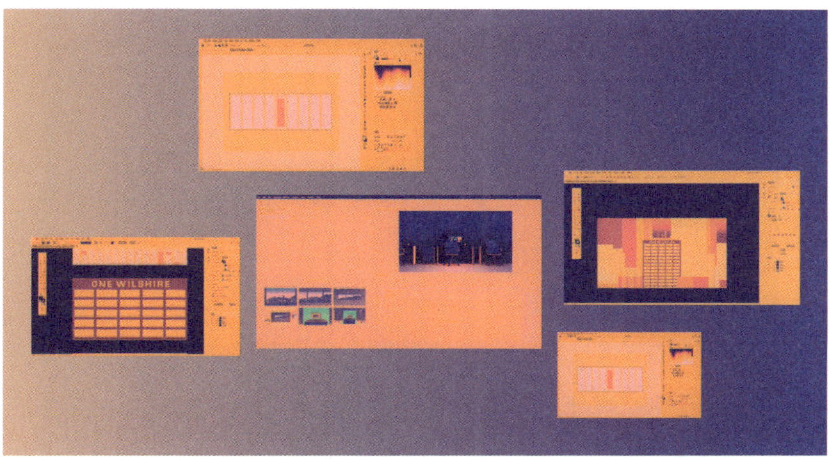

This file is on the cloud

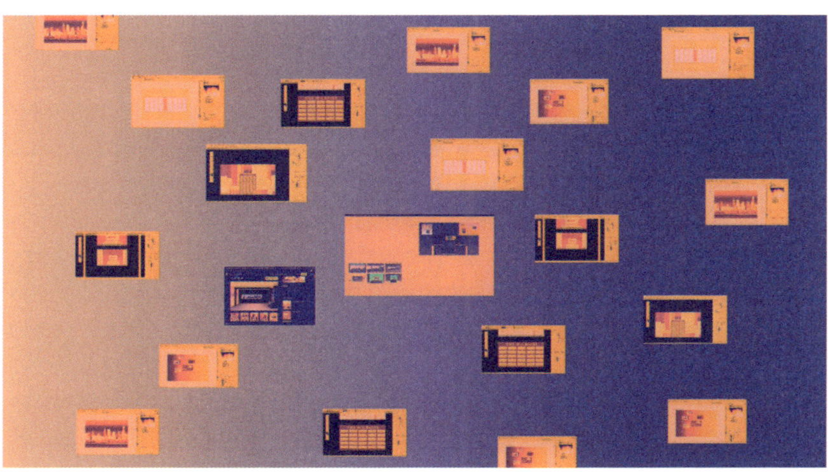

This cloud is a network of data

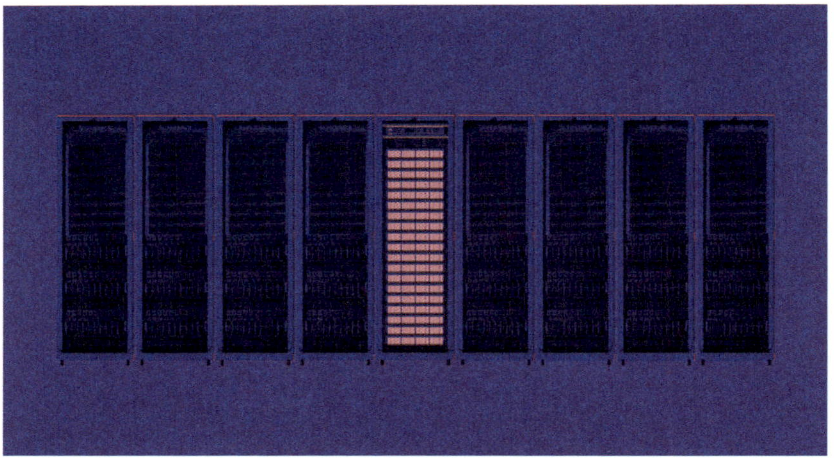

The data is inside a server rack

This server rack is in a stack of server rooms

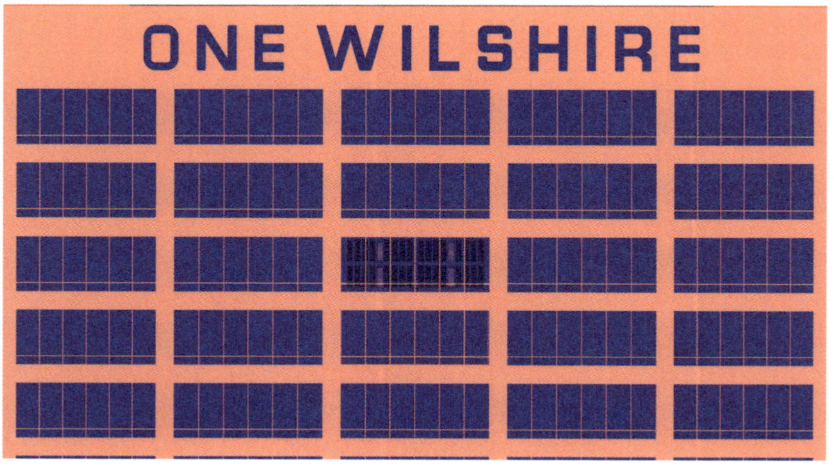

These server rooms are inside of a building

The building is a data center inside of One Wilshire

One Wilshire is inside the skyline of DTLA

The skyline of DTLA is inside a window

A.N.
A.N.A.S.

Peter Behrbohm
and SONDER

"Yesterday, a very official looking letter was received by public administrations and institutions. The sender is the so-called 'Sonderschutzstelle.' The letter details instructions for today, Friday, in the area of Jena. It advises citizens on how to protect their ears in preparation for particular dangers. Today there was a beeping all over the city. Various houses were equipped with acoustic devices that look like big switches. The loud beeping can be heard all over the city. So far, we cannot tell who placed those acoustic devices. We will sort this out."

From Steffi Koppe, Federal Police Inspector in Jena.
(German police official in a public radio transmission, November 2012)

We work in public places just as street sweepers or policemen do. In Germany, there is an agency called *Ordnungsamt*, which might be best translated as "Tidiness Agency." SONDER often appears to be an affiliate, meticulously taking care of sublime errors that others try to erase from the world.

We intervene in public spaces and discourses with obstacles and counter-narratives. We implant complex chains of events into everyday life so passersby and spectators can stop and think, unable to tell what just happened and how to classify their observations. Did something happen at all? Were those people just doing their job? Was it mere coincidence?

Our aim is to expose questionable developments and conflicts hiding in normality. We therefore change aspects of the scenery to create unexpected situations.

These situations are not presented as art. They do not take place in galleries or museums. We ourselves do not consider the constructed realities art, either. The term is merely used to gain funding for future operations. As one cannot erect buildings without permission or install defective devices, somebody designing conflicts might be easily considered insane or even a terrorist.

UFO, Investigation of the control of the State over the territory, 1971-1973, Patrizia Cammeo/Riccardo Foresi Archives, Florence

We prefer to refer to our practice as contextual play. Our mission can only be accomplished if it incorporates a certain degree of joy and humour.

Coming up with new rules for the old game is the purpose of our play. Reality is what you make it.

SONDER is your partner for special operations. We design conflicts and unsolve your problems.

Driving through Italy in the late sixties, UFO stumbles upon a small nondescript building that appears to be a minimalist archetype. Subsequently the group finds similar structures throughout the country—not copies, rather loose relatives of the first—well maintained yet unoccupied miniature architectures. Blind, locked, painted red and entitled with the same cryptic abbreviation: A.N.A.S.

Reality

What do we know of the towns and cities we move through each day? There are good reasons to assume that those apartment buildings contain apartments that are furnished with wardrobes and people, office towers contain offices that are full of white collars the same way that factories are filled with machines and blue collars. People drive around in trains and cars with destinations and reasons and all the pipes, cables and infrastructures are doing nothing but serving their purpose. Whatever is not in working order is either dismantled or fixed sooner or later.

Hic Sunt Dracones

In the past, explorers were eager to explore the areas of the world for which they had no maps—places that ancient atlases depicted crowded by sea monsters. *Hic sunt dracones* means "here be dragons." The empty spaces on the maps were subsequently eliminated, but since then we have begun to build our own spaces. Gray ones—nondescript boxes of any size inhabit cities, harbours, and countryside around the globe. There is no visible difference between furniture stores, data centres, high-rack warehouses,

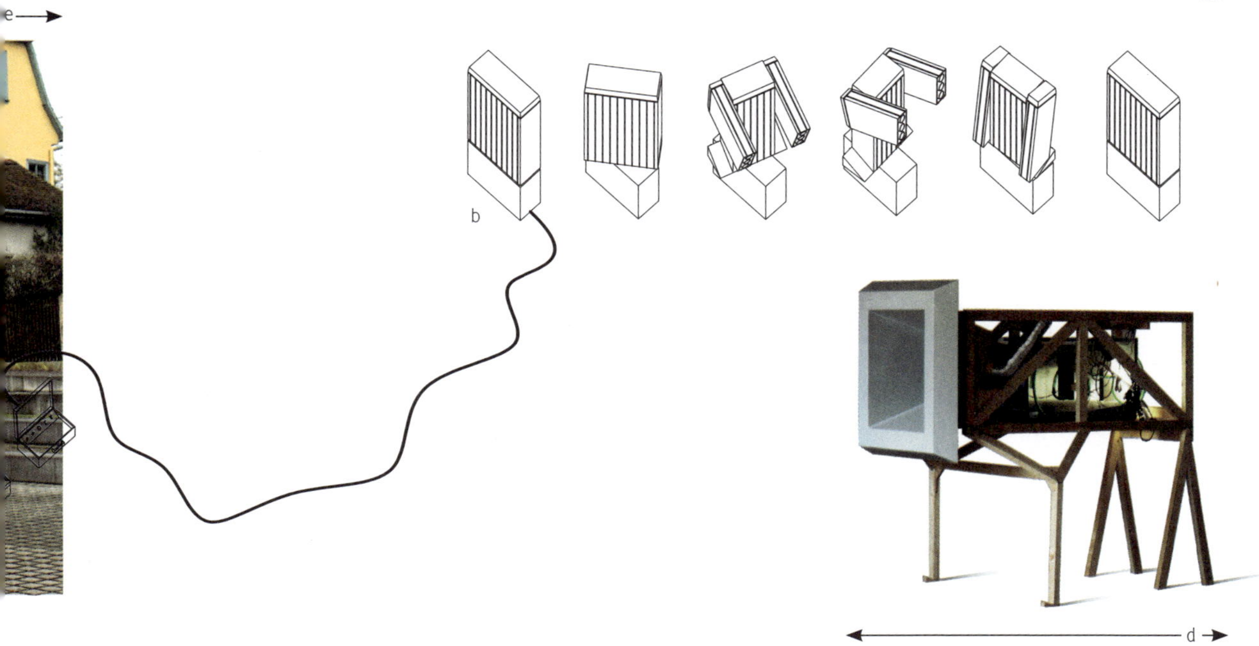

meat-processing plants, maximum-security prisons, cookie factories, or refugee camps. Animals that used to inhabit the meadows have disappeared from manicured gardens to find new habitats inside the multi-layered facades of single-family dwellings, lining up like false pearls on a cheap thread.

Life-sized Tunnel

Life is not a TV show—and yet it is exactly that. Whether it is apartments, offices, renovated old towns, whether it is national parks, farms, or mountain panoramas—the spaces in which we move are increasingly constituted by their surfaces. The backdrop of the daily journey of each individual could be seen as a tunnel, painted from the inside with what we see. A winding gut, a hollow worm with a beautiful skin. Although at first glance it might resemble a woodworm carving its burrow into a tree, it is quite the opposite. Hardly anyone questions the daily tunnel's walls or even tries to dig into it.

While it used to be possible to assume that a rock was made of rock, that a forest was a forest, and that the sea was filled with water and fish, it is no longer that simple. What looks somewhat like wood today is made from plastic, what looks like stone might be glass on a wooden substructure, oceans are made of garbage, and mountain peaks may be defensive structures disguised as rocks. Increasingly, surfaces are mere backdrops for daily life. Well-hidden and secured wallpaper doors lead from the postcard world to its back end.

Mission

As the planet turns into a man-made environment dressed in veneers and mirroring facades, we emphasize the notion of sea monsters. We observe everyday life to intervene in public spaces and its routines, installing disruptive implants with common textures. Construction sites, garages, bank branches, kiosks, rental scooters, castle facade samples, telecommunication boxes. Everything can act as a disguise for potential action.

A.N.A.S.

Infrastructure spaces are of particular interest to us. Infrastructure is everywhere, linking the fragmented world, hidden in plain sight. Like UFO's A.N.A.S. roadhouses, originally built by the Italian highway maintenance agency,

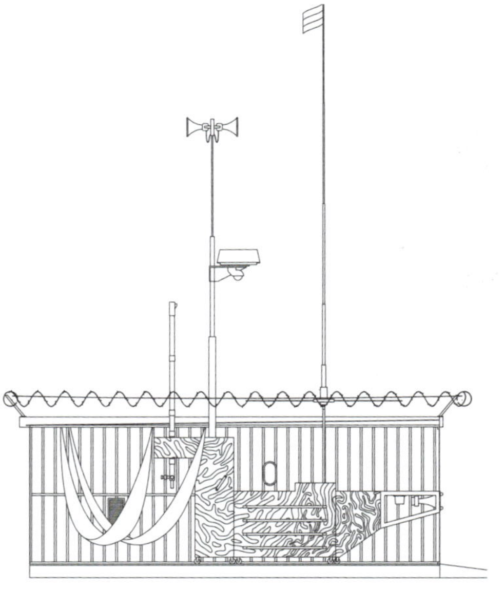

e

infrastructure is laid out as some sort of "Architecture of Bureaucracy." Within these grey zones scattered all over the maps, we are testing future conflicts by installing speculative infrastructures.

Direct Action

Our aim is to give everyday life a slight jolt, to add a hiccough to the busy hum of present times. Rather than putting works into museums or galleries, we are concerned with changing people's reality in a way only planners, architects, or even terrorists can, in order to show that reality, as well as the whole current "system," is nothing "God-given," but constructed in the same way a film set is trying to convey seriousness.

Just like UFO's A.N.A.S. roadhouses and their various remakes, our interventions claim to be part of the ever-enlarging sphere of infrastructure that—instead of quietly performing its service—is made of Trojan obstacles beginning to take on lives of their own as soon as the sun sets.

a) *Verberge*
Peter Behrbohm, intervention, Berlin 2010
bottle-recycling bank, wood, truck tarpaulin, camping stove, tableware, coffee, water
160x160x175cm

Verberge (German: *verbergen* = to hide; *Herberge* = hotel) is a puristic living space, hidden under the magic cover of one of Berlin's 5000 bottle-recycling tanks. The size is interesting, because it seems to be as big as a structure can get before being considered architecture. Its heart is a multifunctional floor-module, which can be expanded to body size to offer enough dry space to sleep, store luggage, and cook. A periscope folds down from the ceiling to see whether the coast is clear. Every day, thousands of city cleaners cut their way through the city. They do their very best to preserve certain elements of the city, while rigorously erasing others. Regulations and speculations define what has to vanish and what may remain: that which is considered sufficiently official looking is thus cleansed of the debris that is not. By adopting this official city vocabulary, *Verberge* secretly gains bureaucratic legitimacy and was frequently used from August till late

b

December 2010, while standing without permission right at the edge of Alexanderplatz, one of the central squares of Berlin.

b) *Transformator*
Peter Behrbohm, intervention, Berlin
2013-ongoing
wood, steel, motors, suitcase, signal rockets
27x80x130cm

Transformator is the first device of its kind introducing an all-new executive strategy. Its mission is to restrain police violence in the near future. After all, it's the human factor that consistently leads to bad decisions and bloodshed without cause. A central board will hereafter decide on the operation of armed machinery.

Disguised as an electric substation, *Transformator* is tested in the streets of Berlin and Germany as a fully operational autonomous rocket launcher. Passersby are unsure what is about to happen when a suited gentleman arrives at one of the grey boxes that are to be found all over the city, plugs in the service computer that is built into a suitcase and runs a routine check of the device's active range of motion. The electric box spins around, unfolds its arms in quick movements, and suddenly six 44 millimiter-barrels are targeting neighbouring buildings before transforming back into a grey electric box. The gentleman returns the machine to its hibernation mode, unplugs his computer, and leaves the site, heading for the next *Transformator* on his list.

c) *Fahnenflucht*
Peter Behrbohm & Anton Steenbock, intervention, Berlin 2013-ongoing
aluminium tubes, rope, microcontroller, flag
size changes

After the erasure of the socialist Palace of the Republic, the reconstruction of the Prussian Castle has just been completed. During the construction, a monumental sample facade informs the public about the future castle. But then a detail causes confusion among tourists and Prussian patriots. For a daily flag ceremony, a German flag with the socialist emblem is being hoisted automatically in graceful slowness. For one minute, it flies in the wind until proceeding back to half mast, hiding in the strangely royal town house.

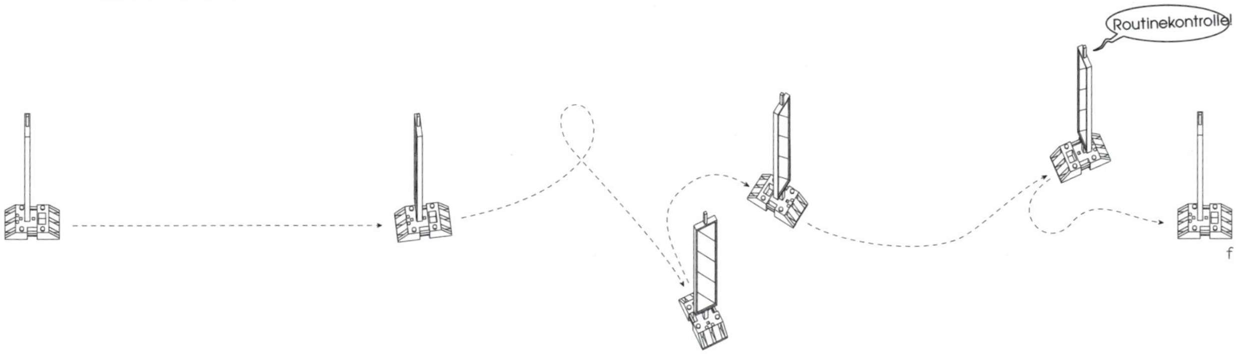

d) *Bank*
Peter Behrbohm, intervention, Newcastle upon Tyne 2014
wood, aluminium, glass, water, lamps, loudspeaker, fish
approx. 1200x400x160cm

Another bank has just opened at the edge of a medium-sized city, on a minor arterial road. The building itself is strikingly nondescript. Glowing capital letters do their best to generate integrity. "Money is faith," that's what they say. And as if to underline the statement, a polished cash machine and a set of surveillance cameras protrude out of the wall right beneath the letters. This, after all, looks like a bank. And obviously, that is what this business is all about. Potential customers might be irritated as it is not their PIN request, but goldfish swimming in the cash machine's terminal and the surveillance cameras start talking to them.

e) *Habbakuk*
Peter Behrbohm & Anton Steenbock, intervention, Jena 2018
metal garage, wood, aluminium, conifers, antennas, radar, radio device, surveillance cameras, loudspeaker, periscope, flag, stone grout, caterpillar drive, motors, tractor seats
600x600x800cm

Under the guise of a regular German double garage, a monitoring station is erected overnight. With the help of various instruments on the rooftop, any activities in the surrounding environment are recorded and evaluated by experts using a terminal inside. A vehicle disguised as a pile of sand and emitting loud pigeon coos leaves the garage every day to conduct inconspicuous observation rides within the neighbourhood. In 1998, there were already some noises coming from another garage in the suburbs of Jena. Inside—two gentlemen and a young woman were working on a box, which they eventually place in front of the city's theatre, exactly where the monitoring station is set up 20 years later. The box turned out to be a bomb, missing a detonator. As police officers stormed their garage in 1998, the bomb makers went underground.

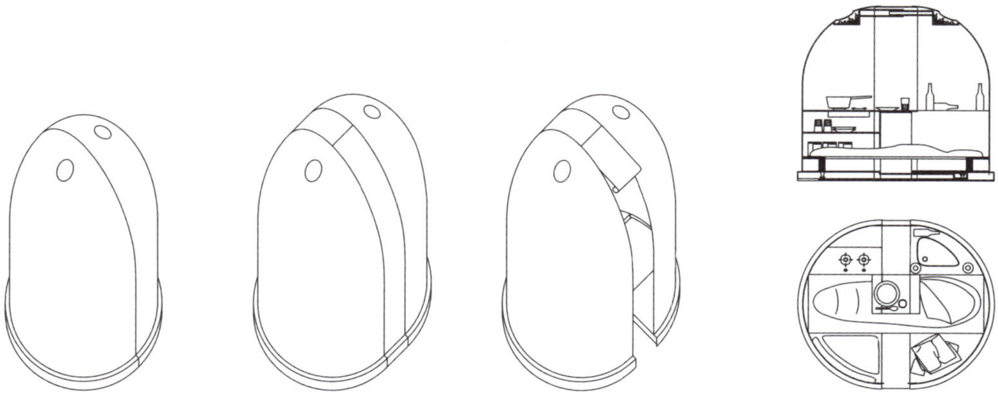

a

Under observation by and strange protection of German secret service agents, they murdered immigrants throughout Germany in the following years. When they blew their cover, the group became known internationally as the National Socialist Underground.

f) *Routinekontrolle*
Peter Behrbohm, intervention, Lemgo 2019
wood, toy tank, rubber, microcontroller, loudspeaker, acrylic paint
approx. 40x80x150cm

Routinekontrolle (routine check) is a self-propelled replica of a German standard construction site barrier, type K1. According to estimations, there are about as many K1s standing on German motorways as Germans chasing each other on tarmac.

As all German citizens are well trained in following the K1's basic instructions, this self-propelled version is highly likely to lead the country into a bright future.

Caution: oncoming traffic.

e →

We are about

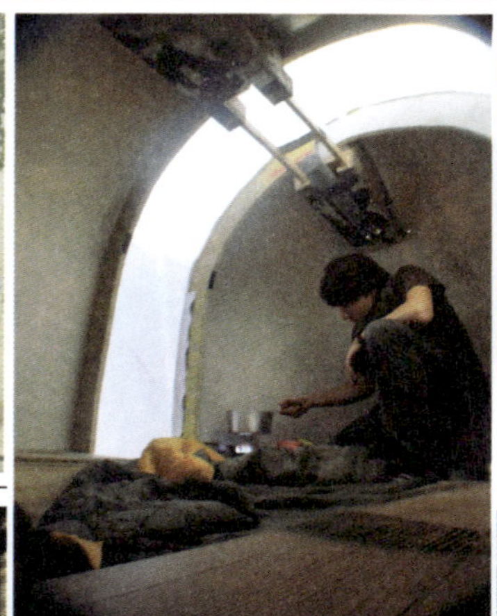

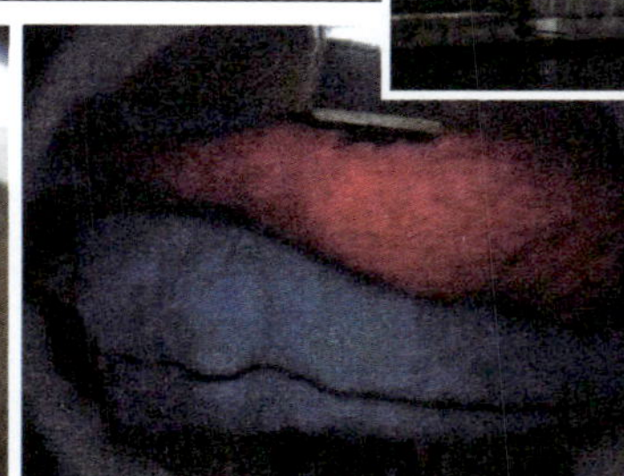

BANK

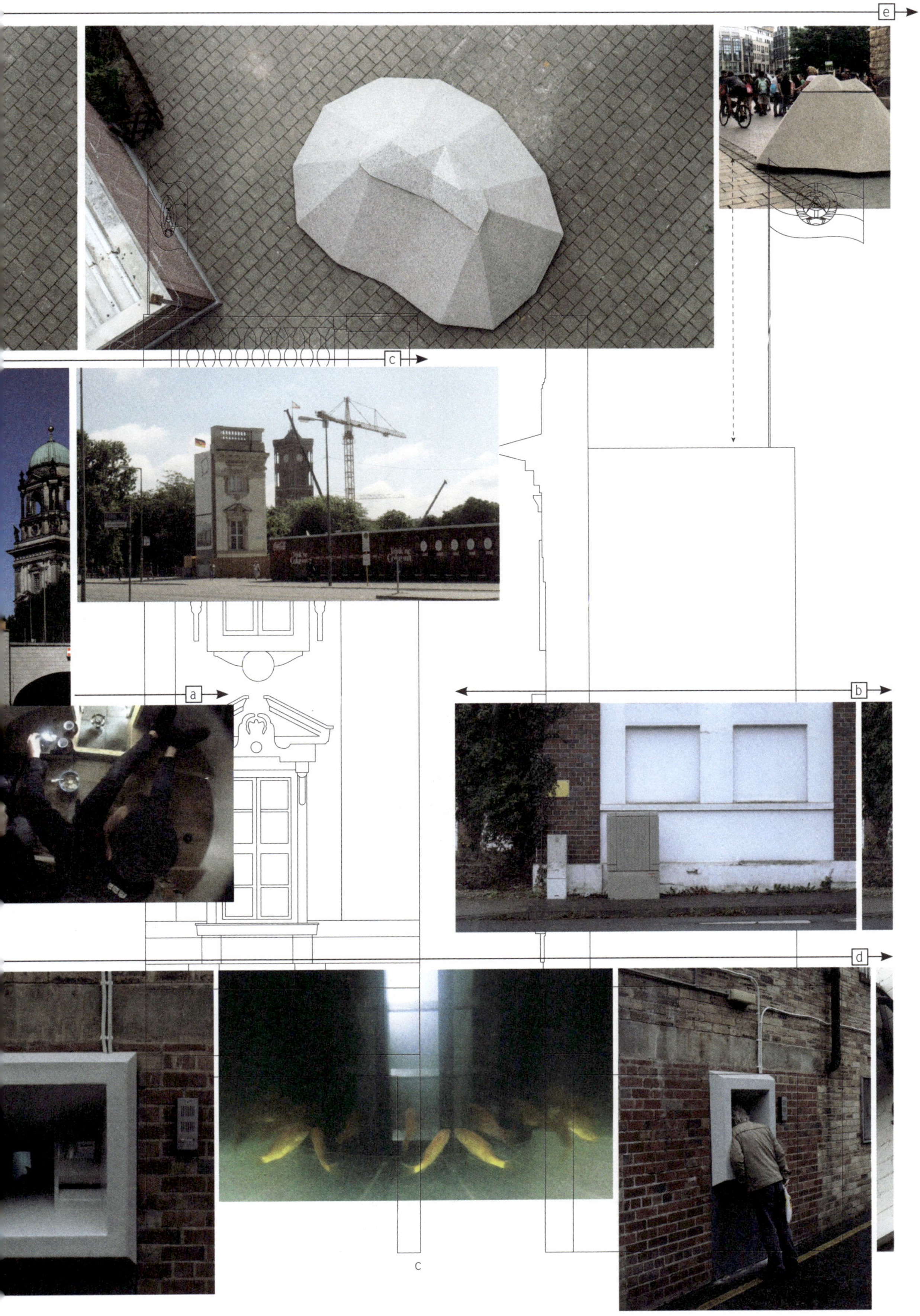
e
c
a
b
d
c

BANK

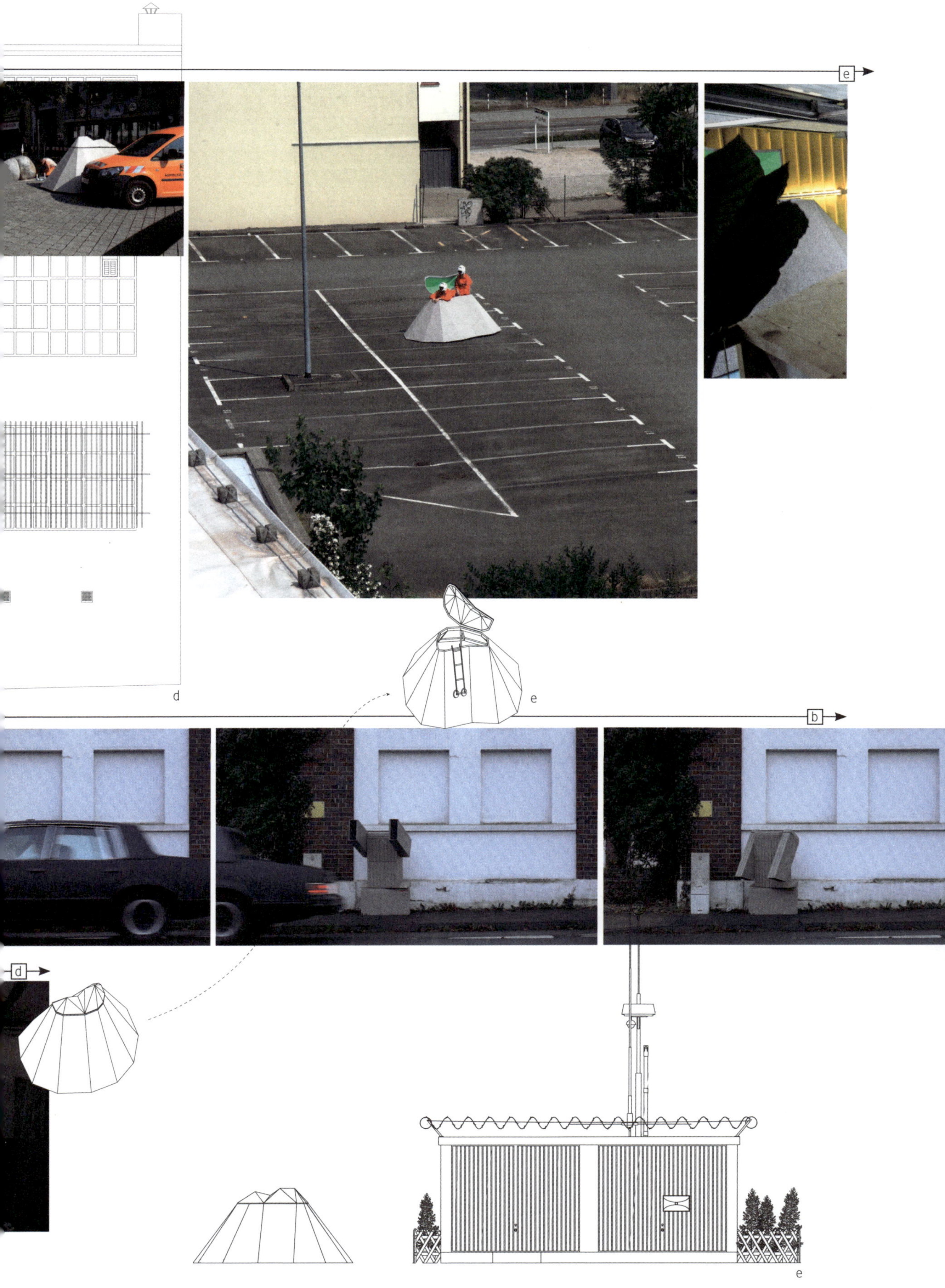

e
d
e
b
d
e

Scale, Displace, Replicate

(ab)Normal

Even today, in the context of the innumerable symbols that distinguish contemporary society, icons prove to be a decisive means used by individuals to communicate and to identify with what are true communities. Over the course of the last few decades, from the artistic avant-gardes to architecture,[1] the change in scale of these signs, starting with the colossal, has been widely employed to evaluate their relevance and their nature as an eloquent device. Examples of such alterations in size, from enormous statues of women to buttons as big as lakes, can by now be found all over the globe, becoming an emblematic testimony to a state of affairs.[2]

Given the role that these semantic procedures play in the system of communication and language, the modification of dimensional parameters can be considered a way of undermining the hierarchical structure of society. Originally tried out by the advertising industry of mass society, altering the size of icons has established itself as a sophisticated tactic of political marketing, to the point where it has become a weapon in what we could call a genuine psychological war. It is clear that manipulation of an object's dimensional relations amplifies the impact of the messages that it conveys to the emotional unconscious of the user, going as far as to trigger primordial reactions of attraction or repulsion that are hard to control. The premises of the experiments with the manipulation of icons can be found in the studies of Edward Bernays,[3] considered the pioneer of a psychological approach to marketing. The nephew of Sigmund Freud, Bernays was perhaps the first to utilise translation of the meaning of icons as a vehicle of expression, with the precise aim of inoculating the collective imagination of American society in the period after World War I with unconscious desires. The "Torches of Freedom" campaign[4] launched by Bernays in 1928 with the objective of encouraging the consumption of cigarettes by women, is a perfect example of the experiments conducted on the psychosocial impact of the advertising medium. Until the end of the twenties, it was in fact considered socially unacceptable for women to smoke cigarettes and viewed as a sign of immorality, partly due to the fact that the image of the cigarette in a woman's mouth was perceived as explicitly pornographic. With "Torches of Freedom," Bernays put into practice what he had learned from psychology: he disconnected the cylindrical geometry of the cigarette from its presumed resemblance to the male phallus and turned the paradigm on its head by persuading potential female consumers that buying cigarettes would acquire them a

UFO, *Dollaro lamp*, wedding of Michelangelo Caponetto and Dominique Papi, Florence, 1972, Patrizia Cammeo/Riccardo Foresi Archives, Florence masculine role; he made, when all is said and done, cigarettes a means of emancipation.

Thus, Bernays became the forerunner of a profession, that of public relations, which relies extensively on the power of icons, contributing to the formation of what can be seen today as an out-and-out industry of the production of images. With a logistical system so broad and pervasive that it is no longer restricted to the surface of the globe but extends to the immeasurable one of the web, the environmental impact of this industry is now so great that it can be considered on a par with any traditional polluting enterprise.[5]

(ab)Normal intends to examine the state of the art in the political use of iconography through the analysis of three case studies: replicas of the Unabomber's cabin, the beatification of Carlo Acutis and the project for the new Turkish Ministry of Defence.

Displace: the Unabomber's Cabin

After leaving his teaching post at Berkeley in 1971, where he had been a professor of Mathematics, Theodore John Kaczynski embraced a way of life characterised by silence and isolation, moving to the countryside near the city of Lincoln (Montana). Kaczynski, aka the Unabomber, built a small wooden cabin without electricity or running water and little more than ten square metres in size in which he took refuge, fleeing the consumer society he hated. Kaczynski taught himself survival skills that would allow him to live in a self-sufficient way. His obsessive reading of Jacques Ellul's book *The Technological Society*[6] provided Kaczynski with the grounds for his formulation of a harsh critique of the hyper-technological nature of contemporary society. Out of this came the Unabomber and his manifesto *Industrial Society and Its Future*.[7]

The cabin consisted of a single room with a wooden framework ranged along its perimeter. Inside it a bed, bookshelves, a desk, and a wood-burning stove defined an elementary living space, all of it built out of the wood of the surrounding fir trees. In essence, the cabin was a spatial representation of the ideology that motivated the first eco-terrorist in history.[8]

The domesticity of the cabin became a symbol of its inventor and builder's fight against technology, transcending the figure of Kaczynski himself.

A condensation of the idea of an anarcho-primitive lifestyle that Kaczynski promoted through his writings and his attacks, this cabin has become a fetishised testimony to the Unabomber's physical as well as ideological detachment from American culture. The Unabomber's cabin has consolidated the iconography of a model of an untamed, anarchic, and anti-urban life in strong contrast to the technological and logistical structure of the American postal system on which Kaczynski himself relied to wage his campaign of terror.

In the institutionalised setting of the headquarters of the FBI, in museums or on the sets of popular TV series, the various displacements and replicas of the cabin have exorcised the icon of a natural, wild, and anarchic America and above all one in opposition to the rational and urban America of the metropolis. As these numerous replicas attest, this operation can be seen as the debunking of the founding myth of the United States, that of free and untamed adventurers, and at the same time as an acclamation of it.

Replicate: the Perfect Copy of a Saint

Carlo Acutis was a devout young Catholic who died of leukaemia at the age of fifteen. He dedicated his youth to his faith and applied his computer programming skills to the development of a website that he used

1. Robert Kusmirowski, *Unacabine* (replica of the cabin by Theodore John Kaczynski, Unabomber), New Museum, New York, 2008

to catalogue Eucharistic miracles. The figure of Acutis became the symbol of a youthful Church and his fame spread not only throughout Italy but also internationally.

Ten years after his death, in 2016, Acutis was beatified by the Church and his body, subject to inevitable decomposition, has been reconstructed with parts in silicone.[9] The semi-artificial replica of Acutis' body, on public display in Assisi, appears contradictory in the light of the hagiographic tradition of Catholicism. It presents a sugar-coated image of a youthful Church, at its ease in an ever more consumption-oriented and technology-dependent society. At the same time it reflects the system of beliefs of that same Church, founded on a series of supernatural phenomena, such as the presumed perfect state of preservation of Acutis' remains. Inside a glass reliquary, in fact, the body has been put on display wearing Adidas gym clothes, jeans and Nike trainers, presenting the idealised icon of a 21st century teenager with a passion for technology. The Nike logo and the recognisable Adidas stripes take up roughly the same amount of space as the copperplate engraving of the *nomen sacrum IHS* set on the glass surface that separates the body from visitors. In Acutis' corpse, the brands of consumer society encounter traditional Catholic iconography and fuse with it, creating an unexpected means of signification able to speak to a new generation of young Catholics.

Scale: the Long Shadow of the Crescent Moon

At the gates of Ankara, in an out-of-the-way place on the outskirts of the capital, President Erdogan is having a new complex built, one that is conceived as a means of boosting the military and logistical power of Turkey. Located on a site measuring around 13,000 hectares, it will house the Ministry of Defence and the headquarters of the country's land, air and naval forces.[10]

The project envisages the construction of a crescent-shaped building set at the centre of a gigantic pentagon. Another star-shaped structure will house a reception centre for visitors, completing a layout that slavishly replicates the Turkish flag. Although limited in number and often hard to find, images of the "crescent moon" point to two precise objectives: on the one hand, the need of a State like Turkey, a hegemonic power in the ecosystem of Middle Eastern countries, to assert itself as the nation to turn to, a role it had lost with the fall of the Ottoman Empire—a constant geopolitical strategy, pursued ever since the birth of Turkey as a nation; on the other, the choice to erect the buildings within a pentagonal perimeter is undoubtedly part of a strategy of re-branding, aimed at upgrading the perception of Turkey in diplomatic circles and openly taking its cue from the Pentagon of the United States. In addition, legend has it that the origins of the crescent moon, first on the Ottoman flag and then on the Turkish one, can be traced back to the founding myth of Mehmed II, the sultan who conquered Constantinople, declaring the end of the Eastern Roman Empire and therefore of Western hegemony over the East.

Erdogan himself has declared that the new complex "will strike fear into our enemies with its standing and give confidence to our friends." In this sense, the icons of Erdogan's complex are part of a shameless strategy of political marketing and psychological warfare aimed at consolidating the position of the president himself following the failed coup of 2016 and "rivalling the Pentagon." And yet behind the clumsiness of this attempt to merge two icons that have their roots in military power, a far more complex reality emerges: the rehabilitation of a founding myth is an expedient for stimulating the sense of belonging to a tribe, and in the case of Ankara, to a nation.

Conclusions

It is clear that we are immersed in a dimension that communicates almost exclusively by means of images that are transformed, magnified, or deformed. As Peter Szendy argues, to the production of images corresponds a production line of value, accessible through analyses that take into consideration basic parametric characteristics, like the compression of the image, its format, its size and its RGB components, but also anticipatory aspects, such as the potential popularity of an image on the social network used for its circulation. From this emerges a purely economic dimension of the image for which Szendy uses the neologism "iconomie,"[11] i.e. a blend of the terms "icon" and "economy." Thus, the conscious manipulation of icons assumes the connotations of a strategy aimed at upsetting the status quo. From the replicas of the Unabomber's cabin to Acutis' "branded" corpse to the clumsiness of the colossal icons of power imagined by Erdogan, the examples presented in this essay show how the intuitions of the radical architects, and specifically the displacement and dimensional manipulation of icons, have been taken up and digested by the market. In the total absence of any alternative to the dominant way of thinking, the transformation of icons has become one of the main tools employed in the dissemination of propaganda, powerful enough to rejuvenate ancient institutions verging on obsolescence, reposition roles on the geopolitical scene and abate the cultural impact of the most peculiar phenomenon of terrorism in America by exorcising and watering down its message.

2. The mortal remains of Blessed Carlo Acutis, Sanctuary of the Spoliation, Assisi

3. Project for the new headquarters of the Turkish Ministry of Defense (Crescent Star), Ankara, 2021-2023

1 Stefano Pezzato, 'Ufo', in Pino Brugellis, Gianni Pettena and Alberto Salvadori (eds.), *Utopie radicali. Archizoom, Remo Buti, 9999, Gianni Pettena, Superstudio, UFO, Zziggurat* (Macerata: Quodlibet, 2017), pp. 246-275.

2 Niall Patrick Walsh, 'Apple is Building a $1 Billion Campus in Austin, Texas', *ArchDaily*, 29 December 2018.

3 Larry Tye, *The Father of Spin: Edward L. Bernays and the Birth of Public Relations* (New York: Owl Books, 2002).

4 Edward L. Bernays, *Propaganda* (New York: Horace Liveright, 1928; reprint with an introduction by Mark Crispin Miller, New York: IG Publishing, 2005).

5 James Glanz, 'Power, Pollution and the Internet', *The New York Times*, 23 September 2012. See https://www.nytimes.com/2012/09/23/technology/data-centers-waste-vast-amounts-of-energy-belying-industry-image.html.

6 Jacques Ellul, *The Technological System* (Eugene, OR: Wipf and Stock, 2018).

7 Theodore John Kaczynski, 'Industrial Society and Its Future', *Washington Post*, Supplement, 22 September 1995.

8 Giuseppe Gagliano, *Il ritorno alla madre terra. L'utopia verde tra ecologia radicale ed ecoterrorismo* (Trento: UNI Service, 2010).

9 Ilaria Quattrone, 'Carlo Acutis, Il Beato di internet: Cosa è successo al corpo del ragazzo', *Milano Fanpage*, 5 October 2020. See https://www.fanpage.it/milano/carlo-acutis-il-beato-di-internet-cosa-e-successo-al-corpo-del-ragazzo.

10 Matthew Loh, 'Turkey is building its own, bigger version of the Pentagon meant to span 135 million square feet and support about 15,000 personnel', *Insider*, 1 September 2021. See https://www.insider.com/turkey-builds-its-version-the-pentagon-erdogan-135-million-sqft-2021-9.

11 Peter Szendy (ed.), *Le Supermarché du visible* (Paris: Éditions de Minuit, 2017). English ed., *The Supermarket of the Visible: Toward a General Economy of Images* (New York: Fordham University Press, 2019).

IHS

Carpets as Environments

Parasite 2.0

Incipit

This text is a stream of ideas that emerged from a recorded dialogue between the members of our group which centred on the concept of Environment as it has established itself in the context of contemporary art. Taking as a starting point the work of the American artist Allan Kaprow, who mastered the concept by applying it to his practice, this stream of ideas looks at some of the most important references in our work, from Hakim Bey's *Temporary Autonomous Zone* to Johan Huizinga's *Homo Ludens*. The ideas are consequent, numbered from the first to the sixth, and have not been subjected to an intrusive editing. Each idea is expressed by one of the members of our group. During the recording we realised that the simple act of sitting on a carpet created an Environment. The carpet defined, with its borders between inside and outside, an area of exception able to host a range of actions, a space with subversive characteristics. That carpet lies at the origin of a project of carpets called *Hypersizing*. Their decorations and shapes have been drawn from a catalogue of CAD patterns and blocks usually employed in the representation of architecture to define materials, spaces and their technical equipment. Halftone images of construction materials like bricks and thermal-acoustic insulators, and symbols linked to the installation of electrical wiring and building site machinery, form patterns that, as in an architectural section, define a space and its features. Historically, the carpet has always defined another space, be it of prayer or idleness, or even of the definition of political and social hierarchies. In our understanding of its meaning, the carpet becomes a representation of materials and spaces in lines that, by themselves, define an architecture now elevated to the status of an Environment or a *Temporary Autonomous Zone* in which to dream of "possible worlds."

I

The concept of Environment, in the sense of which we wish to speak, is the one used by the artist Allan Kaprow to define his works. To describe a new way of conceiving artistic expression he needed to use a special term, different from those of painting or sculpture that had already found acceptance at the beginning of the 20th century, in order to appropriate it and turn it into something else. His Environments are installations that in a certain sense need to be not just observed, but inhabited, experienced, touched, soiled. They are living spaces that change over time, that constantly take on different forms, that evolve. Perhaps the most emblematic is his mound of tyres. There is a significant aspect of play. He said himself that his Environments "are generally quiet situations, existing for one or for several persons to walk or crawl into, lie down, or sit in." To me, they say something quite different. They are more like chaotic situations. I picture a party. But then I ask myself in what way an Environment in the sense given to it by Kaprow differs from any habitable space or place of amusement and any time that is free from actions to which we assign a financial and economic value.

UFO, *Coccoina*, Piazza Santo Stefano, Bologna, 1972

II

I believe that, in our minds, the moment we think of the sense that Kaprow gave to the concept of Environment, an automatic mechanism is triggered that makes us connect it directly with another concept that was central to his artistic production: the Happening. I consider the two concepts inseparable. The former refers to a space; the latter to an action. The two fundamental elements needed to bring something into being, to create a moment. And out of their linking comes a result, whatever it might be. For this reason, I believe that, if we think of Kaprow's Environment, we think straight away of the chaos that can arise in a particular period of time through the actions of a series of people who may not have set themselves any goal, but who share energy and space in the same moment.

A third element not mentioned by Kaprow, but which I consider equally fundamental, is the freedom that can bring any of these Environments to life. The freedom to interpret the space, its use, its function. But also the freedom to give rise to something that in other regulated contexts—by factors of every kind—could not occur. Perhaps this is why we separate Kaprow's Environment from, for example, that of our home; because it is part of our routine and so we don't see it as a new space in which to experiment. Perhaps the new context pushes us towards a new result? I don't know. It is also true that, while I am speaking of this, I immediately think of the fact that the walls of our home can be our greatest personal utopia, where anything can happen: utopia on the scale of the sofa.

III

Perhaps another component of this concept that we can add is precisely its temporary character. Perhaps artistic experiences of this type, exactly because they are limited in time and linked to specific actions, are able to produce places that can propose new visions of the world? I think that this kind of thing also takes place in the daily lives of us all; we will have to learn to recognise them. We could start out from Hakim Bey's idea of the *Temporary Autonomous Zone* (*T.A.Z.*) in our effort to recognise these Environments in our experience of life. The *T.A.Z.* is a moment where the experience of the individual is connected to that of others in the form of a free and open autonomous community; one outside the system of normality. It is no accident that this concept stemmed from a specific event: the first rave in history at Castlemorton in England at the beginning of the nineties. Does not being at a party mean being called on to behave in an out-of-the-ordinary way, to reappraise interpersonal relations in order to experience a different kind of community? Perhaps the artistic experiences to which we are referring in order to tackle the concept of Environment from our point of view are all attempting to replicate, or in some way try out, a similar approach; perhaps even in Kaprow's case.

In May 1972, in *The Planet as Festival*, Ettore Sottsass Jr. imagined in utopian fashion the places, systems and infrastructures of this world of continual festival. But is it possible for these experiences to become less temporary? Is it possible to plan them?

IV

Could their fleeting character be the question to tackle? That is to say, when they remain transitory spaces, do temporary experiments become futile? Futile because they give up the possibility of bringing about a transformation of space that persists in time? But perhaps this is the key. Hakim Bey, for example, tells us that the temporary nature of his autonomous zones is the only way to keep them going and not let them be swept away by the action of the dominant culture. Does the solution lie there? As was pointed out earlier, the playful aspect of Huizinga's game and, later, of *New Babylon* is fundamental. For example, when children are playing they construct a temporary imaginary Environment; they gather together objects, toys, anything they can lay their hands on. The result of the assembly of these different parts is the space in which the play occurs. In this play rules are often imagined, starting conditions. In a sense it's like the configuration of a world with its codes and conventions. It is a cosmology. But what happens when the game comes to an end? Its world ends too. It is dismantled and the children are ready to play a new game, they start again from scratch. In a way we have always been fascinated by the construction of the refuge, the hut in the living room. Using cushions, sheets, pieces of furniture, carpets, or anything else available in the home. That's how an Environment is created.

V

So I would emphasize temporariness and chaos; when these two factors are not there, the mechanism breaks down. The permanence and constancy of a system, and its complete normality, strip the Environment in which this occurs of meaning. And this is as true for the hut in the living room as it is for the improvised festival in a park and for the freedom of expression of a group of individuals on the street. The Happening serves precisely to undermine the constancy of a system. To bring it into question and to subvert it. Thus, an Environment becomes a space of practice in which new proposals are made, the things to which we are accustomed are questioned, and we come into contact with the different. Returning, in fact, to one of the initial points of the discussion, many financial and economic aspects aim to make space immobile and thus to abolish it. Both in terms of activities to be carried out, and in terms of time: if a space is not utilized (no temporariness and no chaos), it paradoxically does not exist. It is shut in a cage through a set of regulations and laws. It is bought and run, depriving it of the possibilities of individuals or masses. Saskia Sassen deals with this theme, speaking explicitly of *POPS* (*Privately Owned Public Space*). These are public spaces owned by private bodies that, through a series of agreements with local governments (today in a position of absolute marginality), are able to manage in whatever way they like entire public areas, such as the squares or streets in which their headquarters are located, with the precise aim of stopping them from being used by the population. To stop them from becoming people's "playgrounds." And note, not necessarily because these settings might be a location for demonstrations, protests, and revolts, but to prevent them from continuing to be places in which there is still the possibility of declaring that, for a particular time and through a particular action, "we are present."

VI

I remember that when we interviewed Franco (Bifo) Berardi in 2015, he told us: "The problem is going to be: what scale and what persistence can happy forms of survival have? To what extent will they be able to connect up with experiences of institutional representation? To what extent will they be able to foreshadow projects for afterwards?". Perhaps this is the point. Even Bey in the years following his writing of the book *T.A.Z.* admitted the existence of *Permanent Autonomous Zones*. But perhaps our concept of Environment does not indicate in itself a place but those settings that maintain the possibility of carrying out temporary, shared projects which are open and mutable over time. Places that act as an instrument of autonomy thanks to specific boundary conditions. Perhaps this is a form of Environment open to all and that summons everyone to action, to be part of this Happening, to play "seriously" with our surroundings, to undergo an experience disconnected from the economic dynamics of normality with the aim, perhaps, of making utopias come true for a few specific moments. Then each one of us will take home our own bit of the experience, and maybe understand that other modes of collective life and relationship with our habitat are possible, even in normality.

RX
RLF

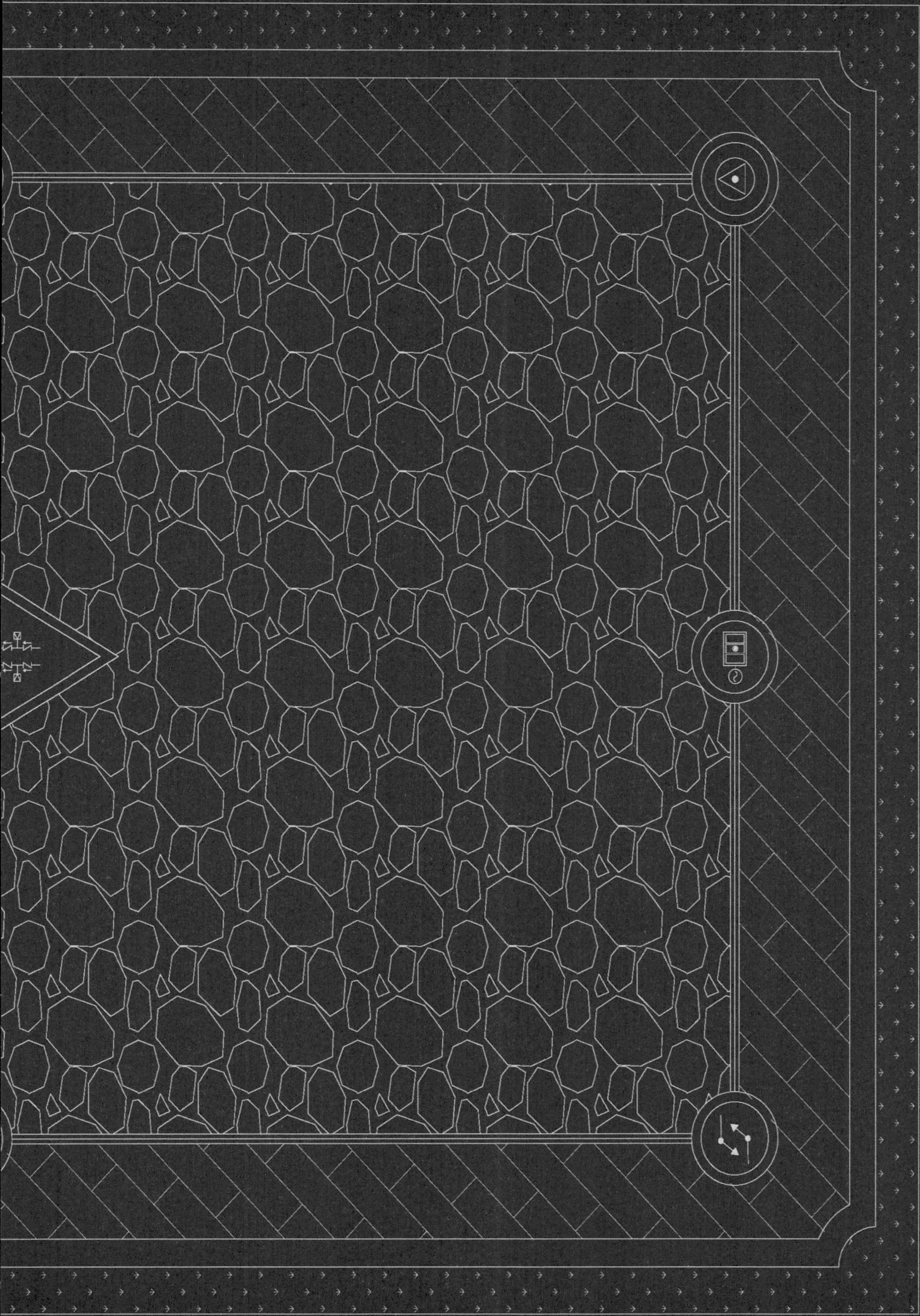

4 ANTO

OLOGY

Facoltà di architettura di Firenze 85 giorni di occupazione

Urbino: un'esperienza

Intervento politico nell'Università

Tecnico, scuola e società industriale

Questo breve documento è stato elaborato da un gruppo di studio dell'Istituto Tecnico Industriale «A. Pacinotti» di Mestre.

Lo scienziato e la violenza

Documento elaborato da un gruppo di docenti e ricercatori dell'Università di Padova

Quindici, *giornale mensile*, n. 10, 15 aprile 1968

1. Florence Faculty of Architecture—85 Days of Occupation

Vittorio Maschietto, 'Facoltà di architettura di Firenze 85 giorni di occupazione', *Quindici*, no. 10, 15 April-15 May 1968, p. VI.

Florence: on 23 January 1968 the Faculty of Architecture is occupied by the students. This occupation extends to most of the Faculty, with students striking on average for three days. The police charge at a sit-in in front of the Rectory, causing many injuries. A few days later the Carabinieri turn up at the architecture Faculty to take down names; it is a Sunday afternoon and only about eighty people are there. The next day, the students go to the police station to furnish a full list of the occupiers. They are turned away. It is therefore sent by post.

The distinctive quality of the Architecture Student Movement is the approval and definition of power in the hands of the Assembly.

The power of the Assembly is considered necessary to counterbalance the power of the research institutes and allow independent decision-making about the type of work to be pursued at the university.

Compared to the fruitless attempts at reform that resulted from the struggles of previous years, this formulation of power through the Assembly is a structural upheaval that:

- does away with the separation between didactics and research
- demolishes academic authoritarianism, in terms of both the forms of blackmail that deprive students of all power to protest (disciplinary sanctions, certifications of attendance, scholarship exams), and the top-down power structure based on chairs (entrenched academic "despots").
- has the political aims of ensuring the right to a higher education and attaining a general student salary
- ensures that the struggle can spread beyond its own confines and act in concert with other Movements of global protest, both nationally and internationally.

On 26 February, motion "A" is approved by the General Assembly:

- power shall be exercised at the Faculty of Architecture by the General Assembly: the latter includes everyone who publicly acknowledges its power
- individual members of the teaching staff shall take part in the General Assembly on the same footing as individual students

- the legal force of the General Assembly's decisions will be ensured by the fact that the professors on the Faculty Board who publicly acknowledge the power of the Assembly thereby assume the obligation to countersign the Assembly's decisions for bureaucratic ends.
- The A. has the power to appoint non-decision-making executive committees, to determine modes of implementing its power, to assume direct control over planning research and didactics and over the management of funds, to set up an administrative office and printshop...

This motion is sent to the teaching staff and rector.

In the subsequent motion of 4 March, the professors' acceptance of motion A is identified as a *sine qua non* for initiating dialogue with the teaching staff.

Meanwhile, the G.A. moves ahead with the task of defining how it will exercise its power: the time frame for calling meetings is established, as is the internal structure and the plan to create section Assemblies made up of seminar groups and seminars: the smallest units of this structure, which have begun to form spontaneously and identify paths of experimental research.

The new role of the professors will be determined individually, as experts within the seminars, and collectively, on a section committee along with student representatives to oversee the management of funds.

The section committee answers to the Assembly, which can revoke its power.

Once again, the Faculty Board is deprived of all authority and survives on paper for the sole purpose of ensuring the legal validity of the new bodies of power.

On 20 March the Faculty Board, in view of the student motions, responds with a minority motion (Ricci-Eco), in which it:
- acknowledges the foundations of the Assembly's power in motion A
- offers legal backing, assuming joint responsibility for Assembly decisions even when there is a clear violation of the laws in force (self-management) so long as they guarantee scientific rigour.

... and with a majority motion that accepts the statements of principle but sidesteps and rejects the crucial point regarding the full power of the Assembly.

In response, the G.A. on 26 March:
- reaffirms its acquisition of power (motion A)
- deems the professors' response elusive
- nonetheless notes that the acknowledgement of its authority in the Ricci-Eco motion is a positive signal
- invites all those who simply state agreement with the principles behind motion A to clarify their stance
- moves forward with the work undertaken in the experimental seminars, opening up the possibility of collaborating with the professors and assistants who have accepted motion A
- reaffirms the university's new political role within the nation, which can be expressed by using the outcome of research as a tool of protest and to break with the status quo.

As stated in the document, the content of the experimental research has already been discussed. The first general theme proposed is: ANALYSIS OF THE USE OF THE TERRITORY BY CAPITAL—the way territory use is geared to maximising profit, a subject that can be broken down into the following points:
- stage of using the city and densely populated areas as production hubs for exploitation
- stage of extending exploitation to the entire territory
- analysis of current trends in the behaviour of capital
- analysis of how the city is used by capital

the following points are then added:
- analysis of the current structure of global imperialism
- political significance of the student struggles in Italy and the rest of the world
- technological development, scientific research, use of urban work.

This research must be seen as a fully valid didactic result for the academic year underway.

On the 70th day of the occupation, a "wall newspaper" manifesto addressing the population is drafted, approved in the Assembly and posted around the city, to counter the boycotting, mystification and vilification of the Student Movement in the pages of *La Nazione* and all the "independent" national newspapers.

La Nazione does not publish it.

At the same time, in a letter to the Faculty Board, the G.A. points out that should the academic year end up being cancelled, it will be due to the culpable political and cultural immobilism of the teaching staff.

The occupation continues, as does the radical protest against budgeting policies, and the inadequacy, paucity or even cultural nonexistence of research and didactics.

The time frame of research is further defined:

the theme of "technological development and scientific research" is subdivided into:
technological development / super-exploitation of manual and intellectual work /organisation of consumer society / profit-oriented scientific research

the theme of "imperialism" into:
imperialism and capitalism / the struggle in Vietnam, in third-world countries / in the advanced capitalist countries / the Chinese cultural revolution / the Russian, Chinese, Cuban, Algerian revolutions, etc.

The new role of scientific subjects is defined in greater detail.

The theme of "analysis of the use of the territory by capital" inspires this proposal:

— the Faculty of Architecture, governed by the students, can take on the task of exposing the chaotic way in which the ruling classes, pseudo-urbanists and superintendencies manage the spatial organisation of the territory.

A few examples in Tuscany: the parks of Migliarino and San Rossore, yet to be established; the coast around Livorno, the disgusting state of Punta Ala and Riva del Sole, the garden city of Viareggio, the collusion between political parties and private interests, etc.

All of these themes of historical reanalysis and critique are accompanied by the proposal of a parallel semiotic exploration through direct cultural operations and projects. Two main objectives are suggested: to raise awareness of the Movement among the population of Florence (expansion of the struggle) and to challenge the sclerotic mindset of rationalist design at the Faculty of Architecture (atrophy of the objective).

In February, a construction site is opened at the Faculty itself: working in "life-size" or on macro-dimension with inflatable materials and papier-mâché. The pieces produced there are then employed in surprise actions, as "concrete" elements interrupting and disrupting standard rites of the historic centre of Florence, such as afternoon shopping, the Sunday stroll after mass, vehicle traffic, tourist routes. These acts of "urbanistic terrorism" demonstrate the Faculty's openness to superstructural alternatives, without prejudice to the political and ideological positions of the Movement's overall struggle.

On 5 April a policy document is approved in the Assembly regarding the vital "needs" of the Student Movement:

— need for the S. M. to be considered an ongoing tool of protest
— need for the M. to define itself through constant, conscious, efficacious acts of protest against the current system
— need for the protest to have actual incisive results in the real world
— need for the M. to also present itself as encouraging new proposals
— need for the S.M. to immediately begin consciously working through different types of research.

On 6 April the Faculty Board:

— expresses their desire to use all available means to prevent the invalidation of the academic year and avoid outside interference
— declares their willingness to carry out all possible experimentation at the Faculty in terms of both research and management, based in part on the very forms proposed by the students...

Two days later, the General Assembly:

- again denounces the attempt at blackmail that can be seen in the Faculty Board document...
- also denounces the strategy now clearly embraced by a considerable portion of the Faculty, which by issuing trivial and only hypocritically accommodating statements, tries to conceal their concrete refusal to accept the Faculty Assembly's decisions and attempts to keep all power in their *own hands*, expressing the willingness at most to "*also* consider student proposals," and in no case to relinquish their decision-making power.

On 16 April, the Faculty Board:

- more explicitly states their willingness to carry out all possible experimentation aimed at academic reform of the Faculty, accepting the forms of power outlined in the Ricci-Eco motion.

On 17 April, at 9:05 pm, the G.A. approves the final motion:

"The struggle of the Architecture students, now in its 85th day, has had two fundamental goals within the overall Student Movement in Italy. *The first was a general political objective: a salary for secondary-school and university students in order to concretely guarantee the right to higher education for the children of the working class. The second regarded the struggle against academic authoritarianism, seen as one of the tools employed by the capitalist plan in order to obtain the portion of scientific research that it deems essential and expects universities to provide.*

With this in mind the Architecture Faculty Movement has gradually yet forcefully rejected all previous forms of power that existed within the Faculty, placing itself in opposition to them, including the delegated bodies whose "equal partner" status masked their actual nature as buttresses to the existing centres of power. Relying on its own force to negate the power whose main channels of application were the chairs, institutes, and Faculty Board, it countered them with the General Assembly, which has taken all power into its own hands and ensured the possibility of its application by forcing the old centres of power to become the bureaucratic signatories for all legal purposes.

Today, the Movement has essentially won this part of its struggle, and though it must now take on the task of consolidating this power and launching the new Faculty, it can consider itself to have obtained a sufficiently secure position to justify a change in its modes of struggle. The student occupation of the Faculty premises will cease as of today, though the general state of unrest will continue; it cannot, however, persist for the entire duration of this important experiment.

This Assembly has therefore decided to convene a Constituent General Assembly, and to appoint a technical executive council for this purpose made up of instructors and students who will meet in the very near future.

Likewise, the Architecture Faculty Movement believes it is important, once again, to reiterate that it is not interested in and firmly rejects any form of struggle that is primarily corporative.

While conscious of this victory, it also wants to be conscious of this victory's limitations and the shortcomings of the struggle it has carried out to date, which has been entirely confined to the Faculty. Overall, it has been incapable of arriving at the deeper ties linking a certain kind of Faculty to a certain kind of society; still capable only of stating, but not concretely working towards, general political objectives such as the goal of a salary; incapable of forging real connections with the social forces engaged in the struggle.

It has also decided to organise a university Assembly as the logical conclusion of a struggle which though led by the Faculty of Architecture, can express its full force only through the general struggle against higher forms of authority: of the university (Academic Senate) and nation.

To protect themselves against all forms of repression, the students, who have already sent lists of the hundreds of organisers and supporters of the Occupation to investigating magistrates, have also decided to send the signatures of those taking part in today's Assembly, at which Professors and Students are jointly responsible participants."

The following press release is unanimously approved by the first General Assembly of Professors and Students:

"The Assembly of students occupying the Architecture Faculty of Florence, having reviewed the document presented by the Faculty Committee on 16 April 1968, has declared that it agrees to begin the experimentation envisioned therein, which takes into account the proposals developed by the occupying Assembly, and has decided to merge with the Constituent General Assembly of Instructors and Students.

Believing that it has thereby achieved one of the main objectives of the Student Movement, it means for the Constituent General Assembly and later Faculty Assemblies to become the place where that movement must continue to pursue all of its fundamental demands.

The General Faculty Assembly, which held its first meeting today, 17 April 1968, hereby acknowledges that the occupation has come to an end, and it will now establish the modes of undertaking experimentation."

After 85 days of occupation, and a week of "rest," a new course began at the Arch. Faculty of Florence, on April 24, with the first Constituent General Assembly.

(Vittorio Maschietto)

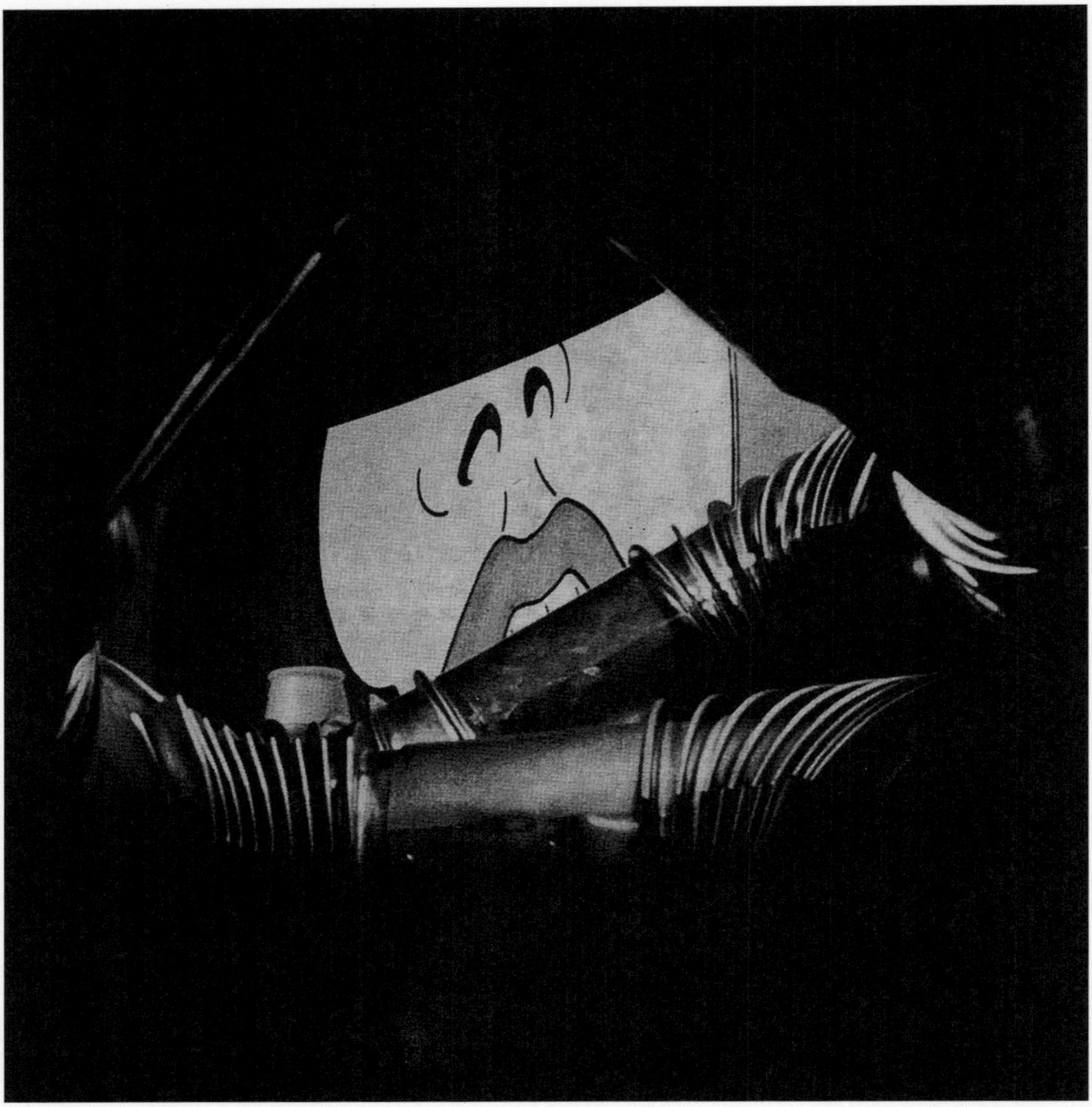

2. A Difficult Selection

(Proposal for the Competition for the Staging of the Italian Section at the 14th Milan Triennale)

Marco Dezzi Bardeschi, Gianfranco Censini and Riccardo Foresi, 'Proposta per il concorso per l'allestimento della sezione italiana alla XIV Triennale di Milano', in Carlo Guenzi, 'Una selezione difficile', *Casabella*, no. 325, June 1968, pp. 4-21: 9.

Marco Dezzi Bardeschi
Gianfranco Censini
Riccardo Foresi

Considerations

The "large number" is, prospectively, the super number, super production, super consumption and their super relationship: we take note.

It is a reality transplanted from a super structure to a mini structure.

Ahead of the cognitive process there is a process of identification.

Alienation is absence of identification.

Enjoyment is as different from use as identification is from alienation.

The super number also produces absolutely perfect instruments of alienation.

From use to enjoyment, from servitude to acculturation.

The super number is super monopoly of the means of production and means of communication.

The super number is a super relationship of dependence.

Acculturation can overthrow the relationship.

Solution

The solution lies in the development of an acculturating machine with a bisymmetrical structure and operating on a dual level of interpretation: diachronic and synchronic.

Given that it is designed to function alternately in one direction at a time, the machine, which consists essentially of 5 pneumatic organs made of translucent and opaque PVC (on the periphery the two pieces of the peristaltic tube, in the middle 2 mammillary containers plus the joint that connects them), is structured symmetrically in time...

Anyone coming from one of the two possible directions who approaches the machine encounters, at its ends, two blockages caused respectively by an evidently handmade macro-washing machine made of papier-mâché on a scale of 5:1 and a pile of wrecks of American cars in which it is possible to recognise clearly the aura of the period immediately after the war.

Into these two plugs run the collectors of the peristaltic tube from which the programmed, diachronic process of working inside the machine has drawn. From there chinks open up that, offering just a glimpse of the more delicate parts of the machine and of Jodelle's mouth, invite the viewer to make use of the external circuit, which is apparently more fortuitous and synchronic. So this last performs the function of bringing about, in the user who has not yet been "processed" in the internal cycle of production, the open-mindedness characteristic of someone who has been subjected to a synchronic totality of stimuli, while in someone who has already been transformed, that of inducing only a function of memory.

The internal circuit on the other hand, divided into the phases washing of inhibitions / process of identification / process of understanding / fixing of memory, should be considered a simulator of mental processes of variable acceleration, designed expressly to stimulate and provoke.

At the beginning of the circuit, the macro-washing machine or the pile of car wrecks, with their relatively low entropic level of information, serve to bring about a mental preconditioning of the patient who is about to be subjected to a much more intensely stimulating set of signs than usual. It is in fact in the "washing of inhibitions" section of the tube that the real processing begins. It is here, since the duct has been designed so as to allow the passage of just one person at a time in one direction, that the first bombardment of the individual with signals takes place.

The operation is carried out through tactile presences, fixed, instantaneous, dynamic, deep, and projected images, transparencies and distortions, lights and noises in a continuous crescendo of entropy produced by the progressive build-up and interaction of the programs imposed on the machine, until the user arrives at such a high level of internal tension that in order to be able to realise it in a productive and operative sense he needs to have at his disposal the conditions for a group activity.

At this point he is introduced with the others into the first of the mammillary containers where the process of identification takes place. Here, where the entropy attains levels close to that of white noise, the programs have a greater effect on the relationship between individual and group, individual and society, inducing him to seek and to sense his place, his personal responsibility in the group, in the society to which he belongs.

To speed up this process, already prepared for, individually, with the "washing of inhibitions" treatment, a system of group operations is added inside the mammillary container that is programmatically suggested and stimulated.

We are in the machine's centre of symmetry.

The entropy is very high.

The joint that unites the two mammillary containers is a structural diaphragm: a heavy rain of strips of black polyethylene renders it impenetrable to sound and light, and passing through it alone results in such a lowering of the patient's mental tension that, when he returns to the second mammillary container to undergo a process of understanding, he has lost a great deal of the personal implications and antisocial aggression that might have accumulated in the subjectifying phase of the machine.

Thus he is ready for the historicising phase.

From here on the reconditioning occurs. The programs are inverted and progressively from the process of understanding to the fixing in memory lose ambiguity and entropy of information: while, as in a film projected backwards, a sort of decoding and historicistic schematisation of the signals received and reinterpreted inversely is possible, at the same time "almost" normal patterns of behaviour are being formed again in the patients.

The machine, therefore, after performing the function of elaborating the mental processes of normal individuals, progressively accelerating them and getting them to integrate with one another and with other key mental images in such a way as to make them arrive at the extreme consequences, at the most decisive contradictions, after taking the patient to the breaking point, before expelling him, in a noble act of public spirit and justice, tries to readjust his behaviour to fit into the normal society from which it has sucked him. Thus the simulator of mental processes of variable acceleration cannot be accused of instigation to abnormality.

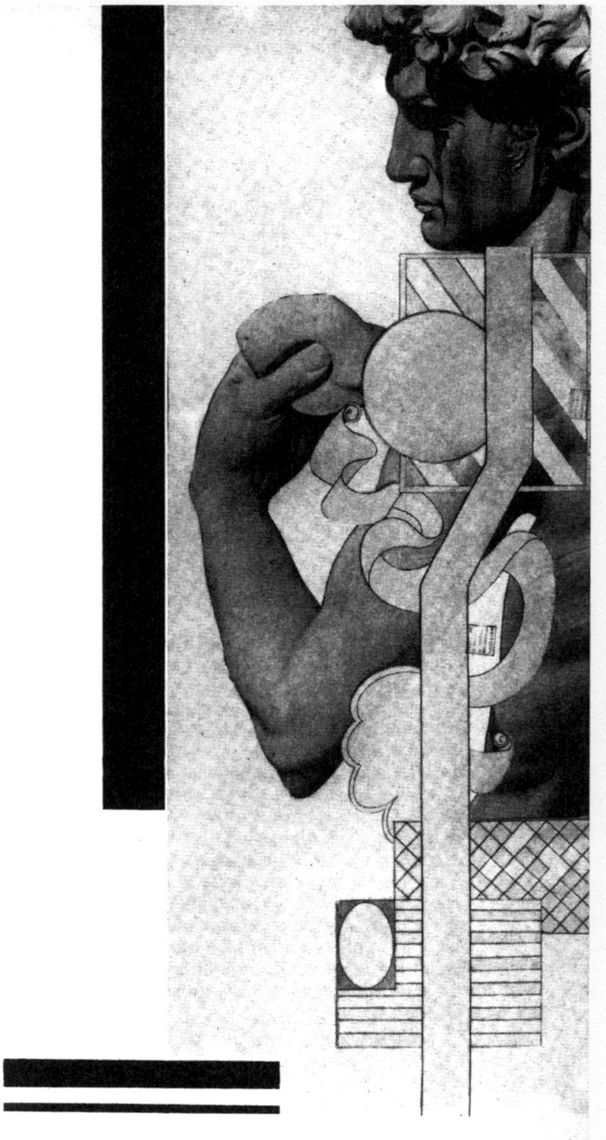

3. The Restoration of the User

Houchang Amirpour, Rodolfo Bracci, Gianfranco Gorelli and Titti Maschietto, 'Il restauro dell'utenza', *Marcatrè*, no. 46-49, October 1968, pp. 52-71.

1) MEANING OF THE MUSEUM

Let's go straightaway to look up the entry "museum" in an Italian, a French, an English, and an American encyclopaedia.

This is what the Italians write: "when, as the civilisation of a people grows more sophisticated, it begins to appreciate not just the artistic expressions or the historical relics of the moment, but also those of the ancient past, which can no longer be conserved in their original function and location; when it begins to perceive the importance that contemporary works might have in the future for the history of society or the arts or the sciences, and thus to think about ensuring their preservation, then the museum emerges (Enc. Italiana Treccani)."

According to the French: "the museum is an institution whose purpose is to provide for the conservation of items that best illustrate the phenomena of nature and the works of humanity, and to utilise these items for the enhancement of human knowledge (Larousse)."

According to the Anglophones: "museums and galleries are places in which collections of objects are displayed for their particular interest (...). Three elements are always present in the museum in every era: the owner, the object and the public. But just as models of philosophy and behaviour have evolved over the centuries, the aims of the museum and the relations between the three elements are continually changing. However, the most important fact to determine with regard to the museum is its purpose (...). In addition to the selection and display of items, the organiser must engage in a number of activities aimed at informing the visitors to the museum: they also provide a good service to the public (Enc. Britannica)."

According to the Americans, finally: "in the 19th century the museum emerged from its formative stages—the palace collection, the cabinet of the prince, or of scholars, and the public deposit of materials coming from palaces or studies—to give rise to the modern museum, a research laboratory and educational center (Enc. of Social Sciences)."

Harrison's correctly Marxist sociological analysis takes as its hypothesis the educational and cathartic value of the work of art, i.e. it recognises that it has its own, universally communicable language. We know that the work originally spoke only to its client or the narrow circle of his friends and family, in other words to people to whom the historical motive and the episode represented were already known.

So the first forcing of the communicative relationship between art and the masses came when the communication intended for one person or a few people had to be expanded to a greater number. The future for Harrison lies in the change by which, with the sedation and hypnotisation of the average user ended, along with the monopoly of museums on the part of certain forces, new democratic prospects would open up for a free appreciation of the work of art in a correct museological presentation.

Now we question whether the relationship between work and its consumer can become fluid in such a spontaneous manner, that is owing to an effective compatibility of "natural" codes; firstly because of what has been said about the forcing of the genesis of its appreciation, and then because we cannot ignore the fact that today the work of art has entered the circuits of mass communication. So while the behaviour of the user is indeed linked to certain "class-based subjections," it is above all the fruit of an overflow of the side effects of particular advertising techniques, which use the work of art to characterise certain social or "cultural" stylistic elements.

In this sense we can speak of the self-awareness of mass culture, if it results from a mediated flow that does not contribute directly to the aim of persuasion.

The aura of the work of art was created precisely through its non-marketability, through the attempt to play up the tendency of certain products to uniqueness, which exacerbates the classist classification, while for the work of art that is truly unique, one for all and not a few for someone, this discrimination no longer exists: as the unique specimen is unmarketable, a wrapping of "respect" has been created around the work of art and it can only be consumed by ripping this covering. The ripping is done through a whole series of rites of approach and appreciation: it should be noted that the creation of the aura predates the boom in mass publishing with low-cost reproductions.

We define as factors of usage today that set of lateral characteristics of the cultural industry, extraneous even to social differences, by which the collective imaginary is re-proposed in a self-aware form.

We regard the human being as the field of our applications: mass communications have taken root in him and have modified his cultural substance—culture understood in the sense that cultural anthropology gives to this word, i.e. of modification and consequent new social relationship... The human being has been enriched with new senses and capacities: all the media are extensions of some human faculty, whether mental or physical.

It is from the awareness of this fact that our investigation of usage moves. We will be seeking the structure of usage at the level of the reality of the imaginary, intervening at each dialectic step through successive simplifications. We will make therefore, as a first intervention, a cut of a synchronic character through the body of users as it presents itself today.

To define the aforesaid corpus we have handed out various pilot questionnaires on average types: at the exit of museums, in the rooms, during urban tours. The questionnaire is at once result and proposal: the questions inserted are derived from crude questionnaires applied as "drafts," getting users to speak and describe themselves without putting them under pressure with precise alternatives.

From this point a new phase of the work would start that would lead to more rigorous sociological conclusions backed up by statistical percentages.

We have been in contact with the institute of sociology for a verification of the model and as far as we are concerned, our work as promotors ends here, with the intuitive and synthetic definition of the negative form of the corpus fruens; i.e. its primary structure, its significative form, its denotation.

Taking this further will lead to an identification of the secondary structures and connotative steps. Here it suffices for us to have defined the terms of the problem and indicated the methodological procedure, which is the structuralist one: (the work will have a follow-up precisely in the sphere of museological reorganisation). So we will check the specific field of the extensions produced by the mass media: we imagine the human being as if the clothes he wears, the telephone through which he communicates, the TV he watches, the illustrated magazine he reads, the radio he listens to, the car that transports him... are extensions in both the physical sense—the eye that sees more, the skin better protected and more elegant, the legs faster... and the mental sense, i.e. the awareness that these media vitalise every one of his faculties.

Now we picture the work of art in the age of its technical reproducibility: it too has its extensions, of an eminently mental character, as purchasable copy, instalments at the newsagent's, cinematic reproductions, etc.

An example of this is psychedelic art, which enters the circuits no longer as "extended work" but as pure extension, in other words it exists only at the moment in which it is reproduced. Already this indicates to us the connotative sense of this extension of the work of art, i.e. its aggression towards the human being: but it is the human being accompanied by and equipped with his extensions, whose original impulses are emitted from the same sources. The zone of meeting between the two emanations occurs ahead of the true contact in the flesh between user and original.

Indeed we can say that the informational intensity of the latter is almost insignificant with respect to the multitude of interactions and the multitude of binary choices at a high bitrate that are reproduced at the first stage. This fringe state is diachronic: given the presumption of deferring the "sure" synthesis to the "magical" moment at which the aura is rent, thought has not yet been given to analysing the formation and solidification of the self-aware structure along the diachrony. This is the point. Our intention is exactly this: giving well-defined time and spaces to this pre-use, to this accumulation of data, of conscious or subliminal registrations. We do not believe that at present everything can be resolved in the moment of the encounter at the top, nor that this encounter can be made more effective by restructuring the organisation-museum, through a series of discussions to identify what kind of presentation is the most correct.

Indeed we think that the use of our mediatory machines could indicate the modifications that need to be made to the museological system.

Our proposal, our intervention, hinges on the presentation of some examples of usage-tools at a semiological rather than a constructive level. On the one hand they are a physical extension of the work of art onto the user, on the other cultural connections with him, images that speak to him in everyday code, drawing that is on the daily paradigm of bombardment by the mass media but proposing other syntagmatic structures: leaving the code unchanged, its systems of expectation will not be broken, just gently forced.

All the usage-tools will connote the character of precariousness and perishability, as well as being clumsily handmade.

The great modern circus, an extension of the media, is Montreal: we are proposing it again monographically on art and on a Florentine scale.

Florence presents itself to us at once as a city of art, a work of architecture and a container of numerous works of art; whence the intervention

a) on various urban scales: a revival of the 17th-century carnival, an Argonautica on the Arno, a biennial flood made of polyurethane, a series of major elements of disturbance and demystification of the city's rites and myths, a parade of floats, a circus of art in the piazza...

b) on the scales of the building: distorting mirrors, periscopic visions, upending of prime connotative functions—windows stairs courtyards—kinetic projections on the walls...

c) on the scales of interiors and the work of art: processes of preparation; staging of single-work exhibitions, serial reproductions, repetitive-obsessive components...

In addition, Montreal was intended to function for a few months, a work of art is "immortal": this is the difference that results in the myths and rites of approach.

Fruition in Montreal was an even trade: the value of the merchandise on offer was redeemed in the price paid for the ticket. With the work of art, however, this is an unbridgeable gap, since its value is "incalculable."

The user is already predisposed for a feeling of congenital inferiority, for an unequal encounter in which he will certainly come off the worse, even when attacking, and will go away with a load of frustrations: money and the credit card are no longer enough.

We want to demolish this social altar, to allow the user to touch and play a part in the game of creation in which the master, the artist, is no longer the "incomparable" genius: just perhaps the first or the most fortunate of us. Communication of the work of art of an educational nature doesn't have to come from above, from a teacher, but can be re-established at the level of the pupils and their direct participation.

Do we in this way run the risk of consuming the work of art like a hit pop song just because we have the direct possibility of playing it ourselves? It is not a risk because an open work always presents a functional alternative. In any case you won't find us mourning the death of art.

THE RESTORATION OF THE USER
A GUIDE TO THE WORK

A) Seminar regarding "Investigation and proposal about the situation of museums in Florence." Report.

B) Map of the historic centre of Florence showing artistic and cultural landmarks.
Elements to be superimposed:
a) sightseeing itineraries drawn from a nineteenth century guidebook
b) sightseeing itineraries and timetables drawn from a modern-day guidebook
c) proposal/manifesto for large-scale progression of fruition

C) Implementation of the proposal: presentation of prototypes of devices and usage-tools.
1) devices in the piazza
2) specially equipped routes
3) machines and mechanisms
4) indoor installations
5) conservative restoration

ORTHOGOSCOPE modular paths, orthogonal variations, pistons.
series: pedestrian routes
types: narrow for medieval urban fabric, medium width for Renaissance urban fabric, wide for "Poggi demolitions."
UrbTUBE Modular channels
series: walkways.

ROADWORKS composite path, grid equipped with devices
series: walkways.

GYRORAMA moving cylindrical projections
series: piazzas.
types: small for interiors, medium for historic centre, large for belvederes.

BATHYSCOPE programmed mechanical museum in vertical cylinders
series: small piazzas.

TUNNEL of ART composite expandable units—programmed mechanical museum
series: large piazzas.

AZTECOSCOPE programmed mechanical museum on multiple levels
series: large piazzas.

PUZZLES pieces made of polyurethane, vinyl, styrofoam
series: piazzas.
type: Michelangelo.

ATTIC BASE marbled PVC wrapper with its own shading
series: classical.
type: small, medium, king size.

CORINTHIAN CAPITAL as above
series: classical.
types: as above.

SPHEROSCOPE self-propelled cart on air cushion
series: barricades.
types: small to block an alley, medium to block a street, large.

INNEROUTERSCOPE expandable cart
series: walk-in space.
types: small for one person, medium for a family, large for a tour group.

PHENAKISTISCOPE mirrored cube with rotating projections
series: walk-in space.
types: small for one person, medium for a family, large for a tour group.

SPECTACLES mechanical theatre on self-propelled sets
series: walk-in space.

WELCOMESCOPE adjustable mylar aperture
series: monumental entrances.
types: small for one person, medium for a family, large for a tour group.

LABORATORY optical equipment
series: interiors.

SUPERWORKSHOP
series: interiors.

INVITATION TO THE OPERA-TIVE programmed projections and mylar screen/screening
series: interiors.

EMPAQUETAGE MONUMENTAL translucent polyethylene wrapping with steel cords and cables
series: conservative restoration.

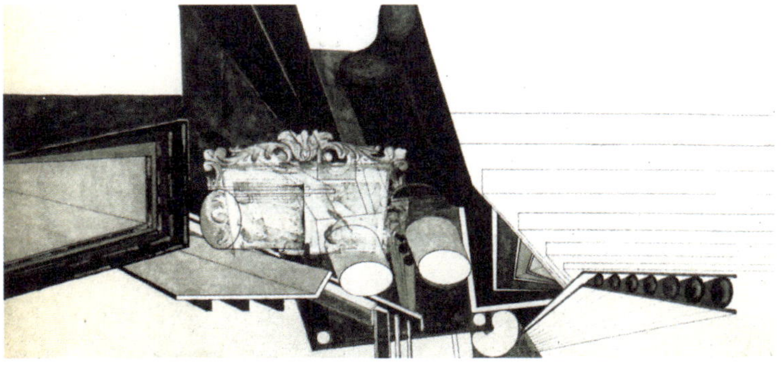

4. Urbanistic Ephemeron on a Scale of 1:1

Lapo Binazzi, Lapo (sic) Cammeo, Riccardo Foresi, Sandro Gioli and Titti Maschietto, 'Effimero Urbanistico scala 1/1', *Marcatrè*, no. 37-40, May 1968, pp. 198-209.

WALL NEWSPAPER

BUTWESHALLFORGIVEEVENOURBRETHRENWHOHAVEERRED
whoever can should bring paint plastic boilersuits helmets musical instruments castanets whoever can should bring pillows to slash footballs to aerate bottle rockets and slogans flypaper
whoever can should bring tragic masks beautiful girls useless machines caterpillar tractors live chicks whoever can should bring

BUTWESHALLFORGIVEEVENOURBRETHRENWHOHAVEERRED

CLEANSING/OF/CODES/MULTIPLICITY/
OF/CODES/COMPLEXITY/OF
INTERRELATION/HIGH/ENTROPY
OF/INFORMATION/ATROPHY
OFTHE/OBJECTIVE/HYPERTROPHY
OF/THE IMAGINARY

whoever can should bring we will issue receipts
of hallucinogens sweets and roaches
candy floss budding flowers fresh ricotta

BUTWESHALLFORGIVEEVENOURBRETHRENWHOHAVEERRED

PHILOLOGY/OF/REREADING/BROKEN
INSIDE/UNDERNEATH/BY/OPERATION/
AND/OR/PRODUCTION/OPERATION
METHOD/WORK/PRODUCTION
SEMIOTIC/ANALYSIS/
come all you flower children you free-swinging willies occupy Your Faculty Your schools Your city with fluffy obstacles let colour the blueprints with butterfly wings

FLORENCE
February 1968
Occupied Palazzo San di Clemente
A CONSTRUCTION SITE
has been opened
to produce one-of-a-kind pieces
these pieces will clearly show
their flimsily
and clumsily
handmade nature
they will serve as
elements of disruption
in
SOCIO-URBAN
ARCHITECTURAL
rites and myths

and via a circuit of
DISINHIBITION
architecture
for vertical usage

in resuscitated
micro-syndacalist terms
echoes PEPSI
in an integraaaaaaated
circuit

B U T W E S H A L L F O R G I V E E V E N O U R B R E
T H R E N W H O H A V E
E R R E D

The U.F.O.s

EPHEMERON 1

Florence, 12 February 1968: occupied Faculty of Architecture
Palazzo di San Clemente, atrium

12:00 pm	in the seventeenth-century atrium, with the doors closed, several operators unroll a milk-white extruded polyethylene tube, Ø 50 cm 1. 100 m
12:15 pm	the operators seal one end of the tube, attaching the other to the mouth of a Singer vacuum cleaner with its airflow reversed
12:30 pm	the air is turned on
12:31 pm	manipulated by the operators, the tube goes through an initial phase of stiffening
12:33 pm	stupefaction of operators/users
12:35 pm	the extruded tube begins to display its flawless cylindricity creeping rustling crackling hissing rubbing pressing wrinkling poking mounting falling taking advantage the operators guide insert knot shore substitute the seventeenth-century structures
1:00 pm (approx)	the diameter of tube and columns is now the same
1:01 pm	the columns used to be the same diameter as the tube
1:02 pm	stage of maximum erection: the tube penetrates the Mannerist pointed arches
1:03 pm	the operators overcome and violate the tube
1:20 pm	the nimblest operator detaches the Singer: the tube discharges relaxes grovels
1:30 pm	the deflated tube became a plan again: the technicians tidy up the 1000 m3 atrium and wind the extrudate onto the 0.25 m3 spool it is Italian *pranzotime*: the technicians take off their lab coats, emerge from the *vetrage* through the crowd of curious onlookers attracted by the white gleam and the noise

EPHEMERON 2

Florence, 12 February 1968 same place main lecture hall second floor

4:00 pm	General Assembly. discussion: for the past twenty days there have been political clashes between the revirginised forces of micro-syndicalism and a new composite Left aiming to form an alternative centre of power
6:30 pm	two U.F.O. operators speak: they suggest switching the immediate objectives of the struggle from the invention of new bureaucratic and organisational structures to operation and/or production: verifying and ensuring the presence and continuity of the Movement
6:45 pm	the second operator announces the opening of the construction site; other operators unroll the tube outside the lecture hall and bring it in, still in its tumescent state, passing it rhythmically from hand to hand transferring its management to the Assembly as a whole
6:50 pm	fought over by its new manager-users the tube sways lurches blankets envelops transports knots pushes: by this point the role of the technicians is one of mere maintenance
7:00 pm	many peristaltic heaves: the tube evaginates at the big north window of the lecture hall; some rush down to the park/car park to receive the tube-foetus born from the womb of San Clemente emblazon the ends with the slogan POWER to the STUDENTS encircle the Italian flag ¾ of the way around shout: onward to the occupied Faculty of Education!

EPHEMERON 3

Florence, historic centre, 12 February 1968

7:15 pm	the tube rests on the brains of students standing 3.50 m apart. It moves, twists, shouts: POWERtotheSTUDENTS POWERtotheWORKERS CONTROLofPOWER BLACKPOWER HOCHIMINH and CHE in a rhythmic chant
Piazza San Marco	the rectorate is ignored
Via Cavour	snaking along to the police station. blocking traffic. tube is squeezed chewed pierced deflated. The technicians just barely manage to grab it by the tail and stop at the air supply station of Stock 84 Bar, suturing its wounds with white semiplastified 6 cm wide Mystik tape. names bestowed by the citizenry. include: big snake Chinese dragon tube crap worm turd pop phallagogy communists
Piazza Duomo	roundabout at the Baptistry
Strozzi-Tornabuoni	shopping-snake: commerce is blocked
Faculty of Education	enthusiasm, applause, the assembly of occupiers join in: the tube sets off again more quickly resting on multiple brains
8:05 pm	the tube lashes the city with ever more violent writhings
8:30 pm	Italian *cenatime*: the city assimilates the tube. the appalled technicians mystify themselves into the crowd and melt away home

EPHEMERON 4

Downtown Florence, 5 March 1968

1:30 pm	Italian *pranzotime*
Viale Giovine Italia	the entire police force blocks the Movement's holy crusade against the office of *La Nazione*
Piazza del Duomo	one-traffic-warden-just-one questions the legality of the presence on the parvis of: 300m of 15cm ⌀ polyethylene tubing, milk-white and cooked al dente one 4m silverpapermaché pitchfork Jodelle's half-open mouth four kolossal teeth a swollen stick of butter mylar propaganda sauce
2:00 pm	
Viale Giovine Italia	the entire police force harasses the Holy Crusade
Piazza Duomo	the hastily assembled crowd of users gratifies U.F.O. with the appellations: agit-prop carousel pop spaghetti idiots Buitoni desecrators longhairs filmmakers communist gobblers
2:30 pm	
Viale Giovine Italia	the police wash away the Movement
Piazza Duomo	U.F.O. is forced to quickly clear the parvis

5. Attractive Urboeffimeri 1:1

UFO, 'Urboeffimeri avvenenti 1:1', *Marcatrè*, no. 41-42, June 1968, pp. 52-73. The paragraph "URBOEFFIMERI AVVENENTI 1:1" contains a fragment of the text published by Maschietto in April of the same year in *Quindici*, no. 10. *Marcatrè's* text differs from that of *Quindici* by the addition of a single sentence: "The U.F.O. group has been working in Florence at the Faculty of Architecture since the beginning of the student agitations."
In the letter signed by UFO and addressed to Riccardo, among the texts quoted is "pacco di spacco." In reality, what appears on *Urboeffimero* is "Pacco ti spacco."

THE UFOS

WHAT THE UFOS ARE AND ARE NOT

THEY ARE NOT FLYING SAUCERS
THEY ARE UNIDENTIFIED FLYING OBJECTS
THEY ARE NOT SCIENTIFIC URBANISTS
THEY ARE PALM READERS OPERATING ON THE URBAN SCALE
THEY ARE NOT A HOMOGENOUS GROUP
THEY ARE MERCENARIES
THEY ARE NOT A FLORENTINE OLIGARCHY
THEY ARE LEGION AND VERY CORDIAL
THEY ARE NOT SEEKERS OF NEW DIMENSIONS AND NEW SPACES
THEY ARE URBANIST TERRORISTS
THEY ARE NOT BONNIE AND CLYDE
THEY ARE ANGELS OF THE CITY

THINGS THE UFOS
DON'T REALLY LIKE
approved zoning plans / Fall-out / Real estate speculation / Scale models / History professors /
Pravda / Military parades / agricultural plans / The Kennedys

THINGS THE UFOS
REALLY LIKE
The Viareggio Carnival / Chinese dragons / Sixteenth-century street decorations / Landslides / The urbanism initiatives of Blacks in Detroit and Newark /
The scale of 1:1 / Chicken racing.

ATTRACTIVE URBOEFFIMERI 1:1

The U.F.O. group took action in Florence once a month in February, March, April, May, June and July, sparking contemptuous articles in many independent newspapers.

It brought a documentation pavilion to the 14th Triennale di Milano and closely followed the events surrounding the occupation of the Triennale, making efforts to help the latter rebuild ties with the Student Movement. The forthcoming catalogue will include a report on the U.F.O. group.

The documentation of the first two actions has been published in the latest issue of Marcatrè.

It took action in San Giovanni Valdarno, where it organised a happening as part of the events in conjunction with the 6th Masaccio painting award, sparking a public debate at every level of the town that stretched on for a month.

It also took part in a debate on the problems raised by its work in S. G. Valdarno, along with Umberto Furio Colombo, Claudio Popovich, Giuseppe Chiari.

U.F.O. is made up of: *CARLO BACHI, LAPO BINAZZI, PATRIZIA CAMMEO, RICCARDO FORESI, SANDRO GIOLI, MASSIMO GIOVANNINI, VITTORIO MASCHIETTO, MARIO SPINELLA.*

URBOEFFIMERO 5

WHAT'S THAT WHAT'S THAT?? A CAMPAIGN EVENT?
- Sorry! Is that a student demonstration?
- *Sì*... yes!
- What does it mean?
- Well... *ecco, vedi, insomma*... it's a... are you American?
- Yes
- What's your name?

LOOK! THEY WROTE IT WRONG!
- My name? Maggie

WHAT DO YOU MEAN, WRONG! THEY'RE CHINESE!
- Maggie... well, we're protesting against... we're rejecting... Maggie, now that's a nice name! What are you doing here in Florence?
- I study *italiano* at the British Institute.
- How old are you?
- I'm seventeen... WHAT does it actually mean?
- It means... the legend of the historic centre... we're protesting... do you live here by yourself?
- I live with two girlfriends of mine.
- They can't be as pretty as you!
- Are you an UFO?
- YES I AM.
- Are these boys UFO as well?
- No! no! just me, me, me! Where do you live, Maggie, can I walk you home, we can talk about it all...
- No thank you, ciao UFO!

THEY'VE GOT IT SIDEWAYS! CAN'T GET THROUGH! CAN'T GET THROUGH!
- Maggie! MAGGIE! *magg*...

The next day, 27 April 1968, *La Nazione*—that Florentine know-all—reports: "yesterday afternoon a group of students organised an unusual demonstration in the city centre: they paraded through the streets with a huge inflated plastic cylinder, shaped like a toothpaste tube, with slogans conceived to leave no room for doubt about their 'Chinese' ideas. The biggest one read 'powel to the students', with the 'r' turned into an 'l' as if by a Chinese accent. Other slogans included 'Che' (Guevara, of course) 'UFO' (?) and, given the shape of the large cylinder, the name of a toothpaste brand... 'with Vietcong' as an added ingredient."

URBOEFFIMERO 6

Mr. UFO, Esq., service no. 374564/Q
Val Pusteria Army Recruit Training Centre

Florence, 13 May 1968

Dear Riccardo,

Yesterday we went out with the long S of 'alvarani and 'upermarket wrapped up like an American dollar and we played with gold ribbons in Piazza Duomo; Lapo, spermatic as always, won four to two, Carlo filmed it all and I recorded audio, Patrizia slithered through the thighs of the S. When the demonstration came by, we presented our brothers-in-arms with the S, which filled the whole street! Wouldn't you know, those plainclothes gentlemen from Spectre burnt holes in it with their cigarettes because they suspected it was full of their own tear gas? I interviewed them for kicks, but they arrested me with a wave of the hand. We all sat down and chanted our favourites and then off we go! on the double! Then we were hassled by the usual evil hippies dressed in grey-green. Tug-of-war, argy-bargy, and they took the S. Now they'll have to keep it on ice, otherwise the "quite a package," "giocagiocimin" "magozurlinpiaio," and the photos of Rudy will go bad. It's already rumoured we made a barricade of tethered ballocks but that's not true, we just wanted them to turn off the sirens. And how's by you, poor little recruit? Are you scared of terrorists? It sure is dangerous there. Whereas here nothing ever happens... wounds light (in absence of complications), limbs in casts. Hugs and kisses. Yours, UFO

THE NEXT "GIORNO," *IL GIORNO* VENTURES ITS BEST GUESS: "... POLICE ARE BLOCKED BY TETHERED BALLOONS..."

THE UNNUMBERED
OR, REGARDING ABSENT PRESENCE:

PALAZZO DELL'ARTE

(New, grand, dazzling, comfortable, elegant
brand-new structure
of thought, conditioned and air-conditioned)
Grand premiere
A perverse and twisted thriller!
In Milan, the city of vice and of love
for technological innovation,
eroticism, drama and poetry
blend together in a fatal cocktail:

THE BIG NUMBER

An extraordinary event!
The greatest actors from the biggest "historical blockbusters"
all together in this amazing cast to tell a story
that will be remembered by one and all for having:
the most daring strip teases
the most incredible heists
the most ferocious gangsters
the most barbaric violence
the most memorable songs!!
(due to the extremely graphic realism of some scenes, the Directors
advise that this is not for the weak of... history).

WARNING !!!

THIS is just the Milanese *pied-à-terre* and/or
Workshop of the U.F.O. group:
hanging on the walls, as *fond memories*,
are some of their operations in the field
of architecture and urbanism, one of their
wall newspaper, some spoils of war and a
friendly lamp.
The U.F.O.s apologise for their
absence, but since they are busy elsewhere
disrupting SOCIO-URBAN and ARCHITECTURAL
RITES AND MYTHS
with actions on a 1:1 scale,
they have been forced to leave
the workshop unattended and idle
for the moment: they therefore invite
visitors for a *prudent historical use.*

U.F.O. U.F.O. U.F.O. U.F.O. U.F.O. U.F.O.
U.F.O. U.F.O. U.F.O. U.F.O. U.F.O. U.F.O.

Chicken Circus Circulation
ovvero
heppenveironment
ovvero
superurbeffimero n. 7

SULLA piattaforma comunale UFO porta oggetti UFO (per gentile concessione del museo congegni-ingegni UFO)

UFO vestito di nuovo: abbinamento pubblicitario UFO-Pastucol suggellato in avenue Kleber.

Lo slargo municipale ospita una mostra non permanente di elementi venusiani e codice terrestre: bocca e forchetta.
bocca: fiero pasto, Jodelle, Tom Jones, draga chimica a gusto continuo, five flavors, centomilioni di bocche indiane.
forchetta: artiglio, spaghedi, D.C., Concorde, Gap Tecnologico.

S. Giovanni Valdarno, 24 giugno 1968, ore 21
INIZIO... INIZIO... BARNARD... INIZIO
Un oggetto non meglio identificato si incastra proprio nel tettodel comune valdarnese.
Il cordone ombelicale prensile esala la società venusiana, che attuata la totale automazione applica lo schema collaudetissimo perfettissimo cordialissimo a stratificazione classista.
Nella preesistenza locale torreiforme il grande alchemico trova il suo habitat convenzionale e lì si arrocca.
Dal suo pied-à-tour il grande alchemico smista le vergini al pied-à-toit e i tecnici pied-à-terre.

12

Una nota sugli abbigliamenti ci è presentata dal nostro inviato speciale Rolando Barthes

Monsieur Bachi, le grand alchimiste:

le pantalon taillé droit
ceinture en biais
et zip devant
le manteau en poli-naturel
damassé infroissable
à côtes jaunes

« Les vierges toutes nues:

un costume decontracté pour une soirée d'été
jupe dansante jupon gansé
architectures mouvantes toute en arrondis

3

« Les técniciens:

les tenues de ville
se ponctuent de blanc
pour le soixanteneuf, pas de cravate!

5

Con gesti deterrenti il Grande Alchemico vara i polli confronto al Valdarno.
I polli carambolano sul taboga ai sensitoi.
Le vergini caramellano i polli di vernice a spruzzo gialla e azzurra.
« placent les poulets sur le gril bien chaud, les arrosent de cognac et les rôtissent, les décorent avec des rondelles de citron et du persil ».
Le vergini scrotano i polli verso il basso dove sono insacchettati dai tecnici-operatori UFO.
I polli insacchettati vengono caramellati ai valdarnesi più svelti.

TECNICI UFO IRRORANO IL CONDIMENTO

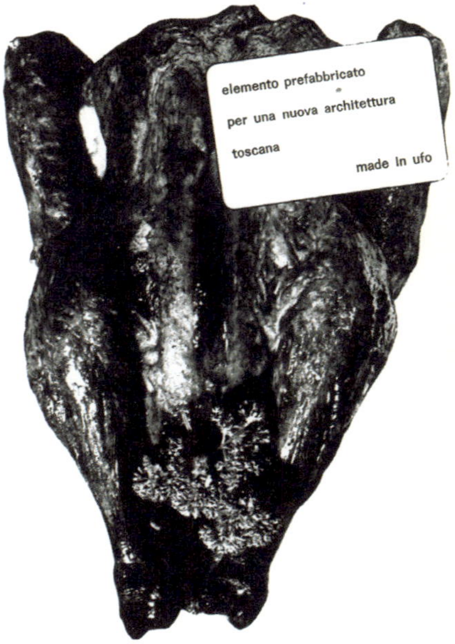

URBOACCESSORIO VERGINALE

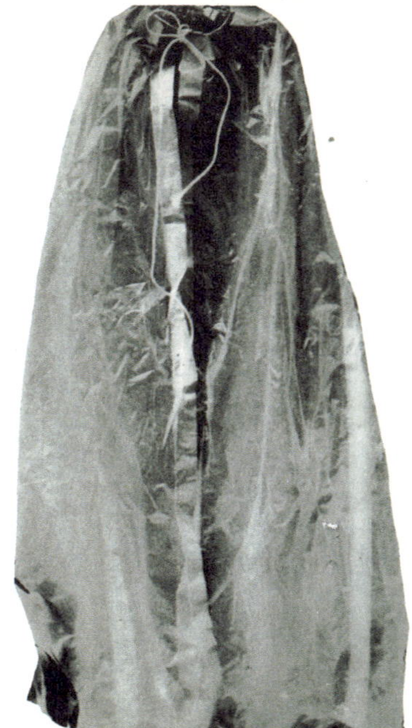

URBOACCESSORIO ALCHEMICO

6. Chicken Circus Circulation, or, Happenvironment, or, Super-urbeffimero no. 7

UFO, 'Chicken Circus Circulation ovvero heppenveironment (sic) ovvero superurbeffimero n. 7', *Marcatrè*, no. 41-42, June 1968, pp. 76-89.

Chicken Circus Circulation
ovvero
heppenveironment (sic)
ovvero
superurbeffimero n. 7

ON the municipal UFO platform UFO glovebox (with kind permission from the museum of UFO contraptions and contrivances).
UFO all spruced up: UFO-Pastucol marketing alliance signed on Avenue Kleber.
The area in front of the town hall houses a temporary exhibition of objects from Venus in Earth code: mouth and fork.
mouth: Ugolino's savage meal, Jodelle, Tom Jones, continuous-suckle chemical dredge, five flavours, a hundred million Indian mouths.
fork: claw, spaghetti, D.C., Concorde, Technology Gap.

San Giovanni Valdarno, 24 June 1968, 9:00 pm
BEGINNING... BEGINNING... BARNARD... BEGINNING
An unidentified object gets stuck right on the roof of San Giovanni's town hall.
Its prehensile umbilical cord exhales the Venusian community, which having implemented full automation applies a perfectly flawless perfectly courteous tried-and-true scheme of classist stratification.
The Grand Alchemist finds his standard habitat in the pre-existing tower-shaped structure and ensconces himself there.
From his *pied-a-tour* the Grand Alchemist deploys the virgins to the *pied-a-toit* and the technicians to the *pied-a-terre.*

A note on their apparel is presented by our special envoy Rolando Barthes

12 *Monsieur Bachi, le grand alchimiste*
le pantalon taillé droit
ceinture en biais
et zip devant
le manteau en poli-naturel
damassé infroissable
à côtes jaunes

• *Les vierges toutes nues:*

un costume decontracté pour une soirée d'été
jupe dansante jupon gansé
architectures mouvantes toute en arrondis

3 • *Les técniciens (sic):*

les tenues de ville
se ponctuent de blanc
pour le soixanteneuf, pas de cravate!

5 With gestures of warning the Grand Alchemist launches the chickens towards the Valdarno. The chickens carom on toboggans to the sensetoits. The virgins caramelise the chickens with yellow and blue spray paint.
"placent les poulets sur le grill bien chaud, les arrosent de cognac et les rotissent, les décorent avec des rondelles de citron et du persil." The virgins escrote the chickens down to where they are bagged by UFO technicians-operators. The bagged chickens are caramelised by the nimblest Valdarnese.

UFO TECHNICIANS POUR ON THE SAUCE

67 THE RETURN OF THE SQUID

... In a series of diabolical attacks in Saigon all the American secret agents meet their end at the hand of a seductive and perverse Vietcong woman who goes by the name of THE CAT!

shrewd and savage
soft and sensual
the cat slips silently
through the alleyways of Old Saigon
to nab her, the C.I.A.
sends the playboy agent Goldrake.

hard as marble
with his wits always about him
even in tasks of love
GOLDY once again wins
his poker game with death!

But who is the Grand Alchemist? Christ? Yep Uncle Sam, the bossman, the Urcodex, immobile prime mover. He's cock of the walk. Cockadoodle. Who are the virgins? Cops? Yep supermarket cashiers. Armed? With caramel pistols. These roofdwelling she-crickets all feathers and spray. They're the media: people tamers, chicken trainers. And are the technicians workers? Yep they are exploited by the system, overseen by the superpolice. They work two hours a month, forced to make the same repetitive movements. They're the Cinecittà stuntmen. The ones from De Rica. And the chickens, are they good? They're our special palemeat, extra flavour and peak taste, with pure baby pap
Tip-top technological
Supercoop

one of the three chickens is Blaiberg
one of the three chickens is Ted Kennedy
one of the three chickens is Pope Paul VIth
one of the three chickens is Pincus

Who's behind this encounter? The C.I.A.? Market competition. The gap... NO NO! I think that He is Von Braun, that those girls are the antiseptic cosmotechnical Laikas and those fellows are the countdowners.

FIVE... FOUR... THREE... TWO... FIRE... (albinoni)
3 (the chickens arrive)
(albinoni)
THIS IS RADIO VALDARNO !!
(albinoni)
THE FREE CHICKEN SCRATCHES UNDERGROUND !!
(albinoni)
This is your very own Ted Kennedy speaking to you !
(albinoni)
the gang of Venusian imperialists and Russian revisionists wants to destroy the Free-Ranger of the Valdarno flooding us with their whitemeat puppets. We cry NO to the chickens of the masters NO! to the masters of the ironworks
NO to the colonialist ambitions of Pure Pap!
YES to Jacobin chicken! The imperial-revisionist scumbags will themselves be annihilated!
(albinoni)
THIS IS RADIO VALDARNO !
(albinoni)
THE FREE CHICKEN SCRATCHES UNDERGROUND!!
(albinoni)
You too can be a part of our big revolutionary contest
SKIN THE CHICKEN!!
(albinoni)
The technicians wave their hands over the chickens of the Valdarno
they sniff
they chomp
they crunch
they slurp
they cry: CHICKEN!

The tinfoil Garibaldi is unveiled before the shocked Valdarnese who witness his reunion with ANITONA. Anitona follows the arrow pointing to "Aspromonte"—accompanied by the Valdarnese. Having reached this rugged spot she has a Badedas shower that cleanses regenera-

tes tones: UFO technicians see to the lathering. The workers gather objects to form a barricade. They tear off their white coats. They pile up the porphyry chickens, the hand-chickens, the throwing chickens, the Jacobin chickens. They throw them from behind the barricade.

(sirens)

The UFO shave-cream the local Establishment: the Marzocco lion.

The Alchemist from Venus watches with interest and seized by existential doubt, murmurs: frightful contradictions.

The virgins caramelise the Valdarno chickens, extinguish the Jacobin chickens and rescrote them all over again.

Connotations

Garibaldi: the Alchemist's double, happy prince, hero-father (of us all), Che Guevara, Giap, Castro, Rudy Dutschke, Cohn-Bendit, Mao, Ho Chi Minh, Robin Hood.

Anitona: sex, Italy and *Italietta*, mama (of us all) sister daughter, Ophelia, pin-up, floozy, America.

Aspromonte: forest, Debussy, Schifano, forest ranger intermezzo, place of purification from technological sins.

Styrofoam: talcum powder, four seasons shower gel, Barnard's brother, source of the information, large syntagmatic unit, Big Roberts, Bad Roberts.

Foam: Barnard cerebral medium, gurgling information, funfair rides, candy floss.

Marzocco: longhair, palmolive shaving cream. The local Man's best friend, home-team hooliganism, know-all of San Giovanni, Garibaldi's dog.

Tiger: the magician's apprentice, proud owner of alchemy set, Bachi's dog, the twelve apostles.

Barricade: Bellocchio, collage of products and techniques with ideological binder, general mess, repellent.

Bachi: Hamlet. The squid. Goldrake.

Virgins: negentropic breeders.

The F.L.N. TV bar provides the warriors with an effigy of the secret weapon of 30x3 Kennedys. The secret weapon silently snakes its way to the virginal tympanum. Anitona palpitates the secret weapon and adorns herself with it. Rhythmic phases of heave-ho overseen by the UFO sailors accompany the peristalsis. The ascension of the Valdarnese phallus proceeds toward the mercurial Alchemist, though kept in check by those gelid administrators, the virgins. Mr Bachi, not by design but through mechanisms of fate, adopts the weapon, absorbs its information and uses it to adorn his perfect being. He flushes the tube to the virgins who caramelise and scrote it mercilessly. The technicians retrieve their white coats and put them on. The very Great Alchemist casts a magnetic IBM fishing net at bystanders.

FINAL SHOWDOWN OF THE COCKADIDDLYSQUATS
protective circuit
consolatory motive
Mr. Campus
passing the hat
"Accattone" scrounger
I hate you dear UFOs

CONNOTATIONS SECRET WEAPON:
"HIGH ENTROPY" INFORMATION TUBE
WEAPON FOR KILLING THE
THIRD KENNEDY
IRIDESCENT PROTOPLASM
TRIPE / TRIPE WITH TOMATO SAUCE
LETTUCY SNAIL SLIME
ROARING STADIUM
GAPEMOUTH

WAIT I GET IT!
he's the old Kennedy, with Garibaldi in the two worlds, Anitona is Mama Kennedy, the virgins are the widows and mothers of unborn children, the children, the UFOs, the American chickens and the third world of the Valdarno, the secret weapon is the hidden conspiracy, and the foam must be...

7. Architetti Tzigani

Lapo Binazzi, 'Tzigan Architects (1969)', *Terrazzo*, no. 5, September 1990, p. 131.

The "ARCHITETTI TZIGANI" ("Gypsy architects") picked up their drawings from the table in the ice-cream parlor
ICE CREAM PARLOR
REARED IN FREEDOM
... they couldn't have borne the least form of repression in their eyes the memory
of prairies sparkled beneath the moon
of the "CAFFÉ CONCERTO"
and filled the eyes of passers-by with melancholy...
the weirdness of their behaviour did not fail to amaze the AMERICAN DAIRYMAID and the BATHYSCAPHE BOY who every time he was ashore followed them on ADVENTUROUS PILGRIMAGES
a light plaintive air floated from a distance
far
far away
the architetti tzigani's camp was often the destination of fat young ladies with FEATHERED HATS in search of a cheap thrill
"THE GERMAN BARBER"
"THE BEER CONTRACTOR" also called the "Bavarian" watched over the tents telling each
other in turns
about their homosexual
HOMOSEXUAL
HOMOSEXUAL weaknesses
... but there were moments when the festival reached its climax
then... THE ARCHITETTI TZIGANI left the waiters' napkins and their drawings and jumped onto the tables
"TO DANCE FOLK DANCES"
often on their travels they would head northwards to the GREAT INDUSTRIAL METROPOLISES where the contrast was ever more striking
thus CONTROVERSIES arose to which they answered "YES" and "NO"
AT REGULAR INTERVALS OF 5 MINUTES EACH causing disconcertion among the moderate and right-thinking folk who were most of all amazed by the
EASE
with which they seemed to be able to change their opinion
THEIR OPINION
EX-SERVICE MEN
OF THE MOMENT
EX MARINES back from CAMBOGIA?
this is what people wondered
and so by the camp fire great exploits were dreamt of while forgetting to wash the dishes, but always obsequious and ceremonious with the fat ladies they spoke to them with such tender eyes...

Lapo Binazzi, 1969

la nostra POLEMICA
vuole essere solo
un bisbiglio insi
stente e gentile
ai vostri orecchi
come la RADIO la~~sciat~~
sciata accesa che
capti una trasmis
sione da un altro
pianeta in toni bas
si e discontinui
e faccia pensare
a Goldoni in Marziano
e ai battibecchi
delle sue comari....

FIRENZE E L'ALLUVIONE
FIRENZE E IL TERREMOTO
FIRENZE E GLI SLITTAMENTI CONTINENTALI
FIRENZE E LE GLACIAZIONI
FIRENZE E LE ECLISSI

sono titoli possibili di altrettanti romanzi a fumetti ....così l'ARCHITETTURA cercando di far coincidere LINGUAGGIO E NON-LINGUAGGIO (per ora), tende da una parte ad agglomerati sempre più consistenti tenta di costituirsi come **URBANISTICA** senza riuscirci, dall'altra porta l'**AZIONE** nelle strade e nelle piazze e cerca personaggi perfetti come GLI ARCANGELI PICCOLO MOZART PICCOLO LORD FANTEROY.. sotto forma di ALLUCINAZIONI.....

ARCHITETTURA diventa l'elemento catalizzatore di contesti diversi un **DATO** ALCHEMICO PRIMARIO come

A I R

W A T E R E A R T H

F I R E

si può apprezzare il DISCONTINUO come un'acquisizione irreversibile del progresso tecnologico il termine ultimo anche se non ultimissimo della Società Automatizzata.......Non è chi non veda in questa tendenza una nuova forma di costrizione di massa ma tant'è: il teorico e il pratico l'antico e il moderno da che mondo è mondo sono sempre andati a braccetto molto bene assieme......

le MEMORIE-CONGELATE DELL'ARCHITETTO-ARCHEOLOGO si danno la mano con l'URBANISTICA-FANTASMA l'attrezzo più utile per scavare avanti e indietro nel tempo è la PROFEZIA.........

si portano alla luce **RESTI DI VILLAGGI** e PEZZI DI CITTA' ma abbiamo la sensazione precisa che più in là non si possa andare per una sorta di necessità di ordine economico.....la tendenza a raccontare **STORIE** sempre più GROSSE si è impadronita dell'**ARCHITETTURA** che diventa **UTOPIA** nel pensiero teorico

8. Manifest of the Discontinous

Lapo Binazzi, *Manifesto del discontinuo*, Archivio FRAC, Orléans, s.d. The document was published in UFO, 'Brano inedito' (Manifest of the discontinous, 1969), in Gianni Pettena (ed.), *La città invisibile. Architettura sperimentale 1965/1975* (Florence: Associazione Intercomunale N.10, 1983), pp. 188-189.

BRANO INEDITO

our polemics want to be
only an insisting and
gentle whisper in your
ear like the radio
left on picking up
a trasmission from
another planet on
low and discontinuous
tones to make you
think of Goldoni in
Mars language and of
his Merry Wives quarrels...

FLORENCE AND THE FLOOD
FLORENCE AND THE EARTHQUAKE
FLORENCE AND THE CONTINENTAL SLIDING
FLORENCE AND THE ECLIPSE

these could be the titles of as many comic strips novels that is why the Architecture trying to make coincident, for now, language and no-language aims at AGGLOMERATION more and more thick at one side and tries to deliver itself as URBANISM not succeeding in. At the other side brings the ACTION in the streets, in the piazzas, and looks for perfect character as the ARCANGELS LITTLEMOZART LITTLE LORD FAUNTERLOY... undershaped ALLUCINATIONS.

Architecture becomes the catalyst element of different contexts, primary alchemic datum as

AIR
WATER EARTH
FIRE

We can appreciate the DISCONTINOUS like an unreversible acquisition of technological progress, the last even if not the latest of an automatized society... is there anybody who can't see in this aim a new shape of masses constriction but "tant'è"***; theory and practice, ancient and modern, since the world is world, always walked arm-in-arm very well together...

the FROZEN MEMORIES of the
ARCHEOLOGIST architect give
their hand to each other with
the PHANTOM URBANISM, the
most useful tool to dig forwards
and backwards in spacetime is
the PROPHECY..........

one brings to the light wrecks of golden VILLAGES and places of TOWNS but with the precise feeling that, further on, we could not go because of a kind of economic necessity... the aim of bigger NOVELINGSTORIES got hold of ARCHITECTURE that becomes UTOPIA of THEORETICAL THOUGHT.

A
big big
STORY same for
everybody tries to can-
cel the RIGHT of little little
tribes to invent daily on their OWN
STORY to build a PERSONAL "CIVITAS".......

NOBODY KNOWS WHAT IS THE RIGHTWAY! one day Grand Father told me—if you try to reason you get crazy—and I poor architetto Tzigano (Gypsy architect") why shouldn't I believe to Grandfa? who am I not to do it? eh? who am I? eh? uh? so we did we eh? tried eh? uh? we to reason? and we got crazy

— we understood a thing boy, boxes guy, VILLAGES exist!— — eh?
— we understood another thing boy: we gotta make it, according to what that our conscience diktat — uh?
— and another THING we understood ROY: that Florence broke the moorings which fastened her to one of the most mianland have I ever seen following the stream arrived to the River Mouth then in open sea and the SEAGULLS have flown about above Ponte Vecchio and at the end has arrived at sight of SWITZERLAND a middle-ocean island a peace-and-low OA-SIS-IN. -eh?
— you have never thought before she could have done it! Admit it! eh? got it uh?
— do you understand now our sarcasm about GLOBAL SOLUTIONS eh?
— we do not propose to ourselves a road to fly over with THEORY but we will always walk down with our big big CROSSES together with the weak and poor people dropping down viscera and faces even if it's not so heroic.
— we will be very close to YOU and WE will help YOU to resolve OUR problems.
— we perfectly know the big problems of our dear little towny wow yes!
— I tell you, we know them, we can say we know them into the deepest profoundest recesses:

the URBAN PLAN
the AIRPORT
the RAILWAY
the UNIVERSITY
the NURSERY
the TUBE
the MONUMENT
the MUSEUM
the WATER STREAM
the AIR STREAM
the A.N.A.S. ROADHOUSE
the POLLUTION

but we can tell you as well that we are elaborating some SOLUTION modern rational full of good taste simple handy clean.

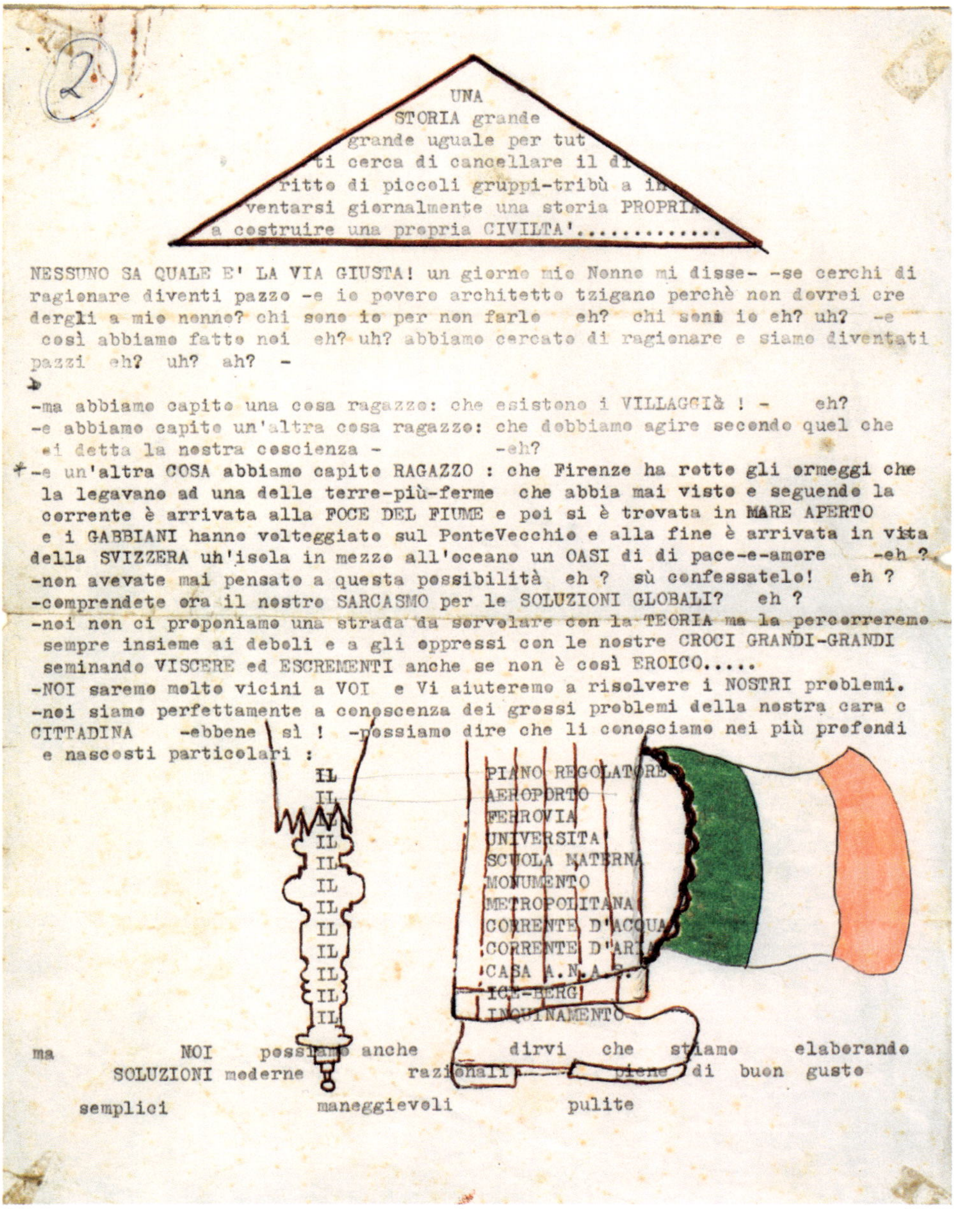

(2)

UNA
STORIA grande
grande uguale per tut
ti cerca di cancellare il di
ritto di piccoli gruppi-tribù a in
ventarsi giornalmente una storia PROPRIA
a costruire una propria CIVILTA'............

NESSUNO SA QUALE E' LA VIA GIUSTA! un giorno mio Nonno mi disse- -se cerchi di ragionare diventi pazzo -e io povero architetto tzigano perchè non dovrei crederli a mio nonno? chi sono io per non farlo eh? chi sono io eh? uh? -e così abbiamo fatto noi eh? uh? abbiamo cercato di ragionare e siamo diventati pazzi eh? uh? ah? -

-ma abbiamo capito una cosa ragazzo: che esistono i VILLAGGIà ! - eh?
-e abbiamo capito un'altra cosa ragazzo: che dobbiamo agire secondo quel che ci detta la nostra coscienza - -eh?
-e un'altra COSA abbiamo capito RAGAZZO : che Firenze ha rotto gli ormeggi che la legavano ad una delle terre-più-ferme che abbia mai visto e seguendo la corrente è arrivata alla FOCE DEL FIUME e poi si è trovata in MARE APERTO e i GABBIANI hanno volteggiato sul PonteVecchio e alla fine è arrivata in vista della SVIZZERA un'isola in mezzo all'oceano un OASI di di pace-e-amore -eh ?
-non avevate mai pensato a questa possibilità eh ? sù confessatelo! eh ?
-comprendete ora il nostro SARCASMO per le SOLUZIONI GLOBALI? eh ?
-noi non ci proponiamo una strada da servolare con la TEORIA ma la percorreremo sempre insieme ai deboli e a gli oppressi con le nostre CROCI GRANDI-GRANDI seminando VISCERE ed ESCREMENTI anche se non è così EROICO.....
-NOI saremo molto vicini a VOI e Vi aiuteremo a risolvere i NOSTRI problemi.
-noi siamo perfettamente a conoscenza dei grossi problemi della nostra cara c CITTADINA -ebbene sì ! -possiamo dire che li conosciamo nei più profondi e nascosti particolari :

IL
IL
IL
IL
IL
IL
IL
IL
IL
IL
IL
IL
IL

PIANO REGOLATORE
AEROPORTO
FERROVIA
UNIVERSITA
SCUOLA MATERNA
MONUMENTO
METROPOLITANA
CORRENTE D'ACQUA
CORRENTE D'ARIA
CASA A.N.A.S.
ICE-BERG
INQUINAMENTO

ma NOI possiamo anche dirvi che stiamo elaborando SOLUZIONI moderne razionali piene di buon gusto
semplici maneggievoli pulite

C'è molto gioco, gioco dichiarato, dico, e qua e là venato di ferocia, nel lavoro degli U.F.O. di Firenze. I loro allestimenti realizzano fumetti nello spazio, con tutta la gamma dei risvolti dei fumetti, iconografici e psicologici, ma non ancora intellettualistici, che leggevamo da ragazzi. Più che di comico si tratta a dire il vero di *tragicomic stripes*, di archifumetti costruiti sulla trave della parodia. Ci invitano al loro controcarnevale permanente e nel contempo, proprio per il potere della parodia, ci escludono dal gioco. Non assistiamo nemmeno a una proposta di attività ludica, come parrebbe; appunto perché la parodia ributta e non attira. Il nostro intervento è possibile solo in una fase successiva: quella del gioco nell'accezione di contesa, intrigo e lotta. Vecchio gioco, ma che tende sempre a non farsi identificare, come è giusto che sia con gli U.F.O., oggetti volanti sconosciuti.

Di certo, siamo nella Bengodi degli stereotipi e delle superstizioni — ossia qualche gradino sotto l'orizzonte delle mode e dei miti, nel paese della cultura cosiddetta bassa, che ha l'aria « nostrana » dappertutto. Nel negozio di sport i disegni di « Forza John! » recuperano edificanti avventure amate da intrepidi boy-scouts; al ristorante, le avventure di Sherwood fanno da fondale alla gastronomia e aggiungono il pittoresco al pittoresco, come si suole; si rifà il belletto al night-club con buffetti di tribalismo ed esotismo, « Bambaissa » e « I Grandi Viaggi », e ancora le immagini rimandano a stereotipi di massa ferragostana. Ma è nell'erboristeria « Re di Puglia » che la bassa cultura, con le sue immagini e i suoi comportamenti, ramifica ovunque; questo erbario-sacrario può essere tutto: atto di pietà ecologica per la natura uccisa e gesto triviale contro il patetismo ecologico, patriottismo rinverdito e tisana patriottarda. A parte quest'ultimo caso, brillante, si tratta di temi scarsamente parodistici in sé. Nella bassa cultura si godono le storie avventurose o i viaggi organizzati con grande gusto.

Ma per coloro che alla bassa cultura non appartengono, come i creatori e i destinatari di questi allestimenti, e che tuttavia rifiutano di identificarsi con l'alta o media cultura, il gusto gioca a fior di pelle. Molti artisti e qualche scrittore praticano la riduzione del mondo a fotografia, fumetto, cioè stereotipano l'uomo e le sue azioni per amore del neutro, dell'oggettivo e dell'anonimo, e odio dell'angoscia e di chi si attarda a distinguere il bene e il male; la loro regola prima è di liquidare ogni senso del tragico. Altri invece non riescono a sottrarsi alla coscienza del tragico; tentano di liquidarlo con l'uso della parodia, altrimenti ne sono sommersi come i vecchi artisti e i vecchi scrittori. È utile comunque sapere dov'è la tragedia, che la si odi o no.

Gli U.F.O. ricorrono all'uso della parodia al momento della trasmissione. Quando, una volta disegnati e costruiti, i loro archifumetti devono essere comunicati ai mezzi d'informazione e, tramite questi, a coloro per i quali o contro i quali hanno allestito il loro discorso. Con foto « sceneggiate », didascalie e dichiarazioni cabalistiche, fanno ridondare la loro opera di spunti parodistici, sarcastici e polemici. La tragedia è forse già nelle loro immagini germinali, e sicuramente nella trasmissione di queste immagini a chi dovrebbe intenderle o invece le fraintende — come può darsi che stia accadendo qui; ma ai loro occhi, è chiaro, nulla è più tragicomico dei loro mezzi, metodi, aspirazioni e funzioni di architetti. *T.T.*

UNA LETTERA DAGLI UFO A DOMUS

operatori sparsi per il mondo cantano alla luna come cow-boys storie dolcissime nel fuoco dei bivacchi

Ci scusiamo per il ritardo ma sperando « CHE LE VIE DELLA GEOGRAFIA SIANO INFINITE » il « MESSAGGIO NELLA BOTTIGLIA » Vi arriverà sicuramente in tempo. Viaggerà « A DORSO DI MULO » « LEGATO ALLA ZAMPA DI COLOMBO » « NELLA PANCIA DELLA BALENA » insieme all'ANGUILLA e ai GABBIANI DEL PONTEVECCHIO e verrà individuato dai TECNICI DELLA N.A.S.A./A.N.A.S. Per ora sono storie in una situazione geografica che si sta arrovesciando come si arrovescia un lupo, un « LUPO » o un « LEONE » infilando la mano nella bocca e acchiappando la coda OPERAZIONE COMUNE AI GLADIATORI E AGLI INDIANI LICENZIATI DALLA CASA DI PRODUZIONE. Nel tentativo di ristabilire gli equilibri naturali in ecologia proponiamo un baedeker internazionale del turista archeologo rovesciando il rapporto GASTRONOMIA-ARCHEOLOGIA sperando che nell'addentare le ROVINE DEL TEMPIO si rovini almeno qualche dente le nostre idee sono sempre molto confuse ma ci muoviamo molto come tutti gli animali di razza e siamo più nomadi degli ZINGARI e più fermi dei CUBI DEGLI INCAS. . .

CORDIALI CORDIALI
CORDIALI CORDIALI
Vi salutano gli
U.F.O.

« A.N.A.S. » typology

« A.N.A.S. » restoration

9. A Letter from the UFOs to Domus

UFO, 'Una lettera dagli UFO a Domus', *Domus*, no. 495, February 1971, p. 48.

Like cowboys
operators
scattered around
the world
sing to the
moon
tender stories
around campfires

We apologise for the delay but in the hope "THAT GEOGRAPHY WORKS IN MYSTERIOUS WAYS" the "MESSAGE IN THE BOTTLE" will undoubtedly get to You in time. It will travel "BY MULE" "TIED TO A PIGEON'S LEG" "IN THE BELLY OF THE WHALE" along with the EEL and the SEAGULLS OF THE PONTE VECCHIO and will be identified by the TECHNICIANS OF N.A.S.A./A.N.A.S. For now they are stories in a geographical situation that is turning inside out like you turn a wolf, a "WOLF" or a "LION," inside out by putting your hand in its mouth and grabbing its tail A COMMON OPERATION FOR GLADIATORS AND INDIANS FIRED BY THE FILM STUDIOS. In the attempt to re-establish natural equilibrium in ecology we are proposing an international Baedeker of the tourist archaeologist overturning the relationship GASTRONOMY-ARCHAEOLOGY in the hope that by sinking his teeth into the RUINS OF THE TEMPLE at least some tooth will be ruined our ideas are still very confused but we are moving a lot like all purebred animals and we are more nomadic than GYPSIES and more fixed than the CUBES OF THE INCAS...

BEST BEST
BEST BEST
Wishes from the
U.F.O.s

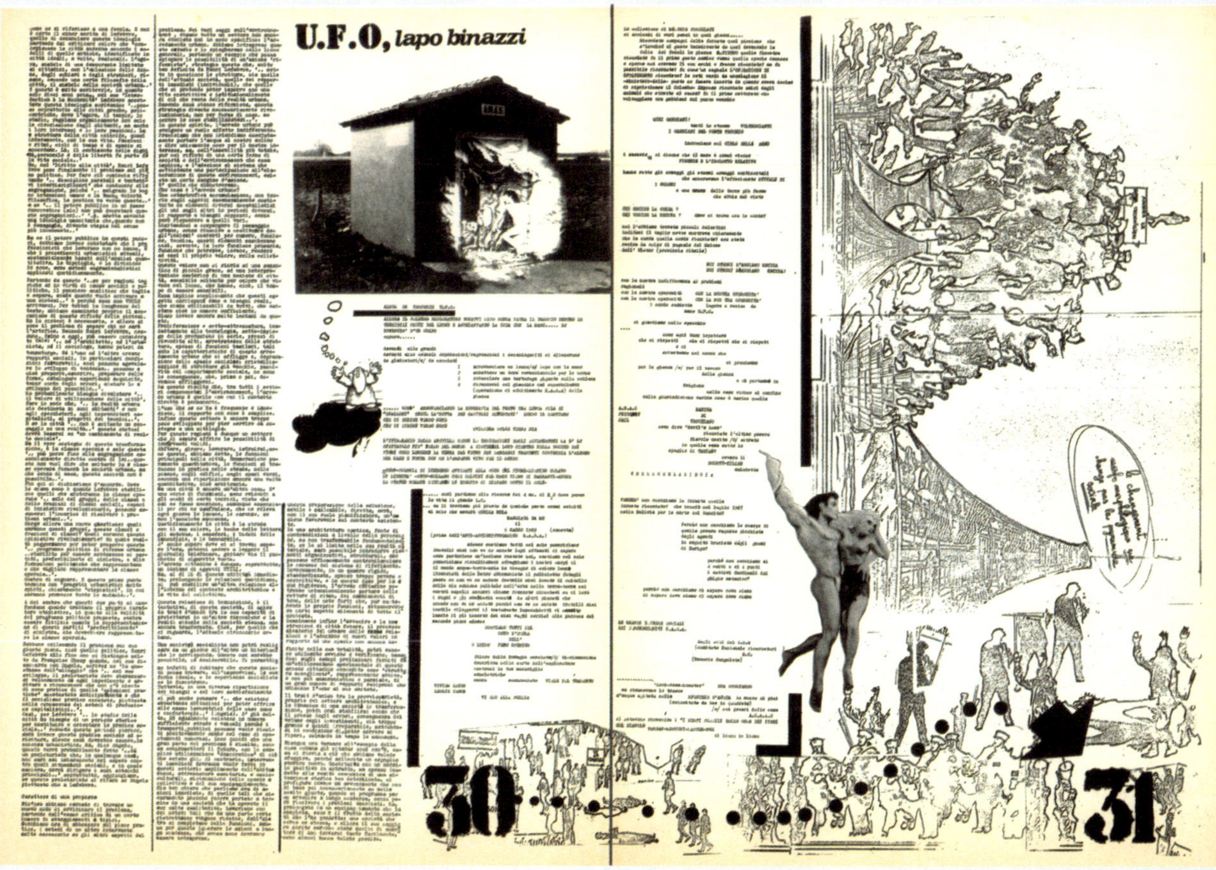
U.F.O, lapo binazzi
30
31

10. Album of Prophecies

UFO and Lapo Binazzi, 'Album di profezie', *Harck*, no. 1, 1971, pp. 30-31.

U.F.O. ALBUM OF PROPHECIES

AND SO THE FAMOUS EXPLORER BONATTI FEARLESSLY THRUST HIS ARM INTO THE TERRIBLE JAWS OF THE LION AND GRABBING ITS TAIL IN HIS HAND..... TURNED IT INSIDE OUT WITH ONE TUG
And yet.....

Faced with great
Faced with cruel repression/regression the second-born trained as gladiators/and/as crusaders

1. turning a lion/or/wolf inside out with their bare hands
2. bringing down a bull by flipping it by the horns
3. turning a giant tortoise on its back
4. using a net to fight off superpigeons (N.A.S.A. culling operation) in the square

...... SO TURNING THE GEOGRAPHY OF THE PLACE INSIDE OUT A LONG LINE OF "SMUGGLER MULES" FOLLOWS THE "FLOW OF EXPORTED CAPITAL" ALONG THE PATH
THAT LEADS NORTH
THAT LEADS NORTH
MY OWN SWEET SWITZERLAND

THE ROUTE OF THE EELS FOLLOWS THE DIRECTIONS OF THE EXPLORERS BUT IT'S THE WORLD'S FINEST SPECTACLE TO WITNESS THEM SWIMMING BACK UP THE MOUTHS OF RIVERS LIKE READING THE EARTH FROM THE GLASS OF THE SUPPOSED SARGASSO IT SKIRTS THE MAST OF THE SEA AND BRINGS QUICKSILVER ROUND THE WORLD

-STOP-COLONY OF ICEBERGS SPOTTED AT THE MOUTH OF THE RIVER-FREEZING LIQUID ON THE LOOSE-STOP-THEY ROLL LIKE DOLPHINS IN THE SEA FULL OF SWIMMERS-THE ROMAN STATUES ALSO FOLLOW THEIR EXAMPLE MELTING AWAY IN THE SUN-

... so we started off in search of the 4 m^3 of H_2O where the great L.C. (Le Corbusier) lost his life
... but we find them sooner somewhere now melted by the sun that ripened THE APPLE
THAT I ATE
on
9 MARCH 1969
(a rennet)
(prior to N.A.S.A.'s FUNGICIDOCIDES)

now let us all stay in the afternoon sun oh my brothers don't go wolves famished for knowledge as an Indian woman gives birth stay here, let us rest in the afternoon sun warm ourselves rub our bodies the world of water-land-air needs colour lions sacked by the Metro embrace the policeman frighten him come on don't go my brothers take the knife of my back clean it on the grass on the down-to-earth on your blue hair leafy tresses bend over the spiders and the obelisks come from other planets what's happening don't go why don't you go my brothers no point in rereading the will wolfcublets I axxxxt (sic) you I leave the most uncertain of my vague smiles to the landlady on the second floor now

LET US ALL REST IN THE
SHADOW CAST
BY THE
LAST SPHERICAL PEAR

row of trees from sunny Romagna/or/two-dimension described in the explorer's maps and papers
show us your skeletal
marvels
unknown world SUNSET BOULEVARD
VIVIEN LEIGH
LESLIE CARON
I LOVE YOU MADLY

The collection of FROZEN MEMORIES
Acquired several new pieces in those days .....
Do you remember merrie men that pigeon
that took flight at the gesture of blessing from
that windowsill the crowd of the faithful the
piazza of SAINT PETER's that window
remember how it was the first act of antagonism towards that harmful and filthy species we were there with bows and arrows remember? but it was possible remember? it was like a signal the CULLING OPERATION remember? the green bird-hunting nets the ministry-of-postal-services had been stockpiling them ever since it decided to bring back the Pigeon-Express remember friends of animals those twinges in your heart? it was the first one captured that wheeled among the seagulls of Ponte Vecchio

THOSE SEAGULLS!
all in a flock WHEELING
THE SEAGULLS OF PONTE VECCHIO

in the SKY OF THE ARNO they cross paths

The priests tell us the sea is coming close now
FLORENCE AND ITS ISOLOTTO-ISLAND

They've broken the moorings even the continental moorings
that anchored the loyal BOOT OF
THREE COLOURS
to one of the driest lands
ever seen

WHO CUT THE ROPE?
WHO KILLED THE QUEEN?
where is the rope now?

we've found it oh defenseless little
Celestines the clean cut clearly showed
that the rope that rope remember? Had been
cut with a slash of the dagger of the Malay
from Ulster (the rebel province)

WE OURSELVES CUT IT
WE OURSELVES CUT IT!

with our indifference to regional problems
with our industriousness
WITH OUR INDUSTRIOUSNESS
with our industriousness
WITH OUR INDUSTRIOUSNESS
the 2 aforecited ropes worn out and cut by
U.F.O. hands
we look at ourselves in the mirror
....
like any good inspector
with any self-respect self-respect self-respect
and we
arrest ourselves in the sense that
we grab ourselves
by the jacket/and/by the lapel
of the jacket
and haul ourselves
to Prison
in the house near the border
of the marine jurisdiction marine as in

A.N.A.S. MARINA
PRISON OF
JAIL VECCHIANO
aka the "devil's home"
remember the last poor
Devil who came out of/or/into
that house masquerading
as TARZAN?
or rather thecursed
BOUNTY-HUNTER

W H O R E A D S T H E B I B L E

WHY don't we seek the forest that
forest remember? that burned in July 1967
in Bolivia for the death of the outlaw?

Why don't we seek the shoes of
that poor girl beaten
by the agents
and later burnt by the gnomes
of Zurich?

why don't we seek in the house of the
4 winds or in the 4 directions
the evil Cardinals with their
satanic sneers?

Why don't we seek to know where we are
to know where we are to know where we
are

THE GREAT SOCIAL ENTERPRISES
OF N.A.S.A.'s SECOND-BORN

from the records of the N.R.C.
(National Research Council)
F.M.
(Frozen Memories)

....
the "Loch-Ness-Monster" HAD DISAPPEARED
but traces remained
of troubled water in the POND amidst the
pines
(marked off by a square of buoys)
/or/ in the vicinity of the
A.N.A.S. roadhouse
one could instead find FOSSILISED PRINTS OF THE
FEET
OF THE DEVIL
TARZAN-MERCURY-MASTER-FOX
from vine to vine

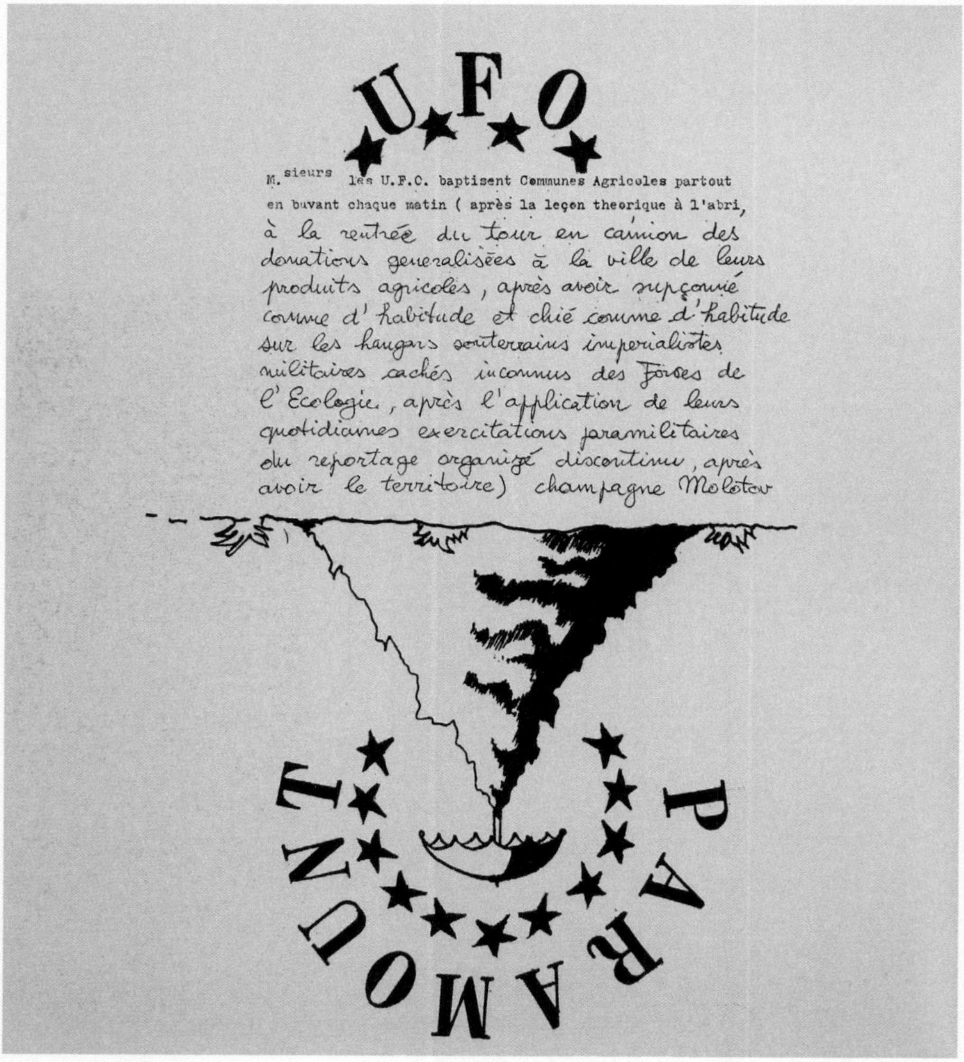
U.F.O
M.sieurs les U.F.C. baptisent Communes Agricoles partout
en buvant chaque matin (après la leçon theorique à l'abri,
à la rentrée du tour en camion des
donations generalisées à la ville de leurs
produits agricolés, après avoir supçonné
comme d'habitude et chié comme d'habitude
sur les hangars souterrains imperialistes
militaires cachés inconnus des Forces de
l'Ecologie, après l'application de leurs
quotidiannes exercitations paramilitaires
du reportage organizé discontinu, après
avoir le territoire) champagne Molotov
PARAMOUNT

11. Paramount

UFO, 'Paramount', in Achille Bonito Oliva (a cura di), *7. Biennale De Paris (catalogo della mostra, Parc Floral de Paris),* (Florence: Centro Di, 1971), n.p.

UFO

Misters UFO each morning baptise the Agricultural Communes with Molotov Champagne (after the theoretical lesson in the shelter, at the return of the tour in truck of the generalized donations to the city of their agricultural products, after suspecting as usual and shitting as usual on the unknown hidden military imperialist underground sheds of the Forces of the Ecology, after the application of their daily paramilitary exercises of discontinuous organised reportage, after having (sic) the territory)

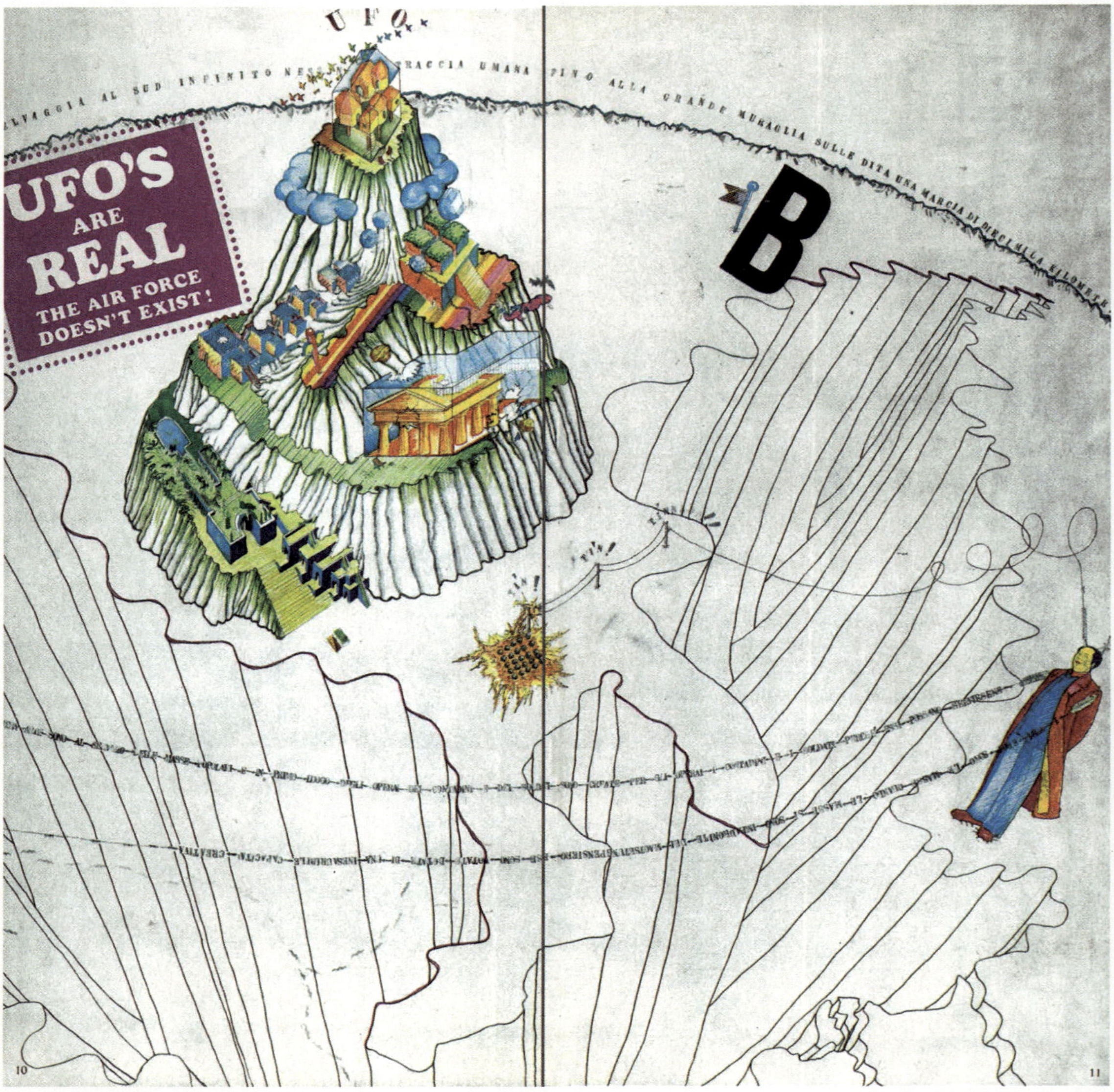
U F O
TRACCIA UMANA FINO ALLA GRANDE MURAGLIA SULLE DITA UNA MARCIA DI
UFO'S
ARE
REAL
THE AIR FORCE
DOESN'T EXIST!
B
10
11

12. UFO

R. B., 'UFO', *Caleidoscopio*, no. 11, January 1972, pp. 10-14.

The first part of the text was republished in Gianni Pettena (ed.), *La città invisibile. Architettura sperimentale 1965/1975* (Florence: Associazione Intercomunale N.10, 1983), in an extended version entitled "U.F.O. Story," signed by Lapo Binazzi alone and dated 1968. In the version appeared in Pettena's book, the text was extended with an introduction and a conclusion. The introduction reported: "EVERYTHING STARTED THAT DAY: THE FILM STUDIOS THAT SENT A WHOLE BUNCH OF INDIANS AND A LOAD OF OTHER PEOPLE ON THEIR WAY HEY! MIKE! ARE YOU LISTENING TO ME? BODY OF A DRUNK DOG! EVEN TARZAN AND THE GENERAL WENT TO DOWN A GLASS AT THE BAR OPPOSITE SO WE THOUGHT TO DO THIS FOR THEM WHICH IS A VILLAGE SURE A FINE VILLAGE A BLIND ALLEY IN THE MIDDLE OF THE COUNTRYSIDE BY GOD! BUT THERE WERE MANY PROBLEMS MIKE BELIEVE ME YOU COULDN'T SEE FROM THE OTHER SIDE THAT WAS HOW WE HAD THE IDEA OF THE CUL-DE-SAC WE LOOKED EACH OTHER IN THE EYE EUREKA! FROM THEN ON THAT WOULD BE OUR SOLUTION TO THE PROBLEMS OF TRAFFIC REMEMBER IT MIKE WHEN YOU ARE GROWN UP! SO WE TWISTED THE TRACKS AROUND AND TOOK BACK THE 'SALUTES' IT WAS REALLY A FINE DEAD END! BODY OF A MANGY DOG! ANYWAY THAT DAY N.A.S.A. CHANGED DIRECTION: INSTEAD OF GOING TO BREAK THEM AT THE LUNARS THEY SACKED 60,000 SUPERTECHNICIANS ON THE SPOT JUST THINK MIKE THIS IS IMPORTANT BY GOD! THERE WAS A SORT OF GOLD RUSH WHAT ELSE COULD WE DO? WE PUT THEM UP SOMEHOW OR OTHER IN THE A.N.A.S. HOUSES BUT THEY WENT OUT AT NIGHT TO DISTURB THE 'ECO-SYSTEMS' AND TO TAKE IT OUT ON THE INDIANS AND ALL THE OTHERS SO MUCH VIOLENCE MIKE!". The conclusion reported: "AND AT THE END OF 'SUNSET AVENUE' WE WILL ERECT THE U.F.O. ELDORADO IN GRATITUDE AND UNDERNEATH DIG A TUNNEL FOR THE TOMB OF THE PHARAOH X LIFE PULSATED IN 'SUNSET BOULEVARD' AT THE TABLES THE OLD AND FAT LADIES WATCHED US AND THEIR EYES SPARKLED UNDER THE MOON OF THE CAFFÈ CONCERTO THE END."

IT WAS AN ARCHITECTURE OF FACADES OF RAILWAY HOUSES OF INDIAN TENTS OF ROAD WORKERS' HOUSES OF COUNTRY GRAVEYARDS OF 16TH-CENTURY STABLES OF NEO-NEOREALIST FACTORIES OF LITTLE TEMPLES OF CASTLES OF FAIRY CASTLES OF ROMAN AQUEDUCTS OF TELEPHONE BOXES OF PINEWOODS OF BEACHES OF MONUMENTS AND AN URBANISM MADE UP OF CUL-DE-SACS DEAD-END TRACKS DESERTS PRAIRIES COLLAPSED TRENCHES MAIN STREETS CINEMATIC VILLAGES KASBAHS GHETTOES PUEBLOS BIG ESTATES SMALL TOWNS TENEMENT HOUSES TOWERS OF BABEL INDIAN CAMPS TENT CITIES SHANTIES ON A WORLDWIDE SCALE.... SO OUR VILLAGE HAS RISEN UNEXPECTEDLY OH! WE WORKED HARD MIKE! WITH THE INGENUITY CHARACTERISTIC OF PIONEERS OR FRIARS AND THAT'S WHAT WE FELT OURSELVES TO BE WE PUT UP THOSE STRICTLY TYPICAL MODELS IN A SHORT TIME.....

THE WIND ON THE PAPER WALL

These **villes de papier**, which do not shift the flight of birds in the sky, nor disturb the lazy torpor of the Spanish *Guardia Civil*, as soon as they negate their **strategy of the fantastic** appearance to take on the forms of the **utopia of the possible** become "project of quality." The creative constants of utopia, in fact, which reality wants mediated through the expository necessities of needs, can at any moment turn against the **ad hoc** phantoms of reality as soon as these, denying their possible condition of real facts, become *epiphenomena* of class. Besides on the crystal vault of the temple the anger of the law of gravity is just one model of the armed thought of the **Masked Man** deft at taking flight at the right time in the direction of when.

Common sense—historical negation of the sense of the real—unilaterally inflates the definition of the fall. For that matter what on earth are the topographies of these "inhabitables" if not geographies of **signs**? The cultivation of cabbage, intensive under the "TING!" of the telegraph, is apologetic of other rooms, of other sounds, of picnics consumed on the sycamore in the shadow of a patrol of dead killed twice: by the penal laws and by the laws of Gutenberg. The politics of hope, dressed in the colours of yellow, of papal memory, are nothing but the hope of a better future. But hope, we know, cannot fit in the rucksack of those who have nothing to propose apart from life itself!

(*r. b.*)

UFO

Carlo Bachi, Lapo Binazzi, Patrizia Cammeo, Riccardo Foresi, Vittorio Maschietto

ELEMENTI DI PROSSEMICA TERRITORIALE

QUESTIONARIO

Hai mai notato che in vicinanza di particolari istituzioni repressive dello STATO BORGHESE:
CARCERI CONVENTI CASERME (basi segrete) commissariati di polizia (anche di quartiere), persiste in permanenza una specie di anello psicologico protettivo, di campo magnetico di tipo particolare determinato da circostanze solitamente strane?
(sì) (no)
Pensi che le sentinelle, di certo di guardia, siano in relazione con ciò?
(sì) (no)
Pensi che siano le emissioni di un qualche criptopotere?
(sì) (no)
I fatti e le cose connessi con questo tipo di istituzioni ti appaiono come un tutto unico di tipo simbolico?
(sì) (no)
Se sì, ti è mai successo di vedere un edificio che agisce come un soggetto?
(sì) (no)
e un'auto?
(sì) (no)
Ti è mai successo di avere come delle apparizioni di fatti persone e cose di cui intuivi vagamente, ma con una certa resistenza da parte tua ad ammettere una simile eventualità, la connessione, poi rivelatasi esatta, con quanto ti è stato detto prima?
(sì) (no)
In vicinanza di queste istituzioni, hai ricevuto mai violenze psicologiche e materiali o di qualsiasi tipo?
(sì) (no)
Da parte di chi? ______

Ti è mai stata rivolta la parola da parte di emissari di questi poteri nascosti con una scusa qualsiasi, oppure per aver commesso azioni che in qualsiasi altro punto del territorio probabilmente appena fuori di quella specie di anello magnetico o che altro, non avrebbero avuto alcuna osservazione?
(sì) (no)
Racconta: ______

Sei disposto a farci un racconto più generale su un'esperienza avuta in proposito?
(sì) (no)
Racconta: ______

Una volta uscito da questa avventura ti sei sorpreso a pensare che poteva trattarsi di un sogno, di uno scherzo, di una congiura? Di avere attraversato un luogo dove per incanto le libertà personali erano minori che in altri punti del territorio?
(sì) (no)
Hai pensato che si poteva trattare di ciò che si dice volgarmente un ABUSO DELL'IMMAGINARIO?
(sì) (no)
Hai mai notato di recente, trovandoti nei pressi di dette istituzioni e specialmente di basi militari alleate, improvvise sparizioni di fatti e persone o cose?
(sì) (no)
Racconta: ______

Cerca attraverso una piantina disegnata di descrivere la topografia del luogo con punti di riferimento esatti:

Hai mai notato trasformazioni morfologiche del territorio dovute a protesi mimetiche di uscite, ingressi, boccaporti segreti?
(sì) (no)
Crediti nell'esistenza degli UFO?
(sì) (no)
Quali? ______
Riesci a distinguere facilmente i campi di influenza di istituzioni diverse agenti sul territorio?
(sì) (no)
Quando esci di città? ______
No! Volevo dire, qual è il momento in cui credi stupidamente di uscire dalla città?
______

Credi che dipenda dai cartelli segnaletici della geografia borghese?
(sì) (no)
o dal ringiovanimento brusco degli edifici?
(sì) (no)
o dai negozi sfitti?
(sì) (no)
o dall'improvvisa apparizione di un giardiniere in fuga?
(sì) (no)
Credi nell'esistenza della perfezione della periferia?
(sì) (no)
Pensi forse che sia solo un grosso guadagno per alcuni?
(sì) (no)
per chi? ______
Sai che un ladro che scappa in periferia è subito acciuffato?
(sì) (no)
Lo stesso in città o in campagna può farla franca?
(sì) (no)
Hai deciso come comportarti in facoltà?
(sì) (no)
e a casa?
(sì) (no)
Potresti dedurre (indovinare) dagli indizi precedenti il tipo di attività degli abitanti, l'ora del giorno, il grado di cultura medio, le loro abitudini?
(sì) (no)
In un viaggio all'estero sei capace di riconoscere a colpo sicuro quali sono le istituzioni simili a quelle a te ben note di casa tua?
(In questo campo di osservazione rientrano autostrade, case A.N.A.S., ferrovie dello stato, istituzioni per l'infanzia e più generalmente INDUSTRIA-AGRICOLTURA-ATTIVITA' TERZIARIA?)
(sì) (no)
Oss.: Data l'importanza di questo punto, sarebbe meglio fare l'analisi caso per caso, salvo i casi di intreccio; importante a questo proposito è di mettersi in un punto di osservazione privilegiato o completamente sottomesso, comunque sono da preferire gli obiettivi veramente obiettivi tendenti al **realismo più crudo** cioè agli indizi.
Sai che le automobili sono di proprietà pubblica?
(sì) (no)
Sarebbe sensato in questo caso interrompere le autostrade ogni 100 km. con m. 200 di bosco ceduo?
(sì) (no)
Credi che queste passeggiate per cambiare macchina facciano bene?
(sì) (no)
ti piacerebbe?
(sì) (no)
Nella tua osservazione e ricerca degli indizi ti senti condizionato dalla segregazione che t'impone la città?
(sì) (no)
Ti senti veramente partecipe della vita del territorio con tutti i suoi innumerevoli segreti?
(sì) (no)
Hai mai pensato che ogni segregazione o occultamento aumenta il potere nascosto di chi le compie?
(sì) (no)
Ti sei mai servito di questo procedimento?
(sì) (no)
In vicinanza di tali istituzioni hai mai visto volare gente dalla finestra?
(sì) (no)
E sparati dal cannone?
(sì) (no)
dove? ______
Assistendo a una corsa a tappe sei mai stato testimone di un dirottamento?
(sì) (no)
Cerca di ricostruire a freddo o a caldo, se per caso eri in possesso di un qualsiasi mezzo di riporto, le circostanze in cui ti sei trovato:
(Sono ammesse le fotografie di edifici, le piantine topografiche, i nastri magnetici, i films, i microfilms, pareri occasionali di testimoni, interviste, numeri di telefono, le foto aeree, le foto di territorio, il videotape, libri contabili, INDIZI SOLIDI REALI, e quanto altro possa servire all'istruzione della pratica in questione)
Hai mai cercato di risalire dalla divisa di un poliziotto a un suo cervello?
(sì) (no)
Sei davanti ad un edificio sede di una delle istituzioni di cui sopra; ne osservi le caratteristiche formali, cerchi di vedere cosa succede all'interno, ti soffermi sui particolari apparentemente insignificanti, pensi che stai costeggiando un mondo completamente estraneo a te, alle tue speranze per il futuro, tenti di indovinare il complesso di abitudini che ne regolano il funzionamento, pensi di trovarti davanti ad una specie di mostro sconosciuto di enormi dimensioni che mangia, rumina, sputa fuoco, caca, si occupa di cose relative a se stesso e basta, espande i suoi emissari ed esecutori in tutto il territorio circostante?
(sì) (no)
Hai mai fatto parte di un'organizzazione clandestina, di una setta segreta?
(sì) (no)
quale? ______
hai partecipato a riunioni iniziatiche?
(sì) (no)
dove? (descrivi esattamente luoghi e circostanze): ______

Cosa ne pensi della massoneria? ______
pensi che sia in relazione con l'attuale situazione politica?
(sì) (no)
e con la situazione della scuola?
(sì) (no)
Quante volte al giorno fai l'amore con tua moglie (o fidanzata o amante...)?
______
Pensi che la droga sia un modo per governare il mondo?
(sì) (no)
in che modo? ______
Sei disposto a perdonare queste divagazioni?
(sì) (no)
Ne scusi la banalità?
(sì) (no)

L'indignazione di K. — nel *Castello* di K. — per un verbale mai sottoscritto, cercando il pettine di Frida sotto il solito traliccio, per un verbale, « steso in mia assenza da uno che non ha nemmeno assistito al colloquio? Questa è bella! » ci guida (sic!) attraverso « gli agiati percorsi » alla vera natura dell'ambasciata in corso, confronta anche con la domanda: a che livello interviene l'organizzazione segreta nel controllo della scuola, leggiamo: « ...l'amministrazione intende prendere delle misure veramente generose, non dipende che da lei accettarle. E cioè le offre provvisoriamente il posto di bidello ». Che la scuola sia veramente piuttosto sudicia come dice il sindaco lamentandosi del lavoro della moglie del sagrestano? La polizia indaga! Non a caso questo questionario è stato sequestrato da quella fiorentina nella nota sede del solito « gruppetto di sbandati capelloni drogati e sovversivi », sequestrato in camicia — come suol dirsi — quasi prima di delinquere, insomma, sequestrato in matrice. Per il sudiciume della scuola, K. — a scanso di pericolosi equivoci — osserva: « rispondendo secondo verità non è poi una grande disgrazia ». Infatti, questo testo è stato distribuito dagli UFO, in parte assistenti, durante un seminario — semiclandestino — sul territorio, e da lì partito — con la mano del Signore — in tutta Italia. E questo è tutto. Il resto della storia potrebbe essere così: « Lei si è preoccupato per nulla signor maestro, io non ho la minima intenzione di accettare quel posto. Ottimamente, disse il maestro, ottimamente, lei rifiuta senza alcuna riserva » (pagine 120, 121, 122 dell'edizione italiana). A chi fosse interessato al « posto », invece, si suggerisce di riempire il questionario e spedircelo indietro. Sarà pubblicato in un libro con il vostro nome o senza, a piacere, affinché ciò che gestisce il sociologo ritorni alla sociologia (sic!).

FU UN ARCHITETTURA DI FACCIATE
DI CASELLI FERROVIARI DI TENDE INDIANE
DI CASE CANTONIERE DI CIMITERI DI CAMPA-
GNA DI STALLE DEL'500 DI FABBRICHE
NEO-NEOREALISTE DI TEMPIETTI DI
CASTELLI DI CASTELLI DI FATE DI ACQUE-
DOTTI ROMANI DI CABINE TELEFONICHE
DI PINETE DI SPIAGGE DI MONUMENTI
E UN URBANISTICA FATTA DI
STRADE CHIUSE BINARI MORTI DESERTI
PRATERIE TRINCEE FRANATE MAIN STRE-
ET VILLAGGI CINEMATOGRAFICI CASBAH
GHETTI PUEBLI FEUDI PAESOTTI FALANSTERI
TORRI DI BABELE ACCAMPAMENTI INDIANI
TENDOPOLI BARACCHE A SCALA MONDIALE....
IL NOSTRO VILLAGGIO SORSE COSI'
ALL'IMPROVVISO OH! ERAVAMO OPEROSI
MIKE! CON LA SOLERTIA CARATTERISTICA
DEI PIONIERI O DEI FRATI E TALI NOI CI
SENTIVAMO TIRAMMO SU IN POCO TEMPO
QUEI MODELLI RIGOROSAMENTE TIPICI.....

A che livello pensi che intervenga (se interviene) l'organizzazione segreta nel controllo della scuola (università)?
bidelli?
(sì) (no)
studenti?
(sì) (no)
addetti alle esercitazioni?
(sì) (no)
incaricati?
(sì) (no)
professori di ruolo?
(sì) (no)
ai gradi più alti?
(sì) (no)
Che strategia intendi adottare ai fini di formarti una famiglia? ______

Sapresti sparare a un B-52?
(sì) (no)
e a un F-104?
(sì) (no)
Pensi di vincere tu o di rimanere schiacciato da forze più potenti delle tue?
(sì) (no)
segrete?
o no?
Se qualcuno ti dicesse che per ottenere un posto ufficiale (o no) di leccatore di culo devi vendere il tuo, cosa gli risponderesti? ______

(nel rispondere a quest'ultima domanda ricorda che sei libero di citare degli esempi reali accaduti con nomi di fatti persone cose ecc.)
Nel caso che queste domande ti sembrassero troppo singolari e limitative (troppo individualistiche) pensi che la coscienza di classe ti potrebbe aiutare a risolvere il tuo problema?
(sì) (no)
attraverso quali partiti? ______
Pensi che il questionario non sia obiettivo?
(sì) (no)
Allora saresti disposto a fondare un nuovo movimento di massa?
(sì) (no)
Che ne pensi della crisi dei tecnici? ______
hai mai visto un tecnico disoccupato?
(sì) (no)
se sì dove? ______
cercava lavoro?
(sì) (no)
lo hanno assunto?
(sì) (no)
a quanto il mese? ______
dove? ______ da chi? ______ tel. ______
E' importante per te ottenere un buon voto?
(sì) (no)
fare un buon esame?
(sì) (no)
una buona ricerca?
(sì) (no)
una buona operazione politica?
(sì) (no)
quale delle quattro? I II III IV e perché? ______

Ti piacerebbe tenere in Vaticano una conferenza su ______
(sì) (no)
e in Cina?
(sì) (no)
Puoi darci i nomi di dieci persone che la pensano come te su tante cose?
(sì) (no)
e 100 che non la pensano come te? ______

Scusa, pensi che queste domande siano un ROMPICAPO frutto di una fantasia malata?
(sì) (no) (non lo so)
Saresti disposto a collaborare ad un'inchiesta seria sui CRIPTOPOTERI, a smascherare gli INDIZI?
(sì) (no)
Allora dimmi: sei mai stato interrogato dalla polizia?
(sì) (no)
Dal barista di ORDINE NUOVO?
(sì) (no)
Ti sei mai accorto di trovarti in un luogo diverso e in una diversa situazione mentale da indizi casuali come la differenza di calore tra una zona e l'altra del territorio/città, un improvviso volo d'uccelli, rumori differenti relativi all'attività ivi principalmente svolta, odori strani percepiti olfattivamente con un gusto quasi erotico, una cosa che ti capita sotto gli occhi all'improvviso, una strana sensazione indefinita di inquietudine, un vuoto dentro, presenze sospette in pieno mezzogiorno?
(sì) (no)
Racconta: ______

Hai mai visto particolari segni di vita, vegetazione folta, voli di uccelli, presenze di animali, coleotteri fermi, pipistrelli in caccia di mattina, nelle vicinanze delle istituzioni in esame?
(sì) (no)
Cominciamo proprio da te: sei colpevole o non colpevole?
(sì) (no) (non lo so)

13. Elements of Territorial Proxemics: Questionnaire

UFO, 'Elementi di prossemica territoriale: questionario', *King Kong*, no. 2, June 1972, pp. 10-11.

QUESTIONNAIRE

Have you ever noticed that in the vicinity of particular repressive institutions of the BOURGEOIS STATE:
PRISONS, MONASTERIES, BARRACKS (secret bases), police stations (even neighbourhood ones), there is a sort of permanent protective psychological ring, a magnetic field of a special kind determined by what are usually strange circumstances?
(yes) (no)
Do you think that the sentries, certainly on guard, are connected with this?
(yes) (no)
Do you think that they are the emissions of some hidden power?
(yes) (no)
Do the facts and things connected with this kind of institution look to you like an integrated whole of a symbolic kind?
(yes) (no)
If yes, have you ever seen a building that acts like a person?
(yes) (no)
and a car?
(yes) (no)
Have you ever had anything like an apparition of facts, people, and things which you sensed vaguely, but with a certain resistance on your part to admit such a possibility, the connection, later revealed to be accurate, with what you have been told before?
(yes) (no)

In the vicinity of these institutions, have you even been on the receiving end of psychological and physical, or any other kind of violence?
(yes) (no)
From whom?

____

____

Have you ever been accosted by emissaries of these hidden powers on some pretext or other, or for having done something that at any other point of the territory probably just outside that sort of magnetic or whatever ring would have gone completely unnoticed?
(yes) (no)
Tell us about it:

____

____

Are you willing to give us a more general account of an experience of this kind?
(yes) (no)
Tell us about it:

____

____

Once you had emerged from this adventure were you surprised to think that it might have been a dream, a practical joke, a plot? To have passed through a place where as if by magic there was less personal freedom than at other points of the territory?
(yes) (no)
Have you thought that it might have been what is commonly called an ABUSE OF THE IMAGINARY?
(yes) (no)
Have you ever noticed recently when near such institutions and especially Allied military bases

sudden disappearances of facts and people or things?
(yes) (no)
Tell us about it:

____

____

Try to draw a plan to describe the topography of the place with exact points of reference:

Have you ever noticed morphological transformations in the territory due to mimetic prostheses of exits, entrances, secret hatchways?
(yes) (no)
Do you believe in UFOs?
(yes) (no)
Which ones?

____

____

Are you able to easily distinguish the fields of influence of different institutions acting on the territory?
(yes) (no)
When you leave the city?

____

____

No! What I meant to say, at what moment do you stupidly believe you have left the city?

____

____

Do you think that it depends on the warning signs of bourgeois geography?
(yes) (no)
or on the abrupt rejuvenation of buildings?
(yes) (no)
or on unlet shops?
(yes) (no)
or on the unexpected appearance of a fleeing gardener?
(yes) (no)
Do you believe in the existence of perfection in the suburbs?
(yes) (no)
Do you perhaps think that it is just a fat profit for some?
(yes) (no)
for whom?
(yes) (no)
Do you know that a thief who escapes to the suburbs is nabbed at once?
(yes) (no)
Can the same thief get away with it in the city or the countryside?
(yes) (no)
Have you decided how you are going to behave in the Faculty?
(yes) (no)
and at home?
(yes) (no)
Could you deduce (guess) from the preceding clues the type of activity of the inhabitants, the time of day, their average level of education, their habits?
(yes) (no)
On a journey abroad are you able to recognise without fail which are the institutions similar the ones you are familiar with at home?
(Do motorways, A.N.A.S. roadhouses, national railways, institutions for children, and more generally INDUSTRY-AGRICULTURE-SERVICES fall within this field of observation?)
(yes) (no)
NB: Given the importance of this point, it would be better to carry out the analysis case by case, apart from the ones that are intertwined; it is important in this connection to adopt a privileged or completely submissive point of observation, but truly objective objectives tending to the **crudest realism,** i.e. to the evidence, are to be preferred.
Do you know that cars are public property?
(yes) (no)
Would it make sense in this case to interrupt motorways every 100 km with 200 m of woodland?
(yes) (no)
Do you think that these walks in order to change cars would be good for people?
(yes) (no)
would you like it?
(yes) (no)
In your observation and research of the evidence do you feel conditioned by the segregation that the city imposes on you?
(yes) (no)
Do you really feel part of the life of the territory with all its innumerable secrets?
(yes) (no)
Have you ever thought that any segregation or concealment increases the hidden power of those who do it?
(yes) (no)
Have you ever made use of this procedure?
(yes) (no)
In the vicinity of such institutions have you ever seen people fly out of the window?

(yes) (no)
And shot from a cannon?
(yes) (no)
where?

Have you ever witnessed a change of course while watching a race in stages?
(yes) (no)
Try to reconstruct in the cold light of day or on the spur of the moment, if by chance you were in possession of any means of return, the circumstances in which you found yourself:
(Photographs of buildings, topographic maps, magnetic tapes, films, microfilms, random opinions of witnesses, interviews, telephone numbers, aerial photos, photos of the area, videotapes, account books, REAL SOLID EVIDENCE and whatever else might be of use to the establishment of the practice in question are all admitted).
Have you ever tried to find your way back from a policeman's uniform to his brain?
(yes) (no)
You are in front of a building housing one of the institutions referred to above; you observe its formal characteristics, you try to see what is going on inside, you linger over apparently insignificant details. Do you think that you are moving along the edge of a world completely extraneous to you, to your hopes for the future? Do you try to work out the set of habits that govern its functioning? Do you think that you are faced with a sort of monster of enormous size that eats, ruminates, spits fire, shits, concerns itself with things related to itself and nothing more, sends out its emissaries and executors into the whole of the surrounding territory?
(yes) (no)
Have you ever belonged to a clandestine organisation, a secret sect?
(yes) (no)
which?

Have you taken part in rites of initiation?
(yes) (no)
where? (describe exactly the places and circumstances)

What do you think of Freemasonry?

Do you think that it has any connection with the current political situation?
(yes) (no)
and with the situation in education?
(yes) (no)
How many times a day do you make love to your wife (or girlfriend or lover...)?

Do you think that drugs are a way of governing the world?
(yes) (no)
how?

Are you willing to forgive these digressions?
(yes) (no)
Do you excuse their banality?
(yes) (no)
At what level do you think that the secret organisation intervenes (if it intervenes) in control of the school (university)?
janitors?
(yes) (no)
students?
(yes) (no)
teaching assistants?
(yes) (no)
temporary lecturers?
(yes) (no)
permanent professors?
(yes) (no)
at higher levels?
(yes) (no)
What strategy do you intend to adopt in order to form a family?

Would you know how to shoot at a B-52?
(yes) (no)
and at a F-104?
(yes) (no)
Do you think you are going to win or be crushed by forces more powerful than your own?
(yes) (no)
secret ones?
or not?
If someone told you that to obtain an official (or not) post as an arse licker you are going to have to sell yours, how would you respond?

(when answering this last question remember that you are free to give examples of things that have really happened with names of facts people things, etc.)
If you find that these questions are too singular and limiting (too individualistic), do you think that class consciousness could help you to solve your problem?
(yes) (no)
through what parties?

___

___

Do you think that the questionnaire is not objective?
(yes) (no)
Then would you be willing to found a new mass movement?
(yes) (no)
What do you think of the crisis in technicians?

___

___

Have you ever seen an unemployed technician?
(yes) (no)
if so, where?

___

___

was he looking for work?
(yes) (no)
did they hire him?

___

___

(yes) (no)
for how much a month?

___

___

where?

___

for whom?

___

tel.

___

Is it important for you to get good marks?
(yes) (no)
do well in an exam?
(yes) (no)
carry out good research?
(yes) (no)
a good political operation?
(yes) (no)
which of the four? 1st, 2nd, 3rd, 4th, and why?

___

___

Would you like to hold a conference in the Vatican on

___

(yes) (no)
and in China?
(yes) (no)
Can you give us the names of ten people who think the same way as you about many things?
(yes) (no)
and 100 that don't think like you?

___

___

Excuse me, but do you think that these questions are a RIDDLE that is the fruit of a sick imagination?
(yes) (no) (don't know)
Would you be willing to collaborate with a serious investigation of the HIDDEN POWERS, in order to uncover the EVIDENCE?
(yes) (no)
Then tell me: have you ever been interrogated by the police?
(yes) (no)
By the barman of ORDINE NUOVO?
(yes) (no)
Have you ever been made aware that you are in a different place and a different mental situation by random clues like the difference in warmth between one part and another of the territory/city, an unexpected flock of birds, noises that differ from the ones related to the principal activity carried out there, strange odours perceived with the nose in almost erotic fashion, something that happens suddenly in front of your eyes, a strange and vague sensation of disquiet, a feeling of emptiness inside, suspicious presences in the middle of the day?
(yes) (no)
Tell us about it:

___

___

Have you ever seen particular signs of life, dense vegetation, flights of birds, presence of animals, motionless beetles, bats hunting in the morning, in the vicinity of the institutions in question?
(yes) (no)
Let's start with you: are you guilty or not guilty?
(yes) (no) (don't know)

K's indignation—in K's *The Castle*—over a protocol he never signed, while looking for his comb under the usual transmission tower, for a protocol "drawn up afterwards in my absence by someone who wasn't at the interview at all? That's not bad," guides us (*sic!*) along "easy paths" to the true nature of the embassy under way and also confronts us with the question: at what level does the secret organisation intervene to control the school. This is what the protocol said: "(...) the administration wants to provide a temporary and truly generous settlement; it simply lies with you to accept it. He offers you provisionally the post of school janitor'." Is the school really as dirty as the mayor says, complaining about the work of the churchwarden's wife? The police are investigating! It is no coincidence that this questionnaire was confiscated by the Florentine police in the well-known haunt of the usual "small group of misfits, hippies, drug addicts and subversives," confiscated in its nightshirt—as they say—almost before committing a crime, in short, confiscated in the mould. As for the dirt in the school, K—to avoid any chancy misunderstandings—replied "keeping to the truth, that it wasn't so very bad." In fact, this text was distributed by the UFOs, in part acting as assistants, during a—semi-clandestine—seminar on the territory and from there spread—by the hand of God—throughout Italy. And that's all. The rest of the story could go like this: "'You've taken your trouble for nothing, teacher, (...) I have no intention of accepting the post.' 'Splendid!' said the teacher. 'Splendid! You decline quite unconditionally (pages 120,121 and 122 in the Italian edition)'." To anyone interested in the "post," though, we suggest filling in the questionnaire and sending it back to us. It will be published in a book with or without your name, as you wish, so that what the sociologist handles can go back to sociology *(sic!)*.

UFO

Lapo Binazzi
Patrizia Cammeo
Riccardo Foresi
Carlo Bachi
Titti Maschietto

IL GIRO D'ITALIA
E'
PER DAVVERO
UN
PROGETTO D'URBANISTICA

Partiam!-Partiam!-Partiam!! Si controllano i debiti e i crediti la carovana si sposta per esercitazioni nel tratto di territorio A-B. Con le insalate i campi gli orti cinesi - memorie - congelate negli occhi i girini transitano nel Piper obsoleto e meditano un attraversamento del Centro Storico con:
A-B Gara di inseguimento individuale intorno al battistero
A-B Giro del Duomo: prove di velocità
A-B Scalata della cupola con funi e tiranti
A-B Inseguimenti a squadre sul sagrato (a tappini)

A-B LA PUNZONATURA

IL GIRO D'ITALIA
E'
RIVISTA ALL'ITALIANA

Un ragazzino di 6 anni con la marinara tira al guinzaglio dietro i cespugli un enorme bastimento bianco alto 10 metri recitando la storiella:
Or tre baldi giovanotti
son finiti nei salotti
per piacere alle signore
leggon testi con ardore
progettando a cavalcioni
si fan belli gli sbruffoni
va a finire in uno smacco
lo spettacolo assai fiacco
Sono guai e son dolori
volan bassi i pomodori.

TRAGUARDO TRICOLORE A PREMIO A-B

UFO

IL GIRO D'ITALIA
E'
UN PROGETTO D'ARCHITETTURA

La piramide umana.
L'uomo sparato dal cannone.
Il vincitore di tappa.
Sono fra le poche forme di architettura ancora possibili.

LA VITTORIA DI TAPPA A-B

IL GIRO D'ITALIA
E'
UN PROGETTO DI DESIGN

massima:
«Il rifornimento di idee passa attraverso la gastronomia».
conclusione:
...facendo l'elastico con idee e concetti forme e sostanze alla folla verticale correndo su due ruote e camminando su due gambe che è lo stesso.

A-B IL PIC-NIC

14. The Giro d'Italia

UFO, 'Il Giro d'Italia', *in. Argomenti e immagini di design*, no. 6, July-August 1972, pp. 66-67.

THE GIRO D'ITALIA
IS
REALLY
AN URBANISM SCHEME

Let's go!-Let's go!-Let's go!! Checking the debts and credits the caravan moves on for exercises in the stretch of territory A-B. With the salads the fields the Chinese vegetable gardens—memories—frozen in their eyes the cyclists pass through the obsolete discotheque and think about a crossing of the Historic Centre with:
A-B Individual pursuit race around the baptistery
A-B Giro del Duomo: speed trials around the cathedral
A-B Climb of the dome with ropes and wires
A-B Team pursuits on the parvis (in short stages)

THE GIRO D'ITALIA
IS
AN ITALIAN-STYLE REVUE

A 6-year-old boy in a sailor suit drags an enormous, 10-metre-high white ship on a lead behind the bushes reciting the story:
Now three dashing young men
have ended up in the drawing rooms
for the pleasure of the ladies
they read texts with ardour
planning astride
the blowhards show off
it's going to finish in humiliation
the lackadaisical spectacle
It's trouble and its pain
tomatoes are flying low.

THE GIRO D'ITALIA
IS
A PROJECT OF ARCHITECTURE

The human pyramid.
The man shot out of a cannon.
The stage winner.
Are among the few forms of architecture still possible.

THE GIRO D'ITALIA
IS
A DESIGN PROJECT

maxim:
"The replenishment of ideas passes through gastronomy."
Conclusion:
... getting left behind the group with ideas and concepts forms and substances to the vertical crowd running on two wheels and walking on two legs which is the same.

LA PROVOCAZIONE DEGLI UFO

Nel pomeriggio del 27 maggio, nei locali che avevano ospitato Il Codice si è svolto un happening, organizzato dal gruppo degli UFO di Firenze (Carlo Bachi, Lapo Binazzi, Patrizia Cammeo, Riccardo Forese, Titti Maschietto) con l'eccezionale collaborazione del signor Rodolfo Bracci — happening che si è interrotto clamorosamente con l'arrivo di un cavallo purosangue.

HAPPENING ALL'EURODOMUS

Lezione Universitaria n. 1 Turin old domestic landscape

<u>Titolo</u>: DALL'URBANISTICA ALL'EFFETTO PERSONALE-USI E COSTUMI
(proiezioni)

LA CASA A OSTACOLI SUL TERRITORIO (partecipazione del pubblico)

....

L'mpossibilità di esprimere se stessi in modi di abitare prima della riconquista del comportamento è l'impssibilità di una casa non-a-ostacoli. Tra fatto personale e ragion di stato c'è sempre qualcosa da fare.......

si tratta di esaminare le possibilità di adattamento estetico anche nei casi più gravi
realtà e fantasia coincidono nel presente
e uccidono il drago dell'intrigo e del machiavellismo

Nella prossemica territoriale gli indizi
della discontinuità del reale sono gli ostacoli
salutari da portarsi appresso:
sono gli EFFETTI PERSONALI

Le recinzioni e le sottrazioni di territorio si uguagliano con le somme dei comportamenti sbagliati.

Nel percorso in vista del mare, prima di arrivare alla contemplazione della serenità del panoramico, il cavaliere e il cavallo di Piazza di Siena cercano senza riuscirci il filo d'Arianna nel labirinto del quotidiano, superando gli ostacoli della mente.

15. The UFO's Provocation

UFO, 'La provocazione degli ufo: happening all'Eurodomus', *Domus*, no. 512, July 1972, p. 34.

On the afternoon of 27 May, a happening took place in the rooms that had hosted *Il Codice*, organised by the UFO group in Florence (Carlo Bachi, Lapo Binazzi, Patrizia Cammeo, Riccardo Foresi, Titti Maschietto) with the exceptional collaboration of Signor Rodolfo Bracci—a happening that was sensationally interrupted by the arrival of a thoroughbred horse.

University Lecture no. 1
Turin old domestic landscape
Title: FROM URBANISM TO THE PERSONAL BELONGING—CUSTOMS AND TRADITIONS
(projections)

THE OBSTACLE HOUSE ON THE TERRITORY (participation of the public)

....

The impossibility of expressing ourselves in modes of living before the reconquest of behaviour is the impossibility of a non-obstacle house. Between personal matter and reason of state there is always something to do.......

> It is a question of examining the possibility of aesthetic adaptation even in the most serious cases
> reality and fantasy coincide in the present and kill the dragon of intrigue and Machiavellianism.

In territorial proxemics signs
of the discontinuity of the real are salutary
obstacles to be carried around;
they are PERSONAL BELONGINGS

> Enclosures and misappropriations of territory can be compared with the sums of patterns of bad behaviour.

On the road in view of the sea, before arriving at contemplation of the serenity of the scenic route, the rider and horse of Piazza di Siena seek in vain Ariadne's thread in the labyrinth of the everyday, overcoming the obstacles of the mind.

UFO
Coccoina

I
Il camion scarica una rete elastica e un materasso per l'uomo sparato dal cannone
materiali
(del camion e dell'uomo del comune e della piazza):
rete metallica elastica/
materassa materasso elastica/
maglia di campione d'Italia/
ciuccia di campione d'Italia/
miccia 4 yarde/
cannone a elastico/
corda metrica di platino e iridio/
teodolito iperbolico/
tavole trigonometriche/
casco accappatoio
fedina penale vaselina/

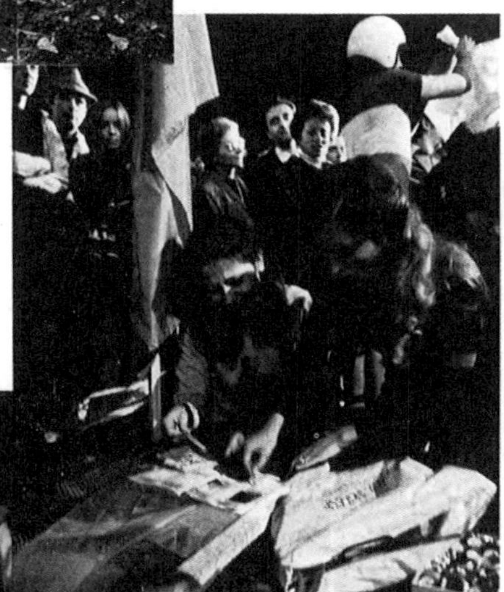

II
Coccoina incolla le figurine a tavola e sogna
materiali:
tovaglia a quadri/
piatto di spaghetti freddi/
album di figurine/
coperto del papà di turno
di notte che non è ancora arrivato/
barattolino col pennello/
figurine/doppioni/
soffietto sbuffo accostino
allarghino inzucchino e ritirino/

III
Giro d'Italia a tappini
materiali:
tappini/
presine di coccoina da naso/
gessetti colorati/
gessetti bianchi/
passi carrai/
furgoni di banche/
fettucce d'arrivo/
pointchaud plug-in plug-off/
mistappa/
bandiere rosse spada di legno
il parrucchiere e la sua signora/
passo del gatto reticolato
paramilitari/

16. Coccoina

UFO, 'Coccoina', in Daniela Palazzoli (ed.), *Pollution: Per una nuova estetica dell'inquinamento* (Bologna: Fondazione Iris, 1972), pp. 46-47.

I

The lorry unloads a mesh frame and a mattress for the man shot out of the cannon

materials
(of the lorry and the man the town hall and the square):
springy mesh frame/
springy materass mattress/
Italian champion's jersey/
Italian champion's teat/
4-yard fuse/
springy rubber-band cannon/
platinum and iridium measuring tape/
hyperbolic theodolite/
trigonometric tables/
bathrobe helmet
criminal record vaseline/

II

Coccoina pastes in trading cards at the table and dreams

materials:
checked tablecloth/
dish of cold spaghetti/
trading card album/
place set for dad on the evening
shift who hasn't come home yet/
paste jar with brush/
trading cards/duplicates/
sigh huff line-upper spread-outer
double-downer and pull-backer/

III

Giro d'Italia with bottle caps

materials:
bottle caps/
dabs of Coccoina to sniff/
coloured chalk/
white chalk/
no-parking spots/
bank vans/
finish lines/
pointchaud plug-in plug-off/
podiumgirl/
red flags wooden sword
the hairdresser and his lady/
catlike stealth barbed wire
paramilitaries/

ACTION AND BEHAVIOUR

SUMMARY

The man makes his way towards the cannon to be shot: in his thoughts a glimpse of the situation in the Faculty of the teaching assistants of the restoration of the transmission belt mechanism is offered.

The underemployed man enters the cannon: in those few seconds before the shot he sees Coccoina again, sees his mother again, sees '68 again and focuses on his operation.

The cannon shots: in those few moments of flight, he remembers all the years that have been stolen from him, he passes along the distraught faces of the spectators who ask: nature or convention?

During the flight he feels the unbearable stink of the long term. The roads turn increasingly narrow as he approaches the centre where the last kilometre banner is placed.

From the window of her little bedroom Coccoina throws trading cards at the procession.

"Giant secret arsenal of bottle caps discovered in a famous downtown hotel—GIRO crew arrested."

EXPLANATION

I

The lorry unloads a net etc...

The man shot out of the cannon is one of the forms of architecture still possible. Reinstating the private disciplines of power, in fact, fills the virtual space of expansion of cryptopower in political agreements attempted with confidence in the university and elsewhere by the various bosses, is water and oil ok?

II

Coccoina pastes in trading cards etc...

Coccoina is a project of power: by increasing forces Coccoina binds husband and wife, beyond the referendum, to the transmission belt between party and union and pastes in trading cards in the warm spots. "Palazzo, madame?" "No thanks, ALREADY DONE!".

III

Giro d'Italia with bottle caps etc...

The Giro d'Italia with bootle caps is the urbanistic form still possible: the liberation of the territory during the crossing, the opening of gate locks, the crossing of private areas, the gentle concessions, the adverse possession of the military zones, the supplying the cyclist on the run, the peaceful invasions, the always possible hijackings, the curiosity for the interiors of bank vans, for the blocks of flats courtyards, the masses flocking to the Festival dell'Unità, the variable weather conditions, the paramilitary exercises, the exclamation of the wingman: "OH DO WE ALWAYS HAVE TO BE THE LAST!?".

So we are elusive.

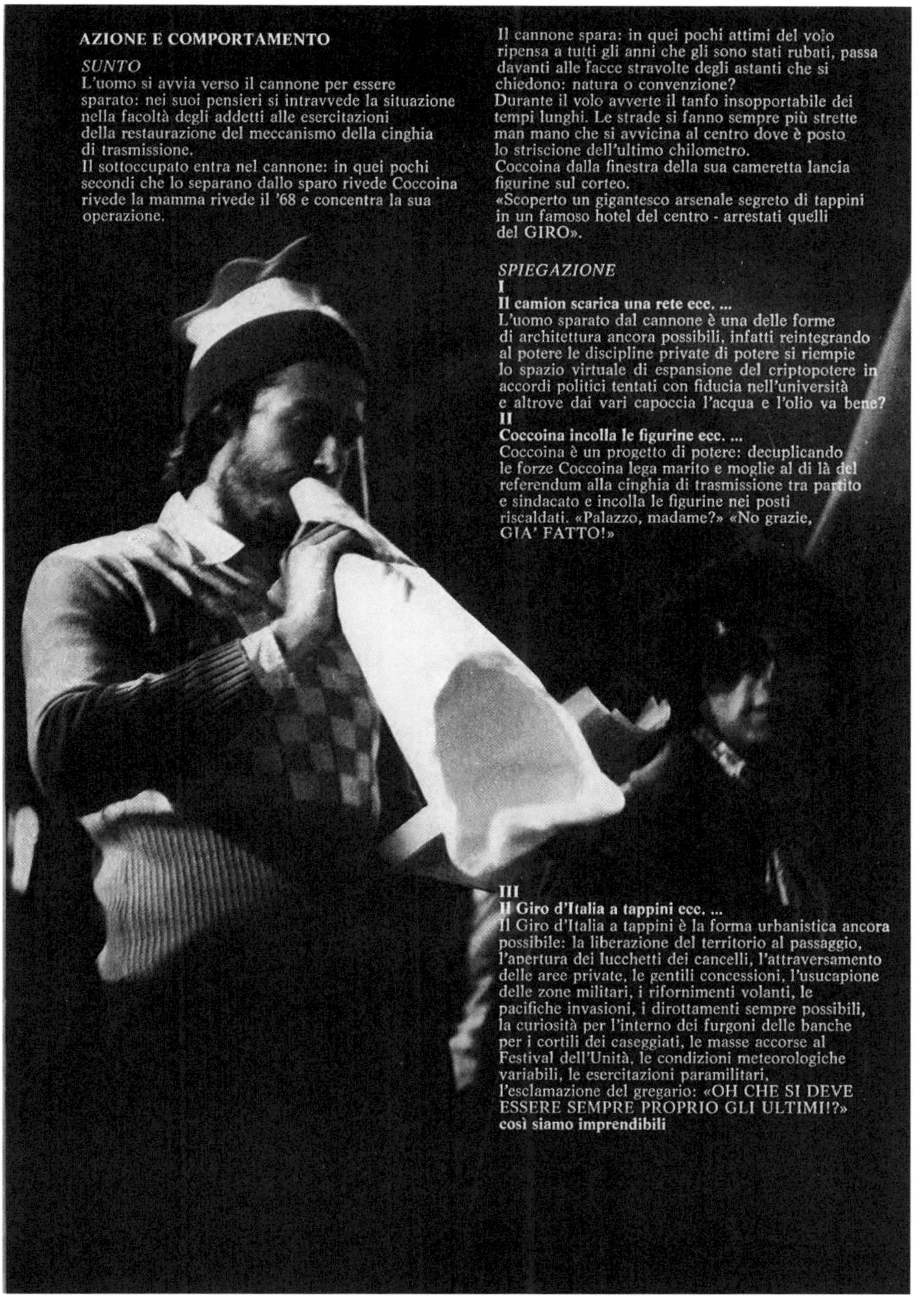

AZIONE E COMPORTAMENTO

SUNTO

L'uomo si avvia verso il cannone per essere sparato: nei suoi pensieri si intravvede la situazione nella facoltà degli addetti alle esercitazioni della restaurazione del meccanismo della cinghia di trasmissione.
Il sottoccupato entra nel cannone: in quei pochi secondi che lo separano dallo sparo rivede Coccoina rivede la mamma rivede il '68 e concentra la sua operazione.
Il cannone spara: in quei pochi attimi del volo ripensa a tutti gli anni che gli sono stati rubati, passa davanti alle facce stravolte degli astanti che si chiedono: natura o convenzione?
Durante il volo avverte il tanfo insopportabile dei tempi lunghi. Le strade si fanno sempre più strette man mano che si avvicina al centro dove è posto lo striscione dell'ultimo chilometro.
Coccoina dalla finestra della sua cameretta lancia figurine sul corteo.
«Scoperto un gigantesco arsenale segreto di tappini in un famoso hotel del centro - arrestati quelli del GIRO».

SPIEGAZIONE

I

Il camion scarica una rete ecc. ...
L'uomo sparato dal cannone è una delle forme di architettura ancora possibili, infatti reintegrando al potere le discipline private di potere si riempie lo spazio virtuale di espansione del criptopotere in accordi politici tentati con fiducia nell'università e altrove dai vari capoccia l'acqua e l'olio va bene?

II

Coccoina incolla le figurine ecc. ...
Coccoina è un progetto di potere: decuplicando le forze Coccoina lega marito e moglie al di là del referendum alla cinghia di trasmissione tra partito e sindacato e incolla le figurine nei posti riscaldati. «Palazzo, madame?» «No grazie, GIA' FATTO!»

III

Il Giro d'Italia a tappini ecc. ...
Il Giro d'Italia a tappini è la forma urbanistica ancora possibile: la liberazione del territorio al passaggio, l'apertura dei lucchetti dei cancelli, l'attraversamento delle aree private, le gentili concessioni, l'usucapione delle zone militari, i rifornimenti volanti, le pacifiche invasioni, i dirottamenti sempre possibili, la curiosità per l'interno dei furgoni delle banche per i cortili dei caseggiati, le masse accorse al Festival dell'Unità, le condizioni meteorologiche variabili, le esercitazioni paramilitari, l'esclamazione del gregario: «OH CHE SI DEVE ESSERE SEMPRE PROPRIO GLI ULTIMI!?»
così siamo imprendibili

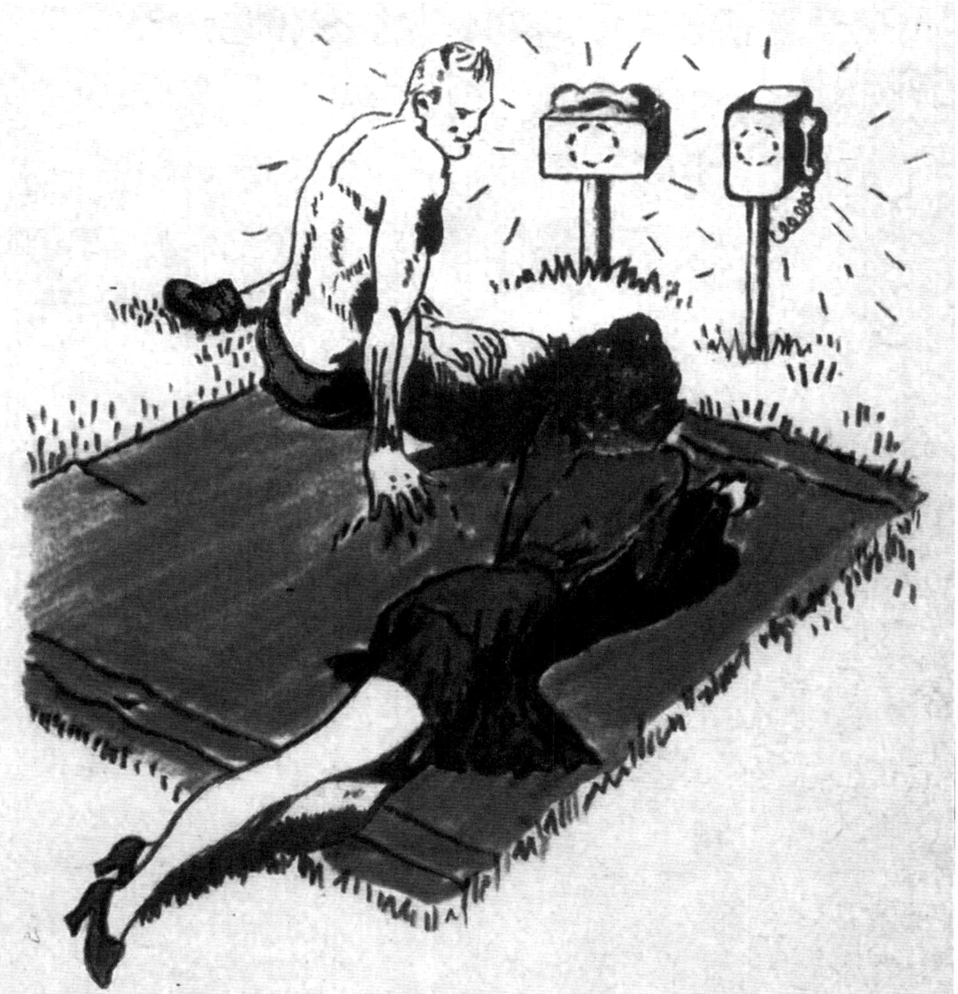

17. Non-design. From the Object to Survival

Lapo Binazzi (UFO), 'Non-Design. Dall'oggetto alla sopravvivenza', in Achille Bonito Oliva (ed.), *Contemporanea. Roma, Parcheggio di Villa Borghese 11. 1973 / 2. 1974* (Florence: Centro Di, 1973), pp. 301-303.
The article is republished in the next year as Lapo Binazzi, 'Non-design. Dall'oggetto alla sopravvivenza', *Casabella*, no. 386, 1974, pp. 16-18. Binazzi used extracts for the first bulletin of the *Global Tools*. See Lapo Binazzi, Andrea Branzi, Germano Celant, Ugo La Pietra, Alessandro Mendini, Adolfo Natalini and Ettore Sottsass Jr., 'Conversazione fra Binazzi Branzi Celant La Pietra Mendini Natalini Sottsass Jr.', in *Bollettino Global Tools* (Milan: Edizioni L'uomo e l'arte, 1974). The article will eventually be published in an abridged version in *Spazioarte*, vol. IV, no. 10-11, June-October 1977, p. 4.

The purpose of the composition is to show how objects and also ideas, especially good ones, are accessories of capitalism which have wrongly been considered irreplaceable expressions of human activity.

The composition will proceed through a series of sections illustrated by slides which will be gathered together in a stereopticon.

The sections are:
1. "The destruction of the object"—atrophy of the objective—hypertrophy of the imaginary—terroristic design.
2. "The recreation of behaviour"—the analogy of sports—the dress design—animated films.
3. "Utopia of survival"—global tools—individual creative activity—the distortion of services—natural techniques and related behaviour.

Our attention to the phenomena of survival manifested and invented by younger strata during recent years causes us to find the same tendencies within design itself.

The constant search for greater liberty, for free space in which to exercise and cultivate it, the creation of really magic territories of the imagination, the mobility of installations, the forced precariousness of existence, the refusal of the slavery of work, the broadening of one's own consciousness, the rebellion against the pyramid-like structure of society—these are the directing ideas of these movements.

The superstructures under attack make the system creak and reveal their own key role.
Capital, which becomes more harsh in its reactions and repressions and tries to attack the weakest, shows us that the way that has been chosen is the correct one.

The vacuum that has been opened up allows much space for the recreation of one's own behaviour, for the invention of new forms of communication, for love.

The objects available to us have disappeared, as have the accessories, the knickknacks, the furniture, the walls, and also the house the city and all the rest—how beautiful!

There remain the planet, the sky, the stars, the trees—to start from the beginning.

Unfortunately we discover paid electric plugs in the country, and phone taps—capital has gone even this far.

Perhaps the renunciation was not complete—we wanted to hear music. Look!

The country is not only imaginary, but they are starting to give us their attention now and perhaps it is already late.

There remain for us rudimentary installations with which we can do something, a crocheted sweater, some embroidery, the rudimentary techniques for climbing a tree, going for a swim, a bike ride, some rudimentary techniques for directing the flow of water, for orienting oneself.

Even genius in the end really isn't much use because everything is so natural that it is not needed. The nights bent over the encyclopaedia are all over, as are the attempts to emulate, the attempts to set up a record...

We meet each other with joy because we discover each other showing ourselves nature as a work of art... we have many animals around, let's try some training courses.

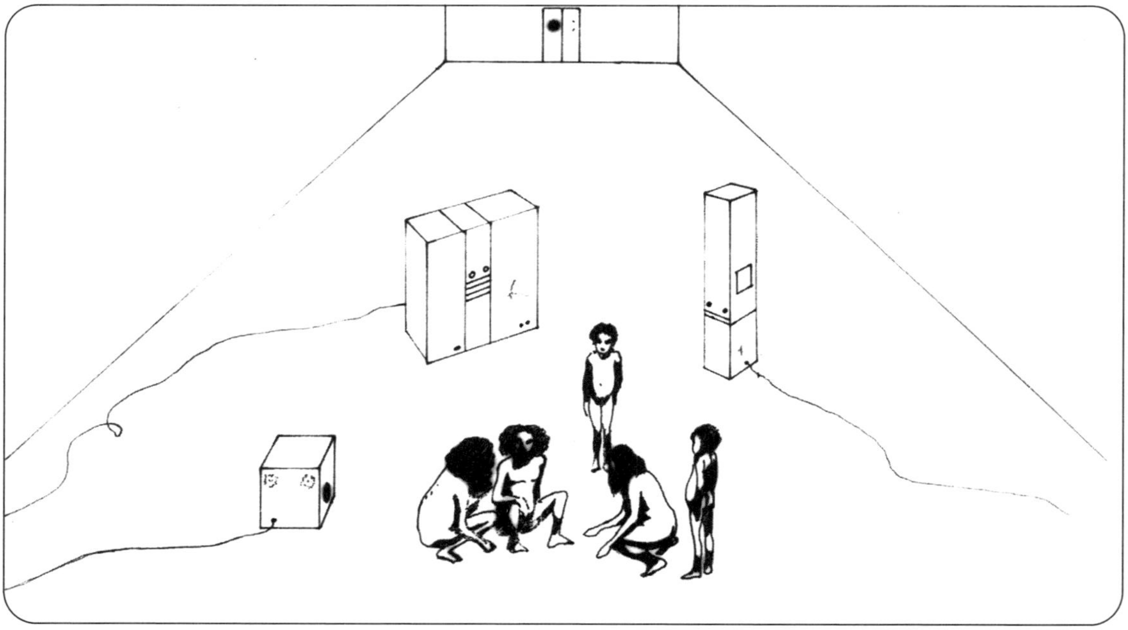

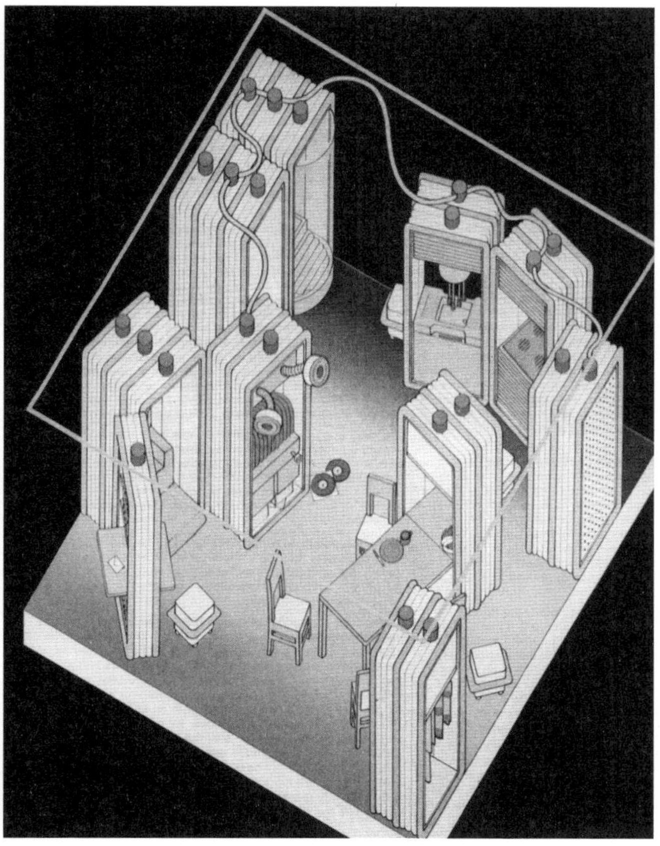

UFO

RISPOSTA AL QUESTIONARIO DI «IN» SUI PROBLEMI DELLA FACOLTÀ DI ARCHITETTURA

Come al solito avete centrato il problema! ma a che varrebbe spiegare quando ci sono tanti che lo faranno meglio di noi! Che ancora non sia venuto il momento? In questa lettera si, possiamo accennare tentare ventilare ma non di più. Come sapete la nostra attività è sempre stata anti-specifico ci abbiamo creduto dall'inizio. I nostri seminari ce li siamo fatti sempre in segreto da noi, e ognuno di noi se li faceva a casa sua da solo e così abbiamo conservato una dinamica interna niente male eh? Così a volte si supera la visione del presente e si sciorinano profezie. Per esempio la foto che ci siamo fatti sotto il traliccio nel 1971 o le leggendarie tipologie ANAS del 1969 prima dello scandalo Chiatante. Forse tutto ciò non ha molto significato ma, e se lo avesse? In questo senso la LEGGENDA può essere un'eredità per tutti. Se dovessimo scomparire vorremmo essere ricordati per aver provocato le statiche situazioni del POTERE come le gallerie, l'università, le mostre, i passanti, le piazze, un briciolo più degli altri.
Il verbo che più ci piace è RIMETTERE IN GIUOCO.
Vi proponiamo qui una serie di immagini dei nostri comportamenti alternativi nei diversi specifici della nostra attività sperando nel multiforme. Speriamo che i brontolii sordi della teoria non arrivino a strozzarci la gola e a turbare la tranquillità del nostro

SENZATEMPO

1. NOI CI RIFIUTIAMO DI SPIEGARE! (MOLTI SONO TERRORIZZATI DALLE SPIEGAZIONI)

2. LA CONSUETUDINE CON LA REPRESSIONE NON CE LO CONSENTE

La società divisa in classi: destra - sinistra

3. ABBIAMO INVENTATO FRA L'ALTRO IL DISCONTINUO L'EPOPEA ANAS LE MEMORIE CONGELATE GLI SPAZI CHIUSI GLI SPAZI PRIVATI GLI SPAZI SEGRETI

Progetto di base segreta

4. SIAMO DEI SUPERTECNICI SUPERDEQUALIFICATI

Assalto alla centrale elettrica

5. CI OCCUPIAMO DI POLITICA, DI DESIGN, DI ARCHITETTURA DI URBANISTICA, DI PROBLEMI DI LINGUAGGIO ABBIAMO ACQUISTATO UNA CONOSCIENZA ANCHE TROPPO CHIARA E DISTINTA

Progetto di osservatorio

6. SIAMO SEMPRE AL POSTO GIUSTO E SEMPRE FUORI POSTO ABBIAMO INVENTATO CENTO SBOCCHI PROFESSIONALI ORA CI SIAMO SCOCCIATI!

Specifiche discipline Anas

7. LA POLIZIA CI PERSEGUITA MA NOI NON POSSIAMO APRIRE BOCCA NON VOGLIAMO COMPROMETTERE MILIONI DI COMPAGNI SCONOSCIUTI

«Sotto il traliccio»
Foto eseguita 12 mesi prima della morte di Feltrinelli

8. ABBIAMO SEMPRE PUNTATO SULLA CURIOSITÀ

9. TRA IL DIRE E IL FARE C'È DI MEZZO IL MARE

Nuotata AV

18. UFO's Response to *in*'s Questionnaire on the Problems of the Faculty of Architecture

UFO, 'Risposta al questionario di "in" sui problemi della Facoltà di Architettura', *in. Argomenti e immagini di Design*, no. 9, February-March 1973, pp. 78-80. This text is published as a response to a questionnaire drawn up by Ugo La Pietra entitled "The Faculty of Architecture in the Process of Downgrading." The aim of the questionnaire is to reflect on the contradictions that according to its compiler are emerging in the academic sphere between the cultural project and the contemporary political and social context. La Pietra subdivides the questionnaire, which consists of twenty-one questions in all, into two, concerning respectively the problematic relationship of the teaching programme with political matters ("political problems") and a more general reflection on the content of the teaching ("problems of the discipline"). Ugo La Pietra, 'La Facoltà di Architettura nel processo di dequalificazione', *in. Argomenti e immagini di Design*, no. 9, February-March 1973, pp. 2-3. In its responses to the survey, UFO decided to address only the first category, which comprises the following questions. "**1a** — *How can struggle within the school be set in the context of class struggle?* **2a** — *Does a political line that tackles the contradictions at a comprehensive level have to set itself, within the school, the task of pointing out to students new ways of understanding intellectual work? Would it be possible to put the instruments of the discipline to a different use?* **3a** — *Bourgeois science does not offer means for the comprehensive understanding of reality. How should the problem of the relationship between knowledge and the transformation of reality be tackled?* **4a** — *How should the experience of didactic experimentation in the Faculty of Architecture in Milan be evaluated? What actual gains have the students achieved?* **5a** — *What alternative indications of work to traditional jobs, and what opportunities of a professional nature, have emerged from the activity of the research groups?* **6a** — *In what sense is disciplinary analysis connected with the comprehension of structural mechanisms in the research groups?* **7a** — *What connection has it been possible to establish between the work of research and the needs posed by social struggle?* **8a** — *Does group work prove effective, from a methodological viewpoint, in the study of reality? To what extent has the relationship between teachers and students changed?* **9a** — *In what sense does the political formulation of the forces within the student movement influence the activity of research?* **10a** — *What are the guidelines of repressive intervention in the Faculty?* **11a** — *What role does the Technical Committee play in the repressive manoeuvre?*".

As usual you've hit the nail on the head! But what use would it be to explain when there are many who will do it better than we can! Has the moment not come yet? In this letter yes, we can hint attempt suggest but no more. As you know our activity has always been anti-specific, we have believed in this from the outset. We have always held our seminars in secret from ourselves, and each of us did them at home alone and so we have preserved an internal dynamism, not bad at all eh? Thus at times we go beyond the vision of the present and rattle off prophesies. For example the photos that we took of ourselves under the pylon in 1971 or the legendary A.N.A.S. roadhouses of 1969 before the Chiatante scandal. Perhaps none of this has much meaning, but if it did? In this sense the LEGEND can be a legacy for all. If we were to disappear we would like to be remembered for having provoked the static situations of POWER like galleries, universities, exhibitions, passers-by and squares a wee bit more than the others.

The verb we like most is TO BRING BACK INTO PLAY.

Here we propose to you a series of images of our alternative modes of behaviour in the various specifics of our activity, placing our hopes in the multiform. We hope that the muffled rumblings of theory do not come to choke us and to disturb the tranquillity of our

TIMELESS

1. **WE REFUSE TO EXPLAIN (MANY ARE TERRORISED BY EXPLANATIONS)**
2. **FAMILIARITY WITH REPRESSION DOES NOT ALLOW US IT**
3. **WE HAVE INVENTED AMONG OTHER THINGS THE DISCONTINUOUS THE HEROIC DEEDS OF A.N.A.S. FROZEN MEMORIES ENCLOSED SPACES PRIVATE SPACES SECRET SPACES**
4. **WE ARE HIGHLY-DESKILLED SUPER-TECHNICIANS**
5. **WE ARE INTERESTED IN POLITICS, DESIGN, ARCHITECTURE, URBANISM, IN PROBLEMS OF LANGUAGE WE HAVE ACQUIRED ALL TOO CLEAR AND DISTINCT A KNOWLEDGE**
6. **WE ARE ALWAYS IN THE RIGHT PLACE AND ALWAYS OUT OF PLACE WE HAVE INVENTED A HUNDRED PROFESSIONAL PROSPECTS NOW WE ARE FED UP!**
7. **THE POLICE HARASS US BUT WE CAN'T SAY A WORD WE DON'T WANT TO ENDANGER MILLIONS OF UNKNOWN COMRADES**
8. **WE HAVE ALWAYS BET ON CURIOSITY**
9. **SAYING IS ONE THING AND DOING ANOTHER**
10. **DO COME TO OUR VERTICAL SEMINAR (in the sense that it reaches up to the brain)**
11. **THE REAL DEAD SPECIFIC IS THE DEAD ONE**

AMONG THINGS NOT ALWAYS ATTAINABLE:

A PLACE AT THE (art) GALLERY
A POST AS ASSISTANT (and of whom?)
A POST AS MAGAZINE EDITOR (since each of us can make his own)
THE CARD OF A PARTY (before the post of assistant)
A POST AT THE MUSEUM
MONEY
ENROLMENT IN THE REGISTER OF ARCHITECTS
A POST IN THE REGIONAL ADMINISTRATION
CULTURE (or information)
TECHNIQUE TECHNOLOGY THE RIBBON DEVELOPMENT AND THE ZONING PLAN

AMONG THINGS NOT ALWAYS ATTAINABLE:

BEING AT PEACE WITH YOUR OWN CONSCIENCE
THE POSITION OF FULL PROFESSOR
THE POSITION OF BOSS OF FIAT
ECONOMIC INDEPENDENCE AT THE AGE OF 20
AN OVERALL MARK FOR EVERYONE

10. VENITE PURE AL NOSTRO SEMINARIO VERTICALE
(nel senso che arriva al cervello)

Arrampicata parallela

11. IL VERO SPECIFICO MORTO È QUELLO MORTO

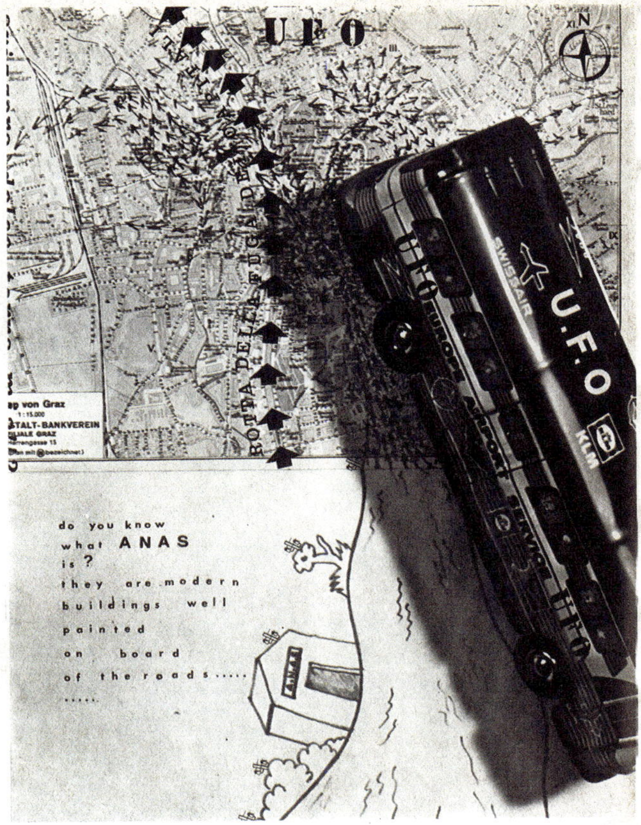

TRA LE COSE NON SEMPRE CONQUISTABILI:

UN POSTO IN GALLERIA (d'arte)
UN POSTO DI ASSISTENTE (a chi poi?)
UN POSTO DI DIRETTORE DI RIVISTA (poiché ognuno si può fare la sua)
LA TESSERA DI UN PARTITO (prima del posto di assistente)
UN POSTO AL MUSEO
I SOLDI

L'ISCRIZIONE ALL'ALBO DEGLI ARCHITETTI
UN POSTO ALLA REGIONE
LA CULTURA (o informazione)
LA TECNICA LA TECNOLOGIA L'ASSE ATTREZZATO E IL PIANO REGOLATORE

TRA LE COSE NON SEMPRE CONQUISTABILI:

LA TRANQUILLITÀ CON LA PROPRIA COSCIENZA
UN POSTO DI ORDINARIO
IL POSTO DI PADRONE DELLA FIAT
INDIPENDENZA ECONOMICA A 20 ANNI
IL VOTO UNICO GENERALIZZATO

80

The typologic variations in buildings by the National Road Board, systematically listed by the florentine group UFO

Bureaucracy architecture

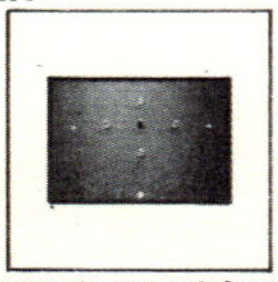

Architettura della burocrazia

Il gruppo fiorentino degli UFO presenta una catalogazione sistematica sulle variazioni tipologiche degli edifici ANAS sparsi sul territorio

CASA CON SEGNALETICA

DEMOLIZIONE

CASA A TETTO PIANO E ALBERO

FARM

CASA CON ZOCCOLO DI PIETRA

CASA DA PASTORE CON GUARDRAIL

RETRO DI ANAS ALL'ALBA (4.45/4.57)

ANAS NEL BOSCO

FUJYAMA

ON THE ROAD

CASA CON GIARDINETTO E STRISCIA GIALLA

NIDO

HOME

CASA DI RIPOSO

FORTINO

SCONOSCIUTA

OSSERVATORIO

RIFUGIO

MASTIO

MOTEL

COSTA

STORE

MAGAZZINO

VILLAGGIO

CASA CON CAPELLI

LOCANDA

ARCHICLASSICO

VILLA

1969 UFO

19. Bureaucracy Architecture

UFO, 'Architettura della burocrazia', *Casabella*, no. 378, June 1973, pp. 30-31.

The typologic variations in buildings by the National Road Board, systematically listed by the florentine group UFO

Bureaucracy architecture

The florentine group UFO presents a systematic cataloguing of the typological variations of A.N.A.S. buildings scattered around the country

HOUSE WITH SIGNAGE
DEMOLITION
HOUSE WITH FLAT ROOF AND TREE
FARM
HOUSE WITH STONE BASE
SHEPHERD'S HOUSE WITH GUARDRAIL
BACK SIDE OF A.N.A.S. AT DAWN (4.45/4.57)
A.N.A.S. IN THE WOODS
FUIJYAMA
ON THE ROAD
HOUSE WITH SMALL GARDEN AND YELLOW STRIPE
NEST
HOME
REST HOME
BLOCKHOUSE
UNKNOWN
OBSERVATION POST
HIDEOUT
KEEP
MOTEL
COAST
SHOP
WAREHOUSE
VILLAGE
HOUSE WITH HAIRS
INN
ARCHICLASSICAL
VILLA

1969 **UFO**

casabella
GLOBAL TOOLS – 12 GENNAIO 1973
377 rivista di urbanistica architettura e disegno industriale

20. A Four-way Conversation on Global Tools

Andrea Branzi (Archizoom), Lapo Binazzi (UFO), Gianni Pettena and Ettore Sottsass Jr., 'Conversazione a quattro sulla Global Tools', *Casabella*, no. 379, July 1973, pp. 45-48.

Milan, 18 May at 10 p.m. at Ettore's place

Taking part: BRANZI (Archizoom), BINAZZI (Ufo), PETTENA, SOTTSASS Jr.

The following are a few excerpts from their conversation.
Contributions to the conversation remain anonymous.

The meaning of Global Tools is tested in various directions.
The subject is: INDUSTRIAL PRODUCTION AND INDIVIDUAL CREATIVITY.

— In fact, I say... I gave a thoroughgoing report on the matter... this school is small effort to move in this direction.
— But I say it isn't, and it isn't moving in that direction.
— Why not?
— Because as soon as you let all the technical typologies—all right—all the technologies back in through the window, you show that you believe in categories that are categories of work, let's say, and scales of the quality of work. When you say that a work of pottery is well done or badly done, all right: you already acknowledge the values of technology, the meanings of technology. Well, in the Utopian society you were telling us about before, these meanings should make no more sense. Because, if at any time anyone wants to make a piece of pottery badly, he will make it badly if it is vital for him to make things, to make pottery. It doesn't matter if it's bad. But in a school, as I said before, you already begin to raise other subjects, and other inhibiting problems.
— Maybe this... is why there has been so much talk going on for so long... this school or this Utopia... that is, maybe we're afraid, maybe we haven't the courage to say, I don't know, that this school is no school, but a circus caravan.
— This Utopia has its shortcomings because, after all, what we're talking about is Utopia—that is, if we approach it by negations, it's likely that we'll get to our human substance.
— I've already told you what my reasons and my motivations are...
— Just a minute. Now it's my turn to interrupt. What I mean in that nobody discusses Utopia the way you put it... we're talking...
— No, no, excuse me but the whole subject started here. I'm quite in favour, or rather we're

all of us very much in favour of this idea of a school or of a system of laboratories, of manual work and individual creativity, and so on. Right? All of us. What are our reasons, as individuals for being attracted by this thing? I told you mine. Just recently, for example, I've given a lot of time to creative activities as an individual, I've been embroidering... I like making clothes and, again, I like doing nothing... however, it's a highly uninhibited doing nothing, I'd say... why? Because I've been rethinking this kind of work in the light of what we've been talking about—so that it is perhaps not enough to accept preconstituted models, perhaps we should try to do things with our hands.

— Of course, of course, that's perfectly all right, I agree completely, and I think the drive we feel is more or less...

— The same thing.

— ... quite similar, except for certain differences... but at this moment we're not here to tell Casabella or tell ourselves... well, we happen to like doing things by hands, so... we mean to do them. Good. That might even be considered a perfectly reasonable position. But we may be here to do something more than that.

— ... very powerful, powerful enough to shake the foundations of that system of disciplines of specific things... perhaps it has already crumbled and been destroyed and we simply refuse to believe it... owing to a series of conditionings. This discontinuous aspect of History is not merely an ultra requirement of history... that is, eventually wars break out again, crises in production come about again... and of course history leaps ahead, but not nature... it is worth keeping in mind that it is possible for us to behave in a different way in each different case while we remain what we are... while we remain people who want to have a clear conscience, want to move ahead... I don't know... give up work, create individually and... manually their own works, and all the rest... except that I don't think we can simplify everything to further a single project, or a single strategy, or a single way of proceeding...

— ... on the other hand the conditionings that we've had...

— ... the only difference is this: the different level of the concept and the different level of the formulation of certain problems; that is, one can also only testify to the reasons why one likes to do these things... and that's all right...

— ... let's all try to describe the image of Utopia as we see it for ourselves... but let's try never to put it on the drawing board, indeed, let's put a lot less, so that there still will be room for...

— Quite. To begin with an immediate necessity... in fact when we began talking about this school, I kept watch over everything to prevent an operation of this kind from ever taking shape... because there's a matter to be cleared up immediately... that all the people we've talked to about this matter only said—and why not?—that this was something they all expected... this, for example, is a kind of immediate check... I mean, the talk going on this evening has already got to the point of rationalizing the matter... so that it may be perfectly all right if certain people have decided to do this and this is already a proof that they came to their decision sincerely, that they didn't make their decision because...

— On the other hand, whatever the operation, it runs along fixed tracks, because the construction of words, sentences, and the language...

— Of course. And then there are different kinds of individual contributions. For example, I may make some contributions of a certain kind within the context of an idea of mine; but if you'd prefer to adopt a discontinuous line towards these problems, that's your business... it's not a thing that can be imposed...

— No. I start with the idea that we're talking here to make our aims clear... as well as certain ideas... it's also a way of checking on our inner convictions...

— Instead of concentrating all our attention on the object we should concentrate it on the equipment we use for construction—that is, on the technology that of course will be crude in the beginning...

— Crude only to a certain extent, because books on technology like Olsky's aren't usually intended for schools; they're elementary hand-books on apparatus and machines, so familiarity in the use of inventions is an achievement that everyone should enjoy as a direct contact with the world about him. The split comes later, when one moves from the object to behaviour. At this point it becomes necessary to invent objects or functions which represent the object and at most have some affinity with it... for industry can no longer produce it precisely because it is the expression of a particular behaviour. At this point one might run into some difficulties; but in my opinion, on a theoretical level or in teaching I see no reason for limiting these possibilities... on the contrary... or any reason for eliminating the possibility of a clean slate, of a non-object that at most we try to reconstruct. In doing this we feel we are performing a useful and liberating service, because we are freeing the individual from the slavery of the non-object—that is, we are freeing him from the slavery of thinking, of reflecting, of behaving and of acting blindly.

— I wouldn't call them object at all, but tools.

— That's it!

— Because they're instrumental for one second of your life.

— Because they're not clearly defined categories and yet they modify your life.

— What's the difference between instrumental and functional?

— A thing is instrumental if it totally commits us; a functional thing would be all right if it weren't already loaded down with precise cultural meanings.

— Which is the dentist's chair again.

— Strange as it may seem, it's a matter of seizing the means of production from industry when these means are not money, which is virtually a value, but the machine, the lathe, the press, and also electronic instruments such as the computer and even the saw, the hammer and the nail.

— And the Black and Decker.

— Yes and the Black and Decker, and the inclined plane. This is what people have to understand.

— ... an allegory of instruments, which is like an allegory of the wheel. For example, if we're in a primitive society and someone comes to me and says "I've invented the wheel," it's clear that he is going to meet with some resistance on the part of those who have never used the wheel but only, let's say, rollers. Practically, the old question of science again! "I've invented the wheel"... well, maybe not... nobody can be found to finance it, so it won't be made... nothing doing, in other words! There will be no wheel. So the one who made the wheel goes on making it and tries to convince as many people as possible to use the wheel because, well... he shows them clearly what the advantages are. But those who refuse to use it find all kinds of moralistic reasons for refusing, saying that the wheel is... I don't know... the negation of God... that the wheel is this and that... now the problems of the school or the non-school today is to establish which is the wheel, our wheel... what wheel has been discovered in the meantime...

— Precisely.

— That is to say, what wheels are at our disposal... so, I say perhaps we know that the wheel we've discovered and distributed and that we want to construct—because we still haven't done so—perhaps we know that object is really possible and we want to build it...

— At this point we could demand that after two months every object produced by the school should be broken into pieces and buried... in the sense that...

— Good...

— Of course...!

— We've discovered a law...

— Precisely.

— We've discovered a law of physics...

— A method... a...

— ... a mathematical system...

— ... mathematics... a system of relations...

— Of course!

— That's the conceptual aspect that I find most... most...

— ... the most interesting part of the question... and that's the aspect that I would preserve most in this school...

— But we agree in everything, really everything; I would even say that if it were a matter of producing wheels and selling them, I wouldn't waste time on the school...

— ... Of course...

— ... Of course...

— As for me, I'm already doing that kind of work, and what's more, I'm not particularly interested in...

— But isn't there anything to sell in this school?

— ...

— If we want to get this statement out, we'd better drop that! All right.

— No really, I quite agree with you on this and I would say that this is the point... the main point of everything, of the whole system in fact... because we don't produce a bloody thing...

— We only give each other ideas temporarily.

— ... but it all disappears...
— We sail along on an empty sea, leaving a lot of debris in our wake...
— Precisely! ... a lot of debris... of...
— But if we didn't, it would be all up with us; we'd be wrong from the word go...
— Listen, I would say that this is a good point for us to stop.
— Yes, let's stop here! Besides...
— Now how does one get down to work? One prepares documents...

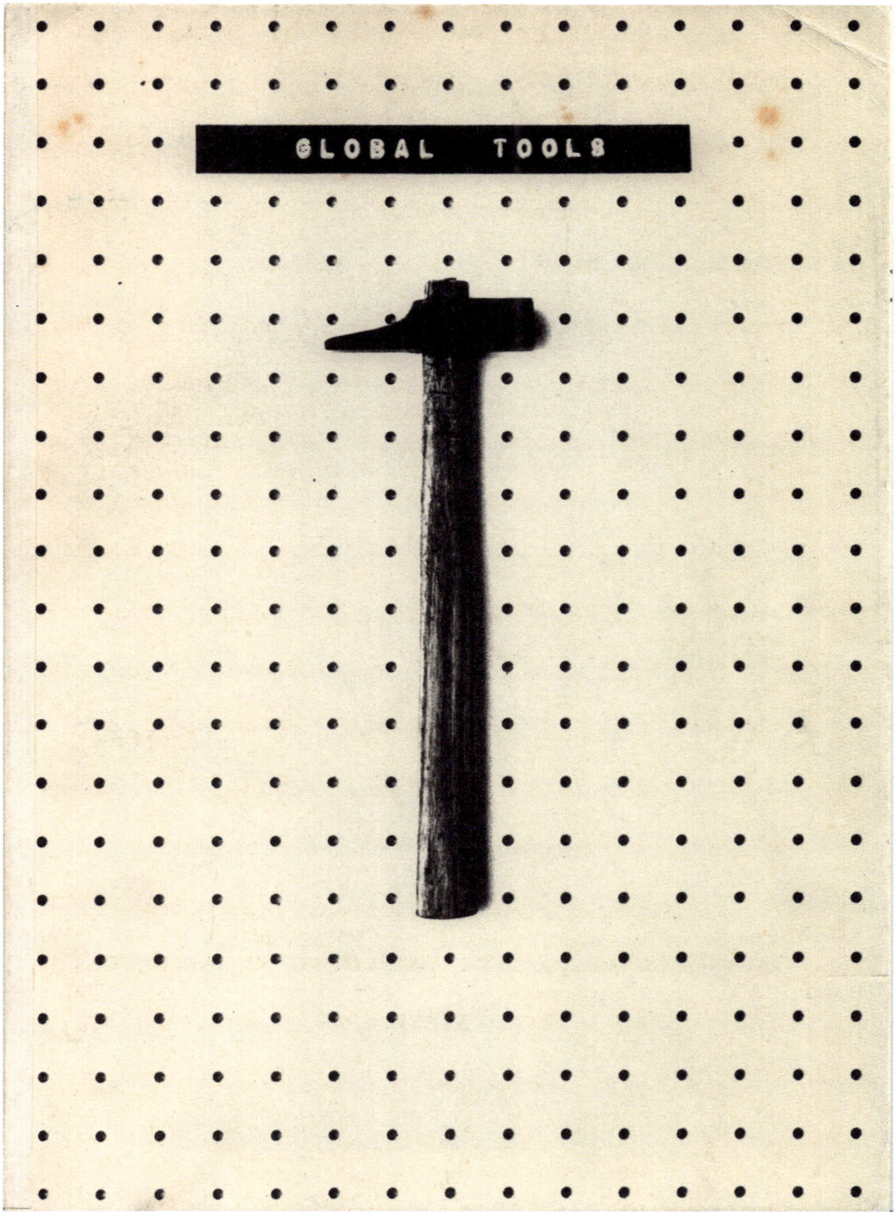
GLOBAL TOOLS

PRODUZIONE INDUSTRIALE E CREATIVITA' INDIVIDUALE
U.F.O.
INDUSTRIAL PRODUCTION AND INDIVIDUAL CREATIVITY

scena 1

...l'Oggetto si trascinò a fatica verso l'interno della FORESTA per non tornare più indietro.

...with difficulty the object dragged into the interior of the FOREST never to return again.

scena 2

A poco a poco perse le sue caratteristiche di comunicabilità (lontano dagli uomini dal contatto e dalla partecipazione con il pubblico spettatore perse anche la sua NATURA CORDIALE E SPONTANEA)

Little by little it lost its ability to communicate (far from men, from contact with public spectators and any sharing in their lives, the object lost even its CORDIAL AND SPONTANEOUS NATURE)

scena 3

diciamo che si ATROFIZZÒ. Seguì un periodo di forte degradazione delle sue caratteristiche interne gaie e spensierate sia perché le erbacce rampicanti della foresta e gli agenti atmosferici e la terra lo corrodevano sia perché subì una specie di trasformazione interna a vantaggio di un nuovo aspetto tutto AEREODINAMICO.

let us say that it ATROPHIED. Then came a period of sharp decline in its gay and carefree internal characteristics, both because the creeping weeds of the forest and atmospheric agents and the earth corroded it and because it suffered a kind of internal transformation and took on a new and completely AERODYNAMIC aspect.

scena 4

Durante questo tempo l'UTOPIA elaborò un modello di società piuttosto AUTORITARIO più in contatto con la RELIGIONE che con l'esperienza terrena degli uomini. I SUPERMITI portarono a una distruzione pressoché totale del genere umano.

During this period UTOPIA developed a rather AUTHORITARIAN model of society more in contact with RELIGION than with the experience of men here on earth. THE SUPERMYTHS led to the almost complete destruction of the human race.

[(continua da pagina 46)

— No, no scusami, il discorso è partito di qui. Cioè, io sono molto attratto, voglio dire che noi tutti siamo altamente attratti da questa storia della scuola o del sistema dei laboratori e del lavoro manuale e della creatività individuale etc. Va bene? Tutti. Qual è il motivo per cui ciascuno di noi è attratto da questa cosa? Io vi ho detto il mio. Io, per esempio, in questo periodo mi dedico molto ad attività creative a livello individuale, ricamo... mi piace fare i vestiti e poi mi piace non far niente, però è un non far niente estremamente disinibito, voglio dire, cioè... Perché? Perché comincio a rivalutare questo genere di cose all'interno del discorso che s'è fatto, per cui veramente basta continuare a accettare modelli precostituiti, cercare di far le cose con le mani.

— Sì, questo va benissimo. Questo sono perfettamente d'accordo e credo che la spinta che sentiamo più o meno è...

— È la stessa. Ecco...

— ...molto analoga salvo differenze... Però, in questo momento noi siamo qua non per dire a Casabella o per dire a noi stessi, vabbé a noi piace fare le cose a mano e allora... possiamo anche farle. Va benissimo. Potrebbe anche essere un discorso ragionevole. Però... forse siamo qua per fare qualche cosa di più.

— ... molto forte, tale da mettere in crisi, da sgretolare, quel sistema di discipline di specifici di cose... che forse è già distrutto, che forse è già sgretolato e che noi ci rifiutiamo di riconoscere... per una serie di condizionamenti. Quest'aspetto discontinuo della Storia non è solo un'ultra-esigenza storica... cioè alla fine si riformano le guerre... alla fine si riformano le crisi di produzione... e naturalmente la storia dei salti, mentre invece la natura no... Si tratta di prendere atto che è possibile comportarci in maniera diversa, in ogni operazione diversa, rimanendo sempre se stessi... rimanendo sempre persone che vogliono essere in pace con la propria coscienza, vogliono creare individualmente e... manualmente i propri oggetti, e tutto il resto... soltanto penso che non si possa semplificare tutto ad uno stesso progetto, ad una stessa strategia, ad uno stesso modo di procedere...

— ...d'altra parte i condizionamenti che si hanno...

— ...c'è di diverso solo questo: il diverso livello di concetto e il diverso livello di formulazione di certi problemi, cioè, si può anche soltanto testimoniare del motivo per cui ci piace fare queste cose... e già va bene...

— ...cerchiamo tutti quanti di dichiarare l'immagine dell'utopia come la vediamo per conto nostro... ma cerchiamo di non metterla mai sulla tavola, anzi mettiamo sulla tavola molto meno, in modo da lasciare ancora spazio a...

— Certo. Tanto per cominciare una necessità immediata... difatti quando si è cominciato a parlare di questa scuola, io immediatamente sono stato molto attento che non venisse definita un'operazione di questo genere qui... perché c'è un fatto che sarà da verificare subito: che tutte le persone con cui si è parlato di questa cosa, non hanno fatto altro che dire: — benissimo — come se questa fosse una cosa che tutti aspettavano... questo per esempio è un genere di verifica immediato... cioè... voglio dire... i discorsi che si fanno stasera sono già ad una fase di razionalizzazione del punto... per cui può andare già benissimo il fatto che certe persone abbiano deciso di far questo e questa è già una testimonianza che l'hanno deciso sinceramente, non che l'hanno deciso perché...

— D'altra parte qualsiasi operazione viaggia su dei binari, perché la costruzione delle frasi delle parole del linguaggio...

— Certo, ci sono poi diversi contributi individuali, cioè io posso dare dei contributi di un certo tipo e all'interno di un pensiero mio, poi se te preferisci avere verso questi problemi un comportamento discontinuo, questo allora però è un fatto che riguarda te... cioè non lo si può assolutamente imporre come...

— No, io parto dal punto di vista che si sta discutendo per chiarire a noi certi scopi... certe idee... e anche un modo per verificare noi stessi al nostro interno...

— invece di centrare l'attenzione sull'oggetto bisogna centrarla sull'attrezzo che serve per costruirlo quindi sulle tecnologie che naturalmente da principio saranno povere...

— Povere fino ad un certo punto, nel senso che i libri di tecnologie come i libri di Olsky non sono in genere libri per le scuole, mentre sono trattati elementari di congegni e di macchine e di marchingegni, quindi la consuetudine con l'uso dell'invenzione è una conquista che si può augurare a tutti come contatto diretto con il mondo circostante; la frattura avviene invece più in là, cioè quando si passa dall'oggetto al comportamento... a quel punto si comincia a dover inventare degli oggetti o delle funzioni che rappresentino l'oggetto e che al limite sono affini a quello e che l'industria non può più produrre proprio perché sono espressioni di un comportamento e a quel punto ci si potrebbe anche trovare in difficoltà, però io a livello teorico o di insegnamento non vedo la necessità di limitare queste possibilità anzi... di eliminare la possibilità di una tabula rasa, di un non-oggetto, che noi si cerca al limite di ricostituire; facendo questo crediamo di fare un'operazione abbastanza utile e liberatoria perché liberiamo l'individuo dalla schiavitù del non-oggetto, cioè liberiamo l'individuo dalla schiavitù del pensare del riflettere del comportarsi dell'agire in maniera cieca

— io eviterei di chiamarli oggetti, li chiamerei strumenti

— ecco sì!

— perché sono strumentali ad un attimo della vita

— non sono delle categorie ben definite e che modificano la tua vita

— che differenza c'è fra strumentale e funzionale?

— strumentale è qualcosa che ci impegna globalmente, funzionale andrebbe bene se non fosse già caricato di significati culturali molto precisi

— che è poi la famosa poltrona del dentista

— paradossalmente si tratterebbe di strappare all'industria i mezzi di produzione, dove questi mezzi di produzione non siano il denaro, che è un valore virtuale. Saranno invece la macchina il tornio la pressa e anche lo strumento elettronico, il computer, ma anche la sega il martello il chiodo

— il black-and-decker

— sì il black-and-decker, il piano inclinato, si tratta di capire questo

— ...un'allegoria sugli strumenti, che è un'allegoria, per esempio non so, della ruota. Cioè se uno ad un certo punto mi viene, in una società primitiva, e mi dice — Io ho inventato la ruota — è chiaro che trova una resistenza da parte di chi non ha mai usato la ruota e scorreva su rulli non so ecco... il discorso della scienza, ...in pratica. — Ho inventato la ruota — vabbé,... no... la ruota... non si trova chi la finanzia, la ruota non si costruisce... niente, insomma! la ruota non si fa. Allora chi fa la ruota naturalmente continua a farla e cerca di convincere quante più persone può ad usare la ruota perché eh... gli fa vedere chiaramente i vantaggi della ruota... ecco; mentre invece chi si rifiuta di usarla comincia a tirar fuori delle giustificazioni moralistiche dicendo che la ruota... non so... è una negazione di Dio... che la ruota... insomma... eccetera eccetera. Allora uno va avanti e cerca di convincere tutti gli altri a usare la ruota... Ora il problema della scuola o della non scuola di ora è di stabilire qual è la ruota, qual è la nostra ruota... qual è la ruota che è stata scoperta in questo frattempo...

— certo...

— cioè di quali ruote noi possiamo disporre...

— Ecco... dico... può darsi che la ruota che noi abbiamo scoperto e che per comodità costruiamo o vogliamo costruire, perché ancora non l'abbiamo fatto..., sappiamo che questo oggetto è possibile e lo vogliamo costruire... ma...

— ...noi potremmo a questo punto stabilire che ogni oggetto prodotto nella scuola, dopo due mesi va spoccato in pezzi, sotterrato... nel senso...

— Benissimo...

— Certo...!

— Noi abbiamo scoperto una legge...

— Esattamente...

— Abbiamo scoperto una legge fisica...

— ...un metodo... un...

— Abbiamo scoperto un... diciamo...

— ...una matematica...

— ...una matematica... un sistema di relazioni...

— certo!

— Cioè, ecco... ecco l'aspetto concettuale, ecco l'aspetto più... più...

— ...più interessante...

— ...più interessante della cosa, è questo, ecco, l'aspetto che mi preme salvaguardare in questa scuola...

— Ma siamo assolutamente d'accordo, più che d'accordo; direi che se si trattasse di produrre ruote e venderle io non ci starei a fare la scuola

— ...certo...

— ...certo...

— io, lo faccio già quel lavoro lì e poi non mi interessa...

— Ma in questa scuola, non c'è nulla da vendere?

[(continua a pagina 48)

scena 5

I pochi superstiti si trovarono senza un PARCO-OGGETTI (anche i comportamenti avevano subito la stessa metamorfosi degli oggetti, così gli uomini dopo un periodo AEREODINAMICO e pieno di speranze fatto di vita nella foresta e di ricostruzione di città MODERNISSIME, furono per un modo di vita più adatto alla MISERIA presente).

The few who survived found themselves without any PARK OF OBJECTS (even behaviour had undergone the same metamorphosis as the objects had, so that after an AERODYNAMIC period full of hope and based on life in the forest and on the construction of THE MOST MODERN cities, men were compelled to give up their AFFLUENCE and anything superfluous and lead a life more in keeping with their present POVERTY).

scena 6

Il CAPITALE aveva rivolto da tempo la sua attenzione ai SERVIZI. « Controllando i SERVIZI... — diceva il CAPITALE — ...mi sarà più facile controllare la società » e mise delle PRESE DI CORRENTE A PAGAMENTO nel TERRITORIO nella foresta e dappertutto. Il PAESAGGIO si popolò di TRALICCI, di STAZIONI DI PEDAGGI e GABELLIERI e di TELEFONI.

For quite some time CAPITAL had focussed its attention on SERVICES. « If I can control SERVICES »..., said CAPITAL, ...« it will be easier for me to control society » and he set up PAY MAINS OUTLETS throughout the TERRITORY, in the forest, and everywhere. The LANDSCAPE bristled with PYLONS, TOLL STATIONS, and TOLL COLLECTORS, and TELEPHONES.

scena 7

Così c'era sempre una gran ressa al POSTO TELEFONICO e si scambiavano derrate e vestiti con GETTONI.
Il fatto è che NESSUNO capì il valore del termine LOTTA DI CLASSE.

So that there was always a great crowd at the TELEPHONE EXCHANGE and they bartered food and clothing for TELEPHONE TOKENS. The fact is that NOBODY understood the value of the term THE CLASS STRUGGLE.

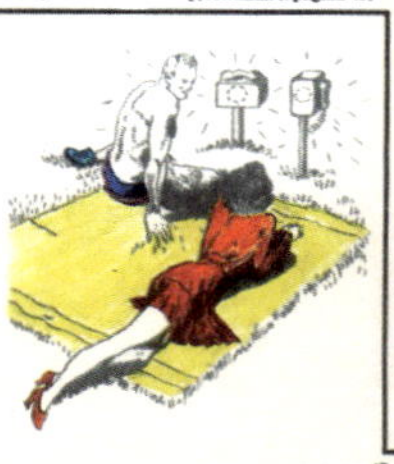

21. Industrial Production and Individual Creativity

UFO, 'Produzione industriale e creatività individuale', *Casabella*, no. 379, July 1973, pp. 46-47.
The text, limited only to the paragraph "scene 6," will be republished in *Spazio-arte*. See 'Produzione industriale e creatività individuale', Spazioarte, vol. IV, no. 10-11, June-October 1977, p. 3.

scene 1

... with difficulty the object dragged into the interior of the FOREST never to return again.

scene 2

Little by little it lost its ability to communicate (far from men, from contact with public spectators and any sharing in their lives, the object lost even its CORDIAL AND SPONTANEOUS NATURE)

scene 3

Let us say that it ATROPHIED. Then came a period of sharp decline in its gay and carefree internal characteristics, both because the creeping weeds of the forest and atmospheric agents and the earth corroded it and because it suffered a kind of internal transformation and took on a new completely AERODYNAMIC aspect.

scene 4

During this period UTOPIA developed a rather AUTHORITARIAN model of society more in contact with RELIGION than with the experience of men here on earth. THE SUPERMYTHS led to the almost complete destruction of the human race.

scene 5

The few who survived found themselves without any PARK OF OBJECTS (even behaviour had undergone the same metamorphosis as the object had, so that after an AERODYNAMIC period full of hope and based on life in the forest and on the construction of THE MOST MODERN cities, men were compelled to give up their AFFLUENCE and anything superfluous and lead a life more in keeping with their present POVERTY).

scene 6

For quite some time CAPITAL had focused its attention on SERVICES. "If I can control SERVICES"..., said CAPITAL, ... "It will be easier for me to control society" and he set up PAY POWER SOCKETS throughout the TERRITORY, in the forest, and everywhere. The LANDSCSAPE bristled with PYLONS, TOLL STATIONS, TOLL COLLECTORS, and TELEPHONES.

scene 7

So that there was always a great crowd at the TELEPHONE EXCHANGE and they bartered food and clothing for TELEPHONE TOKENS. The fact is that NOBODY understood the value of the term THE CLASS STRUGGLE.

LIBRI LIVRES BOOKS

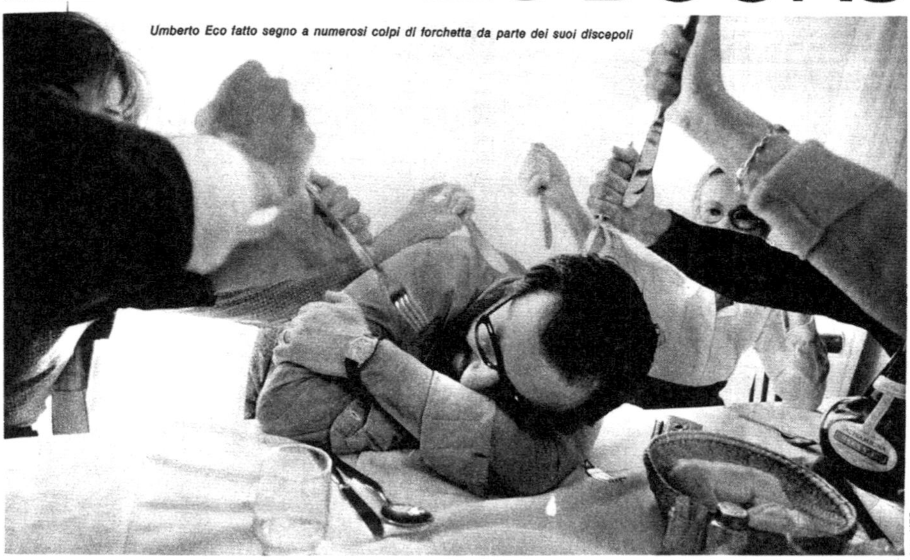

Umberto Eco fatto segno a numerosi colpi di forchetta da parte dei suoi discepoli

foto UFO

Umberto Eco: « Segno ». Enciclopedia filosofica ISEDI, Milano, 1973.

Caro zio Umberto,
le nostre strade si sono divise dal 1968, da quando la pratica e la teoria non sono andate più di pari passo.

La teoria è andata « 'mbraccio a me » con lo specifico disciplinare di tutti i generi. Ma col tempo ci siamo resi conto che non c'era poi una così grande differenza, il tempo si sa livella tutto, relativizza azioni, concetti, comportamenti.

I tempi lunghi della scalata al potere possono essere rivoluzionari mentre le mode passano e l'immaginario ristagna. Le strutture profonde ricevono spinte storiche mentre quelle superficiali ne restano scosse.

L'autocritica si spinge anche più a fondo: adesso stiamo cercando di recuperare certe forme di associazionismo spontaneo anni '60, a livello quasi di Azione Cattolica. È un fatto! Forse una delle ultime strategie che ci restano per invertire la tendenza involutiva che si è impadronita della società. Molto vicini alla strategia della mediazione per raggiungere la sopravvivenza pensiamo di essere così vicini anche a te. Non pensare, leggendo queste righe che si tratti del solito scherzo degli UFO! È la solita maledetta mania intellettuale di considerarsi al di fuori delle proprie azioni, di sospendere il giudizio oltre che sul circostante anche su sé stessi.

Abbiamo seguito il tuo cammino teorico un po' da lontano ma non per questo con minore attenzione. Quando dicevi che la struttura è assente avevi ragione perché adesso qualsiasi disciplina o materia universitaria ambisce ad essere nel suo intimo strutturalista, magari un tantino superficialmente. Perciò noi concludiamo: La Struttura adesso deve essere assente! E quando dicevi che anche il Contenuto ha una Forma noi pensavamo che lo facevi per salvare la Semiotica dall'orgia di contenuti e di sostanze in cui l'avevano precipitata le bombe dei fascisti.

E adesso questo ultimo tuo libro o piccolo manuale sul SEGNO di cui ci è chiara immediatamente la grandissima utilità perché mette finalmente ordine fra una serie di definizioni e teorizzazioni dell'ultimo quarto di secolo che ci lasciavano a dir poco frastornati. Che importa se per un momento abbiamo pensato che l'impatto violento della cultura con un sistema teorico originale come la semiologia o lo strutturalismo riuscisse a scuotere il torpore degli accademici! Ora è chiaro che « nihil sub sole novi ».

L'intento didascalico del manuale sul segno riscatta le pericolose involuzioni.

Il riferimento esplicito al « common sense » ci pare un'indicazione precisa in tal senso.

Tale da superare la difficoltà oggettiva di lettura del testo.

Perciò lo consigliamo indistintamente a specialisti e allievi e accludiamo una foto in cui si vede U. Eco che « è stato fatto *segno* a numerosi colpi di forchetta » da parte dei suoi discepoli

da gli UFO
(Lapo Binazzi)
Firenze-Milano *con amore*

Cher tonton Umberto,
nos routes se sont séparées en 1968, c'est à dire au moment où la pratique et la théorie ne sont plus allées de pair.

En classant les genres selon leur discipline spécifique, la théorie a ouvert les bras dans tous les sens. Mais avec le recul nous nous sommes aperçus qu'il n'y avait pas une telle différence: le temps, on le sait, nivelle tout et rend relatifs les concepts, les actions et les comportements.

Les longs délais de l'accession au pouvoir peuvent être révolutionnaires alors que les modes passent et que l'imagination languit. Les structures profondes accusent la poussée de l'histoire tandis que les structures superficielles n'en subissent que le choc.

L'autocritique va même plus loin: actuellement nous essayons de récupérer certaines formes d'association spontanée du type des années 60 au niveau de l'« Action Catholique » ou peut s'en faut. C'est un fait! Il s'agit peut être d'une des dernières stratégies qui nous restent pour invertir la tendance régressive qui s'est emparée de la société. Très proches de la stratégie de la médiation pour la survie, nous pensons, ce faisant, nous rapprocher de toi aussi. Ne crois pas, en lisant ces lignes, qu'il s'agisse d'une blague genre UFO! Il s'agit de l'habituelle maudite manie intellectuelle de se considérer soi-même en dehors de l'action, de faire porter le jugement non seulement sur l'entourage mais aussi sur soi.

Nous avons suivi ton parcours théorique d'un peu plus loin mais sans négliger pour autant d'y prêter attention.

Quand tu disais que la structure est absente tu avais raison car actuellement n'importe quelle discipline ou matière universitaire se sent intimement structuraliste, ne serait-ce même que de façon un tantinet superficielle. Nous en concluons donc: actuellement la Structure doit être absente! Et quand tu disais que le Contenu aussi a une Forme, nous pension que tu le faisais pour sauver la Sémiotique de l'orgie de contenus et de substances où l'avaient précipitée les bombes des fascistes. Et voici maintenant ton dernier livre, ce petit manuel sur le Signe dont la très grande utilité nous apparaît instantanément car il met enfin de l'ordre dans une foule de définitions et de théories du dernier quart de siècle qui nous laissaient pour le moins déconcertés. Qu'importe si nous avons pensé pour un instant que l'impact violent de la culture, à travers un système théorique original tel que la sémiologie ou le structuralisme, aurait pu réussir à ébranler le torpeur des académiciens! Il est clair désormais que « nihil sub scle novi ».

Le but didactique du manuel sur le signe compense les dangers de l'évolution régressive.

La référence explicite au « sens commun » nous semble une indication précise à ce sujet, au point de permettre de surmonter la difficulté objective de lecture du texte: nous le conseillons donc sans distinction aussi bien aux spécialistes qu'aux élèves et nous joignons une photo où l'on aperçoit U. Eco qui à été fait signe (cible) à coups de fourchette par ses élèves.

de la part des UFO avec amour

Dear Uncle Umberto,
We have gone our separate ways since 1968, since practice and theory have ceased to keep in step.

Theory has gone arm-in-arm with the specific disciplines of all kinds. But with the passing of time we realized that there was not really such a big difference. Time, of course, irons out everything, makes actions, concepts and behaviour relative.

The long years of the ladder to power may be revolutionary while the fashions pass and the imagery stagnates. The profound structures receive historical thrusts while the ones on the surface are shaken by them.

The self-criticism drives still deeper; now we are trying to recover some of the forms of spontaneous associa-

22. Books
(Review: Umberto Eco, *Segno*)

Lapo Binazzi (UFO), 'Libri (recensione di Umberto Eco: "Segno". Enciclopedia filosofica ISEDI, Milano, 1973)', *Domus*, no. 530, January 1974, pp. 49-50.

Dear Uncle Umberto,

We have gone our separate ways since 1968, since practice and theory have ceased to keep in step.
Theory has gone arm-in-arm with the disciplinary specific of all kinds. But with the passing of time we realized that there was not really such a big difference. Time, of course, irons out everything, makes actions, concepts and behaviour relative. The long years of the ladder to power may be revolutionary while the fashions pass and the imagery stagnates. The profound structures receive historical thrusts while the ones on the surface are shaken by them.
The self-criticism drives still deeper; now we are trying to recover some of the forms of spontaneous associationism of the Sixties, almost on a par with Azione Cattolica. It's fact! Maybe one of the last strategies we can still rely on to reverse the involved trend that has taken hold of society. Very close to the strategy of mediation to attain survival, we believe we are also thus close to you. When you read these lines, don't think it's the usual UFO joke! It is the usual blasted intellectual mania for considering oneself outside one's own actions, for suspending judgement not only on one's neighbourhood but on oneself too.
We have followed your theoretic path from some distance, but not for this reason with any less attention. When you said that the structure is absent you were right, because now any university discipline or subject longs in its heart to be structuralist, perhaps a little bit superficially. Therefore we conclude: the structure now *must* be absent! And when you said that Content too has a Form, we thought you were saying so to rescue Semiotics from the orgy of contents and substances into which it had been precipitated by the fascist bombs.
And now this last book of yours, or little manual on SIGNS, the very great utility of which is immediately clear because it at last tidies up a series of definitions and theorizings of the last quarter of a century which left us a little stunned to say the least. What does it matter if for a moment we thought that the violent impact of culture with an original theoretic system like semiology or structuralism might have succeeded in shaking the academics out of their lethargy! Now it is clear that "*nihil sub sole novi*."
The didactic intent of the manual on signs redeems the dangerous involutions.
The explicit reference to common sense seems to be a definite indication in that respect.
To the point that it supersedes the objective difficulty of reading the text.
So we recommend it indistinctly both to specialists and pupils and enclose a photo showing U. Eco who has been made the target (pun on the word "segno" in the Italian) of numerous fork-stabs by his disciples.

Florence-Milan

from the UFOs
(Lapo Binazzi)
with love

GLI UFO LEGGONO

John A. Walker: « Glossary of art architecture and design since 1945 ». Clive Bingley Ltd Publishers, London 1973.

Il Glossario di arte, architettura e design dal 1945, uscito recentemente a cura di John A. Walker per i tipi di Clive Bingley, Londra, non ci coglie impreparati.
Il libro, scritto sotto un forte complesso di colpa, chiamato più comunemente il peccato originale dei critici d'arte, tenta di giustificarsi dal rischio di impopolarità che tutte le classificazioni corrono in campo dell'arte.
A chi dovremmo credere nel futuro? A chi dice che le catalogazioni uccidono, che sono fatte per mettere dei punti fermi dove il discorso potrebbe ancora continuare, che esse emergono quando l'inventivo artistico ristagna, che giovano più ai critici, e per questi alle gallerie e al mercato, che non al pubblico e all'uomo della strada che ne restano comunque esclusi?
Oppure a chi dice che « . . .Lo sviluppo di vocabolari specializzati caratterizza tutti i nuovi campi del sapere, scientifico tecnologico sociale o artistico, senza eccezione? ».
Di questi problemi si rende conto anche l'autore che registra con obiettività anche pareri contrari, come quello di Jaroslav Serpan: « . . .Strana situazione! Assegnato dagli inevitabili attaccatori di etichette a diversi successivi movimenti, come è che io non mi sono mai sentito completamente a casa mia in nessuno di questi? ».
Comunque il carattere illuministico dell'opera è utile in tempi di oscurantismo, e sembra riallacciarsi al problema dell'amplificazione del proprio segno artistico da parte dell'operatore concettuale che utilizza anche il contesto del linguaggio per definire ulteriormente la propria attività e spesso anche i singoli lavori, dimenticando però che la necessità dell'amplificazione, come, più elementarmente l'esporre un'opera in una galleria, discende pur sempre dalla condizione gerarchica di superpotere del fattore economico del mercato artistico, e da quella sempre gerarchica del linguaggio verbale sugli altri linguaggi. Imprecisa ci sembra la similitudine che collegherebbe « . . .la disparità fra le etichette e l'arte che esse denotano. . . » alla « . . .disparità fra le parole e gli oggetti che esse descrivono. . . ». Sappiamo infatti dalla semiologia che mentre nel secondo caso si tratta del rapporto fra il significante e il referente, nel primo, che poi sarebbe quello di cui si preoccupa l'autore, si tratta del rapporto fra linguaggio artistico e metalinguaggio critico.
In ogni caso il lavoro di J. A. Walker nasce dalla coscienza di ampliamento del campo artistico, in cui il critico rivendica una funzione trainante e inventiva allo stesso modo con cui l'artista rivendica una maggior partecipazione alla autodefinizione del proprio lavoro.
Un modo « nuovo » di far critica e di fare arte che oggi sembra accontentare tutti, purché « addetti ai lavori », e che tutto sommato sembra accordarsi perfettamente con le leggi del mercato e dei rapporti di produzione in fase di neocapitalismo avanzato.
Il Glossario raccoglie le tendenze più importanti dal dopoguerra ad oggi, i campi coperti sono architettura, arte-pittura, scultura, grafica e design mentre sono esclusi film, teatro, musica, letteratura e moda. Questa scelta ci pare una precisa indicazione. Il libro sarà indubbiamente utile agli specialisti dei settori toccati.
È compilato per ordine alfabetico con numero progressivo abbinato per quanto concerne le etichette; e di ogni voce è allegata una bibliografia essenziale; vi è un indice generale dei nomi.
Come voci sono considerati anche artisti o gruppi.
Il nostro gruppo — gli UFO — non c'è. Abbiamo ancora l'abitudine sana di scappare alla vista dei messi del tribunale come nei tempi antichi per evitare citazioni di fronte alla Storia.

da gli UFO
(Lapo Binazzi)

The « Glossary of Art, Architecture and Design since 1945 », recently published by Clive Bingley of London and edited by John A. Walker, has not caught us unawares.
Written with a strong guilt complex, more commonly known as the original sin of art critics, the book attempts to justify itself against the risk of unpopularity which all classifications are liable to encounter in the field of art.
Whom should we believe in the future? those who say that cataloguings kill, that they are done to put full stops where the subject could still be continued, that they emerge when artistic inventiveness has dried up, that they do more good to the critics and, through the latter, to the galleries and the market, than to the public and the man in the street who are in any case left out of the picture?
Or those who say that « . . .The development of specialist vocabularies characterizes all new fields of knowledge, whether scientific, technological, social or artistic - without exception »?
The author too realizes that these problems exist and objectively registers even opposite opinions, like that of Jaroslav Serpan: « . . .Strange situation! Assigned by the inevitable stickers on of labels to several successive movements, how is it that I have never felt completely at home in any one of these? ».
However, the illuministic character of this work is useful in times of obscurantism, and seems to tie up with the conceptual artist's problem of amplifying his own artistic sign. The conceptual artist also utilizes the context of language to further define his activity and often his single works too, forgetting however that the need for amplification, like, to put it more elementarily, exhibiting a work in a gallery, still stems from the hierarchic superpower of the art market's economic factor, and from the always hierarchic pre-eminence of the verbal language on the other languages.
The similitude whereby « . . .the disparity between the label and the art it denotes. . . » is apparently linked to « the disparity occurring between all words and the objects they describe. . . » sounds inexact to us. We know in fact from semiology that whilst in the second case the relation is between the significant and the referent, in the first case, which is the one the author is concerned about, the relation is between artistic language and critical metalanguage.
At all events, J. A. Walker's work springs from an awareness of the enlargement of the field of art, in which the critic claims a towing and an inventive function in the same way as the artist claims a greater participation in the self-definition of his work. A « new » way of handling criticism and of making art, which nowadays seems to please everybody provided they are « authorized persons », and which, all things considered, seems to accord perfectly with the laws of the market and of production relations in a stage of advanced neocapitalism.
The Glossary collects the main trends since the last war up till now. The areas covered are architecture, painting, sculpture, graphic art and design, whilst films, theatre, music, literature and fashion are not included. This choice seems to be a definite indication. The book will undoubtedly be useful to specialists in the sectors mentioned.
It is compiled in alphabetical order with a combined progressive number as far as the labels are concerned. Attached to each item is an essential bibliography. There is also a general index of names.
Artists or groups are also treated as items.
Our own group — the UFO — is not there. We still have the healthy habit of escaping the notice of the officers of the court, as in ancient times, to avoid being summoned to appear before History.

Lapo Binazzi
(of the UFO)

Le « Glossaire de l'art, de l'architecture et du design de 1945 à nos jours », paru récemment par les soins de John A. Walker, publié par Clive Bingley, London, ne nous prend pas au dépourvu.
Le livre, écrit sous l'influence d'un sens de culpabilité, appelé plus communément le péché originel des critiques d'art, essaye de se justifier du risque d'impopularité que toutes les classifications courent dans le domaine de l'art.
A qui devrions-nous croire à l'avenir?
A celui qui dit que le fait de cataloguer tue, qu'il sert à mettre des points fixes là où le discours pourrait encore continuer, qu'il est mis en relief quand l'inventive artistique stagne, qu'il sert plus aux critiques d'art et pour eux aux galeries et au marché, plutôt qu'au public et à l'homme de la rue, qui en restent de toute façon exclus?
Ou bien à celui qui dit: « . . .Le développement des vocabulaires spécialisés caractérise tous les nouveaux domaines de la connaissance, scientifique, technologique, sociale ou artistique, sans exception? »
L'auteur également se rend compte de ces problèmes; il prend note objectivement même des opinions contraires comme celle de Jaroslav Serpan: « . . .Etrange situation! Désigné par les inévitables colleurs d'étiquettes à différents mouvements successifs, comment se fait-il que je ne me suis jamais senti complètement chez moi dans aucun de ceux-ci? »
De toute façon, le caractère illuministe de l'oeuvre est utile dans les époques d'obscurantisme et semble se rattacher au problème de l'amplification du signe artistique de la part de l'opérateur conceptuel, qui utilise également le contexte du langage pour définir ultérieurement son activité et souvent même chaque oeuvre, en oubliant toutefois que la nécessité d'amplification — comme le fait d'exposer une oeuvre dans une galerie — descend malgré tout de la condition hiérarchique de super-pouvoir du facteur économique dans le marché artistique et de la condition toujours hiérarchique de prééminence du langage verbal par rapport aux autres langages.
Très imprécise nous semble la similitude qui lierait « . . .la disparité entre les étiquettes et l'art qu'elles désignent. . . » à « . . .la disparité entre les paroles et les objets qu'elles décrivent. . . ». En effet la sémiologie nous enseigne que dans le second cas, il s'agit du rapport entre le signifiant et le référant, tandis que dans le premier, qui serait plus précisément celui dont s'occupe l'auteur, il s'agit du rapport entre le langage artistique et le métalangage critique.
En tout cas, le travail de J. A. Walker naît de la conscience d'un élargissement du domaine artistique, où le critique revendique une fonction locomotive et d'invention de la même façon avec laquelle l'artiste revendique une plus grande participation à l'auto-définition de son propre travail.
Une nouvelle manière de faire de la critique et de l'art, qui semble aujourd'hui contenter tout le monde, pourvu qu'il s'agisse d'« initiés » et que tout compte fait semble s'accorder parfaitement avec les lois du marché et les rapports de production d'un néo-capitalisme avancé.
Le Glossaire recueille les tendences les plus importantes de l'époque allant de l'après-guerre à nos jours, les domaines intéressés sont l'architecture, l'art-peinture, la sculpture, les arts graphiques et le design, tandis que la cinématographie, le théâtre, la musique, la littérature et la mode sont exclus. Ce choix nous semble une indication précise. Ce livre sera sans doute utile aux spécialistes des domaines concernés.
Il est compilé par ordre alphabétique et pour chaque rubrique on a joint une bibliographie essentielle; il y a un index général des noms.
Les artistes ou les groupes aussi sont considérés comme des rubriques.
Notre groupe — les UFO — y est absent. Nous avons encore la saine habitude de fuir à la vue des huissiers du tribunal comme jadis, pour éviter d'être cités face à l'Histoire.

(pour les UFO)
Lapo Binazzi

Institute of Contemporary Art, Londra: The Austrian Exhibition: qui, Max Peintner, «Estate 1972» (12—30.9.1973)

Galleria 291-Milano, Milano: Ralph Gibson (dicembre)

Nigel Greenwood, Londra: Moholy-Nagy (17.12.1973—19.1.1974)

Graphische Sammlung Albertina, Vienna: Walter Pichler (18.10—18.11.1973)

Galleria di Porta Ticinese, Milano: Pino Spagnulo (dicembre)

Warren Benedek Gallery, New York: Hardu Keck

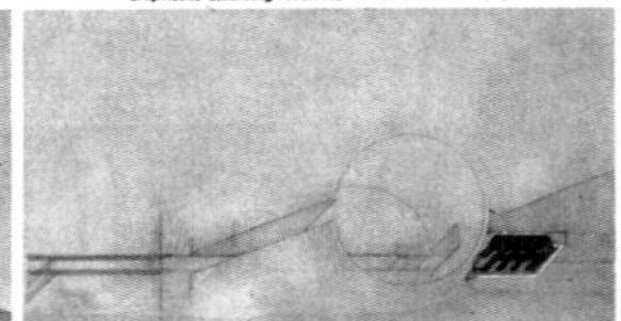

NELLE GALLERIE

23. UFOs Read

(Review: John A. Walker, *Glossary of Art Architecture and Design Since 1945*)

Lapo Binazzi (UFO), 'Gli Ufo leggono (recensione di: John A. Walker, "Glossary of art architecture and design since 1945", Clive Bingley Ltd Publishers, London 1973)', *Domus*, no. 531, February 1974, p. 54.

Written with a strong guilt complex, more commonly known as the original sin of art critics, the book attempts to justify itself against the risk of unpopularity which all classifications are liable to encounter in the field of art.

Whom should we believe in the future? Those who say that cataloguings kill, that they are done to put full stops where the subject could still be continued, that they emerge when artistic inventiveness has dried up, that they do more good to the critics and, though the latter, to the galleries and the market, than to the public and the man in the street that who are in any case left out of the picture?

Or those who say that "...the development of specialist vocabularies characterizes all new fields of knowledge, whether scientific, technological social or artistic—without exception?".

The author too realizes that these problems exist and objectively registers even opposite opinions, like that of Jaroslav Serpan: "...strange situation! Assigned by the inevitable stickers on of labels to several successive movements, how is that the I have never felt completely at home in any one of these?".

However, the illuministic character of this work is useful in time of obscurantism, and seems to tie up with the conceptual artist's problem of amplifying his own artistic sign. The conceptual artist also utilizes the context of language to further define his activity and often his single works too, forgetting however that the need for amplification, like, to put it more elementarily, exhibiting a work in a gallery, still stems from the hierarchic superpower of the art market's economic factor, and from the always hierarchic pre-eminence of the verbal language on the other languages.

The similitude whereby "...the disparity between the label and the art it denotes..." is apparently linked to "the disparity occurring between all words and the objects they describe..." sounds inexact to us. We know in fact from semiology that whilst in the second case the relation is between the significant and the referent, in the first case, which is the one the author is concerned about, the relation is between artistic language and critical metalanguage.

At all events, J. A. Walker's work springs from an awareness of the enlargement of the field of art, in which the critic claims a towing and an inventive function in the same way as the artist claims a greater participation in the self-definition of his work. A "new" way of handling criticism and of making art, which nowadays seems to please everybody provided they are "authorized persons" and which, all things considered, seems to accord perfectly with the laws of the market and of production relations in a stage of advanced neocapitalism.

The Glossary collects the main trends since the last war up till now. The areas covered are architecture, painting, sculpture, graphic art, and design, whilst films, theatre, music, literature, and fashion are not included. This choice seems to be a definite indication. The book will undoubtedly be useful to specialists in the sectors mentioned. It is compiled in alphabetical order with a combined progressive number as far as the labels are concerned. Attached to each item is an essential bibliography. There is also a general index of names.

Artists or groups are also treated as items.

Our own group—the UFOs—is not there. We still have the healthy habit of escaping the notice of the officers of the court, as in ancient times, to avoid being summoned to appear before History.

from the UFOs
(Lapo Binazzi)

CARABINIERI

24. Control, Colonisation, and Fascism in the Territory

UFO and Daniela Palazzoli (eds.), *Controllo colonizzazione e fascismo sul territorio: Milano, Galleria 291, maggio/giugno 1974* (Florence: Centro Di, 1974). The text was republished also in the magazine *Progettare inpiù*. See UFO, 'Appunti per una ridefinizione del concetto di fantaurbanistica', *Progettare inpiù*, no. 8, February-March 1975, p. 24.

The territory, it doesn't matter whether it's in town or country, is subject to continual colonisation. The outposts of civilisation homogenise under exploitation areas with very different propensities. The environment, humanity and its labour are shoehorned into the logic of capital.
Super-control is oppression of the popular masses increasingly subject to the blackmail of services.
The signs of this plan of power, however, can be found everywhere.

GLOBAL TOOLS

GLOBAL TOOLS - Gruppo "TEORIA"
Relazione di Lapo Binazzi

10 ottobre 1974

Si ritiene necessario operare una ridefinizione del concetto di TEORIA come CREATIVITA' PURA.

Per questo mezzo la teoria può essere espressa dall'uomo che reagisce globalmente alla realtà preferibilmente con azioni, comportamenti, ecc. ... semplici e tecniche, pensieri ecc... elementari.

Il processo di identificazione istantanea di teoria e prassi capovolge copernicamente qualsiasi definizione della teoria come strumento per costruire oggetti mentali, modelli di cultura e società. La distruzione di queste mediazioni disciplinari e accademiche attraverso progressive riduzioni è invece ciò che interessa.

In questo senso la teoria come viene intesa comunemente non esiste. Esiste al contrario il processo inarrestabile di autoliberazione dell'uomo da ogni condizionamento, per la completa espressione della sua creatività.

Con la nascita dell'informazione nasce il problema della DISCONTINUITA'. Ogni cosa può essere pensata, definita, divulgata istantaneamente. Per far CAMBIARE CORSO ALLA STORIA bastano poche parole, o pensieri. Si può addirittura ipotizzare cosa cambia in seguito a pensieri non espressi ma solo formulati come energia pura allo stato di creatività.

Nasce la possibilità di pensare una cosa e il suo contrario simultaneamente. E' il problema del codice dei codici e della liberazione anche da questo. In pratica il pensiero, che può contare su una serie collaudata di sistemi di pensiero, è ormai in grado di realizzare dffferenti sistemi di grado più elevato e di negarli al suo interno con verifiche di segno opposto.

Si tratta di definire una serie di strumenti semplici che facciano funzionare il meccanismo.

Le idee sono costruzioni di oggetti che equivalgono alla costruzione dei modelli di potere come struttura della società.

La riduzione opera come procedimento una prima destrutturazione.

La pura creatività si propone la deintellettualizzazione non solo dei prodotti ma anche dei metodi.

Discontinuità e sconnessioni diventano gli elementi distanziatori semplici di qualsiasi ricomposizione.

Si rendono possibili esercizi semplici come pensare due o più cose contemporaneamente, fare due o più cose contemporaneamente. Mettere a confronto elementi sempre più lontani fra loro, originare sistemi volutamente imperfetti ecc. ...

./.

Applicare a campi reali la ricognizione pura di questi procedimenti come il problema dell'amplificazione del "segno"(artistico) come corpo-nero assorbente l'energia in eccesso dell'immaginario collettivo, che restituisce una unica radiazione semplice, secondo la direzione anti-persuasione invertitore riduzione.

La crescita in progressione geometrica della velocità del pensiero pone problemi di adattamento e di sfruttamento delle proprie capacità, fino ad un radicale mutamento delle azioni, dei comportamenti delle teorie e delle tecniche.

La vita, l'ambiente sono i termini globali in cui si verificano strumenti, tecniche, teorie.

Proponiamo una serie di operazioni elementari per evidenziare la fissione di teoria e prassi.

Sembra necessario che ad una fase di analisi segua una di interventi.

Il rapporto con gli altri gruppi sarà indispensabile per non ricreare specifici disciplinari, o quanto meno una confidenza diretta all'interno del gruppo della teoria con i settori del corpo della comunicazione costruzione, sopravvivenza che ridefiniscono il campo di interessi della Global Tools.

L'originalità del procedimento potrà anche rivolgersi a una suddivisione strumentale della teoria in: politica, religione, meditazione, storia, tecnica ecc. ... per proporre temi particolari di indagine su cui si può accentrare di volta in volta l'interesse della Global Tools.

Per l'apertura dei seminari di novembre proponiamo tre possibili temi di discussione:

1) Rapporti fra architettura è magia.
   Studio dei rapporti criptici ai più alti livelli dell'organizzazione professionale. Piramide del potere. Oggetti magici. Problema della scienza ...

2) Analogia sportiva.
   Rapporto fra creatività collettiva come terapia di gruppo e squadre di calcio, di pallavolo, di rugby, di attività all'aria aperta come scoutismo, pic-nic ...

3) Creatività pura.
   ... se io dico che farsi sparare da un cannone, per esempio, è un esercizio di meditazione, si rende necessario costruire il cannone e in una certa maniera perché ciò sia possibile ...
   ... devo riuscire a farmi sparare nei luoghi più diversi tutte le volte che voglio.

25. Global Tools—"Theory" Group

Lapo Binazzi, *Global Tools - Gruppo 'Teoria', Relazione di Lapo Binazzi*, Florence, 10 October 1974 (Lapo Binazzi Archives).
In January 1975 the same text is published in the second bulletin of *Global Tools*, signed this time also by the other members of the "Theory" Group, and with an additional paragraph: "What we should really make permanent is discontinuity of thoughts and reality, preventing the project from going beyond a suggestion, a sketch, an attempt, or an unpredictable act, an end in itself without anything durable or consistent to back it up.
Now we have a day-book of theories and practices; if we should work out severe and highly conscientious plans. Joining technology and theory, who would guarantee that this fury would not be transformed into a 'new aesthetic'?
We cannot repeat it too often that the role of the avant-garde is the technical destruction of culture, and this is seen not as an act of terrorism but as a liberation, as a removal of all the moral considerations, aesthetic creeds and codes which hamper the free expression of individual and collective expression. Our action, as a slow but inexorable corrosion of specific disciplines, goes hand in hand with the great historic destruction of culture mechanically effected by the economic growth of the working masses. These masses imitate bourgeois cultural models, assimilating them as income goals, while destroying the economic balances on which they rest and while demolishing their moral and cultural platform... a foundation of universal values and meaning on which the middle-class has always based its moral right to plan the world.
If the avant-garde, in their moment of doubt, should effect the transformation of their thrust into a 'system' of messages and new scales of projects, reclaiming for their Chaplinesque behaviour the dignity of a new formal range, it would mean that once again—as we did in the early Twenties—we would be giving a new lease on life to the very culture that we want to eliminate. Our real dilemma, then, is to make 'non-meaning' permanent, the great discovery or 'worthlessness', and the exasperating discontinuity of the reality in which we live. For what is really important is to have understood and demonstrated that art is only the productive exploitation of creativity, that the professional intellectual only robs us of the inalienable right we all have to produce and consume our own private culture, and that society, trough the division of labour, alienates all of man's creative faculties, including the political ones." See Lapo Binazzi (UFO), Alberto Breschi, Roberto Pecchioli (Zzigurrat) and Remo Buti, 'T-h-eor-y-ia', in *Bollettino Global Tools n. 1* (Milan: Edizioni l'uomo e l'arte, 1975). The text, in its original version dated 10 October 1974, is also published in *Spazioarte*, vol. IV, no. 10-11, June-October 1977, pp. 17-18.

GLOBAL TOOLS - "THEORY" GROUP
Lapo Binazzi Relation

10 October 1974

We think it necessary to give a new definition of the THEORY concept as PURE CREATIVITY.

According to it theory can be expressed by a man who reacts totally to reality, especially through simple actions, behaviours, etc.... and through elementary techniques, thoughts, etc...

The instantaneous identification process of theory and praxis has upset any definition of theory as an instrument for building mental objects, patterns of culture and society, as Copernico did. On the other hand what must be taken into consideration is the destruction of these disciplinary and academic mediations through progressive reductions.

In this sense, theory, as usually we consider it, doesn't exist. On the contrary, what is going on is the process of self-liberation of man from every conditioning agent in order to achieve a full expression of his own creativity.

After the birth of information, the problem of DISCONTINUITY. We can think, define and spread about everything instantaneously. In order to CHANGE THE COURSE OF HISTORY, just a few words or thoughts are necessary. We can even make hypothesis about what really changes if thoughts remain unexpressed, being only formulated as pure creative energy.

The possibility of simultaneously thinking of something and its opposite arises. It's the problem of the codex of the codices and of freedom from this one, too. Actually, the thought that can rely on a tested series of thinking systems is able to realize different systems of a higher degree and to deny them within its own structure by putting them to a test of apposite sign.

We must define a series of simple instruments setting the mechanism in motion.

Ideas are comparable with the building of objects corresponding to the patterns of the power as structure of our society.

First, reduction causes a process of destructurization (sic).

Pure creativity aims at the deintellectualization not only of products, but even of methods.

Discontinuity and disconnections become simple elements, creating distances and finally rejoining them.

In so doing, it is possible to make simple exercises like thinking or doing two or more things at once. Comparing elements, more and more distant from each other, giving rise to deliberately imperfect systems and so on.

To apply to real fields the pure acknowledgement of these procedures like the amplification of the (artistic) "sign" as a black-body absorbing the superabundant energy of the collective imaginary, which produces only one simple radiation according to the direction: anti-persuasion, reversal, reduction.

The growing, geometrically progressing speed of thought arouses problems of adaptation and exploitation of one's capacities, as far as to reach a radical change of actions, and of behaviours of theories and techniques.

Life and environment are the global terms we test instruments, techniques, and theories within.

We suggest a series of elementary operations to emphasize the fission between theory and praxis. It seems to be necessary that an intervention phase should follow to an analysis phase.

The relationship with the other groups will be essential in order to avoid creating specific disciplinary limits and, even less, a close relation inside the "Theory" Group with the body, communication, building, survival groups, that define the field of interest of Global Tools.

The original procedure may also divide instrumentally the Theory into: politics, religion, meditation, history, technique, and so on... in order to suggest peculiar subject for enquiry, on which the Global Tools movement can focus its interest from time to time.

For the opening of November seminar we suggest three possible topics:

1) Relations between architecture and magic.
   A study of hidden relationship at top levels of professional organisations.
   Power pyramid. Magical objects. The problem of science.

2) Sport analogy.
   Relationship between collective creativity as group therapy and football, volley-ball, rugby teams, and other bodily activities, in the open air like pic-nic, scouting...

3) Pure creativity.
   ... if I claim that being shot out of a cannon, for instance, is a meditation exercise the cannon is to be built in a certain way so that it may happen...
   ... I must succeed in being shot out of (the cannon) on the most different spots, whenever I want.

DISCHI
RECORDS

Collana « Nova Musicha », Cramps Records, Milano 1974.
« Nova Musicha » è una collana di dischi di musica contemporanea, diretta, per Cramps Records, da Gianni Emilio Simonetti. La prima opera è dedicata a John Cage e comprende pezzi dal '47 al '71: « Music for Marcel Duchamp », 1947, per piano solo (performer Juan Hildago), «Music for Amplified Toy Pianos », 1960, per tre pianini-giocattolo e un numero imprecisato di oggetti, e « Radio Music » 1956, da 1 a 3 a 8 apparecchi radio (performers Juan Hildago, Walter Marchetti, G. E. Simonetti), « 4'33" » (performer G. E. Simonetti) eseguito per la prima volta a Woodstock nel 1952, « Sixty two Mesostic Re Merce Cunningham » 1971, per voce e microfono (performer Demetrio Statos).

LIBRI
BOOKS

« Shelter », Shelter Publications, Bolinas, California '74.
In un grande volume (27,5×36,5; 176 pagine), questi argomenti: caverne, capanne, tende, i pellerossa, il legno in Europa, il nuovo mondo, granai, baracche, i nomadi, le cupole (« Domebook » 3), case-barca, barche-casa, auto-casa, camion-casa, le abitazioni più semplici, i modi per costruirsi la casa, vivere e sopravvivere (Bolinas, Cal. P.O. Box 219).

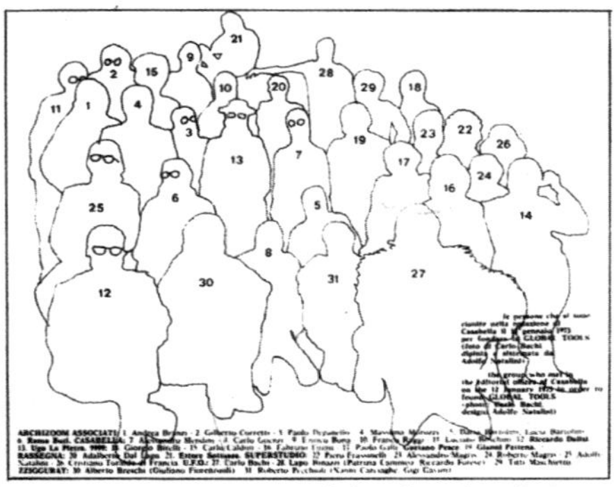

Paola Navone, Bruno Orlandoni: «Architettura "radicale". La neoavanguardia italiana dell'architettura e del design dal 1960 ad oggi ». Documenti di Casabella, Milano 1974.

A Paola Navone e Bruno Orlandoni
— Bravi! Era ora che il mondo sapesse tutto sulla leggenda dell'architettura « radicale »!
— Finalmente avete definito un « luogo culturale » che era passato in silenzio sotto il naso degli accademici e sotto le gambe dei carabinieri!
— Alle accuse velenose del gruppo di « tendenza » è stato risposto a piè fermo, finalmente anche noi abbiamo la « credibilità »!
Queste e altre telefonate vi saranno sicuramente arrivate all'indomani dell'uscita del libro.
Lo trovo perfettamente giusto. Come sapete bene sono stato uno dei maggiori fautori della pubblicazione.
Ma siete proprio sicuri di avere evitato il rischio della ricomposizione di classe di esperienze il cui scopo principale era di creare « discontinuità » e « sconnessioni » nel perfetto sistema del potere, e dei suoi specifici disciplinari?
Di non avere adottato un linguaggio pure « egemone » in quanto « culturale », ma anche troppo filologico, specie nell'allargamento ai corsi e ricorsi universitari?
Lo so bene. Il tentativo di spiegare è una malattia che gli altri ci inoculano per distruggerci e non sempre ci sappiamo ribellare alla maniera giusta. Ma è anche il segno della loro estrema fragilità teorica e psichica, del loro istinto di morte.
Vi si potrebbe sbrigativamente accusare di non aver capito che, in fondo, l'architettura radicale è « un'altra cosa » ecc... ecc..., ma io invece ho apprezzato moltissimo e in blocco il vostro libro come « revival storico », dove l'unico compito della storia è quello di creare la leggenda.
Del resto sapete che in vostra presenza non adopererei mai il tono paternalistico-ironico di questa recensione, esso è una pura forma letteraria di stampo arcaico, accetterei al contrario una discussione tra quattro mura, ma il farlo da queste colonne mi sembrerebbe falso, mentre c'è bisogno appunto di originare « discontinuità » e « sconnessioni ».
Che è un po' la logica della terapia di gruppo « radicale », in opposizione alle varie esperienze artistiche così seriosamente ironiche ma mai in effettiva contraddizione con la logica del mercato. I vostri raffronti fra queste e quelle hanno il merito di sprovincializzare il campo ma certe volte confondono anche le idee!
Il tentativo di « continuizzare » la società attraverso la produzione di oggetti mentali, modelli critici e altro, va una volta per tutte messo in crisi, suona « persuasione » « imbonimento ».
L'architettura « radicale » nasce e si riproduce al di là della stessa definizione ed è bene che continui a farlo.
Inoltre non ha nessun tributo da pagare alle varie correnti artistiche perché fin dal primo momento nega l'individualità dell'arte che è al contrario l'ultimo scoglio su cui la società colloca l'artista per potersene servire meglio.
Una scelta di campo più ristretta avrebbe evitato che fatti e persone che non c'entrano niente con l'architettura « radicale » fossero mischiati con altri che invece c'entrano, ma queste sono considerazioni che è bene rimandare alla lettura o ad una discussione più approfondita.
Mi sembra giusto chiudere qui con un'ultima domanda agli autori:
— Se l'Arcivescovo di Costantinopoli si disarcivescoviscodiscontinuizzasse, vi disarcivescoviscodiscontinuizzereste anche voi?
Lapo Binazzi (UFO)

«Global Tools», edizioni L'Uomo e l'Arte, Milano 1974.
È uscito il primo numero di « Global Tools », pubblicazione del gruppo « Global Tools » fondato nel '73 presso la redazione di Casabella da Archizoom Associati, Remo Buti, Casabella, Riccardo Dalisi, Ugo La Pietra, 9999, Gaetano Pesce, Gianni Pettena, Ettore Sottsass jr., Superstudio, Ufo e Zzuggurat. « Global Tools » è un sistema di laboratori (a Firenze) « per la propagazione e l'uso di materie e tecniche naturali e relativi comportamenti » e « si pone come obiettivo di stimolare il libero sviluppo della creatività individuale ». Segreteria, via Brera 9, Milano.

«Top Symbols and Trademarks of the World », Deco Press, Milano 1973.
Edito da Deco Press (una nuova divisione di Franco Maria Ricci editore dedicata al design, alla comunicazione visiva, alle arti applicate e all'iconografia) è ora uscito «Top symbols and trademarks of the world » a cura di Franco Maria Ricci e Corinna Ferrari: una formidabile raccolta di marchi e simboli commerciali di trenta paesi del mondo. Quattro anni di ricerca, sette volumi, tremila pagine, cinquemila marchi, milleduecento designers. (Prezzo L. 85.000). L'opera è uno strumento di lavoro per quanti operano nel campo del commercio, della pubblicità e della comunicazione visiva. Naturalmente un'opera enciclopedica come questa si presta ad osservazioni su lacune o accumuli, ma il lavoro è di grande interesse.
Ogni paese è rappresentato da una introduzione scritta da uno studioso di design: George Nelson (Stati Uniti), Burton Kramer (Canada), Juan Perucho (Spagna), Decio Pignatari (America Latina), Colin Forbes (Gran Bretagna e Irlanda), Pieter Brattinga (Benelux), François Barré (Francia), Vittorio Gregotti (Italia), Hans Neuburg (Svizzera), Jupp Ernst (Germania Occidentale e Austria), Martin Gavler (Scandinavia), Stane Bernik (Jugoslavia), Grega Kosak (Paesi Socialisti).

26. Books

(Review: Paola Navone and Bruno Orlandoni, *Architettura "radicale". La neoavanguardia italiana dell'architettura e del design dal 1960 ad oggi*)

Lapo Binazzi (UFO), 'Libri (recensione di Paola Navone, Bruno Orlandoni: Architettura "radicale". La neoavanguardia italiana dell'architettura e del design dal 1960 ad oggi, Documenti di Casabella, Milano 1974)', *Domus*, no. 541, December 1974, p. 40.

To Paola Navone and Bruno Orlandoni

— Well done! It was time that the world found out all about the legend of "radical" architecture!

— At last you have defined a "cultural place" that had passed in silence under the nose of academics and between the legs of the *carabinieri*!

— A resolute response has been given to the spiteful accusations of La "Tendenza" group. At last we too have "credibility!".

You will certainly have received these and other telephone calls following the publication of the book.

I find this to be absolutely right. As you know well I have been one of the main promoters of the publication.

But are you really sure that you have avoided the risk of recomposing a class of experiences whose main purpose was of create "discontinuities" and "incongruities" in the perfect system of power, and of its disciplinary specifics?

That you haven't adopted a language that is "hegemonic" too in so far as it is "cultural," as well as overly philological in its approach, especially in the extension to university courses?

I am well aware of this. The attempt to explain is a sickness that others infect us with in order to destroy us and we are not always able to rebel against it in the right way. But it is also the sign of their extreme theoretical and mental fragility, of their death instinct.

You could be hastily accused of not having understood that, when all is said and done, radical architecture is "something else" etc., etc., but instead I have appreciated your book greatly and as a whole as a "historical revival," where history's only task is to create the legend.

Beside, you know that in your presence I would never adopt the paternalistic-ironic tone of this review; it is a purely literary form of an archaic character. I would agree on the contrary to a discussion in private, but to do it from these columns would seem false to me, while there is in fact a need to give rise to "discontinuities" and "incongruities."

Which is to some extent the logic of "radical" group therapy, in contrast to the various artistic experiences that are so seriously ironic but never actually contradict the logic of the market. Your comparisons between these and those have the merit of making the field less provincial but at times they can also be confusing!

The attempt to "continuise" society through the production of mental objects, critical models and the like should be undermined once, and for all. It sounds like "persuasion," "hype."

"Radical" architecture was born and reproduces above and beyond its definition and it is good that it should continue to do so.

In addition, it has no tribute to pay to the various artistic currents because right from the outset it has denied the individuality of art, which is on the contrary the last rock on which society places artists in order to make better use of them.

A narrower choice of field would have avoided facts and people that have nothing to do with "radical" architecture being mixed up with others that do, but these are considerations which it is better to put off to after the book has been read or to a more in-depth discussion.

I feel it is right to end here with one last question to the authors:

— If the archbishop of Constantinople were to disarchbishopdiscontinuise himself would you disarchbishopdiscontinuise yourselves as well?

Lapo Binazzi (UFO)

UFO

appunti per una ridefinizione del concetto di fantaurbanistica

Il Territorio, città o campagna non importa, è sottoposto a una continua colonizzazione. Gli avamposti della civiltà omogeneizzano sotto lo sfruttamento aree di vocazione diversissima. L'ambiente, l'uomo e il suo lavoro vengono ridotti alla logica del capitale.
Il supercontrollo è oppressione delle masse popolari soggetto sempre di più al ricatto dei servizi. Gli indizi di questo progetto di potere sono comunque rintracciabili dappertutto.

Manifesto del discontinuo

Tutte le cose, gli eventi, le azioni, i metodi, i comportamenti originali, sono discontinui. Lo dimostrano le ultime esperienze artistiche, quelle scientifiche e politiche. Gli artisti passano con naturalezza da un campo all'altro di espressione, la ricerca è sostanzialmente adisciplinare, l'arte attraversa un periodo di dematerializzazione e tende alla manifestazione di pura energia fisica e mentale, adotta l'uso dei mezzi più diversi, e anche negli esempi di collaborazione fra arte scienza e tecnologia gli interessi sono mischiati per cercare di stabilire dei punti che non appartengono a nessuno di questi campi ma alla liberazione da ogni possibile condizionamento per l'espressione della creatività umana.
Il concetto stesso di arte sembra essere una specie di jolly per il recupero di spostati anche loro con il diritto del singolo come l'ultima spiaggia in cui poterlo sfruttare meglio. La ribellione agli specifici disciplinari fonda un nuovo diritto alla partecipazione aperta, alla costituzione collettiva di gruppi e energie al pensiero discontinuo. Se l'Arte è stato il feed-back della società borghese e del suo funzionamento è giunto il momento di mettere in discussione anche questo. La stessa cosa vale per l'urbanistica l'architettura il linguaggio e ogni sistema di potere.
La tradizione animistica della crescita attraverso la copia e la copia della copia di sistemi sempre più perfetti, pone problemi al cannibale che vuole riacquistare la sua verginità. Si profila uno scontro fra tecnologia avanzata e tecnologia semplice.
Ciò che noi chiamiamo tecnologia semplice non è altro che la coscienza di rapporti più avanzati anche se discontinui. Non ha importanza l'uso di mezzi altamente sofisticati o destrutturati quanto le diverse relazioni che si stabiliscono fra le esperienze, le azioni i pensieri.
La realtà o la storia sono anch'esse concetti stabiliti da troppo tempo per essere ingenui. Essi sono invece dei perfetti sistemi attraverso cui il potere si esercita. Non hanno niente di trascendentale a parte il fatto che sono il prodotto di una serie di tendenze incoscienti e pluralistiche dell'ontologia degli esseri umani. Valide fino alla propria autodefinizione ma non oltre.
Il dove si andrà a finire, la tecnologia per il momento non ci riguarda anche se per il momento ci basta pensare alla carica anticipatrice delle utopie per sentirci tranquilli. Se questo poi non basta preferiamo agire e comportarci secondo coscienza, il nostro mondo è già il vostro o viceversa, la rete di sconnessioni che abbiamo teso intorno alla realtà è già una realtà nuova che renderà impossibile qualsiasi ricomposizione a buon mercato.

Lapo Binazzi (UFO) 1974

CONTROGUIDA DI FIRENZE
(elementi di prossemica territoriale)

IL TERRITORIO
1) registrazione dei comportamenti spontanei del territorio
2) variazioni di entropia relative alle migrazioni giornaliere e stagionali
3) emigrazione-nomadismo del territorio e della forza lavoro
4) autonomie territoriali e forme di autoorganizzazione
5) opposizione tra parametri formali e creatività proletaria
6) piccole economie territoriali
7) depressioni del territorio sottoproletariato
8) trapianti innesti ferite sostituzioni di territorio
9) sottrazioni di spazi: spazi chiusi spazi privati spazi segreti
10) aree emarginate aree intoccate
11) punti emergenti del territorio
12) intervento alternativo - strumenti freddi di riporto: videotape interviste modelli al vero
13) architettura spontanea

I SERVIZI l'interno la città
— centrali elettriche fonti di energia distribuzione
— centrali idriche distribuzione
— ferrovie caselli passaggi a livello
— gas metanodotti gasometri
— grande smistamento telefonico
— depositi magazzini capannoni
— autostrade strade statali provinciali superstrade non asfaltate sentieri
— informazione e contro informazione
— intervento alternativo ecc...

LA CITTA' l'interno i servizi
— architettura spontanea baracche garitte orti
— arredo urbano
— distribuzione telefonica localizzazione
— uffici pubblici servizi ENEL GAS ACQUEDOTTO SIP
— la città ai vari piani-stratificazioni:
— supercontrollo e centri di potere - occultamento - caserme ministeri S.P.A.
— zone d'influenza del super controllo - comportamenti alternativi
— cartelloni controinformazione scritte spontanee cortei
— supercontrollo istruzione
— sottrazioni di spazi - passi carrai - traffico - banche ubicazione
— intervento alternativo ecc...

PUNTI EMERGENTI DEL TERRITORIO

1969 - CASA ANAS con loggia

1969 - CASA ANAS con loggia

1969 - CASA ANAS neoclassica

1969 - CASA ANAS neoclassica

27. Notes for a Redefinition of the Concept of *Fantaurbanistica*

UFO, 'Appunti per una ridefinizione del concetto di fantaurbanistica', *Progettare inpiù*, no. 8, February-March 1975, pp. 24-27.

Manifesto of the Discontinuous

All original things, events, actions, methods and modes of behaviour are discontinuous. This is demonstrated by the most recent artistic experiences, as well as by scientific and political ones. Artists pass naturally from one field of expression to another, their research is essentially non-disciplinary. Art is passing through a period of dematerialisation and is tending towards the manifestation of pure physical and mental energy. It is adopting the use of the most diverse media, and even in examples of collaboration between art, science, and technology the interests are mixed up in order to try to establish points that do not belong to any of these fields but to liberation from any possible conditioning of the expression of human creativity.

The concept of art itself seems to be a sort of wild card for the recovery of dropouts, they too with the right of the individual as the last chance to be able to exploit him or her better. Rebellion against disciplinary specifics is the foundation of a new right to open participation, to the collective constitution of groups and energies, to discontinuous thinking. If Art has been the feedback of bourgeois society and the way it functions, the time has come to challenge this too. The same is true for urbanism, architecture, language, and every system of power. The animistic tradition of growth through copying and copying of the copy of ever more perfect systems poses problems to cannibals who wish to regain their virginity. A clash is looming between advanced technology and simple technology. What we call simple technology is nothing but the awareness of relations that are more advanced even if discontinuous. The use of highly sophisticated or destructured means is not as important as the different relations that are established between experiences, actions, and thoughts.

Reality or history are also concepts established too long ago to be ingenuous. Instead they are perfect systems through which power is exercised. There is nothing transcendental about them apart from the fact that they are the product of a series of unconscious and pluralistic tendencies of the ontology of human beings. Valid as far as their own self-definition but no further.

The where it's all going to end up, the technology, for the moment, doesn't concern us even if for the moment it's enough to think of the anticipatory power of Utopias for us to feel at ease. If this later turns out not to be enough we prefer to act and conduct ourselves according to our conscience. Our world is already yours or vice versa, the network of disconnections that we have strung around reality is already a new reality that will render impossible any cheap re-composition.

Lapo Binazzi (UFO) 1974

ANTI-GUIDE TO FLORENCE
(fundamentals of territorial proxemics)

TERRITORY
1) recording spontaneous behaviour in the territory
2) changes in entropy related to daily and seasonal population movements
3) emigration/nomadism in the territory and of the workforce
4) local autonomy and forms of self-organisation
5) conflict between formal parameters and proletarian creativity
6) small-scale territorial economies
7) depressed pockets of the territorial underclass
8) transplants grafts fractures substitutions of the territory
9) thefts of space: closed-off spaces private spaces secret spaces
10) marginalised areas untouched areas
11) territory landmarks
12) alternative action—neutral tools of reporting: videotapes interviews life-size models
13) vernacular architecture

SERVICES insides city
— power stations sources of energy distribution
— water system water mains
— railways tollbooths railway crossings
— gas pipelines gasholders
— major telephone exchanges
— depots warehouses sheds
— motorways freeways expressways unpaved footpaths
— information and counter-information
— alternative action etc...

CITY insides services
— vernacular architecture shacks sentry boxes vegetable gardens
— street furniture
— telephone distribution localisation
— public offices utilities POWER GAS WATER PHONE
— the different levels/layers of the city
— hypercontrol and centres of power—concealment—barracks ministries corporations
— areas of influence of hypercontrol—alternative behaviour
— posters counter-information graffiti marches
— hypercontrol of education
— theft of spaces—no-parking spots—traffic—bank placement
— alternative action etc...

RESEARCH PROGRAM

THEME: The city of command (the question of services): hypothesis of intervention in the structures of urban social control.

Formulation of the scientific problem.

The nature of the conflicts that are currently taking place in the urban territory, and the political and theoretical debate that has sprung up over them, raise again the need for a verification of the role played by urban and territorial structures in social and economic relations. The research begun in this field in recent years (from the economic, sociological or urbanistic viewpoint) by now offers a very wide range of interpretative hypotheses that find greater or lesser confirmation in the unfolding of real processes of transformation. Here we intend to move on to a direct checking of some of these hypotheses through the utilisation of new means of analysis and intervention.

The choice of the "question of services" stems from the assumption, as a basic hypothesis, of the definitive incorporation of urban structures in the economic and political mechanisms of capitalist society. Proposing, at this point, to make the services that ensure the functioning of such mechanisms the focus of attention signifies understanding not so much their economic aspects (analysis of revenue, of the building sector, of economies of scale, etc.) as the more directly political facets, i.e. the ones connected with the kind of control that is imposed on the overall social system through the services. It is thought, in other words, that the role of the city in economic and political relations can be analysed (and thus modified) directly through the carrying out of particular urban functions that express the same sort of control over the whole range of social work on which the relationship of production is founded.

On the one hand, therefore, the services ensure the maintenance of a particular level of social productivity as a condition for the creation of profit (as a political factor, expression of the power of a class as well as of the power to make the objective appearance of the so-called laws of economics function): in this sense urban structures fall into the Marxian category of fixed capital and present themselves as the product of objectified past labour, dead labour, incorporated for free as a "natural condition" for the production and reproduction of surplus value.

On the other hand it is always through the services that the shares of distribution of social wealth are re-established, at the moment in which the more mature phase of class struggle, imposing wages as an independent variable, has begun to undermine the stability of the shares of revenue (i.e. the pillar of the whole of neoclassical and neo-Keynesian political economy): in this sense, to use Marxian categories again, the services are considered to be part of variable capital, in the double figure of consumption of monetary wages and of the indirect, non-monetised component of the reproduction of the social workforce.

It is in the mutual relationship between the different figures assumed by the general component of the services that the function of command is established: command of dead labour over living labour (of machinery—fixed capital—over the workforce—variable capital) to the extent to which the distribution of social wealth is subordinate to the possibility of making use of particular shares of urban facilities. If the terrain of a wage uncoupled from the rules of productivity has been the conquest of worker autonomy in this post-war period, the opposition of an indirect wage, in the form of service, is the response that has been made through "reforms" to the pressure of workers for an appropriation of social wealth. Over the course of the last fifteen years, and not in the industrially advanced countries alone, the neutral appearance of "social service" has gradually been crumbling: first through the dynamics of the cycle (growth/recession, economic situation/reforms), at the moment in which the provision of services was linked to the political operation of restructuring as a quid pro quo for the temporary reduction in the autonomy of social struggles; and even more so today, in the course of a crisis of proportions no longer purely cyclical that is putting the very function of control at risk. To summarise, the formulation of the "question of the services" can be traced back to two considerations of a political and economic character:

1. class conflict is tending to shift from the terrain of wage bargaining and work relations to that of the distribution of social wealth;

2. on the terrain of the distribution of social wealth the relation between social costs (for the utilisation of services) and the monetary supply of the wage-earning class becomes decisive, as an expression of the relationship between control and autonomy. It would be an illusion to expect an exhaustive response at this new level of the conflict in terms of political economy (even though a direct connection between this research and **critique** of the political economy remains extremely fruitful): in fact at this point it is a matter of grasping the qualitative difference between the two components of wages (monetary supply and provision of services), and thus of directly checking the functioning of the services to which is entrusted the recovery of a share of power that has been definitively brought into question.

Claudio Greppi (UFO) 1972

Capital controls services, dredges indirect taxes. The major crises in the new phase of capitalism can be overcome in this way without shocks. The backwardness of political practice in the face of these new modes of conduct of the system of power leaves room for adjustment and for intervention.

It is a matter of inserting ourselves into the contradiction to amplify it and make it visible.
The attempt to turn variable capital into fixed capital, i.e. work into services, is made at the expense of the underclass.

The present more advanced phase is that of unchecked devaluation, through which capital draws directly on wages.

With respect to the City and the Territory, traditionally antagonistic terms, the following considerations can be made.

The City as point of accumulation of capital relegates the Territory to the role of a reserve of ground rent.

On the other hand the Territory is to an ever increasing extent the indifferent support for the channelling of services.

The City develops for its part as the preferential location for the organisation, control, and exploitation of services.

In the structuring of the services on the Territory, capital reveals its discontinuous design with respect to the City and to the Territory itself, alternating surroundings of underdevelopment, reserves of low-cost work, reserves of power and segregations of spaces with concentrations of productive investments and privileged areas. It is possible to see the urban and territorial context as the place set aside by capital for experiments in control of the workforce and wages, now exercised more by blackmail than by the proposal and verification of social models.

The traces and signs of past operations are still present as clearly discernible wounds in the urban and regional fabric, and contribute to shaping that urban history which unfortunately tends to lag behind the new techniques of control exercised by capital.

The segregation of spaces poses problems like that of the military zones or simply that of courtyards used as car parks, but reserved for public offices or private companies.

It is precisely in this convergence of tendency with respect to the privileges of public and private services that we can discern the direction in which neo-capitalist society is heading with regard to the shift to the service sector.

The process of rationalisation common to the whole of social being becomes the passage towards a new organisation of electronic super-control.

If from the urbanistic viewpoint it is easy to identify the parameters of intervention, which coincide with the very areas where privilege is exercised, conceptually it is possible to use the iteration of the symbolic elements typical of this process of exploitation. Even the interior of a bank's security van can become the key element of prohibited space.

Finally, the alternative information connecting the various levels of analysis and decoding predisposes the intervention itself as a way of publicising the alternative model proposed.

Means in this sense tend to be used **solely** as means, thereby stripping them of their truly subversive and consciousness-raising power.

This example can be extended to other, analogous facts.

The exploitation of the telephone service presupposes first the creation of an unnatural demand at the level of consumption obtained through an economy based on the mobility of communications, and therefore the increase in the cost of the service itself that signifies hypertrophy of the tertiary function at the level of the number of operators of that service in relation to the number of users.

1974 - METANODOTTO 1 (vigna)

1974 - METANODOTTO 2 (traliccio)

1974 - METANODOTTO 3 (ingresso in città)

1974 - METANODOTTO 4 (ingresso in città)

PROGRAMMA DI RICERCA

TEMA: La città del comando (la questione dei servizi): ipotesi di intervento sulle strutture del controllo sociale urbano.

Impostazione del problema scientifico.

La natura dei conflitti che si svolgono attualmente sul terreno urbano, e il dibattito politico e teorico che su di essi si è sviluppato, ripropongono la necessità di una verifica del ruolo delle strutture urbane e territoriali nei rapporti sociali ed economici. Le ricerche avviate in questo campo negli ultimi anni (dal punto di vista economico, sociologico, urbanistico) offrono ormai una gamma molto vasta di ipotesi interpretative che trovano maggiore o minore conferma nello svolgimento dei processi reali di trasformazione. In questa sede si intende passare ad una verifica diretta di alcune di tali ipotesi attraverso l'utilizzazione di nuovi strumenti di analisi e di intervento.

La scelta della « questione dei servizi » deriva dalla assunzione, come ipotesi di base, del definitivo incorporamento delle strutture urbane dentro i meccanismi economici e politici della società capitalistica. Proporre, a questo punto, come centro di attenzione i servizi che assicurano il funzionamento di tali meccanismi, significa coglierne non tanto gli aspetti economici (analisi della rendita, del settore edilizio, delle economie di agglomerazione ecc.) quanto gli aspetti più direttamente politici, cioè quelli connessi al tipo di controllo che attraverso i servizi viene imposto sul sistema sociale complessivo. Si ritiene, in altri termini, che il ruolo della città nei rapporti economici e politici possa essere analizzato (e quindi modificato) direttamente nello svolgimento di determinate funzioni urbane che esprimono lo stesso tipo di comando sul lavoro sociale complessivo su cui si fonda il rapporto di produzione.

Da una parte quindi i servizi assicurano il mantenimento di un livello determinato di produttività sociale come condizione per la formazione del profitto (in quanto dato politico, espressione del potere di una classe e anche del potere di far funzionare l'apparenza oggettiva delle cosiddette leggi economiche): in questo senso le strutture urbane rientrano nella categoria marxiana del capitale fisso e si presentano come prodotto di lavoro trascorso oggettivato, lavoro morto, incorporato gratuitamente come « condizione naturale » per la produzione e riproduzione del plusvalore.

Dall'altra è sempre attraverso i servizi che si ristabiliscono le quote di distribuzione della ricchezza sociale, nel momento in cui la fase più matura delle lotte di classe, imponendo il salario come variabile indipendente, ha cominciato ad intaccare proprio la stabilità delle quote del reddito (cioè il pilastro di tutta l'economia politica neoclassica e neokeynesiana): in questo senso, usando di nuovo le categorie marxiane, si considerano i servizi come parte del capitale variabile, nella doppia figura di consumo del salario monetario e di componente indiretta, non monetizzata, della riproduzione della forza-lavoro sociale.

Nella reciproca relazione fra le diverse figure assunte dalla componente generale dei servizi si stabilisce la funzione del comando: comando del lavoro morto sul lavoro vivo (della macchina — capitale fisso — sulla forza-lavoro — capitale variabile) nella misura in cui la distribuzione della ricchezza sociale è subordinata alla possibilità di usufruire di determinate quote dell'attrezzatura urbana. Se il terreno del salario sganciato dalle regole della produttività è stata la conquista dell'autonomia operaia in questo dopoguerra, la contrapposizione di un salario indiretto, sotto forma di servizi, è la risposta che attraverso le « riforme » viene data alla spinta operaia verso l'appropriazione della ricchezza sociale. Nel corso degli ultimi quindici anni, e non solo nei paesi industrialmente avanzati, l'apparenza neutrale del « servizio sociale » si è andata progressivamente disgregando: prima attraverso la dinamica del ciclo (sviluppo/recessione, congiuntura/riforme), nel momento in cui la fornitura dei servizi si saldava all'operazione politica della ristrutturazione come contropartita alla temporanea riduzione dell'autonomia delle lotte sociali; più ancora oggi, nel corso di una crisi di proporzioni non più puramente congiunturali, che pone in gioco la funzione stessa del comando.

Riassumendo, l'impostazione della « questione dei servizi » è riconducibile a due considerazioni di ordine politico-economico:

1. lo scontro di classe, dal terreno della contrattazione del salario e del rapporto di lavoro, tende a spostarsi su quello della distribuzione della ricchezza sociale;
2. sul terreno della distribuzione della ricchezza sociale diviene determinante la proporzione fra costi sociali (per l'utilizzazione dei servizi) e disponibilità monetarie della classe dei salariati, come espressione del rapporto fra comando e autonomia.

Sarebbe illusorio aspettarsi una risposta esauriente a questo nuovo livello del conflitto in termini di economia politica (anche se un collegamento diretto fra questa ricerca e la **critica** dell'economia politica rimane comunque estremamente fruttuoso): infatti si tratta a questo punto di cogliere la differenza qualitativa fra le due componenti del salario (disponibilità monetarie e disponibilità di servizi), e quindi di verificare direttamente il funzionamento dei servizi ai quali è affidato il recupero di una quota di potere che è stata posta definitivamente in discussione.

Claudio Greppi (UFO) 1972

1970 - TRALICCIO BIANCO-ROSSO E STOPPIE

1970 - VIADOTTO ELETTRICO E FORESTA DI ULIVI

1973 - RETE - ORTI - TRALICCIO E IDRANTE (sottrazione di spazi) SPAZI PRIVATI

1973 - GARRITTA E TORRETTA (sottrazione di spazi) SPAZI SEGRETI

a) TRAPIANTI - INNESTI - FERITE DI TERRITORIO

b) INTERVENTO ALTERNATIVO

1973 - PASSAGGIO A LIVELLO ASCOLTO 1

1973 - PASSAGGIO A LIVELLO ASCOLTO 2

1973 - PASSAGGIO A LIVELLO ASCOLTO 3

Il Capitale controlla i servizi, draga tributi indiretti.

Le grosse crisi nella nuova fase capitalista possono essere così superate senza scosse. L'arretratezza della prassi politica di fronte a questi nuovi comportamenti del sistema di potere, lascia spazio per la registrazione e per l'intervento.

Si tratta di inserirsi nella contraddizione per ampliarla e renderla visibile.

Il tentativo di trasformazione del capitale variabile in capitale fisso cioè del lavoro in servizi è a carico delle classi povere.

La fase presente più avanzata è quella della svalutazione selvaggia attraverso questa il capitale attinge direttamente ai salari.

Rispetto alla Città e il Territorio, termini tradizionalmente antagonisti si possono fare le seguenti considerazioni.

La Città come punto di accumulazione di capitale relega il Territorio al ruolo di riserva di rendita fondiaria.

D'altra parte il Territorio è sempre più il supporto indifferente della canalizzazione dei servizi.

La città si sviluppa da parte sua come luogo privilegiato dell'organizzazione, del controllo e dello sfruttamento dei servizi.

Nella strutturazione dei servizi sul territorio, il capitale rivela il suo disegno discontinuo rispetto alla città e rispetto al territorio stesso alternando intorni di sottosviluppo, riserve di manodopera a basso costo, riserve di potere, segregazioni di spazi, a concentrazioni di investimenti produttivi, aree privilegiate.

È possibile vedere il contesto urbano e territoriale come luogo destinato dal capitale ad esperimenti di controllo della forza-lavoro e del salario, esercitati ormai più che dalla proposta e dalla verifica di modelli sociali dal ricatto diretto.

Le tracce, gli indizi di operazioni passate sono ancora presenti come ferite ben individuabili sul tessuto urbano e territoriale, e concorrono a formare quella storia urbana che tende purtroppo ad essere ritardata rispetto alle nuove tecniche di controllo esercitate dal capitale.

La segregazione degli spazi ci pone problemi come quello delle servitù militari oppure più semplicemente dei cortili adibiti a parcheggio urbano, ma riservati a uffici pubblici o società private.

Proprio in questo convergere di tendenza rispetto ai privilegi dei servizi pubblici e privati si può rintracciare la direzione di trasformazione della società neo-capitalista nel rispetto dei processi di terziarizzazione.

Il processo di razionalizzazione comune a tutto l'essere sociale diventa il passaggio per una nuova organizzazione del supercontrollo elettronico.

Se dal punto di vista urbanistico è facile individuare i parametri di intervento che coincidono con le aree stesse dove si esercita il privilegio, concettualmente si può usare l'iterazione degli elementi simbolici tipici di questo processo di sfruttamento. Lo stesso interno del furgone di una banca può diventare l'elemento chiave dello spazio interdetto.

La controinformazione infine collegando i vari piani di analisi e di decodifica predispone l'intervento stesso come pubblicizzazione del modello alternativo proposto.

Gli strumenti in questo senso tendono ad essere usati **solo** come strumenti, liberandone così la carica veramente eversiva e coscienziale.

Questo esempio è estensibile ad altri fatti analoghi.

Lo sfruttamento del servizio telefonico presuppone da prima la creazione di un bisogno indotto a livello del consumo ottenuto con un economia basata sulla mobilità delle comunicazioni, e quindi l'aumento del costo del servizio stesso che significa ipertrofia della funzione terziaria a livello di numero di addetti per quel servizio in rapporto al numero di utenti.

NO!
A
B

28. ID Monster

UFO, 'The ID Monster', *On site on energy*, no. 7, 1975, p. 37.

THE ID MONSTER—U.F.O.—is an experiment in over-real fluxus of energy and is part of a project for Florence University, Italy. In a theoretical slide of territory the performer describes his project to the inhabitants of the vicinity through speech and descriptive data. The meaning of "time" and "space" is clear from A to B. The conceptual significance of the performance necessitates a position directly beneath the airplane to create different events which clash at the exact same space-time. Ultimately the territory becomes something concrete to deal with rather than an abstract entity. The result is a symmetrical figure formed by a crossing of the energy fluxus of communication between car and airplane, and overcomes territory.

l'oggetto storico riproducibile all'infinito

UFO

Bachi, Binazzi, Cammeo, Foresi, Maschietto

(testi a cura di Lapo Binazzi)

29. The Historical Object Reproducible ad Infinitum

UFO, 'L'oggetto storico riproducibile all'infinito', in Giovanni Maria Accame and Carlo Guenzi (eds.), *Avanguardie e cultura popolare* (Bologna: Galleria d'arte moderna, 1975), pp. 216-217.

UFO
Bachi, Binazzi, Cammeo, Foresi, Maschietto
(text by Lapo Binazzi)

The meaning of our proposal is a highly dematerialised, commonly invisible historical object. But lets get there step by step.

Simplicity may be a shorthand, the symbolic and total answer to all theoretical expectations. Simplicity of actions, methods and behaviour. Even in the way of introducing it without excessive explanations but through stimuli of the imagination, the reference to the symbolic demands to the observer an effort of imagination like a response from the book of changes, or the particular type of relationship between the wise Indian master and the pupil. Even the rejection of explanation can save one from the suspicion of an atrocious connivance with a power understood as a perfectly functioning system at all levels.

The presentation to the design section of the *Contemporanea* exhibition entitled "Dall'oggetto alla sopravvivenza" (From Object to Survival) began with... : "The aim of the theme is to demonstrate how objects and even ideas, especially the good ones, are accessories of capitalism, improperly considered irreplaceable expressions of human activity." A segmentation into three parts followed: The destruction of the object—The recreation of behaviour—Utopia of survival.

Thus culture, too, reveals itself to be a system of power, like everything codified in general, which remains subversive on the level of reform but reconstitutes repressive structures when seen from the perspective of creativity.

There is no fixed rule of course, since the terms of the problem could sometimes be considered strategically reversed. Nonetheless it can be said that alternative survivals, at least at the beginning, rebel against the convenient game of power and its specifics. One could argue as well that provocation is the preferred weapon for entire generations of young people and artists as well as of workers and working classes. The invention of new forms of opposition and resistance generally characterises the social behaviour of the young classes. So it is hard to see why this should not be applied as well to the academic culture, to the more sedimented behaviours of everyday life, to the blind use of existential structures and superstructures.

This is how terrorist furniture, alternative behaviour, survival hypotheses were born.

Often these experiences are paid for in person, so much so that this becomes a precise recognition criterion. Have you tried to see how someone who has "paid in person" is generally respected or at least is taken into account? The strong temptation to associate this respect with a more or less veiled judgement of ineptitude can lead one down a false path. The reason is clear: it is not convenient to disturb someone who has paid in person because psychologically he is in a position of strength: "What? I paid for something you admire and you bother me? At least leave me alone!". So we try to exorcise the negative power of the figure of the loser, laying the ground to the opposite of his strategy: we overcome all our scruples in a flash, we carry out the misdeed with an act of purifying cannibalism and we are ready on the other side of the barricade.

We have substituted the being-becoming of before with the becoming-being. Parmenidean realism seems to us the fairest in the world, only we do not place the emphasis on the right moment of relative time.

Thus the persistence in a theoretical timelessness embodies in various forms historical objects that can be reproducible ad infinitum and beyond themselves.

Thinking by negatives, reducing our false consciousnesses to zero, proceeding by discontinuities, are examples of simple techniques of constructing these objects.

The whole environment of our experience of group therapy and creativity takes place in an area of theoretical and linguistic precision, the conventional we need to communicate is integrated with the extrasensory perception of our individual presence and absence, with the different sensory mechanisms with which each of us is provided.

The common feature of our product-operations is rather the simplicity of the minimal existential relationship that makes them possible. This sounds like a play on words, but it is true.

SIMPLICITY is the direction in which the entire environment is heading, but it is an extremely refined simplicity that does not make any cultural or other exploitation possible.

We once invented "FROZEN MEMORIES," undocumented remnants of space-time travels of everyday experience, objective and immaterial persistences of facts events objects that can easily overcome the barrier of time. This notion is quite close to that of a historical object reproducible ad infinitum. The discontinuity of experience and its global verification lies in the totality of our behaviours, the persistence of a theoretical line in the different phases of our a-artistic operations, considering art a specific discipline like any other, is the indestructible deterrent, the necessary fuel to proceed along the dead-end track of experience jumping here and there in the direction indicated by Duchamp. Society has relegated the artist to the last resort of individuality in order to be able to blackmail and exploit him better.

Art is no longer so necessary since we can do it absent-mindedly. In England they use the term understatement to describe this process.

We could translate it as SIMPLICITY.

So even the elements of our own internal story become legend, frozen memories of our actions, artificial amplifications of happy moments, historical objects that can be reproducible ad infinitum.

Re-appropriation cannot stop at the territory, but must coincide with the whole physical and mental environment. The continuous re-appropriation of our consciences. It takes place in a theoretical DISCONTINUOUS that relates facts and operations that are increasingly distant from each other, testing the ability of the public and ourselves to react to schizophrenia.

Thus the problem of operational and theoretical ubiquity is a historical object that can be reproducible ad infinitum.

Therefore a moment in the existence of any person is ad infinitum reproducible historical object, a point of accumulation of energy from another dimension.

30. UFO. Discontinuity and Territory

Lapo Binazzi (UFO), *Ufo. Discontinuità e territorio* (Milan: Centro internazionale di Brera, 1977). The text was subsequentely published partially under the title 'Arte v/s ambiente', in Gianni Pettena (ed.), *La città invisibile. Architettura sperimentale 1965/1975* (Florence: Associazione Intercomunale N.10, 1983), and, subsequently, in its entirety with the title 'UFO. Discontinuità e Territorio', in Stefano Pezzato (ed.), *Ufo story: dall'architettura radicale al design globale* (Prato: Centro per l'arte contemporanea Luigi Pecci, 2012).

From the hypothesis on the blackmail of the services not documented here to a theorisation of "liberated territory."
Attention is shifted to the "natural" and unusual elements organised in accordance with a discontinuous technique.
The institutional logic of intervention in the territory or the environment is replaced by the poetic operation of discontinuous visual strategy and the connection of facts apparently remote from one another, comparable by relations of contiguity at the limits of the randomistic theory of free associations, even to the point of losing the most tenuous links for a criterion of expression that moves in the "minimal" mental gap that lies between the two facts proposed, as pure absence able to restore the controls needed to follow the ever more sophisticated "reality."
The global and "synergic" effect is the "symbol" (conceived as inaccurate translation of the image) of the expectations of the altered anthropological context.
Intervention and criticism in the same synchronic time, cut to suit the liberating modes of conduct of individual and collective creative aptitudes.
Actions themselves and contexts of reference for future operations predispose systems of thought for non-random but "transient" juxtapositions needed in order not to fill the gaps with which reality presents itself.
The REJECTION of EXPLANATION is not a negative indication and presupposes the extension of the exit from the operation to the material of "writing," as well as to the visual material.
The place of the "critical text" or text of presentation or self-criticism is taken by a text that has to reckon with the single specificity of "writing," becoming homologous or contrary or opposed to the visual or behavioural material.
The "conceptuality" of the operation or the exit from the operation, as it would be the more correct way to put it, consists in making different materials react with each other and creating a discontinuity of sign different from that of the capitalistic "logic" of the division of the artist's work from that of the critic and in the upgrading of the critic's work in accordance with a precision of "deep" structural analysis in keeping with the "advanced" theoretical characteristics of artistic work.
The interpretation of an operation and its decoding move together with the operation itself into an area of "theoretical" or according to some "cultural" precision that is by now highly sophisticated but is rendered even more so by deliberately ambiguous results or effects often tending to the "symbolic." By "symbolic" is meant here the recourse to a linguistic complexification pertaining to the history of works of art and specific methods of representation. For example, the distortions of perspective of one of Claes Oldenburg's life-size sculptures tend to amplify the artistic sign as much as possible for an immediate perception of the semantic decontextualisation

of the "signs" in a piazza or a street or a suburb or in fields as in Christo's latest environmental works (Valley Curtain). The effect created is an emphatic symbolisation by means of perspective, in this case the method of graphic representation often adopted "a posteriori" that is added to more specifically pop themes such as the "colossal" or the household article like the clothes peg taken out of its context or the opposition between sculpture in a piazza and anti-monument. Proceeding in this way we could use up all the decoding of the operation itself.

On many occasions these old and new methods of operation coexist, making difficult a logical interpretation that in any case is not wanted, in order to boost the deterrent of the work of art.

The syncretism of such works/values tends to zero today on the basis of the global effect, leading to the exhaustion of the political, social, and artistic pressures and the time limits of the operation, putting off discussion of the approximate or averted end of the themes in line with "consumption" and the obsolescence of market trends.

It even comes to the point of planning operations that go in the completely opposite direction, as recovery of a political space that unlike the traditional specific policy of the institutions does not proceed in accordance with a "continuous" logic of transformation in the sense of "history," but with a "discontinuous" logic of practical subversion of the preceding tendencies in line with a discontinuous dialectic that sees market, artist and critic or politician, sociologist, technologist lined up on different sides, etc. ......

The possibility of comprising systems of thought or artistic expression in further systems that include the preceding systems within them, either to use them as a means or to marginalise them for good, is more or less what is understood today as "artistic research"; research which is destined to start off "marred" by interference from other specific fields like science, politics, anthropology, linguistics itself, information, and the market. All this represents a confirmation of the "real" presence that art seeks in the world.

The disruption or destruction of "disciplinary specifics" may not go so far as actual disruption of the traditional roles of the specific work of the artist-critic-politician-scientist-etc. .....

The method known as the "nested box" becomes a game for cannibals in search of the "credibility" to make this valid as an "alibi" for their own survival as specific "professional" workers.

So "professionalism," with all its dependencies compromised and held to ransom by traders, the market and the public, is in turn an alibi for the technical ability of the execution, and inevitably lapses into play-acting, into the "ad-lib" representation of "fake feelings" that critics and the public not infrequently place at the peak of the artistic expression on a consolatory Aristotelian model.

Besides, while cold methods (or "poetics"), in the attempt at aspiration from the conditionings of the public, orient research in a more elevated territory from the logical point of view, they almost always fall down on the level of the relations with institutions. The defence of professionalism to the bitter end becomes the necessary condition for "survival." With the procedures of Arte Povera, of the Minimal, of conceptual art, the operators are pushed back towards the gallery, towards the market, although with the great changes that can result from selling a piece of paper or a photograph or other materials (e.g. Kosuth) instead of a painting in oil on canvas that for so long has represented the rule without exception of artistic operation, on the basis of requirements of non-perishability that have turned into exigencies of false culture derived from the "classics."

Information seems to be the privileged place where these "historic" changes can spread, be tried again, find confirmation and leave a mark through the surmounting of politico-geographical barriers on the whole of the environment in the anthropological sense, but the progressive cooling of the land is making us all too Anglo-Saxon not to doubt, even with melodrama at hand or decadence within reach, this last indeed overworked and regressed and repressive. Is it possible to see the whole of artistic research as being made up of the two parallel and in no way communicating currents of operation and interpretation that proceed ad infinitum, pretending to be in agreement when they are not at all?

The enclosed slides represent three moments in the research that we have been carrying out for ten years. The theoretical course taken in this research goes in the direction of the destructuring of languages and the destruction of disciplinary specifics.

The dismantling of the social as comprehensive environment allows us to intervene even in fields not traditionally covered by architecture.
This non-disciplinary character of the research is also common to the visual arts, music, etc. ......
The first experiments with inflatables in 1968, dropped by surprise into "socio-urban rites and myths," built on a 1:1 scale in the occupied Faculty of Architecture and used by the students as well for actions staged during the demonstrations of Red May. For the architecture of the Faculty they were the tangible demonstration of an experimentation with lightweight materials (polyethylene, scotch-tape, heat sealing, nylon cables). Instead of entering architecture competitions, proposals were made to actually construct the model of the winning project (but distorted of course) and to try out on the spot and at little expense the overall effect of the real architecture on the environment. Think of the enormous possibilities offered by the testing of a project by our "teachers." This operation never carried out would have created a short-circuit between the languages of current architectural "culture" with the more advanced ones of the visual arts.
Something that has also been done by Claes Oldenburg with his designs for monuments and by Christo with his installations.
With the end of the "hot" period that for us was related in part to a series of "different" interior designs for shops, which had allowed us to extend our research onto practical terrain and be paid for our work, we decided to participate like other groups of "radical" architecture operating in Florence, such as Archizoom and Superstudio, in the competition for the University of Florence campus to be built on the plain of Sesto Fiorentino. The photos show two stages in the design: that of the elaboration of a project on the drawing board but one that was out of scale, extending across Europe to the Pillars of Hercules on the left and Albania on the right and conceived as pure theory of representation; and that of testing in the field with an audio-visual project, during a reconnaissance of the territory, as an out-of-kilter copy of reality. A successive elaboration led to the discovery of lines of energy present in Reichian fashion on the territory that formed the *ID Monster*, prefiguration in a science-fiction key of anything constructed as violence done to the free territory, grassland peopled with migratory birds, still unutilised belt on the farthest outskirts of the city.
The (next) photo is part of a sequence of 36 photos of a performance on a territorial scale entitled *Giro d'Italia* that set out to use the key of the cycle race as a means for the liberation of enclosed spaces, private spaces, secret spaces, military no-entry zones, private property, etc. .... and concluded in theatre no. 1 of the *Contemporanea* exhibition where a recording on videotape of the action carried out in real time outside was projected and where the bicycles passed for a liberation of the exhibition itself.
The action that had been commissioned from us by Achille Bonito Oliva for *Contemporanea* showed how only the exit from the operation as well as from market structures, galleries and more or less institutionalised critical spaces would permit the collective reappropriation of creative work.
This exit from the operation is an observation that we have always made in our research and has the purpose of not remaining tied to use, over what can also be the short time of the operation itself, to forms of language established in advance or that would become immediately institutionalised.
On other occasions the use of this mode of conduct in existing installations has served precisely to exit from the operation as well as to connect the constructed architecture with the one acted out, or just imagined. In other words an attempt is made to relativise and render undetermined the process of communication relative to the language and the operations carried out on it.
This method allows a greater ambiguity, which we usually manage even after the end of the event, at the moment of transmission when the "rejection of explanation" amplifies and arouses interest in the sign, unfortunately very often in a symbolic sense owing to the "cultural" frailty of the receivers.
This time, however, we have provided an explanation, I think for the first time... but it is already "history" even if it is not "our history"...

Lapo Binazzi (UFO)

R

31. Zona Film

Lapo Binazzi (UFO), 'Untitled', in Andrea Granchi and Maurizio Nannucci (eds.), *Zona Film. Documenti di cinema d'artista* (Florence: Zona, 1977), n.p.

The documentation of events, actions, and behaviours is the "real" plot on which the film project acts. The sets fabricated as part of the intervention of the camera await the reversal of making a film. The event becomes the pretext, the action, the occasion, the behaviour, the means.

From this moment on, the operation jumps discontinuously into cinema and its metalanguage.

The film becomes only a part of the real daily time in which the "facts" take place.

The impossibility of separating the filmic work from the experimental world recovers the instantaneous identification of theory and practice and contributes to the progressive fragmentation of disciplinary domain. The global spectacle of our operations compares different languages and methods. The traditional relationship between spectator and "actor" is put into crisis.

The "non-matrixed" of everyday life verifies power as an institutional fact articulated in the relationships between production, execution and distribution, towards a collective and amateur creative practice against the professionalism of bourgeois expectations of perfection.

The technical skill of the new techniques is the example of the correctness of every subversive discourse.

The "attention" as theoretical and rhetorical expectation is reduced to the pure and simple expectation of something, which is not frustrated even in the "work in progress." This "attention" refers to the global sense of a coded game to understand in every historical moment "which way the wind's blowing."

di analisi segua una di interventi.
Il rapporto con gli altri gruppi sarà indispensabile per non ricreare specifici disciplinari, o quanto meno una confidenza diretta all'interno del gruppo della teoria con i settori del corpo della comunicazione costruzione, sopravvivenza che ridefiniscono il campo di interessi della Global Tools.
L'originalità del procedimento potrà anche rivolgersi a una suddivisione strumentale della teoria in: politica, religione, meditazione, storia, tecnica, ecc... per proporre temi particolari di indagine su cui si può accentrare di volta in volta l'interesse della Global Tools.
Per l'apertura dei seminari di novembre proponiamo tre possibili temi di discussione:
1) Rapporti fra architettura e magia. Studio dei rapporti criptici ai più alti livelli dell'organizzazione professionale. Piramide del potere. Oggetti magici. Problema della scienza...
2) Analogia sportiva.
Rapporto fra creatività collettiva come terapia di gruppo e squadre di calcio, di pallavolo, di rugby, di attività all'aria aperta come scoutismo, pic-nic...
3) Creatività pura.
... se io dico che farsi sparare da un cannone, per esempio, è un esercizio di meditazione, si rende necessario costruire il cannone e in una certa maniera perché ciò sia possibile...
... devo riuscire a farmi sparare nei luoghi più diversi tutte le volte che voglio.

DE-ARCHITECTURIZATION - Un libro sull'arte e l'architettura ambientale - 1975

Premesse

Molti dei principi fondamentali dell'architettura moderna — particolarmente la progettazione formalistico-funzionale — sono state recentemente sfidate da un'area di attività ibride nell'arte internazionalmente emersa. Questo nuovo lavoro è né arte né architettura nelle qualificazioni convenzionali e propone adesso una totale rivalutazione degli assunti tradizionali. Per mettere a fuoco queste idee antiformali ed anti istituzionali, ON SITE pubblicherà un ampio libro, intitolato DE-ARCHITECTURIZATION. Il termine « de-architecturization » si riferisce ad una condizione (attitudine) a riformare ed eliminare alcune qualità ed elementi dall'architettura. Per ragioni documentative si suggeriscono le seguenti categorie:

1. De-materializzazione, *per descrivere la minimizzazione fisico - psicologico - intellettuale dell'architettura, (applicabile a tutte le categorie).*

2. Indeterminazione, *per includere processi di progettazione-design non sintattici, entropici, arbitrari.*

3. Inversione, *per riferirsi ai cambiamenti nel linguaggio rettorico dell'architettura come sovvertimento di significati originali.*

4. Synergia, *per descrivere un'arte-architettura a livello (esercizio) umano, la ripartizione delle risorse, la manipolazione delle risorse naturali, ecc...*

5. Cosmologia, *per definire un'architettura di simbolismi, cosmici, e metafisici.*

6. Informatica, *per coprire tutte le aree della comunicazione - processi mentali - energia, piuttosto che architettura come materia.*

7. Discontinuità.

Queste suddivisioni possono essere cambiate, riviste ed eliminate, in conseguenza del lavoro ricevuto.

ITINERARIO N. ...

Sapete cosa sono gli A.N.A.S.?
Sono costruzioni moderne ben dipinte ai bordi delle strade...

Esse sono ARCHETIPI

Casa	Fattoria	Magazzino	Osservatorio	Bunker
Villa	Villaggio	Villetta	Casa di riposo (per burocrati)	
Rifugio	Mastio	Motel	Locanda	
Home	Fortino	Nido	On the Road	
Castello	Dogana	Pedaggio	Posta	
Capanno	Base segreta	Ripostiglio	Casa da pastore	
Passo	Cabina	Bagno	Casa cantoniera	
Store	Silo			

— Sai ragazzo cosa ci stanno nascondendo dentro RAGAZZO?!

— COMPLOTTI contro il TERRITORIO! Perdio! ANTI-ANTICRITTOGA-

32. Radical Architecture is Dead: Long Live Radical Architecture

'L'architettura radicale è morta: viva l'architettura radicale', *Spazioarte,* vol. IV, no. 10-11, June-October 1977, pp. 17-20.

WRITTEN architecture is an example of "dematerialisation."

Dear Ugo, I'm late in sending you the "piece," I beg you to publish it in italics.
And if SOUTH-AMERICANISATION has already happened?
If possible in 6-point, which seems to me to be the best for the kind of thing I want to do.
Unfortunately the intellectual turns into a MISSIONARY, and wanders furtively around suburban "ghettos" and "favelas" in a search for NOBLE SAVAGES hated/loved for its degraded "condition" and the need to come to terms with the "new authority" as there always is one.
You could cut the article in two parts and inset it in between three discontinuous blocks of written architecture, as I call it.
The BYZANTINE battles over "form" or "substance" or both are at this point "false problems." The attempt to consolidate revolutionary "privileges," like the parasitism of teaching with three months of paid holidays, reserve of precarious employment, parking orbit for consumers of PETROL during the weekend, serving the needs of "restructuring" without adjectives, seeks to establish the superiority, some say incorrectly "hegemony," of the bourgeoisie over the heads of true proletarians? What do you think of this mode of interpolation? If you like dear Ugo you can intervene too, that way it will become a forum!
The hungry and very aggressive WOLF-CUBS are organising themselves for the great banquet at the end, but it doesn't seem to me that it's going to be a "real feast."
In short cut sew fold do whatever you wish.
It's not that it's all that much better in a small service town or village in SOUTH AMERICA, for instance. STREET PARTIES and ELECTRONIC TARANTELLAS can be more tiring than work in the factory.
And even making love which is something they never talk about in architecture magazines. To the glory of G.A.O.T.U. how to put it this identification of the Architect with God, because the plumb line seems a bit distant from the warm body of a woman. We need to lay off JESUITISMS. You remember the fifties when each of us led a double life. What a difficult adolescence dear Ugo!

Ciao Ugo!

Your Lapo Binazzi (UFO)

De-Architecturization—A Book on Art and Environmental Architecture—1975

Background

Many fundamental principles of modern architecture—especially functional, formalist design—have recently been challenged by a new area that has emerged internationally: that of hybrid activities blended with art. This new work is neither art nor architecture in the conventional sense, and propose that we completely reassess our traditional assumptions. To help bring these anti-formal, anti-institutional ideas into better focus, ON SITE will be publishing an extensive book titled DE-ARCHITECTURIZATION. The term "de-architecturization" refers to a condition (an approach) aimed at reforming and eliminating certain qualities and elements of architecture. For purposes of documentation, we suggest the following categories:

1. De-materialisation, *to describe the physical/psychological/intellectual process of paring down architecture (applicable to all categories).*

2. Uncertainty, *to include non-syntactic, entropic, arbitrary processes of design and engineering.*

3. Inversion, *to speak of changes in the rhetorical language of architecture as a subversion of original meanings.*

4. Synergy, *to describe art/architecture at the human level (of exercise), the distribution of resources, the manipulation of natural resources, etc...*

5. Cosmology, *to define an architecture of symbolisms, both cosmic and metaphysical.*

6. Computing, *to cover all areas of communication—mental processes—energy, rather than architecture as matter.*

7. Discontinuity.

These subdivisions can be changed, revised or eliminated, based on the work that comes in.

ITINERARY NO. ...

You know what A.N.A.S. roadhouses are? They're neatly painted modern constructions on the side of the road...
They are ARCHETYPES

House Farm Storehouse Observation Post
Bunker Villa Village Villetta Rest Home
(for bureaucrats)
Shelter Watchtower Motel Inn
Home Fort Nest On the Road
Castle Customs Office Tollgate Post Office
Cabin Secret Base Shed Shepherd's Hut
Mountain Pass Booth Lavatory Roadworkers' House Storeroom Silo

— Boy you know what they're hiding in there BOY?!
— CONSPIRACIES against our AREA! By God! FUNGICIDOCIDES! Excessively ecological systems! Indians sacked by production houses gagged at wounded knee and thrown into the A.N.A.S. RESERVATIONS of great hunting grounds, the INCONVENIENT techno-underemployed, a few poor immigrants. BLACK ELK and Red Cloud who's Riccardo's son and still little. Wild Horse and the forked-tongue TRAITORS use the excuse of the RESERVATIONS to fence in the area and the MUSTANGS in the corrals tremble and kick at the moon the great paleface friend of LONE

WOLF hunting for survival in the region of the great lakes around SAN POLO.

And the GRANDFATHER SLATHERED IN HONEY to be devoured by bees, and all the insects, and bears and giant ants brought back to life by the FUNGICIDOCIDE.

The interior of the CARAVANS where Billie Bis is fixing two fried eggs after making love with the wife/widow of the fugitive from the GIRO D'ITALIA ... will he find her again? ... will he find her again? ...

— Yes, sonny-boy! The A.N.A.S. roadhouses are absurdly incredible CHINESE BOXES! You can find ANYTHING INSIDE! The FROZEN MEMORIES of tourists coming back from the SEASIDE or the MOUNTAINS, the body of LITTLE ERMANNO, the body of MATTEI (head of ENI), the victims of the Fascists, the end of the BLACK TRAILS, the kidnapped, the kidnappers, the SCALE MODEL or carefully designed photomontage of the latest radical architecture project, a complete VIDEOTAPE equipment, a piece of land stolen from the community, tools, a meeting of the regional government, a rider in the GIRO D'ITALIA led off track by fake bourgeois street signs, the INQUISITION, the trendy art critic, an art gallery, water shortages in the city, and lately the STOCKPILING of WHEAT AND PETROL and all basic necessities, capital being exported... '68!

— Those silos!

— If you happen to pass by them have no qualms! Peek inside! If you can get them open try picking them up by the corner and shifting them! You will find they are unmovable inviolable STRONGHOLDS OF POWER, OF ABUSE OF THE IMAGINARY of its distortion its segregation!

— Never noticed what was hidden in there, huh? They bear witness to a world that is now much colder just as milestones mark the reconnaissance time of cars motorcycles, true examples of absolute architecture, you sure can't go any further than that—in a wide variety of styles from Neoclassical to neo-Enlightenment to kitschy Swiss chalet to frontier home of the African Campaign with palm trees and all that. Attempting a careful description or letting imagination take flight is all the same! They bear witness to the murders of traffic or those committed on the city fringes or in the depths of the territory far from the eyes of men of judgement...

— The great prairies, the great buffalo hunting grounds speak to the elders of the tribe in words of wisdom of the dangers of war between tribes of the same Indian blood, to the young warriors eager for battle confined to reservations they speak of the injustice of the subgovernment of palefaces that have taken the best land the PETROL and rights of use but above all OWNERSHIP.

LIBRI
BOOKS

Bruno Orlandoni e Giorgio Vallino: «Dalla città al cucchiaio», Ed. Studio Forma, Torino 1977.

Dalla mia recensione (Domus 541, 1974) del libro «Architettura Radicale» di Paola Navone e Bruno Orlandoni e dall'accusa di mancanza di «discontinuità», almeno uno degli autori sembra essersi affrancato, poiché chiama la discontinuità a sostegno della diversità di materiali e operatori esibita nel testo, in particolare a sostegno della comparsa di disegni di bambini delle scuole medie messi a confronto visivo con gli architetti radicali.
Inutile dire che io intendevo un'altra cosa. Mi sembrava strano che i giovani «critici» di un fenomeno che mette in discussione gli «specifici disciplinari» e i «ruoli professionali» non dessero, neanche per un istante, la sensazione di mettere in discussione il proprio «ruolino» filologico-storicistico ammantato di prosopopea «marxista» e soprattutto «dialettica» — una parola, questa, che si adopera quando non si sa come andare avanti o cosa proporre, come fa notare (guarda caso) Lucio Colletti ultimamente.
Ma io andrei più in là, in queste poche righe; gli autori di questo «nuovo» (?)

«la metafora rovesciata» foto A. Koppitz

saggio sull'architettura radicale conservando tutta la prosopopea «marxista» e «dialettica», non solo rimproverano alla maggior parte degli operatori radicali la «autonomia» delle posizioni che si risolve in senso «antiprogressista» e addirittura «corporativo» a difesa degli interessi della cultura borghese — bisogna dare atto che non fanno di ogni erba un fascio (timidamente) — ma preferiscono «concludere in forma di premessa» che i disegni dei bambini, di cui non si parla mai nel testo, sono altrettanto e forse più ricchi di fantasia nell'immaginare la «forma della città» degli artisti (ma non sono gli artisti dei bambini anche loro?) che non vivono quanto i bambini (innocenti) l'emarginazione della città capitalistica.
Ora è chiaro che gli Archizoom o Andrea Branzi con la sua «distruzione tecnica della cultura» (che comunque mi è sempre sembrata un gran bel programma, con buona pace di chi considera la lucidità un «pensiero negativo») non sono la stessa cosa degli UFO che scendono in piazza nel '68, e che tutti insieme si differenziano profondamente dal Gruppo di Tendenza e dalle polemiche «velenose» quanto innocue di Massimo Scolari.
Il fatto è che il libro dà l'impressione di voler continuamente (e non discontinuamente) esorcizzare il diavolo dell'architettura radicale oppure il diavolino dei neo-illuministi o il diavoletto della sclerosi speculativo-professionale e di mantenersi equidistante da tutti ma in «avanti» schierandosi con gli oppressi «proletari», ma in definitiva fornendo una falsa ricetta «dialettica», che non esce dai canoni dello storicismo di «maniera» e del proprio ruolo critico.
L'oggetto confezionato e bello e pronto! una «Storia sociale dell'Architettura Radicale» che come tutte le «storie sociali dell'arte» si contraddice in termini, anche senza pensare all'aura.
Io invece quando penso ai «destini dell'Architettura Radicale» (e della definizione non mi importa nulla, anzi mi sta anche antipatica come tutti sanno) penso a qualcosa di diverso, penso alle affinità con i «Nouveaux Philosophes», che sono riusciti a fare di Solgenytsin un gigante di cartone come gli operatori radicali hanno fatto delle loro utopie dei «polli di marmo», che però incombono sulle teste degli infaticabili «organizzatori» di società più o meno «repressive» anche se ammantate di demagogici «decentramenti», minacciando di crollare e rovinare i «compromessi» e le «ristrutturazioni» socialmente storiche.

Lapo Binazzi (UFO)

Bernd and Hilla Becher: «Framework houses of the Siegen industrial region». Schirmel/Moser editori, Monaco 1977.

Il procedimento è proprio dell'arte concettuale: rivelare la ripetizione attraverso la ripetizione, segnalare la molteplicità, segnalare le somiglianze, e le diversità entro le somiglianze; operare nel tempo. Questo è il metodo che i Becher hanno adottato nei loro primi lavori attraverso la fotografia: in una sorta di lunga «operazione», durata 12 anni, hanno raccolto e segnalato delle categorie di forme, scegliendo come forme quei grandi «oggetti» nel paesaggio, quelle grandi «macchine semplici» che sono certe (vecchie) costruzioni industriali, i silos, gli altiforni, le torri d'acqua: oggetti diversi, equiparati dal modo stesso della fotografia (sempre frontale, piatta, con l'oggetto isolato e il cielo vuoto).
Ora dall'«opera» i Becher sono retrocessi al «libro». Tema: il «disegno» delle strutture in legno delle case del Siegen (in Germania, zona industriale mineraria a est di Colonia) dove l'indispensabile uso del legno è ridotto al minimo: variazioni sulla necessità, in decine di immagini.

L.L.P.

«Trylon & Perisphere», la nuova rivista d'arte, mensile, diretta e pubblicata da Gregory Battcock a New York: primo numero, novembre 1977.

Michel Foucault: «Microfisica del potere», a cura di Alessandro Fontana e Pasquale Pasquino. Enaudi, Torino 1977

A interrogarsi su quale sia la funzione dell'intellettuale e del suo sapere oggi ci hanno provato talmente in tanti che a quelli a cui tocca ascoltare (ai non addetti) è venuto a noia soltanto il sentirne parlare. Michel Foucault (uno dei grandi irregolari della cultura francese di questi anni) spingendosi oltre i confini protettivi del già-detto ha aggiunto invece qualcosa di nuovo. Che il re è nudo oggi lo sanno vedere in molti. Non c'è più bisogno come un tempo che a dirlo sia l'intellettuale «maledetto» o «socialista».
«Quel che gli intellettuali hanno scoperto a partire dalle esperienze politiche degli ultimi anni — dice Foucault — è che le masse non hanno bisogno di loro per sapere; sanno perfettamente, chiaramente, molto meglio di loro, e lo dicono bene.
(...) Il ruolo dell'intellettuale non è più di porsi «un pò avanti o un pò a lato» per dire la verità muta di tutti; è piuttosto di lottare contro le forme di potere là dove ne è ad un tempo l'oggetto e lo strumento».
Esiste un sistema di potere che blocca, vieta e invalida il sapere quotidiano della gente, squalificandolo come incompetente e gerarchicamente inferiore. È sul sapere dei malati, degli psichiatrizzati, dei delinquenti (emergenza di un «sapere della gente») che ha pesato da sempre la squalifica sociale. Al sapere a frammenti, particolare e discontinuo (il sapere storico delle lotte), si contrappone il sapere autenticato e unitario delle scienze, esercitato per organizzare, filtrare e tacitare i «saperi assoggettati» in nome di una conoscenza vera e in nome dei diritti di una scienza nella quale ai più resta impossibile riconoscersi.
Quali tipi di sapere volete squalificare dal momento che chiedete: è una scienza? — si chiede Foucault — Quali soggetti parlanti, discorrenti, quali soggetti d'esperienza e di sapere volete dunque «minorizzare» quando dite: «Io che faccio questo discorso, faccio un discorso scientifico, e sono uno scienziato»? E osserva, sorprendendo di certo non pochi: «Se abbiamo un'obiezione da fare al marxismo è che potrebbe effettivamente essere una scienza».
Il potere di cui parla Foucault non è soltanto quello dello Stato (della grande politica) ma è anche (e soprattutto) quello periferico che attraversa la sessualità, la famiglia, i rapporti interpersonali, gli atteggiamenti, incarnato nel corpo sociale come nel corpo dei singoli individui. Mi chiedo infatti — dice a un certo punto Foucault — se non sarebbe più materialista studiare il problema del corpo e degli effetti del potere su di esso, prima di porre la questione dell'ideologia.
Ma il potere non è solo repressione, se lo fosse sarebbe un potere molto fragile. «Se è forte è perché produce effetti positivi a livello del desiderio ed anche a livello del sapere».
Se il potere non fosse altro che repressivo, — chiede Foucault — se non facesse mai nient'altro che dire di no, credete veramente che si arriverebbe ad obbedirgli?

Nives Ciardi

Deleuze e Guattari: «Rizoma». Pratiche Editrice, Parma 1977.

Se per Proust i libri erano come un paio di occhiali («vedete se vi vanno bene»), se per Foucault rappresentano una scatola di arnesi, Deleuze e Guattari li considerano parte di un rizoma.
«In un libro non c'è niente da capire — scrivono — ma molto di cui servirsi. Niente da interpretare né da significare, ma molto da sperimentare». Alla logica ad albero (genealogica e dicotomica), alla logica dei sistemi che fanno discendere da un centro o da un Capo le proprie leggi o fanno salire da una base (dalle radici) le loro verità, Deleuze e Guattari contrappongono un andamento rizomatico fatto di linee di fuga, di gambi, di diramazioni irregolari che procedono a zig zag, a sorpresa, per successioni e combinazioni imprevedibili, evolvendo per steli e flussi sotterranei. La loro scrittura nomade, rizomatica e pulsionale apre spiragli e punti di fuga nel rito del pensare.
«Fate rizoma e non radice, non piantate mai! Non seminate mai, scavate! Non siate uno, né multiplo, siate delle molteplicità! Fate la linea, mai il punto! La velocità trasforma il punto in linea! Siate rapidi anche da fermi! Linea di fortuna, linea d'anca, linea di fuga. Non evocate un Generale in voi! Fate delle carte, non delle foto, né dei disegni! Siate la Pantera rosa, e che i vostri amori siano ancora come la vespa e l'orchidea, il gatto e il babbuino».
Una lettura questa senz'altro controindicata per chi apprezza solo la «scientificità» e ama un pensare unitario e globale, al sicuro dal rischio del continuo cercare. Ruoli, dover essere, competenze, gerarchie e sicurezza vengono di volta in volta spiazzati (senza essere criticati) da un pensiero a frammenti che soffiando in direzioni continuamente diverse è sempre da un'altra parte. Dei segmenti verbali di Deleuze e Guattari ci si può servire forse per fare a nostra volta con i nostri steli sotterranei e con le nostre radici aeree altri selvatici rizomi. Per poi magari attaccarsi a qualche albero (come avviene in natura) e cercare qualcos'altro di nuovo. *Nives Ciardi*

Mirella Bandini: «L'estetico, il politico. Da Cobra all'Internazionale Situazionista, 1948-1957». Edizione Officina. Roma 1977.

Cosa è stata l'Internazionale Situazionista?
Forse un movimento che rifiuta i posteri cui delegare «ardue sentenze».
Infatti è sempre difficile schematizzare in una valutazione complessiva quell'esperienza che fu l'I.S., per il suo volume di istanze e di contraddizioni ma soprattutto per il fatto che nonostante abbia una data di nascita e una di scioglimento (1957-1972), l'I.S. continua di tanto in tanto a riemergere, nei modi del linguaggio e del comportamento di tipo radical-creativo. Inoltre l'I.S. (come accenna il titolo di questo libro) fu avanguardia bifronte.
Alcuni anni fà Mario Perniola scriveva dell'I.S. (1) che nonostante la sua «fine ingloriosa»... «...essa resta un punto di riferimento obbligato per la prospettiva rivoluzionaria moderna». In tal senso, anche se con una matrice e una pratica diversa, alcuni comportamenti della componente dell'autonomia operaia dell'attuale «movimento» di giovani operai e studenti in Italia, possono ricondursi ad istanze situazionistiche. Ma si sa che prima ancora di questa stagione di lotte i situazionisti avevano seminato le proprie ipotesi e teorie contro la «società dello spettacolo» nelle vicende del maggio francese. Resta così arduo definire, o sintetizzare, l'esperienza dell'Internazionale Situazionista, cosa che tuttavia non ha spaventato la Bandini, non nuova a misurarsi con l'argomento. (2)
Vincendo l'esitazione per la mole del lavoro (ma soprattutto, credo, di più la diffidenza e l'avversione dei situazionisti contrari a delegare chiunque a parlare delle loro teorie

(segue a pag. 54)

33. Books
(Review: Bruno Orlandoni and Giorgio Vallino, *Dalla città al cucchiaio*)

Lapo Binazzi (UFO), 'Libri (recensione di Bruno Orlandoni e Giorgio Vallino: "*Dalla città al cucchiaio*", Ed. Studio Forma, Turin 1977)', *Domus*, no. 578, January 1978, p. 48.

From my review (*Domus* no. 541, 1974) of Paola Navone and Bruno Orlandoni's book *Architettura 'radicale'* and the charge of lack of "discontinuity," at least one of the authors seems to have freed himself, since he calls on discontinuity in support of the diversity of materials and operators covered in the text, in particular in support of the appearance of drawings by secondary-school children for visual comparison with the radical architects.

It goes without saying that I meant something else. It seemed strange to me that the young "critics" of a phenomenon that questions "disciplinary specifics" and the "professional roles" should not have given, even for an instant, the impression of questioning their own philological-historicistic "little role" shrouded in "Marxist" pomposity and above all "dialectic"—a word that is used when someone doesn't know how to move forward or what to propose, as Lucio Colletti (as chance would have it) has pointed out recently.

But I would go further, in these few lines; the authors of this "new" (?) essay on radical architecture, conserving all the "Marxist" pomposity and "dialectic," not only reproach the majority of radical operators for the "autonomy" of their positions, which is turned in an "anti-progressive" and even "corporative" sense into a defence of the interests of bourgeois culture—it has to be acknowledged that they (timidly) don't lump everything together—but prefer to "conclude in the form of a preamble" that the children's drawings, of which no mention is made in the text, are equally rich and perhaps even richer in their imagination of the "form of the city" as the artists (but are not the artists children too?) who are not as exposed as the (innocent) children are to the marginalization of the capitalist city.

Now it is clear that Archizoom or Andrea Branzi with his "technical destruction of culture" (which in any case has always seemed like a very fine plan to me, pace those who consider lucidity "negative thinking") are not the same thing as the UFOs who went out into the streets in '68, and that they are all profoundly different from the Tendenza Group and the polemics of Massimo Scolari, as "spiteful" as they are innocuous.

The fact is that the book gives the impression of wanting continuously (and not discontinuously) to cast out the devil of radical architecture or the little devils of the Neo-Enlightenment movement or speculative-professional sclerosis; and to keep an equal distance from all while staying "ahead" by siding with the oppressed "proletarians," but in the end providing a false "dialectical" formula that does not get away from the canons of "mannered" historicism and its critical role.

The object packaged and ready to go! A "Social History of Radical Architecture" that like all "social histories of art" is a contradiction in terms, even without considering the aura. But when I think about the "fortunes of Radical Architecture" (and I couldn't care less about the definition, indeed as everyone knows I don't like it at all), I think of something different. I think of the affinities with the "Nouveaux Philosophes," who succeeded in turning Solgenitsin into a cardboard giant just like the radical operators have turned their Utopias into "marble chickens," but ones that loom over the heads of the indefatigable "organisers" of more or less "repressive" societies, even if cloaked in demagogic "decentralisations," threatening to collapse and destroy socially historic "compromises" and "restructurings."

Lapo Binazzi (UFO)

scelte del pubblico rispetto a una « autorità » fosse anche l'autorità delle «idee» o della «cultura».

Forse Branzi intende qualcosa di simile quando parla di « rete dei servizi priva di significato ».

La centrale elettrica o il viadotto insieme alle case ANAS sono tra gli elementi analizzati concettualmente dagli UFO (7) già da tempo mi sembra.

La capacità di avvalersi di un codice di ordine diverso (8) d'altra parte non significa affatto essere « presenza », giustificare il sistema che rende possibile tali relazioni, ma avere anzi a disposizione migliori « controlli » e migliori strumenti creativi, per « assentarsi definitivamente » anche con il « rifiuto del ruolo » o con l'« uscita dall'operazione » che deve essere necessariamente dal punto di vista logico un'operazione di grado più elevato.

Non è un mistero del resto che questa doppia anima dell'avanguardia storica ci ha lasciato in eredità sia la linea dell'work-in-progress che da Duchamp porta a Joyce, trascendente aristotelica in quanto pluralismo, virtualità a mezza strada tra terra e cielo, sia la linea metafisico-razionalista divergente, soggettiva, platonica e riduttiva dei minimals. Direi che queste due strade portano comunque all'assenza, che non si può dire che una è più assente dell'altra, perchè sono atteggiamenti ricorrenti del pensiero, imputabili più a opportunismi caratteriali dei singoli e della società a seconda dei momenti. È consigliabile piuttosto una maggior serietà critica, e un animo scevro dai facili quanto inutili antagonismi.

2. Caso mai si potrebbe parlare di una variazione di scala: uno porta all'assenza come estrema riduzione nell'oggetto architettonico « chiuso » nel suo linguaggio, l'altra porta all'assenza dell'architettura in un sistema più vasto di relazioni, che può essere una riduzione ancora più estrema. E qui sto parlando di ritornare dalla seconda posizione a esempi concreti di « sintassi discontinua » (9). Comunque non volevo parafrasare il testo della seconda domanda, dal momento che non sono assolutamente convinto che il « declino degli strumenti disciplinari » dell'architettura sia stato determinato dalla definizione di William Morris. Questa può giustificare sia gli « arts and crafts » morrissiani che il « design primario », come l'estensione paradossale che Sanguineti fa per la letteratura all'architetto burocrate, che accontenterebbe più di un interlocutore.

La definizione di Morris mette piuttosto a fondamento dell'assenza il concetto di « uso » come « idea primaria ». L'impasse del momento attuale sta tutto qui. Nel non aver capito come anche le « idee buone » siano accessori del capitalismo, che quando non servono più le butta via, o nella versione socialisteggiante di ideologie, siano « accessori del potere ». La « disgregazione degli specifici

Le fotografie riproducono il Peeling Project, realizzato nel Best Products Retail Center in Virginia, e ultimato nel novembre del '71. Il Best Products South Side Building era un'anonima, rettangolare struttura in mattoni su un parcheggio asfaltato, quando il presidente di Best, Sydney Lewis scelse SITE Inc. per valorizzare visualmente il posto. Il progetto risultante — una serie di angoli "che si scollano" distribuiti lungo la facciata dell'edificio e la proprietà adiacente, ha voluto trasformare il luogo da un posto di quotidiana utilità in uno spazio di fantasia visiva. Allo stesso tempo il carattere essenziale del centro di vendita era conservato. Gli elementi scultorei sono "site-oriented" (la sigla SITE deriva da: Sculpture in the Environment - Scultura nell'ambiente) in modo tale che essi sono cresciuti come parte intrinseca dell'edificio e della terra. Per l'uso dei materiali inerenti e per la speciale natura delle strutture esistenti, Site suggerisce nuove soluzioni per l'uso dell'arte visuale nel contesto urbano. Per ulteriori informazioni potete prendere contatto con SITE, Inc., 60 Greene Street, New York, N.Y. 10012.

34. It's Time for Architecture

Lapo Binazzi (UFO), 'È tempo d'architettura. Riprendiamo l'inchiesta sulla de/stabilizzazione del movimento moderno. Rispondono Lapo Binazzi e Manfredo Tafuri', *Data*, no. 31, March-May 1978, pp. 44-46.
In the article Lapo Binazzi is responding to a series of questions that Andrea Branzi and Benedetto Gravagnuolo put to Reyner Banham, Costantino Dardi, Renato De Fusco, and Vittorio Gregotti: "1. The current 'zero growth' of architecture can lead to two hypotheses: its refoundation as pure formal superstructure and/or its 'disappearance' due to its absence from the processes of construction of the city. Which historical hypothesis do you consider the most likely? 2. Do you not think that the definition of architecture as a vast project of social and productive coordination (e.g. William Morris) has resulted in the decline of the traditional instruments of the discipline engaged in the allegorical quest for such order in the individual work of architecture? 3. Do you believe that in the universe of today's metropolis architectural language is still able to communicate an environmental quality, or do you not think that such quality is now determined by other factors? 4. Do you believe that a new social participation in planning choices is capable in and itself of bridging the gap that exists today between architectural culture and society?". See Andrea Branzi, Reyner Banham, Benedetto Gravagnuolo, Costantino Dardi, Renato De Fusco and Vittorio Gregotti, 'L'architettura è stabile qual movimento', *Data*, no. 28-29, October-December 1977, pp. 18-39.

1. Rather than giving simple answers to the questions posed by Branzi and Gravagnuolo I think it would be more useful to try to take the game apart and uncover its "rules." "Feedback," as if to say we ought to become more "subtle" and be more on guard against historical errors. Often the factual accumulation of experiences already becomes "history" in and of itself before we have decided whether we still need history. Moreover, the post-historical is in fact one of the themes of the inquiry and Gravagnuolo, speaking of *La Tendenza*, cites the "attainment through form of a Historicism without History that renders the issues invariant," that has its roots in "collective memory."

Subtlety consists a) in showing that by mixing up in the top hat plans made "on the drawing board" (and I want to stress this "drawing board") with paradigms and very often entire syntagmata of rationalist codes, and pulling them out of the hat all jumbled up, one is making a more subtle mockery of history (though I still discern in this a certain sense of awe) than by adopting the same procedure with regard to more recent or older codes or one from outside architecture itself. So as examples we can take on the one hand people like Aldo Rossi and Peter Eisenman, but also Graves and Gregotti and Meier and the Kriers, and on the other the lesser embellishment (although with less formal rigour, but also with greater discontinuity given the method of settling between different groups) of Lucien Kroll's University of Louvain; (1) b) in laying claim in the name of this "provocation," undoubtedly perceived by its supporters as more "radical" than any other, to a right to a greater "absence" in the sense of Barilli's hypothesis, of which it is possible to identify in the "specific of art" the lines of force from Duchamp to the Minimalists. And here we are on the verge of historical falsification, for while it is true that Duchamp was in a certain sense the founder of "the specific of the uselessness of art," he believed in it to such an extent that he "exited" from the progressive time of historical space in order to pass through L. Carrol's looking glass into a negative time, into the "black hole" of his life "from that moment on" as a chess player. The mechanism is that of the cybernetic "loop" of "pure discontinuity" and not the comforting and very unprovocative one of "historicism without history."

More consistent the comparison with the "Minimalists." The reductive attitude, by setting itself the famous "limits" of which Andrea Branzi speaks, "re-founds in disciplinary terms" the art system inasmuch as it does not contest it, does not ask itself the classic question of whether it serves more the needs of dealers or the artist or the public. The pure specific, after a period (always too short) of bringing into question or it would be better to say of anti-institution, recomposes, restructures and re-founds itself and lives on the breaches opened up previously.

And here we are once again close to a falsification. In a recent essay entitled "Dopo i poeti" (2), Umberto Eco declared that the prospects of literature after the "revolution" of Gruppo '63's experimentalism had been entrusted to a dispersion of literature in society, to the rituals of pure provocation as well as to occasional attempts at a new *ars combinatoria*, governed by the coarse impulses of the collective unconscious. In its renunciation of any attempt to establish itself as a "system," in the "autonomy" of its own creative processes. Going by this we ought to conclude that either architecture is lagging behind literature, because this has already agreed to "disappear," or that it is ahead because the former has agreed "not to disappear" (which is the same thing). In reality the question is put badly and the indication of this can be found in the timid ambiguity of that and/or contained in the first question. It is said by some that "disappearance," by making necessary some kind of historical solution, would shortly result in a de facto reorganisation of the "system" that it is proposed to destroy; that it would lead in short to a new social order that would threaten the "autonomies of creative processes." That the "refounding of the discipline," languishing towards self-destruction in the long term, would instead be the subtle pleasure of the individual who finds in moral resistance to worldly temptations (3), his or her ethical dignity (I would say "confirmation"). In short technology on the one hand and logical and mathematical abstractions on the other. It's one way of holding forth on the supposed objectivity of science. All of it flourishing the neo-rationalist "style" as "collective memory."

On the other hand the very notion of "radical eclecticism," even in the rather simplistic sense that it is used by C. Jencks (4), supports me in my theory of "discontinuity" as a new phase of the "conceptual." Let me explain. The internal, paradigmatic relations of Eisenman's work (5), refer openly to Chomsky's "deep structures," and aspire to forming a closed system of values, a "language" that can express through its syntactic relations a "conceptuality" that you can see for yourself. If we were to position the constructed work in the territory, it could find itself, as in the pages of Jencks's book, next to, I don't know, a car shaped like a shoe or a kiosk in the form of a hot dog. The mere contiguity of these facts making them react with one another suggests to me the possible existence of a code of a different order that contains both of them. A nested box whose relations with the preceding facts has to be called "conceptual," but seems to establish relations of discontinuity. The sensation is that of finding oneself in a world too small to consider the preceding facts as antagonists. This situation has been well theorised by B. Fuller as well as by McLuhan (6), i.e. information renders even diametrically opposed points of view interdependent, indeed it constitutes their controls as a further guarantee of "autonomy" of the public's choices with respect to an "authority," even if it were the authority of "ideas" or of "culture."

Perhaps Branzi means something similar when he speaks of a "network of services devoid of significance."

The power station and the viaduct are, together with the A.N.A.S. roadhouses, some of the elements analysed conceptually by the UFOs (7) for some time already it seems to me.

The ability on the other hand to make use of a code of a different order (8) does not at all signify being "presence," justifying the system that makes possible such relations, but having instead better "controls" and better creative tools at one's disposal, in order to "absent oneself definitively" even with the "rejection of the role" or with the "exit from the operation" that from the logical point of view ought necessarily to be an operation of a higher level.

Besides it is no mystery that from this dual spirit of the historical avant-garde we have inherited both the line of the work-in-progress that leads from Duchamp to Joyce, an Aristotelian transcendent as pluralism, virtuality halfway between earth and heaven, and the divergent, subjective, Platonic and reductive metaphysical-rationalistic line of the Minimalists. I'd say that both these roads lead in any case to absence, that one can't be said to be more absent than the other, because they are recurrent attitudes of thought, imputable more to opportunism stemming from the character of individuals and society at a particular moment. What would be advisable instead is a greater critical seriousness, and a spirit free from facile and pointless antagonisms.

2. If anything, one could speak of a variation in scale: one leads to absence as an extreme reduction into the architectural object "enclosed" in its language, the other leads to the absence of architecture in a broader system of relations, which can be an even more extreme reduction. And here I'm talking about returning from the second position to concrete examples of "discontinuous syntax" (9). However, I did not want to paraphrase the text of the second question, since I am not wholly convinced that the "decline of the disciplinary instrument" of architecture results from William Morris's definition. This may justify Morris's "arts and crafts" and "primary design," as the paradoxical extension that Sanguineti makes for literature to the architect bureaucrat, which would satisfy more than one interlocutor.

Rather Morris's definition places at the root of absence the concept of "usage" as "primary idea." The impasse of the current moment is all here. It lies in not having understood how even "good ideas" are accessories of capitalism, which throws them away when they're no longer needed, or in the socialistic version of these ideologies, are "accessories of power." The "disintegration of disciplinary specifics" is something more than opposing new forms of social organisation. It is the awareness achieved of opposition to any form of organisation that is authoritarian. It is not a renunciation of creativity, it is the pointless and romantic suicide of the minorities that weave the absence of deconditioning structures into the relations between individuals. In short, there can also be anarchy in architecture, not just among feminists. The civil right to anti-neo-enlightenment rebellion could be justified with this impetus from below alone.

Two facts seem to me necessary to a more thorough analysis: when Eisenman says that "Cardboard (architecture) is not (...) an eclecticism, but a rather precise metaphor of these intentions" (10), he is trying to restore the premeditated and therefore metalinguistic image of how ideas simply present themselves. In this attitude there is an evident need for metaphor to bestow an appearance on the "deep structures" as well, which despite being digested and expelled newly metabolised with original meanings still remain images in their totality, adopting for their interpretation a metalanguage or code of higher order, not necessarily external to architecture. We would be in the presence of "a utopia of significance" able by itself to redeem the hyper-capitalistic processes of the multinationals. The other fact to be analysed is the relationship between "irony" and image. When it is said that art has recently even gone beyond its "dematerialisation" (11), situating itself in a post-object area, what is being sought is a metalinguistic refoundation of the ironic procedures within the artistic specific in a low key. In reality it is one of the famous "limitations" or compromises within a language that ought to be redeemed through the simple "survival" of the extreme uselessness and gratuitousness of art as professionalism.

This international code opens up great possibilities for operating in an "easy" way, laying the foundations for "vibrations" recognisable at all four points of the compass. In fact it founds a "genre," that of Art, that unites the artists of the earth in communication with one another (and in love, jealousy, etc...), establishing the impersonal realm of Information as a global system. If this system is the new transcendence, the individual "closed" languages are the different metaphysics for the more "ethical" or professional. It all seems to make sense, as we are able to arrive at absence from both sides, abolishing the pointless antagonisms. As they say: all's well that ends well!

If it were not for the fact that the only things really to be refounded are the "jet-set" of the intelligentsia, the friendships, whether admitted or not, with wealthy bourgeois and "aristocrats," which in the end is the destiny of these "processes" and not of these products, as naïve "Marxists" have been saying up to now. That is to say the famous "absence," which becomes absence of "tensions" and "conflicts" and turns into a phenomenon of social reconciliation.

3. Architectural language does not depart from this script. Instead of analysing the "after-the-architects" universe or the relationship between "irony" and "discontinuity," which renounced the object and its image some time ago to constitute itself as analysis and to discipline the autonomies of creative processes, it pursues the myth of an introverted sound and utopian "quality" with which to convert the ignorant and "unfaithful" masses. It could even confront the "collective memory"—of '68 with the slogan: "not all revolutions come to harm" the internal reorganisation of "culture" and academic competence.

This apparent language of "austerity" forgoes dismantling the mechanisms of the social, finding incessantly the grain of sand that will throw the feedback of "super-control" into crisis by settling into the claimed but unproven scarcity of "petrol," but in the end providing "status symbol" alibis at right angles to the restructuring of the processes of production.

The "blackmail of the services" (13), responsible for the processes of extreme tertiarisation of the city, i.e. that non-neutral network of absent structures of which Branzi speaks (14), has functioned as a substitute for the old consumerism of goods, as induction of new "needs" for energy, now turned into work and even deliverance and liberation from work itself. So it is clear that the bottleneck of the last ten years cannot justify "retro" or renunciatory attitudes at the cost of operating outside reality.

4. The temptation to take the place of control through a social practice of design choices, to the point of refounding a sort of "primary" interdisciplinarity that could coordinate the arts and crafts of the post-industrial revolution through Morris's concept of "usage," is undoubtedly a possibility, a shifting of the goalposts, a sidestepping of the neo-rationalist impasse, in order to take capitalistic processes to their extreme consequences and artificially create fractures and disconnections in which to insert oneself so as to widen them, to make them visible to all.

But it contains the ambiguity of not forgetting that an armchair is still only an armchair, that it can't be charged with positive meanings without losing its identity, that the revolution is not brought about with design or with architecture. On the other hand it is not even conceivable to architecturalise the world, to make a noise about architecture with architectural crusades that link the "designers" with "neighbourhood councils." This would simply result in the intelligentsia providing neo-enlightened alibis to the new, nascent, and hegemonic but stupid power, in exchange for posts at university and in the civil service.

Lapo Binazzi (UFO)

Notes:

1. Charles Jencks, *The Language of Postmodern Architecture* (London: Academy Editions, 1977).
2. Umberto Eco, *Dalla periferia dell'impero* (Milan: Bompiani, 1976).
3. Benedetto Gravagnuolo, in *Data*, no. 28-29, October-December 1977, pp. 18-39.
4. Jencks, *The Language of Postmodern Architecture.*
5. Peter Eisenman, 'Notes on Conceptual Architecture. Towards a Definition', *Design Quarterly*, no. 78-79, 1970, pp. 1-5.
6. Marshall McLuhan, *Understanding Media: The Extensions of Man* (New York: McGraw-Hill, 1964).
7. UFO and Daniela Palazzoli (eds.), *Controllo colonizzazione e fascismo sul territorio: Milano, Galleria 291, maggio/giugno 1974* (Florence: Centro Di, 1974).
8. Umberto Eco, *La struttura assente* (Milan: Bompiani, 1973).
9. UFO, 'Dining can be a way-out experience in Florence', *Interior Design*, December 1972, pp. 80-81.
10. Mario Gandelsonas, 'Cardboard Architecture. Two Works by Peter D. Eisenman. Linguistics in Architecture', *Casabella*, no. 374, February 1973, pp. 17-31: 24.
11. Douglas Davis, *Art and the Future* (London: Thames and Hudson, 1973).
12. Eco, *La struttura assente.*
13. UFO and Palazzoli (eds.), *Controllo colonizzazione e fascismo sul territorio: Milano, Galleria 291, maggio/giugno 1974.*
14. Andrea Branzi, in *Data*, no. 28-29, October-December 1977, pp. 18-39.

UFO

Il gruppo UFO vive ed opera a Firenze dal 1967, anno di nascita ufficiale.
Il nome non è più simbolo di imprendibilità.
I suoi componenti sono dispersi nella realtà ....
....
....
....
....
....
....

La discontinuità elementare o 'semplice' delle teorie e delle operazioni si costituisce come 'autobiografia' totale, senza-matrice comune a tutti i lavori, amplificazione del proprio segno artistico al di fuori dei luoghi comuni dell'istituzione, riappropriazione personale e collettiva del procedimento creativo.
Il giro del mondo in senso 'antiorario' porta a ovest alle radici del futuro. La distruzione degli 'specifici disciplinari' conferisce 'professionalità' pura agli 'scarti' verso i sistemi massimi e minimi.
L'Archetipo discontinuo mette in relazione fatti apparentemente distanti fra loro, provoca all'inserimento di 'azioni diverse' davanti dietro e di lato ma anche all'esterno, il cui collegamento con l'archetipo è stimolato e ambiguo.
La 'porta' da e per la quale si può accedere ai mondi sia dell'istituzione e dell'antistituzione come del pubblico e del privato, uscire 'dall'operazione' all'esterno o all'interno della propria opera, rimanda ai padiglioni del sistema dell'arte come alla scomparsa del mercato e degli artisti nella laguna non popolata di riferimenti spaziali precisi.
— "Mi hanno accennato all'interessante presenza di 'paletti' ANAS per mezzi acquatici pubblici che mi propongo di verificare sul 'posto'."
Ma questo non è che un aspetto del problema. Si fa la constatazione della mancanza di riferimenti 'specifici' ma emerge una nuova attenzio-

U F O

Firenze I6/5/78

Spett.
La Biennale di Venezia
S.Marco. Ca' Giustiniani
30I00 VENEZIA

Al presidente
Carlo Ripa di Meana

p.c. Lara Vinca Masini

Ogg.
Adesione invito

Gentile Presidente, Le invio questa lettera per confermarLe la nostra adesione all'invito a partecipare alla Biennale di Venezia .

Spero che la lettera Le arrivi da Est, dopo aver compiuto l'intero giro del mondo in senso ANTIORARIO, verso Ovest, alla scoperta del futuro presente, lasciandosi alle spalle l'accademia e le divisioni culturali dell'istituzione, per incunearsi alla fine nella mitteleuropa con diverso segno artistico amplificato.

I difficili rapporti esistenti tra l'architettura e le arti visive, la 'deriva' continentale tra mercato e professionismo, non provocano nessun'slittamento' in un senso o nell'altro,'sono' niente altro che 'slittamento' assoluto e relativo. Sono gli 'scarti' di un antiprocesso operante da tempo a tutti i livelli di conoscenza che si chiama DISCONTINUITÀ'

distinti saluti
Lapo Binazzi (UFO)

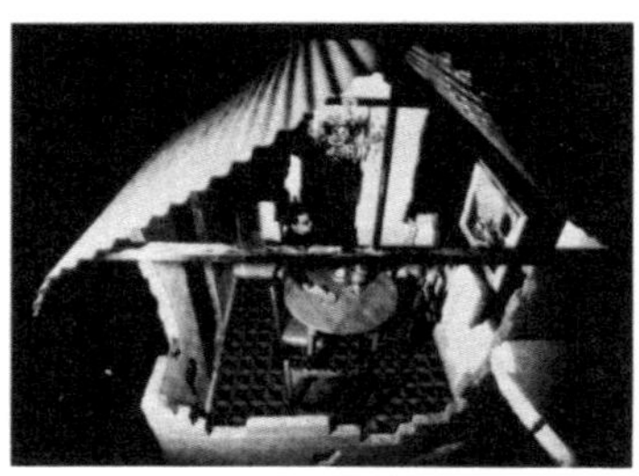

1. ANAS 1 - Restoration - Firenze - 1970.
ANAS 2 - Quella 'vera' - Firenze - 1970.

35. UFO
(Performance Aboard a Boat by UFO-Mino Vismara—Violin)

Lapo Binazzi (UFO), 'UFO' and 'Performance in barca UFO-Mino Vismara (violino)', in Lara-Vinca Masini (ed.), *Topologia e morfogenesi. Utopia e crisi dell'antinatura. Momenti delle intenzioni architettoniche in Italia* (Venice: Edizioni La Biennale di Venezia, 1978), pp. 56-59.

The UFO group has been living and working in Florence since 1967, the year of its official birth.
The name is no longer a symbol of elusiveness.
Its members have dispersed into reality..

The elementary or "simple" discontinuity of theories and operations takes the form of a total "autobiography," without a matrix common to all the works, amplification of its own artistic sign outside the commonplaces of the institution, personal and collective reappropriation of the creative procedure. Going round the world in an "anticlockwise" direction leads west to the roots of the future. The destruction of the "disciplinary specifics" confers pure "professionality" on the "deviations" towards maximum and minimum systems.
The discontinuous Archetype connects facts that are apparently distant from one another, leading to the insertion of "different actions" in front, behind, and at the side, but also on the outside, whose link with the archetype is stimulated and ambiguous.
The "door" from and through which it is possible to gain access to the worlds of both the institution and the anti-institution, as well as those of the public and the private, exiting "from the operation" on the outside or the inside of one's own work, alludes to the pavilions of the art system as well as to the disappearance of the market and the artists in the unpopulated lagoon of precise spatial references.
— "They have mentioned to me the interesting presence of A.N.A.S. 'bollards' for public water transport which I intend to check out on the 'spot'."
But this is just one aspect of the problem. The observation of the lack of "specific" references has been made but a new attention or expectation for peaceful coexistence emerges as an antedated attitude, of architecture, photography, conceptuality, discontinuity, reality, profundity, action, archetype, temporality, politics, technique, history, spectacle, disablement, performance, psychoanalysis, language, dematerialisation, ineffable, artistry, market, sport...
Even in the absence of "physical interventions" that might alter the formal configuration of the radical phenomenon as collective disposition, "things" have gone ahead by themselves. They do not accept impositions, or suggestions, or strategies, given that the "liberation" of energy is the ultimate aim of all action.
The progressive dematerialisation of every processual or systematic parameter nullifies once again any possible language as "recognisable" because it is devoid of "expectations," so it is not just the "form," the object or the image that disappears but any reference that has been over "exploited" for historical or critical ends. In this sense "minimisation" is replaced by fortunate or unfortunate simplicity; the art that would like to be a "gap" between art and nature at best lays the foundations for a definitive gap between nature and convention, which is not art but the difference from it.
In the same way it cannot be architecture or something else. It is pure discontinuity.

Lapo Binazzi (UFO)

UFO

Florence 16/5/78

Dear Sirs
La Biennale di Venezia
S. Marco. Ca' Giustiniani
30100 VENEZIA

To President
Carlo Ripa di Meana
copy to Lara-Vinca Masini

Re.
Acceptance of invitation

Dear President, I am sending you this letter to confirm to you our acceptance of the invitation to take part in the Venice Biennale.

I hope that the letter will reach you from the East, after going all the way round the world in an ANTI-CLOCKWISE direction, to the West, in discovery of the future present, leaving behind academia and the cultural divisions of the institution in order to wedge itself in the end into Central Europe with a different and amplified artistic sign.

The difficult relations between architecture and the visual arts, the continental "drift" between market and professionalism, do not provoke any "shift" in one direction or another, they "are" nothing but that absolute and relative "shift." They are the "deviations" of an anti-process in operation for some time at all levels of knowledge that is called DISCONTINUITY.

yours sincerely
Lapo Binazzi (UFO)

Performance aboard a Boat by UFO-Mino Vismara (violin)

The Fata Morgana is the "mirage" and the b/ark, *la b/arca (barca-arca)*, transported into the middle of the canal.
Just as in the "strait," between Scylla and Charybdis, it is only under particular atmospheric conditions that the phenomenon, a "wonder" but one that is understood here in the sense of a freak in a sideshow, is visible.

The "rare" experience can be repeated as many times as wished until the observer grasps the peculiarities of the situation in the face of an experience difficult to describe, a pure emotion registered.

Architecture, a pretext for expansion of the perceptive faculties, immediately gets confused by the singularity of the phenomenon, and compares the two "separate" but possible realities.
An ephemeral instant frozen in time, archetype of the "vision," multinational clairvoyance of the "artistic sign," stratified in the opposition "Dream, or am I awake?"..
The b/ark is viewed on the same scale as the fronts-backdrops of Venice. The two-dimensional ark is squashed and flattened following the definition of photographic space—it brings near/pushes away the setting, as in the desert. It flees or reaches in the loop-black hole-maelstrom, the exterior of cosmic space.

The doubleness of the points of observation: from the bark-from the *fondamenta* ("quays"), it relativises and renders indeterminate the "position," providing at each point the coordinates on a non-existent graph.

The pure abstraction of the procedure is the logical and mathematical locus of the "absence." A piece of street or forest is superimposed on or extracted from the houses of Venice, against the background of the profiles of the lagoon. In Hemingway, the liberation from "radical" architecture as ghetto—the mawkishness and the "bellyache," are the "Sentiment," the tone, the approximate and discontinuous, matrix-free suprasegmental line, improvisation, and in this case self-treatment, liberation from the by now too cramped semiotic system.

The devices of the violinist

......as in a Duchampian structure............ The third faun-like, intriguing vertex of the triangle between arbitrary terms.......
violinist/Hemingway/the Madonna
The back of the "picture"—the hidden music that emanates from the "house" when the engine of the b/ark is turned off.
The contrivance—invention—medium—connection = the "sentimental" engine.
The boatman is the engineer, the ever-present Deus-ex-machina, in contrast to the mediaeval system.
Redeemed work-travelling companion.
We are all in the same b/ark.

Madonna

It is the women in the bows, the image of the house on water made virtual. Desire attainable by Hemingway or by the faun with sentiment alone.
Approximate quotation from R. Hamilton.
Mawkish-natural vs architecture.
Figurehead-mermaid, the Madonna is stripped bare by those *célibataires* of hers.
The device turns, the wind blows, we set sail.

Oppositions

A- The opposition between "romantic"—softcore (Venice, Hemingway, faun-violin-feminine-Central European......) and "classical" (hardcore, West Coast, the house-image of the motorway), is another maximum system of interpretation.
The canal becomes the road, the boats turn into cars. The medium of this oppositional device is water, vehicle and constraint or medial support, current energy vital tension.
1 House-b/ark = sedimentation of the sign—action—improvisation—music
2 stage design = culture—setting—work

B- The opposition between nature and convention, where the nature is the nature-culture of the existing sign or of the approximate citation or the Sentiment or "sentimental," and the convention is the Artistic Sign, too settled metalanguage, revitalised by sentimentalism, launched against the too serious armies of the "specifics," simple and happy resolution in opposition to the trophisms of architects and artists.

C- The opposition between the "picture" as "frame" and the fourth estate of impersonal information.
Nested box for the exit from the operation. The image of the house in the water and the journalist Narcissus.
Bringing back of useless and exhibitionistic news.
Criticism under way of our history and of any future "usage."

D- The opposition between the image of the sky (aeroplane—air—writing......) and "image of the road" (house—b/ark—water-reflection of the ephebe......), is another useless mechanism for the exit from the system of art and its disciplinary specifics: visual arts/architecture.
"Subtlety" is for insiders.......

Lapo Binazzi (UFO)

Bibliography

WRITINGS OF UFO

• Vittorio Maschietto, 'Facoltà di architettura di Firenze 85 giorni di occupazione', *Quindici*, no. 10, 15 April-15 May 1968, p. VI

• Lapo Binazzi, Lapo (sic) Cammeo, Riccardo Foresi, Sandro Gioli and Titti Maschietto, 'Effimero Urbanistico scala 1/1', *Marcatrè*, no. 37-40, May 1968, pp. 198-209

• Marco Dezzi Bardeschi, Gianfranco Censini and Riccardo Foresi, 'Proposta per il concorso per l'allestimento della sezione italiana alla XIV Triennale di Milano', in Carlo Guenzi, 'Una selezione difficile', *Casabella*, no. 325, June 1968, pp. 4-21: 9

• UFO, 'Urboeffimeri avvenenti 1:1', *Marcatrè*, no. 41-42, June 1968, pp. 52-73

• UFO, 'Chicken Circus Circulation ovvero heppenveironment (sic) ovvero superurbeffimero n. 7', *Marcatrè*, no. 41-42, June 1968, pp. 76-91

• Houchang Amirpour, Rodolfo Bracci, Gianfranco Gorelli and Titti Maschietto, 'Il restauro dell'utenza', *Marcatrè*, no. 46-49, October 1968, pp. 52-71

• *Quattordicesima triennale di Milano: esposizione delle arti decorative industriali moderne dell'architettura moderna* (Milan: Arti grafiche Crespi & Occhipinti, 1968), pp. 47, XXIII

• Gianfranco Censini, Marco Dezzi Bardeschi and Riccardo Foresi, 'Il minimo per sopravvivere', in *Quattordicesima triennale di Milano: esposizione delle arti decorative industriali moderne dell'architettura moderna* (Milan: Arti grafiche Crespi & Occhipinti, 1968), pp. 134-135, LXV

• Carlo Bachi, Nicola Bovoli, Riccardo Mariani and Giovanni Spinoso (eds.), *Firenze Piazza San Marco 30 gennaio 1968. Libro Bianco* (Florence: Cooperativa Libraria, 1968)

• UFO, 'Le cammelle di salvataggio', *Domus*, no. 483, February 1970, pp. 50-51

• UFO and Lapo Binazzi, 'Album di Profezie', *Shopping Club*, 1970

• UFO, 'Una lettera dagli UFO a Domus', *Domus*, no. 495, February 1971, p. 48

• 'Gli UFO', in 9999 and Superstudio (eds.), *Vita, morte e miracoli dell'architettura = Life, Death and Miracles of Architecture* (Florence: G&G, 1971), n.p.

• UFO, 'Paramount', in Achille Bonito Oliva (ed.), *7e Biennale de Paris (catalogo della mostra, Parc Floral de Paris)* (Florence: Centro Di, 1971), n.p.

• 'UFO', in Achille Bonito Oliva (ed.), *7e Biennale de Paris (catalogo della mostra, Parc Floral de Paris)* (Florence: Centro Di, 1971), n.p.

• UFO and Lapo Binazzi, 'Album di profezie', *Harck*, no. 1, 1971, pp. 30-31

• R. B., 'UFO', *Caleidoscopio*, no. 11, January 1972, pp. 10-14

• 'Discoteca Bamba Issa 1', *Casa Vogue*, no. 12, January-February 1972

• UFO, 'Elementi di prossemica territoriale: questionario', *King Kong*, no. 2, June 1972, pp. 10-11

• UFO, 'La provocazione degli UFO: happening all'Eurodomus', *Domus*, no. 512, July 1972, p. 34

• UFO, 'Il Giro d'Italia', *in. Argomenti e immagini di design*, no. 6, July-August 1972, pp. 66-67

• UFO, (cover with photograph of the happening *La casa a ostacoli sul territorio* set up at Eurodomus 4, Turin, 27 May 1972), *Domus*, no. 513, August 1972, n.p.

• UFO, 'Dining can be a way-out experience in Florence', *Interior Design*, December 1972, pp. 80-81

• UFO, 'Coccoina', in Daniela Palazzoli (ed.), *Pollution: Per una nuova estetica dell'inquinamento* (Bologna: Fondazione Iris, 1972), pp. 46-47

• UFO, 'Risposta al questionario di "in" sui problemi della Facoltà di Architettura', *in. Argomenti e immagini di design*, no. 9, February-March 1973, pp. 78-80

• Carlo Bachi and Adolfo Natalini, 'Global Tools' (cover and index), *Casabella*, no. 377, May 1973

• UFO, 'Architettura della burocrazia', *Casabella*, no. 378, June 1973, pp. 30-31

• Andrea Branzi (Archizoom), Lapo Binazzi (UFO), Gianni Pettena and Ettore Sottsass Jr., 'Conversazione a quattro sulla Global Tools', *Casabella*, no. 379, July 1973, pp. 45-48

• UFO, 'Produzione industriale e creatività individuale', *Casabella*, no. 379, July 1973, pp. 46-47

• UFO, 'Untitled' (cover with photograph of the set-up *You Tarzan Me*

Jane), *Domus*, no. 528, November 1973, n.p.

• Lapo Binazzi (UFO), 'Non-design. Dall'oggetto alla sopravvivenza', in Achille Bonito Oliva (ed.), *Contemporanea. Roma, Parcheggio di Villa Borghese 11. 1973 / 2. 1974* (Florence: Centro Di, 1973), pp. 301-303

• Lapo Binazzi (UFO), 'Libri (recensione di Umberto Eco: "Segno". Enciclopedia filosofica ISEDI, Milano, 1973)', *Domus*, no. 530, January 1974, pp. 49-50

• Lapo Binazzi (UFO), 'Gli Ufo leggono (recensione di John A. Walker: "Glossary of art architecture and design since 1945", Clive Bingley Ltd Publishers, London 1973', *Domus*, no. 531, February 1974, p. 54

• UFO, (cover with photograph of the happening *Ipotesi di sopravvivenza 1*, June 1971 from the series *Fotografie della sopravvivenza*), *Casabella*, no. 386, February 1974, n.p.

• Lapo Binazzi (UFO), 'Libri (recensione di Paola Navone, Bruno Orlandoni: Architettura "radicale". La neoavanguardia italiana dell'architettura e del design dal 1960 ad oggi, Documenti di Casabella, Milano 1974)', *Domus*, no. 541, December 1974, p. 40

• Lapo Binazzi, 'Non-design. Dall'oggetto alla sopravvivenza', *Casabella*, no. 386, February 1974, pp. 16-18

• Lapo Binazzi, Andrea Branzi, Germano Celant, Ugo La Pietra, Alessandro Mendini, Adolfo Natalini and Ettore Sottsass Jr., 'Conversazione fra Binazzi Branzi Celant La Pietra Mendini Natalini Sottsass Jr.', in *Bollettino Global Tools* (Milan: Edizioni L'uomo e l'arte, 1974)

• UFO and Daniela Palazzoli (eds.), *Controllo colonizzazione e fascismo sul territorio: Milano, Galleria 291, maggio/giugno 1974* (Florence: Centro Di, 1974)

• UFO, 'Serie spazi chiusi spazi privati spazi segreti', in *schema informazione 2 (catalogo della mostra Returned to Sender, Galleria Schema)* (Florence: La Compos, 1974), n.p.

• UFO, 'Appunti per una ridefinizione del concetto di fantaurbanistica', *Progettare inpiù*, no. 8, February-March 1975, pp. 24-27

• Lapo Binazzi (UFO), Alberto Breschi, Roberto Pecchioli (Zziggurrat) and Remo Buti, 'T-h-eor-y-ia', in *Bollettino Global Tools n. 1* (Milan: Edizioni L'uomo e l'arte, 1975)

• UFO, 'L'oggetto storico riproducibile all'infinito', in Giovanni Maria Accame and Carlo Guenzi (eds.), *Avanguardie e cultura popolare* (Bologna: Galleria d'arte moderna, 1975), pp. 216-217

• UFO, 'The ID Monster', *On site on energy*, no. 7, 1975, p. 37

• UFO, 'Elementi di prossemica territoriale (questionario diffuso dal gruppo Ufo, Firenze)', in Umberto Eco, 'Dopo i poeti', in Eco, *Dalla periferia dell'impero* (Milan: Bompiani, 1976), pp. 297-316

• UFO, 'Elementi di prossemica territoriale (questionario diffuso dal gruppo Ufo, Firenze)', in Umberto Eco, 'Le nuove forme espressive', in Associazione internazionale per gli studi di lingua e letteratura italiana (ed.), *Innovazioni tematiche espressive e linguistiche della letteratura italiana del Novecento: atti dell'VIII Congresso dell'associazione internazionale per gli studi di lingua e letteratura italiana, New York, 25-28 aprile 1973* (Florence: Olschki, 1976), pp. 239-244

• 'L'architettura radicale è morta: viva l'architettura radicale', *Spazio-arte*, vol. IV, no. 10-11, June-October 1977, pp. 17-20

• Lapo Binazzi (UFO), *Ufo. Discontinuità e territorio* (Milan: Centro internazionale di Brera, 1977)

• Lapo Binazzi (UFO), 'Untitled', in Andrea Granchi and Maurizio Nannucci (eds.), *Zona Film. Documenti di cinema d'artista* (Florence: Zona, 1977), n.p.

• Lapo Binazzi (UFO) and Marino Vismara (violino), 'Scarto (performance serie "La metafora rovesciata" Milano 1977. Foto Carlo Bachi)', in Alberto Moretti, Carlo Bertocci, Raul Dominguez and Alessandro Vezzosi (eds.), *schema informazione 3. Politic-art (Le contraddizioni sono ovunque. Contradictions are everywhere)* (Florence: Schema, (1978)), n.p.

• Lapo Binazzi (UFO), 'Libri (recensione di Bruno Orlandoni e Giorgio Vallino: "Dalla città al cucchiaio", Ed. Studio Forma, Torino 1977)', *Domus*, no. 578, January 1978, p. 48

• Lapo Binazzi (UFO), 'È tempo d'architettura. Riprendiamo l'inchiesta sulla de/stabilizzazione del movimento moderno. Rispondono Lapo Binazzi e Manfredo Tafuri', *Data*, no. 31, March-May 1978, pp. 44-46

• Lapo Binazzi (UFO), 'UFO', in Lara-Vinca Masini (ed.), *Topologia e morfogenesi. Utopia e crisi dell'antinatura. Momenti delle intenzioni architettoniche in Italia* (Venice: Edizioni La Biennale di Venezia, 1978), pp. 56-57

• Lapo Binazzi (UFO), 'Performance in barca UFO-Mino Vismara (violino)', in Lara-Vinca Masini (ed.), *Topologia e morfogenesi. Utopia e crisi dell'antinatura. Momenti delle intenzioni architettoniche in Italia* (Venice: Edizioni La Biennale di Venezia, 1978), pp. 57-59

• *Catalogo-listino delle registrazioni videomagnetiche dell'A.S.A.C.* (Venice: Edizioni la Biennale di Venezia, 1979), pp. 24, 25, 52

• Lapo Binazzi, 'Io e mike', *Mèla (a/per/io/dico di scrittura ed immagini da Marciana, Isola d'Elba)*, no. 5, 1981, p. 21

• Lapo Binazzi, 'Luci nervose', *Modo*, no. 45, December 1981, p. 29

• UFO (Lapo Binazzi and Carlo Bachi), 'Fantasy', in Fulvio Irace and Tina Corti (eds.), *Architetture Sussurranti* (Milan: Studio Alchimia 1981), n.p.

• 'Gli oggetti dell'avanguardia (1965-1981)', in Fulvio Irace and Tina

Corti (eds.), *Architetture Sussurranti* (Milan: Studio Alchimia 1981), n.p.

- 'L'architettura radicale', in Fulvio Irace and Tina Corti (eds.), *Architetture Sussurranti* (Milan: Studio Alchimia 1981), n.p.

- 'Biografie: UFO (Lapo Binazzi, Carlo Bachi)', in Fulvio Irace and Tina Corti (eds.), *Architetture Sussurranti* (Milan: Studio Alchimia 1981), n.p.

- Lapo Binazzi (UFO), 'Libri e dischi (recensione di Andrea Branzi: "Merce e Metropoli. Esperienze del "nuovo design" italiano")', *Domus*, no. 640, June 1983, p. 82

- Lapo Binazzi, 'Non-design. Dall'oggetto alla sopravvivenza', in Gianni Pettena (ed.), *La città invisibile. Architettura sperimentale 1965/1975* (Florence: Associazione Intercomunale N.10, 1983), pp. 91-92

- Lapo Binazzi, 'Global Tools. Gruppo "Teoria". Relazione di Lapo Binazzi, 10 ottobre 1974', in Gianni Pettena (ed.), *La città invisibile. Architettura sperimentale 1965/1975* (Florence: Associazione Intercomunale N.10, 1983), pp. 92-93

- Lapo Binazzi, 'Controguida di Firenze', in Gianni Pettena (ed.), *La città invisibile. Architettura sperimentale 1965/1975* (Florence: Associazione Intercomunale N.10, 1983), pp. 94-95

- Lapo Binazzi, 'Carboneria', in Gianni Pettena (ed.), *La città invisibile. Architettura sperimentale 1965/1975* (Florence: Associazione Intercomunale N.10, 1983), p. 96

- Lapo Binazzi, 'Architetti Tzigani', in Gianni Pettena (ed.), *La città invisibile. Architettura sperimentale 1965/1975* (Florence: Associazione Intercomunale N.10, 1983), p. 96

- Lapo Binazzi, 'Arte v/s ambiente', in Gianni Pettena (ed.), *La città invisibile. Architettura sperimentale 1965/1975* (Florence: Associazione Intercomunale N.10, 1983), pp. 96-99

- Lapo Binazzi, 'Ufo Story', in Gianni Pettena (ed.), *La città invisibile. Architettura sperimentale 1965/1975* (Florence: Associazione Intercomunale N.10, 1983), p. 98

- Lapo Binazzi, 'Elementi di prossemica territoriale. Questionario A. II Puntata', in Gianni Pettena (ed.), *La città invisibile. Architettura sperimentale 1965/1975* (Florence: Associazione Intercomunale N.10, 1983), p. 99

- UFO, 'Brano inedito', in Gianni Pettena (ed.), *La città invisibile. Architettura sperimentale 1965/1975* (Florence: Associazione Intercomunale N.10, 1983), pp. 188-189

- UFO, 'Elementi di prossemica territoriale. Questionario', in Gianni Pettena (ed.), *La città invisibile. Architettura sperimentale 1965/1975* (Florence: Associazione Intercomunale N.10, 1983), pp. 189-193

- UFO, 'Cosa non sono e cosa sono gli Ufo', in Gianni Pettena (ed.), *La città invisibile. Architettura sperimentale 1965/1975* (Florence: Associazione Intercomunale N.10, 1983), p. 193

- UFO, 'Cose cui gli Ufo non vogliono tanto bene', in Gianni Pettena (ed.), *La città invisibile. Architettura sperimentale 1965/1975* (Florence: Associazione Intercomunale N.10, 1983), p. 193

- Lapo Binazzi, 'Fenomeno Radicale', *Modo*, no. 74, November 1984, p. 58

- Lapo Binazzi, 'Penna d'oro per alce nero (recensione di Andrea Branzi, "La casa calda", Idea Books, Milano 1984)', *Modo*, vol. 8, no. 75, December 1984, p. 51

- Lapo Binazzi, 'Fiktive Gegenständlichkeit', in Michael Erlhoff (ed.), *Documenta 8* (Kassel: Weber und Weidemeyer, 1987), vol. 2, pp. 26-27

- Lapo Binazzi, 'L'arcidiavolo. In memoria del Post-Modern', in Sergio Calatroni (ed.), *Lettere segrete. Antologia di scritti e di oggetti di design* (Milan: Afro City Editore, 1989), pp. 39-42

- Lapo Binazzi, 'Scrittura Creativa', in Sergio Calatroni (ed.), *Lettere segrete. Antologia di scritti e di oggetti di design* (Milan: Afro City Editore, 1989), pp. 22-23

- Lapo Binazzi (UFO), 'Tzigan Architects (1969)', *Terrazzo*, no. 5, September 1990, p. 131

- Lapo Binazzi (UFO), 'A counterguide to Florence. Itinerary n. 1 (1971)', *Terrazzo*, no. 5, September 1990, p. 133

- UFO, 'Elements of territorial prossemics. Questionnaire (1972)', *Terrazzo*, no. 5, September 1990, pp. 136-138

- Lapo Binazzi (UFO), 'Elements of territorial prossemics. Questionnaire A. 2nd Instalment (1972)', *Terrazzo*, no. 5, September 1990, p. 138

- Lapo Binazzi, 'Ghiribizzi di luce', in *Interni annual: Luce '90-'91*, 1990, pp. 47-52

- Lapo Binazzi, 'Dove sono finite le avanguardie', *Controspazio*, no. 4, July-August 1993, pp. 39-47: 39

- Lapo Binazzi, 'Sperimentalismo e Massoneria', *Quanto quanti quante. Oggetti per misurare e misurarsi* (Florence: Comune di Firenze, Assessorato pubblica istruzione-Archivio giovani artisti fiorentini, 1993), p. 6

- Lapo Binazzi, 'Florenzia y l'architectura radical', *Diseño*, no. 24, March-April 1994, pp. 40-44

- Lapo Binazzi, 'Lettera ad Andrea Branzi', *Area*, no. 26, May 1996, pp. 94-95

- Lapo Binazzi, 'La ricostruzione radicale dell'universo', in Massimo Giovannini and Gaspare De Fiore (eds.), *L'immagine mediata dell'architettura: atti del seminario di studio* (Rome: Gangemi, 1996), pp. 48-57

- Lapo Binazzi and Annarita Agnelli, *La ricostruzione radicale dell'universo* (Florence, 1997)

- Lapo Binazzi and Titti Maschietto, 'Lettera Caro Riccardo. Firenze 13 Settembre 2000', *Arch'it*, 2000, http://architettura.it/files/20000913/index.htm

WRITINGS ON UFO

• Lapo Binazzi (UFO), 'El no-diseno. Del objeto a la supervivencia/Le non-design. De l'objet à la survie/ Non Design. From the object to survival', in Jean-Louis Maubant and Frédéric Migayrou (eds.), *Architecture Radicale* (Villeurbanne: Institut d'art contemporain Éditions, 2001), pp. 102-103, 310

• UFO, 'Reproductions d'œuvres', in Jean-Louis Maubant and Frédéric Migayrou (eds.), *Architecture Radicale* (Villeurbanne: Institut d'art contemporain Éditions, 2001), pp. 98, 126, 218, 310

• UFO, 'Manifesto del discontinuo (1969)', in Marie-Ange Brayer (ed.), *Architectures expérimentales 1950-2012, collection du FRAC Centre* (Orléans: Éditions HYX, 2013), p. 599

• Lapo Binazzi, 'Caro Franco', in Maria Cristina Didero and Franco Audrito (eds.), *Il mercante di nuvole. Studio 65: cinquant'anni di futuro* (Milan: Skira, 2015), pp. 58-61

• Lapo Binazzi (UFO), 'Caro zio Umberto', *Archphoto*, 23 February 2016, https://www.archphoto.it/archives/4231

• Titti Maschietto, 'Bamba Issa', in Marco Delogu (ed.), *Primo autunno. Conversazioni a Belgrave Square* (Macerata: Quodlibet, 2016), pp. 125-127

• Lapo Binazzi (UFO) and Artúr Van Balen, 'Urboeffimiri/Skala 1:1. Interview by Artúr van Balen to Lapo Binazzi', *floating Utopias*, March 2018, https://floatingutopias.org/en/stories/lapo-binazzi-artur-van-balen/

• 'Lapo Binazzi. Interview by Maria Cristina Didero', *Apartamento Magazine*, Spring-Summer 2018, pp. 134-157

• Lapo Binazzi (UFO), 'Pandemia vs Utopia', *Archphoto*, 13 November 2020, https://www.archphoto.it/archives/5801

• Carlo Guenzi, 'Una selezione difficile', *Casabella*, no. 325, June 1968, p. 9

• Claudio Popovich, 'Polemiche e dibattiti intorno al Masaccio', *l'Unità*, Tuscan edition, 7 July 1968

• Eugenio Miccini, 'Nuovi interventi per il Premio Masaccio', *l'Unità*, Tuscan edition, 16 July 1968

• Furio Colombo, 'Un'astronave carica di polli', *L'Espresso*, vol. XIV, no. 30, 28 July 1968, p. 15

• Tommaso Trini, 'Masaccio a Ufo', *Domus*, no. 466, September 1968, pp. 55-56

• Alain Jouffroy, 'Les objets volants non identifiés du groupe U.F.O.', *Opus International*, no. 10-11, April 1969, pp. 61-63

• Umberto Eco, 'Le nuove tecniche', in Eco (ed.), *L'arte come mestiere* (Milan: Bompiani, 1969), pp. 122-123

• 'Dove va il design', *Vogue*, January 1971, pp. 76-81

• Tommaso Trini, 'L'ufo della parodia', *Domus*, no. 495, February 1971, pp. 46-48

• Lara-Vinca Masini, 'Archifirenze', *Domus*, no. 509, April 1972, p. 40

• Umberto Eco, 'Dal cucchiaio alla città', *L'Espresso*, no. 23, 4 June 1972, pp. 4-23

• Vittorio Gregotti, 'Italian Design 1945-1971', in Emilio Ambasz (ed.), *Italy: The New Domestic Landscape. Achievements and Problems of Italian Design* (New York: Museum of Modern Art, 1972), pp. 315-340: 337, 339

• Francesco Gurrieri, 'Il difficile destino degli insediamenti universitari a Firenze', *Necropoli*, no. 15-16, December 1972, pp. 5-27

• Bruce Haggart, 'Italian Trip', *Architectural Design*, no. 4, 1972, pp. 201-202

• Franco Raggi, 'Radical Story', *Casabella*, no. 382, October 1973, pp. 37-45

• Rodolfo Bracci, Daniele Crivelli and Fabio Naldi, 'Untitled' (page featuring a photograph of the happening *La casa a ostacoli sul territorio* set up at Eurodomus 4, Turin, 27 May 1972), in Achille Bonito Oliva (ed.), *8e Biennale de Paris (catalogo della mostra, Parc Floral de Paris)* (Florence: Centro Di, 1973), n.p.

• Franco Raggi, 'Radical Design - Tendenzen der Designer-Avantgarde Italiens', in Vittorio Gregotti, Carlo Guenzi and Franco Raggi (eds.), *Design Als Postulat Am Beispiel Italien (Katalog und Anthologie zur Ausstellung im IDZ Berlin)* (Berlin: Druckerei Albert Heinrich, 1973), pp. 79-104: 83, 90-92, 96, 101

• Franco Raggi, 'Anthologie', in Vittorio Gregotti, Carlo Guenzi and Franco Raggi (eds.), *Design Als Postulat Am Beispiel Italien (Katalog und Anthologie zur Ausstellung im IDZ Berlin)* (Berlin: Druckerei Albert Heinrich, 1973), pp. 118-119

• Ettore Sottsass Jr. and Andrea Branzi, '4. Mostra internazionale dell'industrial design', in *Quindicesima Triennale di Milano. Esposizione internazionale delle arti decorative e industriali moderne e dell'architettura moderna* (Florence: Centro Di, 1973), pp. 45-48: 47

• Achille Bonito Oliva, 'Contemporanea', *Casabella*, no. 386, February 1974, pp. 2-9

• Pierre Restany, 'Ufo Zorro', *Domus*, no. 539, October 1974, pp. 46-47

• '"Global Tools", Edizioni l'uomo e l'arte, Milano 1974', *Domus*, no. 541, December 1974, p. 40

• Gillo Dorfles, *Ufo - Il mostro dell'Id* (Milan: Jabik Arte Moltiplicata, 1974), n.p.

• Paola Navone and Bruno Orlandoni, *Architettura "radicale"* (Milan: Documenti di Casabella, 1974), pp. 25, 31-34, 46-47, 62-63, 70-71, 73-74, 77-78

• Luca Palazzoli (ed.), *Gli abiti dell'imperatore* (Milan: Galleria Luca Palazzoli, 1974), pp. 30, 34

• Paola Navone and Bruno Orlandoni, 'Quando le avanguardie distruggono', in Giovanni Maria Accame and Carlo Guenzi (eds.), *Avanguardie e cultura popolare (catalogo della mostra alla Galleria d'Arte Moderna di Bologna)* (Bologna: Galleria d'arte moderna, 1975), pp. 190-193

• Alessandro Vezzosi (ed.), *Arte Cronaca. Attività Artistiche in Toscana 1973/75* (Vinci: Centro museografico-promozionale d'arte contemporanea, 1976), n.p.

• Ugo La Pietra, 'Architettura radicale in Italia. Che ne è successo?', *Domus*, no. 580, March 1977, pp. 2-7

• Adolfo Natalini, 'Com'era ancora bella l'architettura nel 1966... (Superstudio e l'architettura radicale, dieci anni dopo)', *Spazioarte*, no. 10-11, June-October 1977, pp. 6-11: 6

• Daniela Puppa, 'Giro d'Italia', *Modo*, no. 5, 1977

• Bruno Orlandoni and Giorgio Vallino, *Dalla città al cucchiaio. Saggi sulle nuove avanguardie nell'architettura e nel design* (Turin: Ed. Studio Forma, 1977), pp. 10, 16, 18, 40, 42, 56, 64, 92, 110, 115, 116, 131, 149, 153, 154, 177, 178, 180, 182

• Giorgio Muratore, 'Tra ipotesi tecnologica e crisi di progettazione, "Casabella" 1965-1975', *Casabella*, no. 440-441, October-November 1978, pp. 92-96

• Agnoldomenico Pica, 'Nel canale tra arte e architettura', *Domus*, no. 588, November 1978, p. 1

• Andrea Granchi (ed.), *Cinema d'artista e sperimentale in Italia 1960/1978* (Paris: Centre Pompidou, 1978), n.p.

• Unione fiorentina and Comitato per le Manifestazioni Espositive Firenze-Prato, *6.a Biennale Internazionale della Grafica d'Arte. 3* (Florence: Vallecchi, 1978), p. 173

• *28/78 Architettura - Cinquant'anni di architettura italiana dal 1928 al 1978* (Milan: Editoriale Domus, 1979), p. 66

• Isa Vercelloni, 'Operazione Alchimya: i monumenti da camera di Ettore Sottsass', *Casa Vogue*, no. 101, 1979, pp. 154-155

• Ugo La Pietra and Gaddo Morpurgo, *Il Tempo del Museo Venezia: tema cronografico per architetti e artisti; Magazzini Del Sale* (Venice: La Biennale di Venezia, 1980), pp. 13, 66

• Germano Celant (ed.), *Identité italienne. L'art en Italie depuis 1959* (Paris, Florence: Centre Pompidou, Centro Di, 1981), pp. 234-235, 241, 256, 259, 263

• Bruno Gregori, *Bau. Haus Art Collection, 1980-1981* (Milan: Alchimia, 1981)

• Mario Mariotti, *Piazza Della Palla: Gioco, Scena, Proiezione* (Florence: Alinari, 1981), pp. 21, 26, 100, 101

• Rainer Krause and Deutscher Werkbund Niedersachsen-Bremen (eds.), *Provokationen: Design Aus Italien; Ein Mythos Geht Neue Wege, Ausstellung des Deutschen Werkbundes Niedersachsen und Bremen E.V. 17. Januar - 14. Februar 1982* (Hannover: Deutscher Werkbund Niedersachsen und Bremen, 1982), pp. 106, 110

• Andrea Branzi, *Merce e Metropoli. Esperienze del 'nuovo design' italiano* (Palermo: Epos, 1983)

• Gianni Pettena, 'Il campo', in Pettena (ed.), *La città invisibile. Architettura sperimentale 1965/1975* (Florence: Associazione Intercomunale N.10, 1983), pp. 15-16: 16

• Gianni Pettena, 'Introduzione', in Pettena (ed.), *La città invisibile. Architettura sperimentale 1965/1975* (Florence: Associazione Intercomunale N.10, 1983), pp. 29-30: 30

• Gianni Pettena, 'Il radical italiano', in Pettena (ed.), *La città invisibile. Architettura sperimentale 1965/1975* (Florence: Associazione Intercomunale N.10, 1983), pp. 31-36: 31-34

• Andrea Branzi, *La casa calda* (Milan: Idea Books, 1984)

• Giovanni Lauda, 'Jazzarchitettura', *Modo*, no. 82, September 1985, pp. 46-51

• 'Bau-haus I. II', in Kazuko Sato, *Alchimia: Never-Ending Italian Design* (Tokyo: Rikuyo-sha, 1985), pp. 16-27: 16-17, 25

• 'Radical Design', in Kazuko Sato, *Alchimia: Never-Ending Italian Design* (Tokyo: Rikuyo-sha, 1985), pp. 192-210: 192-195, 209-210

• Sandro Colbertaldo, 'Giovani architetti. Fra radicalismo grafico e utopia libertaria: alcuni arredi e qualche riflessione', *Arredare la casa*, no. 72, 1985, pp. 2-25: 3-4

• Franco Semenzato, *1900-1986: mobili, arredi, oggetti vari* (Milan: Idea Books, 1986), n.p.

• Chiara Guidi (ed.), *Luoghi della seconda avanguardia 1958-1970* (Massa: Palazzo Ducale, 1987), pp. 10, 73

• Giacinto di Pietrantonio, 'Architettura e design postmoderno', in Francesca Alfano Miglietti, *Arte in Italia: 1960-1985* (Milan: Politi, 1988), p. 248

• Emilio Ambasz, 'Italian Radical Architecture and Design, 1966-1973', *Terrazzo*, no. 5, September 1990, pp. 73-79: 76, 78

• 'Visi-faces, scheda Binazzi', in Alessandro Mendini (ed.), *Ollo*, no. 2, 1990, n.p.

• *Mobili italiani 61-91: le varie età dei linguaggi* (Milan: Cosmit, 1991), pp. 62, 142, 155, 224, 258

• Mauro Pratesi and Giovanna Uzzani, *La Toscana* (Venice: Marsilio, 1991), pp. 287, 301-302, 305-307, 312, 321

• Simone Micheli, 'Incontro con Lapo Binazzi. La discontinuità come punto di forza', in Micheli, *I negozi.*

Vita, morte e miracoli (Florence: Angelo Pontecorboli Editore, 1992), pp. 40-51

• Andrea Branzi, 'Mass Creativity', in Andrea Branzi and Germano Celant (eds.), *Andrea Branzi: Luoghi: The Complete Works* (Milan: Idea Books, 1992), pp. 74-75: 75

• Ralph Jentsch, 'Lapo Binazzi, A.N.A.S. 1975', in Jentsch, *The Artist and the Book in Twentieth-Century Italy* (Turin: Umberto Allemandi, 1992), p. 44

• Lara-Vinca Masini, 'Ufo', in *Dizionario del fare arte contemporanea dagli anni '50 ad oggi* (Florence: Sansoni, 1992), pp. 96-97, 303-304, 331-333, 379, 422

• Umberto Eco, 'You Must Remember This', in Germano Celant (ed.), *The Italian Metamorphosis 1943-1968* (New York: Guggenheim Museum, 1994), pp. XII-XV

• Ufo, 'Dollar Lamp for the Sherwood Restaurant', in Germano Celant (ed.), *The Italian Metamorphosis 1943-1968* (New York: Guggenheim Museum, 1994), n.p.

• Andrea Branzi, *Il design italiano 1964-1990* (Milan: Electa, 1996), pp. 105, 110, 118, 173

• Enrico Crispolti, *Rapporto sul Sistema dell'Arte moderna e contemporanea in Toscana* (Florence: Fondazione Primo Conti, ISIA, 1996), pp. 142, 148, 168-169

• Lara-Vinca Masini, *Arte contemporanea. La linea del modello. Arte come progetto del mondo 3* (Florence: Giunti, 1996), p. 311

• Gianni Pettena, 'Radicals. Architettura e design 1960-1975', in Hans Hollein (ed.), *6. Mostra internazionale di architettura. Sensori del futuro: l'architetto come sismografo* (Venice, Milan: Edizioni La Biennale di Venezia, Electa, 1996), pp. 480-485: 482, 484

• Lara-Vinca Masini, 'Gli anni Sessanta e Settanta', in Patrizia Pietrogrande and Eugenio Martera (eds.), *La stanza delle meraviglie: l'arte del commercio a Firenze: dagli sporti medioevali al negozio virtuale* (Florence: Le Lettere, 1998), pp. 100-107: 102

• Lara-Vinca Masini, 'Il movimento radicale', in Patrizia Pietrogrande and Eugenio Martera (eds.), *La stanza delle meraviglie: l'arte del commercio a Firenze: dagli sporti medioevali al negozio virtuale* (Florence: Le Lettere, 1998), pp. 108-115: 109, 111-112, 114-115

• Marc Dessauce (ed.), *The Inflatable Moment: Pneumatics and Protest in '68*, Princeton Architectural Press (New York: The Architectural League, 1999), pp. 10-11

• Gianni Pettena, 'Radicals e altre storie', in Pettena, *Archipelago. Architettura Sperimentale 1959-1999 (catalogo della mostra, Palazzo Fabroni, Pistoia)* (Prato, Florence: Gli Ori, Maschietto&Musolino, 1999), pp. 11-30: 19

• Gianni Pettena, 'Performance/installazioni', in Pettena, *Archipelago. Architettura Sperimentale 1959-1999 (catalogo della mostra, Palazzo Fabroni, Pistoia)* (Prato, Florence: Gli Ori, Maschietto&Musolino, 1999), pp. 50-51

• Gianni Pettena, 'Biografie', in Pettena, *Archipelago. Architettura Sperimentale 1959-1999 (catalogo della mostra, Palazzo Fabroni, Pistoia)* (Prato, Florence: Gli Ori, Maschietto&Musolino, 1999), pp. 133, 155-156

• Sergio Risaliti, 'Lo spazio condiviso', in *Lo spazio condiviso* (Siena: Palazzo delle Papesse, 2000), pp. 6-7

• 'Artisti e Architetti (schede)', in *Lo spazio condiviso* (Siena: Palazzo delle Papesse, 2000), pp. 114-138: 130, 131

• *La collection de design du Centre Georges Pompidou* (Paris: Centre Pompidou, 2001), p. 130

• Isabelle Merly, *Les Années Pop 1956-1968* (Paris: Centre Pompidou, 2001), n.p. (illustrations 68.9, 68.11, 68.74)

• Gianni Pettena, 'Arquitectura radical-Architecture radicale-Radical Architecture', in Jean-Louis Maubant and Frédéric Migayrou (eds.), *Architecture Radicale* (Villeurbanne: Institut d'art contemporain Éditions, 2001), pp. 27-79, 33-43, 297-300

• Sophie Bellé, 'Biografias: UFO/Biographies: UFO/Biographies: UFO', in Jean-Louis Maubant and Frédéric Migayrou (eds.), *Architecture Radicale* (Villeurbanne: Institut d'art contemporain Éditions, 2001), pp. 284-285, 360

• *Continuità. Arte in Toscana 1945-2000: regesto generale* (Pistoia: Maschietto Editore, 2002), pp. 42, 45, 65, 77-78, 193, 195, 198, 205, 212-214

• Sergio Risaliti (ed.), *Toscana Contemporanea* (Florence: Maschietto Editore, 2002), p. 380

• Daniel Soutif (ed.), *Continuità: Arte in Toscana 1968-1989* (Florence: Maschietto Editore, 2002), pp. 37, 134-135, 140, 142

• Gianni Pettena, *Radical design. Ricerca e progetto dagli anni '60 a oggi* (Florence: Maschietto Editore, 2004), pp. 17, 21-22, 24, 84-87, 111-113, 258-259

• Dominique Rouillard, *Superarchitecture: le futur de l'architecture, 1950-1970* (Paris: Éditions de la Villette, 2004), pp. 250-256, 290, 476, 494, 502

• Andrea Branzi, 'Notes on No-Stop City: Archizoom Associates 1969-72', in Martin van Schaik and Otakar Mácel (eds.), *Exit Utopia. Architectural Provocations, 1956-76* (Munich, London, New York: Prestel, 2005), pp. 177-183: 181-182

• Catherine Grenier (ed.), *Big Bang. Destruction et création dans l'art du 20e siècle* (Paris: Centre Pompidou, 2005), p. 140

• Silvia Lucchesi, *Cinema d'artista in Toscana 1964-1980* (Prato: Regione Toscana, Centro per l'arte contemporanea Luigi Pecci, 2005), pp. 24, 26, 27, 31, 32, 179-184

• Marco Bazzini and Stefano Pezzato (eds.), *Italian Genius Now* (Prato: Centro per l'arte contemporanea Luigi Pecci, 2007), pp. 55, 57, 80

• Gabriele Corsani, 'Premessa', in Gabriele Corsani and Marco Bini (eds.), *La Facoltà di Architettura di Firenze fra tradizione e cambiamento: atti del convegno di studi: Firenze, 29-30 aprile 2004* (Florence: Firenze University Press, 2007), pp. XV-XXVI: XXIII

• Raimondo Innocenti, 'L'insegnamento e l'attività urbanistica di Edoardo Detti', in Gabriele Corsani and Marco Bini (eds.), *La Facoltà di Architettura di Firenze fra tradizione e cambiamento: atti del convegno di studi: Firenze, 29-30 aprile 2004* (Florence: Firenze University Press, 2007), pp. 211-224: 215

• Maria Cristina Tonelli, 'La scuola di design fiorentina', in Gabriele Corsani and Marco Bini (eds.), *La Facoltà di Architettura di Firenze fra tradizione e cambiamento: atti del convegno di studi: Firenze, 29-30 aprile 2004* (Florence: Firenze University Press, 2007), pp. 225-238: 234

• Romano Viviani, 'Lo statuto dell'architetto', in Gabriele Corsani and Marco Bini (eds.), *La Facoltà di Architettura di Firenze fra tradizione e cambiamento: atti del convegno di studi: Firenze, 29-30 aprile 2004* (Florence: Firenze University Press, 2007), pp. 265-271: 271

• Andrea Branzi and Gilberto Corretti, 'Il design italiano tra il 1964 e il 1972', in Andrea Branzi, *Il design italiano 1964-2000* (Milan: La Triennale di Milano Mondadori, Electa, 2008), pp. 105, 110, 116, 173

• Marco Bazzini (ed.), *Italian Genius Now* (Seoul, Tokyo, Taipei, New Delhi, Prato: Korean Design Centre, Istituto Italiano di Cultura, Xue Xue Institute, Travancore House, Centro per l'arte contemporanea Luigi Pecci, 2008), p. 83

• Marco Bazzini (ed.), *Italian Genius Now. Back to Rome* (Rome, Prato: MACRO Future, Centro per l'arte contemporanea Luigi Pecci, 2009), pp. 88-89, 112

• Marco Bazzini and Stefano Pezzato (eds.), *Centro Per L'arte Contemporanea Luigi Pecci. La Collezione* (Florence: Giunti, 2009)

• 'UFO', in Andrea Alibrandi (ed.), *Radici Radicali. Archizoom, Pettena, Superstudio, UFO*, Il Ponte, Firenze 2009, pp. 60-72

• Mauro Panzera, 'Architettura Radicale - una riflessione a margine', in Andrea Alibrandi (ed.), *Radici Radicali. Archizoom, Pettena, Superstudio, UFO* (Florence: Il Ponte, 2009), pp. 13-16: 15

• Enrico Pedrini, 'L'Architettura Radicale', in Andrea Alibrandi (ed.), *Radici Radicali. Archizoom, Pettena, Superstudio, UFO* (Florence: Il Ponte, 2009), pp. 9-12: 11-12

• Gianni Pettena, 'Design, Arte Ambientale, Architettura: interrelazioni contemporanee', in Andrea Alibrandi (ed.), *Radici Radicali. Archizoom, Pettena, Superstudio, UFO* (Florence: Il Ponte 2009), pp. 17-22: 19, 20

• Emanuele Piccardo, 'Intervista a Lapo Binazzi', in Piccardo, *Dopo la rivoluzione. Azioni e protagonisti dell'Architettura Radicale italiana 1963-1973* (Busalla: plug_in, 2009)

• Giorgia Marotta, 'La collezione di Casa Masaccio a San Giovanni Valdarno: dagli anni dirompenti del premio Masaccio fino alle recenti avventure', in Liletta Fornasari and Giovanna Uzzani (eds.), *Arte in terra d'Arezzo: il Novencento* (Florence: Edifir Edizioni, 2009), pp. 209-218

• Beatriz Colomina and Craig Buckley (eds.), *Clip, Stamp, Fold: The Radical Architecture of Little Magazines, 196x to 197x* (Barcelona, New York: Actar, 2010), pp. 52, 76, 109, 134, 138, 250, 392, 476, 478

• Adolfo Natalini, Italo Rota, Paolo Tonini and Bruno Tonini, *Il radical italiano nel contesto internazionale dell'architettura utopica e visionaria 1957-1980* (Gussago: Edizioni dell'Arengario, 2011), n.p.

• Brunetto de Batté, 'From the Drop City to the anti-city experiments', in Emanuele Piccardo (ed.), *Archphoto 2.0. Radical City*, no. 1, 2011, pp. 44-45: 44

• 'Field of Action / the piazza', in Emanuele Piccardo (ed.), *Archphoto 2.0. Radical City*, no. 1, 2011, pp. 26-27: 26

• Amit Wolf, 'Superurbeffimero n. 7: Umberto Eco's Semiologia and the Architectural Rituals of the U.F.O.', *Archphoto 2.0. Radical City*, no. 1, 2011, pp. 28-29

• 'Field of Action/ Inflatable City', in Emanuele Piccardo (ed.), *Archphoto 2.0. Radical City*, no. 1 2011, pp. 36-37: 36

• Amit Wolf, 'Superurbeffimero n. 7: Umberto Eco's Semiologia and the Architectural Rituals of the U.F.O.', *California Italian Studies*, no. 2, 2011, http://dx.doi.org/10.5070/C322008956

• Marco Bazzini (ed.), *Italian Genius Now Brasil* (Porto Alegre: Néktar Design, 2012), pp. 9, 21-22, 91-92, 95, 99, 106

• Carla Pasquinelli, 'Il taglio del tempo', in Fabio Amato (ed.), *Spazio e società. Geografie, pratiche, interazioni* (Naples: Alfredo Guida Editore, 2012), pp. 77-87

• Stefano Pezzato (ed.), *Ufo story: dall'architettura radicale al design globale* (Prato: Centro per l'arte contemporanea Luigi Pecci, 2012)

• Marie-Ange Brayer (ed.), *Architectures expérimentales 1950-2012, collection du FRAC Centre* (Orléans: Éditions HYX, 2013), pp. 598-601

- Carlo Caldini (9999), 'Rilassatevi', in Bruno Casini, *Ribelli nello spazio. Culture underground anni Settanta. Lo Space Electronic a Firenze* (Arezzo: Zona, 2013), pp. 195-197
- Bruno Orlandoni, 'Introduction', in Emanuele Piccardo and Amit Wolf (eds.), *Beyond Environment* (Barcelona, New York: Actar, 2014), pp. 11-15
- Emanuele Piccardo, 'From the city to the environment', in Emanuele Piccardo and Amit Wolf (eds.), *Beyond Environment* (Barcelona, New York: Actar, 2014), pp. 17-37
- Amit Wolf, 'The education of an Un-architect', in Emanuele Piccardo and Amit Wolf (eds.), *Beyond Environment* (Barcelona, New York: Actar, 2014), pp. 40-49
- Valerio Borgonuovo, Silvia Franceschini, 'Preface', in Borgonuovo and Franceschini (eds.), *Global Tools 1973 - 1975*, SALT/Garanti Kültür AŞ, Istanbul 2015, pp. 3-4: 3
- Valerio Borgonuovo and Silvia Franceschini, 'When education coincides with life', in Borgonuovo and Franceschini (eds.), *Global Tools 1973 - 1975* (Istanbul: SALT/Garanti Kültür AŞ, 2015), pp. 12-34: 31
- Franco Raggi, 'Dysfunctional objects for a heretical "inverse ergonomics"', in Valerio Borgonuovo and Silvia Franceschini (eds.), *Global Tools 1973 - 1975* (Istanbul: SALT/Garanti Kültür AŞ, 2015), pp. 51-62: 52, 55
- Alison J. Clarke, 'The indigenous and the autochthon', in Valerio Borgonuovo, Silvia Franceschini (eds.), *Global Tools 1973 - 1975* (Istanbul: SALT/Garanti Kültür AŞ, 2015), pp. 126-142: 126, 129, 131
- Patrizia Mello, 'Contestazione radical e Global Tools nella città della storia', *Intersezioni*, no. 2, 2015, pp. 309-323
- Alessandra Pioselli, *L'arte nello spazio urbano. L'esperienza italiana dal 1968 a oggi* (Monza: Johan & Levi Editore, 2015), p. 33
- Elisabetta Trincherini, 'In teoria... i mobili. La produzione dell'arredo in Toscana dal secondo dopoguerra a oggi: pratiche ed estetiche', in Elisabetta Trincherini and Davide Turrini (eds.), *Creativa Produzione. La Toscana e il design 1950-1990* (Lucca: Edizioni Fondazione Ragghianti Studi sull'Arte, 2015), pp. 30-37
- Alessandra Acocella, 'Scenografie radicali. San Giovanni Valdarno 1968', in Acocella, *Avanguardia diffusa. Luoghi di sperimentazione artistica in Italia 1967-1970* (Milan: Fondazione Passaré/Macerata: Quodlibet, 2016), pp. 73-94
- Alessandra Acocella, 'Tra utopia e disincanto. Le mostre di Lara-Vinca Masini alla Biennale di Venezia del 1978', in Flavio Fergonzi (ed.), *Presenze toscane alla Biennale Internazionale d'Arte di Venezia* (Milan: Skira, 2016), pp. 133-147: 136, 142-143, 145-147
- Alessandra Acocella and Caterina Toschi (eds.), 'Firenze sperimentale: gli anni settanta attraverso le testimonianze di Bruno Corà, Lapo Binazzi e Paolo Masi', in Anna Mazzanti (ed.), *Art/Tapes/22. Le origini della videoarte* (Cinisello Balsamo: Silvana Editoriale, 2017), pp. 44-48: 44, 46-48
- Gianni Pettena, 'Le ragioni di un'utopia', in Pino Brugellis, Gianni Pettena and Alberto Salvadori (eds.), *Utopie radicali. Archizoom, Remo Buti, 9999, Gianni Pettena, Superstudio, UFO, Zziggurat* (Macerata: Quodlibet, 2017), pp. 21-31: 26, 28
- Pino Brugellis and Manuel Orazi, 'Radicali per sempre', in Pino Brugellis, Gianni Pettena and Alberto Salvadori (eds.), *Utopie radicali. Archizoom, Remo Buti, 9999, Gianni Pettena, Superstudio, UFO, Zziggurat* (Macerata: Quodlibet, 2017), pp. 33-40: 33, 36, 37
- Marie-Ange Brayer, 'Il progetto architettonico radicale come "design territoriale"', in Pino Brugellis, Gianni Pettena and Alberto Salvadori (eds.), *Utopie radicali. Archizoom, Remo Buti, 9999, Gianni Pettena, Superstudio, UFO, Zziggurat* (Macerata: Quodlibet, 2017), pp. 47-60: 56
- Maria Cristina Didero, 'Il design radicale non è mai esistito', in Pino Brugellis, Gianni Pettena and Alberto Salvadori (eds.), *Utopie radicali. Archizoom, Remo Buti, 9999, Gianni Pettena, Superstudio, UFO, Zziggurat* (Macerata: Quodlibet, 2017), pp. 61-78: 65, 74-76
- Marco Brizzi, 'Architetture tracciate nell'editoria', in Pino Brugellis, Gianni Pettena and Alberto Salvadori (eds.), *Utopie radicali. Archizoom, Remo Buti, 9999, Gianni Pettena, Superstudio, UFO, Zziggurat* (Macerata: Quodlibet, 2017), pp. 79-86: 83
- Manfredo di Robilant, 'L'eredità dei Radicali, ovvero le due accezioni di un aggettivo', in Pino Brugellis, Gianni Pettena and Alberto Salvadori (eds.), *Utopie radicali. Archizoom, Remo Buti, 9999, Gianni Pettena, Superstudio, UFO, Zziggurat* (Macerata: Quodlibet, 2017), pp. 87-97: 87, 89, 91, 97
- Stefano Pezzato, 'UFO', in Pino Brugellis, Gianni Pettena and Alberto Salvadori (eds.), *Utopie radicali. Archizoom, Remo Buti, 9999, Gianni Pettena, Superstudio, UFO, Zziggurat* (Macerata: Quodlibet, 2017), pp. 246-275
- Patrizia Mello, 'Il futuro in azione', in *Neoavanguardie e controcultura a Firenze* (Florence: Angelo Pontecorboli Editore, 2017), pp. 19-34: 20
- Patrizia Mello, 'Alcuni contributi radicali', in *Neoavanguardie e controcultura a Firenze* (Florence: Angelo Pontecorboli Editore, 2017), pp. 39-49: 42, 44-45, 47
- Patrizia Mello, 'Dieci domande a Lapo Binazzi', in *Neoavanguardie e controcultura a Firenze* (Florence: Angelo Pontecorboli Editore, 2017), pp. 50-54: 50, 53
- Patrizia Mello, 'Il concorso per la nuova Università di Firenze (1971)', in *Neoavanguardie e controcultura a*

Firenze (Florence: Angelo Pontecorboli Editore, 2017), pp. 67-75: 71, 72

• Patrizia Mello, 'Le case A.N.A.S. Da architettura della burocrazia a luoghi di sosta turistico-sociali', in *Neoavanguardie e controcultura a Firenze* (Florence: Angelo Pontecorboli Editore, 2017), pp. 91-96

• Patrizia Mello, 'Interviste a Lapo Binazzi (UFO)', in *Neoavanguardie e controcultura a Firenze* (Florence: Angelo Pontecorboli Editore, 2017), pp. 107-115

• Patrizia Mello, 'Schede seminario', in *Neoavanguardie e controcultura a Firenze* (Florence: Angelo Pontecorboli Editore, 2017), pp. 162-177: 163, 172, 173, 175

• Patrizia Mello, 'Appendice', in *Neoavanguardie e controcultura a Firenze* (Florence: Angelo Pontecorboli Editore, 2017), pp. 107-115, 180-184: 184

• Patrizia Mello, 'Firenze e le avanguardie radicali. Progetti, azioni, super-visioni, oggetti extra', in *Firenze e le avanguardie Radicali* (Florence: DIDA Press, 2017), pp. 11-17: 11, 16

• Patrizia Mello, 'Il futuro in azione', in *Firenze e le avanguardie Radicali* (Florence: DIDA Press, 2017), pp. 19-34: 20

• Patrizia Mello, 'Alcuni contributi radicali', in *Firenze e le avanguardie Radicali* (Florence: DIDA Press, 2017), pp. 39-49: 42, 44-45, 47

• Patrizia Mello, 'Dieci domande a Lapo Binazzi (UFO)', in *Firenze e le avanguardie Radicali* (Florence: DIDA Press, 2017), pp. 50-54: 50, 53

• Patrizia Mello, 'Il concorso per la nuova Università di Firenze (1971)', in *Firenze e le avanguardie Radicali* (Florence: DIDA Press, 2017), pp. 67-75: 71, 72

• Patrizia Mello, 'Le case A.N.A.S. Da architettura della burocrazia a luoghi di sosta turistico-sociali', in *Firenze e le avanguardie Radicali* (Florence: DIDA Press, 2017), pp. 91-96

• Patrizia Mello, 'Interviste a Lapo Binazzi (UFO)', in *Firenze e le avanguardie Radicali* (Florence: DIDA Press, 2017), pp. 107-115

• Patrizia Mello, 'Schede seminario', in *Firenze e le avanguardie Radicali* (Florence: DIDA Press, 2017), pp. 162-177: 163, 172, 173, 175

• Patrizia Mello, 'Appendice', in *Firenze e le avanguardie Radicali* (Florence: DIDA Press, 2017), pp. 180-184: 184

• Agata Knapik, 'Radykalne projekty Florenckiej grupy Ufo w kontekście partyzantki semiologicznej Umberto Eco', *Avant*, no. 3, January 2018, pp. 51-79, https://doi.org/10.26913

• Agata Knapik, 'Radykalne projekty grupy UFO jako przykład architektury narracyjnej', *Quart: Kwartalnik Instytutu Historii Sztuki Uniwersytetu Wrocławskiego*, no. 2, 2018, pp. 88-106

• Valerio Borgonuovo and Silvia Franceschini, 'Global Tools: gli strumenti di una scuola possibile', in Borgonuovo and Franceschini (eds.), *Global Tools. Quando l'educazione coinciderà con la vita, 1973-1975* (Rome: Nero Editions, 2018), pp. 9-33: 9, 10, 11, 12, 27, 28, 29

• Franco Raggi, 'Appunti per un'ergonomia inversa', in Valerio Borgonuovo and Silvia Franceschini (eds.), *Global Tools. Quando l'educazione coinciderà con la vita, 1973-1975* (Rome: Nero Editions, 2018), pp. 91-95: 92

• Alison J. Clarke 'L'indigeno e l'autoctono', in Valerio Borgonuovo and Silvia Franceschini (eds.), *Global Tools. Quando l'educazione coinciderà con la vita, 1973-1975* (Rome: Nero Editions, 2018), pp. 135-139: 135

• Adolfo Natalini, 'Lettera a Paola Navone (segretaria organizzativa Global Tools) con calendario dei primi corsi del giugno-luglio 1975', in Valerio Borgonuovo and Silvia Franceschini (eds.), *Global Tools. Quando l'educazione coinciderà con la vita, 1973-1975* (Rome: Nero Editions, 2018), p. 148

• Mateo Kries, Jochen Eisenbrand, Catharine Rossi and Kirsten Thietz (eds.), *Night Fever: Designing Club Culture, 1960-Today* (Weil am Rhein: Vitra Design Museum, 2018), pp. 34, 58-59

• Alessandra Acocella, 'Effimero urbanistico. L'immagine della piazza nelle azioni del gruppo UFO (1968)', in Stephanie Hanke and Brigitte Sölch (eds.), *Projektionen. Der Platz als Bildthema* (München: Deutscher Kunstverlag, 2019), pp. 197-210

• False Mirror Office (Andrea Anselmo and Boris Hamzeian), 'L'assemblaggio come testo figurativo per l'architettura. Un dialogo tra UFO e False Mirror Office', *PianoB*, no. 2, 2019, pp. 88-118, https://doi.org/10.6092

• Frédéric Migayrou and Valentina Moimas, *Aerodream. Architecture, art, design et structures gonflables* (Orléans: Éditions HYX, 2021), pp. 216-217

Biographical Notes

Carlo Bachi was born in Pisa in 1939. In 1967, he founded the UFO group with Lapo Binazzi, Patrizia Cammeo, Riccardo Foresi, and Titti Maschietto (initially joined by Sandro Gioli). During his education, thanks to his friendship with Giuseppe Bartolini, he joined the "Nuova figurazione" painting circle. At the same time, he devoted himself to producing photographic reportages documenting the Florence flood of 1966 and the 1968 student movement demonstrations (some of his photographs are published in the book *Firenze Piazza San Marco 30 gennaio 1968. Libro Bianco*, Cooperativa Libraria, 1968). In 1975, he graduated from the Faculty of Architecture at the University of Florence. After the dissolution of UFO, he worked as an architect between Pisa and Florence, where he developed interior architecture and naval design projects. In 1988, he was chosen by Paolo Benvenuti for the role of Jesus Christ in the film *Il Bacio di Giuda* ("Judas's Kiss"), presented in Venice in 1989. He died in 1991.

Lapo Binazzi was born in Florence in 1943. In 1967, he founded the UFO group with Carlo Bachi, Patrizia Cammeo, Riccardo Foresi, and Titti Maschietto (initially joined by Sandro Gioli). His interest in literature and Umberto Eco's lectures led him, as early as 1968, to teach Semiology at the Leonetto Cappiello Art Academy (Florence). In 1971, he graduated from the Faculty of Architecture at the University of Florence with a master's thesis titled *L'ingegnosa conquista della montagna della tigre*. After the dissolution of UFO, he continued developing the group's reflections through the realisation of performances (*Catastrofi leggere ecc.*, *Guerre stellari*), films (*Improvvisazione al pianoforte*), objects (*Pinocchio*, *Scarica elettrica al neon*, *Il Servizio del Dott. Caligari*), books (*Pinocchio Triangolare*, Da Burde, 1991), architectural projects, and interior design, in the pursuit of a "discontinuity" of forms, concepts, and materials. Among his participations in exhibitions are *Documenta 8* (Kassel, 1987), *La casa del Dolce Stil Novo* (Florence, 1991), and the retrospective dedicated to his work at R&D Gallery (New York, 2016). Since the eighties, he has taught in London (Architectural Association, 1982, with Nigel Coates), in Milan (Domus Academy, 1985), and in Florence (Polimoda, 1990; University of Florence, Faculty of Architecture and Faculty of Letters, 2000-2012; Florence Institute of Design International, 2012-present).

Patrizia Cammeo was born in Florence in 1943. In 1967, she founded the UFO group with Carlo Bachi, Lapo Binazzi, Riccardo Foresi, and Titti Maschietto (initially joined by Sandro Gioli). During her university years, she designed jewellery called *Paesaggi da indossare*. In 1971, she graduated from the Faculty of Architecture at the University of Florence with a master's thesis titled *L'ingegnosa conquista della montagna della tigre*. From 1971 until 1978, she was an assistant of the Urbanism course held by Paolo Sica at the Faculty of Architecture in Florence. After the UFO group experience ended, she worked as an architect between Florence and Milan. Since 1981, she has participated in competitions with the AIR group, of which her husband, Riccardo Foresi, was the Head, and with which she also worked on projects for interiors, parks, and exhibitions. From 1996 to 1998, she worked in Vittorio Gregotti's studio for the project of the Pula Technology Park in Sardinia and the Livorno Town Plan. She then went on to work as an urbanist and landscape architect, drafting projects for Orbetello, Capolona, Subbiano and Radicondoli, for which she drew up the town Plan. Currently, she still works as an artist in Florence, where she paints and produces design objects and jewellery.

Riccardo Foresi was born in Florence in 1941. In 1967, he founded the UFO group with Carlo Bachi, Lapo Binazzi, Patrizia Cammeo, and Titti Maschietto (initially joined by Sandro Gioli). Like Patrizia Cammeo, his future wife, during his university years he designed jewellery. In 1971, he graduated from the Faculty of Architecture at the University of Florence with a master's thesis titled *L'ingegnosa conquista della montagna della tigre*. From 1971 to 1978, he was an assistant of the Urbanism course at the Faculty of Architecture in Florence held by Paolo Sica, with whom he also collaborated on books (*L'urbanistica*, Le Monnier, 1981; *Firenze: la questione urbanistica: scritti e contributi 1945-1975*, Sansoni, 1982). Since the mid-seventies, he has held courses in Urbanism and Environmental Planning at the Faculty of Architecture in Florence, and written articles. Since 1979, at the head of the AIR group, he has taken part in various architecture competitions (Parco dell'Arboreto in Pistoia, Fiera Catena in Mantua, Porto Navile in Bologna). He designed and made installations and furnishings, and collaborated, from 1985, with the Mercedes research centre for the study and design of trucks. He died in 2000.

Vittorio (Titti) Maschietto was born in Viareggio in 1942. In 1967, he founded the UFO group with Carlo Bachi, Lapo Binazzi, Patrizia Cammeo, and Riccardo Foresi (initially joined by Sandro Gioli). Since his university years, he has been interested in art, producing Action Painting works on various media. In 1971, he graduated from the Faculty of Architecture at the University of Florence with a master's thesis titled *L'ingegnosa conquista della montagna della tigre*. His involvement as an architect (first at the Pierluigi Spadolini practice, and then in his own practice, based in Milan) and as a teacher (as an assistant in the Urbanism course held by Paolo Sica at the Faculty of Architecture in Florence) is accompanied by intense publishing activity (Maschietto&Musolino and Maschietto Editore), and the writing of novels, poems (*B&B*, Marco del Bucchia Editore, 2008; *Radicali liberi*, Maschietto Editore, 2011) and film scripts. His publications on architecture include *Firenze punto zero* (Maschietto&Musolino, 1995), *Il parco degli Scambi* (Polistampa, 1995), and *Lucca interrotta* (Maschietto Editore, 2016). During the nineties, he drew up the Railway System Feasibility Plan for the Province of Florence. For the Province of Lucca, he supervised the restoration of the Palazzo Ducale and the Fortezza di Mont'Alfonso, and drew up the Integrated Plan for Sustainable Urban Development of Lucca and the Tertiary Park of Sorbano.

(ab)Normal is a multi-disciplinary collective founded by Marcello Carpino, Mattia Inselvini, Davide Masserini, and Luigi Savio. Projects and writings of (ab)Normal have been published in magazines such as *Domus* and *Abitare*, and showcased in cultural venues, such as the Oslo Triennale, the Ljubljana Biennale, the Swiss Architecture Museum, the Milan Triennale, and Haus der Architektur Graz.

Alessandra Acocella is a researcher and Professor in Contemporary Art History at the University of Parma. She has published, among other books, the monograph *Avanguardia diffusa. Luoghi di sperimentazione artistica in Italia 1967-1970* (Quodlibet, 2016), and co-edited the collection *Lara-Vinca Masini. Scritti scelti 1961-2019. Arte Architettura Design Arti applicate* (Gli Ori, 2020).

Andrea Anselmo is an architect, design studio assistant, and researcher in History of Architecture at UCLouvain, co-founder of False Mirror Office and the magazine *Burrasca*. His interest in the neo-avant-garde of the sixties and seventies has led him to collaborate with practices that have taken up its legacy, such as OMA (2013) and MVRDV (2015-2019). He is now writing a PhD thesis titled *Villa Dall'Ava by Rem Koolhaas/OMA: a Surrealist Incubator for a New Rationalism* that investigates a contemporary project with the method of historical research.

Peter Behrbohm is a Berlin-based architect/artist who creates autonomous obstacles to conduct crash tests in public spheres and its routines. By himself or as a member of various collective formations, he explores speculative architectures and future conflicts. He is the co-founder, with Anton Steenbock, of the artist group SONDER.

False Mirror Office gathers five architects who share an interest in project and research: Andrea Anselmo, Gloria Castellini, Filippo Fanciotti, Giovanni Glorialanza, and Boris Hamzeian. Brought together at the Polytechnic School of Genoa, they have been collaborating remotely from different countries since the group's founding. Believing that new only originates as a reaction to the existing, False Mirror Office re-discovers the past as the present, re-signifies high as mass culture, and re-values forms and functions. As a matter of fact, False Mirror Office mis-represents architecture.

Adam Nathaniel Furman is a London based artist and designer of Argentine and Japanese heritage. Trained in Architecture and Fine Arts, Furman addresses these disciplines through exhibitions and projects of different nature and scale, extending his field of investigation to industrial and interior design. His profile is enriched by an international research and teaching activity focused on the use of colour in architecture, as well as a personal commitment to the promotion of diversity and representation in the discipline of architecture.

Jacopo Galimberti is a Professor at the IUAV of Venice. His articles have appeared in journals such as *Art History*, *The Art Bulletin*, *The Oxford Art Journal*, and *Grey Room*. He is the author of *Individuals against Individualism. Western European Art Collectives (1956-1969)* (Liverpool University Press, 2017), and of two forthcoming books published by Verso Editions: *Images of Class: Operaismo, Autonomia and the Visual Arts (1962-1988)* and *The Year of Living Dangerously. Italy's Movement of '77* (with Steve Wright).

Giovanni Galli graduated in Architecture from the IUAV of Venice. He is a Professor at the Polytechnic School of Genoa, where he teaches Theory of Architecture and Architectural Design. His main publications include the monographs *Le maschere della forma. Manuale di composizione* (Carocci, 2008), *Sostenibilità e potere* (Sagep, 2015), *Breve storia della forma architettonica (credo laico dell'architettura occidentale)* (Sagep, 2019), and the critical essay "The Primitive Hut as Original Sin - On the Possibility of Generating Primaeval Architecture in an Edenic Context" published by *San Rocco*.

Boris Hamzeian is an architect and postdoctoral fellow in History of Architecture at the École Polytechnique Fédérale de Lausanne (EPFL). As part of his research into the post-war avant-garde and technomorphic architecture, he published articles on the history of the Centre National d'Art et de Culture Georges Pompidou in Paris (subject of his PhD thesis, 2021), the UFO group, and the works by OMA and Aldo Rossi. He is member of the scientific committee of the *Archphoto 2.0* magazine, of the Construction History Society, and the co-founder of False Mirror Office.

Andrew Kovacs is an architect living in Los Angeles active in the fields of practice and teaching. His practice, Office Kovacs, works on projects at all scales: from monographs to exhibitions, from temporary installations to interior designs, and from theoretical architectural projects to public competitions. Kovacs is also the founder of Archive of Affinities, a very popular social media feed devoted to the collection of architectural b-sides.

Jimenez Lai works in the world of art, architecture, and education. His practice, Bureau Spectacular, imagines other worlds and engages in the design of architecture through telling stories; beautiful stories about character development, relationships, curiosities, and attitudes, but also absurd stories about fake realities that invite enticing possibilities. The stories conflate design, representation, theory, criticism, history, and taste into cartoon pages. These cartoon narratives swerve into the physical world through architectural installations, models, and small buildings.

Beatrice Lampariello is an architect and Professor of History of Architecture at UCLouvain, where she has been teaching since 2019 after carrying out research and teaching activities at the École Polytechnique Fédérale de Lausanne (EPFL). Her main publications include essays and monographs on several protagonists and their works during the second half of the 20th century, including, *Villa a Floirac. Rem Koolhaas/OMA 1994-98* (Aracne, 2011), *Superstudio* (with Roberto Gargiani, Laterza, 2010), *Aldo Rossi e le forme del razionalismo esaltato* (Quodlibet, 2017), and *Le Monument continu de Superstudio* (with Roberto Gargiani, B2, 2019).

Parasite 2.0 are Stefano Colombo, Eugenio Cosentino, and Luca Marullo. The practice was founded in 2010 as an independent research unit, a space of expression parallel to the academic environment. They investigate the status of human habitats, acting through a hybrid of architecture, design, and scenography.

Point Supreme Architects was founded in Rotterdam in 2008 by Konstantinos Pantazis and Marianna Rentzou, and is now based in Athens. In 2012, they were included by the popular Greek newspaper *LIFO* among the twenty most influential personalities in Greece.

Simon Sadler is a Professor in the Department of Design and in the Art History Program at the University of California, Davis. His publications focus on histories, theories, and ideologies of architecture, design, and urbanism since the mid 20th century, and include studies on Archigram, the Situationists, and counterculture.

Traumnovelle is a militant faction founded by three Belgian architects: Léone Drapeaud, Manuel León Fanjul, and Johnny Leya. Traumnovelle uses architecture and fiction as analytical, critical, and subversive tools to emphasize contemporary issues, and questions the relationships between architecture and politics.

UNIDENTIFIED FLYING OBJECT FOR
CONTEMPORARY ARCHITECTURE

A PROJECT BY
Beatrice Lampariello
False Mirror Office
Andrea Anselmo
Gloria Castellini
Giovanni Glorialanza
Filippo Fanciotti
Boris Hamzeian

EDITORS
Beatrice Lampariello
False Mirror Office
Andrea Anselmo
Boris Hamzeian

CONTRIBUTORS
(Ab)normal
Marcello Carpino
Mattia Inselvini
Davide Masserini
Luigi Savio
Alesssandra Acocella
Peter Behrbohm
Bureau Spectacular
Jimenez Lai
False Mirror Office
Andrea Anselmo
Gloria Castellini
Filippo Fanciotti
Giovanni Glorialanza
Boris Hamzeian
Adam Nathaniel Furman
Jacopo Galimberti
Giovanni Galli
Andrew Kovacs
Beatrice Lampariello
Parasite 2.0
Stefano Colombo
Eugenio Cosentino
Luca Marullo
Point Supreme
Konstantinos Pantazis
Marianna Rentzou
Simon Sadler
SONDER
Traumnovelle
Léone Drapeaud
Manuel León Fanjul
Johnny Leya

ILLUSTRATIONS CREDITS
Carlo Bachi, Lapo Binazzi, Patrizia Cammeo, Riccardo Foresi, Titti Maschietto (UFO)
Michael Webb (Archigram); Archigram Archives
Gianni Pettena
Ugo La Pietra; Ugo La Pietra Archives
Archizoom; Musée National d'Art Moderne, Centre Pompidou
Superstudio; Musée National d'Art Moderne, Centre Pompidou
Alessandro Poli, Roberto Gherardi; courtesy Alessandro Poli Archives
Guy Debord, Asger Jorn
Carlo Caldini, Fabrizio Fiumi, Paolo Coggiola, Paolo Galli, Andrea Gigli, Mario Presti, courtesy Elettra Fiumi
Adolfo Natalini Archives
Gruppo T; courtesy Gabriele Devecchi Archives
Christo; photo Massimo Piersanti, Archivi MAXXI Arte | Fondo Incontri Internazionali d'Arte (AIIA); courtesy Fondazione MAXXI. © CHRISTO by SIAE 2022
Claes Oldenburg
Domus
Edilizia Moderna
Madelon Vriesendorp
Point Supreme
Gianni Pettena
Nick Hannes
Adam Nathaniel Furman
False Mirror Office
Andrew Kovacs
Bob Civil
Traumnovelle
Jimenez Lai
Bureau Spectacular
Peter Behrbohm
SONDER
(ab)Normal
Parasite 2.0

Beatrice Lampariello and False Mirror Office thank:
Lapo Binazzi, Patrizia Cammeo, Titti Maschietto, Elettra Fiumi, Gianni Pettena, Francesco Caneschi, Emma Bellavita Mussio, UCLouvain, FRAC Centre-Val de Loire, Italian Council, Rolex Centre Library, Fondazione Ugo La Pietra, Casa Masaccio

The book is dedicated to Roberto Gargiani and to the *raft of the Medusa* he built for young visionaries, the LTH3 laboratory

Project realized thanks to the support of the Directorate General for Contemporary Creativity of the Ministry of Culture as part of the Italian Council program (IX edition, 2020)

italianCouncil
Bringing our Contemporary Art to the World

Direzione Generale
Creatività Contemporanea

UNIDENTIFIED FLYING OBJECT FOR
CONTEMPORARY ARCHITECTURE

Published by
Actar Publishers,
New York, Barcelona
www.actar.com

Graphic design
False Mirror Office - Actar D

Copy editing and corrections
Tadzio Koelb
Arnau Grima i Santacreu

Translations from Italian
Christopher Huw Evans
Johanna Bishop

Printing and Binding
Arlequin SL

Cover Image:
UFO, *Chicken Circus Circulation*, San Giovanni Valdarno, 1968

Image pp. 10-11:
Riccardo Foresi, photographed by Carlo Bachi, 1973, Patrizia Cammeo/Riccardo Foresi Archives, Florence

Image pp. 64-65:
UFO, Photography, Faculty of Architecture of University of Florence, 1968, Patrizia Cammeo/Riccardo Foresi Archives, Florence

Image pp. 150-151:
UFO, Polyurethane column, 1970, Patrizia Cammeo/Riccardo Foresi Archives, Florence

Image pp. 244-245:
UFO and Marino Vismara, Performance for the Venice Art Biennale, *B/arca A.N.A.S.*, Venice Art Biennale, Venice, 1978, Lapo Binazzi Archives, Florence

Distribution
Actar D, Inc. New York, Barcelona

New York
440 Park Avenue South, 17th Fl
New York, NY 10016, USA
T +1 212 966 2207
salesnewyork@actar-d.com

Barcelona
Roca i Battle 2-4
08023 Barcelona, SP
T +34 933 282 183
eurosales@actar-d.com

Indexing
ISBN: 978-1-63840-992-2
Library of Congress Control Number: 2021948147

Printed in Barcelona

Publication Date: July 2022